Gary Cornell

The Visual Basic 4 for Windows 95 Handbook

Osborne McGraw-Hill
Berkeley New York St. Louis San Francisco Auckland Bogotá Hamburg London Madrid Mexico City
Milan Montreal New Delhi Panama City Paris São Paulo Singapore Sydney Tokyo Toronto

ACQUISITIONS EDITOR
Wendy Rinaldi

PROJECT EDITOR
Mark Karmendy

TECHNICAL EDITORS
David Jezak, Jonathan Zuck

COPY EDITOR
Judith Brown

PROOFREADERS
Pat Mannion, Stefany Otis

COMPUTER DESIGNER
Jirka Vcelak

ILLUSTRATOR
Loretta Lian

SERIES DESIGN
Seventeenth Street Studios

COVER DESIGN
Mason Fong

Osborne **McGraw-Hill**
2600 Tenth Street
Berkeley, California 94710
U.S.A.

For information on translations or book distributors outside the U.S.A., or to arrange bulk purchase discounts for sales promotions, premiums, or fundraisers, please contact Osborne **McGraw-Hill** at the above address.

The Visual Basic 4 for Windows 95 Handbook

1234567890 DOC 99876

ISBN 0-07-882091-X

Contents

13 FINISHING THE INTERFACE 499

14 TOOLS AND TECHNIQUES FOR TESTING AND DEBUGGING 541

15 AN INTRODUCTION TO GRAPHICS 563

19 RECURSION 753

20 A SURVEY OF DATABASE FEATURES 797

21 A CHECKBOOK MANAGEMENT PROGRAM 839

About the Author...

Gary Cornell is a computer programmer and professor of mathematics at the University of Connecticut. He has written or coauthored several acclaimed books on microcomputers, including the best-selling ***The Visual Basic 3 for Windows Handbook*** and ***Delphi Nuts & Bolts: For Experienced Programmers***. He can be reached at 75720.1524@compuserve.com or 75720,1524.

Acknowledgments

One of the best parts of writing a book is when the author gets to thank those who have helped him or her, for rarely (and certainly not in this case) is a book by one author truly produced alone. First and foremost, I have to thank the team at Osborne/McGraw-Hill. Their patience, dedication, help, cheerfulness—you name it—went way beyond the call of duty. To Wendy Rinaldi, Mark Karmendy, and Jirka Vcelak... Thanks! Jonathan Zuck and especially David Jezak combined for a very useful tech review. Next, I have to thank those people at Microsoft (whose names I unfortunately don't know) who created Visual Basic and have now made it even better in version 4. It's a very useful upgrade with a lot of potential for its users. Finally, thanks to all my friends who put up with my strange ways and my occasionally short temper for lo, so many months.

Introduction

When Visual Basic 1.0 was released, Bill Gates, Chairman and CEO of Microsoft, described it as "awesome." Steve Gibson in *Infoworld* said Visual Basic is a "stunning new miracle" and will "dramatically change the way people feel about and use [Microsoft] Windows." Stewart Alsop was quoted in the *New York Times* as saying Visual Basic is "the perfect programming environment for the 1990s."

So what is all the hype about? Exactly what is Visual Basic and what can it do for you? Well, Bill Gates describes Visual Basic as an "easy yet powerful tool for developing Windows applications in Basic." This may not seem like enough to justify all the hoopla until you realize that Microsoft Windows is used by millions of people, and that developing a Microsoft Windows application formerly required an expert C programmer supplied with about 20 pounds worth of documentation for the needed C compiler and the essential add-ons. As Charles Petzold (author of one of the standard books on Windows programming in C) put it in the *New York Times*: "For those of us who make our living explaining the complexities of Windows programming to programmers, Visual Basic poses a real threat to our livelihood."

Visual Basic 2.0 was faster, more powerful and even easier to use than Visual Basic 1.0. Visual Basic 3 added a simple way to control the most powerful databases available. Visual Basic 4 adds support for 32-bit development and begins the process of turning Visual Basic into a fully object oriented programming language. Moreover, unlike earlier versions of Visual Basic, the newest version allows you to seemlessly add in third part tools to make your development easier. So welcome to the latest and best version of Visual Basic, the programming tool of the 1990s!

About This Book

This tutorial is a comprehensive, hands-on guide to all the ins and outs of Visual Basic 4 programming—one that doesn't assume you've programmed before. (However, people familiar with earlier versions of Visual Basic or another structured programming language will, of course, have an easier time.) You'll start at the beginning and quickly move along the road to mastery. Soon you'll be writing sophisticated Windows programs that take full advantage of Visual Basic's exciting and powerful event-driven nature. Finish this book and you will be in a position to write commercial-quality Visual Basic programs!

I've tried hard to stress the new ways of thinking needed to master Visual Basic programming, so even experts in more traditional programming languages can benefit from this book. I've taken this approach because trying to force Visual Basic into the framework of older programming languages is ultimately self-defeating—you can't take advantage of its power if you continue to think within an older paradigm.

To make this book even more useful there are extensive discussions of important topics left out of most other introductory books. There's a whole chapter on objects, including a non-trivial example of building your own objects with Visual Basic. There's a whole chapter on recursion. There are methods of keeping file information secret and ways to add protection to programs you may want to distribute. It also includes an extensive discussion of sorting and searching techniques and lots of tips and tricks. My goal was to make this book a "one stop resource." I even have an appendix on how to use the Internet to get further information about Visual Basic.

Unlike many of the books out there, I not only want to introduce you to a topic but to take you the one step further that leads you to mastery.

The main body of this book ends with a professional quality checkbook management program. This was chosen because, in my opinion, nothing shows off the power of Visual Basic better than a program like this. This program took less than a week to design and implement. It is easy to imagine an entire finance program capable of generating millions of dollars in sales written in only a few weeks using Visual Basic. (This is not simply my imagining what could happen—substantial parts of Quicken are written in Visual Basic, and UnInstaller, the most successful Windows product to come along in quite a while, was written mostly in Visual Basic.)

Finally, since most users of Visual Basic have (or eventually will have) the higher-end versions ("Visual Basic Professional Edition" or "Visual Basic Enterprise Edition," I cover many of the special features of these higher-end products into the text itself rather than relegating them to an appendix.

How This Book Is Organized

This book can be used in a variety of ways depending on your background and needs. People familiar with structured programming techniques can skim the complete discussions of the programming constructs such as loops and Sub and Function procedures in Visual Basic. These appear in Chapters 5 through 11. Beginners will want to work through this material more carefully.

Here are short descriptions of the chapters:

Chapters 1 and 2 introduce you to Visual Basic and help you become familiar with the Visual Basic environment.

Chapters 3 and 4 start you right off with the notion of a customizable window (called a *form*) that is the heart of every Microsoft Windows (and thus, Visual Basic) application. You'll see how to add the Basic controls—such as command buttons, text boxes, and labels—to your forms.

Chapters 5 through 11 discuss the core programming techniques needed to release Visual Basic's powers. You'll see how to take full advantage of Visual Basic 4's various data types and control structures, as well as its many built-in functions. You also learn how to add your own functions to Visual Basic 4. You'll see how to use Visual Basic's implementation of part of the object oriented programming paradigm—including how to build your own objects with Visual Basic. You'll see how to sort and search through data, use the grid control, and use modular programming techniques to make your programs more flexible, powerful, and easier to debug.

Chapters 12 and 13 show you how to finish building the user interface. They take you through most of the rest of the controls you can add to your forms. You'll see how to add list boxes, radio (option) buttons, check boxes, scroll bars, and all the other controls that Microsoft Windows users expect in their Windows applications—and that make Windows applications so much easier to use than their counterparts running under DOS. We cover both the standard controls and those found in the Professional and Enterprise editions (including the Windows 95 specific controls.) Moreover, we indicate workarounds if you want to use a Professional edition feature and only have the standard edition whenever possible.)

Chapter 14 shows you the powerful debugging tools in Visual Basic 4. You'll learn how to isolate bugs (programming errors) and then eradicate them.

Chapter 15 introduces you to the world of graphics. Since Microsoft Windows is a graphically based environment, the powers of Visual Basic in this arena are pretty spectacular.

Chapter 16 shows you how to analyze the way a user is manipulating his or her mouse.

Chapter 17 shows you how to handle files in Visual Basic, including sophisticated methods for encrypting (that is, keeping the contents of files safe from casual probes). We especially emphasize the changes in file handling techniques between Visual Basic 4 and earlier versions of Visual Basic.

Chapter 18 introduces you to the world of dynamic data exchange (DDE), object linking and embedding (OLE), and OLE automation. DDE lets you automate the transfer of information between Windows applications—and you'll be able to have Visual Basic coordinate the transfers! OLE lets you embed other Windows applications within a Visual Basic application so users can take full advantage of many of their other Windows applications. OLE automation lets you control another Windows application using *its* native language.

Chapter 19 is an extensive treatment of *recursion*. Recursion is one of the most powerful programming tools available, and it's too often slighted in introductory books. In addition to powerful methods for sorting data, this chapter gives you a short introduction to recursive graphics, or *fractals*. Fractals are one of the most powerful tools in graphics—for example, they were used in the Genesis sequence in *Star Trek II: The Wrath of Khan*.

Chapter 20 is an introduction to the Data manager and other data access features added to Visual Basic 4. You'll see how to control the most powerful PC databases with only a few lines of code using the new data control.

Chapter 21 is the checkbook manager. It's a long program, but by this stage nothing in it will be foreign to you.

Appendix A shows you how to use the new Setup Wizard that makes distributing your files a breeze.

Appendix B surveys what resources are available for Visual Basic on the Internet.

Appendix C contains, courtesy of Microsoft, answers to what they regard as the most frequently asked questions about Visual Basic. We added this appendix in the hope that it will save you hours of waiting on the line for Microsoft's support services to help you.

Appendix D opens up to you the exciting world of third-party tools and resources.

Conventions Used in This Book

Keys are set in small capital letters in the text. For example, keys such as CTRL and HOME appear as shown here. Arrow and other direction keys are spelled out and also appear in small capital letters. For example, if you need to press the right arrow key, you'll see, "Press RIGHT ARROW."

When you need to use a combination of keys to activate a menu item, the first two keys will be separated by a plus sign and the entire key combination will appear in small capital letters. For example, "Press CTRL A+B" indicates that you should hold down the key marked "Ctrl" on your keyboard while holding down the "A" and the "B." On the other hand, ALT F, P means press the "Alt" key, then the "F" key, and then the "P" key—you don't have to hold down the "Alt" key.

DOS commands, filenames, and file extensions appear in full capital letters: COMMAND.COM, .TXT, and so on. Microsoft Windows 95 is referred to just as Windows most of the time. Earlier versions of Windows are called Windows 3.X when they need to be referred to. Keywords in Visual Basic appear with the first letter of each word capitalized: for example, Print, DeBug, FontSize, and so on.

The syntax for a command in Visual Basic is set in ordinary type except that items the programmer can change appear in italics. For example, the Name command used to rename a file appears as

Name *OldFileName* As *NewFileName*

Also, programs are set in a monospaced font, as shown here:

```
Private Sub Form_Click()
  Print "Hello world!"
End Sub
```

and lines of code that should appear on one line when you program, but which for typographic reasons need to be on more than line in this book, will be outdented or an underscore will be used. (Visual Basic 4 added a line continuation charcter—the underscore—which you can use whenever you are not inside quotes.) Here are some examples:

```
    Print "This line is much too long to fit on one line
but is outdented to indicate it should be entered on one line"

M$ = "This line is also too long but it has an " + _
"underscore so it will be regarded as one line by VB"
```

Finally, menu choices are indicated by writing the menu name, followed by a bar (|), followed by the menu item; for example, "choose File|Open" means open the File menu and then choose the Open option.

Disk Order Form

There are a couple hundred pages of code in this book. You may not want to enter it all. The companion disk contains all the code in *The Visual Basic 4 for Windows Handbook* with more than two lines. It also includes the form files for the figures and the more interesting projects. The disk also includes the commented source code for the version of the checkbook manager given in the text, and also one that uses the more object oriented features of Visual Basic. In addition, the disk contains around fifty bonus procedures with full source code. Here's a sample of what the bonus procedures include:

Business procedures for...

- Calculating internal rate of return
- Analyzing a loan or annuity
- Determining straight-line, sum-of-digits, or double-declining balance depreciations

Procedures for working with arrays...

- Sorting, insertion, and searching

Mathematics procedures for...

- Numerical integration
- Working with vectors
- Matrix algebra

To order your disk, send your name, address, along with a check or money order for **$25.00** for the first copy (**$3.00** for each additional copy—if you have purchased a companion disk to an earlier version of this book the price is only **$10.00**.) to

Books on Science
128 Moulton Road
Storrs, CT 06268

--------------------------------(cut here)---------------------------------

Please rush one companion disk for *The Visual Basic 4 for Windows Handbook* to

Name ____

Address ____

City ____________________ State ___________ ZIP _________

First copy @ $25.00 _________

Additional copies at $3.00 each _________

Upgrade at $10.00 _________

Total enclosed is: _________

(Orders from outside the United States should use a check issued on a bank with an American branch please. Connecticut residents please add the appropriate sales tax.)

We offer a 30-day, money-back guarantee.

This is solely the offering of the author. Osborne/McGraw-Hill takes no responsibility for the fulfillment of this offer.

Chapter One

Getting Started

THIS chapter gives you an overview of Microsoft's Visual Basic version 4. (The full name is rather a mouthful: I will usually just call it Visual Basic from now on. If it is necessary to distinguish the current version of Visual Basic from earlier ones, the earlier version numbers will be given.) Note, however, that since I am assuming you are not a naive user of Windows 95, this chapter (and book) spends only a short time on how to install Visual Basic, or start it, and no time at all on how to manipulate windows within the Windows environment. However, I am *not* assuming any expertise in Visual Basic or even any programming language.

Why Windows and Why Visual Basic?

Graphical user interfaces, or *GUIs* (pronounced "gooies"), have revolutionized the microcomputer industry. They demonstrate that the proverb "a picture is worth a thousand words" hasn't lost its truth to most computer users. Instead of the cryptic C:> prompt that DOS users have long seen (and some have long feared), you are presented with a desktop filled with icons and with programs that use mice and menus.

Perhaps even more important in the long run than the *look* of Microsoft Windows applications is the *feel* that applications developed for it have. Windows applications generally have a consistent user interface. This means that users can spend more time mastering the application and less time worrying about which keystrokes do what within menus and dialog boxes. (Of course, Windows 95 applications look a bit different than Windows 3.1 applications did: the consistency is *within* versions of Windows, not *between* versions of Windows.)

While programmers have long had mixed feelings about GUIs, beginning users seem to like them, and so Windows programs are expected to be based on the GUI model (and to have the right look and feel). Therefore, if you need to develop programs for any version of Windows, you'll want a tool to develop GUI-based applications efficiently.

For a long time there were few such tools for developing Windows applications. Before Visual Basic was introduced in 1991, developing Windows applications was much harder than developing DOS applications. Programmers had too much to worry about, such as what the mouse was doing, where the user was inside a menu, and whether he or she was clicking or double-clicking at a given place. Developing a Windows application required expert C programmers and hundreds of lines of code for the simplest task. Even the experts had trouble. (The Microsoft Windows Software Development Kit that was required in addition to a C compiler weighed in at nine and one-half pounds.)

This is why when Visual Basic 1.0 was released, Bill Gates, chairman and CEO of Microsoft, described it as "awesome." Steve Gibson in *Infoworld* said Visual Basic is a "stunning new miracle" and will "dramatically change the way people feel about and use Microsoft Windows." Stewart Alsop was quoted in the *New York Times* as saying Visual Basic is "the perfect programming environment for the 1990s." As Charles Petzold, author of one of the standard books on Windows programming in C, put it in the *New York Times:* "For those of us who make our living explaining the complexities of Windows programming to programmers, Visual Basic poses a real threat to our livelihood." The latest version of Visual Basic continues in this tradition: sophisticated Windows 95, Windows NT, and even Windows 3.X (which is how we will indicate Windows 3.1, Windows 3.11, and Windows for Workgroups) applications can now be developed in a fraction of the time previously needed. Programming errors (bugs) don't happen as often as they did, and if they do, they're a lot easier to detect and fix. Simply put: *with Visual Basic, programming for Windows has become not only more efficient but it has become fun*—well, most of the time.

In particular, Visual Basic lets you add menus, text boxes, command buttons, option buttons (for making exclusive choices), check boxes (for nonexclusive choices), list boxes, scroll bars, and file and directory boxes to blank windows. You can use grids to handle tabular data, communicate with other Windows applications, and access databases. You can have multiple windows on a screen. These windows have full access to the clipboard and to the information in most other Windows applications running at the same time. You can use Visual Basic to communicate with other applications running under Windows easily, using the most modern version of Microsoft's OLE technology (see Chapter 18).

What You Need to Run Visual Basic

Visual Basic is a sophisticated program. The standard edition requires Windows 95 or version 3.51 (or later) of Windows NT. (It is theoretically possible but rather unusual to use the 16-bit version included in the Professional or

Enterprise edition under Windows 3.1.) So, at the very least, you'll need a machine powerful enough for these 32-bit operating systems. Realistically, you'll want

- A fast 486 or a Pentium and at least 8MB of RAM—16 would be much better.
- A hard disk with at least 60MB free. (If you want to install both the 16- and 32-bit versions of Visual Basic, the amount of space needed increases to more than 70MB.)

What Does the Newest Version of Visual Basic 4 Offer You?

These are some of Visual Basic 4's advantages over the first three versions:

- You can generate 32-bit applications for both Windows 95 and Windows NT with no extra work. (If you have the Professional or Enterprise edition you can also build 16-bit "legacy" Windows 3.X applications from essentially the same code.)
- With Visual Basic you can take advantage of Microsoft's OLE technology—including the ability to build OLE servers (see Chapter 18).
- You can build programs using some of the techniques of object-oriented programming (see Chapter 11).

note: *If you have some familiarity with object-oriented programming (OOP), you should be aware that Visual Basic controls are not quite objects in the sense of OOP, nor does Visual Basic offer a full object-oriented development platform. Please see Chapter 11 for more on object-oriented programming and how Visual Basic's controls fit in with the tenets of OOP.*

- You can extend the Visual Basic programming environment. You can create or use third-party tools that "add in" seamlessly to the Visual Basic environment. (For example, if you have the Enterprise edition, you can have Microsoft's Source Safe product built in. Source Safe makes it easier to use Visual Basic in large group projects by implementing version control.)
- You can use conditional compilation to do multiplatform development more easily (see Chapter 7).

You also don't have to pay too much of a performance penalty: applications developed under Visual Basic run quick enough for most situations (although generally speaking, slightly slower than they did in Visual Basic 3 unless you have lots of RAM). This is not to say that you can eliminate C or C++ programming for Windows; extending Visual Basic still requires tools that, at present, are usually done in these languages.

note: *Although the features of the Enterprise edition that are not part of the Professional edition are not covered in this book, it makes developing both client/server and group projects much easier as well.*

Setting Up Visual Basic

Visual Basic comes in both a disk version and a CD version. (As with all programs, if you have the disk version, the first thing you should do is make backup copies of the original distribution disks.) Send in the registration card. It's true that you'll get a certain amount of junk mail as a result, but it also will be easier to get support and notices of upgrades from Microsoft.

Running the Setup Program

The disks for Visual Basic contain an automated Setup program to install the various versions of Visual Basic. Windows 95 or NT 3.51 or later must be running for the 32-bit Setup program to work. You can run the 16-bit Setup program under Windows 3.X. You can run the Setup program as many times as you want, which means you are not tied into the options you choose the first time. (It's a good idea for first-time users to use the default options.) The first time you set up Visual Basic, the Setup program asks for your name or the name of the company that bought the copy of Visual Basic. It keeps track of this information and uses it to remind you to whom the program is licensed—every time you start Visual Basic.

I won't bother going into the details of using an automated setup program. I assume, by now, that you have installed lots of programs under the Windows environment. Just look for the SETUP.EXE program on the CD or on DISK1 and then start it. Follow the directions, and soon you'll have your copy of Visual Basic up and running. (You will have to install the 16-bit version separately from the 32-bit version if you have the Professional or Enterprise edition.)

note: *If you install Visual Basic 4, in the same directory as older versions of Visual Basic you will overwrite the older version. Since Visual Basic 4 can run programs written using Visual Basic 1.0 and 2.0 with at most minor modifications, this is not usually a problem. If you need to save an earlier version of Visual Basic, install Visual Basic 4 in a different directory.*

After you've completed the installation procedure, Visual Basic is installed in its own program group. You can use the Windows 95 Explorer or standard Windows 95 drag and drop techniques to move Visual Basic to another program group or onto the desktop. Consult the documentation that came with your Windows package or a book such as *Windows 95 Made Easy* by Tom Sheldon (Berkeley, CA: Osborne/McGraw-Hill, 1995) to see how to do this.

If there are any corrections or additions to the documentation, you'll find them in a file called README.TXT. If this file is on the distribution disks, the Setup program automatically copies this file and places an icon to represent it on the Windows desktop in the Visual Basic program group. If you double-click on this icon, Microsoft Windows loads the file into the WordPad. This makes it easy to look through the information.

note: *You don't have to explicitly set up a printer for Visual Basic. Visual Basic uses whatever printer information Windows is currently using.*

Starting Visual Basic

The easiest way to run Visual Basic under Windows 95 is to use the Program option on the Start button. (The Setup program automatically adds it to the Start button.) See Figure 1-1 for an example of what you might see. You would go to the appropriate version of Visual Basic and then a submenu would pop up. You would then choose the Visual Basic item on this submenu. There are, of course, lots of other ways to run Visual Basic: You can also start Visual Basic from the Microsoft Windows desktop by moving to its directory and then double-clicking on the Visual Basic icon. You can start Visual Basic by opening the Run dialog box and entering the path to get to Visual Basic, as shown in Figure 1-2. (C:\VB is where I put my version of Visual Basic. The default installation uses a Windows 95 "long directory name" of Program Files, which becomes PROGRA~1 in a DOS window.) You can add it to the Start menu by dragging; you can create a shortcut to it. (Under Windows 95 the list really does go on and on.)

Figure 1-1
Typical Start button list under Windows 95

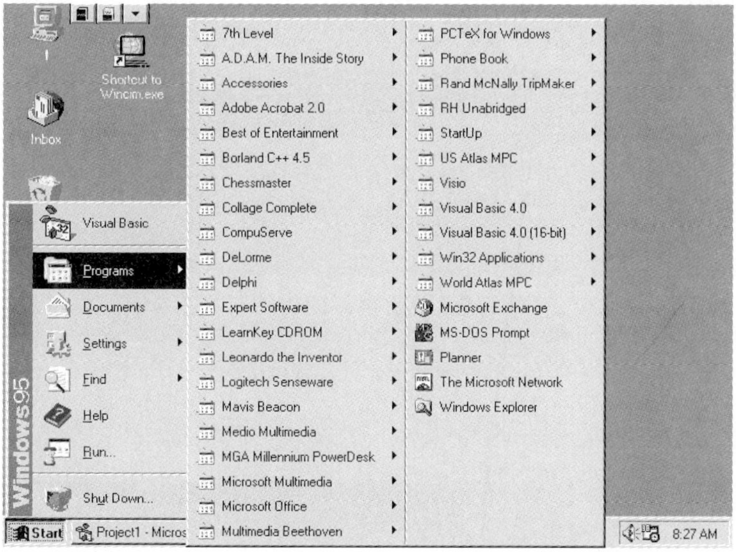

When you start Visual Basic, you see a copyright screen telling you to whom the copy of Visual Basic is licensed. After that you see a screen like the one in Figure 1-3. (The next chapter explains all the parts of this screen in some detail.)

Figure 1-2
Run dialog box for Visual Basic

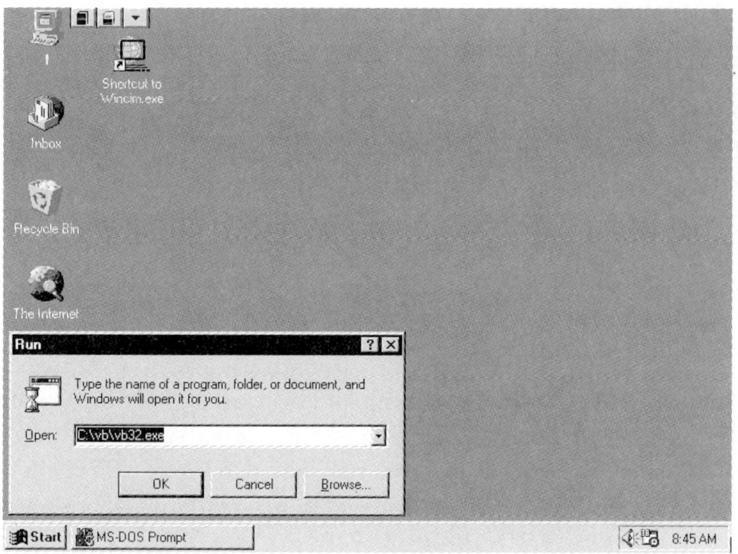

Figure 1-3
Initial Visual Basic screen

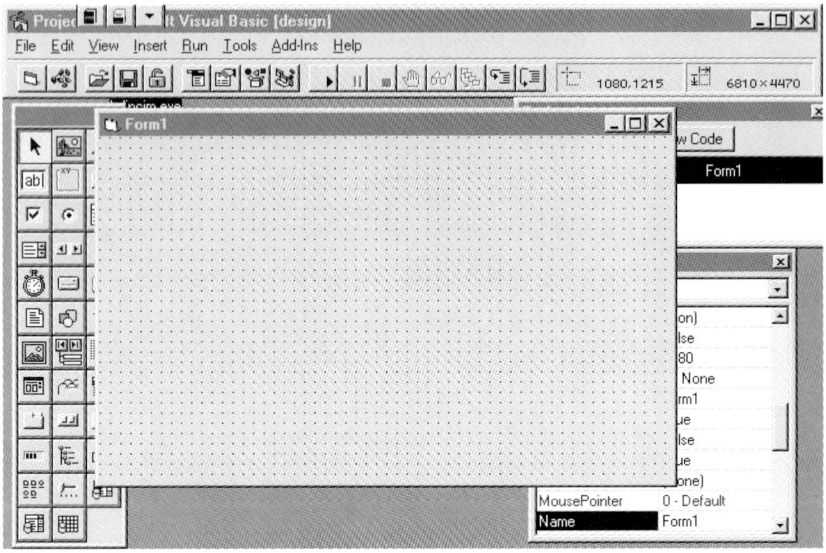

Working with Visual Basic

In this section you'll see a step-by-step process that builds the simplest Windows application: a sizable Window with maximize, minimize, and exit buttons. Although it is a very simple application that really doesn't do anything, following the steps outlined here is a useful way of introducing yourself to Visual Basic.

When you start Visual Basic, your initial screen (if you are using Windows 95) will look something like the one in Figure 1-3. (There will be some minor changes under Windows NT, and depending on your version of Visual Basic your screen may look slightly different. As I said earlier, you'll see a lot more about the Visual Basic environment in the next chapter, but for now it is probably easier if you just follow the steps without worrying too much about the environment.)

Note the blank window in the center of the screen in Figure 1-3, which has a grid of dots. This is the *form* that you will customize. You use the grid to align controls, such as command buttons and list boxes, on the screen (you'll learn more about this in Chapters 3 and 4). When you run your project (or compile it so that it can be run independently of the Visual Basic development environment), forms become the windows that users see.

At the top of the blank form is the title bar with its caption. (*Caption* is the Visual Basic term for what appears in the title bar of the form.) Currently, this form is titled Form1, which is the default caption that Visual Basic gives to a form when you start working on a new project.

To the left of the Form1 window in Figure 1-3 is the toolbox. The toolbox is where you find the controls you will place on the form. *Controls* is the terminology used in Visual Basic for the objects you place on the windows you are designing. (You'll see how to use the toolbox and manipulate controls in Chapter 4. The controls you have available depends on which version of Visual Basic you have.) Partially obscured is the Properties window, which you use to customize the form and the various controls you'll place on it. (You'll see how to use the Properties window in Chapters 3 and 4.)

For now, concentrate on the central window named Form1. In many Visual Basic applications, the size and location of the form at the time you finish the design (usually called *design time*) are the size and shape that the user sees at *run time*. This is not to say that Visual Basic doesn't let you change the size and location of forms as a project runs (see Chapter 4); in fact, an essential feature of Visual Basic is its ability to make dynamic changes in response to user events.

One way to resize a form that is common to all Microsoft Windows applications is to first click inside the form so that it is active. (You can always tell when a window is active because the title bar is highlighted.) Then move the mouse to any part of the border of the form. The mouse pointer changes to a double-headed arrow when you're at a hot spot. At this point, you can drag the form to change its size or shape. Similarly, to move the form, you can click anywhere in the title bar and then drag the form to a new location. The size and location of a form are examples of what Visual Basic calls *properties* of the form.

To start developing the first sample application, simply do the following:

1. Change the form's default size, shape, and location by manipulating it at some of the hot spots or by dragging it around the screen.

2. Run the project by pressing F5 or choosing Start from the Run menu (ALT R, S, or the Run tool).

Notice that what you see is an ordinary-looking Windows window with the same size, shape, and location that you left the form in at design time. Next, notice that when you run this new project, the window that pops up has standard Windows features such as resizable borders, a control box (in the upper-left corner), and maximum, minimum, and exit buttons (in the upper-right corner)

under Windows 95. This shows one of the most important features of Visual Basic: your forms become windows that already behave as they should under the version of Windows you are using, without your having to do anything!

Return to the development environment by pressing ALT+F4, double-clicking on the control box, or clicking on the exit button. Notice that your application automatically responds to these "standard" ways of closing a Windows application. This illustrates the important point that, in many cases, Visual Basic applications behave as Windows users expect, without requiring any special intervention by the programmer (or the user).

Running an Existing Visual Basic Project

Let's start on the road to seeing how powerful Visual Basic is by running one of the sample programs supplied with it. (Visual Basic comes with hundreds of sample programs. As you become more familiar with Visual Basic, you'll find these sample programs a good source of examples and ideas.) The one I want to show you how to run is a simple four function calculator. This project uses only 75 or so lines of code, yet it gives a fully functional, visual-oriented four function calculator.

Here is the general procedure to load an existing project. (Remember, *project* is what Visual Basic calls the files that make up an application under construction—it is a combination of a visual component and code.)

1. Go to the File menu by pressing ALT+F or clicking on the File item on the menu.
2. Choose Open Project.

This opens a dialog box that looks like this:

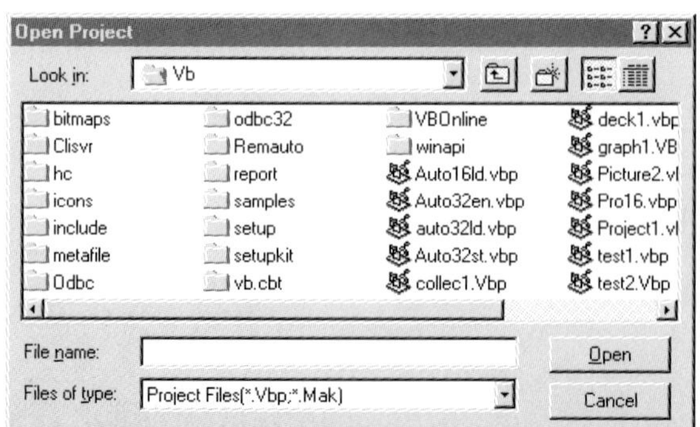

The project you want is in a subdirectory of the SAMPLES subdirectory (as are all the samples supplied with Visual Basic). So move to the SAMPLES subdirectory, and then click on the directory marked CALC. Double-click on the file named CALC.VBP, as shown here:

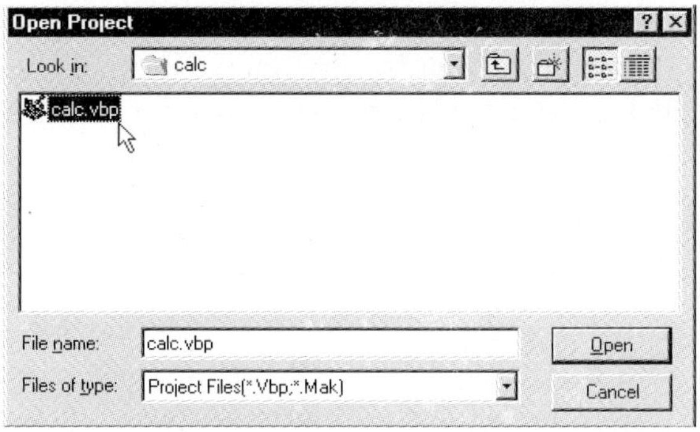

After a short delay, the calculator project loads into Visual Basic. Press F5 to run the project. When you are through playing with the calculator, click on the exit button or press ALT+F4 to go back to the development environment.

The Online Tutorial

At this point, I suggest at least glancing at parts of the online tutorial. Doing this will complement and reinforce the information presented in the next few chapters. To use the online tutorial:

1. Click the Help item on the main menu bar.
2. Click the item marked Learning Microsoft Visual Basic.

(The keyboard shortcut for starting the tutorial is to press ALT+H first. This opens the Help menu. Now press L to select the tutorial.) The following illustration shows the main menu bar with the Help menu pulled down:

Assuming you've installed the tutorial, selecting these items will usually take you directly to it. The main screen for the tutorial is shown in Figure 1-4.

The tutorial is very easy to use. Before you begin, you might want to click the Instructions button. This gives you a screen like the one in Figure 1-5. When you are done with this screen, press ESC to close this pop-up window. The tutorial is a slightly modified version of an ordinary Windows 95 help file, and so you won't have much trouble navigating it. You don't have to cover the lessons in any order, and you can return to them as often as you want. (Click on the Contents button to go back to the main screen.) Once installed, the tutorial is always available to you.

Each lesson covers various topics that you may or may not be interested in; you can skip around. You double-click on a heading or topic to open it, and to move from screen to screen, click the button marked >> in the title bar. If you want to go back to a previous screen, click the button marked <<. To go back to the main screen and choose a different lesson, click the Contents button.

Figure 1-4 Main screen for the Learning Visual Basic tutorial

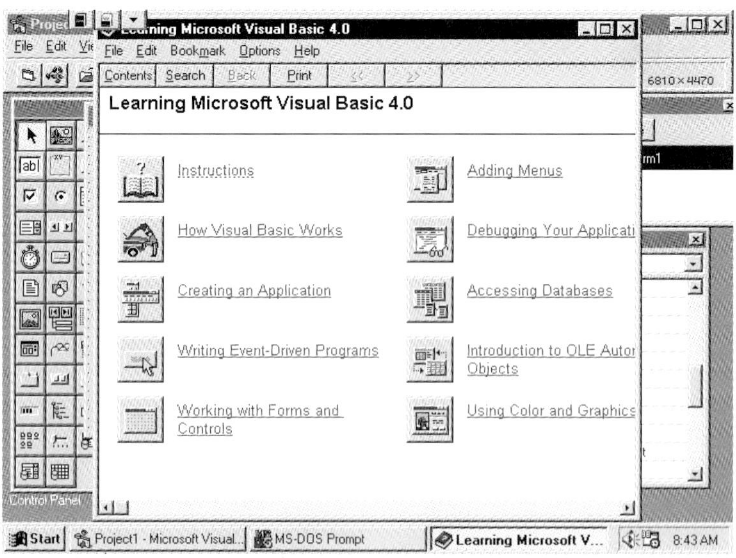

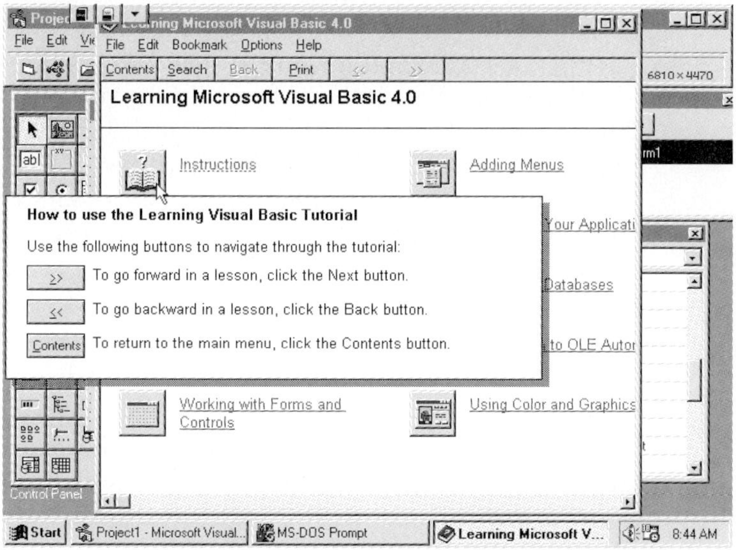

Figure 1-5 Learning tutorial instruction screen

Overview of How You Develop a Visual Basic Application

I want to end this chapter by giving you an overview of how you develop a Visual Basic application. Some of these steps may seem unclear now, but very shortly they will (all) become second nature.

The *first* step in developing a Visual Basic application is to plan what the user will see—in other words, to design the screens. What menus do you want? How large a window should the application use? How many windows should there be? Should the user be able to resize the windows? Where will you place the *command buttons* that the user will click on to activate the applications? Will the applications have places *(text boxes)* in which to enter text?

As mentioned earlier, in Visual Basic, the objects you place on the windows you are designing are called controls. The number of controls you have at your disposal depends on the version of Visual Basic you are using. The standard edition has more than 20, the Professional and Enterprise editions, more than 50. Moreover, since Visual Basic has inspired third-party vendors to create a large number of controls for specialized tasks, you can almost always find a custom control for a specialized task. (See Appendix D.) To create your own controls, you will most often use C or C++.

What makes Visual Basic different from almost any other programming tool is how easy it is to design the screen. You literally draw the user interface, much like using a paint program. In addition, when you're done drawing the interface, the command buttons, text boxes, and other controls that you have placed in a blank window will automatically recognize user actions, such as mouse movements and button clicks. Visual Basic also comes with a menu design feature that makes creating both ordinary and pop-up menus a snap.

Only after you design the interface does anything like traditional programming occur. This leads to the *second* step in building a Visual Basic application: writing the code to activate the visual interface you built in step one. The point is, objects in Visual Basic *will* recognize events like mouse clicks; how the objects respond to them depends on the code you write. You will almost always need to write code in order to make controls respond to events. This makes Visual Basic programming fundamentally different from conventional programming.

Programs in conventional programming languages run from the top, down. For older programming languages, execution starts from the first line and moves with the flow of the program to different parts as needed. A Visual Basic program works completely differently. The core of a Visual Basic program is a set of independent pieces of code that are *activated* by, and so respond to, only the events they have been told to recognize. This is a fundamental shift. Now instead of designing a program to do what the programmer thinks should happen, the user is in control.

Much of the programming code in Visual Basic that tells your program how to respond to events such as mouse clicks occurs in what Visual Basic calls *event procedures*. Essentially, everything executable in a Visual Basic program is either in an event procedure or is used by an event procedure to help the procedure carry out its job. The *third* and *fourth* steps are—of course, and unfortunately—finding the errors in the code (*debugging* in the jargon) and then fixing them.

Here's a summary of the steps you take to design a Visual Basic application:

1. Customize the windows that the user sees.
2. Decide what events the controls on the window should recognize.
3. Write the event procedures for those events (and the subsidiary procedures that make those event procedures work).

Here is what happens when the application is running:

1. Visual Basic monitors the windows and the controls in each window for *all* the events that each control can recognize (mouse movements, clicks, keystrokes, and so on).
2. When Visual Basic detects an event, if there isn't a built-in response to the event, Visual Basic examines the application to see if you've written an event procedure for that event.
3. If you have written an event procedure, Visual Basic executes the code that makes up that event procedure and goes back to step 1.
4. If you have not written an event procedure, Visual Basic waits for the next event and goes back to step 1.

These steps cycle continuously until the application ends. Usually, an event must happen before Visual Basic will do anything. Thus event-driven programs are more *reactive* than *active*—and that makes them more user-friendly.

Let me end this chapter by pointing out that since Visual Basic's programming language is based on a modern structured version of BASIC, it's easy to build large programs by using modern modular and (some) object-oriented techniques. (It is not at all like the condemned BASICs of long ago.) Visual Basic also provides sophisticated error handling for the all-too-common task of preventing users from bombing an application. The Visual Basic compiler is fast, and even lets you do background compilation or compile only the code that is needed to start the application. This means that any changes needed to correct the routine programming and typographical errors that are so common when you begin building an application are a snap. In addition, it has an extensive online help system for quick reference while you're developing an application.

Chapter Two

The Visual Basic Environment

This chapter shows you how to use the menus and windows that make up the Visual Basic environment. Given the power of Visual Basic, with its richness of tools and detailed menus, it's easy to be overwhelmed at first. To help reduce any confusion, this chapter gives you a detailed description of what the environment has to offer. When you're finished, you'll be comfortable with the online help, the editing tools, and the file-handling utilities built into Visual Basic. On the other hand, there's a lot of information in this chapter; you might want to skim it and only return to it as needed.

It is worth noting that if you are not completely comfortable with the look and feel of Microsoft Windows applications, studying its environment and this chapter will help. After all, Visual Basic is itself a well-designed Windows application, and the way its menus and windows respond is typical of Windows programs. (For example, Visual Basic pops up context-sensitive menus when you click the right mouse button.)

Remember, though, that until you are familiar with how a Windows application should look and feel, you can't take full advantage of the power of Visual Basic. Of course, if you are developing an application with Visual Basic for your personal use, conforming to the Windows standard is not essential. However, if others will be using your application, following the Windows standard essentially eliminates the learning curve for using your application. For example, Windows 95 users expect a single click with a mouse to select an item and a double-click to activate it in a dialog box. They want exit buttons on the far right of the title bar, and so on.

The default settings built into the design process of a Visual Basic application make it easy to conform to the Windows guidelines. For example, the windows you build default to having the usual buttons and they are located where you would expect to find them. In particular, if you are using the 32-bit version of Visual Basic under Windows 95, then, for example, you will see an exit button on the far right of the title bar. Windows can also be moved and resized as users expect. Similarly, menus respond the way users expect. Of course, Visual Basic doesn't lock you into these defaults, but it is not a good idea to make changes casually.

note: *I used the Professional edition of Visual Basic for the screen shots. If you have the standard or Enterprise edition, your screens will be slightly different and you may have a few less (for the standard) or a few more (for the Enterprise) items on the menus. The main menu bar remains the same in all three editions.*

An Overview of the Main Screen

As mentioned in Chapter 1, when you start Visual Basic, you are presented with a copyright screen indicating to whom the copy of the program is licensed. After a short delay, you are automatically dropped into the Visual Basic environment, as shown in Figure 2-1.

Figure 2-1 The initial Visual Basic environment

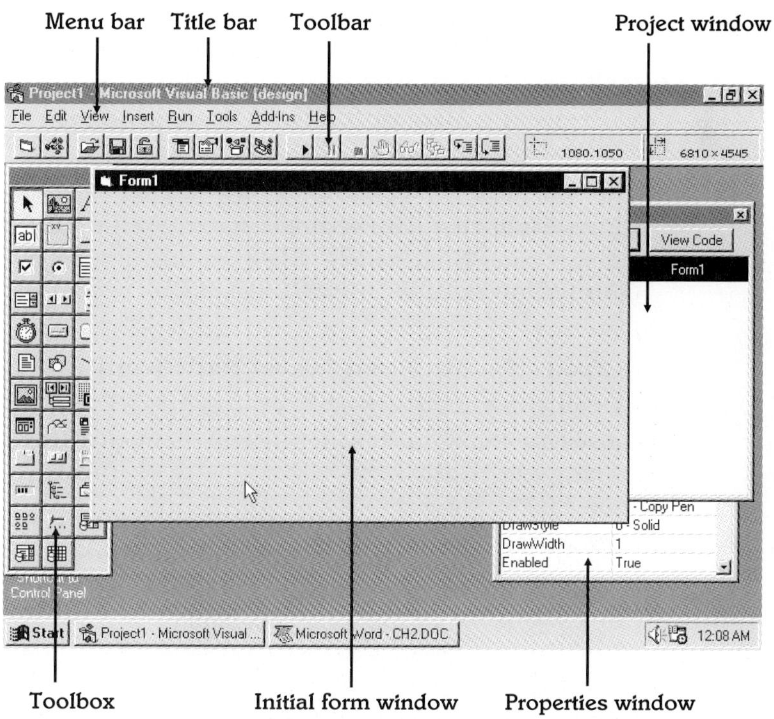

note: *Visual Basic remembers your last screen arrangement when you exit it and reuses it. For this reason, your screen may look different from Figure 2-1.*

The screen is certainly crowded. You can see the six parts in the standard Visual Basic environment, although two windows are partially obscured. The Properties window is used when customizing a form or control and is discussed at length in Chapters 3 and 4. Another window, called the Debug window, shows up when you are running or debugging a program; see Chapter 14.

Following is a description of the other parts of the main screen. Subsequent sections of this chapter cover the most commonly used parts of the menus.

Title Bar

The *title bar* is the horizontal bar located at the top of the screen; it gives the name of the application and is common to all Windows applications. Everything below the title and menu bars in a Windows application is called the *client area*. Your application is completely responsible for the look, feel, and response of the objects you place in this area.

In Visual Basic, the title bar starts out by displaying

Project1 - Microsoft Visual Basic [design]

This is typical of Windows applications: in sophisticated programs (such as Visual Basic) that have multiple states, the title bar changes to indicate the different states. For example, when you are running a program within the Visual Basic environment, the title bar switches to

Project1 - Microsoft Visual Basic [run]

and when you are debugging (having temporarily stopped the program) the title bar switches to

Project1 - Microsoft Visual Basic [break]

(See Chapter 14 for more on debugging.)

Menu Bar

Selecting items from the pull-down menus listed on a *menu bar* is one of the most common ways to unleash the power of a Windows application. The same is true of Visual Basic itself. For Visual Basic, the menu bar gives you the tools needed to develop, test, and save your application. The File menu contains the commands for working with the files that go into your application. The Edit menu contains many of the editing tools that will help you write the code that activates the interface you design for your application, including the search-and-replace editing tools. The View menu gives you fast access to the different parts of your program and to the different parts of the Visual Basic environment. The Insert menu lets you insert external files or new Visual Basic objects into your projects. The Run menu lets you test your application while developing it. The Run menu also gives you access to the tools used to correct (debug) problems, or *bugs,* in computer jargon (Chapter 14 offers a detailed discussion of debugging techniques). The Tools menu gives you access to more debugging tools and is also how you control Visual Basic's environment. The Add-Ins menu gives you access to tools that can be added to the Visual Basic environment. (How many add-ins you start out with depends on your version of Visual Basic. All versions, for example, have an add-in for working with databases (see Chapter 20).) Finally, you use the Help menu to gain access to the detailed online help system provided with the program or to run the very basic tutorial included.

tip: *Many companies provide tools that you can add to Visual Basic to make your work more productive. See Appendix D for more information on third-party tools.*

Notice that all the menus have one letter underlined. Pressing ALT and the underlined letter opens that menu. Another way to access the menu is to press ALT alone to activate the menu bar. When you do, notice that the File menu item is highlighted. You can now use the arrow keys to move around the menu bar. Press ENTER or DOWN ARROW to open the menu. Once a menu is open, all you need is a single *accelerator key* (also called an *access* or *hot key*) to select a menu option. For example, if the Help menu is open, pressing L brings up the tutorial. Accelerator keys are not case-sensitive.

Some menu items have *shortcut keys*. A shortcut key is usually a combination of keys the user can press to perform an action without opening a menu. For example, as is common in Windows applications, pressing ALT+F4 exits Visual Basic without going through the File menu.

note: *Remember, we will describe choosing an item from a menu by using the pipe symbol (|). For example, "choose File | Open Project" means pull down the File menu and then choose the Open Project item.*

Toolbar

The *toolbar* shown in Figure 2-2 is immediately below the menu bar and was added in Visual Basic 2.0. As is becoming more common in Windows applications, Microsoft added toolbar icons to let you activate common tasks without using the menus. Since every item on the toolbar has a keyboard equivalent, which one you choose is a matter of taste. If you can't remember what a tool on the toolbar means, Microsoft has added "ToolTips" that give you a textual description of what the tool does. These tips pop up when you rest the cursor on a tool. They are on by default. If you don't see them, see the section on the Options tabbed dialog box that follows for how to turn them on. (Makes one wonder doesn't it: is the next trend in icons to replace pictures by buttons with words on them?)

Reading from left to right on Figure 2-2, Table 2-1 lists the tools and what they do.

Toolbox

Located at the left of the screen in Figure 2-1, just below the toolbar, the *toolbox* contains the tools for developing your application. How many tools are available

Figure 2-2 The toolbar

Icon	Name	Purpose
	New Form	Lets you add a new form (customizable window) to a project. Same as Insert | Form. See Chapter 5 for information on using multiple forms in your applications.
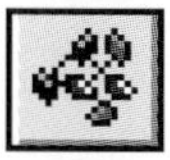	New Module	Lets you open a new module for specialized programming code. You'll see how to use these modules in Chapter 9. This is the same as Insert | Module.
	Open Project	Lets you save an existing Visual Basic project. Same as File | Open.
	Save Project	Lets you save your Visual Basic project. Same As File | Save Project.
	Lock Controls	Locks controls in place to prevent accidental movement. Same as choosing Edit | Lock Controls.
	Menu Editor	Used to design menus (see Chapter 12). Same as Tools | Menu Editor or the shortcut key combination of CTRL+E.
	Properties	Modifies the default size, shape, and color of your Visual Basic objects (see Chapters 3 and 4). This is the same as pressing the F4 shortcut key or choosing View | Properties.
	Object Browser	Opens the Object Browser dialog box. Same as View | Object Browser. The shortcut is F2. The Object Browser is discussed in Chapters 5 and 11.)
	Project	Switches focus to the Project window. This is the same as using the CTRL+R shortcut or choosing View | Project.
	Start	Lets you run the application. After you design an application, this is the same as choosing Run | Start.
	Break	Pauses a running program. (Programs can usually be continued by using the Run tool or SHIFT+F5.) Same as the Run | Break or the CTRL+BREAK combination. (Mostly used as a debugging tool—see Chapter 14.)
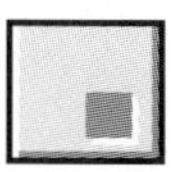	End	Ends the running program. Same as choosing Run | End.
	Toggle Breakpoint	A debugging tool; see Chapter 14. This places a temporary stop sign at a specific place in your program. Available from the Run menu; the shortcut is F9.

Table 2-1
Toolbar Icons

Icon	Name	Purpose
	Instant Watch	Another debugging tool discussed in Chapter 14. This lets you take a snapshot of what is happening to various parts of your program. Also available from the Tools menu; the shortcut is SHIFT+F9.
	Calls	Shows a list of current procedure calls. A debugging tool; see Chapter 14.
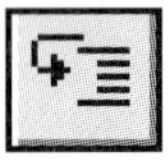	Step Into	Moves through your program one line at a time. Also a debugging tool, discussed in Chapter 14. Available from the Run menu or with the F8 shortcut.
	Step Over	Used when your program has grown more sophisticated by breaking down specific tasks into different procedures (see Chapter 14). Also moves through your program one line at a time, but treats a procedure (Chapters 9 and 10) as a single step. Also a debugging tool, discussed in Chapter 14. Available from the Run menu; the shortcut is SHIFT+F8.

Table 2-1
Toolbar Icons (continued)

depends on your version of Visual Basic and whether you have added anything to Visual Basic (see the section later in the chapter on "Custom Controls" for how to do this). Figure 2-3 shows the default toolboxes supplied with the various editions of Visual Basic. (The Professional and Enterprise editions have the same toolbox.) You use the toolbox to place command buttons, text buttons, and the other controls in your application (see Chapter 4.)

The Initial Form Window

The initial *form window* takes up much of the center of the screen. This is where you customize the window that users will see. (See Chapter 3 for more details on the initial form window.)

note: *This book follows the Visual Basic manual's convention of using the term "form" to describe a customizable window to which you can add objects such as command buttons.*

Figure 2-3 Toolboxes for Visual Basic's different versions

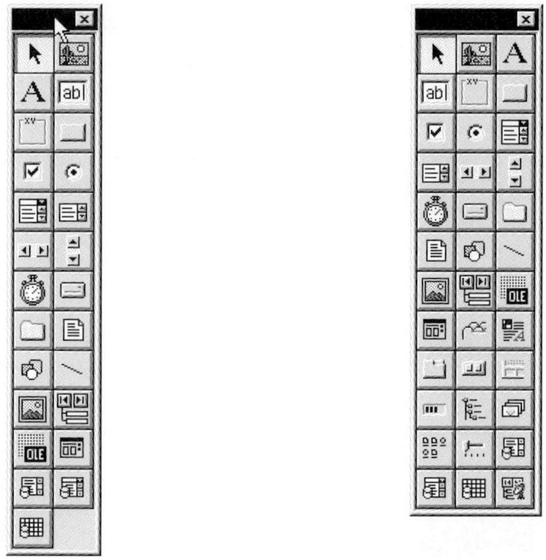

Toolbox for standard edition

Toolbox for Professional and Enterprise editions

Project Window

Since it is quite common for Visual Basic applications to share code or previously customized forms, Visual Basic organizes applications into what it calls *projects*. Each project can have multiple forms, and the code that activates the controls on a form is stored with the form in separate files. General programming code shared by all the forms in your application can be divided into different modules, which are also stored separately. (These are called *Standard* or *code* modules and are described in Chapter 10.) The Project window is usually located at the far right of the screen of Figure 2-1. (It's partially obscured by the initial form window. You can always make it visible by choosing View | Project or CTRL+R or clicking on the Project tool.)

The Project window contains a list of all the customizable forms and general code (modules) that make up your application. Here's what the initial Project window looks like:

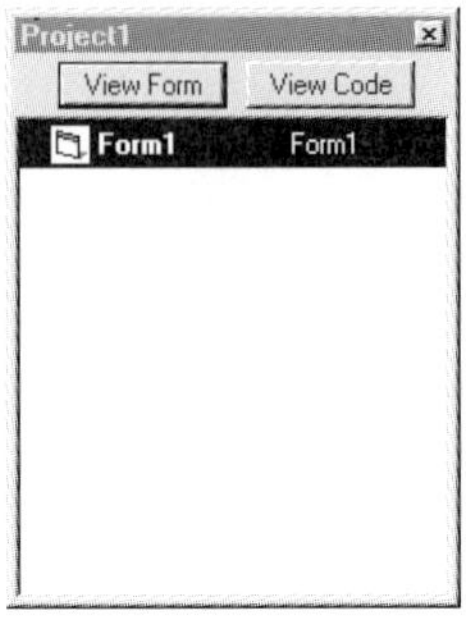

Notice that one item is already listed in the Project window. This is the initial form on which you will build the application. If you can click on the View Form button, you bring the highlighted form to the forefront. Clicking on the View Code button will take you to the code associated to the form.

Although Visual Basic stores all the files that go into making up the project separately, it does keep track of where they are. It creates a file, called the *project file*, that tells it (and you, if you look at the file) where the individual files that make up a project are located. Visual Basic creates the project file whenever you choose Save Project from the File menu (or equivalently, the Save Project tool from the toolbar). It creates a different project file whenever you choose Save Project As. Project files have the extension .VBP in their filename. (Under Windows 95 you can have a long filename if you prefer. It is a good idea however, to continue to use the .VBP extension regardless of the length of the other part of the filename.)

Prior to Visual Basic 4, project files had the extension .MAK. Visual Basic 4 can still use these MAK files to load projects built under earlier versions of Visual Basic. It defaults, however, to a message box asking you if you want to use the Visual Basic 4 versions of any controls used in the project whenever they exist.

Shortcut (Pop-up) Menus

Although you can't see them in Figure 2-1, Visual Basic, like all Windows 95-compliant programs, has context-sensitive pop-up menus that you gain access to by clicking (usually) the right mouse button. (If you have swapped your mouse buttons because you are left-handed, then, of course, you get the shortcut menu by clicking the left mouse button.) These pop-up menus give you another way of getting at common tasks. Here's an example of the pop-up menu you will see when the mouse pointer is in the form window:

In this pop-up menu, like all pop-up menus in Visual Basic, the items on it are also available from the main menu bar. For example, the View Code item is the same as opening the View menu and choosing Code. This means that whether you choose to use the items on a shortcut menu is entirely up to you. Still, as you explore the different parts of the Visual Basic environment, check out the shortcut menu that will usually be available for that locale.

The Help System

The online help system contains essentially all of the information in the *Language Reference* that comes with Visual Basic. In addition, there are hundreds of example programs and dozens of useful tables. The online help system contains a very useful feature: it is context-sensitive for help. This means that you can press F1 and bypass the help menus to go directly to the needed information. You can get information about any keyword in the Visual Basic programming language, about an error message, or about the parts of the Visual Basic environment. For example, the screen in Figure 2-4 shows what you get if you click on F1 when you are on the New Project item on the File menu.

Once you start the help system, you can move the help window anywhere you want. You can resize it or shrink it to an icon as needed or close it when you are through with it.

tip: *If you have enough memory, shrinking the help system to an icon on the Windows 95 task bar makes it quicker to get at the help files.*

Help Menu

Following is a description of each of the items on the Help menu.

Figure 2-4
Help screen for New Project

Contents The Contents option, activated by pressing ALT H, C (or C alone if the Help menu is open), tells you how the Visual Basic help system is organized.

Search The Search option, activated by pressing ALT H, S (or S alone if the Help menu is open), lets you search for help on a specific topic.

Obtaining Technical Support This option tells you how to get help from Microsoft. (ALT H, O is the access key combination if the Help menu isn't open; press O if it is.) This option also contains hints on advanced topics.

tip: *If you are a member of CompuServe, Microsoft is very efficient about giving answers to the questions posted by users in its MSBASIC forum. (Although MSN—the Microsoft Network—hasn't been up long enough to develop a track record, one would suspect that it will be a very good place to go for questions as well.) Other users of CompuServe monitor the questions posted on the MSBASIC forum and often provide helpful advice as well. (For instance, I frequently log on to this forum and sometimes provide advice when I can.)*

Visual Basic Books Online This new feature in Visual Basic 4 launches the Books Online tool, which lets you look—and search—through the entire catalog of Visual Basic documentation. The contents screen for Visual Basic Books Online looks like Figure 2-5. (Visual Basic Books Online has its own help system for teaching you how to use it.)

note: *Unless you had sufficient hard disk space (18MB) to install the Visual Basic Books Online when you installed Visual Basic, you will need to load the Visual Basic CD in order to gain access to this information.*

Learning Microsoft Visual Basic This is a useful orientation to Visual Basic. It nicely complements the material in the first few chapters of this book.

About The About option gives you the copyright notice and serial number of your copy, tells you to whom the copy of Visual Basic is licensed, and shows you the amount of memory your system has available.

Figure 2-5 Contents screen for Visual Basic Books Online

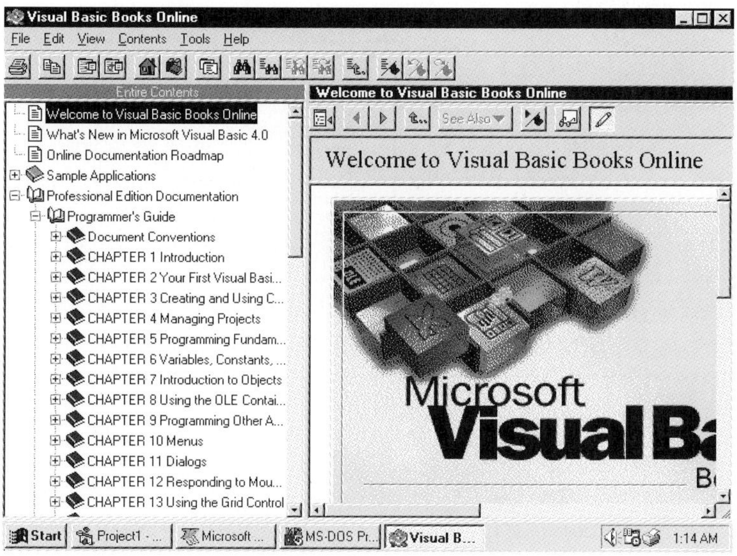

More on the Visual Basic Help System

For those who are not familiar with the Windows help system, this section is designed to give you a quick overview. (The Windows 95 help system is similar to that in Windows 3.X but there are a few differences that are described here as well.) First off, under Windows 95, the main screen of the help system is made up of a three-tabbed dialog box shown in Figure 2-6. As you can see in Figure 2-6, the tabs are named Contents, Index, and Find.

The Contents page for Visual Basic's help system is shown in Figure 2-7. You can move to the different pieces of information described on the Contents page by double-clicking at that item.

The Index page, which is shown in Figure 2-6, lets you search through the entire index of help topics. When you find the topic you are interested in, double-click on it to go to the help page directly, or click on the display button to see the list of topics associated with that index item if there is more than one. For example, Figure 2-8 shows you what happens if you search for the item

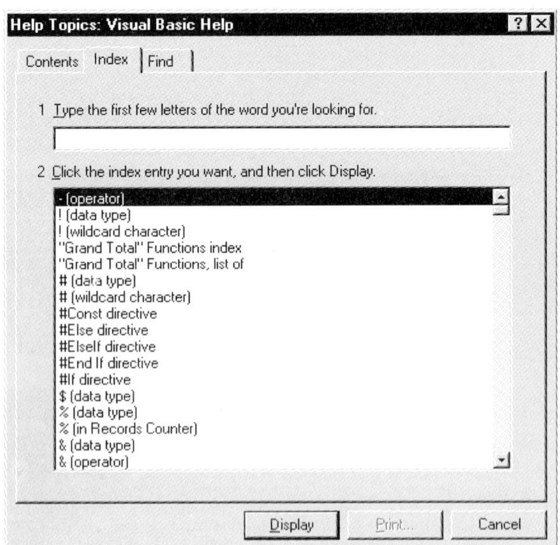

Figure 2-6 Main screen of Visual Basic's help system

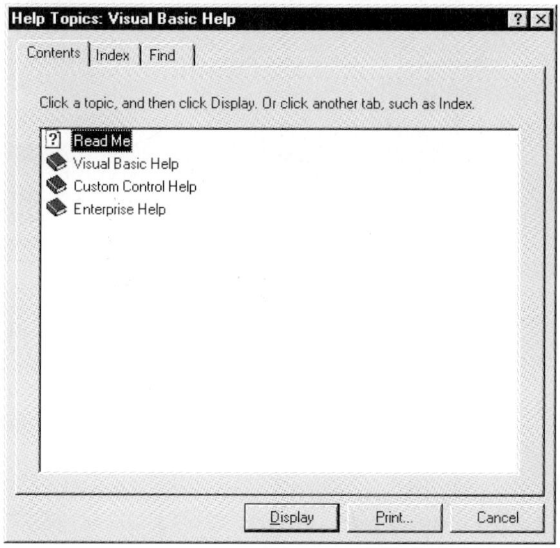

Figure 2-7 Contents page of Visual Basic's help system

marked Toolbar and double-click to go to that help item. (Notice how the help system can include visual elements as well.)

JUMPS WITHIN THE HELP SYSTEM

The Windows help system is an example of a *hypertext* system. This means that you can move around the system by clicking at certain hot spots on the page you are looking at. You already saw this at work when working with the Contents page. In general, if any text is underlined (or colored and underlined on color systems) you get to use that item as a jumping off point to new information. (The cursor changes to a little hand when you are over a jump.)

There are two types of underlines that indicate two different kinds of jumps: solid and dotted.

Solid A solid underline indicates a cross-reference. Clicking on a word with a solid underline takes you directly to the help screen for that topic.

Figure 2-8
Help on Toolbar

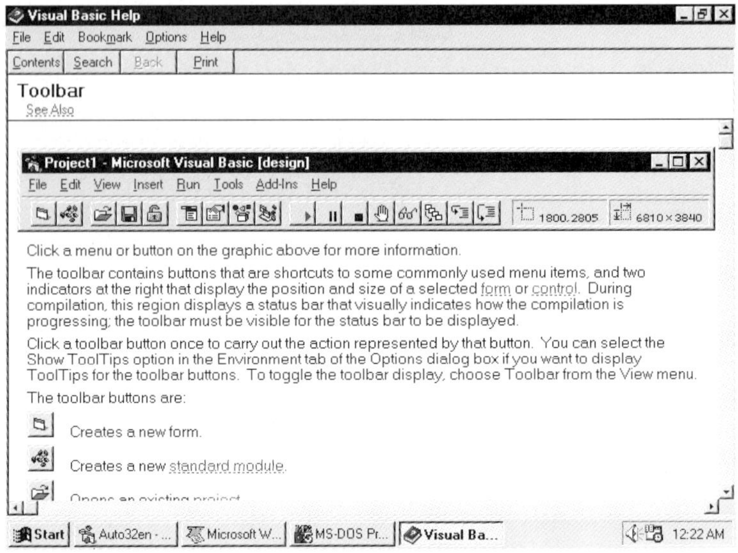

Dotted A dotted underline means that a definition is available for the underlined words. To see the definition, move the cursor to the word that is underlined, press the left mouse button, and keep it down. The definition pops up and stays there until you release the left mouse button.

THE FIND PAGE IN THE HELP SYSTEM

The Find page is new to Windows 95. This lets you do complex searches by (essentially) indexing all the text that appears in the help system. When you use this option for the first time, you see a dialog box like the one shown in Figure 2-9. (Because allowing complex search criteria uses a specially prepared index that takes up a fair amount of space on your hard disk, Visual Basic needs to prepare it. This can take a few minutes.) You can choose to minimize the size of this database by keeping the default "Minimize database size" option checked. If you have disk space galore, choose "Maximize search capabilities."

After Visual Basic builds up the database for searching, you will be presented with the following screen:

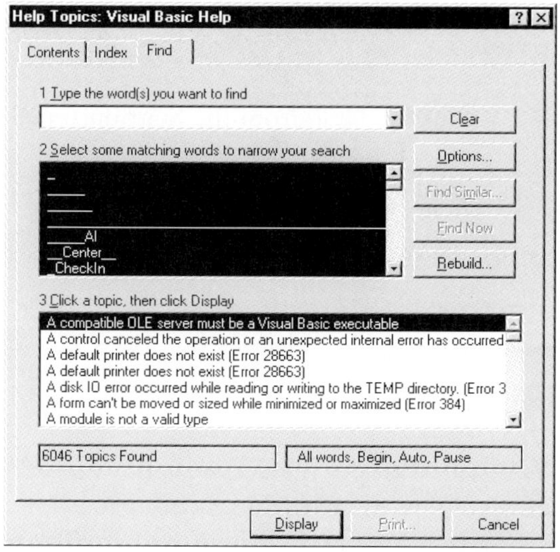

Type the text you want to search for in the first box or choose the items from the list given in the second text box. Then click on the item shown in the third box that satisfies the search criteria you specified. Finally, click on the Display button to actually see the item.

Figure 2-9

Initial screen for setting up a Find database

For more information on using the Find dialog box in a Windows 95 help system:

1. Choose Help from the Start button.
2. Go to the Find command, using items in the general Windows 95 help system.
3. Click on Display to see the list of topics that pertain to Find dialog boxes.

Using the File Menu

You will need the main File menu to work with the files that make up your project. This menu includes commands for saving, loading, and printing files. They are covered briefly here, and you'll learn more about them in Chapter 3. The File menu also lets you exit Visual Basic. As you've seen, the other way to exit Visual Basic is to use ALT+F4 when the focus is on the main menu bar, and like any Windows application, you can also open the control box on the menu bar and choose Close or double-click on the control box.

note: *Under Windows 95 the control box appears as an icon.*

Most of the items on the main File menu are useful only when you've started developing your own applications, as discussed in the later chapters of this book. Figure 2-10 is a picture of the File menu and what follows is a brief look at each of the items, which should help you orient yourself.

New Project The New Project option unloads the current project. If you've made any changes to a project since you last saved it, a dialog box like the following pops up, asking if you want to save your work:

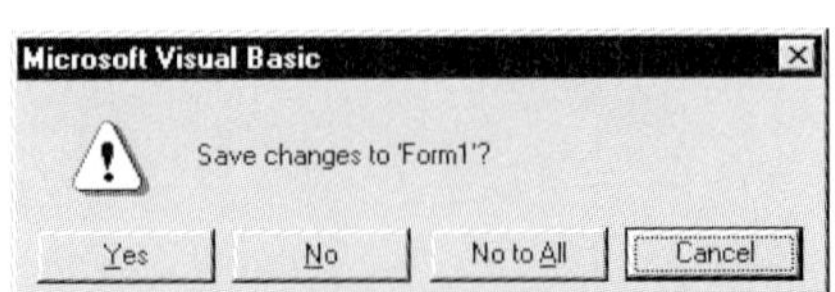

Figure 2-10
File menu

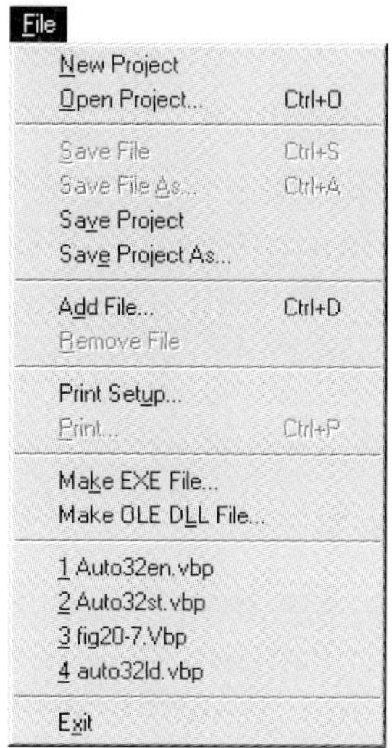

If you answer Yes by pressing ENTER or ALT+Y, you are led to another dialog box for saving files, which we describe later.

Open Project The Open Project option lets you work with an existing Visual Basic application. As the ellipsis after the item indicates, choosing this option opens a dialog box that looks like this:

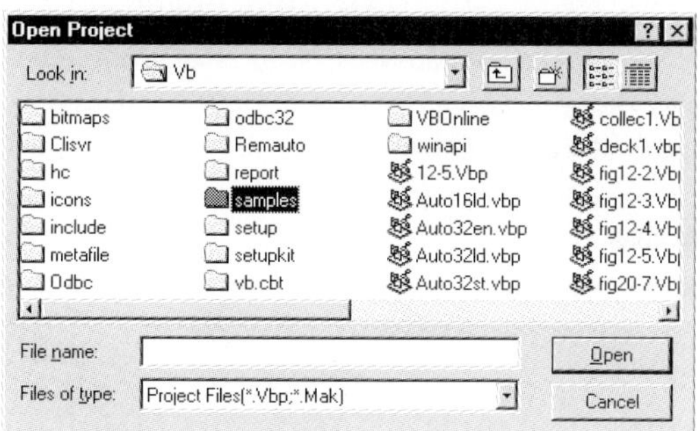

note: *Project names always have a .VBP extension (although long filenames are, of course, permitted under Windows 95).*

Save File The Save File option saves the active object to disk. The first time you choose this option, Visual Basic opens a dialog box identical to the one for the Save File As option discussed next. After the first time you use this, Visual Basic simply saves the file using the previous name. In particular, *no backup of the previous version is kept. You will need to make backups yourself by using the Save File As option described next (and more extensively in Chapter 3).*

Save File As The Save File As option pops up a dialog box that lets you save the active form or Standard module (general-purpose code) to disk, possibly with a new name. Use this option to keep backup copies of a specific piece of a project on a different disk or to save different versions. You also use this option when part of your current application will be useful in other projects. (In that case, you would use the Add File option to add the file to a different project.)

Save Project The Save Project item saves all the files in the current project and creates the project file if one doesn't yet exist. (Recall that a project file is a list of all the files used in the project plus some other information used by Visual Basic.) The first time you choose this option, the program opens a dialog box identical to the one for the Save Project As option.

tip: *In the current version of Visual Basic all the forms that make up your application are stored in ASCII format, which is readable by other applications. (These are called* text-only files *or simply* text files*.) This is a change from earlier versions of Visual Basic in which storing information in text files was an option.*

Save Project As The Save Project As option pops up a dialog box that lets you save all the files that make up the current project with a new name. It does this by creating a new project file and saving the files with their current names. You can also use this option to keep backup copies of the project on a different disk or to save different versions of the project.

note: *The Save Project As option only makes a new project (.VBP) file, it does not make new copies of all the files in your project. (Use Save File As on each file in your project* before *you choose this option if your intention is to make a whole new version of a project with new filenames for all the files in it.)*

Add File The Add File option opens a dialog box that lets you incorporate work previously done into your application. You can add already finished forms, general-purpose code (modules), class modules, or even resource files.

Remove File Use the Remove File option to delete the part of your Visual Basic application you're currently working with from the application. This option does not delete the file from the disk where it was stored. For that you'll need to use the Explorer built into Windows 95 or ordinary DOS commands.

Print Setup This lets you select the printer and set the paper and orientation choices.

Print This lets you print either the current form, code in the form, module (code) that you are working with, or all forms and modules in your application. Choosing it opens a dialog box that looks like this:

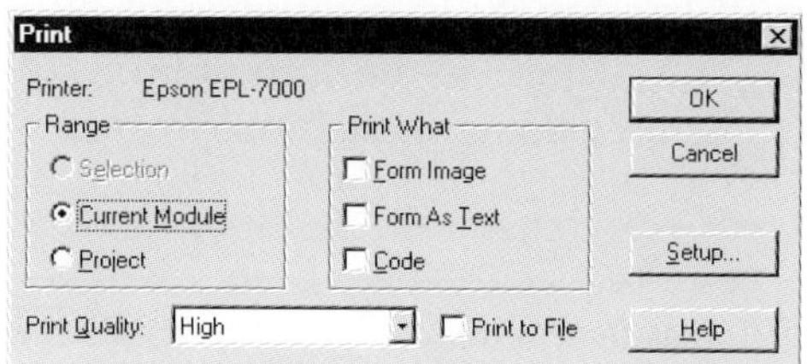

The option (radio) buttons (Selection, Current Module, and Project) determine whether you'll be printing from the part of the application you're currently working with or printing the entire application.

The three check boxes (Form Image, Form As Text, and Code) determine whether you print an image of the forms, the description of the forms that make up all or part of the application (what the user sees), or the code that activates the interface. (See Chapter 3.)

Make EXE File The Make EXE File option opens a dialog box that lets you create Visual Basic applications that can run in the Windows environment independent of Visual Basic. Stand-alone Visual Basic applications require dynamic link library (DLL) files and possibly custom control files. Due to Visual Basic's ability to create OLE applications and to use custom controls, it is best to use the Setup Wizard discussed in Appendix A as well as in the chapter in the *Programmer's Guide* called "Distributing Your Application," rather than try to determine the correct files that your application needs. (For more on this option see Chapters 3 and 9.)

Make OLE DLL File This is covered in Chapter 18.

note: *The Make OLE DLL File menu option is available only in Visual Basic's Professional or Enterprise edition.*

The Most Recently Used (MRU) List This keeps track of the four most recently opened Visual Basic projects. If you click on one of the files listed here, Visual Basic automatically loads the project. This makes returning to work in progress easy.

Exit Choosing the Exit option is the usual way to leave Visual Basic. If you've made any changes to the current project, Visual Basic asks if you want to save them before ending the session.

tip: *Any Visual Basic application that handles files should have a File menu. Also, an important convention for Windows applications is that the last item on this menu should be the Exit command with an ALT+F4 shortcut and an "x" access key.*

See Chapter 13 for how to create a menu and Chapter 17 for how to work with files.

Editing

Visual Basic comes with a full-screen program editor. Since it is a program editor, it lacks features such as word wrap and print formatting that even a primitive word processor, such as WordPad, has. On the other hand, it does add features such as syntax checking that can spot certain common programming typos. The Visual Basic program editor also color-codes the various parts of your code. For example, Visual Basic commands can be one color, comments another. The colors used are customizable via the Editor page from the Tools menu's Options dialog box. The Visual Basic program editor is activated whenever you are writing or viewing code. The font used in the editor can be changed to suit your needs. (See the discussion of the Editor page under "Using the Tools Menu" later, for more on this.)

Edit Menu

The Edit menu contains 15 items. Here are brief descriptions of each of them.

Undo, Redo Undo reverses the last edit you made. Redo reverses the last editing action. The shortcut for Undo is CTRL+Z.

Cut, Copy, Paste You use Cut, Copy, and Paste after you select text. Cut places the text in the Windows clipboard, Copy places a copy of it there, and Paste takes whatever is in the clipboard and pastes it into your Visual Basic application. In particular, you can use this item to exchange information (text or graphics) between another Windows application and Visual Basic. The usual Windows shortcuts apply: CTRL+X (or SHIFT+DEL) for Cut, CTRL+C (or CTRL+INS) for Copy, CTRL+V (or SHIFT+INS) for Paste.

Paste Link Paste Link is used in exchanging information dynamically between Windows applications; see Chapter 18.

Delete The Delete command removes the selected information but does not place a copy in the clipboard. (It's usually easier to just press DEL when text is highlighted.)

Find Choosing the Find option displays a dialog box in which you enter the text (string) you want Visual Basic to search for. Visual Basic searches the entire project for the string. The shortcut is CTRL+F. (After you have used the Find dialog box you can use the F3 (Find Next), or SHIFT+F3 (Find Previous), shortcuts to search for the same text again.)

If a search is successful, the Find dialog box closes and Visual Basic places you at the location in the code where the first occurrence of the text was found. It also selects the text. If no match is found, Visual Basic displays a message stating that the text was not found. Here's a picture of what the Find dialog box looks like:

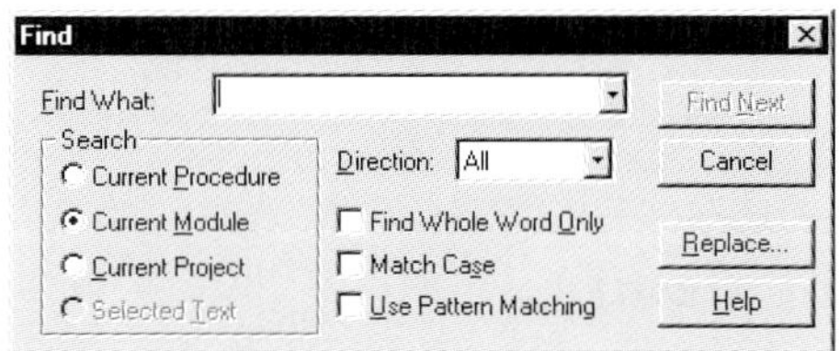

As you can see, this dialog box has a text box for the text to search for and several options. You can decide whether to search all or part of your code and what kind of search it should be (case-sensitive, whole words only) and whether you want to search everything or just from the current insertion point. The pattern matching button allows you to use the normal wildcards: * to match any, and ? to match one character.

Replace The Replace option opens a dialog box with two text boxes but is otherwise similar to the dialog box for Find, as shown here:

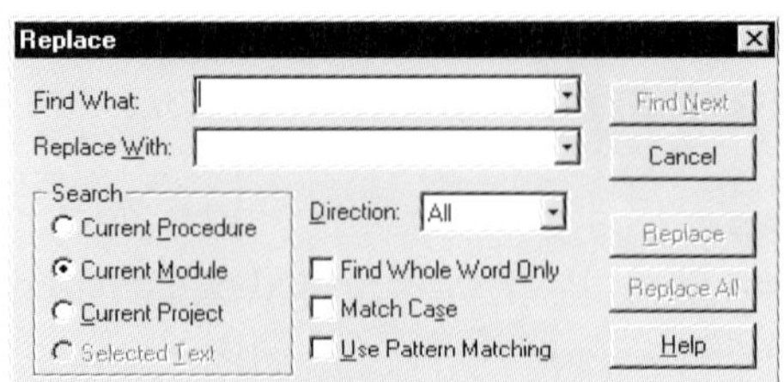

The first of the two text boxes is for the text to be found, and the second is for what should replace it. CTRL+H is the shortcut.

note: *When you click on the Replace button in the Find dialog box you are taken to the Replace dialog box.*

- ***Bring to Front, Send to Back*** The Bring to Front option brings the selected object in front of all other objects; the Send to Back option moves the object back when you are developing the project.

- ***Align to Grid*** Align to Grid is used to accurately position objects on your forms. See Chapter 4 for more on how to use the grid and this option.

- ***Lock Controls*** The Lock Controls option prevents accidental movement of controls when checked. This item is an example of what is usually called a *toggle*: click it once to turn it on (a check mark will show up next to it), click it again to turn it off.

Using the View Menu

The View menu lets you display or hide features of the Visual Basic environment. You also use it to manipulate the objects and controls that make up your application. Here are brief descriptions of each of the menu items.

- ***Code*** You use the Code item to view the program code for the form or module that has the focus. The shortcut is F7.

- ***Form*** You use the Form item to view the form associated to the code that you are working with. The shortcut is SHIFT+F7.

- ***Procedure Definition*** The Procedure Definition option displays the Code window for a called procedure that the cursor is on. The shortcut is SHIFT+F2. See Chapter 10 for more on procedures.

Last Position You use the Last Position item to jump to your previous position in a Code window. The shortcut is CTRL+SHIFT+F2.

Object Browser The Object Browser option displays the Object Browser window. With the Object Browser you can see information about your project and the pieces of Visual Basic itself. (See Chapters 5 and 10 for more on the Object Browser.) The shortcut is F2.

Debug Window You use the Debug Window option to display or bring to the front the Debug window. The shortcut is CTRL+G. See Chapter 14 for more on the Debug window.

Project The Project option displays the Project window. Use this window to view what files make up your application. The shortcut is CTRL+R.

Properties You use the Properties option to display or bring to the front the Properties window. The shortcut is F4, or click on the Properties tool.

Toolbox You use the Toolbox option to display or bring to the front the toolbox.

Toolbar You use the Toolbar option to toggle the toolbar on and off.

Color Palette You use the Color Palette option to display or bring to the front the Color Palette window that lets you change the colors of Visual Basic objects. (See Chapter 3 for how to use the color palette.)

Using the Insert Menu

The Insert menu contains items that let you insert various procedures, windows, code, modules, and so on, into your projects. Here are brief descriptions of each of the menu items.

Procedure You use the Procedure item to add a procedure to the Code window with the focus. (See Chapter 10.)

Form You use the Form item to add multiple windows to your application. See Chapter 5 for more on this option.

MDI Form You use the MDI (multiple document interface) form to make windows act as child windows to a main window. This is discussed in Chapter 12.

Module You use the Module option to add programming code that you'll want to share among all the parts of the application you develop. In Visual Basic, code is attached to a specific window (form) unless you place it in a module. Modules are discussed in Chapter 10.

Class Module You use the Class Module option to add a module containing the definition of a class that you'll want to share among all the parts of the application you develop. See Chapter 12 for more on class modules, which let you use some very basic object-oriented principles in your Visual Basic projects.

File You use File to insert code from another file into the current code module at the point where the cursor is located.

Using the Run Menu

Most of the items on the Run menu are used when debugging (see Chapter 14). The only three items that you will be using until you start learning debugging techniques are described here:

Start This runs your project. (Although most people use the completely equivalent Run tool on the toolbar or press F5.) This menu item is only available at design time, since, for example, when you are actually running a project this item disappears from the Run menu and becomes the Break command (used in debugging).

Start with Full Compile To save time Visual Basic only compiles the part of your code it needs to get the project off and running. If you choose this option Visual Basic will compile all the code in your project before starting. (You will only notice a substantial difference with projects involving multiple forms and/or thousands of lines of code.)

End This ends the program and reclaims all resources used by Visual Basic while running your program. Most people prefer to use the End tool on the toolbar, which is completely equivalent.

Using the Tools Menu

The Add Watch, Edit Watch, Instant Watch, and Calls items on the Tools menu are debugging tools. They are discussed in Chapter 14. The Menu Editor lets you add menus to your Visual Basic projects. It is also discussed in Chapter 14. The References item is used when dealing with objects external to Visual Basic and is discussed in Chapter 12.

note: *If you have the Enterprise edition of Visual Basic and have installed Microsoft's "Source Save" version control package, you will see four more items on this menu: Get, Check Out, Check In, and Undo Check Out. Please consult the Source Safe documentation for these.*

What follows is a short discussion of the two remaining items.

Custom Controls As mentioned previously, Visual Basic is extendible by adding what are usually called *custom controls*. The 32-bit version of Visual Basic must use the newer OLE aware controls—see Chapter 18 for more on OLE.

note: *OLE aware controls are usually called OCX controls because the extension on their filename is always .OCX.*

The 16-bit version of Visual Basic can use both the newer OCX controls and the controls designed for earlier versions of Visual Basic. (Usually called VBX controls—again after the file extension.)

note: *In all cases Visual Basic defaults to popping up a message box asking you if you want to upgrade VBX controls used in an existing project to the newer OCX controls whenever a comparable one exists. This option is controlled from the Advanced page on the Options dialog box (see below). You will have to upgrade VBX controls to make an existing project compile under the 32-bit version of Visual Basic.*

Clicking the Custom Controls item gives you access to the dialog box that lets you choose what items you want to add to Visual Basic's toolbox. Here's a picture of the Custom Controls dialog box (what you see will depend on what is on your system):

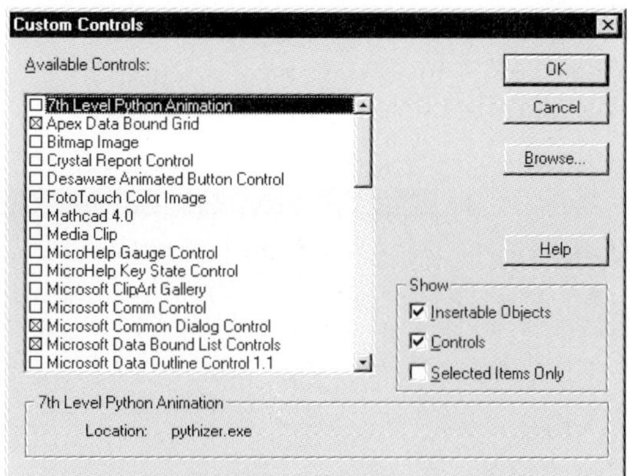

If a box is unchecked, then the control has not yet been added: click in the box next to the item you want to add, or click on a box that is checked to remove the control from the toolbox. Notice how this dialog box gives you the location of the control. (If an item isn't showing up in the Available Controls box, use the Browse button to open up a dialog box that lets you search for it.) As with any dialog box, click on OK to have the new items added, click on ESC to cancel the changes. The controls you choose are added only for the project you are working with. It is possible to make permanent changes to the toolbox (see Chapter 13).

note: *See Appendix A for an explanation of how to distribute an application that uses custom controls.*

Options Clicking on this item opens up a tabbed dialog box shown in Figure 2-11. You'll see more details on how to use the various pages of this dialog box in the chapters that follow. A brief overview of this important item is given in this section.

- The Environment page controls the Visual Basic environment itself. (What happens when you make changes here is that Visual Basic updates a file called VB.INI that stores initialization settings.) Most of the items will be described when coding techniques are discussed. However, the various Save options are worth noting more than once!

Figure 2-11 The Tools|Options tabbed dialog box

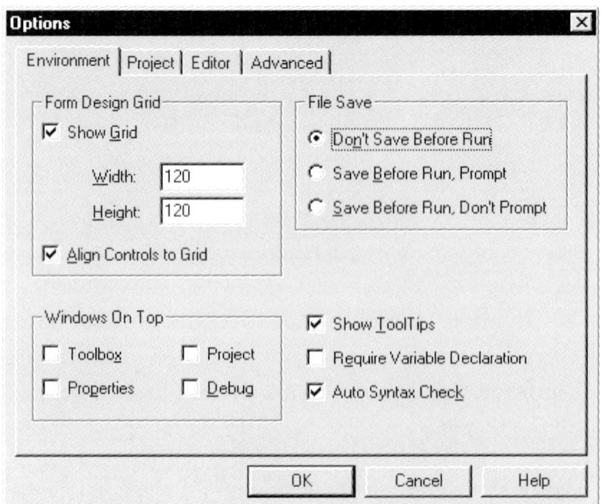

The point is, experienced programmers know by bitter experience that occasionally they will write some code that locks up their machine. If you forget to save the code before this happens, you may lose hours of work. For this reason, I strongly recommend that you check off either the Save Before Run, Prompt or Save Before Run, Don't Prompt option.

note: *If you are not seeing the ToolTips for the controls and toolbar items, you will need to check off the Show ToolTips box on this page.*

Project Options Tab

- The Project page of the Options dialog box specifies settings for the current Visual Basic project. See Chapters 5 and 9 for more on this page.
- The Editor page lets you control how the editor works. Here is a picture of this page:

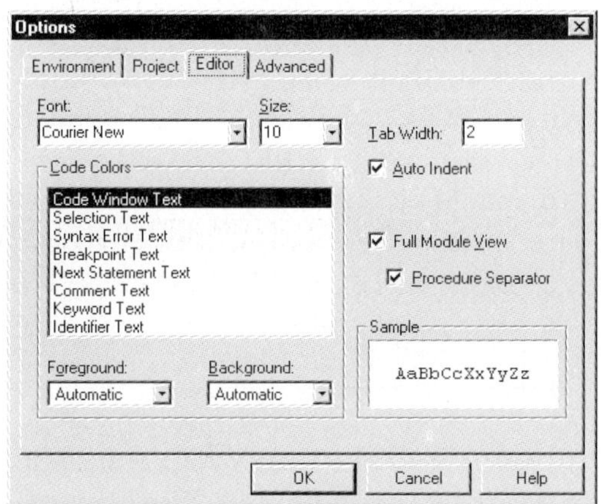

The Font and Size items control how the code appears. (The default is 10-point Courier New. Just enter a new size in the Size box if you have trouble working with this size type.) Code Colors lets you color-code the different parts of your code. This is a useful tool for detecting typos.

note: *The other items in this box are discussed along with coding techniques later in this book.*

The Advanced Page Most of the items on the Advanced page will be discussed later. The only two items that are even remotely relevant now are the ones that pertain to using existing Visual Basic projects. For example, the Upgrade Custom Controls check box determines if Visual Basic should upgrade all the VBX custom controls in an existing project to the corresponding OCX control if they exist. (The default is that it is on.) Similarly, the Background Project Load check box determines whether the project is loaded in the background. The default is that it is on as well.

Using the Add-Ins Menu

The Add-Ins menu gives you access to separate tools that can be seamlessly integrated into Visual Basic. You just check off the item you want to add, and Visual Basic does the rest. Two add-ins are automatically included in a standard installation of the Professional edition of Visual Basic (one in the standard edition). The Report Manager gives you a fairly complete tool for modifying and building reports that you can use in your programs. The other tool included in all versions is the Data Manager, which is used for managing databases (see Chapter 20). You use the Add-In Manager to add and remove add-ins from the menu. (The Enterprise edition of Visual Basic comes with an add-in called Source Safe, which makes it easier to use the team approach to developing Visual Basic projects.)

note: *Although we do not cover it in this book, one of the most amazing features of Visual Basic 4 is that you can write add-ins in Visual Basic itself. This is because the entire Visual Basic environment can be controlled using Visual Basic through OLE automation (see Chapter 18).*

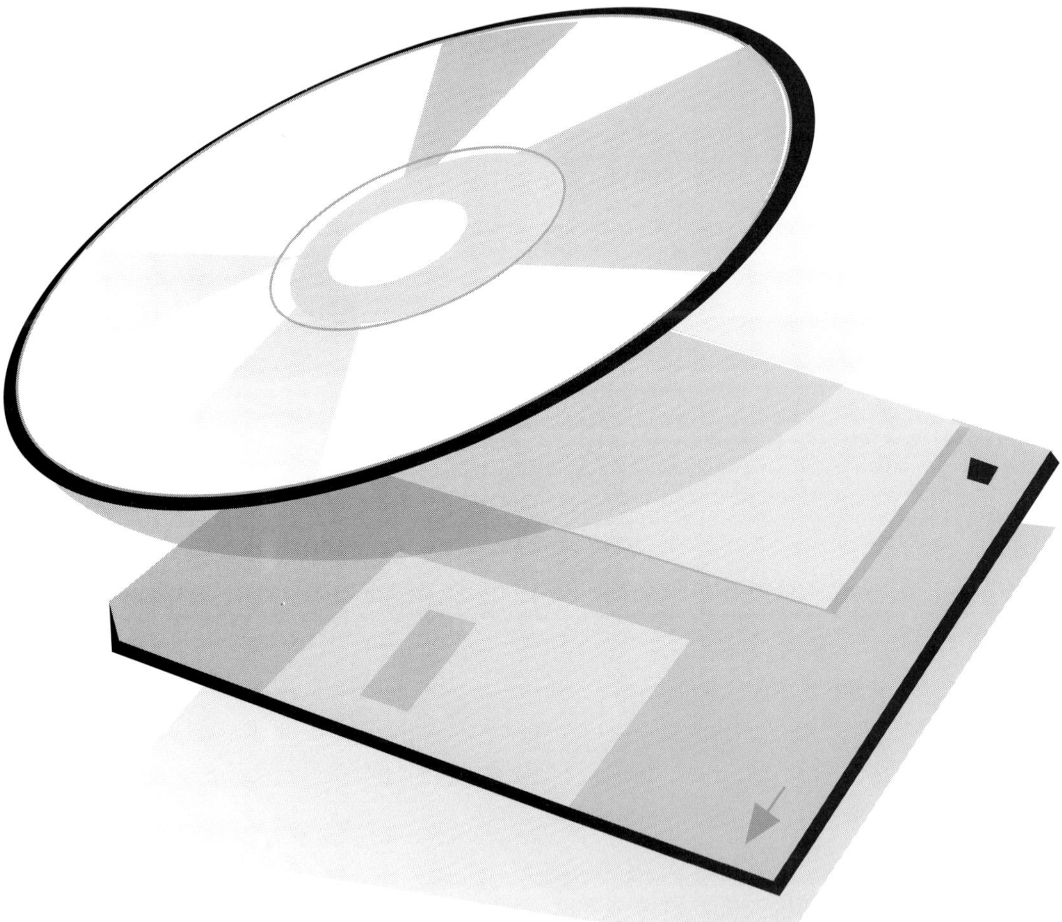

Chapter Three

Customizing a Form

VISUAL BASIC makes it easy to build an application with all the features that a sophisticated Windows program demands. Using user-friendly devices such as list boxes, dialog boxes, message boxes, and command buttons will become routine. Nonetheless, it's best first to become comfortable using Visual Basic to customize a blank form. (Remember that *form* is the term Visual Basic uses for a customizable window.) This chapter shows you how to design forms with a given size, shape, or location. You'll learn how to print text in a form and how to print an image of a form on your printer.

Most important, you'll see how to make a form respond to events such as a mouse click or double-click in the form. (As you saw in Chapter 1, the event-driven nature of Visual Basic is the primary reason it is both extraordinarily powerful and easy to use.)

Starting a New Project

When you start Visual Basic it assumes you want to work with a new *project* (the name Visual Basic uses for an application that is being developed). If you need to throw away your work and start a new project, you can open the File menu and click the New Project item. As you saw in Chapter 2, you can also start Visual Basic by opening an existing project (which you can do from the File menu, the toolbar, or from the Explorer by double-clicking the name of the project file). To make working with an existing project easier, Visual Basic 4 keeps a list of the most recent projects on its File menu. If the File menu is open, you can click on that item to work on that project (or press its number).

When you start Visual Basic, after a short delay, your screen will probably look something like the one in Figure 3-1. There are six elements shown in Figure 3-1. If any are missing, you can reveal them by opening the View menu and clicking on the name of the item.

Figure 3-1
The opening screen

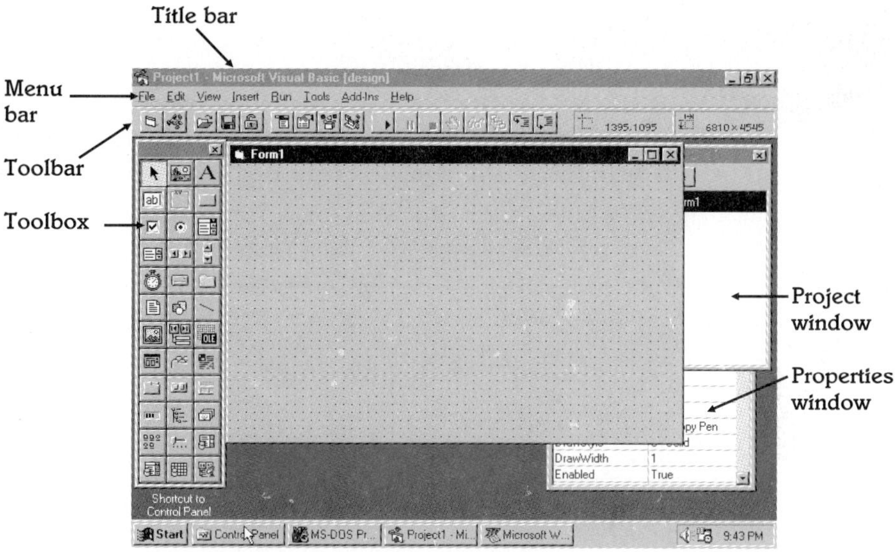

Note the blank window in the center of the screen, which has a grid of dots. This is the form that you will customize. You use the grid to align objects such as command buttons and list boxes on the screen. (You'll learn more about the grid in Chapter 4.) At the top of the blank form is the title bar with its caption. *Caption* is the Visual Basic term for what appears in the title bar of the form. You'll see how to customize the caption shortly so that you can give meaningful titles to your forms. Currently, this form is titled Form1, which is the default name that Visual Basic gives to a form when you start working on a new project.

To the left of the Form1 window is the toolbox. (If it is not available, use ALT V, X to reveal it.) The toolbox contains icons for the various controls, such as command buttons, text boxes, and other controls, needed to customize a form. (The controls on the toolbox are discussed extensively in later chapters of this book. (In particular please see Chapters 4, 9, 12, 13, and 17.) Partially covered at the right of the screen is the Project window (discussed in Chapter 9). Also partially hidden is the Properties window, which you will read about in a moment.

note: *As was mentioned in Chapter 1, you should be completely comfortable with using the mouse to change the size and location of a form before you move on.*

The Properties Window

The size and location of a form are examples of what Visual Basic calls the *properties* of the form. These can be changed from the Properties window, which you can display by pressing F4 or clicking on the Properties tool. The Properties window looks like this:

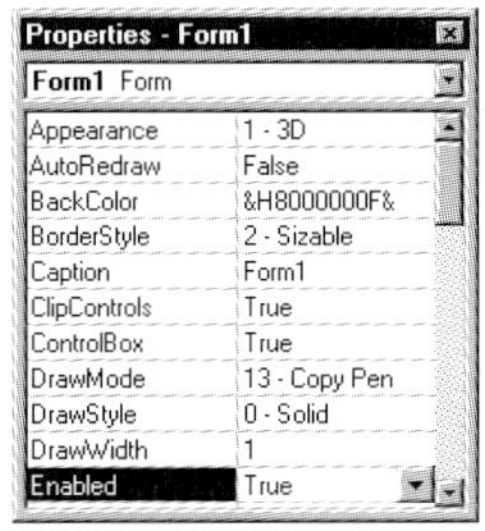

Notice that right below the title bar of the Properties window that says you are working with Form1 is another line that says Form1 Form. This line always tells you the name of the object you are working with and what type of object it is. In this case, the name is the default name, Form1, and, as you might expect, it's a Form object. (When you have other controls on your forms, you can click the down arrow at the far right of this line to see a list of these controls, as discussed in Chapter 4.)

Next, notice the line (near the middle of the screen) that says Caption in the first column and Form1 in the second column. Click on this line to work with the Caption property. The second column of the Properties window always indicates the current setting of the property. (The right-hand column of the Properties window is sometimes called the Settings box.) The Settings box works like an ordinary Windows text box as far as entering or editing information. In this case, whatever you enter in the Caption Settings box becomes the new caption for the form.

tip: *Context-sensitive help works for properties. Pressing F1 when the focus is at a specific line in the Properties window brings up the help file for that property.*

For example, type **First Window App** in the Settings box for the Caption property. Notice that as you do, the caption on the form changes instantly to reflect what you've typed.

In general you must move through the Properties window until you get to the property you want to change. Once you click on a line, whatever you type replaces the setting that was originally there. Another method is to move the mouse until the mouse pointer is in the right column of the correct line in the Properties window, click, and insert the text you want. Note that this method inserts text; it doesn't replace the text originally there. To replace text, you first have to select the text you want to replace. (Remember that under Windows, you select text by holding down the mouse button and dragging the pointer across the text or by using a SHIFT+arrow key combination.)

Use the arrow keys or the mouse to scroll through the Properties window. As you can see, you can set a large number of properties (over 40) for a form. Although you won't learn about them all in this chapter, the next few sections discuss the most useful ones.

As with any Windows list box, you can scroll through the Properties window by repeatedly clicking an arrow in the scroll bars. However, the standard Microsoft Windows shortcut for moving through a list box doesn't work here. You can't press the first letter of the item you want to change to move to the item because anything you type goes into the Settings box.

tip: *To quickly move through the properties in the Properties window, use SHIFT+CTRL+letter key. This moves you to the first property that begins with that letter. Subsequent uses of this combination move to succeeding properties that begin with the letter.*

AN EXAMPLE

Move through the Properties window to the item marked MaxButton (for example by pressing SHIFT+CTRL+M once). Notice that MaxButton replaces Caption in the left-hand column, and True appears in the right-hand column, as shown here:

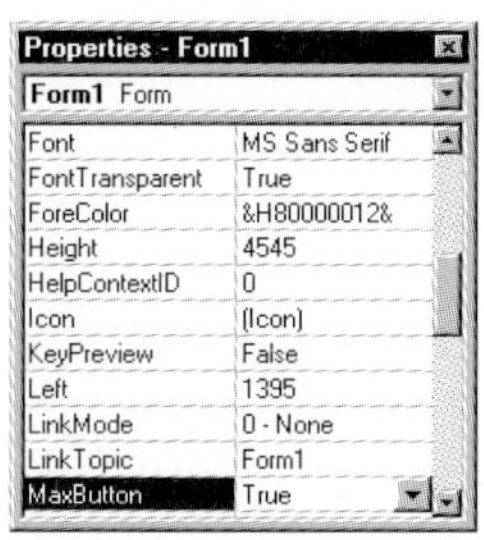

Setting this value to True means that the form you are designing will have a maximize button. (Remember that a maximize button appears in the right corner of a window and lets you maximize the window by clicking the mouse on it once.)

As an experiment, for your first application, change this property to False. There are three ways to do this. The simplest is just to press F. The property changes from True to False. The second is to double-click in the right-hand column. The third is to click the arrow immediately to the right of the Settings box where True appears. A list box drops down with the two options, True and False, as shown here:

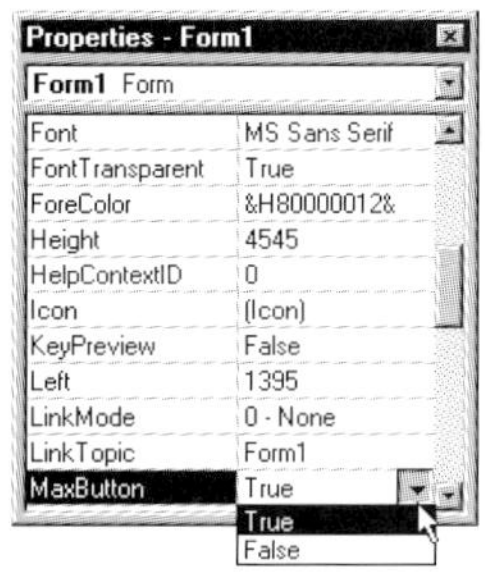

Select the False option by pressing the DOWN ARROW and then pressing ENTER. A general feature in Visual Basic is that whenever a property has a fixed number of options, you'll see an arrow indicating that a drop-down list box is available. You can see the list of options by clicking on the arrow.

Now change the MinButton property to False. (Return to the Properties window, move to the MinButton property, and change its value to False.)

With both of these properties set to False, run this application and see what happens. There are three ways to run a Visual Basic application:

- Select the Start option from the toolbar by clicking the forward (green) arrow (the tenth tool).
- Select the Start option from the Run menu by using the mouse or by pressing ALT R, S.
- Press F5 as a shortcut.

After a short delay, the form will pop up, looking like the one in Figure 3-2. Notice that this form has neither a minimize nor a maximize button. Notice also that, unlike when you changed the caption, these changes show up only at *run time* (that is, when you run the application).

Figure 3-2
Form without maximize or minimize buttons

To return to developing an application, move the mouse to the Run menu and click the Stop option, or use the Stop tool (the tool that looks like a stop button on a cassette recorder). This brings you back to the application you've just developed.

Designing a form that lacks both minimize and maximize buttons may not seem like much, but it does illustrate the absolutely essential process of changing the properties of a Visual Basic object.

SUMMARY OF THE METHODS FOR WORKING WITH THE PROPERTIES WINDOW

Here is a summary of the general method for changing the properties of a Visual Basic form:

1. Display the Properties window by pressing F4, using the Properties tool, or the View menu.
2. Move to the Properties window and select an item from the properties in the list box.
3. Enter the new setting for the property.
4. Press ENTER to accept the new setting.

Following is a table containing the keyboard shortcuts for manipulating the Properties window when it has the focus.

Key	Action
SHIFT+CTRL+letter key	Moves to the first item beginning with that letter
DOWN ARROW	Moves to the next item in the Properties list box
UP ARROW	Moves to the previous item in the Properties list box
PGDN/END	Moves to the last item displayed in the Properties list box or to the last item
PGUP/HOME	Moves to the first item displayed in the Properties list box or to the first item
F4	Brings up the Properties window (you can also use the View menu) or the Properties tool.

After you enter a new setting, press ENTER, click the mouse, or press TAB to accept the changes.

Once you are working with a setting for a property, the usual Windows editing techniques work. You can highlight text with SHIFT+arrow combinations, and the usual editing keys will work: ALT+BACKSPACE undoes the last action, CTRL+C (or CTRL+INS) copies selected text to the clipboard, CTRL+V (or SHIFT+INS) pastes, and so on.

As you saw earlier, when Visual Basic can display a complete list of the settings for a specific property, you can click the down arrow that appears to see the list. (These are sometimes called enumerated properties.) Once you have dropped down the list, you can navigate through it using ordinary Windows techniques. For example, typing the first character moves to the first item beginning with that character, PGDN moves to the last item shown, and so on. (Use F4 to open or close the settings list.)

Common Form Properties

This section gives short descriptions of some of the most common properties of forms. The next two sections discuss other form properties that need more extensive treatment. As you'll see in later chapters, a single property can pertain to many different objects. For example, you will want to set the Font property for text boxes, command buttons, and the like.

Appearance The Appearance property determines whether controls have a three-dimensional look. If you leave it at the default value of 1, controls will look three-dimensional. Change it to 0, and the controls will appear flat.

BorderStyle The BorderStyle property offers only a small number of choices. Because of this, you'll see an arrow to the right of the property setting. You can choose among four values for this property. The default value, 2, allows the user to size and shape the form via the hot spots located on the boundary of the form.

Change this setting to 1 (called *Fixed Single*), and the user will no longer be able to resize the window. All the user will be able to do is minimize or maximize the window (unless, of course, you turn off those options as well when you design the application).

Set this value to 0, and the application will show no border whatsoever and therefore no minimize, maximize, or control box button. Because of this, a form created without a border cannot be moved, resized, or reshaped. This setting is useful for splash screens or when you don't want users to be able to alter your forms.

The fourth setting, 3 (called *Fixed Double*), is not often used for ordinary forms, but it is commonly used for dialog boxes. It gives a nonsizable (it has no hot spots) border that is twice as thick as normal.

A setting of 4 is called Fixed ToolWindow. Under Windows 3.X and Windows NT 3.51 and earlier, this behaves exactly like fixed single. Under Windows 95, use this setting to display the form with a Close button. (The text from the title bar text will appear in a reduced size, and the form does not appear in the Windows 95 task bar.)

A setting of 5, called Sizable ToolWindow, behaves like Sizable under Windows 3.X and Windows NT 3.51. Under Windows 95, as with the Fixed ToolWindow setting, you get the form with a Close button, the text from the title bar text will appear in a reduced size, and the form does not appear in the Windows 95 task bar.

note: *These last two settings are used when you want to create toolbox-style windows.*

Caption As you already know, the Caption property sets the title of the form. The caption is also the title that Microsoft Windows uses for the application icon when the user minimizes the application.

ControlBox The ControlBox property goes into effect only when a user runs the application. As in any Microsoft Windows application, control boxes are located in the far left corner of the title bar. (They show up as an icon under Windows 95, as a box under Windows NT.) Clicking the box displays a list of common window tasks, such as window minimizing, maximizing, and closing, along with keyboard equivalents when they exist.

You have only two choices: You can either have a control box or not. Therefore, there are only two possible settings, so the list box to the right of the settings area is enabled. Note that if your application doesn't have a control box, a user without a mouse is in trouble. He or she won't be able to minimize, maximize, or close the application. Control boxes are generally not a good thing to remove.

Enabled You do not want to change the Enabled property casually. Set Enabled to False, and the form cannot respond to any events. Usually you toggle this property back and forth in response to some event. To make your forms respond dynamically, you must write code. The Properties window is most often used for setting the static properties of your objects.

Font The Font property is the first example you have seen of a property that is set from an ordinary Windows dialog box. If you move the focus to this item and then double-click on the three dots (usually called an ellipsis) you'll see a dialog box that looks something like this:

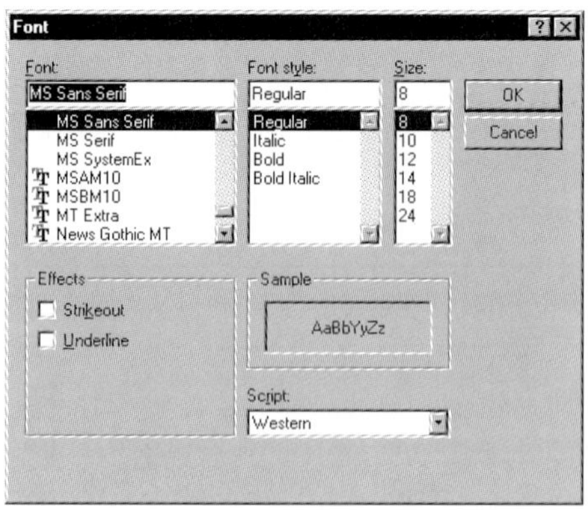

(What you see will depend on the fonts you have installed in your machine.)

In this dialog box, you make changes to the font used for information displayed on the form. It controls how text appears when printed directly on the form.

note: *Visual Basic 4 still supports the various font properties such as FontName, FontBold, and FontSize in code, but you can no longer set these via the Properties window.*

Height, Width Height and Width are interesting properties—and not only because they can be set two ways. They are examples of properties that use the Microsoft Windows *twips* scale to measure the sizes of the objects involved. There are 1440 twips to an inch (567 to a centimeter). The term actually stands for *one twentieth of a point*. (Points are a common measure for printers; this book is set in 11-point type.)

caution: *Twips measure how large the object would be if it were printed; they do not correspond exactly to the size of the object on your screen. For example, on a 15-inch diagonal monitor, the default size of a form is approximately 4.5 inches. (See the section "An Example: The Screen Object and Available Fonts" in Chapter 6 for a discussion of how to adjust your Visual Basic projects for different-sized monitors.)*

Look at the far right of the toolbar, as shown here:

Notice the last box has the value 6810 X 4545. (The numbers you see will depend on your screen resolution.) This box always tells you the current value in twips for the width and height of the form. Now drag your form to change the width and height. Notice that when you change the size of the form by dragging, the value at the far right of the toolbar changes to reflect the new size. If you look in the Properties window, you'll see that the values for these properties change as well.

Of course, using the mouse and dragging to set the height and width is a less precise procedure than you may need. Luckily, since Height and Width are properties, their values can be changed, directly via the Properties window. You just have to enter the value you want in the appropriate line in the right-hand column. For example, if I changed the width to 3420 twips, I would cut my window in half (at least as close to half as the screen can display).

Like the Caption property, any changes you make to the height and width of the form go into effect immediately—they do not wait until the application runs.

note: *Unless you disable the border by changing the Border Style property, a user can size and reshape the various forms in the application regardless of how you set them at design time.*

Icon The Icon property is one you will use frequently. This property determines the icon your application will display when it is minimized on the toolbar or turned into a stand-alone application on the Windows desktop. (It is also the icon used for the control box under Windows 95.) Visual Basic comes with a large library of icons that you can use freely. Pictures of them appear in Appendix B of the *Visual Basic Programmer's Guide*.

note: *The Professional or Enterprise edition of Visual Basic come with programs for creating and modifying icons for both 16-bit and 32-bit applications.*

To see how to choose an icon for your application, go to the Properties window and select the Icon property. Notice that to the right of the Settings box is the ellipsis indicating that a dialog box is available to help you select the value of the property. Click the box containing the three dots, and the following dialog box appears:

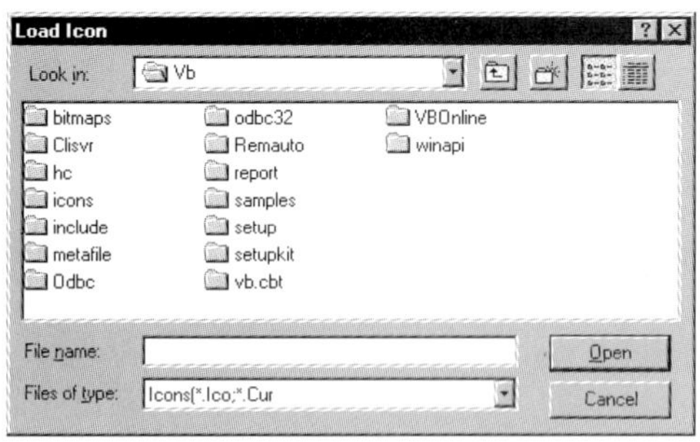

Assuming that you have installed Visual Basic in the ordinary way, the icons supplied with Visual Basic are found in the subdirectories of the Icons directory that is under the directory where Visual Basic is installed. As always, there are many ways to get to this subdirectory; probably the fastest is to move the mouse pointer to the Icons subdirectory in the dialog box and double-click. Of course, you can type the full path name of the file in the File name text box or move the focus to the Directories list and select the name by keystrokes alone.

To see an example of how to set the Icon property, go to the Icons subdirectory and move through the list of its subdirectories until you get to the one marked misc; double-click this name. The Files list box now shows the more than 70 icon files in this directory. (Under Windows 95 you can actually see the icons.) To choose the FACE03 icon, double-click on it. (You can also move the focus to the File name text box and type the name of the icon, or move through the file list until you can select FACE03 and press ENTER. To be sure that you really have changed the icon for the Form1 application:

- Under Windows 95 look at the control box.
- Under Windows NT or Windows 3.X, click the application's minimize button.

Left, Top The Left and Top properties determine the distance between the left or top of the form and the screen. Set the value of the Top property to 0, and the form you're designing is flush with the top. Set the value of the Left property to 0, and it will be flush with the left side of the screen.

These settings work in much the same way as the Height and Width properties. You change them in the same two ways. They are also measured in twips, and changes go into effect when you reset the values, not when the user runs the application.

MousePointer, Mouse Icon MousePointer is a useful property that sets the shape of the mouse pointer. The default value is 0, but as the pull-down list indicates, there are 17 other values. A setting of 4, for example, turns the mouse pointer into a rather pretty square within a square. The settings you will use most often are 11 and 13. A value of 11 changes the mouse pointer to an hourglass and, as in other Microsoft Windows applications, it is useful for telling a user that he or she has to wait until the computer finishes what it is doing. Set the MousePointer property to a value of 99 and you will be able to use a custom icon. This is most commonly done using code when the cursor is over a specific control (see Chapter 16), but you can change it at design time by following these steps:

1. First set the MousePointer property to 99.
2. Then pick the icon you want as the value of the MouseIcon property. (Use the same techniques to select this icon as were described for the Icon property.).

Visible Visible is another property that is dangerous to change by mistake. Set the value of this property to False, and the form will no longer be visible (and, therefore, somewhat difficult for the user to manipulate!). You usually will want to make a form invisible only when you are designing an application with multiple forms. Then you will often want to hide one or more of the forms by using the Visible property. Often, you will reset this property by using code and not at the time you design the application.

WindowState The WindowState property determines how the form will look at run time. There are three possible settings. A setting of 1 reduces the form to an icon, and a setting of 2 maximizes the form. A setting of 0 is the normal default setting. This property is most often changed in code.

Scale Properties

You will often need to position objects or text in a form accurately. Some people are not comfortable thinking in terms of twips. To help you, Visual Basic provides five properties that affect the scale used in a form. (For more information on the scale properties, see Chapter 15.)

ScaleMode The ScaleMode property allows you to change the units used in the form's internal coordinate system. Tired of twips? There are seven other possibilities. You can create your own units (the value of this setting is 0), keep the default twips (this value is 1), or use one of the six remaining choices. An interesting setting—especially for graphics—is 3. This uses one *pixel* (a picture element—the smallest unit of resolution on your monitor) as the scale. And of course, if you are more comfortable with them, you can choose inches (5), millimeters (6), or centimeters (7).

ScaleHeight, ScaleWidth Use the ScaleHeight and ScaleWidth properties when you set up your own scale for the height and width of the form. Resetting these properties has the side effect of setting the value of the ScaleMode property back to 0. For example, if you set the value of each of these properties to 100, then the form uses a scale that has point 50,50 as its center. You will probably reset the values of these properties only when you are writing an application that uses graphics.

ScaleLeft, ScaleTop The ScaleLeft and ScaleTop properties describe what value Visual Basic uses for the left or top corner of the form. The original (default) value for each of these properties is 0. Like ScaleHeight and Scale-Width, these properties are most useful when you are working with graphics. For example, if you are writing a program that works with a graph, you rarely want the top left corner to be at point 0,0.

Color Properties

The colors you use in an application have a dramatic effect on how easy and pleasurable the application is to use and, as a result, how well it is received. You can specify the background color (BackColor) and the foreground color (ForeColor) for text and graphics in the window. Visual Basic has many ways to change the colors of an application dynamically by using code. See Chapter 14 for more information on using code to achieve this effect.

The BackColor and ForeColor Properties via the Color Palette

Suppose you try to set the BackColor property. If you open the Properties window and select BackColor, you'll see the following:

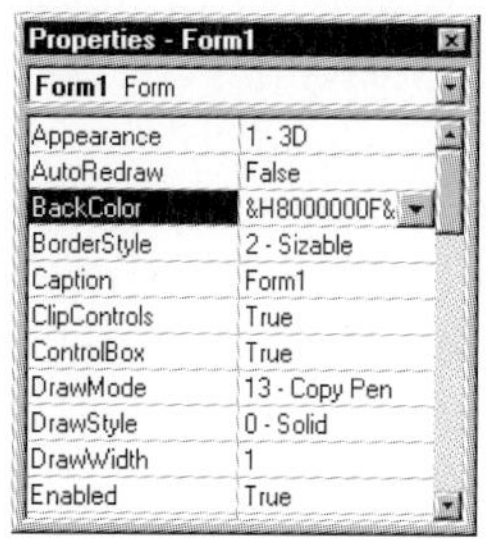

The setting is &H8000000F&, which is rather cryptic to say the least. In fact, Visual Basic describes color codes by using a hexadecimal code (base 16), which is described in the section "Colors and Counting in Base 16" in Chapter 5. In theory, using hexadecimal code allows you to set up to 16,777,216 different colors—usually finer control than one really needs. The most common way to set colors is to choose one of the color properties and click the down arrow in the Settings box. A box filled with small colored boxes opens up, as shown here.

(Although you cannot see the colors here, you can get an idea of what the color palette looks like.)

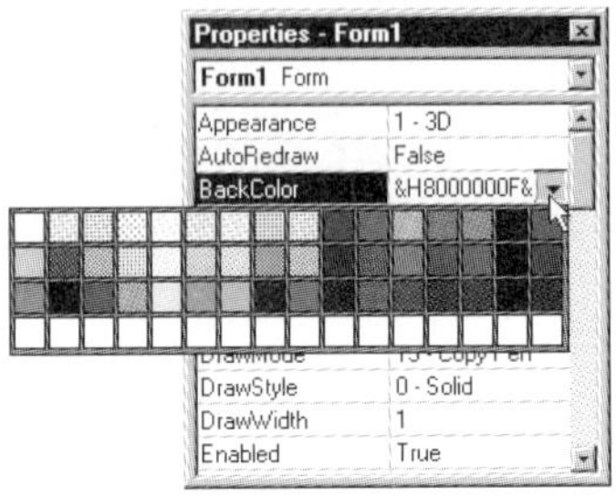

Click whatever color you like, and the color code for that color is placed in the Settings box.

WORKING WITH THE COLOR PALETTE

You can also create your own colors by working with the color palette directly. Open up the color palette by going to the View menu and choosing the color palette (ALT V, L). Here's what you see:

Notice, to the left of the palette, a dark box enclosed in a lighter box. The inner box displays the current foreground color, and the outer box displays the current background color.

You can change the foreground color by clicking the inner box and then clicking any of the colored boxes displayed. To change the background color, click the outer box and then click any of the colored boxes displayed.

The text box in the bottom left corner of the color palette displays the foreground and background colors for any text in the form or control you've selected. To go back to the default colors specified in the Windows control panel, click the Default command button at the right and close the palette by clicking the Exit button.

You can also create your own colors for the color palette. To do this, follow these steps:

1. Click the Custom Colors button on the color palette. Visual Basic adds a line of blank boxes at the bottom of the palette. Each of these boxes represents a possible custom color.

2. Click one of these blank boxes and then click the Define Colors command button (which is now enabled). This opens the Define Color dialog box, shown here:

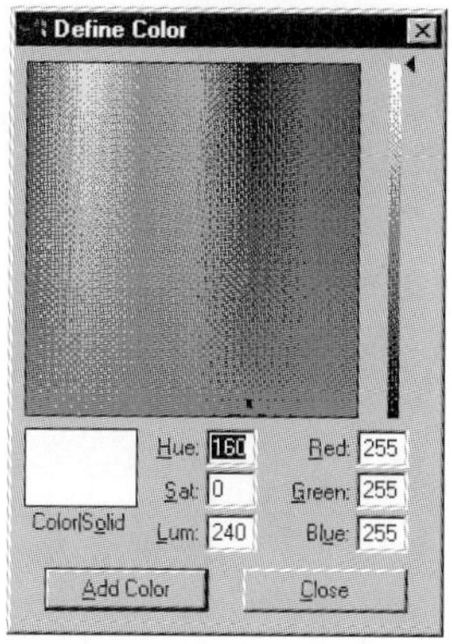

Now you can change the amount of red, green, or blue; color; hue; saturation; or luminosity of your form to suit your needs by adjusting the controls in the dialog box. Press the Add Color button to create the custom color or the Close button to cancel. To make the color palette go away, double-click on its control box or use the ALT+F4 shortcut when the palette has the focus.

Making a Form Responsive

By now, you should be comfortable with designing Visual Basic forms. The essence of a Microsoft Windows program (and, therefore, of Visual Basic) is to make your forms responsive to user actions. Visual Basic objects can recognize many different events. (Forms recognize more than 20.) For example, if a user clicks an area on the screen, you may want a message displayed; if the user clicks a command button, you may want an action performed. To effect these actions, you write programs in Visual Basic's structured programming language.

Although Visual Basic objects can recognize many different events, the objects will basically sit there unless you've written code to tell them what to do when an event occurs. Thus, for any event to which you want a Visual Basic object to respond, you must write an event procedure telling Visual Basic what to do. *Event procedures* are nothing more than the lines of programming code that tell Visual Basic how to respond to a given event.

The Code Window

Here, you will make your form respond to a mouse click. Double-click in any blank part of Form1 (your form may have a different name). A new window opens up, and your screen looks something like the one in Figure 3-3. Double-clicking the form opens the Code window. This is where you enter the code to tell Visual Basic how to respond to the event.

Notice the two combo boxes in the top screen, marked Object and Proc. If you click the arrow next to the Object list box, you pull down a list of all objects in your form, as shown here:

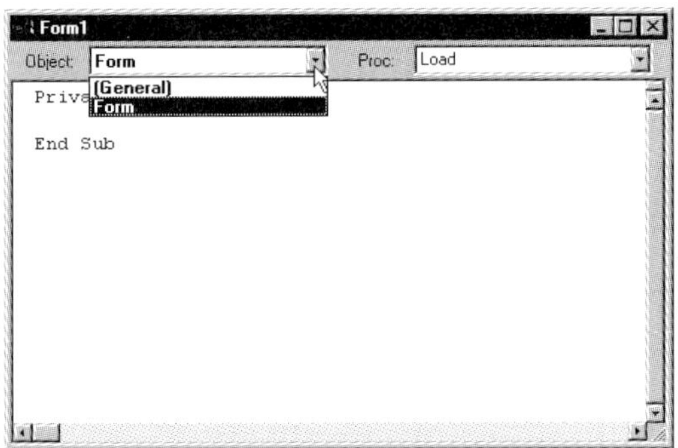

tip: *F7 opens the Code window and SHIFT+F7 brings the Form window back.*

You have yet to put any text boxes, command buttons, or other controls on this form, so no objects except the form itself (and an object called General, discussed in Chapter 5) are listed in this box. If you pull down the Procedure list box (the one abbreviated Proc) at the right, you see a list of all the events that the Visual Basic object named in the Object box can recognize. A form can recognize 25 events, so the Procedure list box has 25 items in it.

In Figure 3-3, below the Object and Procedure list boxes, you see the following code:

```
Private Sub Form_Load ()

End Sub
```

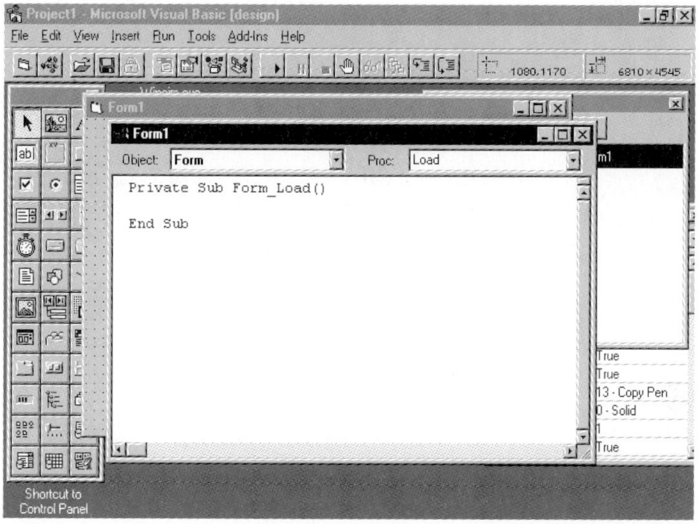

Figure 3-3 The Code window

This code is an example of an *event procedure template.* Like any template, it gives you a framework in which to work. The Form_Load event is invoked whenever Visual Basic brings up a form. It is often used to set initial properties of forms via code; you'll learn more about it in Chapters 4 and 5. (Chapters 4 and 5 discuss in detail how to write code for Visual Basic, so don't worry if you are a novice programmer. If you are an experienced programmer, you can move through these chapters quickly.)

For now, you want to enter the code that tells Visual Basic how to respond to a mouse click. To do this, you have to bring up the template for the Form_Click procedure. Move to the Procedure list box and click the down arrow. The screen will look like Figure 3-4. Move through the box until you get to the Click item. Click on it, and Visual Basic gives you a new event procedure template for the Click event procedure and moves the cursor to the blank line before the End Sub line.

tip: *As in any list box, you can quickly go to an item by pressing the first letter of the item. For example, pressing C will quickly take you to the click procedure.*

Figure 3-4 Code window when working with click event procedure

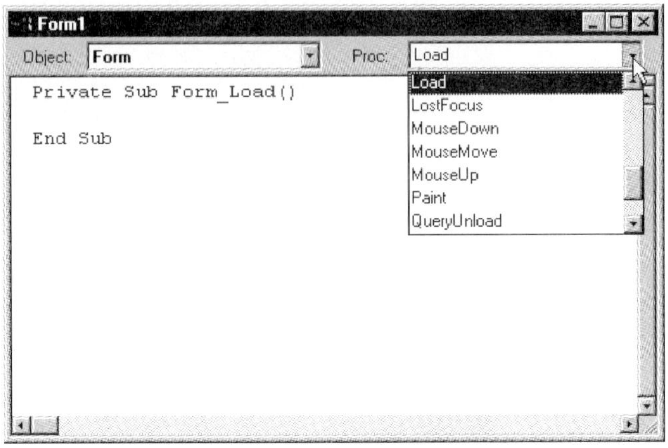

A SIMPLE EVENT PROCEDURE

Suppose you want to write the code necessary for Visual Basic to respond to a mouse click with a message. You can use all the normal Windows editing keys to enter code. For example, you can switch between insert and overstrike modes when you type. You can select text and then copy or cut it.

If the cursor is not at the blank line before the End Sub, move it there by scrolling through the Code window and clicking on the blank line. Press the TAB key or the SPACEBAR a few times (this indentation will improve readability) and type **Print "You clicked the mouse once."** Your Code window will look like this:

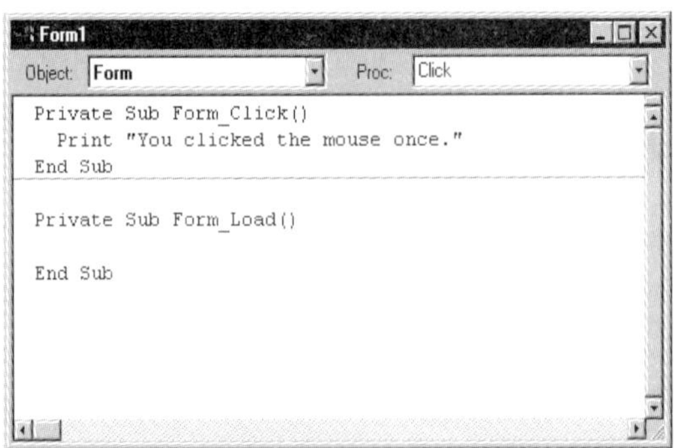

Now press F5 to run the application. As soon as the form pops up, move the mouse until the pointer is inside the form and click once. You'll see something like this:

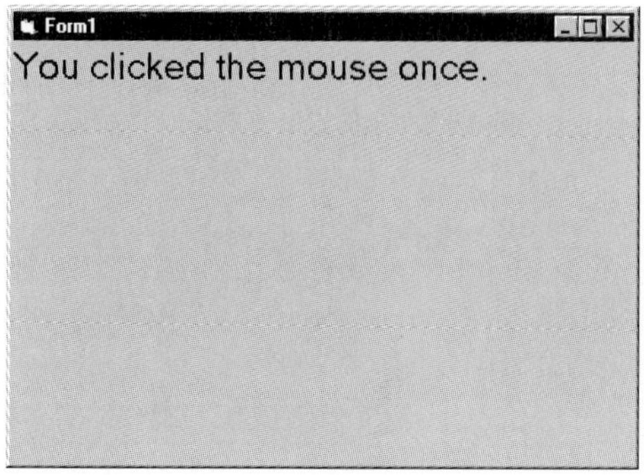

As you've probably guessed, the Print command sends the exact text found between the quotation marks directly to the form. (In the preceding illustration, the font size for the form was set to 18 points to make a larger splash; the default size is 8.25 points.) The default position for text is the top left corner of the screen, but you'll soon see how to change this.

MORE GENERAL EVENT PROCEDURES

In general, no matter what event you want the form to respond to, the code for an event procedure for a form in Visual Basic begins with something that looks like this:

```
Private Sub Form_NameOfTheEvent ( )
```

The following table gives some examples of event procedures and what they mean.

Event Procedure	Tells the Form
Private Sub Form_Click ( )	To respond to a click
Private Sub Form_DblClick ( )	To respond to a double-click
Private Sub Form_GotFocus ( )	To respond when it receives the focus
Private Sub Form_LostFocus ( )	To respond when it loses the focus

MONITORING MULTIPLE EVENTS

Visual Basic is always monitoring your computer for events, but unless you write code for the event, nothing happens. For example, you can add more code to monitor (and print) something when the user double-clicks.

To do this, end the previous program by going to the Run menu and clicking End (or click the Stop tool—the one that looks like the stop button on a cassette recorder). Now open the Code window (if it is not already open) by double-clicking in a blank part of the form. Notice that Visual Basic now displays the code for the Click event. Suppose you want to write code for the Double-Click event. Move the mouse to the arrow that drops down the list box for procedures and click. Your Code window should look something like this:

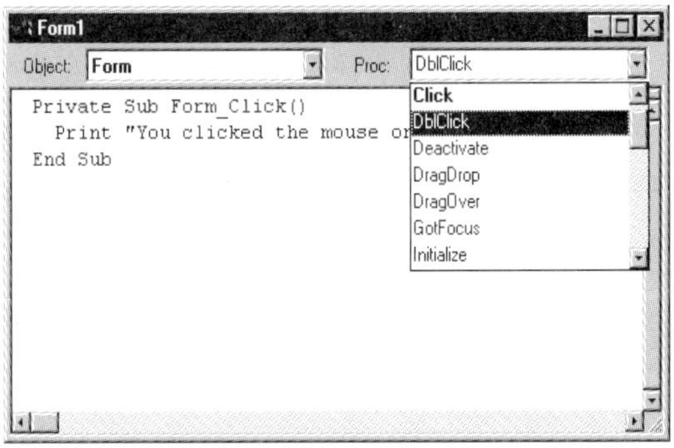

Select the Double-Click event by pressing D. Notice that the Click event procedure is now in bold—this is how Visual Basic indicates that an event procedure already exists for a particular event.

A new event template is added for the Double-Click event. Just as before, you can type between the beginning and ending lines of this event template. For example, type **Print "I said to click once, not twice!"** The Code window will look like this:

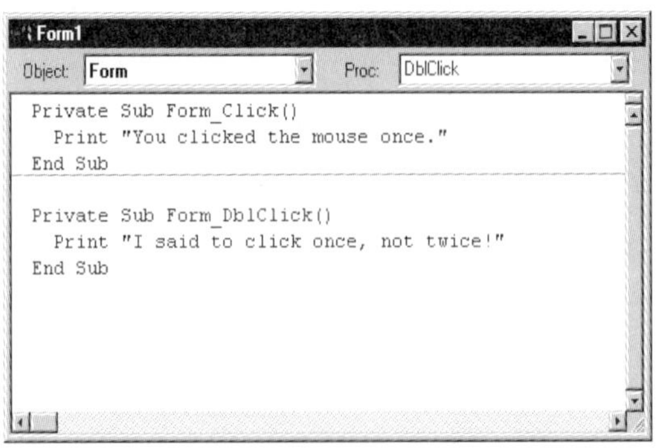

Now run the application and double-click. You'll see something like this:

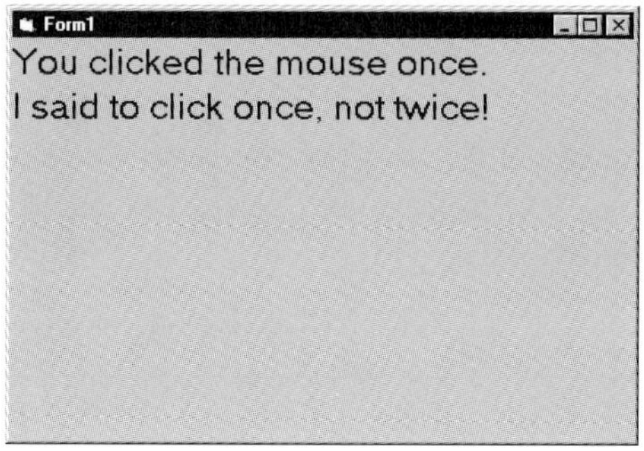

Notice that both lines of text appear on the screen. This is because in monitoring for a double-click, Visual Basic also detected the single click and activated the code for that event as well.

If all you want to do is clear the screen before displaying the second message, you need only make the first line of the double-click procedure the Cls command, which clears any text and graphics in the form. The Double-Click event procedure now looks like this:

```
Private Sub Form_DblClick ()
  Cls
  Print "I said to click once, not twice!"
End Sub
```

The Print and Cls commands are examples of what Visual Basic calls methods. Roughly speaking, *methods* are Visual Basic statements that affect what Visual Basic objects *do* (as opposed to properties, which affect what they are).

You can use another syntax for the Print or Cls command. This syntax is used for other Visual Basic objects, and it follows the general format *Object.Method* (discussed further in Chapter 4). This syntax uses the name of the object, followed by a period, followed by the method, followed by (if applicable) what the method should do:

```
ObjectName.Method WhatToDo
```

The default name for the first form created in a Visual Basic project is Form1, so the double-click procedure in this syntax would be written as follows:

```
Sub Form_DblClick ()
  Form1.Cls
  Form1.Print "I said to click once, not twice!"
End Sub
```

You will need to use the longer version when your projects involve more than one form, because this version lets Visual Basic know which form to apply the method to.

note: *Many programmers like to use the reserved object name of Me. This object name always refers to whatever forms code is being processed. Thus a line of code such as* ***Me.Cls*** *will always clear the screen in the form in which code is being used. I will usually use the* Me *object name.*

Printing a Form

Visual Basic relies on the underlying Windows program to handle its printing needs. For this reason, you should make sure you have configured Windows with the name of your printer when you set up Windows. Most of the time you won't need to get involved with the Windows Print Manager; Visual Basic takes care of the interface pretty well. It uses whatever printer information is contained in the Microsoft Windows environment control panel.

To dump the entire contents of a form to the printer in Visual Basic requires only a single command: PrintForm. Since this also affects what the form does, as opposed to what it is, it is another example of a Visual Basic method. PrintForm tries to send to your printer a dot-for-dot image of the entire form—including those parts of the form that are hidden. As an example, add the line PrintForm to the double-click procedure before the End Sub line; double-click and see what happens.

Typos

Nobody types completely accurately all the time. Visual Basic can point out many typing errors when you enter a line, and it will even correct some (such as leaving off a closing quote). All this happens even before you try to run your program. Moreover, as you'll see in Chapter 5, Visual Basic makes it easier to distinguish the different features of your code by color or size.

Suppose you made a typo when you were writing the Click event procedure presented earlier and misspelled the command word Print by typing Printf instead. Your Code window would look like this:

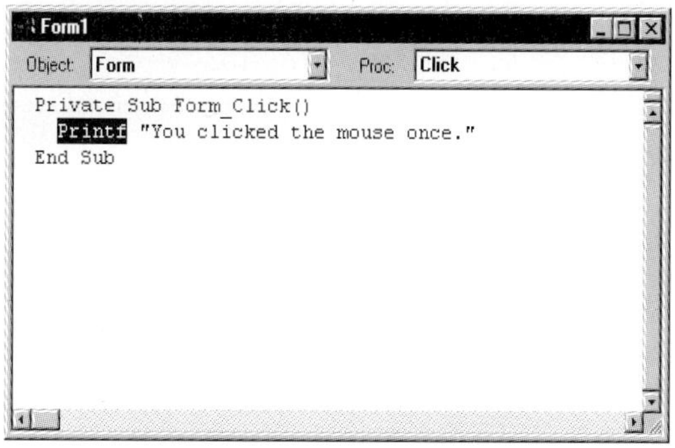

Notice that on your screen Printf should be in a different color than it was when it was correctly spelled (black instead of blue). If you don't notice the color change and try to run the program and click in the form, Visual Basic will immediately respond with an error message box, and your screen will look something like Figure 3-5. Notice that the offending word is highlighted and the message box tells you, "Sub or Function not defined"—what you entered isn't recognizable to Visual Basic. As you'll see in Chapter 9, Visual Basic lets you define your own Functions and Subs (like the event procedure ones) that extend its powers. In this case, Visual Basic thinks you mean one of these user-defined gadgets.

If you press ENTER or click the OK command button, the offending word remains highlighted, and you can either type the correct replacement or move the mouse pointer to the "f" and press DEL. After you make the correction, the program will run as before.

Another common typo with the Print method is to forget it completely—just typing the text. To see what happens when you do this, delete the keyword Print and run the program again. This time Visual Basic responds with a box saying you have made a syntax error—that what you entered doesn't conform to the grammar of a Visual Basic program.

If you need some help determining what is causing the error, press F1 for context-sensitive help when the error message is on the screen. Visual Basic opens the Help window and gives you some general information on the error. For example, the help screen for a syntax error looks like Figure 3-6.

Figure 3-5 Effects of a typo when coding

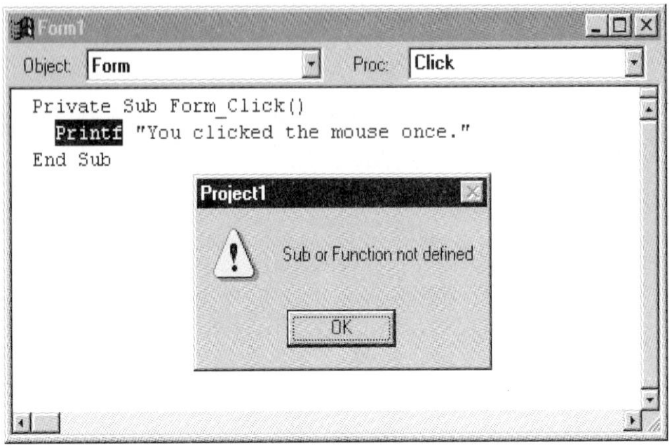

Visual Basic can even find some syntax errors after you finish typing a line. To make sure this feature is on (or to turn it on if it is off), choose Tools | Options

Figure 3-6 Help screen on syntax error

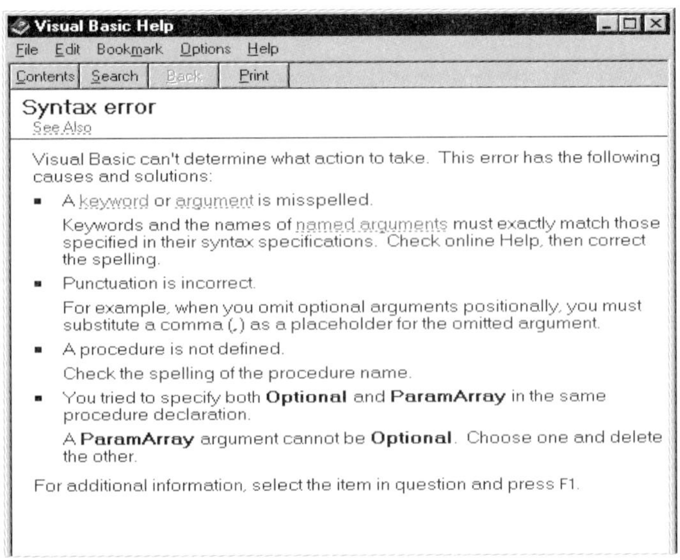

and then go to the Environment page. Move to the item marked Auto Syntax Check and make sure that it is checked (on).

Saving Your Work

You should get into the habit of saving your work frequently. Visual Basic will not let you exit the program or start a new project without asking whether you want to save your work. In fact, Visual Basic lets you automatically save your work before a project runs. This is a useful preventative from the dire effects of system crashes, because you can't save a project while it is running or when you are in break mode. To activate this feature:

1. Choose Tools | Options and go to the Environment page.
2. In the File Save box, change the Save Before Run option to either one of the two Yes options. (I always choose the "Save Before Run, Don't Prompt" option.)

In any case, most of the ways of saving your work are done by working with the File menu, so they are covered next.

Saving from the File Menu

The following sections describe the four save methods that are listed on the File menu.

Save File Use Save File to save the specific form you are working on. To use this option, press CTRL+S (or use ALT F, S). The default extension for form files is .FRM. The first time you choose this option, Visual Basic pops up a dialog box like the one shown in Figure 3-7. Subsequent uses do not pop up a dialog box—the saving occurs almost without your being aware of it.

note: *When you save a form again by using the Save Form option, Visual Basic does not keep a backup copy of the previous version.*

Save File As The Save File As option opens up the same dialog box you saw in Figure 3-7. This box allows you to rename the current form (.FRM) file *and is the only way to make a backup copy or store a copy of the current form on another disk.* To select this option, press CTRL+A (or ALT F, A). The next time you save the project (see the next topic), Visual Basic will update the file it uses for bookkeeping purposes to reflect the new name. (These bookkeeping files are usually called *project files* and have the extension .VBP.)

Save Project Choose the Save Project option in order to save the entire project. To select this option, press ALT F, V or use the Save Project tool. When you first try to save a project by clicking this option, Visual Basic opens a dialog box similar to the one shown in Figure 3-7. It also gives the project a suggested name (a rather prosaic Project1.VBP).What you enter into the Save Project dialog box shown becomes the name of a .VBP file. It then pops up a dialog box for saving all the other files in the project if they haven't been saved already. When you create a stand-alone application, Visual Basic combines all the files in the project by looking for them where the .VBP file tells it to.

If you use the Save Project option to save revised versions of the same project during the course of developing and improving it, Visual Basic no longer provides you with a dialog box; it assumes you want to use the same project name every time.

Figure 3-7
Save File dialog box

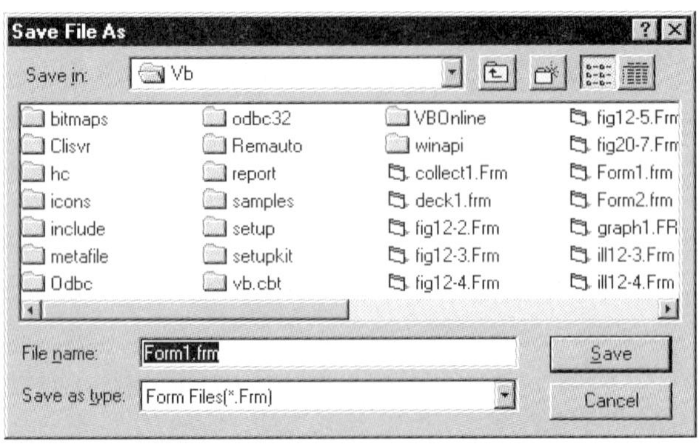

note: *When you save a project using the Save Project option, Visual Basic does not keep a backup copy of the previous version. To save a backup copy of a project, do the following:*

1. Save each of the files on the project with a new name.

2. Choose the Save Project As option and give the project file (.VBP) a new (path) name. (You can also use standard Windows 95 or Windows NT techniques to save these files while still in Visual Basic.)

Save Project As The Save Project As option pops up the same sort of dialog box as you see when you first use the Save Project option, but it asks only for the new name of the .VBP file, unless you've changed the form. If you have, then it opens up a dialog box that looks like this:

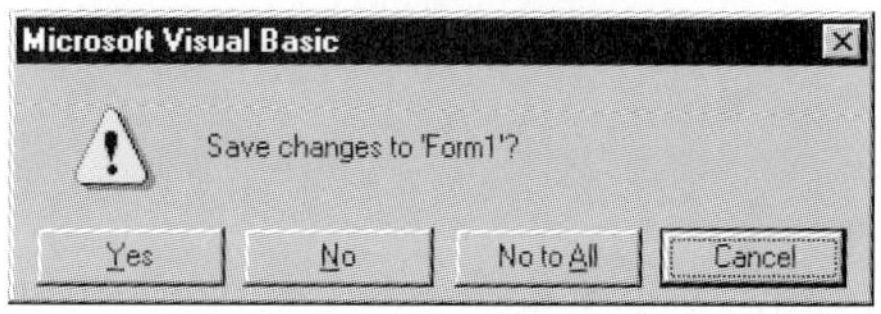

Note that if you click the Yes button, the changes to the Form are saved to a file with the same name as before. This means you will have lost the information contained in the original .FRM file.

caution: *Save Project As does not make a backup copy of the unchanged files in the project. It saves a new project (.VBP) file with the current file names.*

Creating Stand-Alone Windows Programs

One of the most exciting features of Visual Basic is the ability to change your projects into stand-alone Microsoft Windows programs. To do this, simply go to the File menu and choose the Make EXE File option (ALT F, K). This opens a dialog box that looks like Figure 3-8. (See Chapter 9 for more on this dialog box.) For now, notice that the default name for the .EXE version of your file is the project name (the name of the .VBP file with an .EXE extension). For the stand-alone program, the Windows desktop uses the same icon that Visual Basic uses for the executable version of the project.

When you distribute a Visual Basic 4 program, it is also necessary to supply various *dynamic link libraries* to the user. These files come with Visual Basic. (Dynamic link libraries are the cornerstone of Windows programming; among

Figure 3-8
Make EXE File dialog box

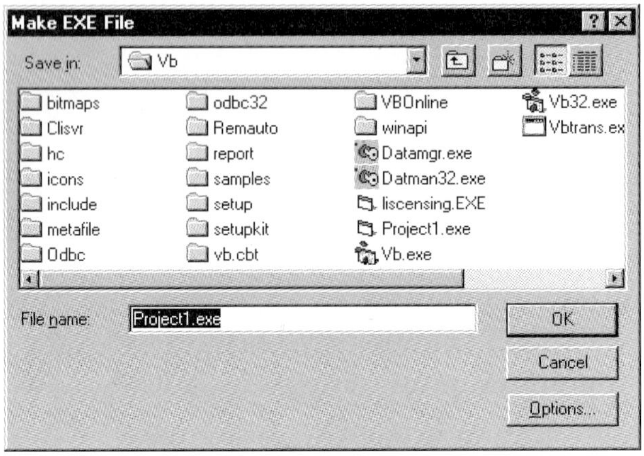

their other features they allow many programs to use the same code simultaneously.) No matter how many different stand-alone Visual Basic applications users have, they need only one copy of the necessary files in a Windows directory accessible to Windows. They also need only one copy of any custom control files used by the Visual Basic applications. (The directory containing the system files for Windows itself is the usual choice.) This file contains various support routines that a Visual Basic program needs to handle the screens, numbers, and other parts of the application. Microsoft freely allows you to distribute the necessary run-time libraries.

Finally, Visual Basic 4 comes with a setup wizard that makes distributing your programs easy. See Appendix A of this book for more information on this as well as information on the various run-time libraries needed for Visual Basic executable files.

Chapter Four

First Steps in Building the User Interface

CHAPTER 3 showed you how to customize a blank form. You saw how to use the Properties window to make a form more visually appealing, as well as how to write simple event procedures to make them responsive to a user. This chapter shows you how to use the toolbox to add controls to a form. You'll see several controls in this chapter: command buttons to initiate actions, text boxes to accept or display data, labels to identify controls and data, and image controls to display pictures.

The techniques for using the Properties window that you saw in Chapter 3 will appear again; it's a good idea to make sure you are completely comfortable with the techniques for setting properties before you continue. Just as with forms, controls remain basically inert until you write event procedures to tell them how to respond, and the techniques for writing event procedures for controls are similar to those you use for writing a form. For example, to have clicking a command button initiate an action requires writing an event procedure almost identical to the one that made a blank form respond to a click. Finally, you'll see how message boxes can make applications more friendly by, for example, warning users of irreversible steps they may be taking.

note: *While the controls discussed in this chapter are among the most commonly used ones for Visual Basic applications, a polished and professional Visual Basic application will likely need the controls that are discussed in Chapters 12, 13, and 17. All this chapter does is give you enough information about manipulating controls so that you can master the underlying programming language. This way you won't be burdened with discussions of dozens of controls and hundred of properties before you can get your programs to actually* ***do*** *anything.*

The Toolbox

As the name suggests, the toolbox is a set of tools you use to embellish a blank form with the controls needed for sophisticated Windows programs. The standard edition of Visual Basic comes with 26 different tools. The Professional edition adds 28 more.

One of the more exciting features of Visual Basic is its extendability by what are called *custom controls*. The 16-bit version of Visual Basic can use two types of custom controls. The first are the custom controls that were used in earlier versions of Visual Basic. These are files having a .VBX extension in their names. (An example might be PEN.VBX.) The newer custom controls have an .OCX extension and are designed to work better with OLE (object linking and embedding—see Chapter 18). The 32-bit version of Visual Basic can only work with the .OCX controls that are designed for it. You will need to upgrade any old Visual Basic controls in this case. Chapter 2 showed you how to add custom controls to your projects. You can also buy custom tools from third-party developers that can extend Visual Basic in even more dramatic ways (see Appendix D).

You can control which custom controls get added to your toolbox automatically. To make a custom control automatically part of your toolbox:

1. Open the appropriate autold*.vbp project (autold16.vbp for 16-bit development, autold32.vbp for 32-bit development).
2. Add the custom control to the toolbox.
3. Save the autold*.vbp project.

Figure 4-1 shows the toolbox supplied with the standard version of Visual Basic, including the custom controls that are loaded automatically. The toolbox is usually located on the far left of the Visual Basic screen, but it need not be visible at all times. If the toolbox isn't visible, you must make it visible in order to work with controls. To open the toolbox, go to the View menu on the main menu bar and choose Toolbox (ALT V, X). You can move the toolbox using ordinary Windows techniques. Following are brief descriptions of the tools covered in this chapter.

Command Buttons Command buttons are sometimes called push buttons. The idea is that when the user moves the mouse to the command button and clicks,

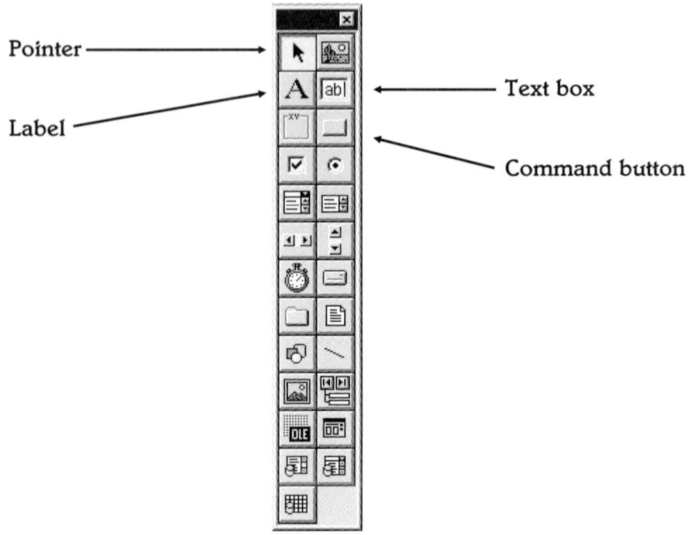

Figure 4-1 The toolbox

something interesting should happen (and will, once you write the event procedure that tells Visual Basic how to respond to the mouse click). When you click a command button, it gives the illusion of being pressed. This optical illusion comes from the shading used by Visual Basic for command buttons and is inherited from Microsoft Windows.

tip: *The Professional and Enterprise editions come with a control for 3-D command buttons. These work in much the same way as ordinary command buttons—but they often look better. 3-D command buttons are a custom control and so may need to be added to your toolbox. (The default installation, though, is that they are available.).*

Image Controls Image controls are one of two types of standard controls that can be used to display pictures. They use the fewest Windows resources for displaying images. (Picture boxes—see Chapters 6 and 15—can do more but use more resources.) Since image controls also recognize the Click event, you can use them as graphical replacements for command buttons. However, unlike command buttons, image controls do not give the user any feedback when they've been pressed, unless you program them to do so in the project.

note: *The Professional edition comes with a control for animated buttons (see Chapter 13) that give you another option when you might consider using an image control for a command button. Animated buttons are a custom control and so must be added to your toolbox (see Chapter 2).*

Text Boxes Text boxes are sometimes called edit fields. You use text boxes to display text or to accept user input. Most of the code you write for text boxes is for processing the information users enter into them. All the ordinary Windows editing tools, such as cutting and pasting, are available when you enter information in a text box. Text boxes can allow word wrap and may have scroll bars for moving through the text. Scroll bars are vital because text boxes can accept large amounts of text. The usual limit for a text box is approximately 32,000 characters.

protip: *For 32-bit versions (Windows 95 and Windows NT development), the Professional and Enterprise editions comes with a RichTextBox control that goes way beyond what an ordinary text box can do. RichTextBoxes are discussed further in Chapter 6.*

Labels Labels are for information that users can't change. They identify objects and occasionally are used to display output. You have almost complete control over how the label displays information—whether the text is boldfaced, what size it is, and so forth. (You cannot mix fonts however.) Although labels do respond to 12 events, usually they are used passively—for display purposes only.

The Pointer The first item on the toolbox is not a control but is used to manipulate controls after you create them. Click the pointer when you want to select, resize, or move an existing control. The pointer is automatically activated after you place a control on a form.

Creating Controls

Most of the methods for using the toolbox are similar to those used in a paint program such as Microsoft Paint, which comes with Windows. You use a combination of pointing, clicking, and dragging to manipulate the toolbox. For example, to draw an item from the toolbox on a form:

1. Move the mouse pointer to the tool you want to use and click. The tool changes color (shade) to indicate that you've selected it. (It also looks pressed in.)
2. Move the mouse pointer to the form. Think of this as the paint area in which you will draw the control. Notice that the mouse pointer has changed from an arrow to a shape like a crosshair.
3. Hold the mouse button down and drag the mouse to create the object. As you drag the mouse pointer, an outline of the control appears on the form.

One corner of the control is determined by where you press the mouse button in step 3, and the other is determined by where you release the button.

Notice as well that when you release the mouse button, the control has eight little boxes, called *sizing handles*, jutting out. (Line controls are one-dimensional and have only two sizing handles.) You will use these to move and resize a control after you've created it. The pointer control is automatically highlighted when you release the left mouse button as well.

Notice that as you manipulate the control, it seems to move or enlarge in fits and starts, not smoothly. As the old computer joke goes, this is not a bug in Visual Basic, it really is a feature. The position of controls on a form in Visual Basic default so that they are located only at grid points. If you are willing to have a control appear off the grid, you can smooth out the motion of the controls. However, doing this makes it more difficult to align the control on a form. If you want to do this, the section called "The Grid" at the end of this chapter shows you how. That section also shows you how to make the design grid even finer, which is often preferable to removing the design grid completely.

tip: *The dotted design grid can help you accurately locate the control.*

There are two reasons why the feature of locating controls only at grid points—called *aligning to the grid or snapping to the grid*—makes positioning controls in Visual Basic a snap. First, the corners and sides of any control will always end up on a grid mark. Second, you have a small amount of leeway when you move the crosshair. Only when the vertical line of the crosshair hits a grid mark does the object move left or right. Similarly, only when the horizontal line of the crosshair hits a grid mark does the object move up or down.

In theory, you can have 254 different control names used on a single form, but you will rarely use this many. One reason to limit the number of controls on a form is that Windows (especially 3.X) is limited in the number of controls and windows it can handle at any one time. If you start adding too many controls or menus to a form, your program will slow down dramatically. As Windows gets closer to its limits, it is possible that Visual Basic will crash and need to be terminated by Windows.

Working with an Existing Control

Let's suppose you've used the techniques described in the previous section to create a command button on a blank form. (When you create a command button, it appears with a centered caption: Command1, Command2, and so on. As you'll soon see, you can easily change these captions via the Properties window.)

The techniques in the last section let you create a control and place it anywhere you like on a form. In Visual Basic you are never forced to keep a control at its original size or at its original location. The techniques needed for moving or resizing controls are the same for all Visual Basic controls. You can also cut and paste controls by cutting out the control and using the Copy item on the Edit menu. (Chapter 9 describes the effect of copying an existing control.)

To work with an existing control, you must first select it. This is done by moving the mouse pointer until it is inside the control and clicking. (Or you may use the TAB key until the focus is at the control. You can tell where the focus is by looking at the sizing handles.)

RESIZING AN EXISTING CONTROL

Suppose you've created a command button but aren't happy with its size. To change the size of an existing command button, you need to use the sizing handles mentioned earlier. Figure 4-2 shows you a command button with a pointer at one of its eight sizing handles on an otherwise blank form.

If the sizing handles no longer appear, you can make them reappear by moving the mouse pointer to the control and clicking once. When the sizing handles are visible, you know the control is selected. The four corner handles let you change the height and width at the same time. The mouse pointer changes to a double-sided diagonal arrow when you move the pointer to one of the corner sizing handles. The four side handles let you change the size in one direction only. At these handles, the mouse pointer changes to a straight double-sided arrow.

Figure 4-2 Command button with sizing handles

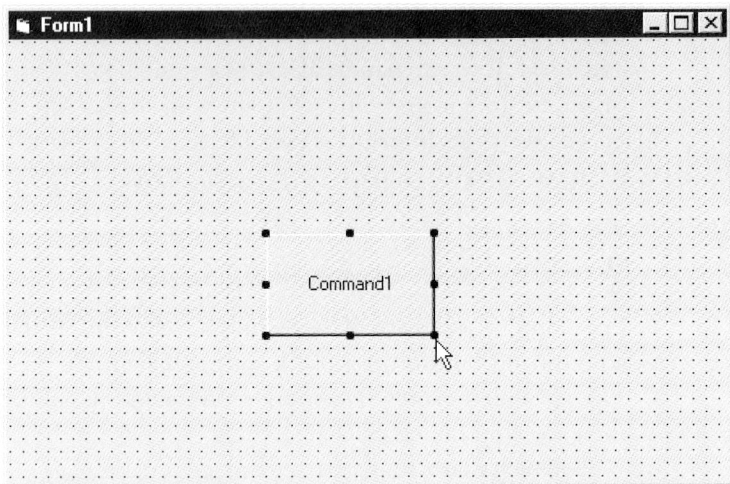

To actually resize a control:

1. Move the mouse pointer to a sizing handle and click and hold down the left mouse button.
2. Drag the mouse until the control is the size you want.

For example, if you want to shrink a control button in from the left side while keeping the right side fixed, move the mouse pointer to the sizing handle in the center of the left side, click, and drag the mouse over to the right. You also can get feedback on the size and position of the control by looking at the far right of the toolbar.

MOVING AN EXISTING CONTROL

In order to move an existing control, the focus must be at that control. Notice that when you move the mouse so that the mouse pointer is inside the form, its shape returns to the form of an arrow. The crosshair shows up only when you are creating a new control. Now, to move an existing control:

1. Move the pointer anywhere inside the control, click the left mouse button, and hold it down.

2. Drag the mouse until the control is at the location you want it to be and then release the left button.

For finer control over the movement of controls:

1. Select the control.
2. Use CTRL+an arrow key to move the control one grid mark at a time.

Shortcut for Creating Controls

Now that you know how to move controls, you may prefer a shortcut for creating them. If you double-click on any of the toolbox icons, that control appears in the center of the screen in its default size. The more controls you double-click on, the higher they get stacked. You then can use the techniques from the previous section for moving controls to reposition and resize the controls on the stack.

For example, suppose you want to create an application with five command buttons symmetrically dispersed, as shown in Figure 4-3. The easiest way to do this is to double-click on the Command Button icon five times. This stacks five command buttons in the center of the form. Then you can easily use the method

Figure 4-3 Form with multiple command buttons

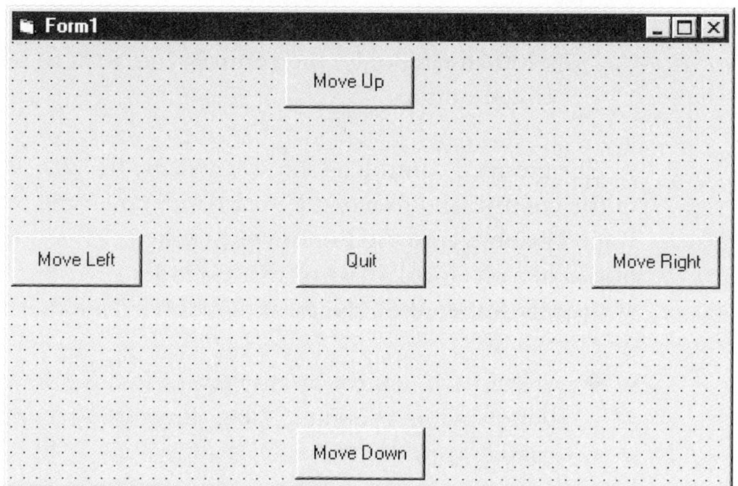

given in the previous section to move the buttons to the locations shown in Figure 4-3.

You may have noticed that the captions are more informative than the usual Command1, Command2, and so on. You change the captions by adjusting the Caption property of the command buttons via the Properties window. You will see how to do this in the section "Properties of Command Buttons," later in this chapter.

note: *See Chapter 12 for another method of creating multiple control at design time. See Chapter 10 for the methods for creating controls at run time.*

Working with Multiple Controls

Occasionally, you'll want to move a group of controls in the same direction. For example, you may have three command buttons lined up and want to keep them aligned but move them up a couple of grid marks. To work with multiple controls as a single unit, you must first tell Visual Basic that you wish the controls to be temporarily treated as a unit. There are two ways to do this. Follow these steps for one method:

1. Imagine a rectangle that hits only those controls you want to select. Move to one corner of this imagined rectangle and click the left mouse button.
2. Hold the left mouse button down and drag the dotted rectangle until it hits all (and only) the controls you want to select. Then release the mouse button.

The grouped controls all show *gray* sizing handles. When you select any one of the controls and move it, Visual Basic moves the other controls in a similar way. The above method only works when the controls to be moved can be placed in a rectangular "lasso" that excludes any other controls. If the controls are widely scattered on the form, you'll need another method:

- Select each control by moving to it and holding down the left mouse button while pressing CTRL. (From the second control on, the sizing handles turn gray.)

Regardless of what method you choose, if you move the mouse pointer to any one of the controls you've selected and drag it to its new location, the other controls move along with it.

To undo the selection process for multiple controls, move the mouse pointer outside the selected controls and click.

Locking Controls

Once you are happy with the position of the controls on your form, you may want to use the new locking feature of Visual Basic 4. By choosing Edit|Lock Controls (ALT E, K), the Lock Control from the toolbar, or the shortcut menu, you stop yourself from inadvertently moving a properly positioned control. Since this item is a toggle, choosing it again frees up controls so that you can move them once more.

Deleting Controls

You may end up with too many controls on your form—especially if you use the double-click method a lot. To delete a control:

1. Move the mouse pointer until it is inside the control and click the left mouse button to select it.
2. Press DEL or open the Edit menu and choose the Delete option by pressing ALT E, D.

The methods for selecting multiple controls so you can move them as a unit, discussed in the previous section, are also used when you want to delete many controls at once. Once you've told Visual Basic that you want the controls considered as a unit, the DEL key or Delete menu option works on all the controls in the group. You can also use the ordinary Windows editing shortcut keys such as CTRL+V (or CTRL+INS) to paste, in addition to the Edit|Paste option.

Properties of Command Buttons

Just as you use the Properties window to customize the size and shape of blank forms, you can use it to customize controls. For example, if you don't like the default values for a control's property, you can open the Properties window and change them.

The next few sections take you through what are the most useful properties of command buttons. But you also may want to scroll through the list of properties and use the online help for any property that has a name that intrigues you, even if that property is not covered in this chapter.

The Caption Property

The Caption property of a form determines the name that shows in the title bar. Similarly, the Caption property on a command button determines what the user sees. Any text you use for the caption on a command button is automatically centered within the button. However, command buttons aren't resized to fit the caption you choose—you have to do that yourself.

Command buttons always start out with captions like Command1, Command2, and so on. The number indicates the order in which the buttons were created. Let's create a simple command button like the one shown in Figure 4-4. This message will not fit inside the default size of a command button. Luckily, you can create a caption first via the Properties window and then resize the control to fit it. More of the message shows up as you enlarge the control, so it's easy to judge when to stop.

Figure 4-4 A long caption on a command button

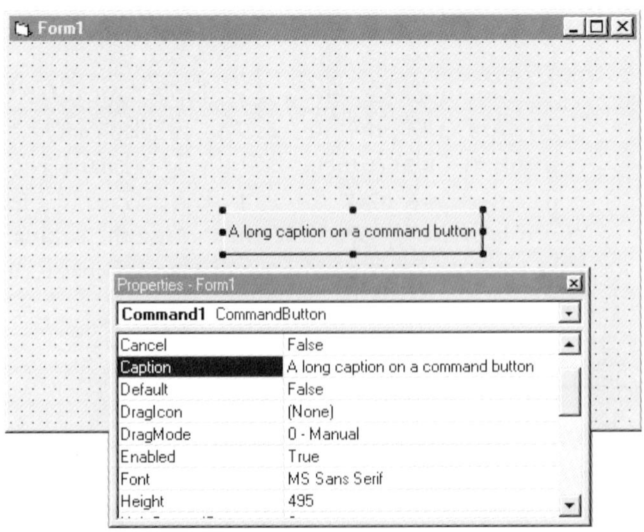

Double-click on the Command Button icon to create the button in the center of the screen. The Properties window should be visible. If the Properties window is not visible, use the F4 shortcut to make it appear.

Let's suppose that you want to change the Caption property of the command button. If for some reason the Caption property isn't showing up on the Properties window for the command button, the method to get to it is similar to the one you learned in Chapter 3:

1. Move to the Properties window.
2. Go to the Caption property by using the mouse or the UP ARROW and DOWN ARROW keys.

tip: *The SHIFT+CTRL+letter combination you saw for moving through the Properties window of a form works for controls as well.*

Now you can type the new setting for the Caption property. If you need to replace the old setting (or part of it), hold down the left mouse button and drag it until all the text you want to use is highlighted. Overwrite the old setting or fill in the blank area by typing the phrase **A long caption on a command button**.

The results are shown in Figure 4-5. Now you can resize the command button to fit the new caption.

Figure 4-5 Designing a long caption

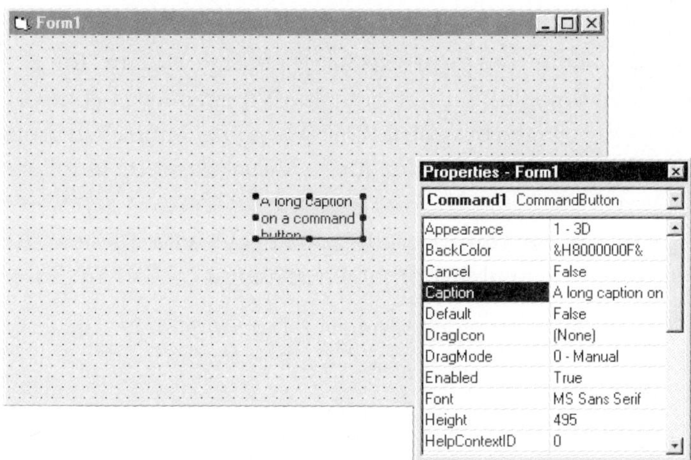

The Name (Control Name) Property

The Name property is very important when you start writing event procedures for controls. This property determines the name Visual Basic uses for the event procedures you write to make a control respond to the user. Picking meaningful names for controls goes a long way toward making the inevitable debugging process for developing an application easier. For example, suppose you are writing the code to make clicking a command button move a form to the left, as you did with the Move Left command button in the form in Figure 4-3. When you have five command buttons in an application, writing code that looks like this

```
Private Sub Command4_Click ()

End Sub
```

to make a form move left is a lot more confusing than writing it like this

```
Private Sub LeftButton_Click ()

End Sub
```

or this:

```
Private Sub btnLeft_Click ()

End Sub
```

Don't go overboard; the setting you use for a control's name should be meaningful but not ridiculous; the names of controls *do* enlarge the size of the file created by Visual Basic when you've finished programming the project. The limits on a control name in Visual Basic are as follows:

- A control name must begin with a letter. (After that, you can use any combination of letters, numbers, and underscores.)
- The name cannot be longer than 40 characters.

Microsoft's convention (see Chapter 3 of the *Programmer's Guide*) is to use an abbreviation for the type of control followed by the meaningful part, as indicated by the btnLeft in the preceding program. (Microsoft also suggests as an alternative using cmd as the prefix for command button names.)

note: *This book uses Microsoft's convention for naming controls most of the time. I actually prefer control names like LeftButton rather than btnLeft or cmdLeft—since it is easier for me to read. The trend—helped along by Microsoft of course—is against this, so in this edition I bowed to the inevitable. Whatever you do, however, follow some convention, or else your code may be unreadable soon after you've written it!*

Other Useful Properties for Command Buttons

There are 33 properties you can control for a command button, although not all can be set from the Properties window. Many of them are similar to the ones you saw for a form in Chapter 3. For example, command buttons have BackColor, Height, and Width properties. What follows is a short discussion of the most basic ones.

BackColor As with forms, the BackColor property sets the background color for the button, but really only changes the colors of the four corners. Because of this, the BackColor property is rarely changed. You can set the background color by using the methods described in Chapter 3 to access the color palette. Command buttons do not have a ForeColor property, so you must accept the default color for this.

Height, Width The Height and Width properties measure the height and width of the command button. Note that the units used are the ones set by the scale properties for the surrounding *container.* Usually the container is the form, but as you'll see in Chapter 10, you can block out regions within a form by using controls such as frames or picture boxes. This means the default measurement for the height and width of a command button is expressed in twips (1/20 of a printer's point, or 1/1440 of an inch). On the other hand, if you set the ScaleMode property of the surrounding form to 5 (inches), the Height and Width properties for command buttons will also be measured in inches.

You can change the settings for these properties directly from the Properties window or by using the sizing handles. As with a form, the current values for the size of the command button are displayed at the far right of the Properties window for the command button.

Left, Top The Left and Top properties determine the distance between the command button and the left edge and top of the container (again, usually the form), respectively. As with the Height and Width properties, these properties use the scale determined by the surrounding form. You can also change them by dragging and, as with forms, the values are displayed to the right of the Settings box on the Properties window.

Visible The Visible property determines whether the command button is visible or not. It's quite common to have your code alternately make a command button visible and invisible, depending on the situation. Like the Visible property for forms, this property can only be set to True or False.

Enabled The Enabled property determines whether the button can respond to any event whatsoever. If you set this property to False, Visual Basic will not respond to any event concerning that button. Unlike the Visible property, the button remains on the form but is inert. The Enabled property is more often temporarily toggled on or off via code in order to maintain flexibility in your program. Changing this property also changes the appearance of an item, usually by graying out the text.

MousePointer Setting the mouse pointer to something different than the usual arrow is a good way to give a user feedback that he or she has moved the focus to the command button. (Recall that "having the focus" is the standard phrase in Microsoft Windows to describe that a control is primed to receive input.) The same 17 settings that are available for the MousePointer on a form are available for a command button—including the ability to make custom cursors by the method discussed in Chapter 3.

Font When you open up the Font dialog box, all the font characteristics—Bold, Italic, Name, and so on—can be set independently for each command button.

These properties allow you to control how the caption appears within the button.

Shortcuts for Setting Properties

Suppose you want to set the Caption property for all the command buttons on your form. If you set it once and immediately select another command button, the Caption property for the new control is the one that appears on the Properties window. In general then, Visual Basic remembers the property just set for a control and, if possible, brings up the same property for the next control you select on the Properties window. (But you still have to change the property.)

Similarly, if you select a group of controls, the Properties window will show only the common properties that the controls in the group share. Change one of them and all of them change.

tip: *The easiest way to work with the different controls on a form is to click the down arrow to the right of the first line of the Properties window (below the title bar). This gives you a list of all the objects on the form. Here's an example of what you'll see:*

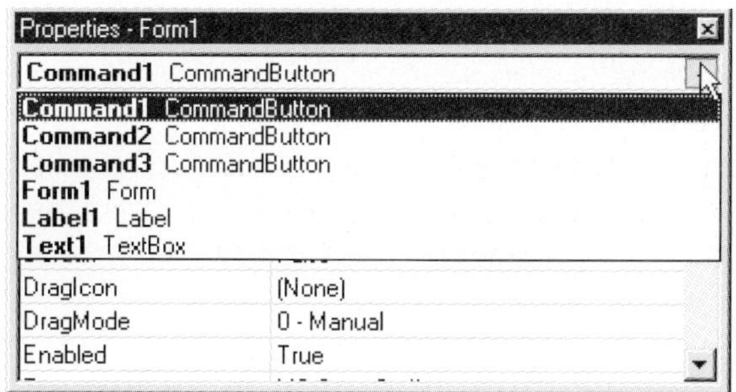

Simple Event Procedures for Command Buttons

Writing an event procedure for a command button is similar to writing one for a form. Whenever you double-click a control or use the F7 shortcut, Visual Basic opens the Code window. Visual Basic presents you with a template for the most common event procedure (usually the Click event) for that object.

Suppose you set up a command button with the caption "Click here for HELP!" Moreover, suppose you set the control name (the Name property) for this control to the more meaningful btnHelp. Figure 4-6 shows what you will see in the Code window. Notice that the event procedure template has a form similar to the ones you saw in Chapter 3. The only difference is that the control name for the object is used, followed by an underscore, followed by the name of the event. This is the general form for the event procedure template for controls:

```
Private Sub ControlName__EventName ( )

End Sub
```

Click the down arrow to the right of btnHelp in the Object box. Your Code window should look like the one in Figure 4-7. Notice that the list of objects in the Object list box has grown to include one named btnHelp. Visual Basic always keeps track of all the objects in your project, and you can write event procedures for any of them by opening the Code window, moving through the Object list box, and selecting the object that interests you.

Let's add a simple Print statement to this event procedure, as shown here:

```
Private Sub btnHelp_Click ()
  Print "No Help is yet available. Sorry."
End Sub
```

Figure 4-6 Code window for setting up a command button

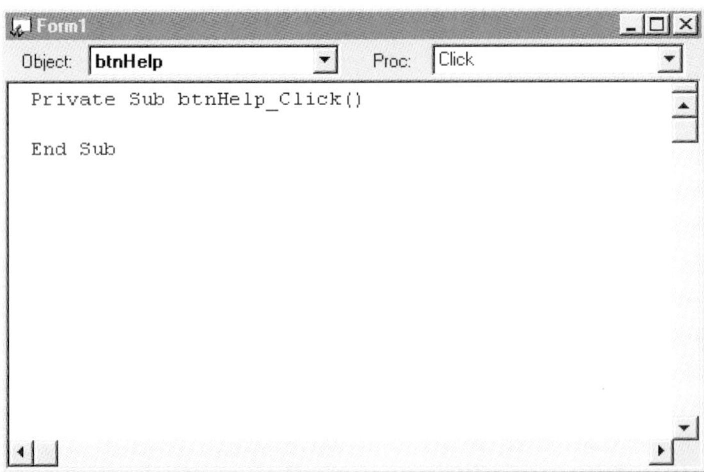

Figure 4-7 Pull-down list showing objects in a project

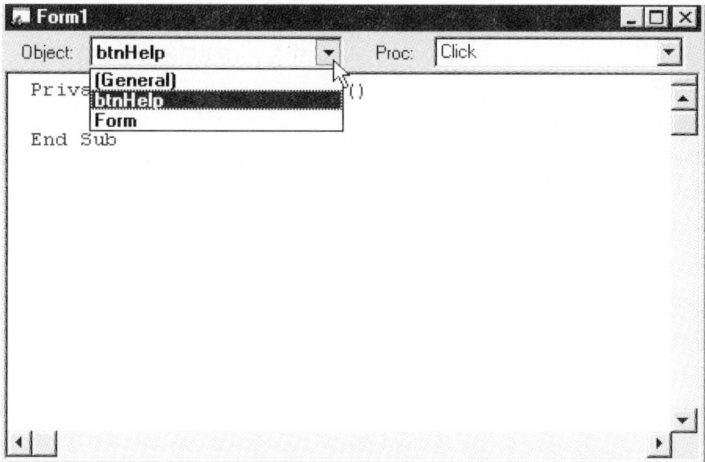

Now if you run this program (for example, by pressing F5) and click the form button, you should see something like what is shown in Figure 4-8.

In general, you have to be aware of the problems of using Print statements with a form that has controls on it already. If a control is located where the text is supposed to appear, the information printed to the form appears behind the control. Figure 4-9 shows an example of this.

Figure 4-8 Results of clicking on the Help button

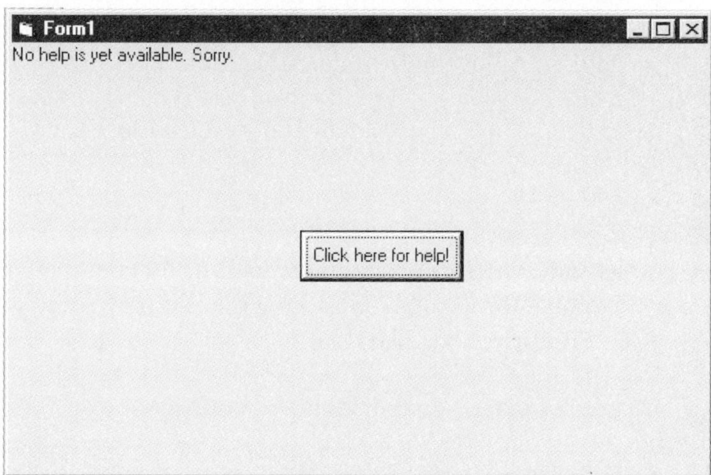

Figure 4-9

Text obscured by an existing control

The usual way to handle help information (or any other information you don't want obscured) is to use a picture box, separate form, or occasionally a message box. You might then have the user close the window when he or she has digested the information. (Chapter 5 shows you how to do this.) Also, you should be aware that if you iconize a window or move another window so that it temporarily covers a form with text on it, the text will disappear. You can overcome this by setting the AutoRedraw property of the form to True. (See the section later in this chapter on this important property.) Another possibility is to rewrite the text as needed. The Paint event procedure is the usual place to do this. This is because Visual Basic generates the Paint event whenever a form is moved, enlarged, or uncovered when AutoRedraw is False.

Other Events for Command Buttons

Command buttons can respond to 11 events, but clicking is by far the most common. Two others you may find useful are GotFocus and LostFocus. Naive users are often inattentive to just where the focus is and may get confused if what they type or click seems to be having no effect. Controls in Visual Basic can monitor whether the person has inadvertently moved the focus. You can then remind users that they've moved the focus and ask if they really want to do that. An event procedure that looks like this

```
Private Sub CommandButton_LostFocus ()

End Sub
```

lets you write the code to respond to users moving the focus away from that button—for example, by asking them if they really want to.

Similarly, code like this

```
Private Sub CommandButton_GotFocus ()

End Sub
```

might include code to generate help about that command button (for example, a "tooltip").

Command buttons can also respond to a user's pressing specific keys (see Chapter 7) and to mouse events (see Chapter 13).

Some Final Points on Command Buttons

Usually, the user of the application you develop chooses a command button by moving the mouse pointer to the button and clicking. However, sometimes you will want more flexibility. One other method for activating a command button is common to all Windows applications: move the focus by pressing TAB, and then press the SPACEBAR when the focus is where you want it to be. Both of these methods generate the Click event for that button. In other words, Visual Basic activates the Click event procedure in either case if one is available for that control. As you'll see in Chapter 5, you can also activate a Click event via code. The user knows a button has received the focus when it gives the appearance of being three-dimensional. What actually happens is Visual Basic draws a thinly dashed box around the text in the button and a fine rectangle around the button itself.

In addition, sometimes you want to give people an escape button for an action. This button cancels an action or otherwise extricates the user from some sort of situation he or she doesn't want to be in. You activate this command button (one to a form) by pressing ESC on the keyboard. A command button that does this is called a *cancel button* in the Visual Basic manuals.

You usually use the Properties window to make a command button the cancel button, although you can use code as well. If you have scrolled through the list of properties available for a command button, you may have noticed the Cancel property. If you set the Cancel property to True, you ensure that pressing ESC generates the Click event for this button, regardless of where the user has moved the focus. Setting the Cancel property to True for one button automatically sets it to False for all the other command buttons on the form.

Another possibility—but one that has its problems for novice users—is to set up a default command button for the form. This generates the Click procedure for the chosen (default) button whenever someone presses ENTER. This can be a problem because unsophisticated users are apt to press ENTER at the strangest times. (This is mostly because it's natural to think that if the focus is at a command button, pressing ENTER will work. Pressing the SPACEBAR is not something Windows neophytes are apt to remember.) In any case, if you want to use this option, set the Default property of the button to True. Also, you can have at most one default command button to a form.

tip: *You can combine the default and cancel buttons into a default cancel button. This feature is especially useful if you are about to take an irreversible action.*

Access Keys

Many Windows applications allow pressing ALT and one other key, the *access key*, to quickly activate a control or a menu item—Visual Basic itself, for example. These access letters are underlined in the caption of the control or name of the menu item.

Visual Basic makes it easy to set up an access key for any object that has a Caption property. When you set the caption, all you have to do is place an ampersand (&) in front of the letter you want to be the access key. For example, look at Figure 4-10. Notice that the *C* in the Caption property is underlined. When the application is running, you can activate this button either by pressing the ALT+C combination or by clicking on the button.

While it is possible to have the same access key for more than one control on a form, doing so is unusual. What happens in this situation is that the focus moves to the next control with an access key, but the control is not activated until you click the mouse or press the SPACEBAR.

Figure 4-10 Caption allowing access key for control

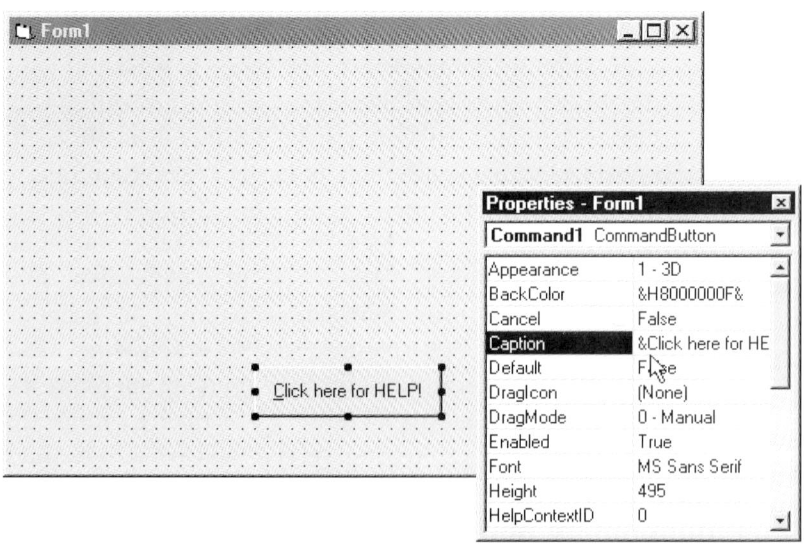

Image Controls

Image controls hold pictures. They can also be used to create toolboxes if you don't have the Professional edition (see Chapter 13). The toolbox icon for an image control is the sun over a mountain (see Figure 4-1). Image controls can be used to display icons or pictures created with a program such as Microsoft Paint. They can also hold Windows metafiles. Here are typical examples of image controls:

Since image controls respond to the Click event, you can use these images (taken from the TRAFFIC icon directory) to substitute for the command buttons in Figure 4-3.

You load a picture into an image control by resetting the value of the Picture property. If you choose the Picture property for the image control, this opens up a dialog box that lets you choose what image file to load.

You can also reset the Picture property directly by copying an image from a graphics program to the Windows clipboard and then using the Copy command on the Edit menu to paste the image into the image control. Visual Basic will attach the graphic to the project when you save it. Finally, you can also change this property via code, as you'll see in Chapter 16.

PROPERTIES OF IMAGE CONTROLS

Many of the properties of image controls are similar to those for command buttons. For example, you can set the Left and Top properties to control where the image control is located. However, unlike forms, the BorderStyle property for an image control has only two possible settings: you can have either no border (setting = 0) or a fixed single border (setting = 1).

note: *Microsoft's suggested prefix for an image control is* img.

The most important new property of an image control is the Stretch property. This determines whether the image control adjusts to fit the picture or the picture adjusts to fit the control. If the Stretch property is left at the default value of False, the control resizes itself to fit the picture. If you change it to True, the picture resizes (as best it can) to fit the control. As a general rule, only Windows metafiles—which essentially store directions for drawing pictures rather than actual bitmaps—can be enlarged without great loss of detail. To see this, start up a new project and place two large image controls on the form. Set the Stretch property to True for one of them and leave it as the default for the other. Load the TRFFC07 "slippery road" icon. Here's what you'll see:

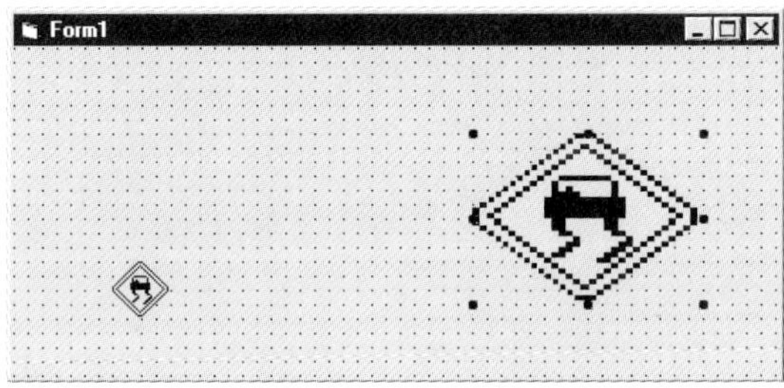

Notice that the detail in the enlarged image is greatly reduced (Stretch property = True).

Text Boxes

Text boxes (and RichTextBoxes if you have the Professional or Enterprise edition—see Chapter 6 for more on them) are the primary method for accepting input and displaying output in Visual Basic. Text boxes automatically allow cutting and pasting via the standard Windows techniques. In fact, printing too many lines of text to a form will often lead to a run-time error and, in any case, you can't scroll back through the form for lines that may have slipped off the top. (The icon in the toolbox for a text box shows the letters *ab*, as shown in Figure 4-1.)

tip: *Use a textbox (or a RichTextBox) for all but the simplest textual displays on a form.*

Text boxes never treat what a user types in as a number; this means that getting numeric information to a Visual Basic program requires transforming a string of digits into a number by using a built-in function or Visual Basic's built-in automatic conversions (see Chapter 5).

Standard Properties of Text Boxes

There are 50 properties for text boxes (36 can be set at design time via the Properties window). Many of them should be familiar to you. As before, the Name property is used only for the code you write; the user never sees it. (Microsoft's prefix for the name of text controls is *txt,* by the way.)

note: *You can set the font properties via the Font dialog box, but all text in the text box will appear the same. A RichTextBox on the other hand allows different text to appear differently.*

Since users can move the focus to a text box and type information there, the font properties also affect what the user places inside the text box. As with command buttons, the Height, Width, Left, and Top properties use the scale determined by the surrounding container.

Unlike command buttons (but like forms), you can set both the BackColor and ForeColor properties for a text box. The ForeColor property affects the color of the text that is displayed. BackColor affects the rest of the text box. Both of these can be set independently of the surrounding container. It is easiest to set them using the color palette from the Properties window. (To control colors directly, please see the section on color codes and hexadecimal notation in Chapter 5.)

As with command buttons, the Enabled property affects whether the text box will respond to events. In particular, if a text box is disabled, the user cannot enter text inside it. When a text box is disabled, it is grayed.

Also as before, it is quite common to toggle the Visible property between True and False with code in order to make a text box appear and disappear.

The MousePointer property has the same 17 possible settings as for forms; you often change this property to dramatize that the focus is now within the control.

Some Special Properties for Text Boxes

There are a few properties for text boxes you have not seen before, and the BorderStyle property works differently than for forms. This section covers these important properties.

Text The Text property is the analog of the Caption property for a command button or a form. The Text property controls the text the user sees. When you create a text box, the default value for this property is set to the default value for the Name property for that control—Text1, Text2, and so on. Because text boxes do not have a Caption property, you will need a trick to give the user an access key for them. You'll see how to do this shortly. If you want a text box to be empty when the application starts up, select the Text property and blank out the original setting.

Alignment The Alignment property controls how text is displayed. The default value is 0, which leaves the text left-aligned. Use a value of 1 and text is right-aligned. Use a value of 2 and text is centered.

ScrollBars The ScrollBars property determines whether a text box has horizontal or vertical scroll bars. These are useful because Visual Basic allows you to accept long or multiple lines of data from a single text box; roughly 32,000 characters is the usual limit. (The 32-bit version of Visual Basic raises this limit to 2 to the 32 power.) Without scroll bars, it becomes much harder for the user to move through the data contained in the text box, thus making editing the information that much more difficult.

There are four possible settings for the ScrollBars property:

Value	Meaning
0	This is the default value. The text box lacks both vertical and horizontal scroll bars.
1	The text box has horizontal scroll bars only (limits text to 255 characters).
2	The text box has vertical bars only.
3	The text box has both horizontal and vertical bars.

MultiLine The MultiLine property determines whether a text box can accept more than one line of text when the user runs the application and is usually combined with resetting the value of the ScrollBars property. In any case, if you set this to True, a user can always use the standard methods in Windows to move through the text box: the arrow keys, HOME, CTRL+HOME, END, and CTRL+END.

Visual Basic automatically word wraps when a user types more than one line of information into a text box—unless you've added horizontal scroll bars to the text box. Also, users can use the ENTER key to separate lines unless you've added a default command button to the form (yet another reason to be careful of this). If you have a default command button, the user has to press CTRL+ENTER to break lines.

Since forms are limited in the amount of text they can display and do not scroll, multiline text boxes are the usual method for displaying large amounts of text in Visual Basic. The limit for a multiline text box is approximately 32,000 characters.

BorderStyle As with the image control, there are only two possible settings for the BorderStyle property for a text box. The default value is 1, which gives you a single-width border, called a *fixed single*. If you change the value of this property to 0, the border disappears.

MaxLength The MaxLength property determines the maximum number of characters the text box will accept. The default value is 0, which (somewhat counter-intuitively) means there is no maximum other than the (roughly) 32,000-character limit for multiline text boxes. Any setting other than 0 will limit the user's ability to enter data into that text box to that number of characters.

PasswordChar As you might expect from the name, PasswordChar lets you limit what the text box displays (although all characters are accepted and stored). The convention is to use an asterisk (*) for the password character. Once you set this property, all the user sees is a row of asterisks. This property is often combined with the MaxLength property to add a password feature to your programs. (See Chapter 7. Also, see the section on Masked Edit boxes in Chapter 13 for another way to work with passwords.)

Locked This true/false property (new to version 4) lets you prevent users from changing the contents of the text box. Users can scroll and highlight text but won't be able to change it. (Because users can highlight text, they will still be able to use ordinary Windows techniques to copy information from the text box—they just won't be able to change it. This property is most commonly toggled on or off via code.)

Event Procedures for Text Boxes

Text boxes can recognize 17 events. Events such as GotFocus and LostFocus work exactly as before. Three others—KeyDown, KeyUp, and KeyPress—are for monitoring exactly what the user types. For example, you would use these events to write a program that allows someone to use dollar signs when entering amounts that ultimately need to be treated as numbers. This type of data processing requires a fair amount of code, which you'll see in Chapter 7.

Although the Change event lacks the flexibility of the key events you'll see in Chapter 7, you may find it very useful. Visual Basic monitors the text box and calls The Change event procedure whenever a user makes any changes in the text box. No matter what the user types, Visual Basic will detect it. One of the most common uses of this event procedure is to warn people that they should not be entering data in a specific text box, blanking out what they typed.

Labels

Use labels to display information you don't want the user to be able to change. Probably the most common use for labels is to identify a text box or other control by describing its contents. Another common use is to display help information. The icon for a label is the bold, capital letter *A*.

There are 34 properties for labels (30 are displayed in the Properties Window). Most of them overlap with the properties for text boxes and forms, and many of them should be familiar to you by now. Like forms (but unlike text boxes), labels have a Caption property that determines what they display. This property is originally set to be Label1 for the first label on your form, Label2 for the second, and so on. At design time you can have at most one line of text as the caption for a label. With code (see Chapter 5) you can add blank lines of text to a caption. As before, the Name property is used only for the code you write; the user never sees it. (Microsoft's naming convention is to use a *lbl* prefix for the name of label controls.)

Double-clicking on the Font property brings up the font dialog box that you have seen before. As with command buttons, the Height, Width, Left, and Top properties use the scale determined by the surrounding container.

Also, as with text boxes, you can set the BackColor and ForeColor properties for a label. The ForeColor property affects the color of the text that is displayed. BackColor affects the rest of the label. Both of these can be set independently of the surrounding container.

The Enabled property is not often used for labels. Its primary role is to determine whether the user can move the focus to the control that follows the label in tab order (see the section a little later in this chapter called "Access Keys for Text Boxes"). As before, it is quite common to toggle the Visible property between True and False to make a label appear and disappear.

The MousePointer property uses the same 17 possible settings. This is rarely changed for labels, but one possibility is to change the icon when the user moves from the label to the control that is being labeled.

Useful Properties for Labels

There are five especially useful properties for labels, one of which you have not seen before: AutoSize. Another, WordWrap, works slightly differently than it does for text boxes. For example, WordWrap can be used only when you set AutoSize to True. Also, the BorderStyle property has one neat use that can give more polish to your applications.

Alignment The Alignment property for a label has three possible settings. The usual (default) value is 0, which means the text in the label is left-justified (flush left). Set the value of this property to 1, and the text inside the label will be right-justified; set the value to 2, and the text is centered.

BorderStyle, BackStyle The BorderStyle property has the same two possible values as text boxes do. The difference is that the default value is 0, so labels do not start out with a border. Set the value to 1, and the label resembles a text box. This is occasionally useful when your program displays results. Using labels with a BorderStyle property value of 1 for displaying output avoids the problem of text boxes being changed by the user. Your form will have a control that looks like a text box, but it will not be responsive to the user. The BackStyle property determines whether the label is transparent or opaque.

AutoSize, WordWrap Unlike command buttons, labels can be made to grow automatically in a horizontal direction to encompass the text you place in them. This is a function of the AutoSize property. The default value for this property, though, is set to False, and you need to change it to True to take advantage of it. If you also set the WordWrap property to True, then the label will grow in the vertical direction to encompass its contents, but the horizontal size will stay the same. In addition, the words will be wrapped so that they are never broken, as indicated here:

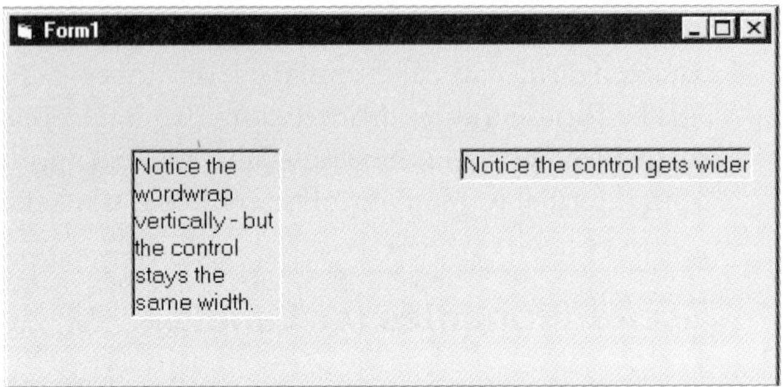

The labels in this example have the BorderStyle set to 1 so that you can see them more easily, and each started out at the same width.

Event Procedures for Labels

Labels respond to 12 events. For example, they can respond to clicking, double-clicking, or the Change event. The most common event procedures for a label are mouse events (see Chapter 16). You can use a click of the right mouse button to provide context-sensitive help or pop up a menu, for example. One problem is that labels do not respond to key events or detect whether the user has shifted the focus. This dramatically restricts the use of event procedures for labels. Labels in Visual Basic remain primarily descriptive and not responsive.

Navigating Between Controls

Using the mouse is the most common way to move from control to control in a Windows application, but your applications have to allow for using the TAB key as well. *Tab order* is the term used in a Windows application for the sequence of controls that pressing TAB moves you through. In a Visual Basic application, the order in which you create the controls is the order used for the tab order. The first control you create at design time is the one that receives the focus when the application starts up. If you press TAB once when the application is running, you move to the second control you created at design time, and so on. If you press TAB when the focus is at the last control you've created, the focus moves back to the first one. (Disabled controls are skipped.)

It's possible to change the setting for the tab order via the Properties window or by writing code. The property you need to set is the TabIndex property. If you set this value to 0 for a control, this control automatically becomes the first control in tab order, and all the other controls move upward in tab order. What used to be the first control in tab order is now the second, the second is now the third, and so on. If you change a control with a higher tab index, then only controls with larger tab indexes are affected. If you create a control and set the TabIndex property at design time, the settings for the TabIndex property are moved higher to make way for the new control. You can also change the TabIndex via code (see Chapter 5).

Access Keys for Text Boxes

Text boxes lack a Caption property, so you need a trick to allow users to move the focus to them quickly via an access key. The trick works like this: labels have captions, so you can set an access key for them by using the ampersand (&) in front of the letter you want to make the access key. However, labels do not respond to the GotFocus or LostFocus event. So what happens when you use the access key? If you press the access key for a control that does not respond to focus events, the focus moves to the next control that will accept it in tab order.

This makes it easy to give an access key for a text box. You create a label for the text box, set up the access key for the label, and then create the text box. (Doing this ensures that the text box follows the label in tab order.)

tip: *If you need to use an ampersand in a label but don't want it to be an access key, set the UseMnemonic property of the label to False.*

Message Boxes

Message boxes display information in a dialog box superimposed on the form. They wait for the user to choose a button before returning to the application. Users cannot switch to another form in your application as long as Visual Basic is displaying a message box. Message boxes should be used for short messages or to give transient feedback. For example, you would not generally use them to provide a help screen. A good example of where an application might display a message box is when the user moves the focus away from a text box before placing information inside it. The simplest form of the message box command looks like this:

```
MsgBox("The message goes in quotes")
```

(The parentheses are optional in this form of the Msgbox statement.)

Message boxes can hold a maximum of 1,024 characters, and Visual Basic automatically breaks them at the right of the dialog box. You can set line breaks yourself, as you will see in Chapter 5.

For example, suppose you wrote an application and thought the user needed to be reminded that nothing would happen until he or she clicked a command button. You might add a LostFocus event procedure that looks something like this:

```
Private Sub Command1_LostFocus ()
   MsgBox ("You have to click the button for anything to happen")
End Sub
```

When you run this application and move the focus away from the command button, you will see a screen like the one shown in Figure 4-11. Notice in Figure 4-11 that the title bar for the message box isn't particularly informative. You can add your own, more informative, title to a message box. For this you have to use the full form of the message box statement by adding two options to it. This is the complete syntax for the MsgBox command:

Figure 4-11 Message box demonstration

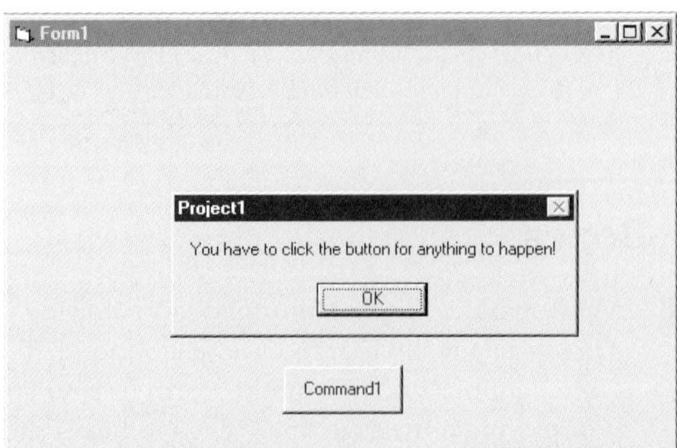

MsgBox (*MessageInBox,TypeOfBox, TitleOfBox*)

You have already seen the item called *MessageInBox*—this gives the text in the box. You combine three different groups of numbers to specify the kind of message box. (In Visual Basic 4 you can use symbolic constants for these numbers—they are indicated in the first column.) The first number controls what kind of buttons appear. The following tables summarize this information.

Symbolic Constant	Value	Meaning
vbOKOnly	0	Display OK button only
vbOKCancel	1	Display OK and Cancel buttons
vbAbortRetryIgnore	2	Display Abort, Retry, and Ignore buttons
vbYesNoCancel	3	Display Yes, No, and Cancel buttons
vbYesNo	4	Display Yes and No buttons
vbRetryCancel	5	Display Retry and Cancel buttons
vbCritical	16	Display Critical Message icon
vbQuestion	32	Display Warning Query icon
vbExclamation	48	Display Warning Message icon
vbInformation	64	Display Information Message icon

For example, the following statement

```
MsgBox("Will Have Yes and No Buttons!", vbYesNo)
```

gives you a message box like this:

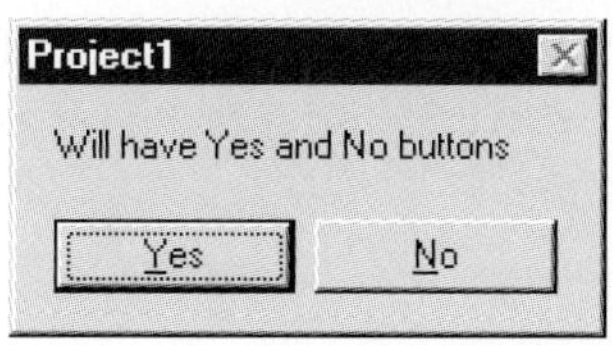

The next group of numbers controls which button is the default button for the box. This is summarized in the following table.

Symbolic Constant	Value	Meaning
vbDefaultButton1	0	First button is default
vbDefaultButton2	256	Second button is default
vbDefaultButton3	512	Third button is default

You can combine these options by adding the values together. For example, the statement

```
MsgBox "Example of buttons", vbOKCancel+ vbExclamation+_
vbDefaultButton2, "Test"
```

displays a message box that looks like this:

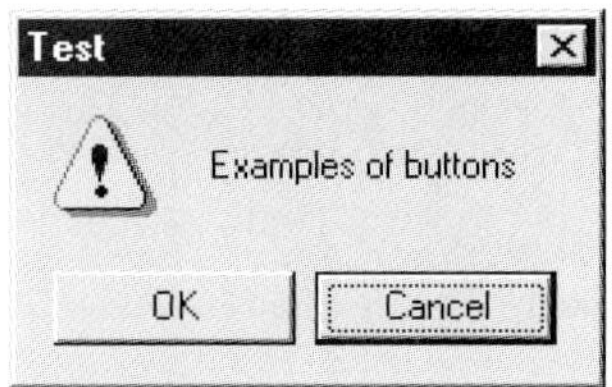

This box contains an exclamation point with OK and Cancel buttons, and the second button, Cancel, would be the default button for this form.

note: *You can arrange for a message box to stop all Windows applications until it is closed by temporarily adding the vbSystemModel constant (or its value 4096) to the value you would otherwise use. This should not be done casually!*

Although message boxes do not have event procedures associated with them, it is possible to determine which button was pressed by assigning the value of the MsgBox to a variable and reading off the value, as you will see in Chapter 7.

The Grid

Since the grid is so important to accurately positioning controls, mastering it will make it easier to give your applications a finished, professional look. In order to control the grid, choose Tools | Options (ALT T, O) and then go to the Environment page on the Options dialog box, as shown in Figure 4-12. The following sections describe four properties you can control.

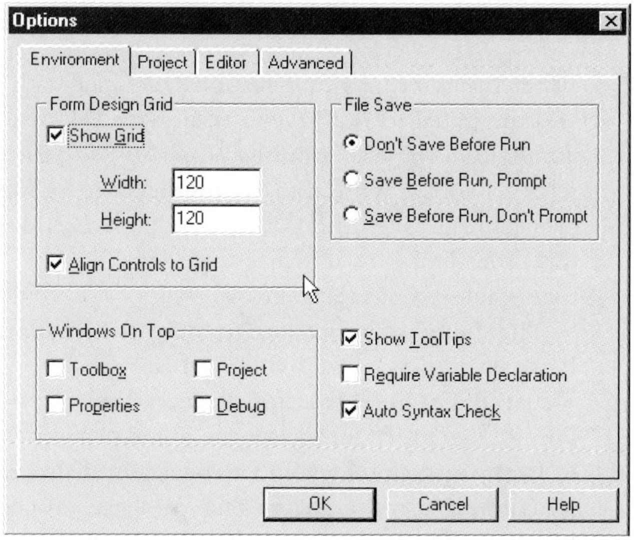

Figure 4-12 Environment page in the Options dialog box

Show Grid You can turn the grid on or off by changing the Show Grid setting. The default setting is on. There is usually little reason to turn the grid off.

Grid Width, Grid Height boxes The Width and Height text boxes let you set the distance (in twips) between grid marks. The default is 120 twips. Change these both to 60, and the grid becomes twice as fine.

Align Controls to Grid The Align Controls to Grid check box determines whether controls automatically move to the next grid mark or whether they can be placed between grid marks. Usually you are better off changing the grid spacing to match your design requirements than turning this option off.

It's possible to align an item to the grid even if you've chosen to turn this option off. To do this, select the control by clicking it once (the sizing handles show up) and choosing Edit|Align to Grid (ALT E, G).

What Happens When a Visual Basic Application Runs

When the user runs an application developed with Visual Basic, he or she usually sees the initial form that you've designed. However, much more than that is going on in the background. When Visual Basic first creates a form, it checks whether you've written an event procedure for initializing the form. This event procedure is called the Form_Initialize procedure. The most common use of this procedure is to initialize form level variables (see Chapter 5) and change the default settings for controls.

The Initialize procedure is new to version 4 and occurs prior to the Form_Load procedure, which was the first procedure that earlier versions of Visual Basic used for initialization. Some people still prefer to use the Form_Load procedure to set the initial properties for a form.

In any case, you may find it easier to initialize the properties of the form and its controls using code in one of these procedures rather than using the Properties window. (See the section in Chapter 5 on resetting properties for more information.)

Since the Form_Load procedure is the default event procedure for a form, all you usually have to do is double-click in any blank area of the form to get to the Form_Load event procedure template. You will have to explicitly choose the Initialize procedure from the Proc box in the Code window to work with it.

```
Private Sub Form_Initialize ()
  'Initialize form level variables
  'Initialize properties
  ' etc.
End Sub
```

Right after Visual Basic processes the Initialize procedure it calls the Form_Load procedure. After that Visual Basic calls four other event procedures—if you've written code for them. Here is the order in which Visual Basic invokes these events:

- Form_Initialize procedure
- Form_Load procedure
- Form_Resize procedure
- Form_Activate procedure
- Form_GotFocus procedure (only if no controls on the form are enabled)

- Form_Paint procedure (only if the AutoRedraw property, discussed in the next section, is False)

Generally speaking, initial information you want printed to the form should be done by placing Print statements in one of the other event procedures rather than in the Form_Initialize or Form_Load procedure. This is because unless you first use the Show method or set the AutoRedraw property to True, nothing will show up!

These events can be confused because they are triggered under similar circumstances. It is important that you keep in mind the order in which they are triggered by Visual Basic. Following are short discussions of these important events.

Form_Initialize Event The Initialize event is triggered first and only once: Visual Basic triggers this event when the form is first created. *The Initialize event occurs before the Load event.* As its name suggests, the Initialize event is where you place code that you use for setting initial properties of the form.

Form_Load Event The Load event is triggered when a form is loaded into memory and occurs after the Initialize event. Usually this code is triggered once only. (However, using code, it is possible to unload and then reload a form, as discussed in Chapter 5, so one can have this event triggered more than once.) When you start a program with a single form, it will generally be loaded automatically—thus triggering this event. (See Chapter 5 for dealing with multiple form applications.)

The Form_Resize Event Visual Basic triggers the Form_Resize event whenever the user resizes a form, or minimizes and then restores the form. For this reason, the most common use of this event procedure is to recalculate (and rescale if necessary) the size and position of any objects on your form. For example, suppose you spent a lot of time positioning controls symmetrically on a form. Without repositioning them in the Form_Resize procedure, a user can, all too easily, spoil your hard work! (See Chapter 12 for an example of how to do this.)

Form_Activate Event Visual Basic triggers the Form_Activate event procedure whenever a form becomes active (that is, when the user moves the focus to it).

However, if you move to a different application running under Windows and then return to the form, Visual Basic does not call the Form_Activate event procedure again. For this reason the Form_Activate event procedure is usually used only in multiple form applications.

Form_GotFocus Event After the Activate event is triggered, Visual Basic will trigger the GetFocus event for the form *only if all visible controls on it are disabled.* (For this reason, people rarely use the GetFocus event for a form.)

Form_Paint Event The Form_Paint procedure is where you put Print methods when the AutoRedraw property is set to False. Visual Basic calls this event whenever the form is moved, enlarged, or newly uncovered. You then use this event procedure to redraw the information on the form. However, when the AutoRedraw property is set to True, this event is *not* called, and you'll need to use the Refresh method directly (see the section on this method later in this chapter).

note: *Visual Basic also generates events when someone tries to close an application by closing the last form. See Chapters 5 and 7 for how to work with the Unload, Query_Unload, and Terminate events.*

The Display in Visual Basic

After Visual Basic processes any statement that affects the display, it calls on Windows to do the work. Windows in turn tells the display adapter how to display the image. When you install Windows, the installation program checks (or you tell it) what hardware and software you have. Then the installation program installs the necessary screen and print drivers.

Since Windows is a graphical environment, all of this means that what you can do with Visual Basic depends on the driver programs that Windows uses for controlling the screen and printer, but using these driver programs is automatic. You do not have to worry about all the possible combinations of hardware a user may have. This is different from what MS-DOS programmers are used to. For programming graphics under DOS, you must have part of the program check what kind of graphics board is installed (or even if there is a graphics board at all) and adjust itself accordingly. You may still want to write the code to adjust your forms to different screen resolutions (see Chapter 12).

This is because a form designed for 640 X 480 resolution will appear rather strange in 1280 X 1040!

Nothing comes for free, however. Windows has to do a lot to manage a graphics environment, and this forces trade-offs. For example, the Visual Basic default is that when you move a form or temporarily hide it, or when one form covers another and moves away, the original text and graphics will probably disappear. This will happen even if the window that covers your form comes from a completely different Windows application. You can arrange for Visual Basic to have *persistent graphics*, but the cost is that Visual Basic must keep a pixel-by-pixel copy of the object in memory. This is called a *bitmap of the screen*. Since many machines will not have enough available memory to store more than a couple of screens, Windows may use your hard disk for temporary storage, but this slows down reaction time dramatically.

The AutoRedraw Property for Forms

As you'd expect, persistent graphics are determined by a Boolean (True or False) property of forms and picture boxes. Like most properties, you can set this at design or run time. Set the AutoRedraw property to True and Visual Basic saves a copy of the object in memory. Set it to False and you will have to manage the redrawing of graphics yourself.

For a resizable form, Visual Basic saves a screen representation of the window. In particular, this means that when you enlarge the form or when it is covered by another form, no text displayed on the form (and no graphics information—see Chapter 15) is lost. This requires by far the most memory.

There is one other problem you must be aware of when you set AutoRedraw to True. When AutoRedraw is True, Visual Basic draws the complete image to memory before displaying it on the screen. Only when the bitmap is complete and Visual Basic is in *idle time* (not responding to a specific event—see Chapter 8) will the image finally show up on your screen. On the other hand, you can use the Refresh method to display the image at different stages. However, each time Visual Basic processes a Refresh statement, it redraws every dot in the image from scratch. This can be painfully slow.

Visual Basic activates the Paint event each time a part of the form is newly exposed. This often happens when the user moves or enlarges the form. You can write the necessary code in the Paint procedure whenever you want to redraw part of a form (or picture box—see Chapter 15). Therefore, the least memory-intensive way to handle the problem of text or graphics disappearing because a user covered a form is to redraw the form or picture box. This again shows the constant trade-off in programming between memory-intensive and

CPU-intensive activities. Set AutoRedraw to True and you use up memory (if you have it), so this, potentially, can speed up the program. Using the Paint event procedure (or the hard disk, if you don't have enough memory) uses up time. You have to choose what's best for the application. At the extremes, the choice is easy: if the amount of drawing to be done is minimal, using the Paint event procedure is better. In any case, Visual Basic calls the Paint procedure for the object only if the AutoRedraw property of the object is set to False.

caution: *Do not put any statements that move or resize the object inside the Paint procedure. This is because Visual Basic will just call the Paint procedure again and again, and you will be stuck in an infinite regression.*

The Refresh Method

The other method you need to get started with Visual Basic programming is the Refresh method. This method applies to forms and controls. It forces an immediate refresh of the form or control and, as mentioned previously, will let you see an image develop even when AutoRedraw is True. If you use the Refresh method, Visual Basic will also call any Paint event procedure you have written for the object. It is quite common to use this method inside the Form_Resize procedure in order to redisplay any graphics that are calculated in the Paint event procedure. Also, while Visual Basic handles refreshing the screen during idle time, occasionally you will want to take control of this yourself. Whenever Visual Basic processes an *Object*.Refresh statement, it will redraw the object immediately and generate the Paint event if the object supports this.

The ASCII Representation of Forms

Visual Basic 4 has stopped using a binary notation to describe its forms. All form information is stored in text format that you can read (and change) using your favorite word processor. (Be sure to save it in text format if you do change it!) Using the text representation of a program makes it easy to check that the properties of the various controls and forms are exactly what you want. To see what the ASCII representation of a form looks like, do the following:

1. Start up a new project.

2. Set the caption to "ASCII".
3. Add a command button in the default size, in the default location, and using the default name of Command1 by double-clicking on the Command Button tool.
4. Add a Click procedure to the command button with the single line of code:

```
Print "You clicked me!"
```

5. Save the form with the name ASCII.FRM. (Use the Save File As option on the File menu.)

Now, if you examine the file in another word processor, such as Windows WordPad, or in a text editor, such as Windows Notepad, here's what you will see. (Don't be intimidated by the length of the following listing; the pieces will be described step by step.) (The values for height and width and such will depend on your machine.)

```
VERSION 4.00
Begin VB.Form Form1
   Caption         =   "ASCII"
   ClientHeight    =   4140
   ClientLeft      =   1140
   ClientTop       =   1515
   ClientWidth     =   6690
   Height          =   4545
   Left            =   1080
   LinkTopic       =   "Form1"
   ScaleHeight     =   4140
   ScaleWidth      =   6690
   Top             =   1170
   Width           =   6810
   Begin VB.CommandButton Command1
      Caption         =   "Command1"
      Height          =   495
      Left            =   2760
      TabIndex        =   0
      Top             =   1800
      Width           =   1215
   End
End
```

```
Attribute VB_Name = "Form1"
Attribute VB_Creatable = False
Attribute VB_Exposed = False
Private Sub Command1_Click()
  Print "You clicked me"
End Sub
```

The idea of the ASCII form representation is simple: it contains a textual description of the form's properties. The listing begins with the version of Visual Basic used, followed by the name of the form. Then come the current settings of all the properties associated with the form. For example, the new caption is reflected by the line of code that looks like this

```
Caption =          "ASCII"
```

because this is what we reset the Caption property to be. The Client properties describe the form's position *vis-à-vis* the desktop. After the properties of the form come the various controls on the forms in the same format, indented slightly for readability. The ASCII format for a Visual Basic control starts like the following:

```
Begin VB.ControlType ControlName
```

In the example this is the line:

```
Begin VB.CommandButton Command1
```

Then come the properties of the control. For example, since we didn't change the control name or any of the other properties, the above listing does not show the default values for the other properties of a command button. Finally, whatever code is attached to the form is listed after an Attribute section that describes properties of the form. (For more on the ASCII representation of a form, please consult Appendix A of the *Programmer's Guide*.)

tip: *You can use a word processor to modify the ASCII representation of the form; then reload the project into Visual Basic and see the changes you've made. Using the various sophisticated search and replace functions available in modern word processors or program editors is often the most efficient method to make wholesale changes to control names or properties.*

Chapter Five

First Steps in Programming

By now you have a feel for what a Visual Basic application looks like. You've seen how to customize forms by adding controls, and you've started writing the event procedures that are the backbone of a Visual Basic application. But as you've probably realized, the event procedures you've seen haven't done much. To do more, you must become comfortable with the sophisticated programming language built into Visual Basic.

If you are familiar with QuickBASIC, Pascal, C, or even QBASIC, you'll have an easier time of it, and the next five chapters will go pretty quickly. If you are familiar only with the older interpreted BASIC found on PCs (GW-BASIC, BASICA), you'll want to read these chapters much more carefully. In any case, there are subtle differences between Visual Basic programming and conventional programming that can trip up even experienced programmers, so you probably don't want to skip these chapters.

Anatomy of a Visual Basic Program

It can't be stressed enough that the key to Visual Basic programming is recognizing that Visual Basic generally processes code only in response to events. If you think of a Visual Basic program as a set of independent pieces that "wake up" only in response to events they have been told to recognize, you won't go far wrong, but if you think of the program as having a starting line and an ending line and moving from top to bottom, you will. In fact, unlike many programming languages, executable lines in a Visual Basic program must be inside procedures or functions. Isolated executable lines of code don't work. For illustration purposes, this book may show you fragments of a program, but they are not meant to work independently (nor can they).

Basically, even if you know a more conventional programming language well, you shouldn't try to force your Visual Basic programs into its framework.

If you impose programming habits learned from older programming languages upon your Visual Basic programs, you're likely to run into problems.

The Code Window

You always write code in a Code window. (When you are dealing with multiple forms or more complicated code, you can have multiple Code windows open at the same time.) Figure 5-1 shows the Code window with the Object list box pulled down for the calculator sample application that comes with Visual Basic. As you have seen, this window opens whenever you double-click a control or form. You can also click View Code from the Project window or View menu, or press F7, to open the Code window.

The Code window has a caption that lists the name of the form, which is the value of the Name property of the form. (It is Calculator in Figure 5-1.) It also has two list boxes and an area for editing your code. Unlike earlier versions of Visual Basic, all code for a form in Visual Basic 4 defaults to being displayed in one continuous stream in the same Code windows—just as it would be if you looked at the text version (see Chapter 4) in another word processor. This is usually called *full module view*. Each procedure in full module view is separated by a dotted line and is listed alphabetically.

Figure 5-1

Code window for Calculator project

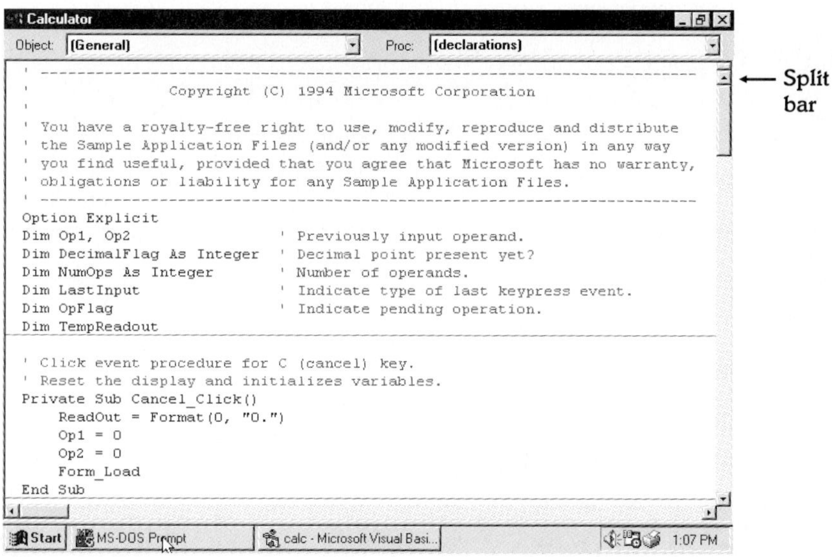

tip: *If you want to use Visual Basic 3's single procedure view, choose Tools | Options and then go to the Editor Options page. Now uncheck the Full Module View check box.*

All the usual Windows editing techniques are available when you enter code (as discussed in Chapter 2), and these are summarized in Table 5-1 if you are using the default editor setting in full module view. (Some of these keys are shortcuts for techniques described in later chapters—don't worry if you don't know what something means yet.)

tip: *The shortcut menu (click the right mouse button) lets you copy, cut, and paste while in the Code Window.*

Description	Shortcut Keys
View Code window	F7
Find	CTRL+F
Replace	CTRL+H
Find Next	F3
Find Previous	SHIFT+F3
Move one word to right	CTRL+RIGHT ARROW
Move one word to left	CTRL+LEFT ARROW
Move to end of line	END
Move to beginning of line	HOME
Insert new line	CTRL+N
Delete current line	CTRL+Y
Delete to end of word	CTRL+DEL
Indent	TAB or CTRL+M
Remove indent	SHIFT+TAB or CTRL+SHIFT+M
Shift one screen down	CTRL+PAGE DOWN (Go to bottom of current screen)
Shift one screen up	CTRL+PAGE UP (Go to top of current screen)
Go to last position	CTRL+SHIFT+F2
Beginning of Code window (module)	CTRL+HOME
End of Code window (module)	CTRL+END
Clear all breakpoints	CTRL+SHIFT+F9
Move focus to Object list box	CTRL+F2
View Object Browser	F2
View Form	SHIFT+F7

Table 5-1
Code Window Shortcut Keys

The Split Bar

As indicated in Figure 5-1, the Code window has a *split bar* located below the title bar at the top of the vertical scroll bar. The idea is that as your code gets more complicated, you'll want to see two parts of the Code window at once. If you drag this bar down, Visual Basic splits the Code window into two horizontal panes. (What you see in the Object box and Procedure box depends on which pane has the focus.) You can then scroll separately through the panes as needed. Dragging the split bar to the top of the window closes a pane.

The Object List Box

The left list box, called the *Object box,* lists all the objects on the form. This includes all the controls on the form, plus an object called General that holds common code that can be used by all the procedures attached to the form. You'll see more about this kind of code in the sections in this chapter titled "Changing the Defaults for Types" and "Constants" and in Chapters 8 and 9. When you click on any item here, the editor takes you to the first piece of code written for that object (if one exists).

The Proc(edure) List Box

The right-hand list box, named Proc, is the *Procedure list box*. As you have seen, this list box gives all the events recognized by the object selected in the Object list box. If you have already written an event procedure, it shows up in bold in the Procedure list box. If you click on any event listed in the Proc box, Visual Basic displays the event procedure or event procedure template in the Code window and moves the cursor to it.

Statements in Visual Basic

When you enter a statement in Visual Basic, the program uses the same advanced technology pioneered in QuickBASIC to analyze and process it. This happens immediately after you press ENTER. Visual Basic will detect many typos at this stage if you have "Auto Syntax Check" on in the Environment page of the Options dialog box. If a statement you enter can't be analyzed, a message box pops up that often helps you find out what caused the problem.

tip: *Remember the context-sensitive help feature of Visual Basic. If you need help on the syntax for functions, statements, properties, events, or methods in the Code window, move the cursor to (or type) the keyword or the property, event, or method name, and press F1. You can also select an event in the Procedure box and press F1 for information about the selected event.*

Visual Basic ignores case and spacing, except within quotation marks. Nonetheless, Visual Basic does try to impose its own conventions. It capitalizes the first letter of command words and often adds extra spaces for readability. For example, no matter how you capitalize the command word Print—PRint, Print, print, and so on—pressing ENTER will change it to Print. It's a good idea to stick to a standard method of spacing and capitalization in your code.

Statements in Visual Basic rarely use line numbers or line labels, and each statement generally occurs on its own line. If you use a line with more characters than can fit in the window, Visual Basic scrolls the window toward the right as needed. Lines are limited to 1023 characters but unlike earlier versions of Visual Basic can be extended to the next line by using an underscore. (Make sure the underscore doesn't appear inside quotation marks though.) Given the line continuation character added in Visual Basic 4, you will only rarely need to have lines that are longer than the width of the screen. Finally, you can combine statements on one line by placing a colon (:) between the statements.

Sometimes in this book you'll see lines that easily fit this limit but are longer than can fit on one line of a printed page. When this happens, we will usually use the underscore line continuation character, and the succeeding line will be "outdented." However, if the split has to take place inside quotation marks, we can't use the underscore in the actual code. In this case not only will the succeeding line will be "outdented" but the double quotation marks or parentheses will be closed on that succeeding line. Here are some examples of these conventions:

```
MsgBox "You have to click a button for anything to happen" _
vbOKOnly, "Test Button"
    Print "This is an example of a line that won't fit on a
single line of the page."
```

If you were entering these lines in Visual Basic, in the first example you could either omit the underscore and continue typing or use the underscore and hit ENTER after it. In the second example you would continue until you reached the closing quote.

Remark Statements

There are two ways to indicate a remark statement. The most common now is to use a single quotation mark (')— not the apostrophe found below the tilde (~~) but the one usually found below the double quotation mark ("). Here is an example:

```
Private Sub Command1_Click ()
  'A comment describing the procedure would go here
  '

End Sub
```

You can also use the older Rem keyword:

```
Private Sub Command1_Click ()
  Rem   Comments describing the procedure would go here
  Rem

End Sub
```

As usual, the programming lines are indented to improve readability. If you want to add comments to the ends of lines, it is easier to use the single quotation mark because the Rem form requires a colon before it. For example:

```
PrintForm  'Dump the current window

PrintForm  :Rem A bit more cumbersome
```

Everything on a line following a Rem statement is ignored, regardless of whether it is an executable Visual Basic statement or not. Commenting out executable statements is a common technique to help debug your programs.

The End Statement

When Visual Basic processes an End statement, the program stops. If you are developing a program, you are dumped back into the development environment. The effect is exactly the same as choosing the End option on the Run menu. In a stand-alone program, after the End statement, all windows opened by the program are closed and the program is cleared from memory.

You can have as many End statements within a Visual Basic program as you want, but it is good programming practice to restrict the number of events that end a program.

Many professional programmers prefer to use only one End statement in their code. They place this End statement in the QueryUnload event for the main form. (One advantage to doing this is that you can then use the QueryUnload event to execute any code needed for cleaning up.) If you choose to write your programs this way, then you replace any End statements with an Unload Me statement. This calls the QueryUnload event for that form. (See the section of this chapter called "Applications That Look Like They Are Over—But Aren't" and Chapter 7 for more on how to use the QueryUnload event.)

Writing Code: The Editor Page on the Options Dialog Box

Good programming builds on code that is easy to read—Visual Basic 4 goes way beyond earlier versions of Visual Basic by letting you control the size, font—even the color—of different pieces of your code. It makes it easy to use a consistent indentation pattern. All these features are controlled by the Editor page in the Options dialog box, which you get to by choosing Tools | Options (ALT+T, O) and then clicking on the Editor tab (see Figure 5-2). Let's go over the items in this important dialog box one by one.

FONT

Click on the down arrow in the Font drop-down list box to see the complete list of fonts that your system knows about. If you don't like the default Courier New font, choose another one by clicking on the font name when the list is dropped down.

SIZE

The Size drop-down list box lets you determine the size of a font. You can type a point size directly in the text box or make a choice of size by clicking on the down arrow and then clicking on the size. You might want to change the font size if you are working with a laptop or if you have trouble seeing smaller print.

Figure 5-2

The Editor page on the Options dialog box

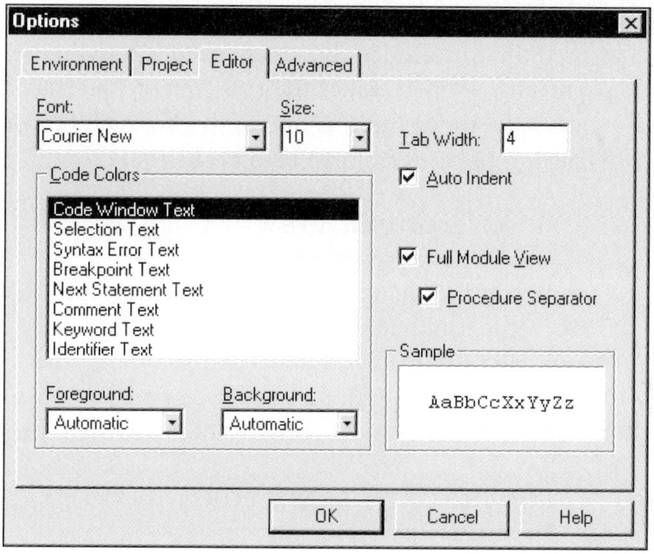

CODE COLORS

In the Code Colors box you determine the foreground and background colors used for each type of code. For example, the default is that comments are green and syntax errors are highlighted in red. If you don't like the defaults, change them by:

1. Clicking on the code element you want to work with in the Code Colors box
2. Clicking on the arrow in the Foreground drop-down list
3. Clicking on the color you like
4. Choosing OK

(Changing the background color is less common but works the same way.)

TAB WIDTH

Use the Tab Width box to set the number of spaces you get when you press the TAB key. This can be anything from 1 to 32 spaces; the default is 4 spaces.

AUTO INDENT CHECK BOX

If the Auto Indent box is checked, after you use the TAB key to indent a line, pressing ENTER makes the subsequent line start at the same place as the line above it. Indentation is one of the best ways to make programming structures clearer. (This defaults to being on.)

FULL MODULE VIEW

When Full Module View is checked (the default), you see all the code as one. You can then scroll through it with the arrow keys, PAGE UP/PAGE DOWN keys, and so on. If you uncheck this, you go back to the Visual Basic 3 way of looking at code: each piece of code pops up in a separate window, and you use CTRL+UP/ DOWN ARROW to cycle through the different pieces of code.

PROCEDURE SEPARATOR

You use the Procedure Separator check box in conjunction with full module view. If you leave this checked, then you see separator bars between the pieces of code in the Code window.

SAMPLE

The Sample box shows you a sample of text in the font, size, and color settings you've currently set.

note: *If you decide to close the Editor Options page without making any changes, click on Cancel or press the ESC key. To have whatever changes you made go into effect, choose OK.*

Assignment and Property Setting

Giving values to variables and resetting properties are two of the most common tasks in Visual Basic code. Visual Basic uses an equal sign for both operations; for example,

```
InterestRate = .05
```

The variable name always appears on the left, and the value always appears on the right. Visual Basic *must* be able to obtain a value from the right side of an assignment statement. It will do any processing needed to make this happen. You can consider an assignment statement as a way for a Visual Basic variable to get a (new) value or as a means of copying information from a source to a destination.

note: *You can also use the older Let notation:*

```
Let InterestRate = .05
```

Assigning to Properties

If you want to change a property setting for a Visual Basic object, place the object's name followed by a period and then the name of the property on the left side of the equal sign, and put the new value on the right-hand side:

object.*property* = *value*

For example, suppose you have a text button (control name of Text1) and want to blank it out in code rather than use the properties bar. You need only have a line like this in an event procedure:

```
Text1.Text = ""
```

Since there is nothing between the quotation marks, the text assigned to this property is blank. Similarly, a line like

```
Text1.Text = "This is the new text."
```

in an event procedure changes the setting for the text property to the text in the quotation marks.

You can change the setting of a property via code as often as necessary. For example, if you wanted to change the caption on a command button called Command1, you would place a line like this in an event procedure:

```
Command1.Caption = "Put new caption here."
```

Similarly, if you wanted to make a button called Command5 the first button in Tab order, you would add a line like this to an event procedure:

```
Command5.TabIndex = 0
```

Now suppose you want a form called Form1 to move around when various command buttons are clicked. Here is an example of one of the event procedures you would need:

```
Private Sub LeftButton_Click ()
  Form1.Left = Form1.Left -75
End Sub
```

Look at the key line: Form1.Left = Form1.Left -75. On the left-hand side of the assignment statement is the property that gets the value, but it seems that the property occurs on the right-hand side as well. What happens is that Visual Basic first analyzes the right-hand side of any assignment to extract a value from it. In this case it looks at the current position of the left side of the form and calculates the number of twips it is from the left. It then subtracts 75 from this number. Only after it has done this does it look to the left side. Visual Basic now changes the old value of the "Left" property to a new one.

All this can be a little confusing. Some people find it helpful to remember that right-hand sides of assignment statements are there only for the values they yield, and only the left-hand side gets changed.

DEFAULT PROPERTIES

Every Visual Basic object has a default property (for example, text boxes have the Text property). When referring to the default property, you don't need to use the property name. For example, you can enter

```
Text1 = "This is new text"
```

Most Visual Basic programmers avoid this because they feel it makes their code less readable. (If you want to see which default properties are assigned to which controls, see Table 3-2 of the *Programmer's Guide*.)

BOOLEAN PROPERTIES

Properties that take only the value True or False are called *Boolean properties,* after the English logician George Boole. Many Boolean properties have already been discussed. Boolean properties specify whether a command button is visible, is enabled, or is the default cancel or command button. Visual Basic 4 has built-in constants for these important property values. A statement such as

```
Command1.Visible = False
```

in an event procedure hides the command button. The control stays hidden until Visual Basic processes the statement:

```
Command1.Visible = True
```

If you want the TAB key to skip over a control while a program is running, change the TabStop property to False:

```
Control.TabStop = False
```

Internally, Visual Basic uses the values 0 for False and -1 for True for property settings (actually, any nonzero value will work for True). The usual way to toggle between Boolean properties is with the Not operator. Suppose you have a statement such as

```
Command1.Visible = Not(Command1.Visible)
```

in an event procedure. This statement works as follows: Visual Basic finds the current value of Command1.Visible, and then the Not operator reverses this value; that is, if the value was True, it changes to False, and vice versa.

note: *For the Not operator to work properly in toggling a Boolean property between on and off, you must use the built-in True constant or a value of -1 for True.*

(For additional information on the Not operator, see the section on "Bit Twiddling" in Chapter 8.)

tip: *Another example of a Boolean property is the Value property of command buttons. Setting this property to True in code has the same effect as the user clicking the button. This feature is useful for self-running demonstrations when combined with the SetFocus method to move the focus to the correct control.*

Variables

Variables in Visual Basic hold information (values). Whenever you use a variable, Visual Basic sets up an area in the computer's memory to store the information. Variable names in Visual Basic can be up to 255 characters long and, provided the first character is a letter, can include any combination of letters, numbers, and underscores. The case of the letters in the variable name is irrelevant. The following table lists some possible variable names and indicates whether they are acceptable.

Base1_Ball	Acceptable
1Base_Ball	Not acceptable—first character is not a letter
Base.1	Not acceptable—uses a period
Base&1	Not acceptable—includes & inside the name
ThisIsLongButOK	Acceptable—only 15 characters long

All characters in a variable name are significant, but case is irrelevant. BASE is the same variable as base. On the other hand, Base is a different variable from Base1, and both are different from Base_1. However, Visual Basic always changes the form of the names of your variables to reflect the capitalization pattern you last used. If you use Mortgageinterest, mortgageinterest, and MortgageInterest successively as variable names, then when you move off the line, Visual Basic will automatically change all occurrences to MortgageInterest because this was the last one you used.

tip: *Visual Basic's capitalization feature is often useful in detecting typos in variable names. If you think a misspelled variable name is causing a problem, change one occurrence to all caps, move off the line, and scan the program to see if all the occurrences of the variable name have been changed. If you find one that wasn't changed, you will know that it contains a typo. Correct the error and then change the variable name back to the form you want; all occurrences of the name will change again as well. For another way to help detect typos and variable names, see the section, "Requiring Declaration of Variables" later in this chapter.*

Choosing meaningful variable names helps document your program and makes the inevitable debugging process easier. Meaningful variable names are an excellent way to clarify the point of many kinds of program statements.

You can't use names reserved by Visual Basic for variable names; for example, Print is not acceptable as a variable name. However, you can embed reserved words within a variable's name. For example, PrintIt is a perfectly acceptable variable name. Visual Basic will present an error message if you try to use a reserved word as a variable name, usually immediately after you press ENTER.

One of the most common conventions for variable names is to use capitals only at the beginning of the words that make up the parts of it (for example, MortgageInterest, not Mortgageinterest). This convention is called *mixed case variable names.* This is the convention used in this book, as most people find it much more readable. Some people add underscores as well (for example, Mortgage_Interest)—this style is not used in this book because it wastes space and occasionally causes problems in debugging.

Variable Types

Visual Basic handles 14 standard types of variables, and it is possible to define your own variable types. This section describes the ones you will use for most data manipulations.

STRING

String variables hold characters. One method to identify variables of this type is to place a dollar sign ($) at the end of the variable name: AStringVariable$. String variables can theoretically hold up to 65,535 characters in the 16-bit version of Visual Basic 4. (The limits grow enormously in the 32-bit versions of Visual Basic, however—to around 2 billion.) In any case a specific machine may hold less due to memory constraints, overhead requirements for Windows, or the number of strings used in the form.

One of the most common uses of string variables is to pick up the information contained in a text box. For example, if you have a text box named Text1, then

```
ContentOfText1$ = Text1.Text
```

assigns the string contained in the text box to the variable named on the left-hand side.

INTEGER

Integer variables hold relatively small integer values (between -32,768 and +32,767). Integer arithmetic is very fast but is restricted to these ranges. The identifier used is the percent sign (%):

```
AnIntegerVariable% = 3
```

LONG INTEGER

The long integer variable is a type that was introduced in QuickBASIC. It holds integers between -2,147,483,648 and +2,147,483,647. The identifier used is the ampersand (&). Long integer arithmetic is also fast, and there is very little performance penalty on 386DX and 486DX machines for using long integers rather than ordinary integers.

```
ALongIntegerVariable& = 123456789
```

SINGLE PRECISION

For single-precision numbers, the identifier is an exclamation point (!). These variables hold numbers that are approximations. They can be fractions, but you can be sure of the accuracy of only seven digits. This means that if an answer comes out as 12,345,678.97, the 8.97 may or may not be accurate. The answer could just as well be 12,345,670.01. Although the accuracy is limited, the size (range) of these numbers is up to 38 digits. Calculations will always be approximate for these types of variables. Moreover, arithmetic with these numbers is slower than with integer or long integer variables.

DOUBLE PRECISION

Double-precision variables hold numbers with 16 places of accuracy and allow more than 300 digits. The identifier used is a pound sign (#). Calculations are also approximate for these variables. You can rely only on the first 16 digits. Calculations are relatively slow with double-precision numbers. Double-precision variables are mainly used in scientific calculations in Visual Basic—because of the data type described next.

CURRENCY

Currency variables are a type that will be new to GW-BASIC and QuickBASIC users. They are designed to avoid certain problems inherent in switching from binary fractions to decimal fractions. (It's impossible to make 1/10 out of combinations of 1/2, 1/4, 1/8, 1/16, and so on.) The currency type can have 4 digits to the right of the decimal place and up to 14 to the left of the decimal point. Arithmetic will be exact within this range. The identifier is an "at" sign (@)—*not* the dollar sign, which identifies strings. While calculations other than addition and subtraction are about as slow as for double-precision numbers, this is the preferred type for financial calculations of reasonable size. (For those who are interested, this type uses 19-digit integers, which are then scaled by a factor of 10,000. This gives you 15 places to the left of the decimal point and 4 places to the right.)

DATE

The date data type gives you a convenient way to store both date and time information for any time between midnight on January 1, 100 to midnight on 31 December 9999. You need to surround any assignment to date variables between the #, for example:

```
Millennium = #January 1, 2000#
```

If you do not include a time in a date, Visual Basic assumes it is midnight.

BYTE

The byte type is new to Visual Basic 4 and can hold integers between 0 and 255. This is a great convenience when you need to save space, and it makes certain arrays (see Chapter 10) much smaller than they would be in earlier versions of Visual Basic. It is also needed for handling binary files in Visual Basic 4.

BOOLEAN

Use the Boolean type when you need variables to be either True or False. It is considered good programming practice to use this data type rather than integers for True/False values.

VARIANT

The variant type was added to Visual Basic way back in version 2.0. The variant data type is designed to store all the different possible Visual Basic data received in one place. If you don't tell Visual Basic what type of information a variable holds, it will use this data type.

It doesn't matter whether the information is numeric, date/time, or string; the variant type can hold it all. Visual Basic automatically performs any necessary conversions, so you don't (usually) have to worry about what type of data is being stored in the variant data type. On the other hand, as you'll see in Chapter 7, you can use a built-in function to determine whether data stored in the variant type is numeric, date/time, or string. This function lets you easily check user entries to see whether they match the format you want.

Using variants rather than a specific type is slower because of the conversions needed and takes up more memory because of additional overhead. In addition, many programmers feel that relying on automatic type conversions leads to sloppy programming. One reason is that relying on the machine to do conversions occasionally leads to some weird behavior in your programs (because the conversion you assumed would be made turns out not to be the one that Visual Basic made).

note: *This book uses the variant data type only when its special properties are needed. I follow the convention that the programmer should be in control at all times and rely on conversions from the variant data type only when he or she is in control of them and thus fully aware of the consequences. If you want to use the variant data type, you will want to study the online help for the VarType function that lets you determine what type of information is stored in a variant variable.*

Fine Points of Variables

Unlike many other versions of BASIC, in Visual Basic you cannot use variables such as A% and A!, which differ only in the type identifier, in the same program. Using them produces a "duplicate definition" error when you try to run your program.

The first time you use a variable, Visual Basic temporarily assigns it a default value of "empty" and gives it the variant type. The "empty" value disappears the moment you assign a value to the variable. Every other type of variable also has a default value. For string variables, this is the null (empty) string—the one you get by assigning "" to a string variable. For numeric variables, the default value is zero. You should only rely on the default values if this is documented (by a Remark statement, for example) in your program. Otherwise, you risk creating a breeding ground for hard-to-find bugs. It is therefore quite common to use the first statements in an event procedure to initialize the variables.

SWAPPING

A common task within a procedure is *swapping,* or interchanging the values of two variables. Surprisingly enough, the designers of Visual Basic left out the command Swap that QuickBASIC has for this. You have to write the code yourself.

Suppose you have two variables, *x* and *y,* and you try the following to swap variables within an event procedure:

```
x = y
y = x
```

This doesn't work, and it is important that you understand why. What goes wrong is that the first assignment gives the current value of *y* to the variable *x, but it wipes out the previous value of x.* The result is that the second statement merely copies the original value of *y*, which is what it was originally anyway. The solution is to use a temporary variable:

```
temp = x        ' copy old value of x to temp
x =  y          ' x now has old value of y
y = temp        ' retrieve original value of x, give to y
```

The Dim Statement for Types

Many people prefer not to use the identifiers to specify the type (and, in any case, variables such as date variables have no distinguishing identifier). Instead they use the Dim statement inside a procedure. The technical term for these statements is *declarations.* Declaring the types of variables used in an event procedure before using them—and commenting as needed, of course—is a good programming habit. It can make your programs more readable since it is easy to skip over the single-character identifiers.

```
Private Sub btnCalculate_Click
  ' This procedure calculates mortgage interest
  Dim Years As Integer
  Dim Rate As Currency
```

```
  Dim Amount As Currency
  Dim I As Integer
  Dim TextBox As String
  Dim Interest As Currency


End Sub
```

You can combine declarations on a single line, for example:

```
Dim Year As Integer, Rate As Currency, Name As String
```

caution: *A common mistake is to use something like*

```
Dim X, Y, Z As Integer
```

on the assumption that all three will be integer variables. In fact, in this example, X and Y default to be variants and only Z is an integer variable. You must use the type identifier each time. (You can also write : Dim Years%, Rate@, and so on, if you prefer using a type identifier.)

If a variable is declared in a Dim statement, then trying to use variables with the same name but a different type identifier at the end of the variable will cause a "duplicate definition" error when the program is run. For example, if you use the statement Dim Count As Integer to declare the integer variable Count, then the variables Count$, Count!, Count#, and Count@ may not be used. Count% may be used, however, and is recognized by Visual Basic as just another way of denoting the variable Count.

Finally, to give a variable the variant data type, just use the Dim statement without any As clause or identifier:

```
Dim Foo     'makes Foo have the variant data type
```

You can also use

```
Dim Foo As Variant 'more explicit easier to read
```

note: *Some programmers like to use the convention of adding a lowercase prefix to variables to indicate what type they are. For example, sngInterestRate, intCount. This book only uses this convention occasionally for illustration purposes.*

Requiring Declaration of Variables

One of the most common bugs in a program is the misspelled variable name. Unless you take steps when you start your program, you'll find Visual Basic programs are prone to this. The problem is that Visual Basic allows you to create variables "on the fly" by merely using a variable name on a line in a program. Misspell the name for a variable that already exists in your program and Visual Basic will just create a new variable that has nothing to do with the one you wanted to work with—giving it a default value that will inevitably cause bugs. This implicit variable creation makes it very difficult to track down bugs because you have to find the misspelled variable name.

The easiest way to avoid this problem is to force all variables to be declared. Then you will be notified if a variable name is spelled incorrectly in a procedure. The designers of Visual Basic give you this option, but do not force you to use it.

The statement needed for this is called Option Explicit. It is the first example of a statement that is not found within event procedures. A good way to remember why this must be so is that you use Option Explicit to change defaults. You would not bother doing this unless you wanted the change to be true for more than one event procedure.

note: *Any information that you want to be usable by all the event procedures attached to a form is placed in the (General) section of the code window for the form.*

To put an Option Explicit in the (General) section, follow these steps:

1. Open the Code window.
2. Select the (General) object from the list of objects presented in the Object list box.
3. Select (declarations) from the Proc list box.
4. Type **Option Explicit**.

note: *You will often need to place form-level declarations in the (General) section when you experiment with the example code found in the help system.*

(In general, to copy a code example from the help system, use the Copy button in the example Code window. Then use the Paste option on the Edit menu to place the sample code in the Code window.)

After Visual Basic processes an Option Explicit command, it will no longer allow you to use a variable unless you declare it first. If you try to use a variable without declaring it, an error message will appear, as shown here:

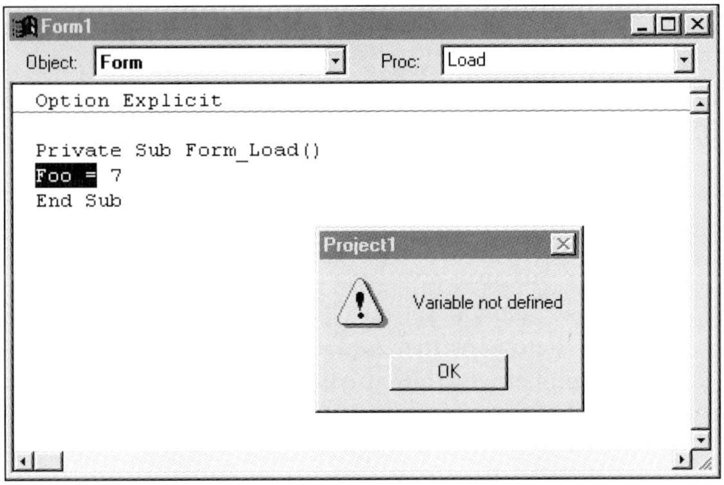

tip: *You can also choose Tools | Options and then go to the Environment page in order to require variable declaration. I (and every other serious Visual Basic programmer I know!) always have this check box set. This inserts an Option Explicit command automatically into your code as needed.*

Changing the Defaults for Types

If you don't want to use Option Explicit, then you will sometimes have a program in which you know it will only (or primarily) use integer variables. In this case it is convenient to change the defaults built into Visual Basic. (Recall that undeclared variables are assumed to be variants.) You change the defaults with what is called a DefType statement. The following table gives some examples:

DefType Statement	What It Does
DefInt A-Z	Changes the default—all variables are assumed to be integers
DefInt I	All variables beginning with I are assumed to be integers
DefStr S-Z	All variables beginning with the letters S through Z are assumed to hold strings

The general forms of the various DefType statements you'll need in this chapter are

DefInt *letter range* (for integers)
DefLng *letter range* (for long integers)
DefSng *letter range* (for single precision)
DefDbl *letter range* (for double precision)
DefCur *letter range* (for currency)
DefStr *letter range* (for strings)
DefVar *letter range* (for variants)
DefBool *letter range* (for Booleans)
DefByte *letter range* (for bytes)
DefDate *letter range* (for dates)

The letters in the ranges need not be caps: DefStr s-Z and DefStr S-Z work equally well. You can always override the default settings by using an identifier or a Dim statement for a specific variable. You put a DefType statement in the (General) section of the code—just as you would (preferably) put the Option Explicit command there.

tip: *Some programmers who don't like Option Explicit put a DefInt A-Z as a form-level declaration in order to ensure that all variables default to integers. This is done because integer variables are handled fastest.*

Scope of Variables

Programmers refer to the *scope* of variables when they want to talk about the availability of a variable used in one part of the program to the other parts of the program. In older programming languages, where *all* variables were available to *all* parts, keeping variable names straight was always a problem. If, in a complicated program, you had two variables named Total, the values could (and would) contaminate each other.

The solution in modern programming languages such as Visual Basic is to isolate variables within procedures. Unless you specifically arrange it, changing the value of a variable named Total in one procedure will not affect another variable with the same name in another procedure. The technical explanation for this is that variables are *local* to procedures unless specified otherwise. In particular, an event procedure will normally not have access to the value of a variable in another event procedure. As always, it is not a good programming practice to rely on defaults. If you want to be sure a variable is local within an event procedure, use the Dim statement inside the event procedure.

Sharing Values Across Procedures

Occasionally you will want to share the values of variables across event procedures. For example, if an application is designed to perform a calculation involving one interest rate at a time, that rate should be available to all the procedures in a form. Variables that allow such sharing are called *form-level* or *module-level variables*. Figure 5-3 shows the scope of variables for a Visual Basic project with a single form.

Just as with the Option Explicit statement, you put the declaration statements for form-level variables in the Declarations section. For example, if you open the Code window, select (declarations) for the (General) object, and enter

```
Dim InterestRate As Currency
```

- The value of the variable named InterestRate will be visible to all the procedures attached to the form.
- Any changes made to this variable in one event procedure will persist.

Obviously, the last point means you have to be careful when assigning values to form-level variables. Any information passed between event procedures is a breeding ground for programming bugs. Moreover, these errors are often hard to pinpoint.

Figure 5-3 Scope of variables

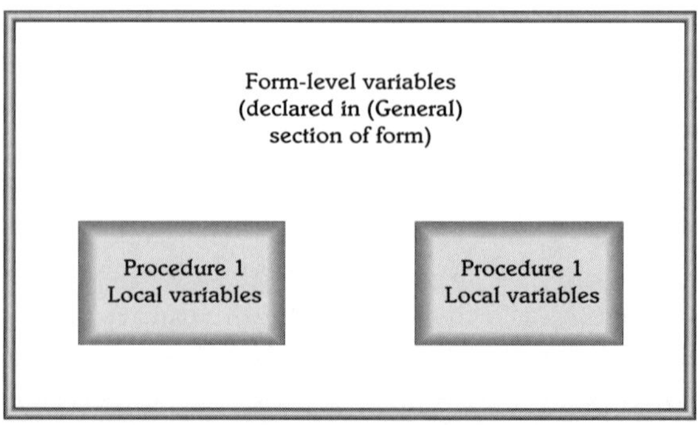

Although most programmers don't think it is a good idea, you can use the same variable name as both a local and a form-level variable. Any Dim statements contained in a procedure take precedence over form-level declarations—they force a variable to be local. Therefore, you lose the ability to use the information contained in the form-level variable. Duplicating the names makes the form-level variable invisible to the procedure. Visual Basic doesn't tell you whether a form-level variable has been defined with the same name as a local variable. This is one more reason to make sure that variables you want to be local really are local by dimensioning them inside the procedure. This forces the variable to be local to that procedure.

tip: *Some programmers like to prefix form-level variables with the letter* f *(for example, fInterest) and global variables with the letter* g *(for example, gInterest). This makes it easier to identify them at a glance. See Chapter 9 for more on global variables.*

The Private Keyword

Visual Basic 4 introduces a new keyword, Private, that you can use to identify form-level variables. Private works the same way as Dim—you use it completely interchangeably with Dim in the (General) section of the form. The idea is to distinguish form-level variables from what are called global (or public) variables. This type of variable is discussed in Chapter 9.

Having Values Persist

When Visual Basic invokes an event procedure, the old values of local variables are wiped out. They go back to their default values. (As mentioned before, you are often better off if they are reinitialized.) Such variables are called *dynamic variables.* However, such variables are not enough for all programming situations. For example, suppose you need to keep track of how many times a command button has been clicked. If the counter is always set back to zero, you're in trouble. You *could* have the values persist by using a form-level variable, but it is generally a good idea to reserve form-level variables only for sharing information. Most programmers choose this method only if other event procedures needed the count.

The solution is to use *static variables.* These variables are not reinitialized each time Visual Basic invokes a procedure. Besides being ideal for counters, they are ideal for making controls alternately visible or invisible (or for switching between any Boolean properties, for that matter) and as a debugging tool.

To make a variable static within a procedure, replace the keyword Dim with the keyword Static:

```
Static Counter As Integer, IsVisible As Integer
```

Here is an example of an event procedure for a command button that counts the clicks and displays the number:

```
Private Sub Command1_Click()
  'This procedure uses a static variable to count clicks
  Static Counter As Integer     ' Counter starts at 0
  Counter = Counter + 1
  Print Counter
End Sub
```

The first time you click, the counter starts out with its default value of zero. Visual Basic then adds 1 to it and prints the result. Notice that by placing the Print statement after the addition, you are not off by 1 in the count.

Occasionally, you want all local variables within a procedure to be static. To do this, add the keyword Static before the words "Private Sub" that start any procedure:

```
Static Private Sub Command1_Click()
```

note: *Form (module) level variables retain their value as well. The problem is that since these variables can communicate any changes made to them to other procedures, they are a breeding ground for bugs. If all you want to do is to preserve the value between uses of the procedure, you are much better off using a static variable inside a procedure than a form (module) level variable.*

Strings

Since information in Visual Basic text boxes is always stored as text, strings are far more important in Visual Basic than in ordinary BASIC. To put two strings together (*concatenate* them), use a plus sign (+). For example, if

```
Title$ = "Queen "
Name$ = "Elizabeth "
Numeral$ = "I"
Title$ + Name$ + Numeral$ = "Queen Elizabeth I"
Title$ + Name$ + Numeral$ + Numeral$ = "Queen Elizabeth II"
```

The + joins the strings together in the order in which you present them. Thus, unlike adding numbers together, the order is important when using the + sign to join two strings together. You can also use the + sign repeatedly to join as many strings together as you want—before Visual Basic makes the assignment statement. Here is an example using the variables defined above:

CurrentQueen$ = Title$ + Name$ + Numeral$ + Numeral$

tip: *If you need to concatenate other Visual Basic data, use an ampersand (&) in place of the +. For example, C = A% & B$ concatenates an integer variable and a string variable by changing them both to variants. (You can also use the & for concatenating strings if you want.)*

ASCII/ANSI Code

A computer doesn't have one kind of memory for text and another for numbers. Anything stored in a computer's memory is changed into a number (actually, a binary representation of a number). The program keeps track of whether the memory patterns are codes for text or not. Usually, the code for translating text to numbers is called the ASCII code (American Standard Code for Information Interchange). The ASCII code associates with each number from 0 through 255 a displayable or control character; although Windows cannot display all 255 ASCII characters and uses a more limited set of characters called the ANSI (American National Standards Institute) character set. The control characters, and such special keys as TAB and line feed, have numbers less than 32. The value of the function Chr(n) is the string consisting of the character of ASCII value *n*. The statement

```
Print Chr(n)
```

either displays the character numbered *n* in the ASCII sequence *for the font currently in use* or produces the specified effect that the control code will have on your screen—or both. For instance, the statement

```
Print Chr(227)
```

prints the Greek letter pi (π) on the screen if you have previously set the FontType to be MS LineDraw by using the Properties window or via code.

The following code uses the ASCII/ANSI value for the quotation mark, 34, to display a sentence surrounded with quotation marks.

```
Print Chr(34);
Print "Quoth the raven, nevermore.";
Print Chr(34)
```

tip: *You can still use the older Chr$ if you want.*

The output of this is

```
"Quoth the raven, nevermore."
```

note: *The preceding output also can be produced by the statement*

```
Print """Quoth the raven, nevermore.""";
```

since Visual Basic—unlike many forms of BASIC—interprets three consecutive quotation marks as a literal quotation mark inside Print statements.

Visual Basic has a function that takes a string expression and returns the ASCII/ANSI value of the first character. If the string is empty (the null string), using this function generates a run-time error.

As you'll see in Chapter 7, ASCII/ANSI order is what Visual Basic uses by default to compare strings when you use relational operators such as < or >. The most important use of the ASCII/ANSI codes is for the KeyPress event procedure, which is also covered in Chapter 7.

note: *Internally the 32-bit version of Visual Basic uses Unicode—a system designed for generating all possible languages. It has more than 65,000 possible character codes. For more on Visual Basic's use of Unicode see the appendix to the* Programmer's Guide. *Except for some special situations involving binary files (Chapter 16), the switch from ASCII/ANSI to Unicode is transparent to the programmer.*

THE NEWLINE CODE

In earlier versions of Visual Basic, one of the most important uses of the Chr function is to set up a newline code for use in your programs. If you want to place separate lines in a multiline text box or add breaks in a message box, you need this code for a new line. As in an old-fashioned typewriter, new lines are made up of two parts: a carriage return to bring the cursor to the first column and the line feed to move it to the next line. In terms of the Chr function, the newline code is

```
vbCrLf = Chr(13) + Chr(10)
```

But now you can just use the built-in constant vbCrLf.

For example, suppose you want to add line breaks in message boxes or multiline text boxes. The fastest way to do this is to first set up a string variable that includes the newline character:

```
TextString$ = "Visual Basic For Windows" + vbCrLf
TextString$ = TextString$ + "Osborne McGraw-Hill" + vbCrLf
TextString$ = TextString$ + "Berkeley, CA"
Text1.Text = TextString$
```

tip: *If you neglect to set the multiline property to True and try to use a newline character, you'll see two funny looking vertical bars in your text box.*

By the way, you might ask why the string is built up first and then assigned to the Text property. This is a general way to speed up a Visual Basic program.

tip: *It is much faster to build up the string first and then change the Text property once than to change the Text property repeatedly.*

Similarly, you can force a break in a message box by setting up the message string using the vbCrLf built-in constant:

```
Message$ = "This will be on line 1."
Message$ = Message$ + vbCrLf + "This will be on line 2."
MsgBox Message$
```

OTHER USEFUL STRING CONSTANTS

Besides the vbCrLf constant for the carriage return/line feed combination, you might find the following built-in constants for various strings useful.

Character(s)	Symbolic Constant
Null character	vbNullChar = Chr$(0)
Carriage return	vbCr = Chr$(13)
Line feed	vbLf = Chr$(10)
Backspace	vbBack = Chr$(8)
Tab	vbTab = Chr$(9)
Vertical tab	vbVerticalTab = Chr$(11)
Form feed	vbFormFeed = Chr$(12)

You can use any of these constants in code rather than making the equivalent Chr (or Chr$) statement. However, only the codes for a carriage return, line feed, tab, and backspace are meaningful in Microsoft Windows.

Fixed-Length Strings

A fixed-length string is a special type of string that plays an important role in later chapters (Chapter 10 and 17). These variables are created with a Dim statement. Here is an example:

```
Dim ShortString As String * 10
Dim strShort As String * 10
```

Both of these statements set up string variables (in spite of not using the identifier). However, this variable will always hold strings of length 10. If you assign a longer string to ShortString, as shown here,

```
ShortString = "antidisestablishment"
```

what you get is the same thing as

```
ShortString = "antidisest"
```

As you can see, the contents of the variable are changed because the right part of the string is cut off. Similarly, if you assign a shorter string to ShortString, like this,

```
ShortString = "a"
```

you still get a string of length 10, only this time the variable is padded on the right so that the string is really stored in the same way as:

```
ShortString = "a          "
```

Thus, fixed-length strings are "right padded" if necessary.

note: *Chapter 17 explains how fixed-length strings are used with random-access files. People whose only experience is with the clumsy method of handling random-access files in interpreted BASIC are in for a very pleasant surprise.*

Input Boxes

Text boxes are the normal way for a Visual Basic application to accept data. (For those who know ordinary BASIC, there is no direct analog of the INPUT statement.) There is one other method that is occasionally useful. The InputBox$ function displays a modal dialog box on the screen. This is the principal advantage of input boxes; it is sometimes necessary to insist that a user supply some necessary data before letting him or her move on in the application. The disadvantages are that the dimensions of the input box are fixed beforehand and you lose the flexibility that text boxes provide. Here is an example of an input box:

As you can see, input boxes have a title bar and four components, three of which are controls. The first may have the prompt, "Please enter your name." There are always two command buttons labeled OK and Cancel. Finally, there is a text box at the bottom. Visual Basic always places the focus here when it processes a statement containing an InputBox function. The simplest syntax for the InputBox function is

VariantVariable = InputBox(prompt$)

This returns a variant. Use

StringVariable = InputBox$(prompt)

to get a string.

Now the user types whatever he or she wants in the text box. Pressing ENTER or clicking the OK button causes whatever is in the text box to become the value of the string variable. Pressing ESC or clicking the Cancel box causes Visual Basic to assign the null string to the variable. The full syntax for the InputBox function is

Variable = InputBox(*prompt*[, *title*][, *default*][, *xpos*][, *ypos*][, *helpfile*, *context*])

Here are short descriptions of these items (they are often called *parameters* or *arguments* in the jargon).

- The *prompt* parameter is a string or string variable whose value Visual Basic displays in the dialog box. It is limited to roughly 1,024 characters. The prompt doesn't wrap, and you have to explicitly add line separators using the vbCrLf characters, as described earlier.
- The *title* parameter is optional and gives the caption used in the title bar. There is no default value; if you leave this out, the application's name is used in the title bar.
- The *default* parameter is also optional. It lets you display default text in the Edit box where the user will be entering information. If you omit this, the box starts out empty.
- Also optional, both *xpos* and *ypos* are integral numeric expressions. *xpos* is the distance in twips between the left edge of the input box and the left edge of the screen. *ypos* gives the distance in twips between the top of the box and the top of the screen. (If you omit *xpos*, the box is horizontally centered, if you omit *ypos*, it will show up around one-third of the way down the screen.)
- The two parameters *helpfile* and *context* are used together when you have a help screen attached to the box—see Chapter 13.

Note that the notation presented in the syntax statement may seem cryptic at first, but it is a good idea to get used to it. It is the notation used in both the manuals and the online documentation. With this notation, anything in square brackets is optional. In this case, the parentheses are outside the square brackets, so they are required. The commas separate the optional elements (the parameters or *arguments*) in this function. If you skip one of the arguments, you still have to use a comma as a separator. (How else would Visual Basic know which argument belongs where? However, see the section on named arguments that follows for one way around this.)

For example,

```
MyInput$ = InputBox("Example", , "A default string", 100, 200)
```

leaves the title bar as the default value (the project name) but starts the box out with the string "A default string" inside of it.

NAMED ARGUMENTS

The InputBox function is one of the many Visual Basic built-in functions that support what are called *named arguments*. Named arguments give you more elegant ways of dealing with functions that have many possibilities. (Unfortunately, not every Visual Basic built-in function supports named arguments—check the online help for those that do.)

For example, you could rewrite the InputBox example above as:

```
MyInput = InputBox(prompt:="Example", Default:= "A default value", _
xpos:=100, ypos:=200)
```

In general, as this example shows, named arguments use a colon plus an equal sign (:=) together with the name of the argument. (The spelling of the argument must match perfectly, but case is irrelevant.) As with any argument, you separate named arguments from each other by a comma.

note: *Even with named arguments you can still only omit optional arguments.*

Numbers

Numbers in Visual Basic cannot use commas to delineate thousands. They *can* use a decimal point, unless they are integers. If you need to give a numeric value to a variable, place the number on the right-hand side of the assignment statement. If you assign a number with a decimal point to an integer variable, it is automatically rounded off. If you assign a number larger than the limits for the given variable, Visual Basic gives you an error message at run time.

Here are some examples:

Number	Acceptable Variable Type
3001	Okay for all numeric variables
3000001	Okay for all but short integer variables
30000.01	Okay for all but integer variables (rounded off for them and long integer variables)
3,001	Illegal because it uses a comma

To change a string of digits to a number, use the built-in function Val:

```
Val("3001") = 3001
```

The Val function reads through the string until it encounters a non-numeric character (or a second period). The number you get from it is determined by where it stopped searching:

```
Val ("30Something") = 30
```

Similarly, you will have to change a number back to a string of digits when you want to display it in a text box. There are many ways to do this, depending on the form you want the number to take. The function Str$ is the simplest. It converts a number to a string but doesn't clean it up in any way. It also leaves a space in front of positive numbers:

```
Str(123)                = "123"
Str(123.4567)           = "123.4567"
Str(-987654321)         = "-987654321"
```

(You can also use the older Str$ function which has the same effect.)

To polish the display, the Str function is often replaced by the Format function. (See the section "The Format Command" in the next chapter.) The Format function is very versatile. Among its many features, this function lets you cut off extraneous digits and display a (large) number with commas or a leading dollar sign.

Another possibility is storing information in the variant data type. If you assign a variable that holds numeric information currently stored in the variant data type to a numeric variable, then Visual Basic will perform the conversion automatically. However (unlike when you use the Val command, for example), you must be careful that the variable of the variant data type holds something with no extraneous characters or extra periods beyond the one allowed. Otherwise, an error message will appear. Visual Basic has built-in functions to check the variable; see the section "What Is It?" in Chapter 7.

Operations on Numbers

The following table gives you the symbols for the five fundamental arithmetic operations:

Operator	Operation
+	Addition
–	Subtraction (and to denote negative numbers)
/	Division
*	Multiplication
^	Exponentiation

For integers and long integers, there is one symbol and one keyword for the arithmetic operations unique to numbers of these types:

Operator	Operation
\	Integer division (this symbol is a backslash)
Mod	The remainder after integer division

The ordinary division symbol (/) gives you a value that is a single-precision, double-precision, or currency answer, depending on the objects involved. The backslash (\), on the other hand, throws away the remainder in order to give you an integer. For example, 7\3 = 2. Since a / gives either a single- or double-precision answer, use a \ or the Mod operator if you really want to work with integers or long integers.

The Mod operator is the other half of integer division. This operator gives you the remainder after integer division. For example, 7 Mod 3 = 1. When one integer perfectly divides another, there is no remainder, so the Mod operator gives zero: 8 Mod 4 = 0.

The usual term for a combination of numbers, variables, and operators from which Visual Basic can extract a value is a *numeric expression.*

ARITHMETIC ON DATE VARIABLES

Visual Basic makes it easy to do calculations with date variables. If you subtract or add an integer, you subtract or add that many days. Adding a fraction changes the time within a day. For example,

```
Dim foo As Date
foo = Now
Print foo
Print foo - 1000
```

prints today's date and time and then prints the day and time 1,000 days ago. (See Chapter 8 for more on the functions that Visual Basic has for dealing with dates.)

PARENTHESES AND PRECEDENCE

When you do calculations, you have two ways to indicate the order in which you want operations to occur. The first way is by using parentheses, and you may well prefer this method. Parentheses let you easily specify the order in which operations occur. Something like 3 + (4 * 5) gives 23 because Visual Basic does the operation within the parentheses (4 times 5) first and only then adds the 3. On the other hand, (3 + 4) * 5 gives 35 because Visual Basic adds the 4 and the 3 first to get 7 and only then multiplies by 5.

Here's another example:

((6 * 5) + 4) * 3

Visual Basic allows you to avoid parentheses, provided you carefully follow rules that determine the precedence of the mathematical operations. For example, multiplication has higher precedence than addition. This means 3 + 4 * 5 is 23 rather than 35 because the multiplication (4 * 5) is done before the addition.

The following list gives the order (hierarchy) of operations:

Exponentiation (^)
Negation (making a number negative)
Multiplication and division
Integer division
The remainder (Mod) function
Addition and subtraction

For example, -4 ^ 2 gives -16 because Visual Basic first does the exponentiation (4 ^ 2 = 4 * 4 = 16) and only then makes the number negative.

Think of these as levels. Operations on the same level are done from left to right, so 96 / 4 * 2 is 48. Because division and multiplication are on the same level, first the division is done, giving 24, and then the multiplication is done. On the other hand, 96 / 4 ^ 2 is 6. This is because the exponentiation is done first, yielding 16, and only then is the division done.

To show you how obscure using the hierarchy of operations can make your programs, try to figure out what Visual Basic would do with this:

```
4 * 2 + 16 / 8 + 2 ^ 3 ^ 4
```

Here's what happens: first the exponents (level 1) are computed left to right (2 ^ 3 = 8, 8 ^ 4 = 8 * 8 * 8 * 8 = 4096), then the multiplication and division from left to right (4 * 2 = 8, 16 / 8 = 2), and then the addition (8 + 2 + 4096 = 4106).

Examples like this one should convince you that a judicious use of parentheses will make your programs clearer and your life easier as a result.

More on Numbers in Visual Basic

If you've tried any calculations involving large numbers in Visual Basic, you've probably discovered that the program often doesn't bother printing out large numbers. Instead, it uses a variant on *scientific notation.* For example, if you ask Visual Basic to print a 1 followed by 25 zeros using a statement like Print 10 ^ 25, what you see is 1E+25.

If you are not familiar with this notation, think of the E+ as meaning: move the decimal place to the right, adding zeros if necessary. The number of places is exactly the number following the E. If a negative number follows the E, move the decimal point to the left. For example, 2.1E-5 gives you .000021. You can enter a number using the E notation if it's convenient; Visual Basic doesn't care whether you enter 1000, 1E3, or 1E+3. To make a number double precision, use a D instead of an E.

If you assign the value of a single-precision variable to a double-precision variable, you do not suddenly increase its accuracy. The number may have more (or even different) digits, but only the first six or seven can be trusted. When you assign a value of one type to a variable of a different type, Visual Basic does a type conversion if it can. If it cannot figure out a way to do this that makes sense, it generates an error at run time.

When you use numbers in your program and do not assign them to a variable of the variant type, Visual Basic assumes the following:

- If a number has no decimal point and is in the range -32,768 to 32,767, it's an integer.
- If a number has no decimal point and is in the range for a long integer (-2,147,483,648 to 2,147,483,647), it's a long integer.
- If a number has a decimal point and is in the range for a single-precision number, it is assumed to be single precision.
- If a number has a decimal point and is outside the range for a single-precision number, it is assumed to be double precision.

These built-in assumptions occasionally lead to problems. This is because the realm in which an answer lives is determined by where the questions live. If you start out with two integers, Visual Basic assumes the answer is also an integer. For example, a statement such as

```
Print 123451*6789
```

starts with two integers, so the answer is assumed also to be an integer. But the answer is too large for an integer, so you would get an overflow error. The solution is to add the appropriate identifier to at least one of the numbers. Use the statement:

```
Print 12345&*6789
```

You can also use a built-in function to force a type conversion if the values are compatible. In particular, Visual Basic will do numeric conversions only if the numbers you're trying to convert are in the range of the new type; otherwise, Visual Basic generates an error message. Using the numeric conversion functions has the same effect as assigning the numeric expression to a variable of the type specified. The following table summarizes these functions.

Conversion Function	What It Does
CInt	Makes a numeric expression an integer by rounding
CLng	Makes a numeric expression a long integer by rounding
CSng	Makes a numeric expression single precision

CDbl	Makes a numeric expression double precision
CCur	Makes a numeric expression of the currency type
CStr	Makes any expression a string
CVar	Makes any expression a variant
CBool	Makes a numeric expression a Boolean
CByte	Makes a numeric expression into a byte
CDate	Makes a compatible expression into a date

note: *It is possible to rely on storing numeric information in variant variables. You can then use the ordinary arithmetic operations on these variant variables. This trusts Visual Basic to make the right kind of conversion—something most programmers won't do.*

Bits, Bytes, and Hexadecimal (Base 16) Numbers in Visual Basic

You may have wondered what cryptic notations such as &HFFFFFF meant for a color code when you looked at the Properties window. It turns out that to set colors directly from the Properties window, you'll need to know a bit about counting in *binary* (base 2) and *hexadecimal* (base 16) formats. (This information is also useful in various other contexts in Visual Basic; although you may want to skip this section now, you will probably want to return to it later if you do decide to skip it.)

Roughly speaking, a computer is ultimately a giant collection of on-off switches, and a disk is a collection of particles that can either be magnetized or not. Think of each memory location in your PC as being made up of eight on-off switches. This affects the internal representation of numbers inside a PC. For example, when you write 255, you ordinarily think two hundreds, five tens, and five ones. The digits are arranged in decimal notation, or base-10 notation, with each position holding numbers 10 times as large as the position to the right. However, your computer thinks in binary notation (base-2 notation) and stores the number 255 in a single-memory location as 11111111, meaning one 128, one 64, one 32, one 16, one 8, one 4, one 2, and one 1. Each of the eight switches mentioned above represents a *bit* (for *binary digit*). When a switch stores a 1, the bit is said to be on, and the value stored in that position is twice the value of the digit in the place to the right (instead of 10 times the value, as in decimal notation). Eight bits form a *byte* (which is one memory location), and half a byte forms a *nibble*.

The following table shows you how to count to 15 in binary notation.

Binary	Decimal
0	0
1	1
10	2
11	3
100	4
101	5
110	6
111	7
1000	8
1001	9
1010	10
1011	11
1100	12
1101	13
1110	14
1111	15

Fifteen is the largest number that can be stored in a single nibble, and 255 is the largest number that can be stored in a byte. Bits are numbered with the leftmost bit called the *most significant* and the rightmost (or zero) bit called the *least significant.*

Binary numbers are difficult for most people to handle. Hexadecimal numbers (base 16) are much easier. Each place in a hexadecimal numbering scheme is 16 times the previous place. So instead of saying "1's place, 10's place, 100's place," as you learned in grade school (for decimal notation), in hexadecimal (hex) notation you say, "1's place, 16's place, 256's place," and so on. For example, hexadecimal 10 is decimal 16. Hexadecimal notation uses A for decimal 10, B for decimal 11, C for decimal 12, D for decimal 13, E for decimal 14, and F for decimal 15. In Visual Basic programs, you prefix a number with &H to indicate that it is a hexadecimal number. Thus, you would write decimal 49 as &H31. Each hexadecimal digit represents four binary digits, or one nibble.

To convert binary numbers to hexadecimal format, group the digits from right to left in groups of four and convert. For example, 11010111 (1101 0111, in two groups of four) is hexadecimal D7: 1101 is 13 in decimal format and D in hexadecimal format, and 0111 is 7 in both decimal and hexadecimal formats.

HOW COLOR WORKS IN VISUAL BASIC

The settings for the color properties are indicated by hexadecimal coding. Every color code in Visual Basic is made up of six hexadecimal digits, from

&H000000& (0) to &HFFFFFF& (16,777,215). This might seem awkward, but the code actually is fairly simple to use—if you understand hexadecimal notation.

Finally, it's a good idea to get into the habit of adding another ampersand to the end of a color code—for example: &HFFFFFF&. This tells Visual Basic to treat the color code as a long integer. As you have seen, long integers are integers that can be greater than 32,767 or less than -32,768, and color codes are usually outside these limits. Forgetting the identifier doesn't usually cause problems, but it's best not to take chances.

To understand the code, think of RGB (red, green, and blue) color monitors as being told to send out a specific amount of redness, greenness, and blueness. The combination of these primary colors gives you all the remaining ones. In the coding used by Visual Basic, the last two hexadecimal digits give you the amount of redness, the middle two give you the amount of greenness, and the first two, the most significant, give you the amount of blueness. Here are a few examples of hexadecimal color codes and the colors they produce:

Hex Color Code	Color
&H0000FF&	Maximum red (no green or blue)
&H00FF00&	Maximum green (no red or blue)
&HFF0000&	Maximum blue (no red or green)
&H000000&	Black (no color)
&HFFFFFF&	White (all colors)
&H00FFFF&	Yellow (red and green)
&H808080&	Gray (equal mixtures of all colors)

The reason that &H808080& is an equal mixture of all colors is that half of &HFF& is about &H80&, because half of 255 is about 128; 128 is equal to 8 *16, which is equal to &H80&.

note: *Some people find it convenient to think of the color code as &HBBGGRR& (B for blue, G for green, and R for red).*

Now you can change color settings directly:

1. Move to the Properties window, select BackColor or ForeColor.
2. Decide how much red, green, or blue you want.
3. Enter the appropriate hexadecimal code.

Example Program: A Mortgage Calculator

You now have seen enough of Visual Basic to write a really useful program: a mortgage calculator. At this stage, what this program will do is allow a user to enter the amount of the mortgage, the interest rate, and the term in years in three text boxes. Then the program will calculate the monthly mortgage payment from scratch using a standard formula.

note: *Visual Basic 4 actually has many financial functions available. These functions are discussed in Chapter 8. In particular, there's a function for doing calculations that are even more sophisticated than mortgage analysis.*

The first thing to do is design the form. Figure 5-4 shows the form with the caption not yet changed. This form has two command buttons, four labels, and four text boxes. It uses the default sizes for all the controls. This lets you use the double-click method for generating them. You then need to move the controls around by using the sizing handles until you are happy with the locations. Table 5-2 lists the controls in this project, following the Tab order.

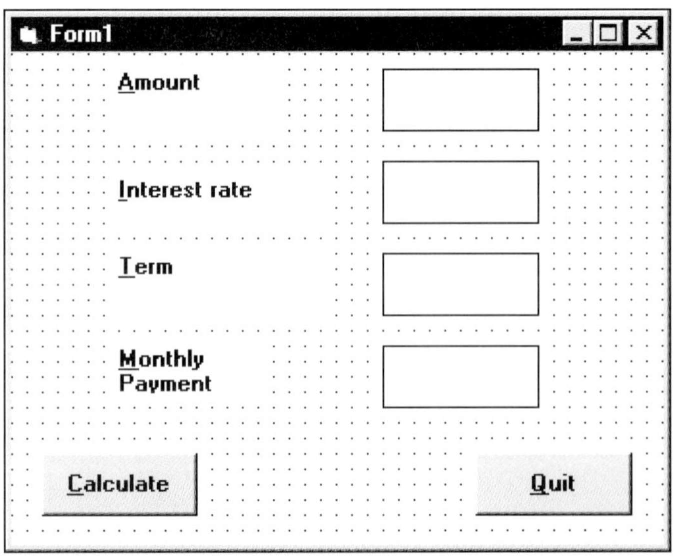

Figure 5-4 Form for the mortgage calculator

Control	Control Name	Caption (or Text)
Form		Mortgage Calculator
1st label	Label1	&Amount
1st text box	txtMortgageAmount	
2nd label	Label2	&Interest Rate
2nd text box	txtInterestRate	
3rd label	Label3	&Term
3rd text box	txtMortgageTerm	
4th label	Label4	&Monthly Payment
4th text box	txtMortgagePayment	
Left command button	btnCalculate	&Calculate
Right command button	btnQuit	&Quit

Table 5-2
Controls for the Mortgage Calculator Program in Tab Order

As you can see in Figure 5-4 or by looking at the ampersands in Table 5-2, this form has many access keys for the controls. There are even access keys for the labels. As you saw in Chapter 4, this gives quick access to the text boxes. For this to work, though, the text box must follow the label in Tab order when you design the form. The TabStop property for the MortgagePayment text box has been changed to False since there is no reason in this application to allow the user to move the focus to this box. The Locked property is also changed to True since you don't want the user to be able to change the contents of this box. (Other possibilities are using a bordered label or setting the Enabled property to False, although this has the side effect of dimming the box.)

Let's go over one way to code this application. All the code is attached to the two command buttons. The code for the Quit button is simple:

```
Private Sub btnQuit_Click ()
  End
End Sub
```

The code to actually calculate the mortgage payment is a little more complicated. First, you need a formula for mortgage payments. The formula for monthly mortgage payments is a bit complicated. It is

Principal**MonthInt*/(1-(1/(1+*MonthInt*))^(*Years* *12))

where *MonthInt* is the annual interest rate divided by 12. Since entering this formula is prone to error, it is broken up into a numerator and denominator in the following code sample.

```
Private Sub btnCalculate_Click ()
  'This calculates the mortgage
  'Using the formula
  'Principal*MonthInt/(1-(1/(1+MonthInt))^(Years*12))

  Dim Years As Integer, Payment As Currency
  Dim MonthInt As Single, Amount As Currency
  Dim Percent As Single, Principal As Currency
  Dim Numerator As Currency, Denominator As Currency
  ' Get info
  Years = Val(MortgageTerm.Text)
  Principal = Val(MortgageAmount.Text)
  Percent = Val(InterestRate.Text) / 100
  MonthInt = Percent/12

  Numerator = Principal * MonthInt
  Denominator = 1 - (1 / (1 + MonthInt))^ (Years * 12)
  Payment = Numerator/Denominator
  MortgagePayment.Text = Str(Payment)
End Sub
```

For more accuracy, this program keeps the years in an integer variable, the interest rate and percent as a single-precision number, and all the others as currency variables. (The program will run a little more quickly if it uses single-precision variables instead of currency variables.) The next point to remember is that text boxes do not give numbers; it is good programming to convert the data inside them by using the Val command instead of relying on variants. This program assumes that the user enters the interest rate as a percent. Because the Val function stops when it encounters a non-numeric character, the user may use a percent sign at the end of what he or she types. (Converting a percent to a decimal means dividing by 100.) To make the logic of the program clearer, there is a separate calculation for the monthly interest, and the formula is separated into its numerator and denominator.

Finally, the program converts the data back to a string in order to assign it to the text property of the MortgagePayment text box instead of using the automatic conversion provided by variants.

Improvements to the Mortgage Calculator

There are lots of ways to improve the mortgage calculator program. Probably the most important would be to make the program more "bulletproof." Inexperienced users often enter information in the wrong form or use the wrong kind of information. For example, they might use commas or dollar signs for the mortgage amounts. In the next chapter you'll see how to write the code to either allow or prevent this as you see fit.

For now, though, suppose you want to add two command buttons that either increase or decrease the interest rate (say by 1/8% = .00125) and then redo the calculations. Here's a simple way to write the code for a button to increase the interest rate:

```
Sub btnIncrease_Click()
  Dim NewRate As Single

  Percent = Val(InterestRate.Text) / 100
  NewRate = (Percent + .00125)*100
  InterestRate.Text = Str(NewRate)
  btnCalculate_Click
End Sub
```

Before getting to the question of why this program may not be the best solution, take a look at the key statement, btnCalculate_Click. This is the first example you've seen of one event procedure using (the technical term is *calling*) another event procedure. As your programs get more sophisticated, event procedures become more and more interrelated. Chapter 9 discusses this in depth. What happens here is that when Visual Basic calls the Click procedure you wrote earlier, it uses the current contents of the text boxes. Because the line

```
InterestRate.Text = Str(NewRate)
```

changes the contents of the text box directly, the Click procedure has new data to work with.

note: *As this example indicates, you call an event procedure with its name. More complicated event procedures (those having arguments) are still called by using their name—you just need to supply the required arguments.*

CODING PROBLEMS IN THE PREVIOUS EXAMPLE

Now why would some people think this version of the mortgage program is not the most efficient programming solution? The offending line is

```
Percent = Val(InterestRate.Text) / 100
```

What this line does is recalculate something that has been calculated once already. While not a mistake, it is inefficient. In a more complicated program, these inefficiencies might grow until they really put a drag on the performance of your application. The problem is, in Visual Basic there is no way to pass information to an event procedure *except through form-level variables.* So some programmers would advocate making all the numeric information derived from the text boxes in this example the values of form-level variables.

If you want to make the information from the text boxes form-level variables, you can do this by adding one of the following to the (declarations) section of the form and removing the corresponding declarations from the event procedures,

```
Dim Principal As Single, Percent as Single
Dim Years As Integer, Payment As Currency
```

or:

```
Private Principal As Single, Percent as Single
Private Years As Integer, Payment As Currency
```

Unfortunately, form-level variables are also a breeding ground for bugs, so many programmers prefer to use them only when they have to. (And they would not be needed in this example once you have mastered Visual Basic!) At this point, given what has been covered about Visual Basic, there is no good solution. (Once you have seen how to use non-event procedures, there will be quite a few possible solutions.)

The moral is that inefficiencies and bug breeding are common when you modify an old program for new uses. You can end up forcing the original program into a frame in which it was never supposed to appear. You're likely to introduce bugs as well. Often, you're better off rewriting the program from scratch—unless you have designed the program well in the first place.

In any case, debugging a program will always be necessary, but it will never be fun. Programs rarely run perfectly the first time. One way to cut down on debugging time is to get into the habit of "thinking first and coding later" (sometimes described as "the sooner you start coding, the longer it takes"). If you think through the possibilities carefully first—for example, deciding which variables should be global and which should be local—you'll go a long way toward "bug proofing" your programs.

Constants

A program is easiest to debug when it's readable. Try to prevent the MEGO ("my eyes glaze over") syndrome that is all too common when a program has lots of mysterious numbers sprinkled about. It's a lot easier to read a line of code such as

```
Calculate.Visible = True
```

than if you use

```
Calculate.Visible = -1
```

even though both will have the same effect.

caution: *True and False are now reserved words. Visual Basic 1.0 code that made them user-defined constants will need to be changed so that these offending lines are removed.*

More generally, Visual Basic's *named constant* feature allows you to use mnemonic names for values that never change. Constants are declared just like variables, and the rules for their names are also the same: 255 characters, first character a letter, and then any combination of letters, underscores, and numerals. The older convention was to use all capitals for constants; now the manuals suggest going to the same mixed case format that is being used for variables. Just as some people like to use a prefix for the variable type, some people like to use the prefix "con" for constants. (I particularly don't like this convention for constants because something like Pi (3.14159...) seems to make a lot more sense than conPi!)

If you have only one form or want the constants visible to the event procedures for only one form, put them in the (declarations) section for the

(General) object, just as you did with the definers that change Visual Basic's default types or for form-level variables. Some people like to use the Private keyword for form-level constants that you saw for form-level variables as well—although it is not needed. Finally, you can also define a constant within a procedure, but this is less common, and only that procedure would have access to the constant.

Set up a constant by using the keyword Const followed by the name of the constant, an equal sign, and then the value:

```
Const Pie = 3.14159
```

You can also set up string constants:

```
Const UserName = "Bill Smith"
Const Language = "Visual Basic Version 4.0"
```

You can even use numeric expressions for constants—or define new constants in terms of previously defined constants:

```
Const PieOver2 = Pie/2
```

What you can't do is define a constant in terms of Visual Basic's built-in functions or the exponentiation operator. If you need the square root of ten in a program, you need to calculate it before you can write

```
Const SquareRootOfTen = 3.16227766
```

Visual Basic uses the simplest type it can for a constant, but you can override this by adding a type identifier to a constant. For example:

```
Const ThisWillBeALongInteger& = 37
```

As mentioned, the convention is to use mixed case for constants, but this is not required. Moreover, references to constants don't depend on the case.

The Supplied Constant File

Visual Basic 4 comes with hundreds of useful constants for working with the built-in functions, objects, and methods. You have seen a few already; for example, the vbCrLf constant that replaces the older Chr(13) + Chr(10). The built-in constants are available for pasting into the Code window from the *Object Browser*. The Object Browser pops up when you press F2 or choose the Object Browser from the View menu (ALT V, O). It is shown in Figure 5-5.

Each different component of Visual Basic 4, such as the database features or the ones coming from Visual Basic for Applications, has its own built-in constants that are available from the Object Browser. Moreover, you can paste these constants into your code and they will automatically be recognized. Visual Basic constants begin with a "vb," database constants (Chapter 20) with a "db," and so on.

To see the constants (there are a few hundred of them!) available in Visual Basic itself, follow these steps:

1. Drop down the Libraries/Project drop-down list box.
2. Choose VB—Visual Basic objects and procedures.
3. Choose the type of constants from the (now filled) Classes/Modules box.
4. Choose the actual constant from the Methods/Properties box.

Figure 5-5
The Object Browser

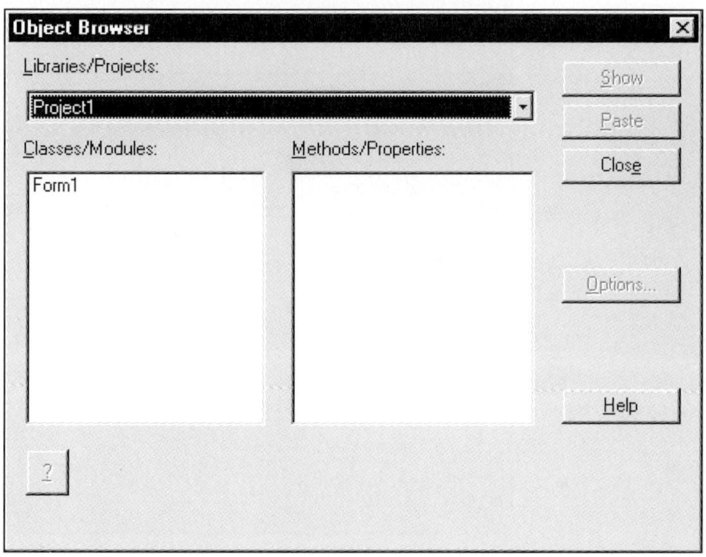

The result looks like Figure 5-6. Note that as you move through the Methods/Properties box, Visual Basic gives you a short description of the constant—including its value.

(To choose a constant from a different part of Visual Basic 4, choose the library you want to work with in step 2 above. The most common other place you will be looking for constants is in the Visual Basic for Applications Object Library.)

To paste a constant into your code:

1. Make sure the cursor is where you want the constant to appear in the Code window.
2. Select the constant from the Methods/Properties box.
3. Click on the Paste button.

tip: *If you are unsure of what constants you need, the online help system will tell you which one you need for a specific function, action, or method.*

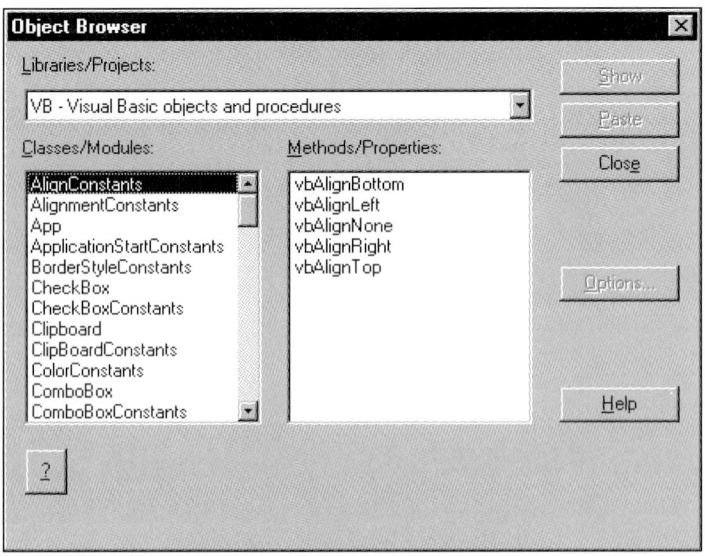

Figure 5-6

Constants in the Visual Basic library

Projects with Multiple Forms

As your applications grow more complicated, you won't want to restrict yourself to applications that are contained in only a single form. Multiple forms will add flexibility and power to your applications. This is over and above solving the problems you've already seen with controls blocking out text that you've printed to a form. To add more forms to an application you're designing, open the Insert menu and choose Form by pressing ALT I, F.

The Project window lists all the forms by name with an .FRM extension. (To make the Project window visible, use the CTRL+R shortcut or choose View | Project.) Visual Basic stores each form as a separate file and uses the .vbp (project) file to keep track of where they are stored. The following illustration shows the Project window with an application that has three forms:

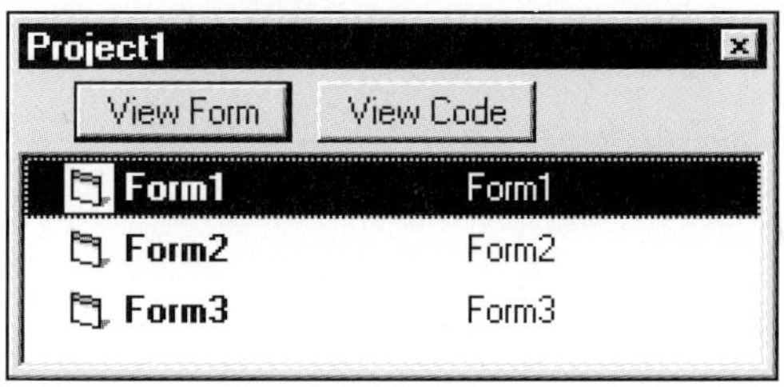

tip: *The easiest way to bring a form to the foreground so you can work with it is to open the Project window and double-click the form's name or select the form by name and click the View Form button.*

Writing Code for Multiple Forms

Although forms do not have a control name that you use for writing code for event procedures, they do have a Name property that you can use to refer to other properties of the form. Setting this property to something meaningful via the properties bar makes it easier to refer to the different properties or apply a method to the form. The default value for this property starts at Form1 for the first form, Form2 for the second form, and so on. Using the default value means you have to refer to properties when you code, like this:

```
Form3.Height = Screen.Height/2    'cut the default height in 2
```

If Form3 was your "Help Form," for example, the code will be a lot easier to read if you set the form name to HelpForm and write

```
HelpForm.Height = Screen.Height/2  'set HelpForm height to
                                   'half normal
```

Microsoft's convention is to use an frm as the prefix to the form name:

```
frmHelp.Heigh = Screen.Height/2
```

Form names are used only in code to refer to properties and methods; they are not used for event procedures. For example, to apply the Cls (clear screen method) to the preceding form, you would write

```
HelpForm.Cls
```

On the other hand, regardless of how you name a form, the Click procedure template for the form itself will always look like this in the Code window:

```
Private Sub Form_Click ()

End Sub
```

Although you do not need the form's name to refer to properties of the current form, using it sometimes makes your code cleaner. This is because code for one form can affect controls on another form. Suppose your HelpForm had a Quit button you wanted to disable via code within an event procedure attached to a different form. It is safer (and clearer) to write

```
HelpForm.Quit.Enabled = False
```

than

```
Quit.Enabled = False
```

although both have the same effect. The general syntax is

FormName.ControlName.Property = Value

Finally, you may need to have variables and user-defined constants available to all the code attached to the project (regardless of how many forms you may have in the project). These are the public or global variables and constants mentioned earlier and are discussed in Chapter 9.

How to Handle Multiple Forms at Run Time

Visual Basic displays at most one form when an application starts running. This is called the *startup form*. Any other forms in your application must be explicitly loaded and displayed via code. The startup form is usually the initial form that appears when you begin a new project. If you want to change this, select Tools | Options and then click on the Project page. Choosing this option gives you the following dialog box:

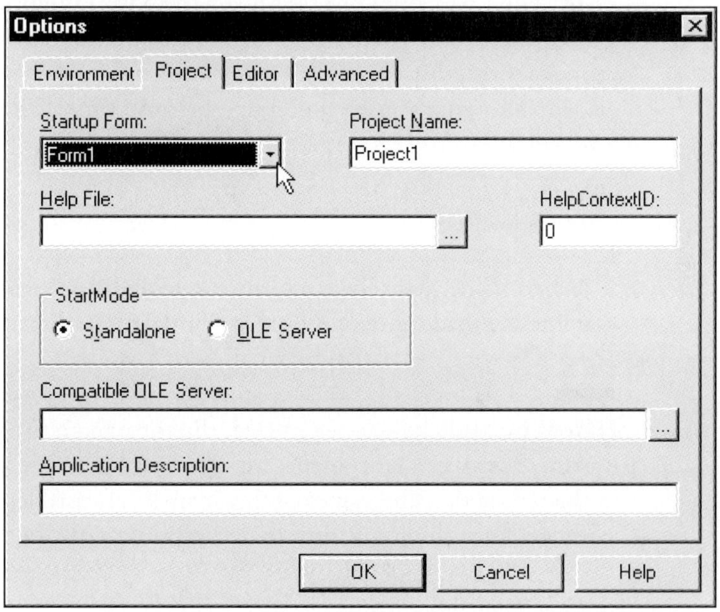

All you need to do now is select the form (by name) that you want to be the startup form by clicking on the down arrow (indicated by the pointer) in the Startup Form option and choosing the form you want.

METHODS FOR FORMS

There are four methods for forms described in this section. You will be using these methods constantly when you work with multiple form applications.

Show The Show keyword shows the form on the screen. To do this, Visual Basic first checks that the form is loaded into memory. If it is not, then it loads the form first. The basic syntax for the Show method is

FormName.Show

The Show method also moves the form to the top of the desktop if it was covered by another form. Show can also be used in the Form_Load event of any form to display information without needing to set Auto Redraw to True. (If you forget to use Show in the Form_Load event procedure before you try to Print to the form, nothing will happen!)

Load The Load keyword places the form into memory but does not display it. Visual Basic also loads the form into memory whenever you refer to its properties or controls in code. Because of this, the main reason to load a form prior to showing it is to speed up response time. The trade-off is that you use up more memory. Its syntax is

Load *FormName*

When Visual Basic loads a form, it sets all the properties of the form to the ones you initially made at design time and invokes the Form_Load event procedure.

Hide The Hide keyword removes the form from the screen but doesn't unload it from memory. The controls are not available to the user, but you can still refer to them in code. The values of the form-level variables do not disappear. As with loading a form, hiding a form trades response time for memory. The syntax is

FormName.Hide

For example, to hide the current form, you can use the Me keyword:

```
Me.Hide
```

Unload The Unload keyword removes the form from memory. (It has the same effect as someone clicking the exit button or double-clicking the control box.)

All information contained in its form-level variables is lost. The syntax for this command is

Unload *FormName*

tip: *When Visual Basic starts the process of unloading a form, Visual Basic generates the QueryUnload event. This event procedure is a good place to put code you want to be activated at the end of the useful life of the form; for example, when the user chooses Close from the control box or the ALT+F4 combination. For more on this event, see the next section in this chapter and Chapter 7.*

APPLICATIONS THAT LOOK LIKE THEY ARE OVER—BUT AREN'T

One of the most common problems when dealing with a multiple form application is when users close a form by accident—but no other form is visible. At this point they would have to know enough to use the Windows Task Manager to kill the project. Since naive users are unlikely to know this, you need to be aware of the possibility—so you can deal with it.

The easiest way to deal with this (all too) common problem is to write code in the QueryUnload event that either:

- Prevents the user from closing down the form

or

- Ends the project if that form is closed

Both of these depend on the QueryUnload event being triggered before the form is purged from memory. The syntax for this event procedure is

```
Private Sub Form_QueryUnload(Cancel As Integer, UnloadMode As Integer)

End Sub
```

To prevent someone from closing down a form, you just need to set the Cancel argument in the QueryUnload event to True. To end the program, place an Unload Me followed by an End statement in the QueryUnload event. (In general, you will want to unload all the forms in your project before ending the project.)

THE ACTIVATE/DEACTIVATE EVENTS

When you start working with projects that involve multiple forms, you may want to take advantage of the Activate/Deactivate events. Visual Basic invokes the Activate event for a form whenever a form becomes the active window. In general, forms become active and thus Visual Basic calls the Activate event when a user clicks on the form or you use the Show or SetFocus method in code. The Activate event occurs before the GotFocus event. Note that Visual Basic will call the Activate event only when a form is visible. This means that if you load the form using the Load method, Visual Basic won't call the Activate event until the form becomes visible (for example, by using the Show event or setting the form's Visible property to True).

Visual Basic invokes the Deactivate event when the Form stops being the active window; it doesn't call it when you unload a form (use the Unload or QueryUnload events for this). Visual Basic also calls the LostFocus event before the Deactivate event.

Finally, the Activate and Deactivate events occur only when the user moves the focus within an application. If she or he moves the focus to another application, these events are *not* triggered.

An Example Using Multiple Forms

To see an example of an application with multiple forms, create a project with two forms and add a command button to each form. The command button on the first form will move the second form to the left and bring it to the forefront. The command button on the second form will bring the first form back to the top without moving it from its original place. You will also prevent the second form from closing down and having the application end when the first form is closed. For illustration purposes, the default names for all the objects are left unchanged.

First off, let's begin with a way to close the project. This is simply the Unload statement along with an End statement in the QueryUnload event for the main form:

```
Private Sub Form_QueryUnload(Cancel As Integer, UnloadMode As Integer)
Unload Me
   End
End Sub
```

The command button for the first form needs the following code:

```
Private Sub Command1_Click ()
  ' Moves the second form around and displays it
  Form2.Show
  Form2.Left = Form2.Left - 75
End Sub
```

Because the control's name is deliberately not set to be more meaningful, the event procedure for the second command button starts off just like the first:

```
Private Sub Command1_Click ()
  ' Show original form
  Form1.Show
End Sub
```

The control names are left unchanged here to make the point that this is sloppy programming. Although Visual Basic will know which Command1_Click procedure belongs where, in a more sophisticated program, this sloppiness would be an obvious breeding ground for confusion. Even if the form names seem clear enough, it is better to use control names such as Form2Shift (or Microsoft's convention cmdForm2Shift) for the first command button and Form1ToTop for the second (cmdForm2Shift). You will probably also want to set the caption properties to explain what actions the buttons perform.

Finally, since you don't want someone to be able to close the second form, you use the following QueryUnload event procedure for the second form:

```
Private Sub Form_QueryUnload(Cancel As Integer, UnloadMode As Integer)
  Cancel = True
End Sub
```

Keeping the Focus in a Form (Modality)

Message boxes require that users close them before they can work with a form. This property is often useful for a form as well. For example, you may want to make sure a user has digested the information contained in a form before he or she shifts the focus to another form in the application. (Users can switch to a completely different application within the Windows environment, unless you are using a system modal message box. See Chapter 4 for more details.) This property is called *modality* in the Microsoft Windows documentation. You make a form modal by adding an option to the Show method that displays the form. If you have a line of code in a procedure that reads

```
FormName.Show 1
```

then Visual Basic displays the form rigidly. No user input to any other form in the application will be accepted until the modal form is hidden or unloaded. Once a form is shown by using the modal setting, a user cannot move the focus to any other form until the modal form is hidden or unloaded. In particular, neither mouse clicks nor keypresses will register in any other form. Usually you have a default command or cancel button on a modal form.

tip: *A dialog box is usually a modal form with a fixed double border.*

Forms default to be nonmodal, but you can also use the following code to force them to be nonmodal:

```
FormName.Show 0
```

Chapter Six

Displaying Information

VISUAL Basic gives you extraordinary control over the appearance of what you place on a form and what you print on a page. The purpose of this chapter is to introduce you to the methods, functions, and properties you use to display your data in a professional way. First, you will work with data that goes on a form. Then you will learn about picture boxes, which work in much the same way as forms. Next, it's on to the RichTextBox control, which lets you display information in multiple fonts and multiple sizes. The chapter ends with a short introduction to using the printer.

Displaying Information on a Form

Since you now know how to add other blank forms to your applications, you are in a better position to display information in an application. You will want to do this because, as you've already seen, controls on a form can obscure any information Visual Basic displays on that form using the Print method.

The general syntax for the Print method applied to a form is

FormName.Print *expression*

where *expression* is any Visual Basic expression. (You can use the Me keyword for the current form or leave it out.)

tip: *Remember to set the AutoRedraw property of the form to be True if there is a possibility that your form will be covered and then uncovered.*

Where Visual Basic displays the information depends on the current value of two properties of a form, called CurrentX and CurrentY. CurrentX refers to the horizontal position where Visual Basic will display information. CurrentY refers to the vertical position where it will display the information. The units used are determined by the scale set up with the various scale methods you saw in Chapter 3.

Whenever you use the Cls method to clear a form, Visual Basic resets the CurrentX and CurrentY values to zero. After clearing the form using the Cls method, then using the default setting for the various scale properties, the next Print statement puts information in the top left corner. If you have changed the scale (for example, by using the ScaleLeft and ScaleTop properties), Visual Basic will use whatever location on the form now represents 0,0. (For more information on the scale properties, see Chapter 15.)

You set CurrentX and CurrentY the same way you'd set any property:

FormName.CurrentX = *Value*
FormName.CurrentY = *Value*

The value may be any numeric expression from which Visual Basic can extract a single-precision value.

note: *Many Visual Basic programmers prefer to use picture boxes or RichTextBoxes instead of printing directly to a form because they can combine fonts in these controls as well. (Even labels and ordinary text boxes can be preferable.) For example, information on a form can't be scrolled without a lot of work. Information in any kind of text box can be made to scroll up and down or left and right with essentially no work, by adding scroll bars at design time or run time.*

Example: Centering Text Inside a Form

Suppose you want to display a message in the exact center of a form. This turns out to be not as easy as it sounds. As a first approximation, here is an outline of what you need to do to find the coordinates of the exact center of the form:

1. Find the current value of the ScaleHeight and ScaleWidth properties. These properties (unlike Height and Width) tell you how large the internal area of the form (without the borders and title bar) is.
2. Divide these values in half.
3. Find the values of the ScaleLeft and ScaleTop properties for the form.
4. Add the results from step 2 to the values from step 3. This gives you the coordinates of the exact center of the form.

The problem is that this doesn't quite finish the job. If you reset the values CurrentX and CurrentY to the results from step 4 of this outline, you would start printing at the center of the screen, but the message wouldn't be centered. What you also need to do is take into account the font size and the length of the message. Once you know this information, you then could shift over and up by half the length and width of the message. The key to doing this is two built-in methods: TextWidth and TextHeight. The syntax for the TextWidth method is

FormName.TextWidth(*string*)

After processing this statement, Visual Basic returns the value for the width of the string inside the parentheses, using the current font and reporting the results in the current scale. So, to the preceding outline, you need to add:

5. Use the TextWidth method on the string you want to center.
6. Now subtract half the value Visual Basic obtains from this method from the value in step 4, and make this the value of CurrentX.

Similarly, the syntax for the TextHeight method is

FormName.TextHeight(*string*)

and it gives the width of the string inside the parentheses. Subtracting half this number from the value of CurrentY obtained in step 4 gives you the location where you should start printing the message.

In general, TextHeight is used to determine the amount of vertical space and TextWidth the amount of horizontal space you need to display a string.

Here is another example in which these methods are useful. Suppose you want to display information at the beginning of the tenth line of text as it would appear in the ordinary coordinate system (0,0 as the top left). Use the following fragment:

```
CurrentY = FormName.TextHeight("I") * 9
CurrentX = 0
```

You use a capital letter to take into account that TextHeight gives the height of the text used. You also have to multiply by 9 rather than 10 to take into account that Visual Basic starts with 0,0 for the top left corner.

note: *To position text inside a multiline text box, you need to insert spaces and newline characters (vbCrLf) as needed. Text boxes do not support direct positioning of text.*

The Font Properties in Code

Which fonts and font sizes you can use depend on what kind of hardware and software is available to the system that is running the application. Visual Basic lets you find out this information; Chapter 7 shows you how. To assign a font name in code, place the name in quotation marks on the right-hand side of an assignment statement using the Name property of the Font object:

ObjectName.Font.Name = "Modern"
Object.Font.Name = "Helv"   'Helvetica

(If the target system doesn't have the font you select, it uses its best approximation.)

All objects that display text let you set the Name property of the Font object. These include forms, command buttons, labels, and the various kinds of text boxes. Of these, only forms, picture boxes, and RichTextBoxes let you combine different fonts. If you change these properties at run time for any other control, all the old text switches to the new font as well. The rule is that if text is specified by a property (for example, the Caption property for command buttons), changing a font changes the previous text. On the other hand, if you display text by using the Print method, the changes are not retroactive and therefore go into effect only for subsequent Print statements.

You can change all the properties of the Font object via code. Except for Font.Size, they are all Boolean properties (True or False). As with Font.Name, any control that displays text lets you set the following:

```
ObjectName.Font.Size = 18              '18 point type
ObjectName.Font.Bold = True
ObjectName.Font.Italic = True
ObjectName.Font.Strikethru = False
ObjectName.Font.Underline = False
```

As with changing fonts, only forms, RichTextBoxes, and picture boxes let you mix these font properties.

Forms (and picture boxes) have one other font property you may occasionally find useful: FontTransparent. If you leave this at its default setting of True, background graphics and background text will show through the text displayed in the transparent font. Here's an example of this property at work:

You can combine the properties of the Font object almost any way you want. If your hardware and software support it, you can have 18-point bold italic script type in a control if that seems appropriate.

Displaying Tabular Data

Although the CurrentX and CurrentY properties give you absolute control over the placement of text in a form, often it will not be worth the trouble to use them for tabular data. When you want to display a table on a blank form, for example, you should probably use the grid control (see Chapter 10). On the other hand, if you just have lots of text and intend to use a nonproportionally spaced font such as Courier, you might want to consider using the built-in *print zones* on a form. (In a nonproportionally spaced font, all characters have the same width.) Print zones are always set 14 columns apart, and Visual Basic recalculates this distance depending on the font characteristics in effect. Each column is the width of the average character in the font. This is why print zones do not work well for the majority of Windows fonts. Most fonts in Windows applications are proportional. (This means that characters like an "m" take up more space than characters like an "i". Proportional spacing gives a more polished look to the screen.)

Each time you use a comma in a Print method (statement), Visual Basic displays the data to the next print zone. For example, a statement like

```
Me.Print FirstName$, MiddleInit$, LastName$
```

tries to have the value of the string variable FirstName$ printed in the first zone, the value of the variable MiddleInit$ at the beginning of the second zone, and the value of the variable LastName$ printed at the beginning of the third zone.

However, if a previous expression runs over into the next print zone, Visual Basic moves to the beginning of the next zone for the next Print statement.

The Tab and Spc Commands and Semicolons

Normally, after Visual Basic processes a statement involving the Print method, it moves to the next line. You also use an empty Print statement to add a blank line. If you want to suppress the automatic carriage return, place a semicolon at the end of the statement. For example:

```
Sub Form_Click ()
  ' demonstrates the difference between using a ; and not
  Me.Font.Name = "Courier"
  Me.Print "This is a test"
  Me.Print "of the Print method"
  Me.Print                              'blank line

  Me.Print "This is a test";
  Me.Print "of the Print method"
  Me.Print                              'blank line
End Sub
```

The Tab function lets you move to a specific column and start printing there. The Tab function also uses the average size of a character in the current font to determine where the columns are. Its syntax is

Print Tab(*ColumnNumber%*);

ColumnNumber% is an integral expression. If the current column position is greater than its value, Tab skips to this column on the next line. If the value is less than 1, Visual Basic moves to the first column. In theory, you can have values as large as 32,767 for the column. But since Visual Basic doesn't wrap around to the next line, you wouldn't really want to do this.

The Spc function has a syntax similar to the Tab function:

Spc(*Integer%*)

This function inserts the specified number of spaces into a line starting at the current print position. The value inside the parentheses can't be negative.

The Format Command

If you've run the mortgage program or have been experimenting on your own, you have probably decided that the answers to simple calculations look strange. You may end up with 16 decimal digits when you really want the answer to look like 1.01, for example. You overcome this problem by replacing the Str function with a new function called the Format function. This function works with a number and a template (also called a format string). The syntax is

Format(*NumericExpression*,*FormatString$*)

(You can also use Visual Basic 3's Format$ version.)

For example,

```
Me.Print Format(123.456789,"###.##")
```

yields 123.46. Visual Basic rounds the number off so there are only two digits after the decimal point.

The Format function, unlike the Str function, does not leave room for an implied + sign. This means that in a statement like

```
Me.Print "The interest rate is ";Format(Payment,"####.##")
```

the extra space after the word "is" is essential.

In general, a # is the placeholder for a digit, except that leading and trailing zeros are ignored. For example,

```
Me.Print Format(123.450,"###.###")
```

yields 123.45. Unlike with QuickBASIC, you don't have to worry about having too few #s before the decimal point in the format string. Visual Basic will print all the digits to the left of the decimal point. This way you can concentrate on deciding the number of decimals you want displayed and adjust the format string accordingly.

If you want to have Visual Basic display leading and trailing zeros, you use a zero in place of the # in the format string. For example,

```
Me.Print Format(123.450,"000.000")
```

yields 123.450.

You may want to display numbers with commas every three digits. For this, place a comma between any two-digit placeholders, for example,

```
Me.Print Format(123456789.991,"#,#.##")
```

yields 123,456,789.99.

One subtle point about the comma: if you place the comma immediately to the left of the decimal point (or use two commas), Visual Basic interprets this to mean it should skip the three digits that fall between the comma and the decimal point (or between the two commas). This is occasionally useful in scaling numbers. If your program deals with Japanese yen and you need to display one hundred million yen, you might want to write 100 million yen rather than 100,000,000 yen. To do this, you use the following statement:

```
Me.Print Format(100000000,"#00,,");" million yen"
```

Combining the # with the zero in the format string ensures that trailing zeros aren't suppressed.

If you need to display a -, +, $, (,), or spaces, you use them in the format string exactly in the place you want them to occur. For example, if you want to have a dollar sign in front of a value, use this:

```
Me.Print Format(Amount,"$###.##")
```

note: *You can use Format in any Visual Basic statement that expects a string, not only with the Print method. For example:*

```
M$ = "Your balance is " & Format(CurrentBalance, "$###.##")
MsgBox M$
```

PREDEFINED FORMAT STRINGS

Visual Basic 4 makes it easier to deal with the most common formatting situations by adding what are called *named formats* to the Format function. For example, you can use a statement like

```
Me.Print Format(Amount, "Currency")
```

instead of

```
Me.Print Format(Amount, "###,###.##")
```

and you will get the same results in the United States. This is because the Currency named format is (in the United States) defined to be the same as the ###,###.## format (that is, commas when needed and always two places to the right of the decimal point).

note: *One advantage to using named formats is that Visual Basic automatically adjusts things like the thousands separator to reflect the country in which the program is being run.*

In particular, using Format(Amount, "Currency") works better for products that are going to be used in more than one country!

The following table summarizes the predefined numeric formats.

Name of Format	Description
General Number	Gives you a string of digits with no thousands separator.
Currency	Uses the appropriate thousands separator and displays two digits to the right of the decimal point.
Fixed	Displays at least one digit to the left and two digits to the right of the decimal point.
Standard	Uses the appropriate thousands separator, at least one digit to the left and two digits to the right of the decimal point.
Percent	Gives you the number in percentage form (that is, multiplied by 100 and a % sign after it). Always displays two digits to the right of the decimal point.
Scientific	Uses Visual Basic's version of scientific notation.
Yes/No	Displays No if the number is 0; otherwise, displays Yes.
True/False	Displays False if the number is 0; otherwise, displays True.
On/Off	Displays Off if the number is 0; otherwise, displays On.

The following table gives you the various formats for date and times. Again, the advantage to using them is that Visual Basic will automatically adjust the format for the current locality.

Name of Format	Description
General Date	Displays a date and/or time. If there is no fractional part, you get a date. If there is no integer part, you get a time. If there is both, you get both.
Long Date	Displays a date using the format that Windows uses for full dates.
Medium Date	Displays a date using the middle date format.
Short Date	Displays a date using the short date format.
Long Time	Displays a time with the hours, minutes, seconds.
Medium Time	Displays time in 12-hour format using only hours and minutes and AM/PM.
Short Time	Displays the time using a 24-hour clock.

If you run the following demo program, you can see the various date and time formats at work, as shown in Figure 6-1. (Of course, since the demo program uses the Now function, what you see depends on when you run it.)

```
Private Sub Form_Click()
Me.Font.Size = 12
Me.Print Format(Now, "General Date")
Me.Print Format(Now, "Long Date")
Me.Print Format(Now, "Medium Date")
Me.Print Format(Now, "Short Date")
Me.Print Format(Now, "Long Time")
Me.Print Format(Now, "Medium Time")
Me.Print Format(Now, "Short Time")
End Sub
```

In earlier versions of Visual Basic it was often useful to set up string constants for the various format strings. This is still useful if you have a custom format that is not one of the named formats. For example, when you have to format values repeatedly, it's worth first setting up a constant such as:

```
Const INFLATION_MONEY = "#00,,"
```

From that point on you can write

```
Format(Amount, INFLATION_MONEY)
```

which is far more readable, less prone to typos, and will be easier to modify in the future.

Figure 6-1 Demonstration of named date/time formats

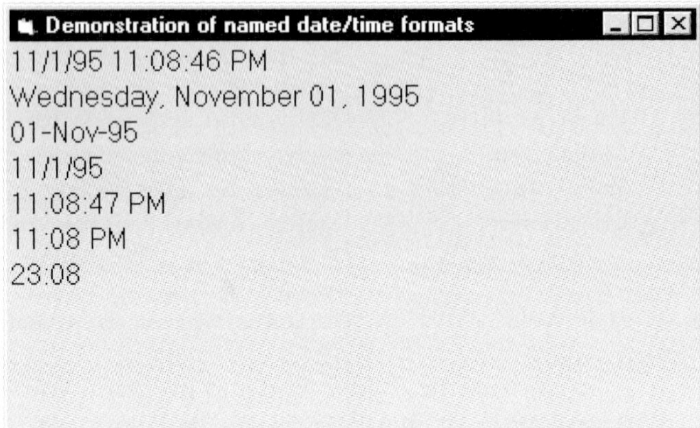

Picture Boxes

You can use picture boxes in many different contexts, not just as passive containers for graphics or icons. For example, because they respond to the Click and Double-Click events, you can use them exactly as you would use a command button, although image controls would be a better choice if that is all you are doing with them. On the other hand, for display purposes at least, you can think of picture boxes as being "forms within forms." For example, you can print text directly to a picture box. You can mix fonts and font sizes as well. Moreover, because picture boxes have the CurrentX and CurrentY properties, as well as the same Scale properties as forms, you can accurately position text inside them. The icon for picture boxes looks like a desert scene and reminds you that this control holds graphical images.

The main difference between picture boxes and forms is that you use the Height and Width properties of the picture box rather than the ScaleHeight and ScaleWidth properties. For example,

```
Picture1.CurrentX = Picture1.Height/2 - TextHeight("A")/2
```

would let you center a line of text vertically in a picture box.

The main advantages to using a picture box rather than the form to display data are

- Picture boxes are less memory hungry.
- You can have more than one picture box on the same form (for example, this means you can display multiple images).

Picture boxes, like forms, can hold three types of graphics: bitmaps, icons, and Windows metafiles.

- Bitmaps are graphical images of the screen (or part of the screen). Each dot (or pixel) corresponds to one bit for black-and-white displays and many bits for color or gray-scale displays. Image controls are often used for bitmaps. When bitmaps are stored in a file, the convention is to use a .BMP extension for the filename. The Windows Paintbrush program generates bitmaps, so this is a convenient source for them.
- You already saw icon files in Chapters 3 and 4. The appendix to the *Programmer's Guide* lists the 400 or so icons supplied with Visual Basic.
- Instead of a dot-by-dot description of the graphical image, think of Windows metafiles as containing descriptions of how and where to draw the object. Because they describe the picture in terms of circles, lines, and the like, they work much better than bitmaps that require you to shrink or enlarge a graphical image. Many publishing programs (such as Microsoft Publisher) come with libraries of Windows metafiles. No metafiles are supplied with the standard edition of Visual Basic, but over 80 are supplied with Visual Basic Professional or Enterprise edition.

Working with Picture Boxes

Picture boxes have over 50 properties and respond to 19 events, and you can use any one of 22 methods for them. Many of the properties are already familiar to you: the font properties control how text appears, Visible and Enabled control whether the control is responsive or even visible, and so on. One property, AutoSize, which you've seen for labels, is even more important for picture boxes. This is because how much of the image your picture box will show depends on how large you design it—unless you set the AutoSize property to True. If AutoSize is True, the picture box will automatically resize itself to fit the image. Of course, like text boxes, labels, and command buttons, you can also resize the picture box by manipulating the sizing handles when you select the control at design time.

The Cls method works in much the same way for picture boxes as it does for forms: it erases whatever image and text were placed on the picture box while the program was running. (You will see shortly how to clear graphics that were placed in a picture box or form at design time by using the LoadPicture statement.)

The Move method lets you move the picture box around at run time. The TextHeight and TextWidth methods are used, as with forms, to accurately size text in order to position it better (using the Scale and CurrentX and CurrentY properties). For the methods for picture boxes that are used for graphics (Circle, Line, and so on), see Chapter 12.

The picture box events that respond to mouse movements or clicks are covered in Chapter 16, and those for Link events are covered in Chapter 18. All the remaining events are those like Click, Double-Click, or the Key events you've already seen.

There are two ways to display an image inside a picture box (or form) at design time. The first is to load a picture by setting the Picture property via the Properties window, just like you did for an image control.

Another possibility is to paste a picture directly into the picture box (or form). For example, you may be enamored of a picture you just drew using Paintbrush and want to bring this image inside a Visual Basic project. You do this by using the clipboard. For example, if the picture box is the active control, copy the picture from Paintbrush to the clipboard. Then choose Edit|Paste (ALT E, P). Visual Basic then attaches the bitmap to the picture box or form. In particular, when you save the Visual Basic project, the image is saved at the same time. Pictures added at design time do not need to be supplied as individual files, as they would if you wanted to load the picture while the project was running.

Nonetheless, you will occasionally want to add (or allow the user to add) a picture while a Visual Basic project is running. There are also two ways to do this. The first requires you to have the picture already loaded in a form or a picture box on some form in the project. If this is true, you need only assign the Picture property of one object to the Picture property of the other. For example, suppose you have two picture boxes, Picture1 and Picture2. Picture1 has an image attached to it, and Picture2 does not. Then a line of code like

```
Picture2.Picture = Picture1.Picture
```

copies the image from the first picture box to the second.

More common, however, is to use the LoadPicture function to attach a file containing a graphical image to a picture box. The syntax for this function is

PictureBoxName.Picture = LoadPicture([filename])

or, for forms:

[*FormName.*]Picture = LoadPicture([*filename*])

If you leave out the optional filename, the current image is cleared from the form or picture box. The filename should include the full path name if the file isn't in the current directory. Unlike the Cls method, which clears images and text placed only while the project is running, the LoadPicture statement without a filename will also clear a picture that was added at design time.

RichTextBoxes

The RichTextBox control is an exciting addition to Visual Basic's toolbox. It is only available for 32-bit development, unfortunately. The RichTextBox control is a custom control, so you will need to add it to the toolbox if it is not already there. It looks like this:

The RichTextBox control lets you display text with multiple fonts and sizes without having to go out and buy a third-party custom control. Moreover, the RichTextBox is not limited to 64K characters like an ordinary text box.

note: *See Chapter 17 for how to save (and retrieve) the information in a RichTextBox control to (and from) a file.*

Properties for RichTextBoxes

Many of the properties of a RichTextBox are the same as for the standard TextBox control, which you saw in Chapter 4 (for example, MultiLine, ScrollBars, and the like). This section explains the new properties that you will need to manipulate with code in order to take full advantage of the RichTextBox.

The trick in using a RichTextBox control is that you must always remember that you first have to select text (or have the user select it) before you can format it. The three properties that tell you what text is selected are described in the following table.

Property	What It Does
SelLength	Returns or sets the number of characters selected.
SelStart	Returns or sets the starting point of the selected text. (It will tell you the current insertion point if no text is selected.)
SelText	Returns or sets a string equal to the currently selected text. (It gives you a "" if no characters are currently selected.)

For example, if the value of RichTextBox.SelLength is 0, then no text is selected. (See Chapter 18 for more on working with these properties.)

The properties described next all work with the selected text in a RichTextBox and thereby let you change its format. You can also use these properties to read off the format of the currently selected text if necessary. (For the properties of the RichTextBox not covered here, please see the online help.)

All these properties work the same way. They affect the currently selected text and *all text added after the current insertion point until they are changed.*

SelBold, SelItalic, SelStrikethru, SelUnderline As you might expect, these properties let you control whether text is bold, italic, and so on. For example, to change the currently selected text to bold in a RichTextBox named RichText1, you might use

```
RichTextBox1.SelBold = True
```

This would also make all selected text (and all text added after the current insertion point) bold. And text would continue to be bold until the SelBold property was toggled off with the subsequent statement:

```
RichTextBox1.SelBold = False
```

SelColor This property sets the color of the currently selected text and all text added after the current insertion point. For example,

```
RichText1.SelColor = vbRed
```

would change the color of the selected text to red. (You can also use the &HBBGGRR& codes you saw in Chapter 5.)

SelFontName This property lets you change the font. For example:

```
RichText1.SelFontName = "Courier"
```

(The next chapter shows you how to find out what fonts are available in your system.)

SelFontSize This property lets you change the size of the currently selected text. The syntax is

object.SelFontSize = Size

(The theoretical maximum value for SelFontSize is 2,160 points.)

A RichTextBox Example

As an example of using a RichTextBox control, consider the code needed to activate Figure 6-2. The idea is pretty simple: all you need to do is modify the currently selected text. For example, to toggle italic text on and off, you need only a single line of code:

```
RichTextBox1.SelItalic = Not (RichTextBox1.SelItalic)
```

One tricky feature comes from the fact that Visual Basic defaults to removing the highlighting from selected text when the focus is removed from a control. (The text still remains selected when the focus returns—you just can't see that it is still selected.)

You cure this by changing the design time property called HideSelection to False from its default value of True. This property controls whether Visual Basic removes the highlighting from selected text when the focus shifts from the control.

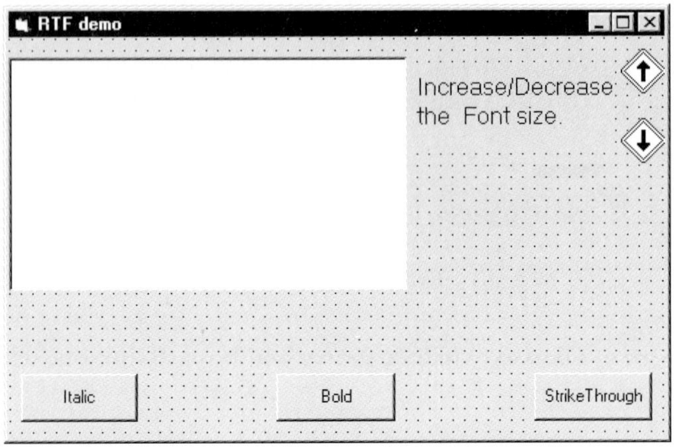

Figure 6-2 A sample RichTextBox project

note: *Moving the focus doesn't affect which text is selected, you just lose the highlighting (unless HideSelection is changed to False).*

Here are the ASCII descriptions of the form, its controls, and the code needed to activate Figure 6-2.

```
VERSION 4.00
Begin VB.Form Form1
   Caption         =   "RTF demo"
   ClientHeight    =   4140
   ClientLeft      =   1800
   ClientTop       =   1500
   ClientWidth     =   6750
   Height          =   4545
   Left            =   1740
   LinkTopic       =   "Form1"
   ScaleHeight     =   4140
   ScaleWidth      =   6750
   Top             =   1155
   Width           =   6870
   Begin VB.CommandButton btnStrikeThru
      Caption         =   "StrikeThrough"
      Height          =   495
      Left            =   5400
```

```
    TabIndex        =   3
    Top             =   3480
    Width           =   1215
End
Begin VB.CommandButton btnBold
    Caption         =   "Bold"
    Height          =   495
    Left            =   2760
    TabIndex        =   2
    Top             =   3480
    Width           =   1215
End
Begin VB.CommandButton btnItalic
    Caption         =   "Italic"
    Height          =   495
    Left            =   120
    TabIndex        =   1
    Top             =   3480
    Width           =   1215
End
Begin VB.Label Label1
    Caption         =   "Increase/Decrease the Font size."
    BeginProperty Font
       name            =   "MS Sans Serif"
       charset         =   0
       weight          =   400
       size            =   12
       underline       =   0   'False
       italic          =   0   'False
       strikethrough   =   0   'False
    EndProperty
    Height          =   735
    Left            =   4200
    TabIndex        =   4
    Top             =   360
    Width           =   2040
End
Begin VB.Image imgFontDecrease
    Height          =   480
    Left            =   6300
    Picture         =   "rtf.frx":0000
    Top             =   840
    Width           =   480
End
```

```
   Begin VB.Image imfFontIncrease
      Height          =   480
      Left            =   6300
      Picture         =   "rtf.frx":0442
      Top             =   120
      Width           =   480
   End
   Begin RichTextLib.RichTextBox RichTextBox1
      Height          =   2415
      Left            =   0
      TabIndex        =   0
      Top             =   200
      Width           =   4095
      _Version        =   65536
      _ExtentX        =   7223
      _ExtentY        =   4260
      _StockProps     =   69
      BackColor       =   -2147483643
      HideSelection   =   0   'False
      ScrollBars      =   2
      TextRTF         =   $"rtf.frx":0884
   End
End
Attribute VB_Name = "Form1"
Attribute VB_Creatable = False
Attribute VB_Exposed = False
Option Explicit

Private Sub Command1_Click()
  RichTextBox1.SelItalic = Not (RichTextBox1.SelItalic)
End Sub

Private Sub btnBold_Click()
  RichTextBox1.SelBold = Not (RichTextBox1.SelBold)
End Sub

Private Sub btnItalic_Click()
    RichTextBox1.SelItalic = Not (RichTextBox1.SelStrikeThru)
End Sub

Private Sub btnStrikeThru_Click()
  RichTextBox1.SelStrikeThru = Not(RichTextBox1.SelStrikeThru)
End Sub
```

```
Private Sub imfFontIncrease_Click()
  RichTextBox1.SelFontSize = RichTextBox1.SelFontSize + 1
End Sub

Private Sub imgFontDecrease_Click()
  RichTextBox1.SelFontSize = RichTextBox1.SelFontSize - 1
End Sub

Private Sub Form_QueryUnload(Cancel As Integer, UnloadMode As_
Integer)
  Unload Me
  End
End Sub
```

The Printer Object

Visual Basic uses the printer you set up when you installed Microsoft Windows. Visual Basic makes it easy to use whatever resolution, font properties, and so on, that the printer driver in Windows can coax from the printer.

First, you have already seen the PrintForm command, which sends a screen dump of a form to the printer. If your application has more than one form, you have to use the form name in this command:

FormName.PrintForm

Because this command does a bit-by-bit dump of the whole form (including captions and borders), it lacks flexibility. Moreover, most printers have higher resolution than the screen.

Most of the printer commands in Visual Basic are page oriented. This means that Visual Basic calculates all the characters (actually dots) that will appear on a page before it sends the information to the printer. This allows you to have complete control over the appearance of the printed page.

The usual way to send information to a printer is the Print method applied to the Printer object. For example, because the Print method is page oriented, you can set the CurrentX and CurrentY properties to precisely position text or even dots on a page.

The syntax used to send text to the printer is similar:

Printer.Print text

Semicolons and commas also work the same way they do for forms. The semicolon suppresses the automatic carriage return; the comma moves to the next free print zone (still 14 columns apart). The Tab and Spc functions also work the same.

You control the font properties in the same way. For example:

```
Printer.Font.Name = "Script"             'Use script font
Printer.Font.Size = 18                   '18 point type
```

As with printing to forms, font changes on a printer are not retroactive. They affect only text printed after Visual Basic processes the change.

Useful Properties and Methods for the Printer

If you check the online help, you'll see that there are 40 properties and 12 methods for the Printer object. Most of the ones that are unfamiliar to you, such as DrawMode, apply to graphics (see Chapter 15). The vast majority, however, should be familiar to you since you've seen them for forms. What follows are short descriptions of some printer properties and methods you will use most often. (Check the online help for the printer properties not covered here as well as for the symbolic constants you need to work with the various printer properties not discussed here.)

ColorMode This property lets you determine whether a color printer prints in color or monochrome. There are two possibilities, as shown in the following table.

Symbolic Constant	Value	Description
vbPRCMMonochrome	1	Prints output in monochrome
vbPRCMColor	2	Prints output in color

Copies This property lets you set the number of copies to be printed.

Height, Width These properties give you the height and width of the paper in the printer as reported by Windows. This is measured in twips, regardless of how you set the scale properties. You can't change these at run time; they are read-only properties. One example of how you might use these properties is to make sure that someone has switched to wider paper before printing something that would not fit on the usual 8 1/2 x 11-inch paper. (For 8 1/2 x 11-inch paper, Visual Basic reports an available width of 12,288 twips and an available height of 15,744 twips.)

EndDoc This method tells Windows that a document is finished. The syntax is

```
Printer.EndDoc
```

This releases whatever information there is about the page or pages still in memory and sends it to the Windows Print Manager for printing.

NewPage This method ends the current page and tells the printer to move to the next page. The syntax is

```
Printer.NewPage
```

Page This property keeps track of the number of pages printed in the current document. The counter starts over at 1 after Visual Basic processes a statement with EndDoc. It increases by 1 every time you use the NewPage method or when the information you send to the printer with the Print method didn't fit on the previous page. A common use of this property is to print a header at the top of each page.

PrintQuality This property is used to set the quality of the printed output—if the printer driver supports it. The syntax is

Printer.PrintQuality = *value*

where you can use four built-in constants, as described in the following table.

Constant	Value	Description
vbPRPQDraft	-1	Draft resolution
vbPRPQLow	-2	Low resolution
vbPRPQMedium	-3	Medium resolution
vbPRPQHigh	-4	High resolution

note: *You can also set the value to the number of dots per inch if the printer (and its driver) supports this.*

The Printers Collection

The Printer object is defined to be the current default printer. The Printers collection, on the other hand, lets you access all the printer drivers stored in the system. (For example, there might be a fax driver installed.) The number of printers installed is

```
Printers.Count
```

The syntax for accessing an element of the Printers collection is simply,

Printers(*index*)

where *index* is a number from 0 to Printers.Count-1.

note: *You can actually change the default printer directly from Visual Basic. This is done with the Set command that you will see in Chapter 12.*

For example, the following code uses the For-Next statement that you will see in the next chapter to find out if any of the printers in a user's system are set up to print in color. If one is, a message box pops up that notifies the user of this fact. (Once you learn a few more commands, you could easily add the code necessary to allow the user to change the default printer to the color printer.)

```
For I = 0 To Printers.Count -1
    If Printers(I).ColorMode = vbPRCMColor Then
         MsgBox"At least one printer has a color mode"
    End If
Next I
```

note: *You can only set the properties of the current default printer.*

Printing Information in a RichTextBox

The SelPrint method of a RichTextBox lets you print the current *formatted* contents of a RichTextBox on the current printer. If the user has selected text in the RichTextBox control, then the SelPrint method sends only the selected text to the printer. If no text is selected, the entire contents of the RichTextBox are sent to the printer. The syntax is a little silly. You first have to print a null string to the Printer in order to "wake it up." You then have to use something called the *device context* of the current printer to tell Windows where to send the information. (A device context is just an integer that Windows uses to identify the object.)

The actual code you need looks like this:

```
Printer.Print ""
RichTextBox1.SelPrint(Printer.hDC)
```

(The hDC property of the Printer object gets its device context ID. It is needed here for some arcane reasons specific to Windows that aren't worth getting into.)

Chapter Seven

Controlling Program Flow

THIS chapter shows you how to make a program repeat operations (loops) and check whether a condition is True or False (conditionals). The parts of a programming language that let you do this are called *control structures*. (This term has nothing to do with the controls you place on forms in Visual Basic.) You'll also see how to control which parts of your programs compile depending on which version of Windows is your target platform (conditional compilation).

Repeating Operations

Suppose you need to repeat an operation. In programming (as in real life), you may want to repeat the operation a fixed number of times, continue until you reach a predetermined specific goal, or continue until certain initial conditions have finally changed. In programming, the first situation is called a *determinate loop* and the latter two are called *indeterminate loops*. Visual Basic allows all three kinds of loops, so there are three different control structures in Visual Basic for repeating operations.

Determinate Loops

Suppose you want to print the numbers 1 to 10 on the current form inside an event procedure. The simplest way to do this is to place the following lines of code inside the procedure:

```
For I% = 1 To 10
  Print I%
Next I%
```

In the preceding example, the line with the For and To keywords is shorthand for "for every value of I% from 1 to 10." You can think of a For-Next loop as winding up a wheel inside the computer so the wheel will spin a fixed number of times. You can tell the computer what you want it to do during each spin of the wheel.

For and Next are keywords that must be used together. The statements between the For and the Next are usually called the body of the loop, and the whole control structure is called, naturally enough, a For-Next loop.

The keyword For sets up a counter variable. In the preceding example, the counter is an integer variable: I%. In this example, the starting value for the counter is set to 1. The ending value is set to 10. Visual Basic first sets the counter variable to the starting value. Then it checks whether the value for the counter is less than the ending value. If the value is greater than the ending value, nothing is done. If the starting value is less than the ending value, Visual Basic processes subsequent statements until it comes to the keyword Next. At that point it adds 1 to the counter variable and starts the process again. This process continues until the counter variable is larger than the ending value. At that point, the loop is finished, and Visual Basic moves past it. Figure 7-1 shows a flow diagram for the For-Next loop.

tip: *Whenever possible, choose integer variables for the counter in a For-Next loop. This allows Visual Basic to spend as little time as possible on the arithmetic needed to change the counter and so speeds up the loop.*

Finally, you may have noticed that the body of the For-Next loop is indented. As always, the purpose of the spacing in a program is to make the program more readable and therefore easier to debug. The designers of Visual Basic made it easy to consistently indent code. The Visual Basic editor defaults to remembering the indentation of the previous line, and every time you press ENTER, the cursor returns to the spot directly below the beginning of the previous line. To move the cursor back, you can use the LEFT ARROW key. Or if you get into the habit of using the TAB key to start each level of indentation, you can use the SHIFT+TAB combination to move backward one tab stop. Each tab stop is set five spaces in from the previous one, although as you saw in Chapter 2, you can change this setting by choosing Tools | Options and then going to the Editor page in this dialog box.

Figure 7-1
Flow diagram of For-Next loop

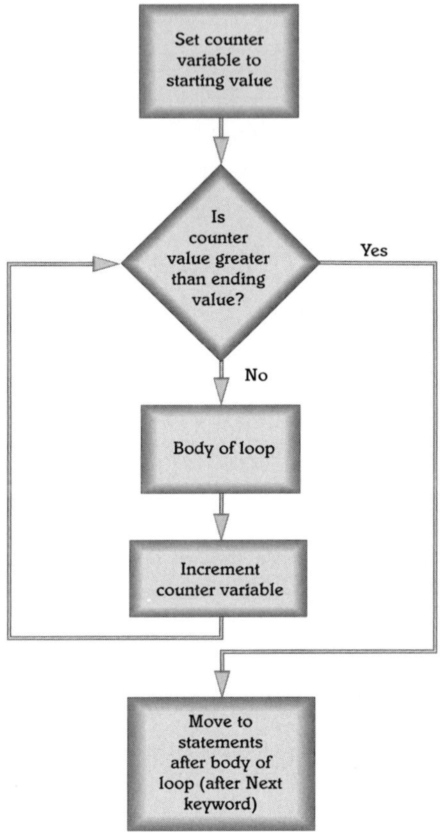

tip: *If you use the TAB key to indent, you can undo the indentation pattern by selecting the block of text and then pressing SHIFT+TAB.*

The most common type of error in using loops is the *off-by-one error.* When this error occurs, instead of performing an operation, say, 500 times as you had planned, the program seems to perform it 499 or 501 times. If your program suffers from this problem, the debugging techniques in Chapter 14 can help you pinpoint the fault in the loop that is causing the off-by-one error. Obviously, it's best to avoid off-by-one errors in the first place. One way to do this is to keep in mind that the loop terminates only when the counter exceeds (not equals) the test value (that is, the range is inclusive).

AN EXAMPLE: A RETIREMENT CALCULATOR

With a For-Next loop, you can compute many financial quantities without knowing a formula. For example, suppose you wanted to write a program that would allow users to enter the following:

- The fixed amount of money they think they can put away for retirement each year
- The interest rate they expect to get each year
- The number of years until retirement

The program would then tell them how much money they will have when they retire. There are sophisticated formulas involving geometric progressions for this sort of calculation, but common sense (and a very simple For-Next loop) suffices. What happens is that each year you get interest on the previous amount, and you add the new amount to it.

Assume that the interest is compounded annually. Then this program will need four text boxes, four labels, and two command buttons. The screen in Figure 7-2 shows the form.

The control names for the text controls in the program should be self-documenting: txtAmountPerYear, txtInterestRate, txtNumberOfYears, and txtNestEgg. (Set the Locked property of the txtNestEgg button to True.) The command buttons should be named btnCalculate and btnQuit.

Figure 7-2 Form for calculating retirement income

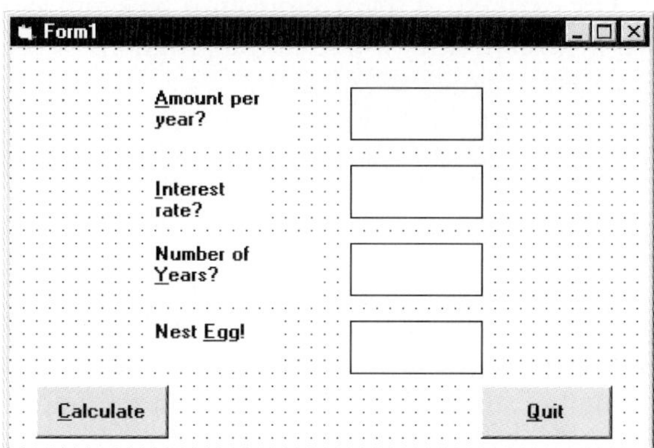

Here is the btnCalculate_Click procedure that does everything:

```
Private Sub btnCalculate_Click()
  'Calculate retirement value assuming fixed
  'deposit and fixed interest rate

  Dim Amount As Currency, Total As Currency
  Dim Interest As Single
  Dim Years As Integer, I As Integer

  Total = 0
  Amount = Val(txtAmountPerYear.Text)
  Interest = Val(txtInterestRate.Text)/100
  Years = Val(txtNumberOfYears.Text)
  For I = 1 To Years
    Total = Amount + Total + (Total*Interest)
  Next I
  txtNestEgg.Text = Format(Total,"###,###.##")
End Sub
```

The new total is derived from the previous year by adding the interest earned to the previous total amount.

MORE ON FOR-NEXT LOOPS

You don't always count by ones. Sometimes it's necessary to count by twos, by fractions, or backward. You do this by adding the Step keyword to a For-Next loop. The Step keyword tells Visual Basic to change the counter by the specified amount rather than by 1, as was done previously.

For example, a space simulation program would not be complete without the inclusion, somewhere in the program, of the fragment:

```
For I% = 10 To 1 Step -1
  Print "It's t minus"; I%; "and counting."
Next I%
Print "Blastoff!"
```

When you use a negative step, the body of the For-Next loop is bypassed if the starting value for the counter is smaller than the ending value, and continues until the counter is less than the ending value.

caution: *Loops with fractional Step values will run more slowly than loops with integer Step values, as will loops with Variants for counters—even if they are integers.*

AN EXAMPLE: IMPROVING THE MORTGAGE CALCULATOR

Here's a more serious example. Let's modify the mortgage program from Chapter 5 to add another form showing a table with various interest rates. You can add another button to the original form to bring up a form with a multiline text box showing the mortgage payments for a rate 1 percent above and below the rate initially selected. (Let's name the new button btnShowTable.)

This new form (see Figure 7-3) will contain a labeled, multiline text box with vertical scroll bars added at design time. Let's call the new form frmTable and the text box on it txtMortgageTable. Call the label lblTable and place it right above the multiline text box. You will use this label to describe what the user will see. You will also add a command button for returning to the original form.

All the work is done in the btnShowTable_Click procedure attached to the added command button on the original form. The code for this example may seem long, but most of the complications relate to formatting the display nicely. Essentially, what you need to do is enclose the original formula in a For-Next loop with a step of 1/8% = 1/800 = .00125.

Figure 7-3 Form for mortgage calculator

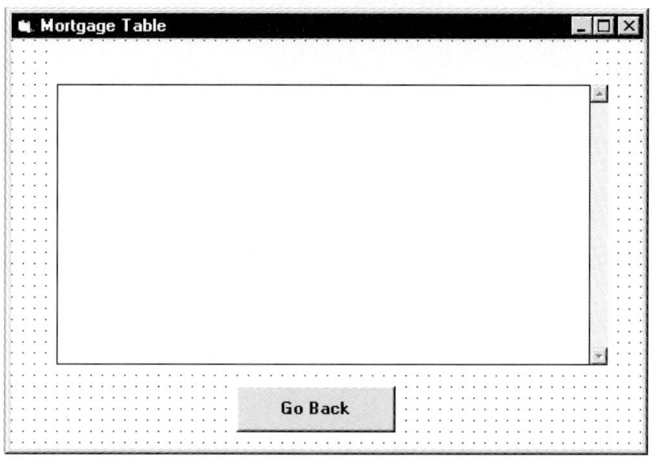

note: *Ideally, this kind of application should be written using a grid control. You'll see how to do this in Chapter 10. Because you haven't seen the grid control yet, this program uses a nonproportionally spaced (Courier) font to make positioning easier.*

Here's the code:

```
Private Sub btnShowTable_Click ()
  'Calculates a mortgage table using original amounts
  'but having the interest rate move up by 1/8%
  'local variables and constants
  Dim SpaceChar As String, T$
  Dim Years As Integer, Payment As Currency
  Dim MonthInt As Single, Principal As Currency
  Dim Percent As Single, Interest  As Single
  Dim StartInterest As Single, EndInterest As Single
  Const DAMOUNT = "###.00"
  Const IRATE = "00.00%"

 'Get info
  Years = Val(txtMortgageTerm.Text)
  Principal = Val(txtMortgageAmount.Text)
  Percent = Val(txtInterestRate.Text) / 100
  StartInterest = Percent - .01             '1% change
  EndInterest = Percent + .01

  'Make new form visible and change to Courier font
  Me.Hide
  frmTable.Show
  frmTable.Font.Name = "Courier"

  frmTable.lblTable.Caption = "Interest Rate" + Space$(18) +_
"Payment"
  For Interest = StartInterest To EndInterest Step .00125
    MonthInt = Interest / 12
    Payment = Principal * MonthInt / (1 - (1 / (1 + MonthInt))_
^ (Years * 12))
    T$ = T$ + Format$(Interest, IRate) + Space$(25) +_
Format$(Payment, DAmount) + vbCrLf
  Next Interest
  frmTable.tblMortgage.Text = T$
End Sub
```

The program starts with the Dim statements that define the variables. Next come the string constants for the Format$ command; for example, the IRATE constant displays the interest rate as a two-place decimal percent. Next comes the code for extracting the information from the text boxes on the original form and for hiding the original form (using the Me keyword). You then show the form named frmTable that will be used for displaying the table and change its font to Courier. Next comes the "." character, which lets you refer to a control on the frmTable form within code attached to the original form.

Finally, there's the For-Next loop that does all the work. Because it is much faster to build a string up rather than to change the text property of a text box repeatedly, the code inside the For-Next loop adds to the string T$. After the For-Next loop finishes, the text property of the multiline text box is changed to T$.

NESTED FOR-NEXT LOOPS

Suppose you want to allow not only a range of interest rates in the mortgage table but also a range of dollar amounts—say with horizontal scroll bars to move through the information. For each dollar amount, you want to run through an entire range of interest rates. This is a typical situation: you have an inner loop that does something interesting in a particular case, and you want to alter the situation to address a slightly different case. Placing one loop inside another is called *nesting* loops.

You'll see how to solve the mortgage problem a little later in this section. For now though, let's look at a simpler example of a multiplication table. A fragment such as

```
For I% = 2 To 12
  Print 2*I%
Next I%
```

gives you the "twos table." To get an entire multiplication table, you need to enclose this loop with another one that changes the 2 to a 3, the 3 to a 4, and so on. The loop looks like this:

```
For J% = 2 To 12
  For I% = 2 To 12
    Print I%*J%,
  Next I%
  Print
Next J%
```

Here's what is happening: The value of J% starts out at 2, and then Visual Basic enters the inner loop. The value of I% starts out at 2 as well. Now Visual Basic makes 11 passes through the loop before it finishes. Once it does this, it processes the extra Print statement before it processes the Next J% statement. At this point Visual Basic changes the value of J% to 3 and starts the process all over again.

Sometimes it's helpful to think of the inner loop in a nested For-Next loop as really doing one thing—that is, as a statement in Visual Basic a bit more complicated than the usual ones. If you keep in mind the idea of the inner loop of a nested For-Next loop as accomplishing one task, then an outline for the nested loops to modify the mortgage program given in the previous section is easy. Here it is:

For *Principal* = *StartingAmount* To *EndingAmount* Step 1000
  The original loop with new display statements & principal modified
Next *Principal*

Nested loops have a reputation for being hard to program, hard to understand, and a breeding ground for bugs. This need not be true. If you are careful about outlining the loops, they won't be hard to program. If you are careful about your indentation pattern, they won't be hard to understand (or, therefore, to debug).

The rule for nesting For-Next loops is simple: the inner loop must be completed before the Next statement for the outer loop is encountered. You can have triple-nested loops, quadruple-nested loops, or even more. You are limited only by how well you understand the logic of the program, not by Visual Basic.

AN EXAMPLE: THE SCREEN OBJECT, AVAILABLE FONTS, AND POSITIONING FORMS

Another good example of a For-Next loop gives you a list of the fonts available to Windows. You can do this by using a simple For-Next loop to analyze a property of the Screen object. The Screen object is one that you will use frequently within Visual Basic. For example, it will let you manipulate forms by their placement on the screen. For our example you need two properties of the Screen object. The first is the FontCount property, which gives you the number of available fonts that the printer or screen has available:

```
NumberOfScreenFonts = Screen.FontCount
NumberOfPrinterFonts = Printer.FontCount
```

The second property that you need is the Fonts property. Screen.Fonts(0) is the first font for your display, Screen.Fonts(1) is the second, and so on, up to Screen.Fonts(FontCount -1), which is the last. All this information is determined by how Windows was set up and by the hardware and software you have.

To run this program, create a new project with a blank form. Add the Click procedure given here, press F5, and then click anywhere in the form.

```
Sub Form_Click()
  Dim I As Integer

  Print "Here is a list of the fonts for your display."
  For I = 0 To Screen.FontCount - 1
    Font.Name = Screen.Fonts(I)
    Print "This is displayed in ";Screen.Fonts(I)
  Next I
End Sub
```

To report on the fonts that Windows can pull out of your printer, change the keyword Screen to the keyword Printer.

tip: *The Screen object also supports the Height and Width properties. These give you the height and width of the physical screen, in twips, as reported by Windows. You can use these properties to adjust the size of a window to fit the screen on which it is running. For example, use the following code if you want to have the Form_Load( ) procedure initialize the size of the form that Visual Basic is loading to be 50 percent of the full screen:*

```
Sub Form_Load()
  Me.Width = Screen.Width/2
  Me.Height = Screen.Height/2
End Sub
```

Indeterminate Loops

Let's go back to the retirement problem discussed earlier. Instead of asking how much money a person will have at the end of a specified number of years, let's ask how long until the person has $1,000,000—again assuming that the same amount of money is put in each year and that the interest rate doesn't change. You could use the previous program and try trial and error, but there is a more direct approach. You'll soon see how to resolve this and many similar problems.

The modified retirement program offers a good example of a task that comes up repeatedly in programming. Loops must either keep on repeating an operation or not, depending on the results obtained within the loop. Such loops are indeterminate—that is, not executed a fixed number of times—by their very nature. You use the following pattern when you write this type of loop in Visual Basic:

Do
    Visual Basic statements
Until *condition is met*

Figure 7-4 shows what Visual Basic does in a Do loop.

Figure 7-4
Flow diagram for Do loop (test at end)

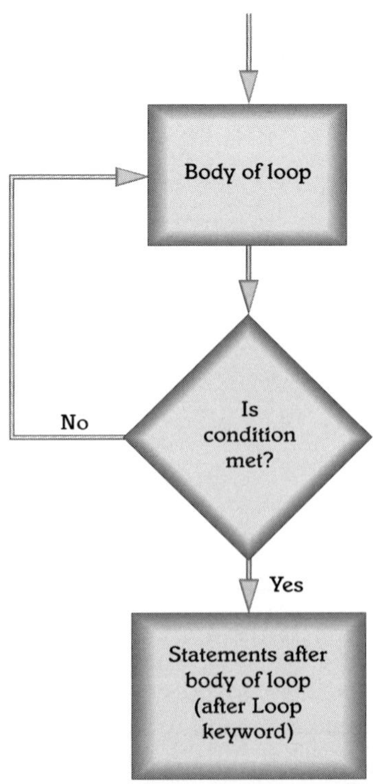

A simple example of this is a password fragment in a Form_Load procedure that starts an application. If you compiled a project to a stand-alone program with a Form_Load procedure that looked like this,

```
Sub Form_Load()
'Password protection

  Do
    X$ = InputBox$("Password please?")
  Loop Until X$ = "Vanilla Orange"
End Sub
```

it would be more difficult for anyone who didn't know the password to use this program. (It would not be impossible, however; a very experienced programmer could find the password by carefully examining the .EXE file, but it wouldn't be easy.)

It's important to remember that the test for equality is strict: typing **VANILLA ORANGE** would not work, nor would **Vanilla orange**. Another point worth keeping in mind is that the test is done only at the end of the loop, when Visual Basic processes the Until statement. If you change the fragment to

```
Sub Form_Load()
 Do
   X$ = "Vanilla Orange"
   X$ = InputBox$("Password please?")
 Loop Until X$ = "Vanilla Orange"
End Sub
```

then, whether you break out of the loop still depends on what the user types in the input box. Initializing the variable to the correct value is irrelevant.

When you write an indeterminate loop, something must change; otherwise the test will always fail and you'll be stuck in an infinite loop. To stop an infinite loop, you can use the CTRL+BREAK combination, or choose End from the Run menu, or use the toolbar. You can also close the application, of course.

RELATIONAL OPERATORS

In more sophisticated programs, you need ways to check for something besides equality. You do this by means of the relational operators. The relational operators are listed here:

Symbol	Checks (Tests For)
< >	Not equal to
<	Less than
<=	Less than or equal to
>	Greater than
>=	Greater than or equal to

For strings, these operators test for ANSI order. This means that "A" comes before "B," but "B" comes before "a" (and a space comes before any typewriter character). The string "aBCD" comes after the string "CDE" because uppercase letters come before lowercase letters. (The online help contains a complete ANSI table that you can find by using the Search button and looking for the ANSI character set.) The ANSI codes from 0 to 31 are for control combinations and include the BACKSPACE and ENTER keys.

note: *You can make all comparisons in the code attached to a form insensitive to case by putting the statement*

```
Option Compare Text
```

in the Declarations section of the form. The Option Compare Text statement uses an order determined by the country set when you install Windows. Use Option Compare Binary to return to the default method of comparing strings by ANSI order.

As another example, suppose you wanted to prevent a "divide-by-zero" error when a user enters data in a text box. Use a fragment like this:

```
Do
  N$ = InputBox$("Non-zero number? Please!")
  Number = Val(N$)
Loop Until Number <> 0
```

Or, to test that the first character of a string in a text box is not a space or a control code, use this:

```
Do
  Text$ = Text1.Text
Loop Until Text$ > Chr$(32)
```

These kinds of loops are the first steps for stopping a user from entering the wrong kind of data. Testing input data is one way to begin to bulletproof a program. In fact, a large part of bulletproofing programs (the jargon is "making them robust") requires making them tolerant of input errors. Instead of blowing up because of a typo, they check that the data entered is usable. If not, they warn the user. The more robust a program is, the less likely it is to behave strangely for an inexperienced user. (The section on "What Is It?" in this chapter has more on checking input.)

You can even monitor keystrokes as they are made inside any control that accepts input. For this, see the section "An Example: The KeyPress Procedure" later in this chapter.

You now can write the program mentioned in the beginning of this section. Here is the btnCalculate_Click procedure that will determine how long it takes to accumulate $1,000,000:

```
Private Sub btnCalculate_Click()
  '  Calculate retirement value assuming fixed
  ' deposit and fixed interest rate

  Dim Amount As Currency, Total As Currency
  Dim Interest as Single
  Dim Years As Integer, I as Integer

  Amount = Val(txtAmountPerYear.Text)
  Interest = Val(txtInterestRate.Text)/100
  Do
    Total = Amount + Total + (Total*Interest)
    Years = Years + 1
  Loop Until Total >= 1000000
  txtNumberOfYears.Text = Str$(Years)
End Sub
```

The body of the loop is much like the one in the retirement program from the beginning of the chapter—figure the yearly change and add it to the previous total to get a new total. This time, however, another counter (Years) keeps track of the number of years. Finally, the loop continues as long as the value of the variable Total is less than 1,000,000. The moment the total equals or exceeds this target, the loop ends and Visual Basic reports the results.

You should be aware of a problem that frequently occurs with these new kinds of loops. Consider this fragment:

```
Total = 0
PassNumber = 0
Do
  Total = Total + .1
  PassNumber = PassNumber + 1
  Print PassNumber, Total
Loop Until Total = 1
```

You might think this program would end after ten passes through the loop, but it doesn't. In fact, this fragment results in an infinite loop, and you need to press the CTRL+BREAK combination or use the toolbar to stop it. This infinite loop occurs for a subtle but important reason. In this fragment, by default, the variant variables get transformed into single-precision variables, and as discussed in Chapter 5, these numbers are only approximations. Visual Basic's internal characterization of .1 is off by a little in, say, the seventh place. As Visual Basic adds .1 to the total, tiny errors accumulate, and the resulting total, although it comes very close to 1, never exactly equals 1. Thus, in loops, check only integer and long integer variables for equality.

This program should be rewritten to allow for a tiny error by changing the test to read

```
Loop Until Total > .99999999
```

or, to be sure that the number is at least 1:

```
Loop Until Total >= 1
```

Changing the test to either case ensures that the program really will stop after ten passes through the loop. Single, double, and currency variables, or variants that can be transformed into one of these types, can be checked only to see if they are close (within a certain tolerance).

SOPHISTICATED INDETERMINATE LOOPS

A common task is reading in a list of names until the last one is encountered, keeping count all the while. Suppose you are looking through the dictionary and happen to notice that the last entry is the name of an insect: the zyzzyva. You decide you want to add up the number of different types of insects that occur in North America. You take out your entomology book and start running the following code:

```
InsectCount = 0
 Do
   InsectName$ = InputBox("The next insect name")
   InsectCount = InsectCount + 1
 Loop Until InsectName$ = "zyzzyva"
Print "The number of different types of insects is ";InsectCount
```

Although this fragment may seem like a prototype for code that reads in a list of items until the last one is encountered, you won't always know what the last entry of the list is. It's only a coincidence that the last word in many dictionaries is the name of an American insect. In general, you won't know the last entry, so you're likely to use a group of strange characters (like "ZZZ") to act as a flag. Instead of testing for zyzzyva, you test for a flag.

It's easy to modify the "InsectCount" fragment to test for a flag. Here is a program that does this (but beware, it has a subtle bug):

```
NameCount = 0
Do
  Entry$ = InputBox$("Name - type ZZZ when done")
  NameCount = NameCount + 1
Loop Until Entry$ = "ZZZ"
Print "The total number of names is ";NameCount
```

The problem with this fragment is that it suffers from an off-by-one error. Imagine that the list consists of only one name besides the flag. What happens? Let's work through this program by hand. The user types the first name and the count increases to 1. Next the user types **ZZZ**. However, because the test is only done at the end of the loop, the count increases to 2 before the test is done. Therefore, when the loop ends, the count is 2 when it ought to be 1. One possible cure is to subtract 1 from the count once the loop ends. The trouble with this type of ad hoc solution (in the jargon, a *kludge*—pronounced "klooge") is that the programmer is stuck with constantly figuring out how far off the results of the loops are when they finish in order to move backward.

Moving backward is a bit silly when Visual Basic makes the cure for this so easy: move the test to the top. Consider this:

```
NameCount = 0
Entry$ = InputBox$("Name - ZZZ to end")
Do Until Entry$ = "ZZZ"
   NameCount = NameCount + 1
```

```
   Entry$ = InputBox$("Name - ZZZ to end")
Loop
```

Now the user types the first name before the loop starts. Once this is done, the program does an initial test. The loop is entered, and 1 starts being added to the counter only if this test fails. (Notice that this kind of loop also works if there is nothing in the list except the flag.) Figure 7-5 shows a picture of what Visual Basic does for this type of loop.

tip: *A good rule of thumb is that if you are going to use the flag, put the test at the end; if not, put the test at the beginning.*

Figure 7-5
Flow diagram for Do loop (test at beginning)

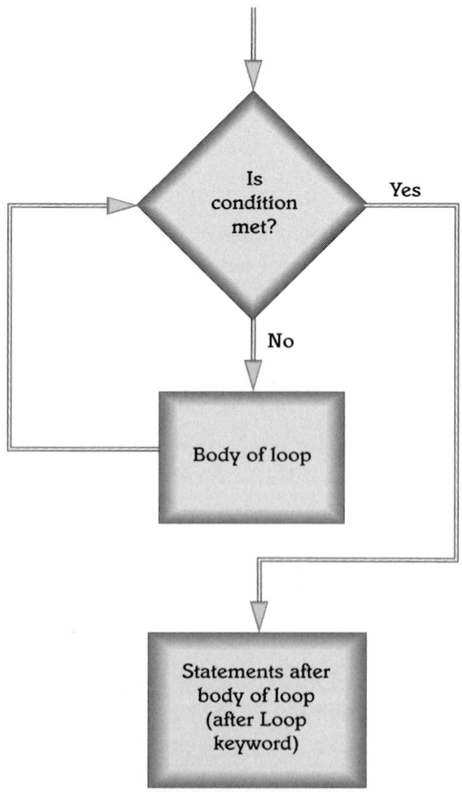

With the test at the end, the loop is always executed at least once; with the test at the beginning, the loop may not be executed at all. Also remember that when the test is at the top, you obviously must have something to test. Therefore, when the test is done at the beginning, initialize all variables to be tested before the loop starts. Finally, don't forget that you usually need two assignment statements when the test is at the top—the first before the test and the second (to keep the process going) inside the loop.

You must follow a similar rule, when nesting Do loops together or when nesting them with For-Next loops, to the rule you follow for nesting For-Next loops alone: inner loops must be finished before the outer loops are tested. Choose a reasonable indenting pattern and you will not have any problems.

Keep in mind that Visual Basic is always asking a True-False question in a Do loop; it's just hidden sometimes. Luckily, all arithmetic operators are done first (they have higher precedence than the relational operators). Visual Basic has no trouble interpreting

```
Loop Until Number*5 > 10
```

as meaning first do the calculation and then do the test (but as always, parentheses make things clearer).

note: *In situations where the user is entering data by using a click on a command button after each entry, you usually don't have to worry about off-by-one errors in the count at the end if you start the count at 0 before the first piece of data is entered.*

THE DO WHILE LOOP

Visual Basic has other kinds of loops. These loops consist of replacing the keyword Until with the keyword While. This new loop may seem superfluous since you can always change a Do Until into a Do While by reversing the relational operator. For example,

```
Do
Loop Until X$ <>""
```

is the same as

```
Do
Loop While X$ = ""
```

and

```
Do
Loop Until Number > 5
```

is the same as

```
Do
Loop While Number <= 5
```

Given this, why bother learning this new type of loop? There are two reasons why the While loop isn't superfluous. The first is that, as much as possible, you want to write a program conforming to the way your mind works. Sometimes you will think of an operation as going on until something happens, while other times you think of it as continuing while, as the saying goes, "the status is quo." The richness of Visual Basic's programming language makes the fit better between your thought patterns and the computer program you're trying to write. In fact, psychologists have found that tests with positive conditions are easier to understand. Do While Number = 0 is easier to process for most people than its counterpart, Do Until Number <> 0.

DO LOOPS WITH AND, OR, NOT

The previous section gave you one reason to use both Do Until and Do While loops, but this is not the only reason. Probably the best reason to use both kinds of loops comes when you have to combine conditions. This is most commonly done with the Or, Not, and And keywords. These three keywords work just like they do in English. You can continue a process as long as both conditions are True or stop it when one turns False. However, it becomes increasingly confusing to try to force combinations of the And, Or, and Not operators into loops that they don't seem to fit. For example, suppose you want to continue a process while a number is greater than zero and a text box is empty. It is much easier to say

```
Do While Number > 0 And Text1.Text = ""
```

than to say

```
Do Until Number <=0 Or Text1.Text <> ""
```

although they both mean the same thing.

THE WHILE/WEND LOOP

There is one other loop possible in Visual Basic. To preserve compatibility with interpreted BASIC, Visual Basic allows a variant on the Do While loop (that is, the test at the top). Instead of saying

```
Do While X = 0

Loop
```

you can say

```
While X = 0

Wend
```

Making Decisions

At this point, your programs can only decide whether to repeat a group of statements or not. They can't, as yet, change which statements are processed depending on what the program has already done or what it has just encountered. The next few sections take care of this. All the commands in these sections deal with turning an outline containing a phrase such as

If *condition* Then *do something else...*

into Visual Basic code. Visual Basic uses the If-Then statement in much the same way that you do in normal English. For example, to warn a user that a number must be positive, use a line like this:

```
If X < 0 Then MsgBox "Number must be positive!"
```

More generally, when Visual Basic encounters an If-Then statement, it checks whether the first clause (called, naturally enough, the If clause) is True. If that clause is True, the computer does whatever follows (called the Then clause). If the test fails, processing skips to the next statement.

Just as in the loops from the previous sections, you can use the If-Then statement to compare numbers or strings. For example, a statement such as

```
If A$ < B$  Then Print A$;" comes before ";B$;"
```

tests for ANSI order (unless an Option Compare Text statement has been processed), and

```
If A <= B  Then Print A; " is no more than "; B
```

tests for numerical order if A and B are numeric variables.

Suppose you need to write a Social Security calculator. The way this tax works is that you pay (in 1995) 6.20 percent of the amount you make up to $57,600. After that, whether you make $60,000 or $5,550,000 per year, you pay no more social security tax. To write code that would activate this type of calculator, you need to write

```
If Wages < 57600 Then STax=.062*Wages Else STax=57600*.062
```

When Visual Basic processes an If-Then-Else, if the test succeeds, Visual Basic processes the statement that follows the keyword Then (the Then clause). If the test fails, Visual Basic processes the statement that follows the keyword Else (called the Else clause). Figure 7-6 shows you what Visual Basic does with an If-Then-Else in flow-diagram style.

Figure 7-6 Flow diagram for If-Then-Else

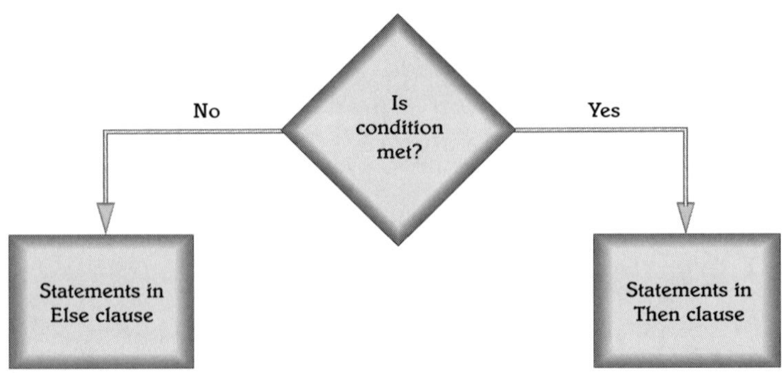

You can also use the keywords And, Or, and Not in an If-Then. These let you check two conditions at once. For example, suppose you have to check whether a number is between zero and 9:

```
If Digit >=0 And Digit <= 9 Then Print "Ok"
```

The ways of using the And operator should be pretty clear by now, but one word of caution. In both speaking and writing, we sometimes say, "If my average is greater than 80 and less than 90, then . . ." Translating this sentence construction directly into code won't work. You must repeat the variable each time you want to test something. To do the translation from English to Visual Basic, say, "If my average is greater than 80 and my average is less than 90, then . . . "

A final note on And: you do not have to use the same variable. A statement such as

```
If (Grade4>Grade3) And Average >60 Then Print "Improving!"
```

is a perfectly good Visual Basic statement. (The parentheses are there only to improve readability; they are not necessary. As you saw earlier, Visual Basic calculates relational operators before worrying about the logical connectors such as And.)

Using the keyword Or in an If-Then is similar. The test is successful if either one of the conditions is True. Suppose you had to test whether at least one of two numbers was nonzero:

```
If A <> 0 Or B <> 0 Then ...
```

There are other, somewhat less common ways of combining tests. For example, you can use the Eqv (equivalence) operator. This test asks whether two conditions are both True or both False. For example,

```
If (X = True And Y = True) or (X = False And Y = False) ...
```

is the same as

```
If X Eqv Y ...
```

Another useful operator (especially for graphics and file security programs) is the Xor (exclusive Or). This corresponds to the English "if A or B but not both."

Similarly, there's the Not that you've already seen. Choosing to use this depends a lot on personal taste (like deciding between Do While and Do Until). Most people find it easier just to change the relational operators. For example,

```
If Not (A$ = "Big Blue")
```

is harder to write than

```
If A$ <> "Big Blue"
```

Similarly,

```
If Not (A > 50)
```

is exactly like

```
If A <= 50
```

If you prefer to use the Not, you'll need parentheses; without them your program is apt to be unreadable.

Since Visual Basic is really testing for a Boolean (True-False) relation in the If clause, you can actually have any Boolean property. For example, in the statement

```
If Text1.Enabled Then ...
```

Visual Basic processes the Then clause only when the Text1 box is enabled.

The Block If-Then

More often than not, you will want to process multiple statements if a condition is True or False. For this you need the most powerful form of the If-Then-Else, called the *block If-Then*. This lets you process as many statements as you like in response to a True condition, as in this example:

If I win the lottery Then
I'm happy
My family is happy
And, the tax man is happy.

Here, there are three statements in response to something being True. To write this statement in Visual Basic, you use a slightly different format than the usual If-Then. The block If-Then looks like this:

If *thing to test* Then
lots of statements
Else
more statements
End If

Now, you do not put anything on the line following the keyword Then; press ENTER immediately after typing it. This bare Then is how Visual Basic knows it's beginning a block. The Else is optional; putting it there (again alone on a line) means that another block will follow, to be processed only if the If clause is False. However, whether the Else is there or not, the block If must end with the keywords End If.

For an example of this, let's modify the original mortgage program in Chapter 5 so the program checks whether the user wants to calculate the payment or the maximum he or she can borrow depending on which text box is empty. The comments in the following program give the formula you need for this. (You have to do a little algebra on the original formula.)

```
Sub btnCalculate_Click ()
  ' This calculates the mortgage
  ' Using the formula, Payment =
  ' Principal*MonthInt/(1-(1/(1+MonthInt))^(Years*12))
  ' Principal =
  ' Payment * (MonthInt / (1 - (1 / (1 + MonthInt))^_
  ' (Years * 12)))-1

  Dim Years As Integer, Payment As Currency
  Dim MonthInt As Single, Amount As Currency
  Dim Percent as Single

  ' Get info
  Years = Val(txtMortgageTerm.Text)
```

```
  Principal = Val(txtMortgageAmount.Text)
  Payment = Val(txtMortgagePayment.Text)
  Percent = Val(txtInterestRate.Text) / 100
  MonthInt = Percent/12
  If Payment = 0 Then
    Payment = Principal * MonthInt / (1 - (1 / (1 + _
MonthInt))^ (Years * 12))
    txtMortgagePayment.Text = Format$(Payment,"###,###.##")
  Else
    Principal =  Payment * (MonthInt / (1 - (1 / (1 + _
MonthInt))^ (Years * 12)))^-1
    txtMortgageAmount.Text = Format$(Principal,"###,###.##")
  End If
End Sub
```

As usual, the indentation is there to make the program more readable; Visual Basic doesn't care.

What Is It?

You can easily use If-Then to determine whether the user has entered a string in the form of a date or a number. The procedure depends on the variant data type combined with two new Boolean functions (functions that return either True or False). For example, the built-in function IsDate tells you whether an expression can be converted to a date. Consider the following code that checks whether the contents of a text box are in the right form to be used as a date:

```
Dim DT    ' DT is a variant
DT = Text1.Text
If IsDate(DT) Then
  ' do whatever you want with the date
Else
  MsgBox "Please enter the text in the form of a date!"
End If
```

Similarly, you can use the IsNumeric function to determine whether a variable can be converted to a number. This gives you a quick way of checking for extraneous characters in a string of digits:

```
Dim NT     'NT is a variant
NT =Text1.Text
If IsNumeric(NT) Then
```

```
  ' do whatever you want with the number
Else
  MsgBox "Please enter the data in the box as a number!"
End If
```

Similarly, you can use the Like operator in an If-Then to do pattern matching.

Using the If-Then with a Message Box

The If-Then is also used to determine which button was pressed in a message box. For instance, assign the value of the MsgBox function to a variable and then use If-Then to check the value. For example:

```
X% = MsgBox ("Yes/No?",vbYesNo)
If X% =vbYes Then Print "Yes button clicked."
```

Notice that you need to use parentheses when using MsgBox in this way. The following table lists the constants you might need for working with the return values from a message box.

Symbolic Constant	Value	Button Chosen
vbOK	1	OK
vbCancel	2	Cancel
vbAbort	3	Abort
vbRetry	4	Retry
vbIgnore	5	Ignore
vbYes	6	Yes
vbNo	7	No

An Example: The Dir$ Command

Another good example of where you'll need an If-Then-Else is when, during a program, you have to find out whether a file or files exist with a specific extension. (You can also use a file list box—see Chapter 17.) The function needed is

Dir$(*filespec*)

where *filespec* is a string expression that contains the filename or file pattern. It is not case sensitive. You can use the two DOS wildcards (? for a single character match and * to allow more characters). You can also include path name information. Each time Visual Basic encounters a Dir$ command with a filespec, it returns the first filename it finds that matches the pattern. When no filenames match, Visual Basic returns the empty string. To continue searching for the same pattern, you call the Dir$ function with no pattern.

Here is a program fragment that checks whether the current directory contains any .TXT files:

```
Dir$("*.TXT")
If X$ = ""  Then
  Print "No text files found"
Else
 Print "First file found is "; X$
End If
```

To find all the files with a .TXT extension, use this:

```
Dir$("*.TXT")
Do While X$ <> ""  'or While Len(X$)
   Print "Text File found is "; X$
   X$ = Dir$                          'Don't reuse the file spec
Loop
```

Combining the If-Then with Loops

Suppose you need to check that there is exactly one file with a .TXT extension in the current directory. To do this, you have to use the Dir$ function, but you need to allow two ways to leave the loop. Here is a fragment that does this:

```
NameOfFile$ = Dir$("*.TXT")
NumberOfFiles = 0
Do Until NameOfFile$ = "" Or NumberOfFiles > 1
  NumberOfFiles = NumberOfFiles + 1
  NameOfFile$ = Dir$
Loop
If NumberOfFiles = 0 Then Print "No Files Found"
If NumberOfFiles > 1 Then Print "Too Many Files"
```

Notice that Visual Basic enters the loop only if it finds an example of the file. You have to allow for the loop never being entered at all. Once the loop is entered, you have Visual Basic add 1 to the file count.

These kinds of loops are so common that computer scientists gave them a special name, *Eureka loops*, after Archimedes' famous bathtub experience. You set up a loop to end if either one of two situations prevails. Then you follow the loop by a test for what actually took place.

Another example of this type of loop would occur if you modified the program that calculated how long it would take to build up a $1,000,000 nest egg to end either if the number of years until you retired was exceeded or you reached the $1,000,000 goal.

You can use the If-Then to give you a way to write a loop that "tests in the middle." For this, you combine the If-Then with a new command: the Exit Do. Whenever Visual Basic processes the Exit Do statement, it pops you out of the loop, directly to the statement following the keyword Loop.

More generally, Visual Basic allows you to set up a potentially infinite loop at any time; just leave off the tests in a Do loop (an unadorned Do at the top and an equally unadorned Loop at the bottom). Once you've done this, the loop will end only when Visual Basic processes an Exit Do statement. (During program development, you can always end the program prematurely from the Run menu, and you can also use the toolbar or CTRL-BREAK combination, of course.) There is a version of the Exit command for leaving a For-Next loop as well; in this case, it takes the form Exit For.

Visual Basic places no restriction on the number of Exit statements you place inside a loop, but loops that have 37 different ways to end are awfully hard to debug. As a general rule, most programmers aim for programs that have only "single entry/single exit" loops. They also find it easier to debug programs that have the loop test at the beginning or end of the loop. Most programmers use the Exit Do (or Exit For) only for abnormal exits from loops, such as when a program is about to divide by zero and leave the loop rather than generate a divide-by-zero error.

Select Case

Suppose you were designing a program to compute grades based on the average of four exams. If the average was 90 or higher, the person should get an A, 80 to 89, a B, and so on. This is such a common situation that Visual Basic has another control structure designed exactly for it. It's called the Select Case. For example, instead of

```
If Grade > 90 Then YourGrade = "A"
If Grade > 80 and Grade < 90 then YourGrade = "B"
```

Using the Select Case control structure, you can write

```
Select Case Grade
   Case > 90
     YourGrade = "A"
   Case > 80
     YourGrade = "B"
 End Select
```

The Select Case command makes it clear that a program has reached a point with many branches; multiple If-Thens do not. (And the clearer a program is, the easier it is to debug.)

note: *Only one clause of a Select Case can be activated in each Select Case.*

That's why you could use the line Grade > 80, whereas two consecutive lines, like this,

```
If Grade > 90 Then YourGrade = "A"
If Grade > 80 Then YourGrade = "B"
```

won't work.

What follows the keywords Select Case is a variable or expression, and what Visual Basic is going to do depends on the value of the variable or expression. The keyword Case is shorthand for "In the case that the variable (expression) is," and you usually follow it by a relational operator. For example, to begin to check that the value of the variable is a letter, you can add the Is keyword:

```
Case Is < "A"
  Print "Character is not a letter."
  Print "Meaningless question"
```

To eliminate all possible nonletter values, you have to consult, for example, the ASCII chart available online via the Help menu. By looking at that, you can see that you also need to eliminate those characters whose ASCII codes are between 91 and 95. You do this as follows:

```
Case Chr$(91) To Chr$(95)
  Print "Character is not a letter."
  Print "Meaningless question"
```

Here, the keyword To allows you to give a range of values. Therefore, this statement is shorthand for, "In the case that the variable is in the range from Chr$(91) to Chr$(95) inclusive, do the following."

Having eliminated the case when the character was not a letter, you may want to print out the message that it is a consonant. You do this with the Case Else, which is shorthand for "Do this case if none of the other situations holds." (The Case Else should always be the last Case in a Select Case.)

```
Select Case Grade
   Case > 90
     YourGrade = "A"
   Case > 80
     YourGrade = "B"
   Case > 70
     YourGrade = "C"
   Case Else
     "Please retake the final."
 End Select
```

Finally, the Select Case control structure allows you to combine many tests for equality on one line. You could write, for example,

```
Case "A", "E", "I", "O", "U"
  Print "letter is a vowel"
```

instead of the obvious five different cases.

Finishing Up with the If-Then

The Select Case command allows you multiple branches but allows you to test only one expression—ultimately one number or string. Suppose you have two numbers, A and B, and your outline looks like this:

```
If A=B  Do ....
If A>B  Do ....
If A<B  Do ....
```

One way to program this is to set up a variable,

```
Difference = A - B
```

and then select whether the value of Difference was zero (when A = B), greater than zero (in which case A > B), or less than zero (A < B). But now suppose someone throws in one or two extra conditions:

```
If A > B And A < 2*B
If A > 2*B
```

Now it's no longer obvious how to use the Select Case command. You could write four block If-Thens corresponding to each of the different conditions in the outline, and most of the time this wouldn't cause any problems. Problems may happen if (as in the preceding example) you have to do something to A or B in one of the blocks. From that point on you're in trouble. All further tests are off. More precisely, suppose the outline was to do one of the following:

```
If A = B
   Print A
If A < B
    Print A and add two to A
If A > B
    Print B and add two to B
```

Here is a translation of this outline:

```
If A = B Then Print A
If A < B Then
  Print A
  A = A + 2
End If
If A > B Then
  Print B
  B = B + 2
End If
```

Suppose the value of A was 4 and the value of B was 5. Then the second option is taken, and the program prints out 4 and makes A = 6. But now the third option is activated—contrary to the outline, which says do only one of the possibilities.

This situation is similar to when you first used the Else command. You need to continue testing within the confines of the original If-Then. This is done with the keywords ElseIf-Then.

Here is the correct translation of the outline:

```
If A = B Then
  Print A
ElseIf A < B Then
  Print A
  A = A + 2
ElseIf A > B Then
  Print B
  B = B + 2
End If
```

Now everything is tied together. And just like in the If-Then-Else or the Select command, Visual Basic activates, at most, one clause. In particular, if A < B, then Visual Basic processes only the second clause. And when Visual Basic is finished doing that, it bypasses any other ElseIfs that may be contained in the block; it goes immediately to the statement following the End If. (By the way, you could replace the final ElseIf with a simple Else; you've eliminated all the other possibilities.)

A block If-Then can have as many ElseIfs as you like but only one Else (as the last clause). The limits are determined by how much you can process rather than what Visual Basic can do. (That's why it's often preferable to use Select Case. Although any Select Case can be transformed into an If-Then-ElseIf, the latter can be much harder to read and hence to debug.)

The final point worth noting is that the block If-Then is extremely flexible. You can put any Visual Basic statement following the keyword Then—in particular, another If-Then-Else. Consider the following, which a teacher might use if he or she regarded the final exam as being not all-important:

```
If FinalExam < 65 Then
  Print "You failed the final exam."
  If Average > 70 Then
    Print "You pass because your average is"
    Print "high enough to overcome failing the final"
  Else
    Print "I'm sorry failing the final and a marginal ";
    Print " passing average means failing the course"
  End If
End If
```

Is it clear (forgetting the indentation pattern for a moment) that the Else belongs to the inner If-Then? The way to see this is to "play computer." For the Else to belong to the outer If-Then, the inner If-Then must have already finished. But it hasn't because, to that point, no End If has shown up. Therefore, the first End If finishes the inner If-Then and the second finishes the outer one, and so the Else must belong to the inner If-Then. Of course, you should, as in the preceding example, use a consistent indentation pattern to make it obvious at a glance where nested If-Thens belong.

An Example: The KeyPress Procedure

Almost all Visual Basic objects will recognize when a user presses and then releases a key. If the key that was pressed generates an ordinary ASCII/ANSI code, it triggers the KeyPress event procedure. Not only can this procedure detect what the user types, but you can also use it to change or restrict what the control will accept.

The syntax for this event procedure is a little different than all the event procedures you've seen up to now. The template for the KeyPress event procedure looks like this:

```
Private Sub ControlName_KeyPress(KeyAscii As Integer)

End Sub
```

Inside the parentheses is the first example of a parameter—the formal name for a placeholder. When Visual Basic detects the user pressing an ASCII key inside a control that recognizes this event, you get a call to this event procedure. Visual Basic replaces the parameter with the ASCII code of the key that generated the event.

For example, a form can detect the KeyPress event if all the controls on it are disabled or invisible, or if the form's KeyPreview property is set to True. If you start a new project with a blank form and attach the following event procedure to it,

```
Sub Form_KeyPress(KeyAscii As Integer)
  Print "The ASCII code of the key you pressed is ";KeyAscii
  Print "The character itself is ";Chr$(KeyAscii)
End Sub
```

you'll be able to explore the ASCII codes for characters until you end the program.

On the other hand, if you want to cancel a keystroke, you need only reassign the parameter KeyAscii to be zero. For example, use the following to force the user to type a digit between zero and 9 into a text block:

```
Sub Text1_KeyPress(KeyAscii As Integer)
  If KeyAscii < Asc("0") Or KeyAscii > Asc("9") Then
     Beep
     KeyAscii = 0
  End If
End Sub
```

This event procedure absolutely prevents the user from typing anything but a digit inside the text box. The procedure blanks out any other character the user may have typed.

Since you can detect whether a user has typed a comma or more than one decimal point, you can use the KeyPress event procedure to check what he or she types in a text box. The next chapter shows you how to write a procedure that accepts a number but disregards commas, extraneous decimal points, and non-numeric characters.

An Example: Working with the QueryUnload Event

One of the most common times you will combine the If-Then with a message box is inside the QueryUnload event. (Recall that this event is triggered whenever someone tries to unload a form. As mentioned in Chapter 5, especially with multiform applications, you will want to put cleanup code in this event.)

The syntax for this event is

Private Sub Form_QueryUnload(*cancel* As Integer, *unloadmode* As Integer)

If you set the *cancel* parameter to a nonzero integer, you prevent the form from closing. Thus you will often need code like this:

```
Private Sub Form_QueryUnload(cancel As Integer, unloadmode_
As Integer)
X% = MsgBox ("Are you sure you want to end the
program?",vbYesNo)
If X% =vbNo Then
  Cancel = True
 'cleanup code goes here
Else
```

```
  'Cancel = False
  'cleanup code goes here
End If
End Sub
```

The *unloadmode* parameter is used to tell you why the form is unloading. Its values are summarized in the following table.

Constant	Value	Description
vbFormControlMenu	0	The user chose the Close command from the Control menu on the form.
vbFormCode	1	The Unload statement is invoked from code.
vbAppWindows	2	Windows is ending.
vbAppTaskManager	3	The Task Manager is closing the application.
vbFormMDIForm	4	An MDI child form is closing because the MDI form is closing (see Chapter 15).

Conditional Compilation

If you have the Professional or Enterprise edition of Visual Basic, you can write code for both 16- and 32-bit Windows. It would obviously be nice if you could maintain only one file with the source code and have Visual Basic do the bookkeeping in the various cases. The key to this is what is usually called *conditional compilation*. For example, suppose you get to a point where you need to write different code for Windows 3.x than for Windows 95 or Windows NT. Your code needs to include a block like this at that point:

```
#If Win16 Then
   ' Place statements that will work only under
    '16-bit Windows statements here.
    '
#ElseIf Win32 Then
   'Place statements that will work only under
   '32-bit Windows here.
#Else
   'Place other platform statements here.
#End If
```

(Notice the similarity to an ordinary If-Then-Else.)

note: *The Option Compare statement doesn't affect the tests in a #If. Visual Basic always uses case-insensitive (Option Compare Text) comparisons.*

In the example, Win16 and Win32 are built-in *compiler constants*. They have the values you expect: the Win16 constant is True when you are using the 16-bit version of Visual Basic; otherwise it is False. The Win32 constant is True when you are developing on the 32-bit version of Visual Basic but is False otherwise.

You can define your own compiler constants at any point you would define an ordinary constant. Here's an example:

```
#Const DebugVersion = True
```

Notice that you use the # to define a conditional compiler constant. Conditional compiler constants defined in code belong to the form or module in which they appear—they cannot be global (public) in scope. Notice as well that a constant like this would be very useful when adding debugging code (see Chapter 14) to your project while it is under development. This is because code that is excluded using conditional compilation is omitted from the final executable file. In particular, it has no size or performance effect.

note: *If you need to define conditional compiler constants that affect the whole project, choose Tools | Options and then fill in the appropriate line of the Project dialog page. An example of a few switches set globally is shown here:*

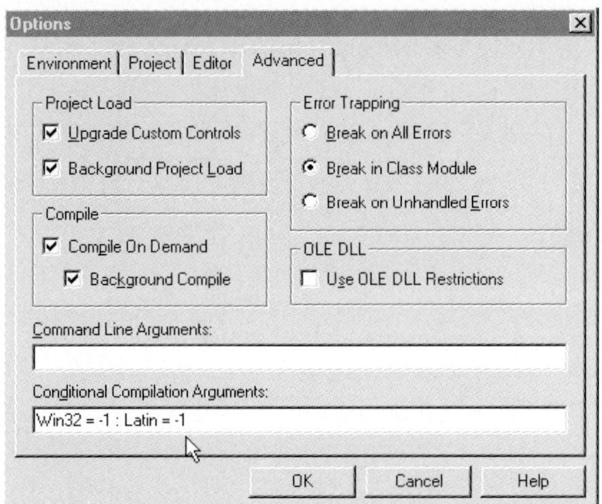

This example would set the conditional compiler constants for 32-bit Windows to be True (and also for using Latin to be true). Notice that you separate multiple constants by colons and that you use -1 for True and not the Symbolic constant True. (Use 0 when you want a compiler constant to be False.)

The GoTo

Like most programming languages, Visual Basic retains the unconditional jump or GoTo. To paraphrase the old joke about split infinitives—modern programmers may be divided into three groups: those who neither know nor care about when they should use the GoTo, those who do not know but seem to care very much, and those who know *when* to use it.

Obviously, routine use of the GoTo leads to *spaghetti code*: code that is hard to read and harder to debug. On the other hand, there are times when using the GoTo actually makes your code cleaner and easier to understand. (In Visual Basic this situation typically comes up when you are deeply inside a nested loop and some condition forces you to leave all the loops simultaneously. You can't use the various forms of the Exit command because all that does is get you out of the loop you are currently in.)

To use a GoTo in Visual Basic, you must label a line. Labels must begin with a letter and end with a colon. They must also start in the *first* column. (Obviously, you should use as descriptive a label as possible.) Here's an example:

```
BadInput:
  'Code we want to process can GoTo here
```

For example, suppose you are using a nested For loop to input data and want to leave the loop if the user enters **ZZZ**.

```
For i = 1 to 10
    For j = 1 to 100
    GetData := InputBox("Data Input", "Enter data, ZZZ to end", "")
    If GetData =  "ZZZ" then
        GoTo BadInput
    Else
       'Process data
    End If;
Exit Sub
```

```
BadInput:
  MsgBox("Data entry ended at user request");
```

Notice how using the Exit For keywords would be cumbersome here. For example, it would require extra code in order to break completely out of the nested loop. Also notice the Exit Sub keywords that prevent you from "falling into" the labeled code.

Chapter Eight

Built-in Functions

This chapter covers Visual Basic's built-in functions. These commands transform raw data into the form you need. For example, there are functions that take strings apart as well as ones that put them together. You'll also see how the pseudo-random number generator lets you build an element of indeterminacy (chance) into your programs, a necessary tool for programming games of chance or simulations.

As always, be prepared to check the online help about specific functions. The examples given there complement the ones given in this chapter.

String Functions

Because information in Visual Basic text boxes is usually kept as text or variants, string functions are far more important in Visual Basic than in ordinary BASIC languages. (Relying on implicit conversions from the Variant data type can occasionally lead to problems and in all cases is slower.) In Chapter 5 you saw how two strings can be joined together (concatenated) using the plus sign (+) or ampersand (&). In this section you'll see the functions available in Visual Basic that let you examine the characters in a string, take strings apart, place one string inside another, and put strings together.

For example, suppose you need a string variable that contains the lowercase alphabet. Just combine the + with a For-Next loop:

```
Lowercase$=""
For I% = Asc("a") To Asc("z")
  Lowercase$ = Lowercase$ + Chr$(I%)
Next I%
```

You can also look up the ASCII/ANSI codes for "a" (97) and "z" (122) in the help files.

You will often use two built-in functions when building up strings. The function

```
Space(NumberOfSpaces)
```

yields a string consisting of only spaces, with the number of spaces determined by the value inside the parentheses. The function

```
String(Number,StringExpression$)
```

yields a string of repeated characters. The character repeated is the first character of the string expression in the second position of the function, and the number of times the characters are repeated is determined by the value in the first position. You can also use the extended ASCII/ANSI code in the second position. The following examples all yield the same string of 10 z's:

```
X$ = String(10,"z")
X$ = String(10,"zyzzavaa")       'only first character is used
X$ = String(10,122)              '  122 = Asc("z")
```

tip: *You can still use the older Space$ and String$ functions.*

Analyzing Strings

Suppose you want to examine an expression character-by-character. For example, you might want to check how many periods (decimal points) are in a string expression before you convert it to a number with the Val function, rather than use the IsNumeric function you saw in Chapter 7. The code for this calls for a For-Next loop with the ending value set to the length of the string. In Visual Basic, the function that does this is Len( ), where the parentheses following the function hold a string expression. Unlike the TextWidth function, this function counts all spaces and nonprinting characters that appear in the string.

Next, you need a function that lets you extract a copy of individual letters or larger chunks out of a string. The most important of these functions is the Mid function. The syntax for this function is

Mid(*string*, start[, *length*])

note: *The Mid function supports named arguments.*

The first entry holds the string (or string expression) you want to cut up. Next comes the starting position of the characters you want cut out of the string. The optional last position specifies the number of characters you want to pull out. These last two options can be either integers or long integers or an expression that Visual Basic can round off to lie in this range. Here are some examples of this function:

```
Mid("Visual Basic", 1, 5) = "Visua"
Mid("Visual Basic", 1, 6) = "Visual"
Mid("Visual Basic", 8, 5) = "Basic"
```

If you leave out the last entry (the one telling how many letters to pull out), as shown here,

```
Mid("Visual Basic", 8, 5) = Mid("Visual Basic", 8)= "Basic"
```

Visual Basic retrieves a copy of the rest of the string—starting, of course, from the position determined by the second entry. You also get a copy of the rest of the string if the third entry is too large (greater than the number of characters remaining).

Programmers say that Mid is a function of three (or occasionally two) parameters, or arguments. Both terms are borrowed from mathematics. Think of them as meaning "the number of pieces of information to be massaged." In a function, each argument is separated from the next by commas. The Mid function usually uses three pieces of information: a string in the first position and integers or long integers in the remaining two positions. (Of course, you can use expressions that evaluate to these as well.)

For example, a fragment that would count the number of periods in a string expression might look like this:

```
PeriodCount% = 0
Length% = Len(StringExpression$)
For I% = 1 To Length%
  If Mid(StringExpression$, I%, 1) = "." Then
     PeriodCount% = PeriodCount% + 1
  End If
Next I%
```

On each pass through the loop, the position (the value of I%) where the Mid function starts working increases. The number of characters pulled out remains the same (one).

The Mid function has two cousins that are occasionally useful: Left and Right. As the names suggest, Left makes a copy of characters from the beginning of a word and Right picks them out from the end. Of the two, Right is the more common. It avoids a subtraction inside the Mid function and can work a bit faster as a result. For example, the following lines all have the same effect:

```
Mid(A$, Len(A$) - 3, 4)
Mid(A$, Len(A$) - 3)
Right(A$, 4)
```

Left works the same way but only saves you from putting a 1 in the second position in the Mid function. If you want the first five characters in a string, use one of the following:

```
Mid(A$, 1, 5)
Left(A$, 5)
```

Mid has one other useful feature. You can use it as a statement to make changes inside a string. For example, if

```
BestBasicForDos$ = "PowerBasic"
```

then the statement

```
Mid(BestBasicForDos$, 1, 5) = "Quick"
```

gives the string variable BestBasicForDos$ the value "QuickBasic". When you use Mid this way, the second position controls where the change will start and the third position controls how many letters to pull out from the string on the right-hand side. These are the letters that will be switched into the original string. For example,

```
Mid(BestBasicForDos$, 1, 5) = "QuickBasic by Microsoft"
```

gives the same result as before. If the right-hand side has fewer characters than the number given in the third position of the left-hand side demands, Visual Basic changes as many characters as occur on the right-hand side. Therefore,

```
Mid(BestBasic$, 1, 5) = "VB"
```

gives BestBasicForDos$ the value "VBwerBasic".

tip: *You can still use the older Mid$, Left$, and Right$ versions.*

MORE ON THE MID STATEMENT

The Mid statement makes changes within a string but never changes the length of the original string. If the number in the third position is too large relative to the number in the second position—that is, greater than the remaining number of characters—then only the characters remaining can change. Finally, just as with the Mid function, you can leave out the last position. For example,

```
Mid("In the beginning ",8) = "middle was"
```

changes the string to

```
"In the middle was"
```

In this case, there's just enough room to fit the string on the right-hand side into the string on the left, starting at the eighth position. Counting from the eighth position, there are ten characters left in the phrase "In the beginning ". (The space counts as a character.)

If you want to change the size of a string, the Mid statement is of little use. Instead, you need to follow a procedure that's a bit like splicing tape. For example, suppose you want to change the string

"QuickBASIC is the best programming language."

to read

"Visual Basic is the best programming language."

Since the string "QuickBASIC" has 10 letters and the string "Visual Basic" has 12 (counting the space), you cannot use the Mid statement. Instead, you must follow the splicing analogy:

1. Cut out the phrase "QuickBASIC".
2. Hold the phrase "is the best programming language".
3. Splice in the phrase "Visual Basic" and reassemble.

Here's the fragment:

```
Phrase$ = "QuickBASIC is the best programming language"
Begin$ = "Visual Basic"
EndPhrase$ = Mid(Phrase$, 11)
Phrase$ = Begin$ + EndPhrase$
```

Programming this kind of change can be a bit painful if you always have to go in and count characters in order to find the position where a character was located. As usual, this task is simplified by one of Visual Basic's built-in functions. Like the Mid function, Instr also works with three (and occasionally two) pieces of information; that is, it's a function of three (occasionally two) arguments.

Instr tells you whether a string is part of another string (the jargon is "is a substring of"). And if it is, Instr tells you the position at which the substring starts. Using the same variable, Phrase$, as in the beginning of the last example, in the line of code

```
X% = Instr(1, Phrase$, "BASIC")
```

the value of X% is 6 because the string "BASIC" occurs in the phrase "QuickBASIC is the best programming language", starting at the sixth position.

In this case, Visual Basic searches the string starting from the first position until it finds the substring. If it doesn't find the string, it gives back a value of zero. Therefore, if

```
X% =Instr(1, Phrase$, "basic")
```

then the value of X% is zero because "basic" isn't a substring of the phrase "QuickBASIC is the best programming language". Remember that case is important inside quotation marks; the Instr function is case sensitive.

The usual form of the Instr function is

Instr(*[where to start,] string to search*, *string to find*)

In this case, the optional first position specifies from which position to start the search. If you leave this entry out, the search automatically starts from the first position.

The full form is actually a bit more powerful (using Microsoft's notation); it is

InStr(*[start,]string1, string2[, compare]*)

where the *compare* parameter specifies the type of string comparison. If you omit it or set it to 0 (the default), it gives you a case-sensitive comparison. Specify 1 to use a case-insensitive comparison. If the *compare* parameter is omitted, the current setting for the Option Compare function determines the type of comparison.

tip: *By using the previous value obtained by Instr you can search for repeated occurrences of a string.*

Since the Instr function returns the value zero (that is, False) when Visual Basic doesn't find a character, or a nonzero value (True) when it does, you will often find yourself writing If-Then or Do loops using the Instr function to do the test. For example, you can write an If-Then:

```
If Instr(Expression$,".") Then
   Print "Decimal point found."
Else
   Print "No decimal point found."
End If
```

rather than

```
If Instr(Expression$,".") <> 0 Then
   Print "Decimal point found."
Else
   Print "No decimal point found."
End If
```

PARSING A STRING

Another good example of how to use the Instr command is a program that parses a string, which means to take it apart into logical pieces and examine the components—for example, to break a name into its component parts. Suppose you had a string made up of individual words, each separated from the next by a single space. Here is a simple outline for pulling out the individual words:

1. Find the first occurrence of a space. Everything up to the first space is a word.
2. Find the second space. Everything between these two spaces is a word.
3. Find the third space. Everything between the second and third spaces is a word.
4. Continue until there are no more spaces.

Now everything between the last space and the end of the word is the last word.

Here is a fragment that implements this outline for the contents of a text box with a control name of Text1:

```
' This fragment uses Instr to parse a phrase
' by searching for a space as the separator

Dim LenPhrase As Integer, BeforeSpace As Integer
Dim AfterSpace As Integer, SizeOfWord As Integer

Phrase$ = Text1.Text
LenPhrase = Len(Phrase$)
If LenPhrase = 0 Then
   MsgBox("No string entered!")
Else
   Separate$ = Chr$(32)                  '= space
   BeforeSpace = 0
   AfterSpace = Instr(BeforeSpace + 1, Phrase$, Separate$)
   Do Until AfterSpace = 0
     SizeOfWord = AfterSpace - BeforeSpace - 1
     NextWord$ = Mid(Phrase$, BeforeSpace + 1, SizeOfWord)
     Print NextWord$
     BeforeSpace = AfterSpace
     AfterSpace = Instr(BeforeSpace + 1, Phrase$, Separate$)
   Loop
End If
Print Mid(Phrase$, BeforeSpace + 1)
```

This fragment of code would usually be inside an event procedure or a general procedure (see Chapter 9). The initialization makes it easy to start the process. Without this, the fragment would have to treat the first word separately.

The next space is found starting one position in from the previous space. At the beginning of the process, this must be the first position because the If-Then-Else ends if the string is not empty.

The Do loop stops when no more spaces are left. By testing at the top of the loop, you take care of the case when there is only a single word. If you are puzzled by why the word is given by one less than the value of AfterSpace - BeforeSpace, it is easy to work out an example. Suppose spaces are at the 5th and 9th positions; this means the actual word takes up positions 6, 7, and 8 (that is, it is three characters long). Setting up a variable for the size of the word makes the Mid statement cleaner. There's rarely a need to combine many statements into one.

Next, the program sets the new value of BeforeSpace to be the old value of AfterSpace, which moves you along to the position of the next space. This sets Visual Basic up to look for the next space. If it finds a space, the cycle continues; if not, Visual Basic moves to whatever is left since there are no more spaces. The rest of the string must be a word.

The program assumes that there is no period or other stop at the end. Another problem with this program is that it doesn't handle multiple spaces within the phrase. The problem, as usual, stems from the outline, which assumes that a word is bounded by no more than one space. How can you take care of the quite common possibility of a double space or even more? You need to change the outline for the previous program. The second step in the previous outline assumes that a word is always located between two spaces, one on either side of it. What you need to do is find the next space as you did before, but what is between these two spaces is a word only if it is not an empty space.

But what really happens if there are two consecutive spaces? As always, an example helps. Suppose the string Phrase$ was given by the following line of code:

```
Phrase$ = "This" + Space$(2) + "is" + Space$(3) + "a test"
```

This puts two spaces between the first and second words in the phrase, three spaces between the second and third words in the phrase, and one space between the third and fourth words.

Let's "play computer." Especially when dealing with loops, this is often best done by setting up a chart detailing the values the important variables are supposed to have on each pass, as shown here:

Pass Number	Value of (Key) Variables
0 (Before entering loop)	BeforeSpace = 0 AfterSpace = 5
(start of) 1st pass through loop	SizeOfWord = 4
(end of) 1st pass through loop	BeforeSpace = 5 AfterSpace = 6
(start of) 2nd pass through loop	SizeOfWord = 0
(end of) 2nd pass through loop	BeforeSpace = 6 AfterSpace = 9
(start of) 3rd pass through loop	SizeOfWord = 2
(end of) 3rd pass through loop	BeforeSpace = 9 AfterSpace = 10
(start of) 4th pass through loop	SizeOfWord = 0

You will often use a table like this when you debug a program. Watch the values of the variables in the Debug window (see Chapter 14), and then check the values Visual Basic displays against your table. Examining the values of variables is of little use unless you know what the values are supposed to be.

As you can see, the table indicates that whenever you have two spaces together, the variable SizeOfWord has the value zero. Does this always have to be true? Yes, it does, because if you have two consecutive spaces, the value of AfterSpace is always one more than the value of BeforeSpace. And so the value of

AfterSpace - BeforeSpace - 1 = SizeOfWord

must be zero.

Knowing this makes it easy to modify the program. (Change the Print statements to read "If SizeOf Word > 0 Then..."). The example program that follows this discussion shows a version of this program that takes this into account and also checks for other word separators, such as commas, periods, and question marks.

As another example, suppose you need to decide on the number of digits before the decimal point in a number. This is easy to do if you combine the Str command with the Instr command. Here's an outline for this:

1. Change the number to a string.
2. Find the decimal point using Instr.
3. If the value from the previous step is zero, there's no decimal point and the number of digits is one less than the length of the converted number (because of the extra space that Str adds).

4. Otherwise, the number of digits in front of the decimal point is two less (because of the extra space that Str sticks on for the sign and the decimal point) than the value given by the Instr function.

Here's the Visual Basic fragment:

```
' find the number of digits
Dim Numeral$, Digits As Integer

Numeral$ = Str(Number)
Digits = Instr(Numeral$, ".")
If Digits = 0 Then
   NumOfDigits = Len(Numeral$) - 1
Else
  NumOfDigits = Digits - 2
End If
```

AN EXAMPLE: CHECKING INPUT

Probably the most important way to bulletproof a program is to check user input. This task was discussed to some extent in Chapter 7 (using the IsNumeric function), but now you have the tools to go much further. Check what the user enters before you start processing the data; don't wait until it's too late. This section shows you how to write the code that will accept a number but disregard commas, extraneous decimal points, and so on. Exactly what is extraneous is determined by the international number setting when you set up Windows. The general procedure for writing this code is as follows:

1. Examine a character.
2. If the character is a digit, place it on the right.
3. If the character is the first decimal point, accept that too and also place it on the right. Otherwise, disregard the character.
4. All other characters are canceled.

As you saw in Chapter 7, the KeyPress event lets you examine characters as they are entered, wiping out the extraneous characters.

The main issue you have to decide is how to store the information. The two most common possibilities are

- Set up a form-level or global variable (see Chapter 9) for the number.
- Leave the text as the (variant) contents of the control and convert the contents of the box to a number inside whatever procedures need it.

The advantage of the first option is that you don't have to cancel out commas, which users might prefer. The advantage of the second is that you may not need to do the extra analysis at all.

The following fragment stores the information as the contents of a form-level variable called Numeral$:

```
Private Sub Text1_KeyPress(KeyAscii As Integer)
  ' This fragment accepts only a number
  Static DecimalPointUsed As Integer

  Select Case KeyAscii
    Case Asc("0") To Asc("9")
      Numeral$ = Numeral$ + Chr$(KeyAscii)
    Case Asc(".")
      If DecimalPointUsed Then
        KeyAscii = 0
        Beep
       Else
        DecimalPointUsed = TRUE
        Numeral$ = Numeral$ + Chr$(KeyAscii)
      End If
    Case Asc(",")
      ' Comma - do nothing to Numeral$
    Case Else
      KeyAscii = 0
      Beep
  End Select
End Sub
```

Since DecimalPointUsed is set up as a static variable, this information is preserved by Visual Basic during each subsequent call to the KeyPress event procedure. On the other hand, if you wanted to allow more than one number to be entered in the control, the situation would be a bit more complicated. You could make this a form or global variable and reset it to False each time you wanted to reuse the information, or you could leave it as a static variable and set it to False whenever the text box started out blank.

If a character is in the range from 0 to 9, then it's a digit. Therefore, it's concatenated at the right of the global variable Numeral$. Next, the fragment moves to the case that accepts a single decimal point in the number. However, entering a decimal point flips the DecimalPointUsed flag to True.

The fragment leaves the commas intact in the display but, of course, doesn't add them to the Numeral$ variable, which will be turned into a number. Any other characters are canceled and the computer beeps to provide some feedback. You might also use a message box here.

The Like Operator and Fuzzy Searching

The Like operator lets you compare strings using ordinary DOS wildcards but goes far beyond that. For example, it can tell you if any digits are inside a string or even if a group of characters is not inside a string. For non-null strings this operator returns True if there is a match and False if not. The case sensitivity of the Like operator depends on the current setting of Option Compare in the form or module. (Of course, you could program all these features using the Instr function, but the Like operator is faster and, of course, saves you programming time.)

As with DOS, a question mark (?) matches one character only and an asterisk (*) allows matches with zero, one, or more characters. For example, an If-Then like this

```
If "QuickBasic" Like "*Basic" Then
    Print "a Basic language"
Else
    Print "not a Basic language"
End If
```

will print "a Basic language". But change the If clause to

```
If "QuickBasic" Like "?Basic" Then
```

and you'll see "not a Basic language".

The following table summarizes the possible patterns:

Pattern Character	Match
?	Any single character
*	Zero or more characters
#	Any single digit
[list of characters]	Any single character in the list
[!list of characters]	Any single character not in the list

For example, if X = ("###" Like "123"), then X is True; but if X = ("[ABC]" Like "123"), then X is False. (But X = ("[!ABC]" Like "123") is True!)

You can also use a hyphen inside the brackets to show an ascending range. For example, "If "[0-9]" Like A$" would tell you whether a digit occurred inside A$.

note: *To match a left bracket ([), question mark (?), number sign (#), or asterisk (*), enclose them in brackets. For example: "*[?]" would check for the occurrence of a question mark.*

Other String Functions

Visual Basic has quite a few functions for handling strings. This section goes through the most important remaining ones.

note: *All these functions can be used both with and without the $. The $ is still accepted to preserve compatibility with earlier Visual Basic code.*

LCase (LCase$), UCase (UCase$) As you might expect from the name, the LCase function forces all the characters in a string to be lowercase. (LCase$ is the older way—it still works.) Similarly, UCase switches all the characters in a string to uppercase. These functions are used when you want to disregard the case inside a string.

StrComp This function can be used instead of the relational operators (such as < or >) to compare strings. Unlike the relational operators, this returns a value, so you usually use it together with an assignment statement. For example, if you set X = StrComp(A$, B$), then the value of X is -1 if A$ is less than B$,

0 if A$ equals B$, and 1 if A$ is greater than B$. It is the reserved constant NULL if one of the strings is empty.

By adding a third option to StrComp, you can control case sensitivity of the comparison. If you use StrComp(A$, B$, 1), then the comparison is not case sensitive; for StrComp(A$, B$, 0), it is. Using StrComp this way is sometimes preferable to using the Option Compare Text feature that globally controls comparisons.

Trim (Trim$), LTrim (LTrim$), RTrim (RTrim$) Although, as you saw earlier in this chapter, you have to work a little bit to pull out extra spaces from inside a string; you don't have to do much for spaces at the beginning or end of a string. The Trim function removes spaces from both the left and right of a string. For example:

```
A$ = "     This has far too many spaces.      "
Trim(A$) = "This has far too many spaces."
```

Similarly, LTrim removes spaces from the left and RTrim removes spaces from the right.

note: *None of the Visual Basic string functions except the Mid statement ever change the string. They all make a copy of the string and modify that copy.*

The Rnd Function

The Solitaire program provided with Windows 3.X shuffles a deck of cards whenever you ask it to. In card games and most other games, the play is unpredictable. This is exactly what is meant by a game of chance. On the other hand, computers are machines, and the behavior of machines should be predictable. To write a program in Visual Basic that allows you, for example, to simulate the throwing of a die, you need a function that makes the behavior of the computer seem random. You do this by means of the function Rnd. For example, run the following Form_Click procedure on a blank form:

```
Private Sub Form_Click()
  Cls
  Dim I As Integer
  For I = 1 To 5
    Print Rnd
  Next I
End Sub
```

What you'll see will look something like the screen in Figure 8-1. As you can see, five numbers between zero and 1, each having six or seven digits, roll down the screen. These numbers seem to follow no pattern: that's what is usually meant by random. They'll also have many, but not all, of the sophisticated statistical properties that scientists expect of random numbers. Without some changes, for example, they would not be very useful in simulation programs. See Chapter 10 for how to modify the built-in random number generator for simulations.

Each time the computer processes a line containing the statement "Print Rnd", a different number between zero and 1 pops out. In theory, the number can be zero but can't ever be 1. (You can also use the Rnd(1) version that is necessary in QuickBASIC.)

It's natural to wonder what a number with up to seven decimal places is good for. Suppose, for example, you wanted to write a program that simulated a coin

Figure 8-1 Demonstration of (pseudo) random numbers

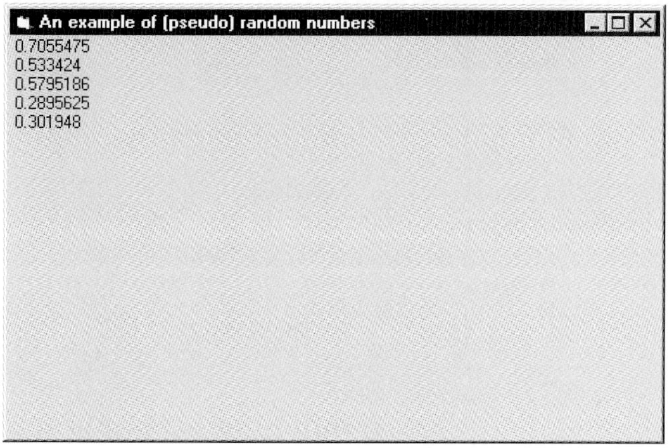

toss. There are three possibilities: it could be heads, it could be tails—or it could stand on edge (don't wait up for this to happen). A fragment to simulate a coin toss might look like this:

```
' A coin toss simulator

CoinToss = Rnd

Select Case CoinToss
  Case Is < .5
    Print "Heads"
  Case .5
    Print "Stood on edge!!!!"
  Case Else
    Print "Tails"
End Select
```

Suppose you incorporate this fragment into a Form_Click procedure:

```
Private Sub Form_Click ()
  ' A multiple coin toss simulator

  Dim Trials As Integer, NumOfHeads As Integer
  Dim NumOfTails As Integer, I As Integer
  Dim CoinToss As Single

  Trials = Val(InputBox$("How many trials?"))
  NumOfHeads = 0
  NumOfTails = 0
  Unbelievable = 0

  For I = 1 To Trials
    CoinToss = Rnd
    Select Case CoinToss
      Case Is < .5
        NumOfHeads = NumOfHeads + 1
      Case .5
        Print "Stood on edge!!!!"     'maybe in a couple of
                                      'years
        Beep: Beep
        Unbelievable = Unbelievable + 1
      Case Else
        NumOfTails = NumOfTails + 1
```

```
      End Select
    Next I
    Cls
    Print "Number of heads was"; NumOfHeads
    Print "Number of tails was"; NumOfTails
    If Unbelievable > 0 Then
      Print "The coin stood on edge!"
    End If
End Sub
```

Try this program with a different number of trials. You should get roughly the same number of heads as tails and no "standing on edges." (For a large number of trials, it would be very unlikely that you'd get equal numbers of heads and tails.) Now end the program and run it again, using the same number of trials as before. If you do, you'll notice that you will get exactly the same number of heads and tails as you did before. This would certainly be unusual behavior for an honest coin. What is happening?

In fact, the numbers you get using the Rnd function are only pseudo-random. Pseudo generally means false, and you've just seen one of the problems of pseudo-random numbers. Every time you start a program that uses pseudo-random numbers, you will get the same sequence of pseudo-random numbers. The program operates as if the computer's memory contains a book of these numbers, and after each program is over, the book gets turned back to page 1. The book always starts at the same place and the numbers are always in the same order, therefore, the results are fixed. You need a way to shuffle the pages each time the program starts. You can do this in many ways, but the easiest way is to add a parameter to the Rnd function.

First, suppose you issue a Rnd(0). Then you get the last pseudo-random number generated. This is useful when trying to debug a program. Rnd(0) gives you a way of checking which pseudo-random number the machine just used. (Imagine trying to debug a program if an important number changes each time and you have no way of knowing its value.) Suppose next there is a negative number inside the parentheses. (The number inside the parentheses is usually called the *seed*.) Each time you give the command

```
Rnd(negative number)
```

that is, use a negative seed, you get the same pseudo-random number. This is another important debugging tool. It lets you rerun a program keeping the pseudo-random numbers temporarily stable. A good way to think about what a negative seed does is to imagine that there is a different list of pseudo-random numbers, each one corresponding to a different negative seed. You can think of the seed as the number from which the random numbers grow. This is done by transforming the seed using the linear congruential method, which transforms the number using the Mod function.

The easiest way to understand what Visual Basic is doing for its random number generator is to imagine you are working only with integers. The random number generator would then use the built-in Mod function to generate the next pseudo-random number roughly as follows:

NextNumber = (A*PreviousNumber + B) mod M

Here, A, B, and M are fixed integers and the PreviousNumber starts from the seed. This method is very fast. But because A, B, and M are fixed by Visual Basic designers, this method can be unreliable if you need many random numbers for a simulation program. If you need thousands of random numbers for a program, see Chapter 10, which gives you one way of improving the built-in random number generator. The cost is that the program will run slightly more slowly and need slightly more memory.

note: *From this point on, this book will stop using the term "pseudo-random" and refer to the numbers coming from the Rnd function as being "random"; this follows the usual terminology in programming.*

The best way not to stack the cards at the outset is to use the exact time of the system clock to reseed the random number generator. (Since the clock is accurate to around a tenth of a second, it's quite unlikely that a program will start at exactly the same moment each time it is run.) You do this by using a new command: Randomize.

The Randomize statement can also be a useful debugging tool. This is because you can use any numeric expression in the Randomize statement. After a Randomize Number command, your program will always be using the same set of random numbers.

Numbers between zero and 1 may (with a little work) be good for imitating a coin toss, but the method used earlier would be cumbersome for, say, a dice simulation. The outline would be something like this:

- If the random number is less than 1/6, make it a 1.
- If more than 1/6 but less than 2/6 (= 1/3), make it a 2.

- If more than 2/6 but less than 3/6 (= 1/2), make it a 3, and so on.

Thinking about this outline leads to a simple trick called *scaling* that more or less automates this process. Suppose you take a number between zero and 1 and multiply it by 6. If it was less than 1/6 to start with, it will now be less than 1; if it was between 1/6 and 2/6 (1/3), it will now be between 1 and 2; and so on. All you need to do then is multiply the number by 6 and move up to the next integer. In general, if the number was between zero and 1 (but never quite getting to 1), the result of multiplying by 6 goes from zero not quite up to 6.

Unfortunately, there's no command in Visual Basic to move up to the next integer. Instead, the Fix function throws away the decimal part of a number. For example:

Fix(3.456) = 3 Fix(-7.9998) = -7 Fix(8) = 8

However, by adding 1 to the result of "fixing" a positive number, you will, in effect, move to the next highest positive integer. For example, look at the following fragment:

```
' A dice simulation using Fix

Randomize
Cls
Die% = Fix(6 * Rnd) + 1
Print "I rolled a"; Die%
```

The key to the fragment is that the number inside the parentheses—6*Rnd—is always between zero and 6, but it can't be 6 because Rnd is never 1. Applying the Fix function gives you an integer between zero and 5 (that is, 0, 1, 2, 3, 4, or 5), and now you only have to add 1 to make it a proper-looking die.

There's another function that works much the same way as Fix: Int. Int gives the *floor* of a number—the first integer that's smaller than or equal to the number. It's usually called the *greatest integer function*. However, thinking of it as the floor function makes it easy to remember what happens for negative numbers. With negative numbers, you move down. For example, Int(-3.5) is -4, Int(-4.1) is -5, and so on. You can see that Fix and Int work the same way for positive numbers but are different for negative ones. Using Int and adding 1 always moves to the next largest integer.

The Int and Fix functions have other uses. For example, the post office charges for first-class mail are 32 cents for the first ounce and 23 cents for each additional ounce (or fraction thereof). Suppose an item weighed 3.4 ounces. Then the cost would be 32 cents for the first ounce and 69 (3*23) for the additional ounces, counting the fraction. The cost is

.32 + Int(3.4)*.23

In general, it's given by the following fragment:

```
If Int(WeightOfObject) = WeightOfObject Then
  Cost = .32 + .23*(WeightOfObject - 1)
Else
  Cost = .32 + .23*(Int(WeightOfObject))
EndIf
```

An Example Using the Random Number Generator

Suppose you wanted to write a "jumble" program. This would take a string and shuffle the letters around. It's a prototype for many other types of operations—for example, shuffling a deck of cards. Here's an outline for one way to do it:

1. Start at the first character.
2. Swap it with a randomly chosen character.
3. Do the same for the second character until there are no more characters left.

The swapping can be done with the Mid statement since you are never changing the size of the string. The screen in Figure 8-2 shows what the form might look like. Suppose the command button is given a control name of btnJumbleIt, the top text box is called txtOriginal, and the destination text box is called txtJumbled. Then the Click procedure looks like this:

```
Private Sub btnJumbleIt_Click ()
  ' a Jumble program demonstrates Mid as a statement
  ' and the Rnd function

  Dim Phrase$, HoldChar$, I As Integer
  Dim LenPhrase As Integer, INum As Integer

  Randomize
  Phrase$ = txtOriginal.Text
```

```
  LenPhrase = Len(Phrase$)
  For I = 1 To LenPhrase
   INum = Int(LenPhrase * Rnd) + 1
   HoldChar$ = Mid(Phrase$, I, 1)
   Mid(Phrase$, I, 1) = Mid(Phrase, INum, 1)
   Mid(Phrase$, INum, 1) = HoldChar$
  Next I
  txtJumbled.Text = Phrase$
End Sub
```

Since values inside the string commands start at 1 and range up to the length of the string, you need to add 1 to Int(LenPhrase*Rnd). Using this value gives you a random position within the string. Once you have the random character, you swap it with the current character in the string, as determined by the counter in the For-Next loop.

Since there is no Swap statement like this,

```
SWAP Mid(Phrase$,INum,1), Mid(Phrase$,I,1)
```

you need to remember both the old and new characters in order to program the interchange.

To make this program into a card shuffler, all you need to do is give Phrase$ the right value. You can do this by using the Chr command. You'll see how to do this in Chapter 9.

Up to this point, all the random integers you've used have started from zero or 1. Sometimes it's convenient to have random integers that span a range. For

Figure 8-2 Form for a Jumble program

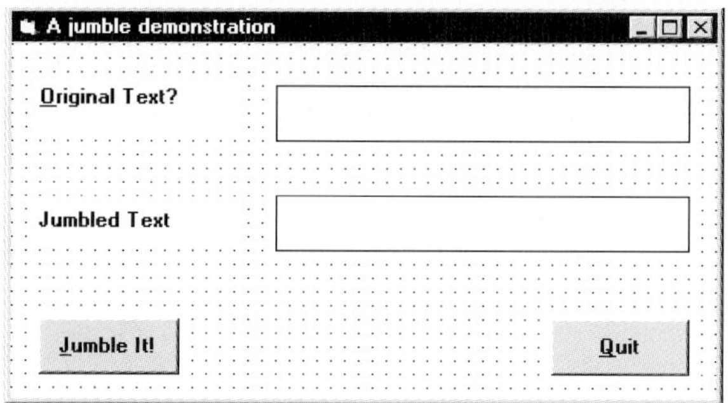

example, take a random four-letter combination; how likely is it to be a word in English? To try this out, you need to generate four random letters and string them together. An obvious way to do this is to apply the Chr$ command to a random integer between 65 and 90 (the range of ASCII codes for the uppercase alphabet). To get a random integer in this range:

1. Generate a random integer between 0 and 25.
2. Add it to 65 to get the ASCII value of a lowercase letter.

Here is a translation of this into code:

```
CharNum = Int(26*Rnd) + 65
```

And here is a fragment that uses this code to continuously generate random four-letter combinations:

```
' Random 4 letter 'words'
' demonstrates Rnd for a range

Dim I As Integer, CharNum As Integer

Randomize
Cls
Do
  Word$ = ""
  For I = 1 To 4
    CharNum = Int(26 * Rnd) + 65
    Word$ = Word$ + Chr$(CharNum)
  Next I
  Print Word$
Loop
```

The key, as explained in the outline for this program given previously, is the statement defining the value of CharNum that gives you a random integer in the correct range. The next statement turns it into a random uppercase letter. As usual, these two statements can be combined into one:

```
Word$ + Chr$(Int(26*Rnd) + 65)
```

However, this code is clearly less readable than the preceding code.

Finally, this fragment creates an infinite loop because no way to end it was programmed. You can use the CTRL+Break combination to end it, but a way more in keeping with the spirit of Visual Basic is to use a Form_Click procedure to start the process and a Form_DblClick procedure or command button to end it (and possibly to use a multiline text box to display the "words").

Bit Twiddling

Bit twiddling refers to looking at the individual bits that make up a number and possibly resetting them if necessary. You need to do this in order to use the KeyUp and KeyDown event procedures that let you detect the non-ASCII coded keys, such as the function and arrow keys. Knowing how the logical operators work on the bit level also makes it easy to program powerful systems for encrypting your data (see Chapter 17). This section builds on the section in Chapter 5 where you saw how binary arithmetic works. (Recall that this was needed to set the background and foreground colors via the Properties box.)

First, Visual Basic has built-in functions to convert a number to a string of hexadecimal (base 16) or octal (base 8) digits. They are

```
Hex ' for hexadecimal
Oct ' for octal
```

Surprisingly, Visual Basic does not have a built-in function for converting a number to binary. There are many ways to write such a program. As usual, it's best to take an example and work through it step-by-step. The easiest examples are, of course, zero and 1, which are the same in decimal and binary. What about 3? This is 11 in binary (1 * 2 + 1). In general, the rightmost (least significant) binary digit is given by checking whether the number is even or odd. The built-in Mod function tells this. For example, the last binary digit is the number Mod 2.

To move to the next binary digit, you have to divide by 2 and throw away the remainder (which you just took into account by using the Mod function). You continue this process until there's nothing left to divide.

As a more serious example, suppose you want to convert the number 43 to binary:

Last binary digit = 43 Mod 2 = 1

Now you divide by 2, using the integer division function (the backslash), and continue the process:

Next binary digit = (43 \ 2) Mod 2 = 21 Mod 2 = 1

And then you continue this process:

Next binary digit = (21 \ 2) Mod 2 = 10 Mod 2 = 0
Next binary digit = (10 \ 2) Mod 2 = 5 Mod 2 = 1
Next binary digit = (5 \ 2) Mod 2 = 2 Mod 2 = 0
Next binary digit = (2 \ 2) Mod 2 = 1 Mod 2 = 1

Since 1 \ 2 is zero, you stop here. Stringing these digits together from bottom to top gives you 101011 (which is 43 in binary).

Here's a program that implements this outline attached to a ConvertTo-Binary_Click event procedure. The program assumes there are two text boxes— Text1 for the number and Text2 for the string of binary digits.

```
Private Sub btnConvertToBinary_Click ()
  Dim Number As Integer
  Dim BinaryForm As String

  Number = Val(Text1.Text)
  BinaryForm = ""
  Do
   Digit = Number Mod 2
     If Digit = 0 Then
       BinaryForm = "0" + BinaryForm
     Else
       BinaryForm = "1" + BinaryForm
     End If
    Number = Number \ 2
  Loop Until Number = 0
  Text2.Text = BinaryForm
End Sub
```

If the number to be converted is zero, you don't want to start the loop. On the other hand, you do want to give the representation of zero in binary, as "0". The real work in this procedure is done in the Else clause. You could use a Select Case statement inside the procedure, but with two options this seems like overkill. Finally, as the example shows, when integer division gives you zero, you stop.

The next section shows you another way to write a binary conversion routine.

Logical Operators at the Bit Level

You may think that Visual Basic's using zero for False makes sense, but why -1 for True? To understand this, you have to know that all the logical operators (Not, And, Or, and so on) are really functions that work on the bit (binary digit) level. Suppose you are given two integers, X and Y. Then X And Y makes a binary digit 1 only if both binary digits are 1; otherwise, it is zero. For example, if

X = 7 in decimal	= 0111 in binary
Y = 12 in decimal	= 1100 in binary

then X And Y = 0100 in binary (4 in decimal) because only in the third position are both bits 1. Because And gives a 1 only if both digits are 1, Anding with a number whose binary digit is a single 1 and whose remaining digits are all zero lets you isolate the binary digits of any integer. For example:

X And 1	Tells you whether the least significant (rightmost) binary digit is on. You get a zero if it is not on.
X And 2	Since 2 in decimal is 10 in binary, a zero tells you that the next significant (second from the right) binary digit is off.
X And 4	Since 4 in decimal is 100 in binary, this tells you whether the next significant (third from the right) binary digit is on.

This process is called *masking* and is the key to using the KeyUp and KeyDown event procedures described in the next section. You can also easily adapt this process to write another binary conversion routine:

```
Private Sub btnConvertToBinary_Click ()
  Dim BitPattern, Number As Integer
  Dim BinaryForm As String

  Number = Val(Text1.Text)
  BinaryForm = ""
  BitPattern = 1
  Do
    Digit = Number And BitPattern
    If Digit = 0 Then
```

```
      BinaryForm = "0" + BinaryForm
    Else
      BinaryForm = "1" + BinaryForm
    End If
    BitPattern = BitPattern * 2     'next bit
  Loop Until BitPattern > Number
  Text2.Text = BinaryForm
End Sub
```

The Or operator, as opposed to the And operator, gives a 1 if either or both of the binary digits is 1. Therefore:

7 Or 12 = 15 (= 0111 Or 1100 = 1111 in binary)

Use Or to make sure specific bits are 1's (the on state). For example, X Or 4 makes sure that the third bit is on, X Or 64, the seventh bit, and so on.

One of the most interesting operators on the bit level is Xor (exclusive Or—X or Y but not both). This gives a 1 in a specific position if exactly one of the bits is on. Here's an example:

7 Xor 12 = 11 (= 0111 Xor 1100 = 1011 in binary)

Xoring has the useful property that Xoring twice with the same number does nothing. For example,

(7 Xor 12) Xor 12 = 11 Xor 12 = 7

or, on the bit level,

0111 Xor 1100 = 1011
1011 Xor 1100 = 0111

That the Xor command brings you back to where you started from if you use it twice, is the key to a popular animation technique. This is because you can restore the previous display exactly as it was before (see Chapter 15). This property of the Xor operator is also the key to a popular method of encrypting information (see Chapter 17).

There are three other logical operators: Imp, Eqv, and Not. X Imp Y gives 1 except when X is 1 and Y is zero. X Eqv Y is 1 only when both bits are the same—both 1 or both zero. The Not operator, on the other hand, works on a number by reversing the bits—a 1 becomes a zero and a zero becomes a 1.

Finally, for those who are curious, here's the answer to the question posed at the beginning of the section as to why -1 is True in Visual Basic. Each integer takes 16 bits. Not 0 is then

Not (0000 0000 0000 0000) = 1111 1111 1111 1111

You might expect this to be the largest integer that can be represented in 16 bits (65,535 in decimal), but Visual Basic uses the leftmost bit for the sign. A 1 there means the number is negative. However, Visual Basic uses what is called *two's-complement notation* for negative numbers. In two's-complement notation, to represent a negative number, you do the following:

1. Apply Not to the 15 bits that represent the number.
2. Set the leftmost bit to 1.
3. Add 1 to the result.

Therefore, for -1, take the bit pattern for 1:

000 0000 0000 0001

Apply Not:

111 1111 1111 1110

Add the leftmost bit as a 1:

1111 1111 1111 1110

Now add 1:

1111 1111 1111 1111

The result is that Not(0) is -1!

For an explanation of why this system really is useful, consult any book on microcomputer architecture.

KeyUp and KeyDown

The KeyPress event reports on which ASCII-coded key a user pressed. The two events described in this section report much lower level information. They will tell exactly what the user did to the keyboard. If you need to determine whether he or she pressed CTRL, a function key, or the like, these are the event procedures to use. For example, if you want your application to supply context-sensitive help when the user presses the F1 key, these are the event procedures to use.

However, these event procedures are a bit more complicated to use because you must distinguish, for example, between lowercase and uppercase letters. The syntax for both of these event procedures is the same:

Private Sub Control_KeyUp(*KeyCode As Integer, Shift As Integer*)
Private Sub Control_KeyDown(*KeyCode As Integer, Shift As Integer*)

Only the control that has the focus can respond to keyboard events. The active form has the focus if no control on the form does, unless you set the KeyPreview property to True. In this case, the form's keyboard events take precedence.

First, you have to use bit masking on the *Shift* parameter to determine whether the SHIFT key, the CTRL key, or the ALT key (or some combination of the three) was pressed. The three constants that you can use are summarized in the following table:

Symbolic Constant	Value	Key
vbShiftMask	1	SHIFT key bit mask
vbCtrlMask	2	CTRL key bit mask
vbAltMask	4	ALT key bit mask

For example:

```
If Shift And vbShiftMask = vbShiftMask Then Print "Shift key pressed"
If Shift And vbCtrlMask = vbCtrlMask Then Print "Ctrl key pressed"
If Shift And VbAltMask = vbAltMask Then Print "Alt key pressed"
```

You can also use the numbers directly, of course:

```
If Shift And 1 = 1 Then Print "Shift key pressed"
```

This means there are eight possibilities. For example, set up a blank form and add the following event procedure:

```
Private Sub Form_KeyDown(KeyCode As Integer, Shift As Integer)
  Select Case Shift
    Case 0
      Print "Neither Ctrl nor Alt nor Shift key pressed"
    Case vbShiftMask
      Print "Only Shift key pressed"
    Case vbCtrlMask
      Print "Only Ctrl key pressed"
    Case 3
      Print "Shift + Ctrl keys pressed"
    Case 4  'or vbShift+Mask + vbCtrl,Mask
      Print "Only Alt key pressed"
    Case 5
      Print "Alt + Shift keys pressed"
    Case 6
      Print "Alt + Ctrl keys pressed"
    Case 7
      Print "Alt, Shift, and Ctrl keys pressed"
  End Select
End Sub
```

(You can simply add the symbolic constants if you wish.)

This procedure assumes that only the first three bits of the *Shift* parameter are used. Since Microsoft reserves the right to use the higher order bits, it may be preferable to start by setting the following

```
LowerThreeBits = Shift And 7        '7 = 0111 in binary
```

and using this new variable in the Select Case statement.

The *KeyCode* integer parameter tells you what physical key was pressed. The code does not distinguish between the key and its shifted sibling. "A" and "a," "1" and "!" have the same codes. The codes for these integers follow the ASCII/ANSII codes only for A-Z and hence a-z and 0-9 on the keyboard. Therefore, ! through all the remaining codes, whether for the arrow keys, the function keys, or the numeric keypad, are given in the library of constants supplied with Visual Basic. (Use the Object Browser to search the Visual Basic library for "Key code constants.")

For example, suppose you want to detect whether a user pressed F1. The code for this turns out to be &H70 and is given by the symbolic constant vbKeyF1. A statement inside a KeyDown event procedure such as

```
If KeyCode = vbKeyF1 Then          'easier the &H70!
   ' perhaps put a msg box with help information here
   ' or show a form until the F1 key was released
   ' check this with KeyUp!
End If
```

is all it takes. (You could use this to start context-sensitive help, for example.)

note: *If the KeyPreview property of the form is set to True, then the form receives the key events before controls on the form receive the event. Set the KeyPreview property to True when you want to create a global keyboard handler. Also, the KeyDown and KeyUp events aren't triggered if someone presses ENTER when the form has a command button control with the Default property set to True, or the ESC key when a form has a command button control with the Cancel property set to True. It is never invoked for the user pressing the TAB key—there is no way strictly within Visual Basic to trap this key.*

Numeric Functions

If you don't do a lot of scientific work, it's unlikely that you will use the information in this section very much. (One surprising use of the numeric functions is to draw curves. Chapter 15 shows you how to do this.)

Sgn( ) The Sgn( ) function gives you a +1 if what is inside the parentheses is positive, -1 if negative, and a zero if it's zero. One non-obvious use of this for integers or long integers is a For-Next loop in this form,

```
For I = A To B Step Sgn(A - B)
```

which, as long as A <> B, runs through the For-Next loop the correct number of times, regardless of whether A is greater than B or not.

Abs( ) The Abs function gives the absolute value of whatever is inside the parentheses. All this function does is remove minus signs:

```
Abs(-1) = 1 = Abs(1)
```

One common use of the absolute value function is Abs(B-A). This gives the distance between the numbers A and B. For example, suppose

```
3 and B = 4
```

Then,

```
Abs(A-B) = Abs(B-A) = 1
```

because 3 and 4 are one unit apart. As another example,

```
Abs(ASC(A$) - ASC(B$))
```

gives the "distance" between the first two characters of the strings A$ and B$.

You often use the Abs function to set up a tolerance test in a Do loop.

Sqr( ) The Sqr function returns the square root of the numeric expression inside the parentheses, which must be non-negative, or a run-time error follows.

Exp( ) The Exp function gives *e* (*e* is roughly 2.7182) to the power *x*, where *e* is the base for natural logarithms. The answer is single precision if *x* is an integer or is itself a single-precision number; otherwise, the answer is a double-precision number.

Log( ) The Log function gives the natural logarithm of a number. To find the common log (log to base 10) use

```
Log10(x)=Log(x)/Log(10)
```

which gives the common logarithm of the value (which must be positive) inside the parentheses. Another way to find the number of digits in a number is to use, for a number greater than 1:

```
Int(Log10(x)) + 1
```

For example, Log10(197) is between 2 and 3 because Log10(100) is 2 and Log10(1000) is 3.

As with the Exp function, the answer is single precision if *x* is an integer or is itself a single-precision number; otherwise, the answer is a double-precision number.

Trig Functions Also for those who need them, Visual Basic has the built-in trigonometric functions Sin (sine), Cos (cosine), and Tan (tangent). The only problem is that Visual Basic expects the angle inside the parentheses following the functions to be in radian measure. To convert from degrees to radians, you need the value of π. The formula is

radians = degrees* π/180

tip: *The easiest way to find the value of π is to set up, early in your program, a form level (or even a global variable—see Chapter 9) PI# using the Atn (arctangent) function in the form:*

*Pi = 4 * Atn(1#)*

This procedure works because the arctangent of 1 is π/4. You can also use the Atn function to find all the other inverse trigonometric functions.

The following table summarizes the inverse trigonometric functions as well as some other useful functions you may want to build from the built-in ones.

Function	Result
pi = 4*Atn(1#)	Value of π in double precision
e = Exp(1#)	Value of e in double precision
Degrees to radians	Radians = degree * π/180
Radians to degrees	Degrees = radians * 180/π
Sec (x)	1/Cos (x)
Csc (x)	1/Sin (x)
Cot (x)	1/Tan (x)
ArcCos (x)	Atn (x/Sqr(-x * x + 1)) + π/2
ArcSin (x)	Atn (x/Sqr(-x * x + 1))
ArcCot (x)	Atn (x) + π/2
Cosh (x)	(Exp(x) + Exp(-x))/2
Sinh (x)	(Exp(x) - Exp(-x))/2
Log $_{10}$(x)	Log(x)/Log(10)
Log $_{a}$(x)	Log(x)/Log(a)

Date and Time Functions

Visual Basic has many built-in functions you can use to read the information contained in the system clock about the time, day, and year. If you combine this with built-in functions for converting dates to numbers, financial calculations become much easier.

note: *All Date functions support named arguments.*

The Date Function

The Date function returns a date of the form month-day-year (mm-dd-yyyy) for the current date. The month and day always use two digits; the year uses four (for example, 01-01-1996 for 1 January 1996). You can also use this function as a statement to reset the current date in the system. The least ambiguous way to do this is by assigning a string to Date in one of the following forms,

```
Date = "mm-dd-yyyy"
Date = "mm/dd/yyyy"
```

where *mm* are numerals between 01 and 12, *dd* are days between 01 and 31, and *yyyy* are years between 100 and 9999.

If you try to reset the date to an illegal date, such as 31 February, you get an "Illegal function call" message box when you run the program. You can also use a two-digit year, but this is not practical for forward-looking programs; Visual Basic assumes you mean 20th-century and not 21st-century dates when there is an ambiguity.

One point to remember: if your computer has a built-in clock calendar, then to permanently reset the clock, you may have to use the setup program that came with the computer. The changes made by Date may remain only until you reboot your computer.

You can also read the time in the system clock or temporarily (see the preceding paragraph) reset it with the Time function. The Time function returns an eight-character date of the form hh:mm:ss. To reset it, assign a string of the correct form to Time, as shown in the following table. The hours range between 00 for midnight and 23 for 11:00 P.M.

Example of Time Command	Effect
Time ="hh"	Sets the hour; minutes, seconds are set to 0
Time ="hh:mm"	Sets the hour, minutes; seconds are set to 0
Time ="hh:mm:ss"	Sets the hour, minutes, seconds

Numeric Calendar Functions

To do financial calculations accurately, your programs must be able to calculate the number of days that have passed between two dates—taking leap years into account, if possible! Visual Basic makes this easy. You simply store the information in two variables of Date type, subtract them, and you're done. (Remember, you surround a date variable with #.)

Sometimes it isn't convenient to use the # notation. When it isn't, Visual Basic supplies the function DateValue(String). This function yields an expression of Date type representing the date defined by the string expression inside the parentheses. Besides accepting strings in the expected form of mm-dd-yyyy, this function can also accept the name of the month or any unambiguous abbreviation for the month. For example, all of the following give the same value to the variable PreMillennium:

```
Dim PreMillennium As Date
PreMillennium = DateValue("12-31-1999")
PreMillennium = DateValue("December 31, 1999")
PreMillennium = DateValue("Dec 31, 1999")
PreMillennium = DateValue("31 December 1999")
PreMillennium = DateValue("31-Dec-1999")
```

You cannot use this function if the date doesn't make sense. For example,

DateValue("2-30-1996")

gives a "Type mismatch" message at run time.

Of course, you will usually need to know what today's date is. For this, Visual Basic has three functions, as summarized in the following table.

Function	Description
Now	Returns the date and time as stored in the system clock
Date	Returns the current date
Time	Returns the current time

For example, suppose you want to write a program that uses these functions to calculate how many days someone has been alive. The form might look like Figure 8-3. It has two text boxes, one label, and a command button named btnCalculate. Let's call the first text button txtBirthDate and the other txtDaysAlive. Set the Text property of both text boxes to be "" and set the Locked property of the second button to True. The code is simply:

```
Private Sub btnCalculate_Click()
Dim BirthDate As Date, CurrentDate As Date
If Not IsDate(txtBirthDate.Text) Then
    MsgBox ("I don't recognize that format, please retry.")
    txtBirthDate = ""
Else
    BirthDate = txtBirthDate
    txtDaysAlive.Text = "You have been alive " & Date - _
BirthDate & " days."
End If

End Sub
```

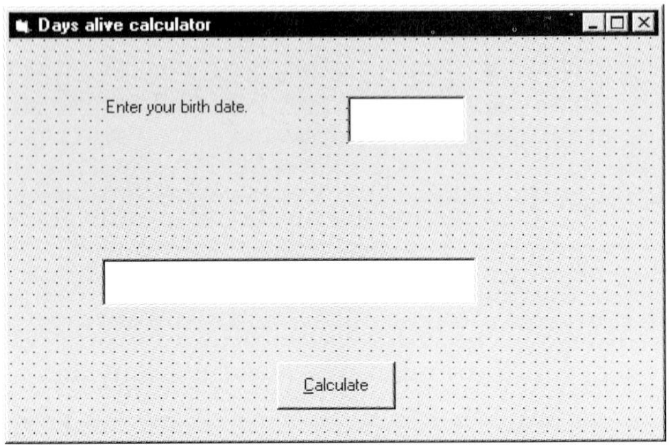

Figure 8-3
Form for days alive program

You will occasionally need the DateSerial function. Its syntax is

DateSerial(*Year*, *Month*, *Day*)

Year is an integer between 0 and 9999 inclusive (or an integral expression that Visual Basic can reduce to this form). *Month* is an integer (or integral expression) with a value between 1 and 12, and *Day* should be some number between 1 and 31 depending on the month. (If you go beyond these limits, Visual Basic wraps into the next month!) For example,

DateSerial(1996,1, 35)

will give you a date in February!

You can apply the Format function to any date expression to display the information contained in the number. For example, if it is now 10:01 P.M. on January 1, 1996, the results are as follows:

Form	Display
Format(Now,"m/d-yy")	1/1/95
Format(Now,"hh:mm")	22:01
Format(Now,"hh:mm AM/PM")	10:01 PM
Format(Now,"hh:mm AM/PM mm/dd/yy")	10:01 PM 01/01/95

There are many other possibilities for format strings for dates. The online documentation is very useful if you need some special form.

OTHER NUMERIC CALENDAR FUNCTIONS

A handful of other functions let you analyze the information contained in a date expression. These are occasionally useful when you need to write applications that work on a day-to-day or even a minute-to-minute basis. The following table lists all the date functions.

Function	Description
Date	Returns the current date (what is shown in the system clock)
DateAdd	Lets you add a specified interval to a date
DateDiff	Lets you subtract a specified interval from a date
DateSerial	Returns a Date corresponding to the specified day, month, and year
DateValue	Takes a string and returns a date
Day	Tells you what day a string or number represents
Hour	Tells you what hour a string or number represents
Minute	Tells you what minute a string or number represents
Month	Tells you what month a string or number represents
Now	Returns the current time and date
Second	Tells you what second a string or number represents
Time	Tells you the current time in the system clock
TimeSerial	Returns a variable of date type for the given time
Weekday	Tells you what day of the week a date corresponds to
Year	Tells you what year a date corresponds to

Financial Functions

Visual Basic comes with a library of financial functions for handling standard calculations that everyone will occasionally need to do. (In fact, some of the financial example programs in Chapters 5 and 7 could have fewer lines of code and run faster if you use these functions.) Source code, however, is not supplied for these functions, which are installed in compiled form as part of the Visual Basic for Applications library.

note: *Since all these functions come from the Visual Basic for Applications library, they all support named arguments.*

Since the terminology in the help files may be obscure to people with no accounting or economics training, this section describes the functions most often used and the terms used in the help files to describe them.

Let's start with the function that will let you do a mortgage calculation. First off, if you look in the help file for financial functions, all you see is a list as follows:

DDB Function
FV Function
IPmt Function
IRR Function
MIRR Function
NPer Function
NPV Function
Pmt Function
PPmt Function
PV Function
Rate Function
SLN Function
SYD Function

None of these seem to have anything to do with a mortgage calculation. It turns out that the function you need is the Pmt function. In the online help it is described as follows:

"Returns the payment for an annuity based on periodic, constant payments and a constant interest rate."

The keyword here (in fact the keyword for most of the financial functions) is "annuity." An *annuity* is a fancy term for a series of payments made over time. For example, when you have a mortgage, you start out with a (large) amount, make (many) payments over time, and end up with a zero balance. (There are also balloon mortgages in which the balance isn't zero.) In the retirement calculator from Chapter 7, you made periodic deposits over time and thereby ended up with a (large) amount of money at the end.

The syntax for the Pmt function is best explained as:

Pmt(*RatePerPeriod*, *NumPeriods*, *WhatYouStartWith*, *WhatYouEndUpWith*, *WhenDoYouPay*)

For example, to calculate a 30-year $100,000 mortgage at 8%, use

```
MortgagePayment = Pmt(.08/12, 30*12, 100000, 0, 1)
```

note: *In all the entries (and the result as well), moneys paid out are represented by negative numbers; moneys received are represented by positive numbers.*

Here's a description of what the parameters in the Pmt function stand for:

- *RatePerPeriod*: Usually the interest rate is quoted per year but you pay every month. This entry needs the interest rate per payment rate. You can ask Visual Basic to do the calculation. So if the yearly rate for the mortgage was 8%, the RatePerPeriod would be .08/12, and you would use this in the first position.
- *NumPeriods*: This is the number of periods. For example, for a 30-year mortgage, this would be 30*12. For a 20-year biweekly mortgage, this would be 20*26.
- *WhatYouStartWith*: In a mortgage, this would start out as the balance. If you were saving money for college, it would be what your initial balance was.
- *WhatYouEndUpWith*: In a mortgage, this would be zero. (In a balloon mortgage, this would be the "balloon payment.") For a savings plan, this would be the amount you wanted to end up with for retirement or college.
- *WhenDoYouPay*: Do you pay at the beginning of the period or at the end? Use a 0 for the end of the month and a 1 for the beginning. (For a $100,000 mortgage at 8%, it costs about $5 more per month to pay at the end of the month. Not that many banks allow you to do this, though.)

note: *In the help files, this function is described as:*

Pmt(*rate, nper, pv*[, *fv*[, *type*]])

Although you need to use these names for the parameters if you use them as named arguments, Microsoft's notation does not stress enough that the units you use for the various entries must be the same. For example, if rate *is calculated using months,* nper *must also be calculated using months.*

Other Financial Functions

Now that you know the key terms and how one of these functions works, here are short descriptions of the other financial functions.

FV This is the function used, for example, for a retirement calculation because it gives you the future value of an annuity based on periodic payments (or withdrawals) and a constant interest rate.

The syntax in the online help is

FV(*rate*, *nper*, *pmt*[, *pv*[, *type*]])

and can be thought of as:

FV(*InterestRatePerPeriod*, *NumPeriods*, *PaymentPerPeriod* [, *StartAmount*[, *WhenDue*]])

Again, the first two arguments must be expressed using the same units. And, as for all financial functions, moneys paid out are given by negative numbers; moneys received are given by positive numbers.

IPmt This gives the interest paid over a given period of an annuity based on periodic, equal payments and a constant interest rate. For example, you could use this to check that your mortgage company's computers are reporting to the IRS the interest paid in a given year.

The syntax (using Microsoft's notation this time) is

IPmt(*rate*, *per*, *nper*, *pv*, *fv*, *due*)

where *rate* is the interest rate per period, and *per* is the period in the range 1 through the number of periods (*nper*). For example, the interest paid in the first month of the third year of a 30-year $100,000 mortgage at 8% is

IPmt(.08/12, 25, 360, 100000, 0, 1)

(So you would use this in a loop to calculate the interest over a given year.)

NPer This function tells you how long (the number of periodic deposits/withdrawals) it will take to accumulate (disburse) an annuity. The syntax is

NPer(*rate*, *pmt*, *pv*, *fv*, *due*)

For example, suppose you are getting 5% on your money and you have $100,000 in the bank. To calculate how long it would take to spend the $100,000 that you have saved if you withdraw the money at a rate of $1,000 a month, use

NPer(.05/12, -1000, 100000, 0, 1)

PV This is the functional equivalent of "a bird in the hand is worth two in the bush." Getting $1,000 ten years from now is not the same as getting $1,000 now. How bad it is depends on the prevailing interest rates. What this function does is tell you how much periodic payments made over the future are worth now. (The technical term for this is *present value*.)

The syntax is

PV(*rate*, *nper*, *pmt*, *fv*, *due*)

The *rate* is, as usual, the interest rate per period, *nper* is the total number of payments made, *pmt* is the number of payments made each period. The *fv* entry is the future value or cash balance you want after you've received (made) the final payment.

For example, if someone agrees to pay you $1,000 a month for ten years and the assumed prevailing interest rate is 6%, then this deal is worth

PV(.06/12, 120, -1000, 0, 1)

to you now. (This is why lotteries can advertise big prizes but pay out relatively little. A $10,000,000 prize paid out over 20 years if the prevailing interest rate is 6% is worth about $6 million.)

NPV This is the net present value function. This function is used, for example, if you start out by paying money as startup costs but then get money in succeeding years. The syntax is

NPV(*RatePerPeriod*, *ArrayOf*( ))

You have to fill the array with the appropriate values in the correct order. For example, the first entry could be a negative number representing startup costs and the remaining entries a positive number representing value received. At least one entry must be positive and one entry must be negative. This function is more general than the PV function because using an array allows the amounts received or disbursed to change over time.

Rate This function gives the interest rate per period for an annuity. You would use this to check on the interest rate you would really be paying if you actually responded to the standard advertising come-on of "Only $49.95 a month for three years will buy you this gadget." (Use the cost today for the *pv* parameter.)

The syntax is

Rate(*nper*, *pmt*, *pv*, *fv*, *due*, *guess*)

The only entry you haven't seen is *guess*. The Rate function uses an iterative procedure to arrive at the true interest rate. You can usually just guess .01 and let Visual Basic do the rest. What happens is, the answer Rate is calculated by iteration. Visual Basic starts with the value of *guess* and repeats the calculation until the result is accurate to within 0.00001%. If, after 20 tries, it can't find a result, the function fails. If the function fails, try a different value for *guess*.

The Remaining Financial Functions

The remaining financial functions are mostly used by business. Explaining them would take us too far afield.

SLN and DDB These functions return the straight line and double declining balance depreciation of an asset over a given period. The syntaxes are

SLN(*Cost*, *SalvageValue*, *LifeExpectancy*)

and

DDB(*Cost*, *SalvageValue*, *LifeExpectancy*, *PeriodOfCalculation*)

IRR, MIRR These give versions of the internal rate of return for a series of payments and receipts. IRR gives the ordinary internal rate of return, and MIRR gives the modified rate in which you allow payments and receipts to have different interest rates. The syntax for the IRR function is

IRR(*valuearray*( ), *guess*)

As with the NPV function, the *valuearray*( ) contains the receipts and disbursements and must contain at least one negative value (a payment) and one positive value (a receipt). Also, as before, the value of *guess* is your best estimate for the value returned by IRR. In most cases, start with a guess of 1% (.01).

The MIRR function has the following syntax:

MIRR(*ValueArray*( ), *FinanceRate*, *ReinvestRate*)

The Most Useful Functions

This chapter ends with some tables that summarize the functions I use most. You can check the online help for more details on them if they are not covered in this chapter. Table 8-1 lists the most common functions, Table 8-2 lists the most common string functions, and Table 8-3 gives you the functions for handling dates and times.

Function	Purpose
Abs	Finds the absolute value of a number
Atn	Finds the arctangent
Cos	Finds the cosine
Exp	Raises e (2.7182...) to the given power
Fix	Returns the integer part of a number
FV	Future value
Hex	Gives the hex equivalent
Int	Finds the greatest integer
Ipmt	Interest paid over time
IRR	Internal rate of return
Log	Common logarithm
MIRR	Modified internal rate of return
Nper	Time to accumulate (disburse) an annuity
NPV	Net present value
Pmt	Pay out for annuity
Ppmt	Returns the principal paid out in an annuity payment
PV	Present value
Rate	Interest rate per period for an annuity
Rnd	Calls the random number generator
Sgn	Returns the sign of a number
Sin	Returns the sine of the number
SLN	Straight line depreciation
Sqr	The square root function
SYD	Sum of years depreciation
Tan	The tangent of an angle in radians
Timer	Returns the number of seconds since midnight

Table 8-1
Common Functions

Function	Description
Asc	Returns the character code corresponding to the first letter in a string
InStr	Returns the position of the first occurrence of one string within another
LCase	Converts a string to lowercase
Left	Finds or removes a specified number of characters from the beginning of a string
Len	Gives the length of a string
LTrim	Removes spaces from the beginning of a string
Mid	Finds or removes characters from a string
Right	Finds or removes a specified number of characters from the end of a string
RTrim	Removes spaces from the end of a string
Str	Returns the string equivalent of a number (the numeral)
StrComp	Another way to do string comparisons
StrConv	Converts a string from one form to another
String	Returns a repeated string of identical characters
Trim	Trims spaces from both the beginning and end of a string
UCase	Converts a string to uppercase

Table 8-2
The Most Common String Functions

Function	Description
Date	Returns the current date (what is shown in the system clock)
DateAdd	Lets you add a specified interval to a date
DateDiff	Lets you subtract a specified interval from a date
DateSerial	Returns a Date corresponding to the specified day, month, and year
DateValue	Takes a string and returns a date
Day	Tells you what day a string or number represents
Hour	Tells you what hour a string or number represents
Minute	Tells you what minute a string or number represents
Month	Tells you what month a string or number represents
Now	Returns the current time and date
Second	Tells you what second a string or number represents
Time	Tells you the current time in the system clock
TimeSerial	Returns a variable of date type for the given time
Weekday	Tells you what day of the week a date corresponds to
Year	Tells you what year a date corresponds to

Table 8-3
Date and Time Functions

Chapter Nine

Building Larger Projects: Projects, Procedures, and Error Trapping

This chapter takes you further along the road to mastering Visual Basic. Once projects become nontrivial, you will no longer want to rely solely on code in event procedures. For this reason, the chapter starts with the techniques needed to create user-defined functions and procedures. Occasionally, you will need to use a function internal to Windows and not part of Visual Basic itself; you'll learn the techniques for this as well. Then it's on to error trapping. These techniques are necessary if you want your program to be able to respond to errors (both internally and externally generated) without just rolling over and dying. The chapter ends by spending a bit more time on the anatomy of a project. For example, you'll see how to add modules for code alone and true global (Public) code to a project. Finally, there's a short discussion of what you need to know to use Visual Basic's compiler more efficiently when you generate stand-alone programs.

User-Defined Functions and Procedures

You've already seen how to use many of Visual Basic's event procedures. Event procedures are the core of Visual Basic programming, but they shouldn't be made too complicated. If an event procedure is much longer than one page—or even one screen length—it may be too long to debug easily. Consider doing some of the work in one or more of Visual Basic's general procedures. There are two kinds of general procedures in Visual Basic. The first type, Function procedures, lets you create new functions, thus extending the built-in Visual Basic functions that you saw in Chapter 8. Sub procedures, on the other hand, are smaller "helper programs" that are used ("called," in the jargon) as needed. Sub and Function procedures help break down large tasks into smaller ones or automate repeated operations.

note: *People generally use the term* subprogram *when they want to refer to both functions and procedures at once.*

Function Procedures

Start thinking about defining your own functions when you use a complicated expression more than once in a project. For example, suppose you need a random integer between 1 and 10. You could write

```
Int((10 * Rnd) + 1)
```

each time you needed it, but this would eventually grow tiresome. Now suppose that the same program needs a random integer between 1 and 40, between 1 and 100, and so on. The statements needed for these are so similar to the preceding statement that you would want to automate the process—that is, to have Visual Basic do some of the work. Suppose you want to attach this function to the current form. To do this, open the Code window by double-clicking anywhere in the form or by pressing F7. Now choose Insert|New Procedure from the Insert menu (ALT I, N), and the Insert Procedure dialog box will pop up, as shown here:

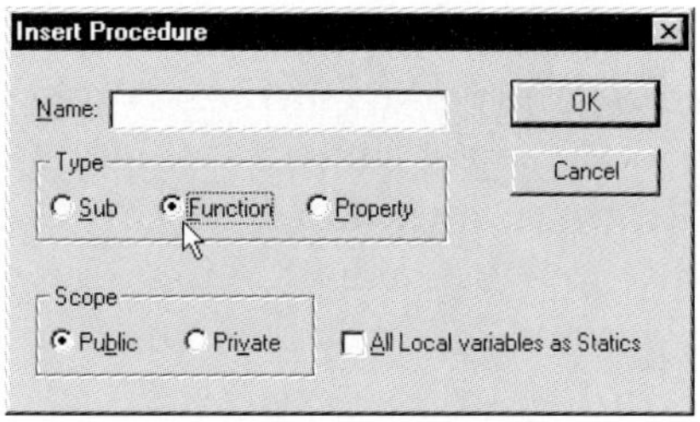

Click the Function radio button (or use the ALT+F shortcut) and type a name. (The example uses RandomRange.) Click on OK, and a function template for the form, shown in Figure 9-1, pops up in the Code window.

tip: *Remember that on top of the vertical scroll bar in the Code window, is the split bar. When you are writing subprograms, being able to look at different parts of your code is very handy. As you drag the split bar with the mouse, the screen splits into two parts. The size of the parts depends on how far you've dragged the mouse. You can then use the direction keys to cycle independently through all the procedures attached to a specific form or module. (Press CTRL+ an arrow key if you are not in full module view.)*

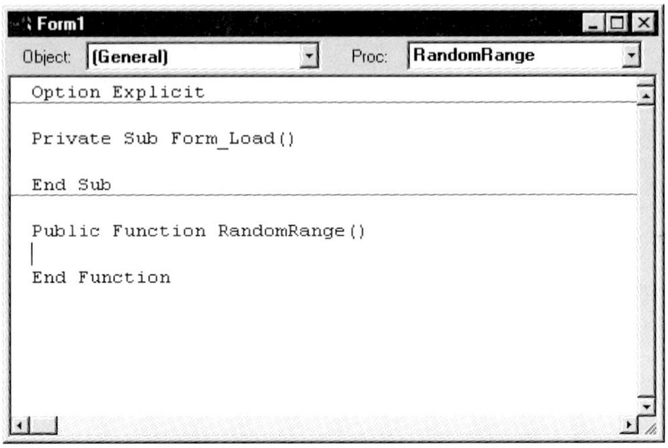

Figure 9-1 Function template in Code window

The whole function will look like this:

```
Private Function RandomRange(X) As Integer
  RandomRange = Int(X * Rnd) + 1
End Function
```

(The code inside the function is sometimes called the *body* of the function.)

Notice that the function template left out the X inside the parentheses—you'll need to enter that as well.

Now you can use RandomRange just like a built-in function in any procedure attached to the current form. If you need to print a random integer between 1 and 10, you can write

```
Print RandomRange(10)
```

When naming the function (in this case, RandomRange), you must follow the same rules as you would for naming variables in Visual Basic. If you prefer, you can add a type identifier at the end of the name of a function or use the As identifier. For example, you could write

```
Function RandomRange% (X)
Function RandomRange (X) As Integer
```

In both cases, Visual Basic knows that the function returns integer values. The key to this function's smooth operation is the X. It's called a *formal parameter*, but it is easiest to think of it as a placeholder. In this case the parameter is a variant variable. You have seen parameters in various Key event procedures, such as KeyUp. To use (or call) this random integer function, you replace the formal parameter (the placeholder) with a numeric expression (a variable, number, or calculation) called an argument of a compatible type. Variant parameters allow you to use any types in your arguments. Visual Basic then replaces all occurrences of the placeholder in the definition of the function with the value of the argument. In particular, Visual Basic does any necessary calculations. Therefore, if

A = 3 and B = 2

then

```
N% = RandomRange(A * B + 37)
```

has the same effect as

```
N% = RandomRange(43)
```

which in turn is the same as writing

```
N% = Int(43 * Rnd) + 1
```

The value you send the function is sometimes called the *actual parameter.*

caution: *You shouldn't expect to get too large a random integer out of the RandomRange function. This is because RandomRange, like any integer expression, can't be larger than 32,767.*

The X used as a parameter (placeholder) in the definition of the function has no independent existence. If you used X as a variable somewhere earlier—even as a global variable—no assignment to its value ever affects the value of the function.

caution: *Be very careful about having a formal parameter on the left side of an assignment statement in the body of the function. Visual Basic defaults to sending the memory location of the actual parameters to the function. This means that any changes you make inside the body of the function to the parameters will affect the original variables. (See the section later in the chapter on "Advanced Uses of Procedures and Functions: Passing by Reference/Passing by Value" for more on this.)*

MORE ON PARAMETERS IN FUNCTIONS

The function RandomRange works with one piece of information; that is, it's a function of one variable (or one argument). You frequently want the value of a function to depend on more than one piece of information. For example, suppose you want a range of random integers between X and Y. You can modify RandomRange as follows:

```
Private Function RandomRangeXToY (X, Y) As Integer
  RandomRangeXToY = Int((Y - X + 1) * Rnd) + X
End Function
```

This may seem a little tricky. If so, try to see what happens with numbers like X = 5 and Y = 37. Multiplying Rnd by Y - X + 1 (33) and using Int gives a range between 0 and 32 (= Y - X). Finally, add X to get the desired range (5 through 37).

If you want to make sure that the function uses only integer values, rewrite it as follows:

```
Private Function RandomRangeXToY (X As Integer, Y As Integer) _
As Integer
  RandomRangeXToY = Int((Y - X + 1) * Rnd) + X
End Function
```

Now the placeholders can only have integer values. For example, if you try to use an argument that is a single precision variable in this example, you will get an error message. If you set

```
Number% = RandomRangeXToY (2.7, 39.2)
```

then 2.7 is rounded up to 3 and 39.2 is rounded down to 39 when Visual Basic substitutes their values into the function definition. If you wrote

```
Number% = RandomRangeXToY(3, 300000)
```

you'd get an overflow error.

AN EXAMPLE

The following program calculates the cost of mailing a letter (notice the parameter is of the single type):

```
Private Function Postage% (Weight As Single)
  'Calculate the cost, in cents, of mailing
  'a first-class letter of a given weight in ounces

  Postage% = 32 - 23 * (Int(-Weight) + 1)
End Function
```

(A trick is used here to take into account the fact that if a letter weighs, for example, 3.25 ounces, you have to pay for 4 ounces. This means that in situations like this, you must move to the next largest integer. Now imagine that you apply the Int function to -3.25. The result is -4. So you need to flip the sign again to make it positive. This trick is the basis of the previous program.)

Now, executing

```
Private Sub Form_Click ()
  'local variables:
  Dim WeightOfLetter As Single

  WeightOfLetter = Val(InputBox("Enter the weight in ounces:"))
  Print "The cost is"; Postage%(WeightOfLetter); "cents."
End Sub
```

and responding to the input prompt by entering 4.7 will produce this output:

The cost is 124 cents.

(or you could use the Format function of course.)

To make the program robust, you must check the information you send to a function before you call the function. Otherwise, you risk a meaningless result. With the Postage function, you need to check whether the weight is a positive number. The following fragment does this:

```
If WeightOfLetter > 0 Then
  Print Postage%(WeightOfLetter)
```

```
Else
  Beep
  MsgBox "A letter must have positive weight."
End If
```

Advanced Uses of Functions

Since the name of a function follows the same rules as the names of variables, choose meaningful function names; they will certainly make your program more readable as well as easier to debug. Keep in mind that unless you give it an explicit type identifier, the type of the function defaults to the Variant data type (or to whatever DefType statement is currently in effect).

The general form of a Function definition is as follows,

(Public/Private) Function *FunctionName* (*parameter1*, *parameter2*, ...)
 statements
 FunctionName = *expression*
End Function

where *parameter1*, *parameter2*, and so on, are variables. These variables are referred to as the parameters of the function. The types of the parameters can be specified by type-declaration tags or with phrases of the form As type; otherwise they default to be variants.

Finally, if a function is declared to be Private, it can only be seen by the code in the form to which it is attached. If declared to be Public, other parts of your project can call it by using the form's name and the name of the function. For example, Form1.Test("it") would call a public function named Test attached to Form1 from any part of your project.

If FunctionName (*argument1*, *argument2*, ...) appears in a Visual Basic statement, then the value of argument1 is assigned to parameter1, the value of argument2 is assigned to parameter2, and so on if the types are compatible; otherwise an error results. After this, Visual Basic executes the statements in the function definition; the last value assigned to FunctionName inside the body of the function definition is the one used for the statement involving the FunctionName (argument1, argument2, ...). The argument entries argument1, argument2, and so on, can be either constants, variables, or expressions.

A Visual Basic statement using (some people say accessing) a function is said to *call* the function and to *pass* the arguments to the parameters. The function is said to return its value. For instance, in the example in the previous section, the statement

```
Print "The cost is"; Postage(WeightOfLetter); "cents."
```

calls the function Postage and passes the argument WeightOfLetter to the parameter Weight. The function returns the value 121. You can even have a statement like this one,

```
Print "The cost is"; Postage(Weight); "cents."
```

only this time, Visual Basic looks for the variable named Weight and substitutes it for the parameter Weight. (Remember, parameters are placeholders—they have no real existence outside of that role.)

The type of value returned by the function is specified with a type-declaration tag (%, !, &, #, or $) appended to the function name, an As clause at the end of the Function line, or a DefType statement appearing above the Function definition.

---

note: *In Visual Basic 4 (unlike earlier versions of Visual Basic), lines in your programs can simply use a form such as:*

FunctionName *(arg1, arg2, arg3)*

but this ("C" style function calling) is unusual. What would happen is that the statements inside the function would be executed, but no value would be returned—only the side-effects caused by the function would occur. Generally speaking, most Visual Basic programmers prefer to make the call to a function part of an expression or statement. (It is most often placed in an assignment statement.)

You can only call a function when you use the same number of arguments as there are parameters in the function definition. Each variable argument can have the same name or a different name than its corresponding parameter, but must be of the same type (integer, long integer, and so on). If an argument is not a variable, its value must be of a type that can be converted to that of its corresponding parameter. For instance, an integer variable argument can be passed to an integer parameter, but not to a long integer parameter. However, an integer constant can be passed to a long integer parameter.

Nothing prevents a function from calling another function. You'll find yourself doing this frequently in order to increase the power of your Function procedures. Visual Basic allows you to call as many functions as you want from within a given function, but you can't nest function definitions. Only one function can be defined at any one time. However, functions can call themselves. This is called *recursion*; the subject is so fascinating and useful that Chapter 19 is devoted to it.

At this point, your functions in Visual Basic are manipulating the values of variables assigned to parameters; they haven't changed the values. (You have made no assignments to parameters within the body of the example functions.) As you saw in the KeyPress event, it's possible to change the values of variables assigned to parameters. This is because by default, as mentioned earlier, Visual Basic passes the memory locations for the variables assigned to parameters to the function. This lets Visual Basic make changes to the values of the variables. (See the section "Advanced Uses of Procedures and Functions: Passing by Reference/Passing by Value" later in this chapter for more on the subject.) In practice, however, you should rarely have to change the value of a parameter in a Function procedure. Generally, a function should simply manipulate existing values and return a new value.

As in event procedures, you can set up your own local variables inside Function procedures and have them be static or not, depending on the application. You can make all the variables in a Function procedure static by putting the keyword Static before the name of the function,

(Public/Private) Static *FunctionName* (*parameter list*)

or by using the Static button on the Insert Procedure dialog box.

Form-level variables are visible to all the functions attached to that module or form. The purpose of using local variables is to avoid inadvertent side effects. A side effect means that something done in the procedure affects the rest of the program. If you use the Cls method in a function attached to a form, then every time the function is used, the form will clear; this is an obvious side effect. Anytime you change the value of a parameter or a global, module, or form-level variable, you cause side effects.

There's certainly nothing wrong with controlled side effects. The key, though, is the word "controlled." You must know exactly when they're going to happen and what the fallout will be for the rest of the project.

LEAVING FUNCTIONS PREMATURELY

You don't have to give every function an explicit value. Sometimes you are forced to exit a function prematurely:

```
Private Function BailOut (X) As Single
  If X < 0 Then
   Exit Function
  Else
.
.
  End If
End Function
```

This function bails out if a negative value is sent to it. Now calling the function with a negative value gives the function the value 0—the default value of any numeric variable. A string function that you bail out of returns the null string "" as its value.

You should rarely find yourself needing the Exit Function statement, and you probably wouldn't use it as in the preceding example. Check out the information you want to send to a function before you call the function (possibly by another function). You should only use the Exit Function statement if it makes the program clearer, or in emergencies. For example, some people may rewrite the FindSeparator function from Chapter 8 using an Exit Function because they feel it makes the program easier to follow.

SOME EXAMPLE STRING FUNCTIONS

Suppose you want to write a function that would allow you to chop out any substring. You saw how to do this in Chapter 8; you use Instr to find out where the string is and then use Right, Left, and Mid to do the cutting. Here's the public function:

```
Public Function CutSmall$ (Big$, Small$)
  'local variables
  Dim Place As Integer, Length As Integer

  Place = Instr(Big$, Small$)
  Length = Len(Small$)
  If Place = 0 Then
    CutSmall$ = Big$
  Else
    CutSmall$ = Left(Big$, Place-1)+Mid(Big$, Place+Length)
  End If
End Function
```

The local variables Place and Length defined here will have no effect on any other variable named Place or Length that might occur elsewhere within the program. Once you've finished defining a function, you can also use the Immediate window to test it if the form (module) to which it is attached is active, or since it is a public function by using the name of the form and then a dot followed by the function name.

As another example, suppose you want to write a function that counts the number of times a character appears in a string. This would be a function of two string variables, and it should return an integer. Let's call it CharCount%:

```
Public Function CharCount% (X$, Y$)
  'This public function counts the number of times
  'the character Y$ is inside the string X$
  'If Y$ is not a character or Y$ does not occur in
  'X$ then this function returns zero
  'local variables: I, Count

  Dim Count As Integer, I As Integer

  Count = 0
  For I = 1 To Len(X$)
    If Mid(X$, I%, 1) = Y$ Then Count = Count + 1
  Next I
  CharCount% = Count
End Function
```

First, notice the extended remark section. In defining a complicated function, it's best to explain what's supposed to happen; explain what kind of information the function expects to deal with, which local variables it uses, and what it is supposed to send out. (If users know what the function expects, they're more likely to check what they send it before the program blows up.) Most of the example programs in this book have, up to this point, been sparsely commented, mostly because the surrounding text explained them. However, when you are hired to write a program, this is the way you would be expected to comment on it. In fact, you might explain what the local variables are doing as well.

The CharCount% function uses two local integer variables: Count and I. As you've seen, it's good programming practice to Dim the local variables before going on to the main business of the function. Being local variables, they have no connection with any variables that might share the same name elsewhere in the program. The advantages this gives over the older Def FN in interpreted BASICs can't be stressed enough. (A complicated string-handling program might have 17 different functions with 17 different variables named I or Count, and you wouldn't want their values contaminating each other.)

Next, notice that the function initializes the Count variable to 0. This is done for the same reason that you would initialize a variable in the main part of a program: relying on default values is sloppy and occasionally dangerous unless you make it clear by a Remark statement that you are doing so deliberately.

The For-Next loop runs through the string character-by-character, checking for a match and adding 1 to the value of the Count variable if it finds one. Finally, the value of the local variable Count is what this function will return. In this case, the body of the function ends with the assignment that defines the function. Using a variable such as Count to accumulate information as a function works is quite common. When you're done, you use the "accumulator" that determines the value of the function in the final assignment.

As another example, let's return to the "find the next word" program from Chapter 8. Suppose you want to modify this program so it gives the next word, no matter what separator you use. Using a user-defined function makes this easy. All you have to do is replace the statement

```
AfterSpace = Instr(BeforeSpace+1, Phrase$, Separate$)
```

with a function that finds the next separator.

Before you look at an outline for this function, think about the information this function needs to massage (manipulate). Is it clear that it will work much like Instr except that the separators will be built into the function? Once you convince yourself of this, you will be able to understand the following outline for the function:

- The function works with a string and a position number.
- The function should search starting at the position after the position number and look character-by-character until it finds a separator.
- If successful, the function should return its position number.
- If not successful, the function should return 0.

Here's a function definition that follows this outline:

```
Public Function FindSeparator% (Phrase$, Position%)
  'local variables
  Dim Afterspace%, Answer%, LenString%, NxtChar$
```

```
  AfterSpace% = Position% + 1
  Answer% = 0
  LenString% = Len(Phrase$)
  Do Until (Answer% < > 0) Or (AfterSpace% > LenString%)
    NxtChar$ = Mid(Phrase$, AfterSpace%, 1)
    Select Case NxtChar$
      Case Chr(32), "!", "?", ".", ";", ":", ","
        Answer% = AfterSpace%
      Case Else
        AfterSpace% = AfterSpace% + 1
    End Select
  Loop
  FindSeparator% = Answer%
End Function
```

This function starts by looking from one position farther along in the string than the position passed as a parameter. This takes into account any previous uses of the function.

The local variable Answer% plays a key role in what follows. As Visual Basic moves through the loop, this variable accumulates information either by staying equal to zero (in which case no separator was found) or becoming positive (the value is the location of the separator).

The Do loop has to stop if either the accumulator (the value of Answer%) signals that the hunt was successful or there's no place else to look (the loop has finished searching all the characters in the string). Notice that instead of using a Do loop with two conditions (a Eureka loop, if you recall from Chapter 7), you could have used multiple Exit Loop commands.

note: *The function could have put all the tests on more than one line. However, by putting the tests on the same line, you speed up the program. For example, if you used three lines, the program would look a little cleaner, but if the separator were a comma, you would be asking Visual Basic to process three lines of code instead of one.*

Using a Select Case statement makes it easy to add another separator to this function; you need only add the appropriate case to the function. In any case, if the character isn't a separator, you move on to the next character.

Finally, the value of the accumulator variable Answer% will be 0 if no separator is found; otherwise, it will be the position of the separator. (You also could have written this as a function of three variables, much like Instr itself.)

Figure 9-2
Form for More Words program

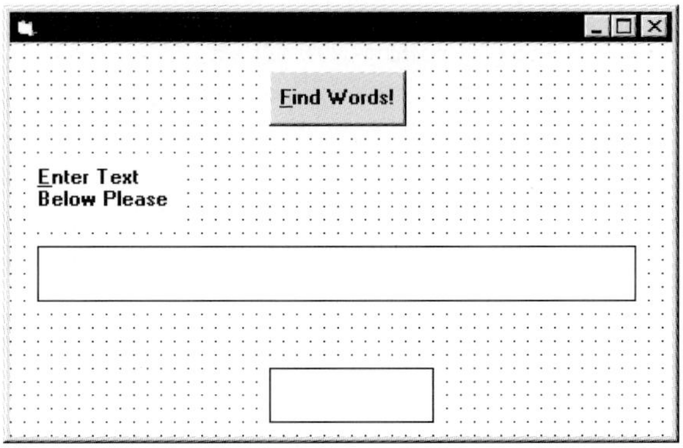

PARSING TEXT

Next, suppose you want to examine the contents of a text box and print out the words one-by-one in a second text box in response to each click on a command button. The screen might look like the one in Figure 9-2. You want each click to print the next word. Supposing the command button is called FindWords, here's how the whole program might go. (Notice that this uses the FindSeparator function from the last section.)

```
Private Sub FindWords_Click ()
  'This event program uses the function FindSeparator
  ' to parse a phrase by searching for the separators
  ' . , : ? ; ! and the space it finds all words
  'contained in the phrase

  ' local variables
   Static BeforeSpace%, AfterSpace%
   Dim Phrase$, LenPhrase%, SizeOfWord%

  Phrase$ = Text1.Text
  LenPhrase% = Len(Phrase$)
  AfterSpace% = FindSeparator%(Phrase$, BeforeSpace%)
  SizeOfWord% = AfterSpace% - BeforeSpace% - 1
  Do Until (SizeOfWord% > 0) Or (AfterSpace% = 0)
    BeforeSpace% = AfterSpace%
```

```
    AfterSpace% = FindSeparator%(Phrase$, BeforeSpace%)
    SizeOfWord% = AfterSpace% - BeforeSpace% - 1
  Loop
  If SizeOfWord% > 0 Then
    NextWord$ = Mid(Phrase$, BeforeSpace% + 1, SizeOfWord%)
    BeforeSpace% = AfterSpace%
    Text2.Text = NextWord$
  Else
    Text2.Text = Mid(Phrase$, BeforeSpace% + 1)
    MsgBox "No more words!"
    Text1.Text = ""
    BeforeSpace% = 0
  End If
End Sub
```

First, notice that the variables BeforeSpace% and AfterSpace% are static variables in order to preserve the information between clicks. If AfterSpace% = 0, then you've finished the text and won't enter the Do loop at all. If SizeOfWord% is also 0, then this small loop eliminates multiple spaces—another example of a Eureka loop.

The If clause changes the value of the static variables in preparation for the next function call and displays the word found in the second text box. The Else clause gives the last word and then a message box. Once the user clears the message box, the last line clears out the original text.

EXAMPLE: A PIG LATIN GENERATOR

This section shows you how to write a "pig latin converter" that demonstrates many of the techniques you've learned so far. Pig latin is a well-known variant on English that children often use: Ancay ouyay understandway isthay?

The rules are simple:

- All one-letter words stay the same.
- Words beginning with vowels get the suffix "way."
- Words beginning with a string of consonants have the consonants shifted to the end and the suffix "ay" added.
- Any *q* moved because of the preceding rule carries its *u* along with it.
- *Y* is a consonant.
- There are no more rules.

Here is an outline for a pig latin converter in its simplest form:

While there are still words
"pig latinize" the next word

To "pig latinize" a word, follow the rules just given. You will need two text boxes (Source and Translation) and a command button (with the control name Translate) to start the process:

```
' A pig latin generator
' This program translates a phrase into
' pig latin. It modifies the 'find word'
' program by adding a 'latinize' function
' Phrase$ is a form-level variable

Private Sub Translate_Click()

  Dim BeforeSpace As Integer, AfterSpace As Integer
  Dim SizeOfWord As Integer
  Dim NextWord$, PigWord$, FinalWord$, T$

  Phrase$ = Source.Text
  If Len(Phrase$) = 0 Then Exit Sub
  BeforeSpace = 0
  AfterSpace = FindSeparator (Phrase$, BeforeSpace)
  Do Until AfterSpace = 0
    SizeOfWord = AfterSpace - BeforeSpace - 1
    NextWord$ = Mid(Phrase$, BeforeSpace + 1, SizeOfWord)
    If SizeOfWord > 0 Then
      PigWord$ = Latinfy$(NextWord$)
      T$ = T$ + PigWord$ + Space$(1)
    End If
    BeforeSpace = AfterSpace
    AfterSpace = FindSeparator(Phrase$, BeforeSpace)
  Loop
  FinalWord$ = Mid(Phrase$, BeforeSpace + 1)
  PigWord$ = Latinfy(FinalWord$)
  Translation.Text = T$ + PigWord$ + Space$(1)
End Sub

Private Function FindSeparator (Phrase$, Position% ) As Integer
  ' local variables are:
  Dim AfterSpace As Integer, Answer As Integer
```

```
  Dim LenString As Integer, NxtChar$

  AfterSpace  = Position  + 1
  Answer  = 0
  LenString  = Len(Phrase$)
  Do Until (Answer <> 0) Or (AfterSpace  > LenString)
    NxtChar$ = Mid(Phrase$, AfterSpace, 1)
    Select Case NxtChar$
       Case Chr(32), "!", "?", ".", ";", ":", ","
         Answer  = AfterSpace
       Case Else
         AfterSpace = AfterSpace  + 1
     End Select
  Loop
  FindSeparator  = Answer
End Function

Private Function Latinfy$ (A$)
  Dim FirstChar$
  If Len(A$) = 1 Then
    Latinfy$ = A$
  Else
    FirstChar$ = UCase$(Left(A$, 1))
    Select Case FirstChar$
      Case "A", "E", "I", "O", "U"
        Latinfy$ = A$ + "way"
      Case Is < "A"
        Latinfy$ = A$
      Case Is > "Z"
        Latinfy$ = A$
      Case Else
        Latinfy$ = ShiftCons$(A$) + "ay"
    End Select
  End If
End Function

Private Function ShiftCons$ (A$)
  ' local variables
  Dim Count As Integer, Done As Integer
  Dim NextChar As String

  Count = 1
  Done = False
  Do
```

```
    NextChar = UCase$(Mid(A$, Count, 1))
    Select Case NextChar
      Case "A", "E", "I", "O", "U"
        Done = True
      Case "Q"
        Count = Count + 2
      Case Else
        Count = Count + 1
    End Select
  Loop Until Done
  ShiftCons$ = Mid(A$, Count) + Left(A$, Count - 1)
End Function
```

As mentioned earlier, all you have to do is change the "find the next word" program to one that, instead of printing the next word, prints the converted form. (Along the way, this function strips out all punctuation and spaces. It is left to you to change the program so that the converted phrase retains the original punctuation.)

The Latinfy function starts out by dealing with the special case of one-letter words and follows the first rule: it does nothing to them. The first case in the Select Case deals with vowels: words with a leading vowel add "way." The next case makes sure numbers and other special characters are not transformed. The Else case calls the most complicated function—the one that shifts consonants to the end.

The ShiftCons$ function works by using a flag to detect when, moving letter-by-letter, Visual Basic finally hits a vowel. By adding 2 to the count, you carry the *u* along with the *q* for this special case. The trick is that by starting with the count equal to 1 and incrementing the count every time a consonant shows up, Left(A$, Count - 1) must, when the loop ends, contain the leading consonants.

This program is a good demonstration of how longer programs can be built from "building blocks." You'll see more about this later in the chapter under the section "Some General Words on Program Design."

Sub Procedures

Function procedures can be made to do almost anything, provided that what you want to do is get an answer—a value—out of them. As mentioned before, although functions can change properties of a form or affect the value of the variables or form-level variables or even the variables passed to them, it's not a good idea to do so unless the change is somehow related to what the function is designed to do. In any case, a function takes raw data, massages it, and then returns a single value. For example, although you can write a function that will walk through a list and return the smallest or the largest value, it can't return both. A function would not usually be used to return a sorted list. (You'll see many ways to sort lists in Chapters 11 and 19.)

You tell Visual Basic you want to define a Sub procedure in much the same way you would with a Function procedure: use Insert | New Procedure, only this time, click the Sub option button.

Suppose, for example, you want to print a song—one with many verses but only a single chorus. The outline is clear:

```
While there are verses left
— —    print verse
— —    print chorus
Loop
```

Unless you wrote a truly bizarre function, you could not easily translate this outline into Visual Basic by using a function. You would need to include many statements of the form,

```
X = Chorus ()
```

or

```
Chorus ()  'in Visual Basic 4
```

even though the Chorus function would not have any value to return. Unless you want to repeatedly type useless statements or place the entire chorus in an event procedure, you'll need a new structure: the Sub procedure.

The structure of the simplest kind of Sub procedure—although one powerful enough to translate the outline—looks like this:

```
Sub Chorus( )
— —  'many print statements
End Sub
```

The first line has the Public or Private keywords followed by the word Sub followed by the procedure's name. A procedure name must follow the rules for variable names. Next comes the parameter list, enclosed in parentheses, for the information the function will use. In this case, the Sub procedure uses no parameters. Even if your procedure uses no parameters, you must have the parentheses. After the parameter list comes the statements that make up the procedure. Finally, there are the keywords End Sub, which, as you've seen, end all event procedures; they are used to indicate the end of general procedures as well. As with Function procedures, if you need to exit the Sub procedure prematurely, you can use the Exit Sub command in the body of the procedure as often as necessary.

If you imagine an event procedure as one of the main verses and the Sub and Function procedures as the choruses, then thinking of a program as a song with many choruses would be a good metaphor for designing any program, except that it misses one key point: each time you need the procedure, it's likely to be in a different situation. The procedure must change to meet new requirements. You need a way to transfer information between the main program and the procedure. You do this in much the same way as you did for functions: by using the parameter list. This parameter list is used to communicate between the main program and the procedure. When you call the procedure, you use the name of the function followed by the arguments (parameters), separated by commas if there is more than one:

```
NameOfProcedure argument1, argument2,...
```

You can also use the QuickBASIC version:

```
Call NameOfProcedure(Argument1, Argument2,...)
```

When you use the Call keyword, you must use parentheses around the argument list; when you omit the Call keyword, you must omit the parentheses.

note: *Only public procedures can be called from outside their forms.*

tip: *Remember, you can also call an event procedure directly in this way. For example, the line Command1_Click calls the Click event procedure for the button named Command1 on the current form. Form1.Command1_Click would do it for the Command1 button on the form named Form1 if you changed Private to Public in the event procedure for Form1.Command1_Click.*

For example, suppose you want to print the old song "A Hundred Bottles of Beer on the Wall" on a blank form in response to a click. It begins this way,

100 bottles of beer on the wall,
100 bottles of beer,
If one of those bottles should happen to fall,
99 bottles of beer on the wall.

99 bottles of beer on the wall,
99 bottles of beer,
If one of those bottles should happen to fall,
98 bottles of beer on the wall.

98 bottles of beer on the wall,
98 bottles of beer,
If one of those bottles should happen to fall,
97 bottles of beer on the wall.

and so on.

Here's what you can write in the event procedure:

```
Private Sub Form_Click()
  Dim I As Integer

  For I = 100 To 1 Step -1
    Chorus I
  Next I
  Print "There are no more bottles of beer on the wall."
End Sub
```

The chorus Sub procedure looks like this:

```
Private Sub Chorus (X As Integer)
  Print X; " bottles of beer on the wall,"
  Print X; " bottles of beer,"
  Print "If one of those bottles should happen to fall,"
  Print (X - 1); " bottles of beer on the wall."
  Print
End Sub
```

On each pass through the loop, the current value of the variable I is sent to the procedure, where it replaces the formal parameter X. The I is also called the actual parameter, as was the case for functions. Also, just as with functions, the names you choose for your formal parameters are irrelevant; they just serve as placeholders. Finally, note that you do not use a type identifier for a Sub procedure.

note: *In practice, you would use a multiline text box for printing so much information on a form. If you rewrite it this way, remember that it is faster to build up the string first than to make assignments to a property repeatedly.*

You may be thinking that this particular example seems a little forced; it's easy to rewrite the program using a For-Next loop. Of course this is true, but writing the program using a Sub procedure changes the emphasis a little; it's a lot closer to the outline. Now think about a more complicated program. Imagine a For-Next loop that surrounds 50 lines of code. In this situation, it's too easy to forget what the loop is doing. Most programmers prefer loops to be "digestible"—the whole loop ideally should not be more than a single screen of code.

Notice how in this program most of the nitty-gritty details have been pushed under the rug. This is quite common when you use procedures. Your event procedures will often have a fairly clean look, containing directions and repeated procedure and function calls. (In fact, some people would even put the directions into procedure calls and so make an event procedure into one long sequence of procedure and function calls. This too is a matter of taste.) In any case, it's unlikely that any event procedure will need to be very long.

In general, a Sub procedure is a part of a program that performs one or more related tasks, has its own name, is written as a separate part of the program, and is accessed by using its name followed by the correct number of parameters separated by commas.

A procedure must have the form

(Public/Private) Sub *SubprocedureName(parameter1, parameter2, ...)*
 statement(s)
End Sub

When Visual Basic executes statements of the form

SubprocedureName argument1, argument2,...
Call *SubprocedureName* (*argument1*, *argument2*, ...)

the values (actually the memory locations) of the arguments are passed to the corresponding parameters, and the statements inside the Sub procedure are executed. (Again, these are usually called the body of the procedure.) When the End Sub statement is reached, execution continues with the line following the call to the Sub procedure. As with Function procedures, you must use the same number of arguments as parameters and they must be of compatible types.

Using the Call keyword, the song program would look like this:

```
Private Sub Form_Click()
  Dim I As Integer

  For I = 100 To 1 Step -1
    Call Chorus(I)
  Next I
  Print "There are no more bottles of beer on the wall."
End Sub
```

QuickBASIC users should note that the DECLARE housekeeping statement is not normally used in Visual Basic and will usually not be accepted. The only time you need a version of the DECLARE statement is when you use Windows' Application Programming Interface (API) functions within a Visual Basic program. (See "Accessing Windows Functions" later in this chapter and Appendix B and C for more on these functions.)

note: *If you delete a control from a form, then any event procedures you may have written for that control become general Sub procedures for that form, using the same procedure names as before. For example, suppose you had a command button with a control name of Command1 and have written a Command1_Click procedure for it. Now you delete the command button from the form. The general procedure part of your form will now have a procedure called Command1_Click. This will also happen if you change the name of the control.*

USING THE OBJECT BROWSER TO NAVIGATE AMONG SUBPROGRAMS

As your programs become more complicated, navigating among the procedures and functions in it will become more complicated as well. The easiest way to navigate among the code in your project is with the Object Browser. For example, Figure 9-3 shows the Object Browser for the sample Calculator project. Notice that all the subprograms for this project are listed in the right (Methods/Properties) column. Sub procedures are listed with a [Sub] after them, Function procedures are listed with a [Function] after them. To quickly go to the code for a specific function or procedure, all you have to do is double-click at the appropriate line in the Methods/Properties column.

In general, follow these steps:

1. Bring up the Object Browser.
2. Choose your project from the Libraries/Projects list box.
3. Choose the form or module whose code you want to inspect from the Classes/Modules list box.
4. Double-click on the name of the subprogram whose code you want to work with.

Figure 9-3 Object Browser for the Calculator project

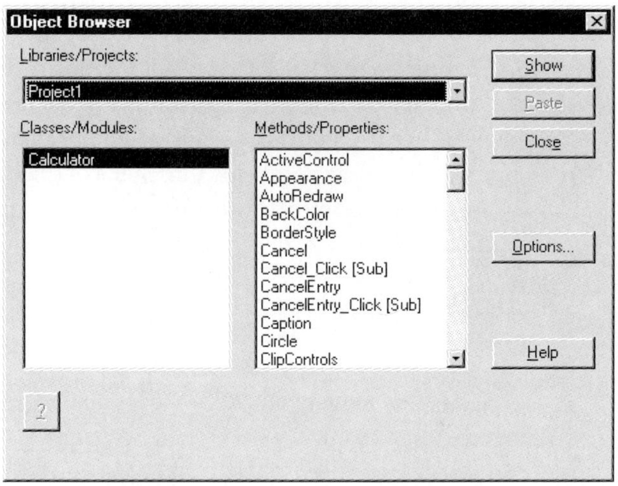

SOME SIMPLE BUT USEFUL PROCEDURES

A sophisticated program may need to beep at the user to give feedback—more beeps may indicate more feedback. Having a general procedure called ManyBeeps in a program is quite common:

```
Public Sub ManyBeeps (X As Integer)
  Dim I As Integer

  For I = 1 To X
    Beep
  Next I
End Sub
```

Since I is dimensioned inside the procedure, it is a local variable. Now you can write

```
ManyBeeps 10
Call ManyBeeps(10)
```

for ten beeps and

```
ManyBeeps 100
Call ManyBeeps(100)
```

for overkill.

Visual Basic lets you set up an event procedure that triggers itself after a set period of time has gone by (the Timer event is discussed in Chapter 12). You may need to write a timer loop inside a procedure that stops processing for a fixed length of time. This is occasionally a useful debugging tool to use, rather than putting in a breakpoint (see Chapter 14) that stops the program in its tracks. To set up a timer loop to waste a fixed number of seconds in a Sub procedure, call the following:

```
Private Sub WasteTime(X As Single)
  Dim StartTime As Single

  StartTime = Timer
  Do Until (Timer - StartTime) > X
  Loop
End Sub
```

(Please see the section "The DoEvents Function" later in this chapter for more on this type of procedure.)

Since the Timer function returns only the number of seconds since midnight, this procedure will run into problems near midnight. One way around this is to use the DateValue function. Another way is to use the Mod function and the fact that there are 86,400 seconds in a day. Just change the Do statement in the preceding code to:

```
Do Until (Timer - StartTime + 86400) Mod 86400 > X
```

To see that this works, assume that it is 2 seconds before midnight and that X is 3. StartTime will be 86398. Consider for now just the whole-number values that Timer will be taking on: 86399, 0 (midnight), 1, 2, and so on. For these values, the expression involving Mod will be as follows:

```
(86399 - 86398 + 86400) Mod 86400 = 86401 Mod 86400 = 1;

    (0 - 86398 + 86400) Mod 86400 =     2 Mod 86400 = 2;

    (1 - 86398 + 86400) Mod 86400 =     3 Mod 86400 = 3;

    (2 - 86398 + 86400) Mod 86400 =     4 Mod 86400 = 4;
```

You can see from this that the expression involving Mod will equal X (3) after 3 seconds and exceed X after 3 seconds, thus ending the loop.

tip: *If you need to have a discernible time between beeps, place a short time interval between them with the Beep statement in the ManyBeeps procedure. You can do this by combining the ManyBeeps procedure with a call to the preceding WasteTime procedure.*

Advanced Uses of Procedures and Functions: Passing by Reference/Passing by Value

There are two ways to pass a variable argument to a procedure: passing by value and passing by reference. When an argument variable is passed by reference, any changes to the corresponding parameter inside the procedure will change the value of the original argument when the procedure finishes. When passed by value, the argument variable retains its original value after the procedure terminates—regardless of what was done to the corresponding parameter inside the procedure. Argument variables are always passed by reference unless surrounded by an extra pair of parentheses.

For example, the statements

```
Display Variable1, (Variable2)
Call Display (Variable1, (Variable2))
```

for a Sub procedure named Display pass Variable1 by reference and Variable2 by value. That is, the compiler creates a temporary copy of Variable2, passes that, and then abandons the copy after the routine finishes.

Consider the Sub procedure Triple, which triples the value of any argument passed to it:

```
Private Sub Triple (Num As Integer)
  Num = 3 * Num
  Print Num
End Sub
```

Notice the assignment to the parameter Num inside the procedure.

When the following lines of code are executed, the variable named Amt is passed by reference to the parameter Num.

```
Private Sub Form_Click ()
  'local variables:
  Dim Amt As Integer

  Amt = 2
  Print Amt
  Triple Amt
  Print Amt
End Sub
```

What you see is

```
2
6
6
```

In this case, only one memory location is involved. Initially, the first line of code inside the Click procedure allocates a memory location to store the value of Amt. (See Figure 9-4*a*.) When the Sub procedure is called, the parameter Num becomes the procedure's name for this memory location (Figure 9-4*b*). When the value of Num is tripled, the value in this memory location becomes 6 (Figure 9-4*c*). After the completion of the procedure, the parameter Num is forgotten. However, its value lives on in Amt (Figure 9-4*d*). (Note: Naming the parameter Amt produces the same result.)

Now consider the same Form_Click procedure as you just saw with the statement changed to Triple (Amt) so that the variable Amt is passed by value. The outcome of the revised code is shown here:

```
2
6
2
```

This time two memory locations are involved. Initially, the first line of code allocates a memory location to store the value of Amt (Figure 9-5*a*). When the Sub procedure is called, a temporary second memory location for the parameter Num is set aside for the procedure's use and the value of Amt is copied into this location (Figure 9-5*b*). When the value of Num is tripled, the value of Num becomes 6 (Figure 9-5*c*). After the completion of the procedure, Num's memory location disappears (Figure 9-5*d*). Since only the value in the procedure's memory location is tripled, the value of the variable Amt remains the same. When the procedure is exited, the memory location for Num is released

Figure 9-4 Passing a variable to a procedure by reference

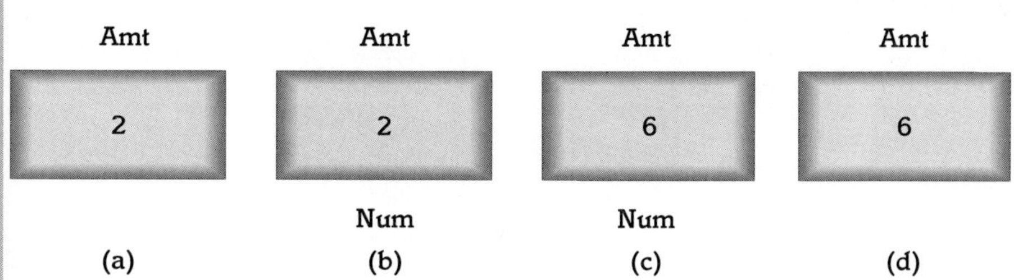

Figure 9-5 Passing a variable to a procedure by value

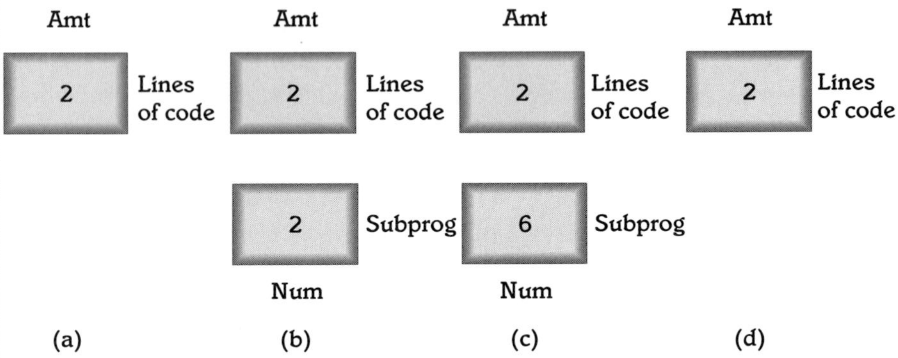

and the variable Num is forgotten. (Note: The outcome of the program would be the same even if the parameter in the subprogram also was named Amt. There would still be two memory locations when the procedure was called—one for the argument Amt and the other for the parameter Amt.)

Here's another example. The following Form_Click event procedure and its associated general procedure use passing by reference to validate what has been entered in an InputBox. Here the value of the variable PhoneNum$ is changed.

```
Private Sub Form_Click ()
  'local variables:
  Dim PhoneNum$

  PhoneNum$ = InputBox("Enter phone number (xxx-xxx-xxxx):")
  Validate PhoneNum$
  Print "Your phone number is "; PhoneNum$
End Sub

Private Sub Validate (Num$)
  Do While Len(Num$) <> 12
    MsgBox "Don't forget your area code."
    Num$ = InputBox("Enter phone number (xxx-xxx-xxxx):")
  Loop
End Sub
```

note: *You can use a marked edit box (Chapter 13) if you really want to accept a number in normal phone format.*

As another example, suppose you want to change a phrase by stripping out all the spaces inside a phrase—in other words, a more powerful version of the built-in function Trim$. The outline is clear: Find out where the spaces are and remove them.

You can use the Mid command to extract the nonspace character in the string. The code that strips out spaces is easy:

```
For Count = 1 To LenPhrase
  If Mid(Phrase$, Count, 1) <>[{|"|}]" Then
    Temp$ = Temp$ + Mid(Phrase$, Count, 1)
  End If
Next Count
```

When this loop ends, the value of Temp$ is the original phrase stripped of all its spaces. Now you have to decide whether you want to change the phrase or set up a new phrase. If you want the original phrase to change, incorporate the preceding fragment into a procedure:

```
Private Sub StripSpaces (X$)
  'local variables:
  Dim Count As Integer, LenPhrase As Integer, Temp$

  LenPhrase = Len(X$)
  For Count = 1 To LenPhrase
    If Mid(X$, Count, 1) <>[{|"|}]" Then
      Temp$ = Temp$ + Mid(X$, Count, 1)
    End If
  Next Count
  X$ = Temp$
End Sub
```

Now whenever you call the procedure via StripSpaces Phrase$, the original string Phrase$ changes. If you rewrite the preceding Sub procedure as a Function procedure, as in the following listing,

```
Private FunctionStripSpaces$ (X$)
  'local variables:
  Dim Count As Integer, LenPhrase As Integer, Temp$
```

```
  LenPhrase = Len(X$)
  For Count = 1 To LenPhrase
    If Mid(X$, Count, 1) <>[{|"|}]" Then
      Temp$ = Temp$ + Mid(X$, Count, 1)
    End If
  Next Count
  StripSpaces$ = Temp$
End Function
```

then the value of the function StripSpaces$(Phrase$) is the phrase stripped of all its internal spaces, but the original Phrase$ is still intact. Of course, you can add a line to the function to make it equivalent to the subprogram; all you need to do is add the statement X$ = Temp$ at the end of the function.

In the following code fragment and function, the variable Bal is passed by value to the function. The outcome is

8667.0178 is the future value of 1000

How would removing the parentheses surrounding Bal affect the outcome?

```
' Calculate future value after Yrs years with interest rate
' IntRate when Bal dollars is deposited and Dep dollars
' is added to the account at the end of each year
Dim Bal As Currency
Bal = 1000
IntRate = .05
Dep = 100
Yrs = 26
' in a non-example program you would use Format (, "Currency")!
Print NewBal((Bal), IntRate, Yrs, Dep);
Print "is the future value of"; Bal

Private Function NewBal (Bal, IntRate, Yrs, Dep)
  'local variables:
  Dim I As Integer

  For I = 1 To Yrs
    Bal = Bal + IntRate * Bal + Dep
  Next I
  NewBal = Bal
End Function
```

If you know that variables sent to a procedure should never be passed by reference, you can specify that some or all of the parameters inside Function and Sub procedures are to be passed only by value. For this, add the ByVal keyword before the parameter in the argument list. Here's an example of the syntax:

(Public/Private) Function *Example* (*X* As Integer, ByVal *Y* As Single)

In this example, an integer variable passed to *X* may be passed by reference (the default) or by value (when enclosed in parentheses), but a single-precision variable passed to *Y* will always be passed by value, whether or not it is enclosed in parentheses.

Since procedures and functions can change the values of the variables used as actual parameters, how do you decide whether to make a variable a form-level variable or send it as a parameter to a procedure? Most programmers follow the convention that form-level variables are for information that should be available to the whole form (for example, the value of π).

caution: *Unfortunately, when you pass variables or expressions by value, Visual Basic may change the type of the expression. This leads to subtle bugs and is usually referred to "evil type coersion."*

Subprograms with an Optional Number of Arguments

Visual Basic permits you to have optional arguments in functions and procedures you define yourself. Optional arguments must be of the variant data type and must be the last arguments in a function or procedure. For example, you might have a Sub procedure that looks like this:

```
Public Sub ProcessAddress(Name As String, Address As String, _
City As String, State As String, ZipCode As String, Option _
ZipPlus4 As Variant)
```

In this case, the last argument (for a Zip+Four code) is optional.

note: *You can have as many optional arguments as you want. They all must be variants, and they must be listed after all the required arguments in the procedure (or function) declaration.*

(You can also have procedures and functions that accept an arbitrary number of arguments. See the next chapter for more on these.)

tip: *Functions and procedures that use the Optional keyword or that accept an arbitrary number of arguments will work slower than those with a fixed number of arguments of a specific type. Save these kinds of procedures and functions for when you really need them.*

AN EXAMPLE: SHUFFLING A DECK OF CARDS

Suppose you want to write a program to create and then shuffle a computer deck of cards. You can think of a deck of cards as being a string variable, as shown here,

```
DeckOfCard$ = "2C3C4C5C6C7C8C9C0CJCQCKCAC2D..."
```

where a 0 is used for the 10—to keep all the cards the same length—and a C is used for clubs, a D for diamonds, and so on. (Windows doesn't support the low-order ASCII codes that give the clubs, hearts, diamonds, and spades symbols.) Obviously, since this string variable will have 104 characters, you'll want the computer to do some of the work. You'll see one slightly awkward method now and much better methods later, in Chapter 10.

In any case, since you want to change this variable when you shuffle the cards, you should write a Sub Shuffle(X$) Sub procedure, not a Function procedure. This procedure will be similar to the Jumble event procedure from Chapter 8. The only difference is that you have to move characters two at a time. (That's why a 0 was used for the 10.)

Here's the Jumble program rewritten as a procedure to do this:

```
Private Sub Shuffle (Phrase$)
  ' a Jumble program converted to a procedure
  ' jumbles by twos

' local variables are: LenPhrase,I
  Dim I As Integer, LenPhrase As Integer

  Randomize
  LenPhrase = Len(Phrase$) / 2
  For I = 1 To LenPhrase
    INum = Int((LenPhrase * Rnd) + 1)
```

```
    NewChar$ = Mid(Phrase$, 2 * INum - 1, 2)
    OldChar$ = Mid(Phrase$, 2 * I - 1, 2)
    Mid(Phrase$, 2 * I - 1, 2) = NewChar$
    Mid(Phrase$, 2 * INum - 1, 2) = OldChar$
  Next I
End Sub
```

In this case, the number of cards is half the length of the phrase, so you set the limits of the For-Next loop by taking half the length of the card string. Since the cards are located starting in the 1, 3, 5, 7... positions, you need to move two characters at a time inside the phrase in order to move to the next card. Otherwise, the Jumble procedure works exactly as before.

Now suppose you want to deal the cards in the course of writing a card program. You make the DeckOfCards$ variable a form-level variable:

```
Private Sub Deal ()
 'Form-level variable assumed to be DeckOfCards$
' local variable is Cards

  Dim Cards As Integer
  Call Shuffle(DeckOfCards$)
  For Cards = 1 To 52
    Print( Mid(DeckOfCards$, 2*Cards - 1, 2) )
  Next Cards
End Sub
```

(Notice the Call syntax in this example.) Again, the point of the 2 as the last parameter of the Mid function is that cards start in the first, third, and fifth positions, and so on.

Standard (Code) Modules: Global Procedures and Global Variables

When you start building larger projects with Visual Basic, you will probably want to reuse code as much as possible. For this reason you will often want to store procedures and functions you create in their own modules rather than leave them attached to a form. The next section explains the techniques needed for doing this.

tip: *Standard modules were called code modules in Visual Basic 3. (Most people still call them that!)*

In general, the Project window gives you access to all the project's form modules, Standard (code) modules, and Class modules (see Chapter 11). If you are using a resource file, this is listed here as well. Each time you click on the View Code button in the Project window you open up a Code window for the highlighted form or Standard module. You can open individual Code windows for as many forms or modules as you want. (You can also double-click on the name of the module in the Class/Modules list box in the Object Browser.)

A Standard (code) module is where you put code that you want to be accessible to all code in a project. Standard modules have no visual components. They are also useful for reusing code. (Just save the code in a Standard module and then add it to another project.) You add a new Standard module by choosing Insert | Module; you add an existing one by using File | Add File. By convention, Standard modules have a .BAS extension.

The Code window for a Standard module looks much like the Code window attached to a form. You can have two types of declarations for variables in the General section of a Standard module:

- For variables visible only to procedures in the Standard module
- For variables you want to be visible everywhere in the project

For the former, use the Private keyword; for the latter, use the Public keyword. (You can leave the Public keyword out, since this is the default.)

```
Private LocalToStandardModule As Integer
Public GlobalToProject As Integer
```

tip: *You can use the older Global keyword instead of Public if you want.*

Of course, just as form-level declarations can be superseded by declarations in procedures, public (global) declarations will be superseded by declaring a form- or procedural-level variable.

The Sub and Function procedures in code modules default so that they are available to the whole project. To make them available only to the code in the

Standard module, you must use the Private keyword before the subprogram header. (It is a good idea to use the Public keyword even though, strictly speaking, it isn't needed.) For example:

```
Private AProcedureLocal (Foo As Variant)
Public AGlobalProcedure(Foo As Variant)
```

tip: *Although you may have many code modules and put global variables in each of them, it makes debugging easier if you keep all global (Public) variables in a single code module.*

The Code window for a Standard (code) looks much like the Code window attached to a form. Below the title bar, to the upper left of the Module window, is the Object list box. To the right of the Object box is the Procedure list box, which gives a list of all the procedures for that module and the Declarations section.

The Sub and Function procedures in code modules default so that they are available to the whole project. This is because where you place a procedure or declare a variable or constant determines which parts of the project can use it. If you attach a procedure to a form, the procedure will be usable only by procedures attached to the form. If you put the procedure in a module, the procedure will be available to the whole project. (Event procedures can be attached only to forms, and Sub and Function procedures can be placed anywhere.)

Similarly, to make a variable into a global variable and so visible to every part of a project, place a statement of the form

Public *VariableName* As *VariableType*

or

Global *VariableName* As *VariableType*

in the Declarations section of any code module. (Both have the same effect.) For example:

```
Public Interest As Single
Global Years As Integer
```

The Public (or equivalently, the Global) declaration for variables is used only in Standard (code) modules; it has no effect in code attached to a form. Variables attached to a form are visible only within that form.

Variables declared in a code module can be local variables. To make a variable a global variable requires the Public (or Global keyword). If you use the ordinary Private (Dim) declaration syntax that you are familiar with in the Declarations section of a code module, then the variable is visible only to the procedures attached to that code module. Similarly, if you use the Private (Dim) statement inside a procedure attached to a code module, then that variable is local to the procedure. Figure 9-6 shows you the scope for variables within a Visual Basic project.

You can also open up a code module window for any code module in the current project. To open an existing module, bring the Project window to the top of the screen and double-click on the name of the module, or use the Object Browser.

Once you create a code module, saving it to disk is easy. When you are working with the module, open the File menu and choose Save File As (press CTRL+A or use ALT F, A). You'll be presented with a dialog box. Enter the path name under which you want the module saved and press ENTER. Visual Basic will do the work.

Figure 9-6 Scope of variables in a Visual Basic project

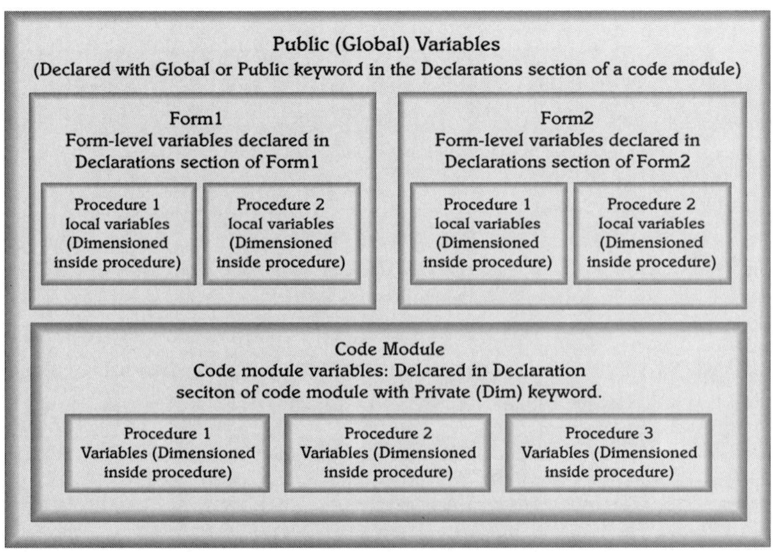

Adding or Removing Code Modules

Just as you can add a form module to your project, you can add text or complete Standard (code) modules that are stored on a disk. This lets you share code between projects (and often means you won't have to reinvent the wheel). On the other hand, code from one module may conflict with code from another module, especially if you are incorporating other people's code. (For example, names of procedures in Standard modules must be unique, regardless of how many modules you have.)

To add an existing code module, open the File menu and choose the Add File option. A dialog box opens, asking for the name of the file. Remember, the convention is that code modules have a .BAS extension and form modules use .FRM. To add code in a file to an existing module, choose Insert | File and then work with the dialog box that pops up. (The file will be inserted at the current cursor location.)

Occasionally, you will need to remove a code or form module from a project. Follow these steps:

1. Open the Project window by clicking on any part that's visible or by choosing View | Project.
2. Select the code module or form module you want to remove in the Project window.
3. From the File menu, choose Remove File (ALT F, R).

Fine Points About the Scope of Procedures

When you use a Sub or Function procedure inside another procedure, Visual Basic follows these simple steps to determine where to look for it:

1. Visual Basic first looks at procedures attached to the current form or module.
2. If the procedure is not found in the current form or module, Visual Basic looks at all the Public procedures in the code attached to the project.

The second of these options explains why the name of a procedure must be unique throughout all code modules. On the other hand, you certainly can have the same procedure name attached to two different forms; otherwise, forms could not have their own Form_Load procedures.

note: *Of course, you can use a Public procedure attached to a form by using the form's name first.*

Accessing Windows Functions

You have already seen that when you create a stand-alone Visual Basic program, you must include the VB32400.DLL file (or VB16400.DLL for 16-bit development). A dynamic link library such as VB32400.DLL contains specialized functions that a Windows program can call on as needed. Windows itself can be thought of as an interlocking set of DLLs containing hundreds of specialized functions. These are called Application Programming Interface (API) functions. Most of the time, Visual Basic is rich enough in functionality that you don't need to bother with API functions. But some tasks, such as learning whether users have swapped their mouse buttons or whether they have a numeric coprocessor, must be done with an API function. You can even use an API function to reboot a user's computer and start a program when Windows reboots.

note: *This book covers the barest basics of using the API. Completely covering the Windows API would require another book roughly this size. The one I recommend is Daniel Appleman's* Visual Basic Programmer's Guide to the Windows 32 Bit API *(Emeryville, CA: Ziff-Davis Press, 1995).*

caution: *If you use API functions at all carelessly, your system is likely to crash.*

Since you may have to reboot frequently, set the "Save before run" option when experimenting with API functions.

As a first example of using an API call, consider the plight of left-handed users of Windows. They might like to swap the left and right buttons via the Windows Control Panel. If you wanted to make your programs truly user friendly, you might want to take this into account. Before you can do this, you need to find out if the buttons have been swapped. The only way to do this is by using a Windows API function called the GetSystem Metrics function. To use this function in the 32-bit version of Windows, add the following Declare statement to the general section of a Standard module.

tip: *In Visual Basic 4 all Declares must be in code modules.*

```
Declare Function GetSystemMetrics Lib "user32" Alias _
"GetSystemMetrics" (ByVal nIndex As Long) As Long
```

As the Declare statement indicates, you send this function a long integer value that tells the function what information you want reported back. This function returns a long integer that you can analyze. For example, here's how to use this API function to find out if the mouse buttons have been swapped: First off, you need a constant for the GetSystemMetric function parameter that tells it you want to know the status of the mouse buttons. The constant must have the value 23 and is usually called SM_SWAPBUTTON. Here's some code that will detect a mouse swap:

```
Private Sub Form_Load
Const SM_SWAPBUTTON = 23
If GetSystemMetrics(SM_SWAPBUTTON) Then
  MsgBox "Mouse buttons switched."
End If
End Sub
```

note: *Most API functions expect the parameters used to be passed by value. As the preceding example indicates, you specify this in the Declare statement that specifies which API function you will be using.*

There are two possibilities for the general form of the Declare statement. For a Sub program in a DLL (one that doesn't return a value), use

[*Public* | *Private*] Declare Sub *name* Lib "*libname*" [Alias " _
aliasname"][([*arglist*])]

For a function (something that returns a value) use

[*Public* | *Private*] Declare Function *name* Lib "libname" [Alias " _
aliasname"] [([*arglist*])][As *type*]

Most of the elements in a Declare statement should be familiar to you (Public, Private, and so on). For the new ones, the Lib argument is just bookkeeping—it tells Visual Basic that a DLL is being called. The libname argument is the name of the DLL that contains the procedure you will be calling. The Alias keyword is used when the procedure has another name in the DLL but you don't (or can't) use it.

For example, to go beyond the built-in beep command, you can use the Windows API version of Beep. The API version allows you to set the frequency and duration. Since Beep is a reserved word in Visual Basic, you probably want to use an alias here. The Declare statement for the Windows API version of the Beep function looks like this:

```
Declare Function APIBeep Lib "kernel32" Alias "Beep" (ByVal _
dwFreq As Long, ByVal dwDuration As Long) As Long
```

(APIBeep is used because Beep is a reserved word.)

As you might expect, the dwFreq parameter gives the frequency of the beep, and the dwDuration parameter gives the duration in milliseconds.

It is extremely important that the Declare statement for an API function be exactly as Windows expects. Leaving off a ByVal keyword will almost certainly lock your system. One nice feature of the Professional and Enterprise editions of Visual Basic is that both come with a file with all the Declare statements and values of the constants needed for the Windows API functions—and an API Viewer program for dealing with this file. The API Viewer can be found in the WINAPI subdirectory of the VB directory, and is shown in Figure 9-7. You can use the appropriate API Viewer to copy and paste the necessary information about an API function directly in your program. There are two versions of the API Viewer: one for 32-bit systems and the other for 16-bit systems. They are called APILOD32.EXE and APILOD16.EXE, respectively.

To use the API Viewer, follow these steps:

1. Open the File menu in the API Viewer and choose the file you want to look at. (The 32-bit API functions are in a file called WIN32API.TXT, the 16-bit information is in WIN31.TXT). Figure 9-8 shows what you will see if you load WIN32API.TXT.

2. After the text file loads, choose what part of the API you need to look at (Declares, Constants, and so on) from the API Type list box.

3. Choose the item you want by scrolling through the Available Items list box.

Figure 9-7
API Viewer main screen

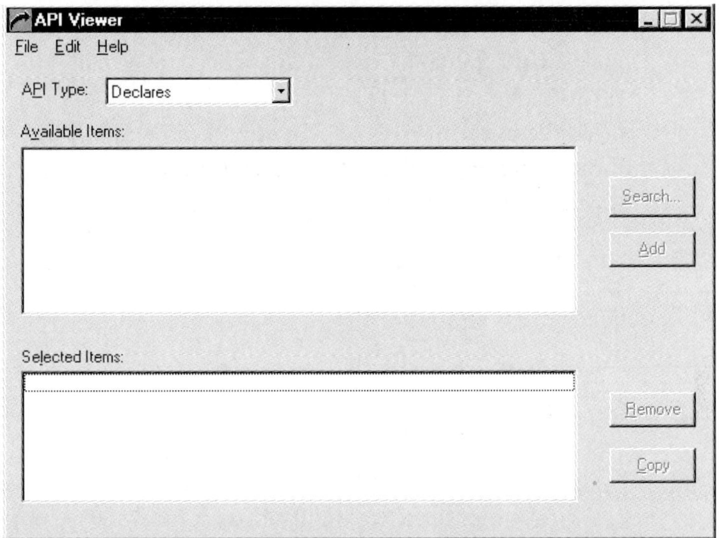

4. Click on the Copy button to place the item in the clipboard.

Figure 9-8
API Viewer for WIN32API.TXT

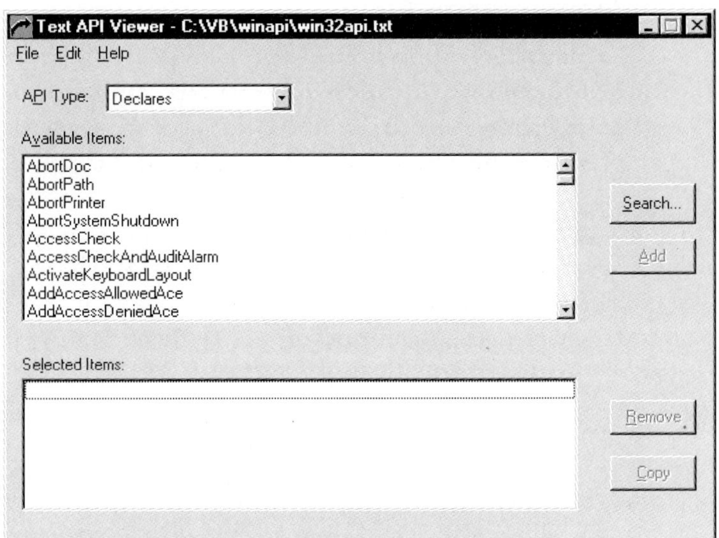

5. Move the insertion point inside your Code window where you want the item to appear, and choose Edit | Paste (or CTRL+V) to copy the item from the clipboard.

For any serious use of API functions, having the necessary documentation about what the API call does is essential.

note: *Many API functions require a Window handle. In Visual Basic, this is the value of the hWnd property.*

The DoEvents Function

Usually you want Windows (and Visual Basic) to monitor the environment constantly for events to respond to. On the other hand, there can be a lot of idle time that you can use to do, for example, time-consuming numeric calculations or sorts. However, you don't want a Visual Basic application to stop responding to events completely. When you write a procedure that wastes time, as you saw earlier in this chapter, you need a way to tell Visual Basic to respond periodically to events in the environment and return to the calculation when nothing else needs to be done.

The function that does this is called DoEvents. Whenever Visual Basic processes a statement containing this function, it releases control to the Windows operating system to process all the events that have occurred. (Windows keeps track of events in an events queue and keypresses in the SendKeys queue.) You should not use the DoEvents function inside an event procedure if it is possible to reenter the same event procedure again. For example, a Click event procedure may be called again by the user's clicking the mouse. If you forget about this possibility, your program may be caught in an infinite regression.

A loop that is processed only when no events are occurring is called an *idle loop*. Idle loops are written inside a special Sub procedure called Main that may be attached to any code module. You can have only one Sub Main procedure in any project. The format looks like this:

```
Public Sub Main ()
  Do While DoEvents()
    'Code you want to be processed during idle time
  Loop
End Sub
```

Next, you have to make the code module containing the Main procedure the startup module. To do this, choose Tools|Options and then choose the Project page. On this page, drop down the StartUp Form list box and choose Sub Main instead of a form. Once you've set a Sub Main as the startup object, Visual Basic does not load any forms automatically. You will have to write the code for this yourself using the Load and Show keywords.

Here's a simple example of an idle loop at work. Start a new project and add a code module. Next, add a global variable Count as a long integer by adding the statement

```
Public Counter As Long
```

to the code module. Next, add this code to the code module:

```
Public Sub Main ()

  Form1.Show  'load Form1 and show it
  Do While DoEvents()
    Counter = Counter + 1
  Loop
End Sub
```

Finally, make Sub Main the startup module and add a Form_Click procedure:

```
Private Sub Form_Click()
  Print Counter
End Sub
```

When you run this program, you'll notice that the number gets larger each time you click inside the form. The reason is that during the idle time (when you are not clicking), Visual Basic moves to the Main procedure and keeps adding 1 to the count. Since Count is a global variable, Visual Basic preserves the value for each call.

The DoEvents function actually gives you the number of forms loaded for the application. Idle loops stop when all forms are unloaded (or when Visual Basic processes an End statement).

Another common use of the DoEvents function is inside a Function procedure that is making a time-consuming numeric computation. Set up a timing loop so that Visual Basic periodically processes a DoEvents function to check what events may have taken place while it was calculating. The little extra time that Visual Basic uses to manage the timing loop inside the function is well worth it.

note: *Using DoEvents is especially important when older 16-bit programs are around. (Most 32-bit programs will not use cooperative multitasking.) Moreover, you still need to use DoEvents with 32-bit code in order to allow the user to cancel what is going on inside a loop of code. (In the jargon, people say "Visual Basic is not multithreaded.")*

Error Trapping

Regardless of how carefully you debug your own program, it's impossible to anticipate all the crazy things an inexperienced user may do. If you want your program to "degrade gracefully" and not just roll over, you'll want to prevent fatal errors. The command that activates (enables) error trapping within a given procedure is

```
On Error GoTo...
```

where the three dots stand for the label (line number) that defines the error trap. The labeled code must be in the current procedure. You cannot jump out of a procedure using an On Error GoTo command. On the other hand, the code for the error trap will often use other Sub or Function procedures to process the error information.

A label for an error trap is exactly like one for the GoTo from Chapter 7. It is any identifier ending with a colon that satisfies the rules for variables. The label identifies the island of code starting on the next line, as shown here:

```
ErrorTrap:
  ' error code goes here
```

Since you don't want Visual Basic to inadvertently "fall" into the error-trapping code, it is a good idea to have an Exit (Sub or Function) on the line immediately preceding the label for the error trap.

The On Error GoTo command can occur anywhere in an event, Sub, or Function procedure. Usually, the error-trapping code is inside that procedure. The only exception to this is when one procedure has been called by another.

In this case, Visual Basic will look to see if an error trap was enabled in the earlier procedure if one does not exist in the second procedure.

Once you start error trapping with the On Error GoTo command, a run-time error will no longer bomb the program. (Operating system errors cannot be helped, of course; Windows 95 will have fewer of them than Windows 3.X had.) In any case, the On Error GoTo command should transfer control to a piece of code that identifies the problem and, if possible, fix it.

If the error can be corrected, the Resume statement takes you back to the statement that caused the error in the first place. However, you can't correct an error if you don't know why it happened. You identify the problem by means of either the Err function or the Err object. This gives you an integer that you can assign to a variable. For example, if you write

```
ErrorNumber = Err
```

the value of the variable ErrorNumber is the error number. Similarly, you can use the Err object:

Err.Number

so the value of the Number property is the current error number.

note: *The Err function is inherited from earlier versions of Visual Basic. Microsoft suggests that you not mix the two methods. Either use the Err object and its properties (see the next section) or use the various error functions.*

Visual Basic can identify more than 80 run-time errors. (Search for "trappable errors" in the online help.) Here are a couple examples:

Error Code	Explanation
57	Device I/O error (for example, trying to print when the printer is offline)
68	Device unavailable (the device may not exist or is currently unavailable)

The way you use this information is simple. Suppose an event procedure will be using the printer. Somewhere in the procedure, before the error can occur, place a statement such as this:

```
On Error GoTo PrinterCheck
```

Now, before the End Sub, add code that looks like this:

```
Exit Sub
PrinterCheck:
  ErrorNumber = Err 'or Err.Value
  Beep
  Select Case ErrorNumber
    Case 25
      MsgBox "Your printer may be off-line."
    Case 27
      MsgBox "Is there a printer available?"
    Case Else
      M$ = "Please tell the operator (= program author?) that"
      M$ = M$ & vbCrLf '=  Chr$(10) + Chr$(13) New Line
      M$ = M$ & "error number " &ErrorNumber & " occurred."
      MsgBox M$
      End
  End Select

M$ = "If the error has been corrected click on OK."
M$ = M$ & vbCrLf
M$ = M$ & "Otherwise click on Cancel."
Continue = MsgBox(M$, vbOKCancel)
If Continue = vbOK Then Resume Else End
```

The idea of this error trap is simple, and the Select Case statement is ideal. Each case tries to give some indication of where the problem is and, if possible, how to correct it. If you reach the Case Else, the error number has to be reported. In any case, the final block gives you the option of continuing or not by using a message box with two buttons. You might want to get into the habit of writing a general procedure that analyzes the error code. The error trap inside a procedure just sends control to the general procedure. If you do this, you can reuse the general procedure in many different projects.

Error trapping isn't a cure-all. For example, very little can be done about a hard disk crash or running out of paper.

A variant on the Resume command lets you bypass the statement that may have caused the problem. If you use

```
Resume Next
```

Visual Basic begins processing at the statement following the one that caused the error. You can also resume execution at any line of code that has been previously identified with a label. For this, use

Resume *Label*

It is unusual to have labels in Visual Basic except in connection with error trapping. Nonetheless, for compatibility with older BASICs, Visual Basic does let you use the unconditional GoTo (see Chapter 7) or GoSub to transfer to the line of code following the label. But there is rarely any reason to use an unconditional GoTo, and GoSubs are far less flexible than procedures.

Both the Resume and Resume Next commands behave differently if Visual Basic has to move backward to find the error trap in another procedure. Recall that this happens when one procedure is invoked by a previous procedure and the current procedure doesn't have an error trap. In both cases, the statement executed by Visual Basic will not be in the procedure where the error occurred. For the Resume command, Visual Basic will call the original procedure again. For the Resume Next command, Visual Basic will execute the statement after the call to the original procedure. You will never get back to the original procedure.

Suppose the chain of procedural calls goes back even further: Procedure1 calls Procedure2, which calls Function3. Now an error occurs in Function3, but the only error handler is in Procedure1. If there is a Resume command in the error handler in Procedure1, Visual Basic actually goes to the statement that called Procedure2.

Because this is unwieldy and so prone to problems, it is probably better to rely only on error handlers that occur in a specific procedure. If one procedure calls another, turn off the error handler in the calling routine.

There's one other error-handling function, Erl (Error Line). If you get really desperate and need to find the line that caused the error and Visual Basic isn't stopping the program at that line, you can do the following:

1. Add line numbers before every statement in the procedure.
2. Add a Debug.Print Erl statement inside the error trap.

When developing a program, you may want to test how your error handler works. Visual Basic includes the statement

```
Error(errorcode number)
```

which, when processed, makes Visual Basic behave as if the error described by the given error number had actually occurred. This makes it easier to develop the trap.

If you are confident that you will no longer need an error trap, you can disable error trapping with the statement

```
On Error GoTo 0
```

(although strictly speaking the 0 is not needed). Similarly, you can change which error trap is in effect by using another On Error GoTo statement. Be sure to have an Exit command between the error traps. Visual Basic uses the last processed On Error GoTo statement to decide where to go.

More on the Err Object

To provide somewhat more centralized error handling when this is necessary, Visual Basic provides the special Err object that can be analyzed when an error occurs. You have already seen how the Number property of the Err object (Err.Number) gives you the error number. Microsoft recommends that except for legacy code you switch to using the properties and methods of the Err object instead of using the various error functions.

All the Err object's properties are reset to zero or zero-length strings ("") after Visual Basic processes either a Resume or a new On Error statement. The properties of the Err object are also reset after you leave the function or procedure. You can also use

Err.Clear

to reset the Err object's properties.

note: *Setting up a centralized error handler is very useful. However, you must pass that procedure the current values of the various Err object's properties. If you call the Err object from a new procedure, all its values will have been reset.*

If you want to generate an error for testing purposes, use the Raise method of the Err object. Its syntax is

Err.Raise(*Number*)

tip: *You can use the Raise method to define your own custom errors.*

If you need to find a description of the current error, use

Err.Description

Some General Words on Program Design

The usual improved methods for writing programs—often called modular, top-down, structured program design—were developed in the 1970s and 1980s from rules of thumb that programmers learned through experience in using conventional programming languages. An event-driven language such as Visual Basic requires some obvious shifts. For one thing, there is no "top" of the program. Nonetheless, when you have something hard to do, you first divide it into several smaller jobs. Moreover, with most jobs, the subtasks (the smaller jobs) have a natural order in which they should be done. (You dig a hole for the foundation before you call the cement truck.) Write programs from the general to the particular. Stub out the code that you'll later implement more fully. After you design the interface for your Visual Basic project, start by looking at the big picture (what are the event procedures supposed to do?) and then, in stages, break that down. This lets you keep track of the forest even when there are lots of trees.

Your first outline lists the event procedures and the jobs they have to do. Keep refining your outline by adding helper Sub and Function procedures for the jobs the event procedures are supposed to do until the pieces to be coded for all the procedures are well within your limits. Stop massaging the problem (breaking down the jobs) when you can shut your eyes and visualize the code for the procedure to accomplish the task you set out for it. Sometimes this "step-wise refinement" is described as "relentless massage." Since programmers often say "massage a problem" when they mean "chew it over and analyze it," the metaphor is striking—and useful.

Even if you can see how to program two completely separate jobs in one Sub or Function procedure, it's usually better not to do so. Sticking to one job per procedure makes it easier both to debug the procedure and to optimize the code in it.

Often, professional programmers are hired to modify programs written by other people. Imagine trying to modify a big program that wasn't written cleanly—if, for example, no distinction was made between local and global variables (all variables were global) and no attempt was made to write the program in digestible pieces with clear lines of communication between the pieces.

What happens? Because all variables are global, a little change you make in a small module could foul up the whole program. Because the pieces of the program aren't digestible and the way they communicate is unclear, you can't be sure how they relate. Anything you do, even to one line of code, may introduce side effects—possibly disastrous ones.

This kind of disaster was common until the late 1960s or early 1970s. Companies first spent millions of dollars having programs modified; then they spent more money trying to anticipate the potential side effects the changes they just paid for might cause. Finally, they hoped that more time (and more money) would fix the side effects. No matter where they stopped, they never could be certain that the programs were free of bugs. Top-down design, when combined with programming languages that allow local and global variables, can stop side effects completely; programs still have bugs, but these bugs don't cause epidemics. If you fix a small module in a giant but well-designed program, then you know how the changes affect everything; it is clear how the parts of the program communicate with each other. Only global form-level variables and parameters need to be checked.

Ultimately, you will develop your own style for writing Visual Basic programs, and what works for one person may not work for another. Still, just as artists benefit from knowing what techniques have worked in the past, programmers can learn from what programmers have done before them.

The first rule is still: Think first—code later. You have some idea of what needs to be done, so you design the interface and start writing code. When your first attempt doesn't work, you keep on modifying your project until it does (or seems to) work. This is usually referred to (sometimes with pride, sometimes with disdain) as "hacking away at the keyboard."

Of course, almost everyone will occasionally write programs with little or no preparation (you may need a ten-line program to print out a label or something); that's one of the virtues of any BASIC, and Visual Basic is no exception. Where do you draw the line? How long must a program be before it can benefit from some paper and pencil? The answer is to know your own limits. You may find it hard to write a program longer than one screen or with more than one event procedure without some sort of outline. If you try to do it without an outline, it might end up taking longer than if you had written an outline first.

Outlines don't have to be complicated. The complete outline for the pig latin program was as follows:

Two text boxes and a command button

text1 for text
text2 for translation

Command button starts process

While there are still words
  latinize the next word

To latinize a word
  one-letter words stay the same
  beginning vowels -> add way
  beginning consonants (y, qu = conson) -> ROTATE and add ay
ROTATE
  find conson
  move it to end

This may be a little hard for others to use, but that's not the point of an outline. Your outlines are for you. In particular, outlines should help you fix the concepts that you'll use in the program. You may find it a good rule that when each line in your outline corresponds to ten or fewer lines of code, you've done enough outlining and should start writing. (Of course, only practice will let you see at a glance how long the coded version is likely to be.)

Some people like to expand their outlines to pseudocode. This is especially common if you are developing a program with or for someone else. Pseudocode is an ill-defined cross between a programming language and English. While everyone seems to have his or her own idea of what pseudocode should look like, most programmers do agree that a pseudocode description (unlike an outline) should be sufficiently clear and detailed that any competent programmer can translate it into a running program.

Here's a pseudocode version of part of the preceding outline:

```
Function(latinize NEXT WORD)
  IF Length(NEXT WORD) = 1 THEN do nothing
  IF FirstLetter(NEXT WORD) = a,i,e,o,u THEN
      latinize(NEXT WORD)  = NEXT WORD + WAY
  ELSE
    Find(leading consonants of NEXT WORD)  ' (qu a consonant)
 latinize(NEXT WORD) = NEXT WORD - leading consonants + ay
```

The point is that, although a phrase such as

latinize(NEXT WORD) = NEXT WORD - leading consonants + ay

doesn't seem on the surface to be very close to Visual Basic code, it is for an experienced programmer.

note: *Probably the key technique development for making code less bug prone is to make sure that the information being passed is exactly what you want—and no unwanted side effects happen. Object-oriented programming techniques (see Chapter 11) make this easier.*

Chapter Ten

Arrays, Grids, and Records

SUPPOSE you need to create a new control with different event procedures attached to it at run time. Visual Basic does this by grouping related controls in a structure called a *control array*. The controls in a control array share common properties but use a parameter to distinguish among them. This parameter identifies the specific control and gives you the flexibility you will need. You'll see how to handle control arrays in the first part of this chapter.

Next, you'll see *variable arrays*. You use a variable array (most people simply say an array) when you need to set aside space in the computer's memory that you can use in a systematic way while a program is running. You use these arrays to store lists and tables. Once you have a list, of course, you'll need to have fast and effective ways to search and sort the contents. This chapter covers some of the many methods known for searching and sorting. (Chapter 19 covers some more sophisticated methods.)

You'll also see how to use one of the custom controls supplied with all editions of Visual Basic: the *grid control*. This control makes it easy to display tabular information. Finally, you'll see how to create *records* (user-defined types). Records let you create variables that combine variables of many types into one.

Control Arrays

You may have inadvertently given two controls of the same type the same control name or tried to copy a control using the Edit menu. If you did, then you saw a dialog box that looks like the one in Figure 10-1. Anytime you use the same control name (the value of the Name property) more than once while designing a Visual Basic application, Visual Basic asks you whether you really want to create a control array. Click the Yes button (or press ENTER), and, as you will see soon, you will be able to add more controls of the same type while the application is running. Each new control in a control array is called an *element* of the control array. (To more easily follow this discussion, you might want to create two text boxes with the control name of Money and set up the same control array as in Figure 10-1.)

Since both controls now have the same name, Visual Basic needs a way to distinguish them. This is done with an new property called the Index property. When Visual Basic creates a control array, it gives the first control an Index property of zero, the second control an Index property of 1, and so on. Like any properties of Visual Basic objects, you can change the Index property at design time using the Properties window. In fact, if you assign any number to the Index property of a control at design time, Visual Basic automatically creates a control array. This lets you create a control array without having to use two controls at design time. In theory, you can have up to 255 elements in a control array, but that would be very unusual—as it would waste too many Windows resources.

Suppose you want to work with the Change procedure for an element of the text box control array, created as in Figure 10-1. When you move to the Code window by, say, double-clicking one of these text boxes from the control array, you'll see something like the screen in Figure 10-2. Notice that the Change event procedure template looks a little different from anything you've seen before. Instead of having no parameters, as the Change procedure ordinarily does, this event procedure now uses a new parameter, Index As Integer.

Figure 10-1 Message box to create a control array

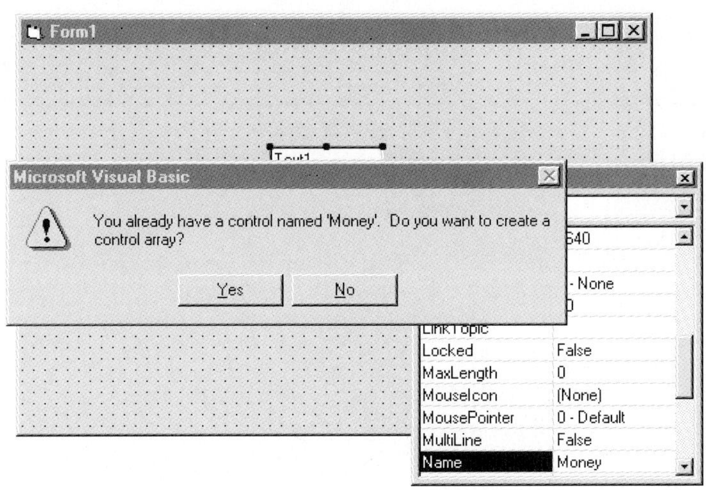

This index parameter is the key to the smooth functioning of control arrays. For example, add the following code to the event procedure template shown in Figure 10-2:

```
Private Sub Money_Change (Index As Integer)
  If Index = 0 Then
    MsgBox "You typed in text box 0"
  Else
    MsgBox "You typed in text box 1"
  End If
End Sub
```

Now, when you type in one of the text boxes, Visual Basic calls this event procedure and passes the index parameter to the procedure. In this way, the event procedure can use the index to determine what to do. When you type in the text box with the Index property of zero, Visual Basic activates the If clause inside this event procedure and so displays text telling you where you typed. Otherwise, Visual Basic processes the Else clause. The If-Then-Else, combined with the index parameter, lets the event procedure determine where you typed. (By the way, do you see why changing the Text1.Text property instead of using ordinary Print statements, as in the example, would not work?)

Figure 10-2 Event procedure template with an index parameter

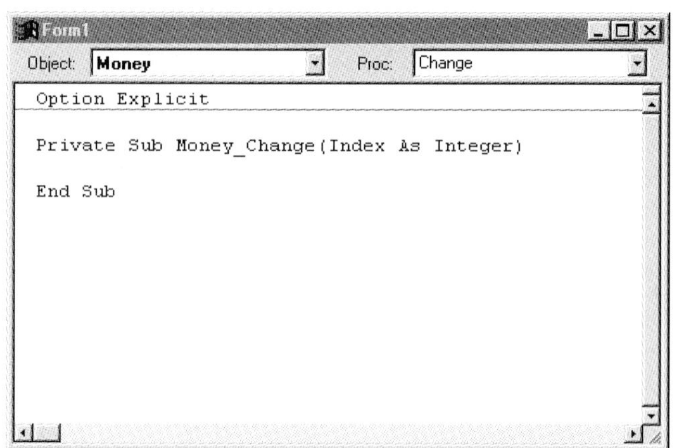

Any event procedure that would work for a single control can be used for a control array of that type while a program is running. Visual Basic adds an index parameter as the first parameter to the parameter list for the given event procedure. For example, the KeyPress event procedure for the control array of Money text boxes now starts out as

```
Private Sub Money_KeyPress(Index As Integer, KeyAscii As _
Integer)
```

instead of

```
Private Sub Money_KeyPress(KeyAscii As Integer)
```

as it would for an ordinary text box.

If you inadvertently add a control to a control array at design time, you can remove it by changing the control name or deleting the control. However, once Visual Basic creates a control array, you must change all the names of the controls before Visual Basic will let you change the Index property. (You can of course delete all the controls in the array in order to eliminate the control array.)

Adding and Removing Controls in a Control Array

Once you've created a control array at design time, you can add controls while the application is running. To do this, you use a variation of the Load command that you have already used to load a new form in an application with multiple forms. For example, suppose you want to add four new text boxes to the Money text box control array created in the previous section. To do this when the startup form loads, all you need to do is add the following code to the Form_Load event procedure for the startup form:

```
Private Sub Form_Load()
  Dim I As Integer

  For I = 2 To 5
    Load Money(I)
    Money(I).Text = "Text box #" + Str$(I)
  Next I
End Sub
```

Whenever Visual Basic loads a new element of a control array, the object is invisible—the Visible property is set to False. All other properties (except the Tab Index and Control Array Index) are copied from the object that has the lowest index in the array. In particular, even if you modify the preceding Form_Load procedure to read

```
Private Sub Form_Load()
  For I = 2 To 5
    Load Money(I)
    Money(I).Text = "Text Box #" + Str$(I)
    Money(I).Visible = True
  Next I
End Sub
```

you will only see the fifth text box. This is because the Left and Top properties start out the same for all the newly created controls. They are the same as Money(0).Left and Money(0).Top. This means that newly created controls in a control array default to being stacked one on top of the other. Because of this, you'll often find yourself applying the Move method to controls in a control array after you tell Visual Basic to load them. For example, suppose you want to place the newly loaded text boxes on the far left. Then, using the default size for the height of a text box, you might write

```
Private Sub Form_Load()
  Dim I As Integer

  For I = 2 To 5
    Load Money(I)
    Money(I).Text = "Text Box in control array #" + Str$(I)
    Money(I).Move 0, 495*(I-2)
    Money(I).Visible = True
  Next I
End Sub
```

The key line

```
Money(I).Move 0, 495*(I-2)
```

starts at the top left when I = 2, because the command is then:

```
Money(I).Move = 0, 0
```

On each pass through the loop, the location for the top of the newly loaded text box moves down by the default height of a text box (495 twips), as shown in Figure 10-3. (We have made the text boxes wider in order to see the caption more clearly. Notice as well that the text in the two original text boxes remains what it was at design time.)

You can use the Unload statement to remove any element of a control array that you added at run time. You cannot use the Unload statement to remove the original elements of the control array that you created at design time. For example, if you add the Click procedure,

```
Private Sub Form_Click()
  Static I As Integer

  If I < 4 Then
    Unload Money(I+2)
    I = I + 1
  Else
    Exit Private Sub
  End If
End Sub
```

Figure 10-3

Demonstration of loading a control array

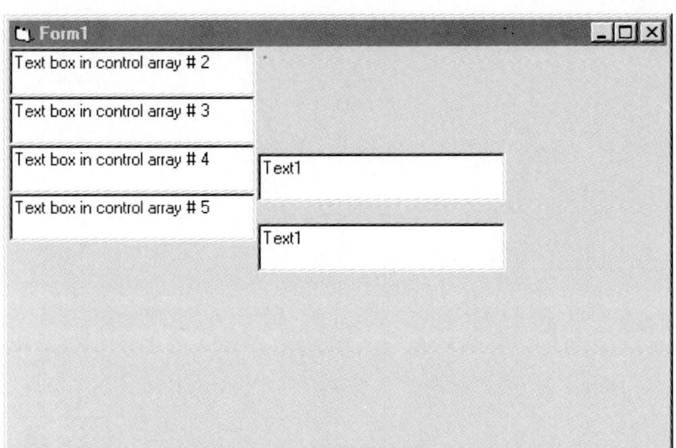

each click on an empty place in the form removes the next control in the control array, but this routine will not remove the initial element in the control array.

You must be careful, of course; you can only load or unload an element of a control array once. If you try to load or unload a control array element twice in succession, Visual Basic gives a run-time error you can trap (Err = 360).

Example: A Square Array of Labels via Control Arrays

The ability to position elements of a control array precisely is important. For example, later in the chapter, in the section " Example: Magic Squares," you'll see a program that creates magic squares. (A magic square is one in which the sums of all the rows, columns, and diagonals are all the same number.) For that version, you'll need a control array of bordered labels on a blank form with maximal size. Moreover, the labels should be square with a size in twips determined by a variable called LabelSize. You'll also need an odd number of rows and columns. Figure 10-4 shows an example of a magic square created by the program from this section.

Figure 10-4 7 X 7 magic square

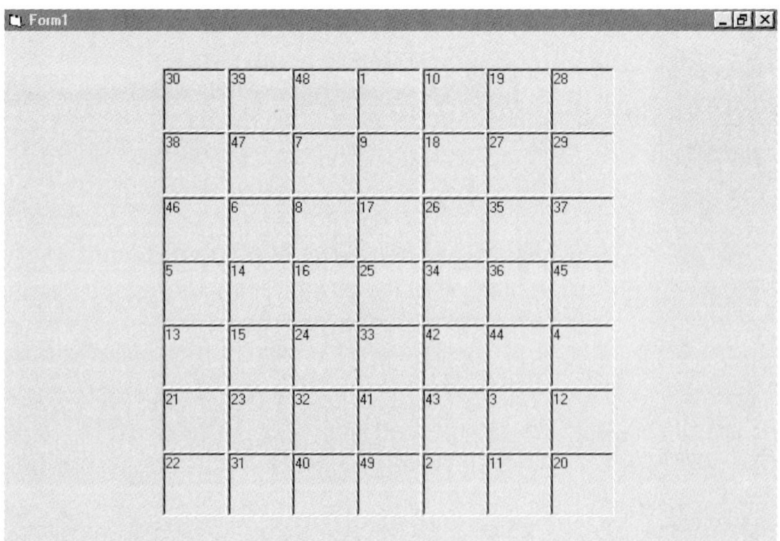

note: *This program is being given as an example to show you how to position controls in a control array. It is much more efficient to use the grid control when you need to display tabular data than to use a control array. (See the section on the "the Grid Control" later on in this chapter, which gives another version of the Magic Square program. Compare the speed of the two, for example!)*

Here's a basic outline for the steps needed to put a square array of labels on a maximized form for the magic square program:

1. Add a label to the form and set the Border property of the label to 1 (fixed single). Set its Index property to be) to make it the first element of a control array. (We suppose its name is lblBox in what follows.)
2. Maximize the form and find its usable height and width using the ScaleHeight and ScaleWidth properties.
3. Get the number *n* of labels and the size. Check that these numbers make sense.
4. The program loads the labels.
5. Then the program arranges the labels in a square on the form by moving them to the correct places.

Where should the labels be moved? Since ScaleWidth/2 is the center of a horizontal line and ScaleHeight/2 is the center of a vertical line, for the horizontal you start at

ScaleWidth/2 – (*n*/2) * LabelSize

where *n* is the number of controls in a row. You use

ScaleHeight/2 – (*n*/2) * LabelSize

for the vertical positioning.

The program is a bit more elaborate than the simple outline would suggest in order to make the various messages users see if they enter unusable data more informative. The extra things the code includes will be discussed as the code is presented.

First, you'll need some form-level variables and, of course, the Option Explicit command. For these, enter

```
Option Explicit
Dim NumberOfDim As Integer, Size As Integer, LabelSize As Integer
```

Here's the Form_Load procedure:

```
Private Sub Form_Load()
 Show
 WindowState = 2                          'maximal
'   Call the GetDimensions procedure
GetDimensions
Me.Print "Please click on the form in order to see the control array."
End Sub
```

Here's the GetDimensions procedure that asks for the size of the box and insists that the size fit the form:

```
Sub GetDimensions()
'Local variables
  Dim I As Integer, BoxSize As Single
  Dim X As String, L As String
  Dim LabelSizeMessage As String

  'get number of rows/columns
  X = InputBox("Number of dimensions?")
  NumberOfDim = Val(X)
  'call a function to check the number of dimensions
  'this will return a message that we use for the loop
  LabelSizeMessage = CheckDimensionNumber(NumberOfDim)
  Do Until LabelSizeMessage = "OK"
     X = InputBox(LabelSizeMessage & "Renter the number of dimensions.")
     NumberOfDim = Val(X)
     LabelSizeMessage = CheckDimensionNumber(NumberOfDim)
  Loop

  'similarly we call a function for the size
  L = InputBox("Size of Labels?")
  LabelSize = Val(L)
  LabelSizeMessage = LabelSizeOk(LabelSize)
  Do Until LabelSizeMessage = "OK"
    L = InputBox(LabelSizeMessage & " Please renter label size")
    LabelSize = Val(L)
```

```
    LabelSizeMessage = LabelSizeOk(LabelSize)
  Loop

End Sub
```

Notice that the GetDimensions procedure uses two string functions that return messages that depend on whether the data entered will work.

Here is the code for these functions. Notice that both these functions return strings that tell the program whether the data was usable or not. The Check-DimensionNumber function is the easiest. It just checks whether the number entered is odd (remember, you will need this for your magic square program) and whether it's less than 16.

```
Function CheckDimensionNumber(X As Integer) As String
    If X Mod 2 <> 1 Then
      CheckDimensionNumber = "Number of rows/columns must be odd. "
    ElseIf X > 15 Then
       CheckDimensionNumber = "Number of rows/columns must be < 16. "
    Else
       CheckDimensionNumber = "OK"
    End If
 End Function
```

The LabelSizeOk routine is a bit more complicated, as you want to be sure that you have enough room on the labels for the numerals. It looks like this:

```
Function LabelSizeOk(X As Integer) As String
  Dim SpacedUsed As Integer, MaximumWidth As Integer
  MaximumWidth = NumberOfDim*NumberOfDim

'MaximumWidth is the width of the largest number that we use
  MaximumWidth = TextWidth(Trim(Str$(MaximumWidth)))
  SpacedUsed = X * NumberOfDim
  If SpacedUsed > ScaleHeight Or SpacedUsed > ScaleWidth Then
     LabelSizeOk = "Labels too large. "
  ElseIf X < MaximumWidth Or X < TextHeight("1") Then
    LabelSizeOk = "Labels too small. "
  Else
     LabelSizeOk = "OK"
  End If
End Function
```

Here's the Form_Click procedure that actually does the work. It calls a procedure for making the boxes and then one for locating them.

```
Private Sub Form_Click()
  Static BoxesMade As Integer
  Cls
  If Not (BoxesMade) Then
    MakeBoxes LabelSize
    BoxesMade = True
  End If
  LocateBoxes LabelSize, NumberOfDim
End Sub
```

Here's the procedure that makes the boxes:

```
Private Sub MakeBoxes(HowBig)
  Dim I As Integer

  lblBox(0).Visible = 0    'temp hide original label
  lblBox(0).Height = HowBig
  lblBox(0).Width = HowBig
  Size = NumberOfDim * NumberOfDim
  For I = 1 To Size - 1      'already have one label lblBox(0)
    Load lblBox(I)
    lblBox(I).Height = HowBig
    lblBox(I).Width = HowBig
  Next I
End Sub
```

Finally, the procedure that locates the labels is shown next. Inside the procedure, the For-Next loop does all the work. By setting the starting width and height as indicated, you can use integer division to find the row. For example, when I is between 0 and NumberOfDim, then Row = 0; and when I is between NumberOfDim and one less than twice the number of dimensions, then Row = 1. Columns are given by the remainder. The line

BoxLabel(I).Caption=Trim(Str$(I+1))

was put in to display the ordering of the boxes.

```
Private Sub LocateBoxes(HowBig As Integer, Number As Integer)

  Dim I As Integer, Row As Integer
  Dim Column As Integer
  Dim StartWidth As Integer, StartHeight As Integer
  Dim CurrentHeight As Integer, CurrentWidth As Integer

  StartHeight = ScaleHeight / 2 - ((Number / 2) * HowBig)
  StartWidth = ScaleWidth / 2 - ((Number / 2) * HowBig)
  For I = 0 To Size - 1
    Row = I \ Number
    Column = I Mod Number
    CurrentHeight = StartHeight + (Row * HowBig)
    CurrentWidth = StartWidth + (Column * HowBig)
    lblBox(I).Move CurrentWidth, CurrentHeight
    lblBox(I).Caption = Trim(Str$(I + 1))
    lblBox(I).Visible = True
  Next I
End Sub
```

Of course, you need a way to end the program, so:

```
Private Sub Form_QueryUnload(Cancel As Integer, UnloadMode As Integer)
UnloadMe
  End
End Sub
```

One nice point about the procedures in this program is that you can easily adapt them to many situations. For example, minor changes to the Locate procedure allow you to use it whenever you'll need to load and position multiple controls on a form.

Lists: One-Dimensional Arrays

Suppose you need data for a 12-month period. You would like to say something like this:

```
For I = 1 to 12
  MonthI = Val(InputBox$(Data for MonthI))
Next I
```

If this kind of loop were possible, the information entered would still be available in the various MonthI variables. Unfortunately, this is not quite correct. In Visual Basic, MonthI is a perfectly good variable name—for a single variable. Visual Basic cannot separate the I from the Month. After you see a systematic way to name groups of related variables that are part of a list, it's easy to take care of this problem.

To Visual Basic, a *list* (often called a one-dimensional array) is just a collection of variables, each one of which is identified by two things:

- The name of the list
- The position of the item on the list

For example, you've already seen in Chapter 5 the Fonts list that Visual Basic uses to store font names. As another example, suppose you are writing a program that lets a user enter an "errand list" at the beginning of each day. You would probably choose to store the information on a list. The third errand might be stored as Errand$(3). The name of this list is Errand$. Notice the dollar sign ($) that indicates that the variables on this list will hold words (strings).

The number in the parentheses is usually called a subscript, pointer, or index. The term subscript comes from mathematics, where the item M(5) is more likely to be written M_5. The term pointer is used because the 5 "points" to the row holding the information. To Visual Basic, M5 is the name of a single variable, but M(5) is the name of the fifth element on a list called M. As you saw with the Fonts list, lists in Visual Basic default to having a zeroth entry.

Fixed Versus Dynamic Lists

Lists can't be open-ended in Visual Basic. While the limits are quite large—they depend pretty much on the amount of memory you have—you must tell Visual Basic how much memory to set aside for the list before you use it.

There are two kinds of lists in Visual Basic: *fixed lists*, in which the memory allocation never changes, and *dynamic lists*, in which you can change size on the fly. The advantage of a fixed list is that memory is set aside at the beginning of the program; you run a much smaller risk of running out of memory while the program is running. The advantage of dynamic lists is the flexibility they give. You can change the size in response to what the program encounters.

note: *List boxes give you another way to store information (see Chapter 12). In many situations using them can be the preferred way to store small amounts of data.*

Both kinds of lists may be made visible to either the whole application, to a specific form or module, or only within an event procedure. To set up a fixed list in a form or module, place a statement such as

```
Dim Errand(13) As String
```

in the Declarations section of the form or module. This sets up a 14-element list for strings visible to every procedure on that form or module. The items would be stored in Errand(0) through Errand(13). (All lists in Visual Basic default to having an entry in the zeroth position.)

To set up a dynamic list in a form or module, place a statement such as

```
Dim Errand() As String
```

in the Declarations section of the form or module. You then use the ReDim statement inside a procedure to allocate the space:

```
Private Sub NameOfProcedure()
..Dim Number As Integer
  ReDim Errand(Number) As String
.
.
End Sub
```

Each time Visual Basic processes a ReDim statement, the information in the array is lost. The advantage, though, is clear: you can calculate how much space you need before issuing the ReDim command. In the preceding example, the value of the variable Number can change depending on the circumstances.

You can also use the ReDim statement in a procedure without needing a Dim statement in the Declarations section of the form or module first. In this case, space is allocated for that list only while the procedure is active and disappears as soon as the procedure is exited.

You can use a variation of the ReDim statement to increase or decrease the size of a dynamic list while retaining any information already stored in the list. For example, suppose the current maximum index for the Errand list is given by OldSize, then the statement

```
ReDim Preserve Errand(OldSize + 1) As String
```

can be placed in a procedure to increase the number of entries in the array Errand( ) by one. All the current information remains intact. Similarly, the statement

```
ReDim Preserve Errand(OldSize - 1) As String
```

drops off the last entry in the Errand list but preserves all the others.

To set up a fixed list that is global and therefore visible to the entire project, place a statement like

```
Public Errand(13) As String
'or
Global Errand(13) As String
```

in a Standard (code) module. This sets up a 14-element global list for strings. The items would be stored in Errand(0) through Errand(13).

To set up a dynamic list that is global, and therefore visible to the entire project, place a statement like

```
Public Errand() As String
Global Errand() As String
```

in a standard module.

You can then use the ReDim statement in any procedure in the whole project in order to resize the list. (Or you could size it once in, say, an Initialize procedure and then deal with the elements of the list from any procedure in the project.)

note: *Each time you use ReDim on a global list, you will erase the contents. Use the ReDim Preserve command to change the size while retaining the information in the list.*

As before, Visual Basic actually reallocates the space each time it encounters a ReDim Errand(Number) statement inside a procedure.

Finally, you can set up a local fixed array inside a procedure by using the Static keyword:

```
Private Sub ProcedureName()

  Static Errand(13) As String
.
.
End Sub
```

As with static variables, the information you store in a list defined by static dimensioning remains intact. You cannot use a variable inside the parentheses when you do static dimensioning. Similarly, the information in a form or global list remains intact until you redimension it.

When you dynamically dimension a list or array, Visual Basic sets aside space at that time. If the program is very large, it's possible that you won't have enough room. If this happens, you'll get the dreaded "out of memory" error. Given Windows' memory-management skills, this is a much more rarely encountered error than you might think.

Some Ways of Working with Lists

Values inside lists are most often assigned by using a For-Next loop or, since you often want to allow someone to stop before entering all the data, by using a Do loop, as in the following fragment:

```
Static Errand(30) as String
Index = 0

Do
  M$ = "You've entered"+ Str$(Index)+ " entries so far."
  M$ = M$ + "Enter the next errand - ZZZ when done"
  NextErrand$ =InputBox(M$)
  If NextErrand$ <> "ZZZ" Then
    Index = Index + 1
    Errand(Index) = NextErrand$
  End If
Loop Until Index = 30 Or NextErrand$ = "ZZZ"

NumberOfItems = Index
```

Notice that a temporary variable, NextErrand$, is set up to hold the information before it is added to the list. This keeps the flag off the list. Once you know the entry is acceptable, you first move the pointer (add 1 to the index) and only then fill in the entry. Do you see why the order is important? Notice as well that this If-Then is completely skipped when "**ZZZ**" is entered. This keeps the flag off the list. Enter **ZZZ**, and you move immediately to the loop test and leave the loop. The variable NumberOfItems keeps track of the number of items on the list. In a program that will manipulate this list in many ways, this variable is a good candidate for a global or form-level variable. (Of course, it is not really in keeping with the Visual Basic spirit to use so many input boxes. This is just a programming example to illustrate a concept. Most likely, in a situation like this, you'd use a command button and a text box.)

However, there are other ways to pass the information around than by using a global variable like NumberOfItems. For this, recall that in Visual Basic all lists default to having a zeroth entry. In the example, when you wrote

```
Static Errand(30) As String
```

Visual Basic actually set aside 31 slots, the extra one being Errand(0). This zeroth slot is useful for things like the number of significant items on the list. What you might want to do (rather than set up a new variable) is enter

```
Errand(0) = Str$(Index)
```

Now, to find the number of items (for example, to set up a For-Next loop), you can convert this entry back to a number by using the Val command.

Another, perhaps even more popular alternative is to keep a flag (like the "ZZZ") right after the last usable item on a list. This lets you use an indeterminate loop to manipulate the list (test for the flag). To do this, modify the previous fragment as follows:

```
' A simple list demo revisited and revised

Static Errand(30) As String
Index = 0
Do
  M$ = "You've entered"+ Str$(Index)+ " entries so far."
  M$ = M$ + "Enter the next errand - ZZZ when done"
  NextErrand$ =InputBox$(M$)
  If NextErrand$ = "ZZZ" Then
    Errand$(Index) = "ZZZ"
  Else
    Errand$(Index) = Next Errand$
    Index = Index + 1
```

```
  End If
Loop Until Index = 30 Or Errand$(Index) = "ZZZ"
```

Notice that here, the If-Then-Else deals with the two possibilities—a real entry or the flag. Notice as well that the last entry could hold the flag. Of the two methods, the idea of keeping the number of items currently used in the zeroth entry (when possible) may be the most appealing, but this is clearly a matter of taste. You may find it comforting to always know how many entries are on a list. It makes debugging easier and, like most programmers, you may find For-Next loops easier to use than Do loops.

Example: Improving the Built-in Random Number Generator

The built-in random number generator (see Chapter 8) in Visual Basic doesn't give good results for some type of simulations and is not a particularly good method for developing encryption programs (see Chapter 17). If you find that the random number generator is a problem, there is a simple method of improving it by using a list. This gives you a way of generating numbers that seem even more random. (Technically, what the method does is eliminate sequential correlations.) All you need to do is the following:

1. Set up an array of random numbers.
2. Use the built-in random number generator to pick one element of the array.
3. Replace the element chosen with a new random number generated by the built-in random number generator.

If you use this method instead of the built-in random number generator, you should eliminate most of the problems of the built-in random number generator, with very few performance penalties. Essentially, what these steps do is shuffle the cards one more time. An array of about 100 works very well. (Actually, 101 works a bit better because 101 is a prime number—you can't factor 101 like you can 100 = 4 * 25.) To implement the method outlined previously, first set up a Public (global) array in a Standard (code) module and fill it with 100 random numbers in an Initialize procedure:

```
Public RandomList(100)  'gives 101 entries
```

```
Public Sub Initialize()
  Dim I As Integer

  Randomize
  For I = 0 To 100
    RandomList(I) = Rnd
  Next I
End Sub
```

Now, call the Initialize procedure in the Form_Load for the startup form (or the Sub Main). Finally, whenever you need a random number, use the following function that you also should place in a Standard module.

```
Public Function NewRandom()
  Dim Foo As Single, X As Integer
  Randomize
  Foo = Rnd
  X = Int(101*Foo)
  NewRandom=RandomList(X)
  RandomList(X) = Foo         'Replace used up entry
End Function
```

Lists with Index Ranges

Some people never use the zeroth entry of a list; they just find it confusing. (And if you are not going to use it in a program, it certainly wastes space.) For this reason, Visual Basic (to keep compatibility with interpreted BASICs) has a command that eliminates the zeroth entry in all lists dimensioned in the module or form. It is the Option Base 1 statement. This statement is used in the Declarations section of a form or module and affects all lists in the module. All new lists dimensioned in that form or module now begin with item 1. After Option Base 1, Dim Errand$(30) sets aside 30 spots rather than 31.

As usual, Visual Basic goes one step beyond interpreted BASICs. Suppose you want to write the input routine for a bar graph program for sales in the years 1980 through 1995. You could write something like

```
Static SalesInYear(15) As Single
For I = 0 To 15
  Sales$=InputBox$("Enter the sales in year"+ Str$(1980 + I))
  SalesInYear(I) = Val(Sales$)
Next I
```

However, this program requires 16 additions (one for each pass through the loop) and is more complicated to boot. This situation is so common that QuickBASIC and Visual Basic enhance the language by allowing subscript ranges. Instead of writing

```
Dim SalesInYear(15)
```

you can now write

```
Dim SalesInYears(1980 To 1995)
```

The keyword To marks the range, smaller number first (from 1980 to 1995, in this case), for this extension of array dimensioning. (You can use Dim, ReDim, ReDim Preserve, and static dimensioning using an index range.) Using an index range, you can rewrite the preceding fragment as:

```
Static SalesInYear(1980 To 1995) As Single
Dim I As Integer

For I = 1980 To 1995
  Sales$=InputBox$("Enter the sales in year"+ Str$(I))
  SalesInYear(I) = Val(Sales$)
Next I
```

Besides being much cleaner, this new fragment runs more quickly. In a large program with lists with thousands of entries, the savings can be substantial.

The Erase Statement

As your programs grow longer, the possibility that you'll run out of space increases (although, given Visual Basic's rather large limits and Windows' memory management, it's never very likely). Visual Basic allows you to reclaim the space used by a dynamically dimensioned array (that is, with ReDim or ReDim Preserve). You do this with the Erase command. For example, if the array Errand was dynamically dimensioned,

```
Erase Errands
```

would erase the Errands array and free up the space it occupied.

If an array was not dimensioned dynamically (that is, was not dimensioned using the ReDim or ReDim Preserve statement inside a procedure), then the Erase command would simply reset all the entries back to zero for numeric lists (and to the null string for string lists or to null for variants). Using the Erase command on a fixed or static list gives a fast method to "zero out" the entries. (It sets them to the null string for string arrays.)

Arrays with More Than One Dimension

You can also have arrays with more than one dimension; they're usually called *multidimensional arrays*. Just as lists of data lead to a single subscript (one-dimensional arrays), tables of data lead to double subscripts (two-dimensional arrays). For example, suppose you want to store a multiplication table in memory—as a table. You could do this as

```
Static MultTable(1 To 12, 1 To 12) As Integer
Dim I As Integer, J As Integer

For I = 1 To 12
 For J = 1 To 12
  MultTable(I, J) = I*J
 Next J
Next I
```

To compute the number of items in a multidimensional array, multiply the number of entries. The dimension statement here sets aside 144 elements.

The convention is to refer to the first entry as giving the number of rows and the second as giving the number of columns. Following this convention, you would describe this fragment as filling an entire row, column by column, before moving to the next row.

Visual Basic allows you up to 60 dimensions with the Dim statement and 8 with the ReDim statement. A statement like

```
Dim LargeArray%(2,2,2,2,2,2,2,2)
```

would set aside either 2^8 = 256 or 3^8 = 6,561 entries (depending on whether an Option Base 1 statement has been processed). But you almost never see more than 4 dimensions in a program, and even a 3-dimensional array is uncommon.

Finally, note that you can use ReDim for multidimensional arrays in exactly the same way.

Assigning Arrays to Variants: The Array Function

Occasionally you will want to store an array in a variant. It is a little less than elegant to do this, but since you can't assign one array to another, this technique can be very useful. For example, this technique gives you a quick way to swap the contents of two arrays, as shown here:

```
Dim I As Integer
ReDim A(1 To 20000) As Long
ReDim B(1 To 20000)
For I = 1 To 20000
  A(I) = I
  B(I) = 2 * I
Next I
Dim Array1 As Variant, Array2 As Variant, Temp As Variant
Array1 = A(): Erase A()
Array2 = B(): Erase B()
Temp = Array1
Array1 = Array2
Array2 = Temp
```

At this point the variants Array1 and Array2 contain the original arrays in reverse order, and the memory for the original arrays has been reclaimed. Since momentarily you have two objects instead of one, this technique can be a bit memory hungry. On the other hand, if you need to swap two arrays, this is a whole lot faster than copying the 20,000 entries one by one!

note: *If you store an array in a variant, use the ordinary index to get at it. For example, after you run the example just shown, Array1(5) would have the value 10.*

Occasionally, you need to create an array in a variant directly. For this you use the Array function whose syntax is

Array(*arglist*)

where the *arglist* argument consists of an arbitrary list of items separated by commas.

Example: Magic Squares

For a more serious example of a program using arrays, consider the following program, which constructs a magic square. A magic square is one in which all the rows, columns, and long diagonals add up to the same number. These squares were once thought to have magical properties. Many people have devised rules for constructing magic squares. The one used in this section is called Loubère's rule and works only for odd-order magic squares—those with an odd number of rows and columns. Here's the method:

1. Place a 1 in the center of the first row.
2. The numbers now go into the square in order by moving up on the diagonal to the right.

Of course, you're immediately met with the problem of where to put the 2. If you've placed a 1 in the top row, going up takes you off the square. The solution is:

3. If you go off the top, wrap around to the corresponding place in the bottom row.

On the other hand, going to the right eventually drops you off the side.

4. If you go off to the right end, wrap around to the left column.
5. Finally, if a square is already filled, or the upper-right corner is reached, move down one row and continue applying these rules.

Here's a 5 X 5 magic square constructed with this rule.

```
17  24   1   8  15
23   5   7  14  16
 4   6  13  20  22
10  12  19  21   3
11  18  25   2   9
```

Suppose you store the numbers that will appear in the magic square in an array called Magic(,), where the first index is the row number and the second the column number. You can use all the procedures in the original program except that you need a form-level array Magic(,) of integers and:

- The Form_Click program will also call the program that fills the Magic(,) array
- The line that placed a number in the labels now uses the numbers stored in the Magic(,) array

Here are the form-level declarations for the magic square program:

```
Option Explicit
Dim NumberOfDim As Integer, Size As Integer
Dim LabelSize As Integer, Magic() As Integer
```

Here's the modified Form_Load:

```
Private Sub Form_Load()
'Local variables
  Dim I As Integer, BoxSize As Single
  Dim X As String, L As String
  Dim LabelSizeMessage As String

 Show
 WindowState = 2                          'maximal

  'get number of rows/columns
  X = InputBox("Number of dimensions?")
  NumberOfDim = Val(X)
  LabelSizeMessage = CheckDimensionNumber(NumberOfDim)
  Do Until LabelSizeMessage = "OK"
     X = InputBox(LabelSizeMessage & "Renter the number of dimensions.")
     NumberOfDim = Val(X)
     LabelSizeMessage = CheckDimensionNumber(NumberOfDim)
  Loop
  ' get size
  L = InputBox("Size of Labels?")
  LabelSize = Val(L)
  LabelSizeMessage = LabelSizeOk(LabelSize)
  Do Until LabelSizeMessage = "OK"
    L = InputBox(LabelSizeMessage & " Please reenter label size")
```

```
    LabelSize = Val(L)
    LabelSizeMessage = LabelSizeOk(LabelSize)
  Loop

 Me.Print "Please click on the form in order to see the magic square."
 End Sub
```

The functions

```
Function CheckDimensionNumber(X As Integer) As String
```

and

```
Function LabelSizeOk(X As Integer) As String
```

are identical to the ones in the previous program, as is the Procedure to make the labels:

```
Private Sub MakeBoxes(HowBig)
```

The only change in the Locate procedure is to change the caption of the labels to reflect the value of the Magic array:

```
Private Sub LocateBoxes(HowBig As Integer, Number As Integer)

  Dim I As Integer, Row As Integer
  Dim Column As Integer
  Dim StartWidth As Integer, StartHeight As Integer
  Dim CurrentHeight As Integer, CurrentWidth As Integer

  StartHeight = ScaleHeight / 2 - ((Number / 2) * HowBig)
  StartWidth = ScaleWidth / 2 - ((Number / 2) * HowBig)
  For I = 0 To Size - 1
    Row = I \ Number
    Column = I Mod Number
    CurrentHeight = StartHeight + (Row * HowBig)
    CurrentWidth = StartWidth + (Column * HowBig)
    lblBox(I).Move CurrentWidth, CurrentHeight
'this is the changed line
    lblBox(I).Caption = Trim(Str$(Magic(Row + 1, Column + 1)))
    lblBox(I).Visible = True
```

```
  Next I
End Sub
```

The Form_Click program now looks like this:

```
Private Sub Form_Click()
  Static BoxesMade As Integer
  Cls
  If Not (BoxesMade) Then
    MakeBoxes LabelSize
    BoxesMade = True
  End If
  MakeMagic ' calls the MakeMagic routine
  LocateBoxes LabelSize, NumberOfDim
End Sub
```

Finally, the key MakeMagic routine that implements Loubère's rule looks like this:

```
Private Sub MakeMagic()
  'local variables
  Dim I As Integer, RowNumber As Integer, ColNumber As Integer
  Dim NewRow As Integer, NewCol As Integer
  ReDim Magic(1 To NumberOfDim, 1 To NumberOfDim)

  RowNumber = 1
  ColNumber = (NumberOfDim \ 2) + 1
  Magic(RowNumber, ColNumber) = 1
  For I = 2 To Size
    If RowNumber = 1 And ColNumber = NumberOfDim Then
    ' at right hand corner
      NewRow = 2
      NewCol = ColNumber
    Else
     NewRow = RowNumber - 1
     NewCol = ColNumber + 1 'move up one row and to the right
     If NewRow < 1 Then NewRow = NewRow + NumberOfDim
' above line means gone off the top
     If NewCol > NumberOfDim Then NewCol = NewCol - NumberOfDim
'above line means gone off the right
   End If
  ' find empty slot by going down row by row
  Do Until Magic(NewRow, NewCol) = 0
```

```
      NewRow = RowNumber + 1
      NewCol = ColNumber
   Loop
   RowNumber = NewRow
   ColNumber = NewCol
   Magic(RowNumber, ColNumber) = I
Next I
End Sub
```

Notice that the If clause inside the For-Next loop corresponds to the special case of the upper-right corner. The two If statements inside the Else clause correspond to the first rule, "up and to the right." Of course, this row may be off the square, and the If-Thens take care of this.

The Do loop stops when you get to an unoccupied square. One of the nice properties of Loubère's method of constructing magic squares is that you know this will always work.

Using Lists and Arrays with Procedures

Visual Basic has an extraordinary facility to use lists and arrays in procedures and functions. Unlike languages like standard Pascal, it's easy to send any size list or array to a procedure. One way to do this, of course, is to make the list or array a form or global variable, as you saw in the section "Example: Improving the Built-in Random Number Generator" earlier in this chapter. However, using lists and arrays as parameters for procedures and functions is much more common.

The reasons for doing this are similar to why one usually prefers parameters to shared variables—they increase your flexibility. To send an array parameter to a procedure or function, put the name of the array followed by ( ) in the parameter list. For example, assume that List# is a one-dimensional array of double-precision variables. Array$ is a two-dimensional string array and BigArray% a three-dimensional array of integers. Then,

```
Private Sub Example(List#(), Array$(), BigArray%(), X%)
```

would allow this Example procedure to use (and change) a list of double-precision variables, an array of strings, a three-dimensional array of integers, and a final integer variable. Note that just as with variables, list and array parameters are placeholders; they have no independent existence. To call the procedure, you might have a fragment like this:

```
Dim PopChange#(50), CityState$(3,10), TotalPop%(2,2,2)
```

Now,

```
Example PopChange#(), CityState$(), TotalPop%(), X1#
```

would call this procedure by sending it the current location (passed by reference) of the three arrays and the integer variable. And just as before, since the compiler knows where the variable, list, or array is located, it can change the contents.

Suppose you want to write a function procedure that would take a list of numbers and return the maximum entry. Since you may want to do this for many different lists, you decide to write a procedure that follows this outline:

Function FindMaximum(List( ))
    Start at the top of the list
    If an entry is bigger than the current Max "swap it"
Until you finish the list.
Set the value of the function to the final "Max"

This kind of outline obviously calls for a For-Next loop. But the problem with translating this outline to a program is, how do you know where the list starts or ends? You could arrange for every list to have a flag at the end, but then you would have trouble combining this with Visual Basic's Range feature. Or you could use the trick of reserving one entry in the list for the number of items in the list.

Visual Basic makes this process easier with the commands LBound and UBound, which are not part of interpreted BASIC. LBound gives the lowest possible index and UBound the highest in a list. For example, you can easily translate the preceding outline to the following:

```
Function FindMax(A() As Single)
  ' local variables Start, Finish, I
  Dim Start As Integer, Finish As Integer, I As Integer

  Start = LBound(A)
  Finish = UBound(A)
```

```
  Max = A(Start)
  For I = Start  To Finish
    If A(I) > Max Then Max = A(I)
  Next I
  FindMax = Max
End Function
```

When this procedure is finished, the value of this function would be the largest entry on the list of single-precision variables.

In general, the command

LBound(NameOfArray,I)

gives the lower bound for the I'th dimension. (For a list (one-dimensional array), the I is optional, as in the preceding example.) Therefore,

```
Dim Test%(1 To 5,6 To 10,7 To 12)
Print LBound(Test%,2)
```

gives a 6 and

```
Print UBound(Test%,3)
```

gives a 12.

Here's another example. Suppose you want to write a general procedure to copy one two-dimensional string array to another. The LBound and UBound commands allow you to copy lists or arrays with different ranges, provided the total number of rows and columns is the same. (Subtract the LBound from the UBound for each dimension and see if they match.)

It's hard to stress enough the flexibility that Visual Basic's method for handling lists and arrays within procedures gives, especially when combined with the LBound and UBound commands. For example, you may have learned about matrices in math or engineering courses. It is close to impossible to write a general matrix package in standard Pascal, yet it's almost trivial in Visual Basic.

One last point: using LBound and UBound is not a cure-all. If part of the list or array hasn't yet been filled, these commands may not help. Therefore, although using a flag or adding the number of items on a list as the zeroth item on the list was a more common programming trick for earlier BASICs (that didn't have UBound and LBound), it is still sometimes useful in Visual Basic.

tip: *You cannot use LBound and UBound with control arrays. Instead, store this information in the Tag property of the original element of the control array.*

The Grid Control

The grid control lets you build spreadsheet-like features into your projects. As the screen in Figure 10-5 shows, this control displays a rectangular grid of rows and columns. How many rows and columns you see at design time depends both on the number of rows and columns you have set *and* the current size of the grid. (For example, in Figure 10-5 there is not enough room to see all of the eight rows and all of the five columns.)

note: *If the GridControl (pointed to in Figure 10-5) is not part of your toolbox, choose Tools | Custom Controls and check off the Microsoft Grid Control in that dialog box.*

Each grid member is usually called a *cell*. Cells can hold text, bitmaps, or icons or even mix text and graphics. You can specify the contents as well as the

Figure 10-5 Sample grid control with eight rows and five columns

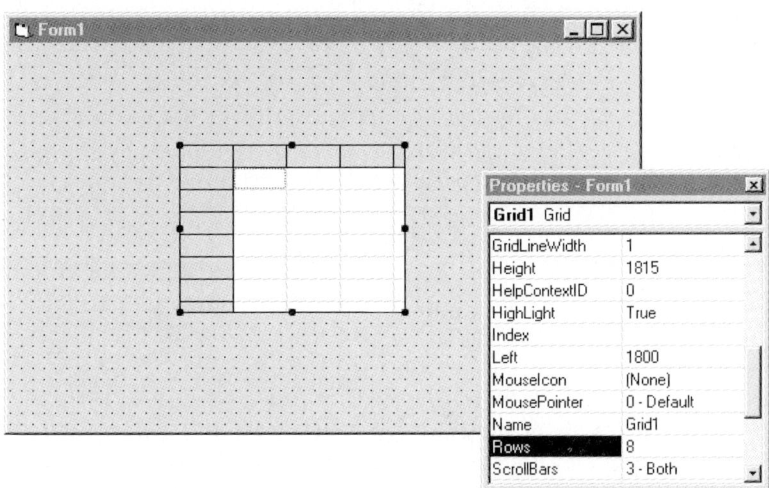

width and height of a row or column individually, and of course, you can use code to control each cell individually while your project is running. Users can move from cell to cell by using the arrow keys or the mouse; Visual Basic handles such movement automatically. The grid control even includes a built-in word-wrap feature so users can enter text more easily, but you must program in the ability for cells to actually accept text. In any case, a grid control, like a text box, can hold only text in a single font. Numbers must be translated back and forth using the Val and Str$ functions or the Variant data type.

Grids let you easily display the information stored in arrays neatly and efficiently. For example, as you will see later in this chapter, you can use a grid control to display larger magic squares than the control array of labels allowed you to do earlier. Moreover, the grid version works faster and uses fewer Windows resources.

Users can work with contiguous groups of cells in the grid, usually called *regions*, by clicking a cell and dragging the mouse or by pressing SHIFT plus an arrow key to select the region. Once a region is selected, code can be used to analyze or change the contents.

The grid control is automatically added to your toolbox unless you modify the AUTO*LD.VBP file that controls the initial startup features of Visual Basic.

note: *If you give someone an application that uses the grid control, you must install the GRID16.OCX or GRID32.OCX file in their \WINDOWS\SYSTEM directory or some other place that Windows knows about. See Appendix A on the Setup Wizard.*

tip: *If you need to build sophisticated spreadsheet features into your grids, consider getting a custom control. Both Farpoint Technologies and Visual Tools make powerful grid controls that come equipped with most (if not all) of the spreadsheet functions one would want. (See Appendix D for information on how to contact these companies.)*

General Properties of the Grid Control

Many of the properties of the grid control are the same as those for the controls that you're already familiar with. For example, the Height and Width properties tell you how large the grid will appear. As another example, the Enabled property determines whether the grid will notice keystrokes or mouse activity. You can even use the Picture property to place a bitmap or icon inside the currently active cell.

tip: *If you set the ScrollBar property to a nonzero value (1 for Horizontal, 2 for Vertical, 3 for both), then Visual Basic automatically adds the appropriate scroll bars when there is information on the grid that cannot be seen.*

The remainder of this section takes you through the most important of the properties that are special to grids.

COLS, ROWS

These properties determine the number of rows and columns in the grid. The default value for each of these properties is 2, but you can reset them in code or via the Properties Window as needed. They obviously must be integers, and the syntax is

GridName.Cols = *NumOfCols%*
GridName.Rows = *NumOfRows%*

You can also add an optional form name. For example,

```
frmDisplay.Cols = 10
```

COLWIDTH, ROWHEIGHT

These two properties specify the width of a specific column or height of a specific row. They can only be set via code. Both are measured in twips. The syntax is

GridName.ColWidth(*ColNumber%*) = *Width%*
GridName.RowHeight(*RowNumber%*) = *Height%*

You can also add an optional form name.

tip: *If text has been automatically word wrapped, then adjust the ColWidth or RowHeight to display the text by checking its TextWidth and TextHeight properties.*

COL, ROW

These properties (which shouldn't be confused with Cols and Rows!) set or return the current cell inside the grid. For this reason they are only available at run time. As the user moves around the grid, the values of these properties change. You then would use their values to determine where inside the grid the user is. By adjusting their values via code, you can specify the current cell directly. Since both Col and Row start out at zero, the top left corner cell has Col index 0 and Row index 0.

TEXT

The Text property sets or returns the text inside the current cell (the one given by the values of the Col and Row properties). You can place up to 255 characters in an individual cell.

For example, if a grid (control name Grid1) has four rows and four columns, the following code fragment places text directly in the bottom right corner and displays the contents of the top left corner cell:

```
Grid1.Col = 3
Grid1.Row = 3
Grid1.Text = "This would go in the bottom right corner"
Grid1.Col = 0
Grid1.Row = 0
Print Grid1.Text
```

(Note that because rows and columns in grids are numbered from 0, the bottom right corner of a 4 X 4 grid has col (and row) index 3.)

COLALIGNMENT

There are three possible settings for data inside a column. You can left-justify (value = 0), right-justify (value = 1), or center the text (value = 2). The syntax is

GridName.ColAlignment(*Index%*) = *Setting%*

FIXEDCOLS, FIXEDROWS, FIXEDALIGNMENT

Often when you are working with a grid, you will want to use certain cells to display information at all times. For example, regardless of how the user scrolls through a spreadsheet, you may want to display the column headings. Fixed rows and columns are always displayed in gray and must be at the top and left side of the grid. The FixedAlignment property works exactly as does the ColAlignment property, but applies only to fixed columns. The syntax for these three properties is

GridName.FixedCols = *NumberOfFixedCols%*
GridName.FixedRows = *NumberOfFixedRows%*
GridName.FixedAlignment = *SettingNumber%*

where, as before, the setting for the alignment property has the possible values 0, 1, and 2. And you can add an optional form name, of course.

GRIDLINES, SCROLLBARS

These two properties control whether grid lines (these make it easier to see cell boundaries) and scroll bars appear. The default is to show grid lines and to have both horizontal and vertical scroll bars.

LEFTCOL, TOPROW

These two properties control what is the leftmost column and highest row displayed from a grid. You use these properties when the entire grid is too large to fit on the form. These properties can only be set in code, and the syntax for both of these properties is similar:

GridName.LeftCol = *LeftmostCol%*
GridName.TopRow = *HighestRow%*

Properties of Selected Cells Inside Grids

Although grids are often used passively to display data (or pictures), it is even more common to make them responsive to the user. Users can select cells or regions and change their contents. This section takes you through the properties that let you work with regions selected by the user.

CELLSELECTED

This is a Boolean (True/False) property that tells you whether the cell specified by the current value of the Row and Col properties is within the region selected by the user. You can use this property to check whether the user has selected a region that includes the current cell.

SELSTARTCOL, SELENDCOL, SELSTARTROW, SELENDROW

These properties are determined by the region currently selected. If all these values are the same, then a single cell was selected.

CLIP

The Clip property is among the most important when dealing with selected regions. This sets or returns the contents of the selected region. The syntax is

GridName.Clip = *String$*

The string expression on the right-hand side contains the entire contents of the selected region. The contents of each cell on the same row are separated from the adjacent cell by the tab character (ASCII 9), and each row is separated from the next by the carriage return character (ASCII 13). For example, the following code fills up the first three columns and two rows with the string equivalents of the numbers 1 through 6.

```
TabChar$ = Chr$(9)
CR$ = Chr$(13)
Grid1.SelStartCol = 0: Grid1.SelEndCol = 2
Grid1.SelStartRow = 0: Grid1.SelEndRow = 1
S$ = Str$(1) + TabChar$ + Str$(2) + TabChar$ + Str$(3)
S$ = S$ + CR$ + Str$(4) + TabChar$ + Str$(5) + TabChar$ + Str$(6)
Grid1.Clip = S$
```

FILLSTYLE

Sometimes you want what the user enters into one cell of the selected region to fill up the entire region. You can control this by changing the FillStyle property from its default value of 0 to the value 1. In addition, when FillStyle is 1, any image assigned to the Picture property automatically fills all cells whose CellSelected property is True.

HIGHLIGHT

This True/False property determines whether the cells selected are highlighted. The default value (True) is that selected cells are highlighted.

Events and Methods for Grid Controls

Grids respond to many of the standard events; for example, you can use the Click event to determine whether the user has clicked inside the grid and the KeyPress event to send what a user is typing inside the grid directly to the currently selected cell. Using the KeyPress event to accumulate keystrokes with a static variable and then testing for the ENTER key is a common way to allow direct entry of data into the grid. All you need to do after the ENTER key is pressed is assign the data accumulated by the static variable to the Text property of the grid. However, since the code to activate a grid control must constantly monitor when the selected region changes, Visual Basic provides you with two events unique to grids that you might want to consider allowing along with (or instead of) the ENTER key. They are described next.

tip: *A common trick for allowing users to enter data is to position a text box directly over a cell. Make it* exactly *the same width and height as the cell. The user can't tell it's not a cell, and so you can give the illusion of direct entry into the grid.*

ROWCOLCHANGE

This event is activated when the current cell changes—either because the user has moved around in the grid or you've used code to change one of the properties given in the previous section. If you make the variable used in the KeyPress event procedure a form-level variable instead of a static variable, you can use an assignment to the Text property of the grid in this event procedure to make the changes.

SELCHANGE

This event is activated when the selected region changes—either because the user has moved around in the grid or the code has directly changed one of the properties given in the previous section.

METHODS FOR RESIZING A GRID

There are also two methods that are unique to grids. These let you insert or delete rows from a grid. The syntax to add a row is

GridName.AddItem *Item$* [,*Index%*]

The string given by *Item$* is placed in the first column of the new row. The optional index parameter gives the position where the row is added.

RemoveItem, on the other hand, removes a row from a grid. Its syntax is

GridName.RemoveItem *Index%*

For example, to remove the first row of a grid you might use

```
Grid1.RemoveItem 0
```

(because the first index starts out at zero).

Magic Squares Using a Grid Control

You can easily modify the magic square program to use a grid rather than a control array. However, let's change the program so that the user can scroll through the grid. This will allow extraordinarily large magic squares. First off, you will need a form with a grid control that has both vertical and horizontal scroll bars enabled. Let's leave it at the default name of Grid1. Once you do this, here is the code that gives this version of the magic square program. To begin with, you need fewer form-level variables:

```
Dim NumberOfDim As Integer
Dim CellSize As Integer, Magic() As Integer
```

Next, the Form_Load is much simpler, as you don't have to check the size (because the user can now scroll through the grid).

```
Private Sub Form_Load()
'Local variables
  Dim I As Integer
  Dim X As String
```

```
 Show
 WindowState = 2                              'maximal

 'get number of rows/columns
  X = InputBox("Number of rows/columns?")
  NumberOfDim = Val(X)
  Do Until NumberOfDim Mod 2 = 1
     X = InputBox("The number of rows/columns must be odd.")
     NumberOfDim = Val(X)
  Loop
 ' the next two lines calculate how wide a cell should be based on
 ' the largest number that is going into it
 'this line finds the number of digits
  CellSize = Len(Trim(Str$(NumberOfDim * NumberOfDim)))
 'this one multiplies it by the width of a digit
  CellSize = CellSize * (TextWidth("1"))
  Me.Print "Please click on the form in order to see the magic square."
 End Sub
```

This routine makes the grid the correct size. To make the scroll bars easier to see, make the grid 90% of the size of the form. It also makes each row and column the correct height and width (as measured by the HowBig parameter).

```
Private Sub MakeGrid(HowBig)
  Dim I As Integer

  Grid1.Cols = NumberOfDim
  Grid1.Rows = NumberOfDim
  Grid1.Height = 0.9 * ScaleHeight
  Grid1.Width = 0.9 * ScaleWidth
  Grid1.Move ScaleWidth / 2 - (Grid1.Width / 2), ScaleHeight / 2 - _
(Grid1.Height / 2)
  For I = 1 To Grid1.Cols
  Grid1.ColWidth(I - 1) = HowBig
  Grid1.RowHeight(I - 1) = HowBig
  Next I
  End Sub
```

As before, the Form_Click calls the procedure that builds the array for the magic square. In this case you also fill the cells in the grid using the array and then make the Grid visible.

```
Private Sub Form_Click()
Dim I As Integer, J As Integer
    Cls
    MakeGrid CellSize
    MakeMagic
    MousePointer = 11
    For I = 1 To NumberOfDim
     For J = 1 To NumberOfDim
        Grid1.Col = J - 1
       Grid1.Row = I - 1
      Grid1.ColAlignment(J - 1) = 2 'centered
      Grid1.Text = Str$(Magic(I, J))
     Next J
    Next I
    Grid1.Visible = True
   MousePointer = 0
End Sub
```

The MakeMagic routine is the same as before, as is the QueryUnload event.

Sorting and Searching

Sorting and searching through lists of names is one of the most common tasks people use computers for. Let's start with the techniques needed for searching through a list.

Searching

Suppose a long list of names is stored in the computer's memory. Now you want to find out whether a certain name is on the list. You can do this easily: just write a program to compare the name you want with all the names on the list. Visual Basic generates code quickly, so this method is effective for short lists.

However, if the list has 5,000 names, all in alphabetical order, this method would be a waste of time. If you are looking in a telephone book for a name beginning with K, you don't start at page 1; you open the book roughly in the middle and proceed from there. When the information in the list you're searching is already ordered, you can speed things up by using an extension of this method: each time, the program will look at a list that is only half the size of the previous list. This procedure speeds up a search almost beyond belief.

Here's an outline for a program that searches through a list that is already in alphabetical order:

1. Divide the list in half.
2. Determine whether you have gone too far. (Is the entry at the halfway mark before or after the name you're looking for?)
3. If you have gone too far, look at the first half of the list; otherwise, look at the second half.
4. Go back to step 1 as long as there are names left to look at.

Suppose your list has 5,000 names. After completing step 4, you will go back to step 1 with a list of 2,500 names. Complete step 4 again and you will have only 1,250 names, then only 625, and so on. By the 12th time, you will have only 2 names to search. This type of search is called a *binary search.*

An extraordinary feature of the binary search is that it works almost as quickly for large lists as for small. For example, suppose you are searching through the New York City telephone directory, with roughly 10,000,000 entries, to find a name. Just by following this outline (and not doing any estimating of where the letters are), you would find the name, if it is in the directory, in no more than 25 applications of step 4.

The procedure is a bit tricky, so it's worth spending time on. What follows is a first attempt. (It has a subtle bug.)

```
Private Sub BinarySearch (X$(), Target$)
  ' LOCAL variables are Low, High, Middle
  ' A global variable called TargetPosition
  Dim Low As Integer, High As Integer, Middle As Integer
  TargetPosition = 0
  Low = LBound(X$)
  High = UBound(X$)

  Do
    Middle = (Low + High) \ 2
    Select Case X$(Middle)
      Case Is = Target$
        TargetPosition = Middle
      Case Is > Target$
        High = Middle - 1
      Case Is < Target$
        Low = Middle + 1
```

```
    End Select
  Loop Until TargetPosition <> 0
  Print TargetPosition
End Sub
```

Setting the variable TargetPosition to zero initializes the global variable at the beginning of the list. At the end of the procedure, this variable will contain the position of the target. (You also could set up another parameter for this information, and an even better idea would be to turn the whole procedure into a function whose value is the location of the target.)

Notice that this procedure uses the UBound/LBound method of finding the limits. The method described earlier for storing the number of entries in the list as the zeroth entry is not needed here because this procedure assumes that the entire list is ordered.

The Do loop does the work. First it finds the middle of the list by using the integer division operator. (List indexes are always integers.) There are three possibilities in the search, so we chose to use the Select Case command. (You can also use If-Then-ElseIf, of course, but see the next try for another way.) If the entry in the middle position is too large, you know that you should look at the first half of the list. Your target can't be the middle entry (you eliminated that in the first case), so you can move the "High" index down by one. (A similar situation holds in the next case.)

Now comes the problem in this preliminary version of a binary search routine: the loop stops only if TargetPosition has a nonzero value—in other words, if the function finds the target. But suppose the target isn't in the list? The loop never stops; the program is stuck in an infinite loop.

How can you fix this procedure so it stops when there are no more entries left to check? Consider the following example. Suppose you are down to a list that consists of two names, say in the 42nd and 43rd positions, and the 42nd entry is too small and the 43rd entry too large. What happens? The first time you're in this situation, the value of Middle is set to (42+43)\2 = 42. Since the value in the 42nd position is too small, the value of Low is set to one more than Middle—that is, to 43. The values of Low and High are now the same. What happens next? Both Low and High are the same, and the value of Middle is also the same. Now the entry in the Middle position is too large, so the value of High shrinks by one, to 42—less than the value of Low. This gives you one way to end the loop. Change it to read

```
Loop Until (TargetPosition <> 0) Or (High < Low)
```

There's another way to write this loop that some people find easier to understand. This method is based on the assumption that something special happens in small lists when the difference between the High and Low indices is 1. Arrange to leave the loop when the list has size 1 and add a few lines to take care of this special case:

```
If (High - Low) < = 1 Then
  If A$(High) = Target$ Then TargetPosition = High
Else
  If A$(Low) = Target$ Then TargetPosition = Low
End If
```

Notice that both these possibilities take care of the case when the list has only one entry, or even no entries. Remember: it's the boundary cases that often cause the most subtle bugs in a program.

SIMPLIFYING THE SEARCH: THE STRCOMP FUNCTION

The situation in which you need to know whether some string is less than, equal to, or greater than another is so common that Visual Basic has a special function for this: the StrComp function. (It works a little faster than the three tests.) Its syntax is

StrComp(*string1*, *string2*[, *compare*])

(StrComp supports named arguments, by the way.)

The optional *compare* argument specifies whether the comparison is case sensitive or not. Use a 0 (the default) for a case-sensitive comparison and 1 for one that is not case sensitive. The point of StrComp is the return values, which are described in the following table:

The Comparison Gives	StrComp Returns
string1 is less than string2	–1
string1 is equal to string2	0
string1 is greater than string2	1
string1 or string2 is Null	Null

Using StrComp, you can rewrite the comparison part of the binary search routine as:

```
Select Case StrComp(X$(Middle), Target)
      Case 0
        TargetPosition = Middle
      Case 1
        High = Middle - 1
      Case -1
        Low = Middle + 1
End Select
```

HOW DO YOU TEST A BINARY SEARCH ROUTINE?

On the subject of bugs, how would you write a test module for a binary search module in order to determine what was wrong with the preliminary program given earlier? You need a long, ordered list. One way to test the program is to use a list that consists of all possible two-letter strings:

AA, AB, AC,...BA, BB,...ZZ

There are 26 * 26 = 676 two-letter combinations. (Using three-letter combinations allows a list of 26^3 = 17,576 entries.)

To create this list, you can use this fragment:

```
Dim A$(1 To 676)
Dim Index As Integer, I As Integer, J As Integer
Index = 1
For I = 65 To 90
  For J = 65 To 90
    A$(Index) = Chr$(I) + Chr$(J)
    Index = Index + 1
  Next J
Next I
```

Now you can test the binary search module by trying various possibilities, such as searching for a two-letter string that is on the list and another two-letter string that is not on the list, or searching for the first entry and the last.

Sorting

Programmers prefer ordered lists, just as people prefer alphabetized lists, such as dictionaries and telephone books, because techniques such as binary searching work so quickly. Sorting data is one of the most common jobs a computer is asked to do. Unfortunately, sorting is also one of the most time-consuming tasks for a computer. Because of this, computer scientists have developed literally hundreds of different ways to sort lists, and it's impossible to say which is best in all possible circumstances. This section discusses four methods. The first two are useful for short lists. The third is often the method of choice, even for lists having thousands of entries. The last sort method is called the *bubble sort* and seems to be the sort most commonly given in elementary books. Unfortunately, it has few, if any, redeeming features, and you may find it better not to use it even if you are adapting code already written. It is usually better to switch to one of the other three sort procedures given here. Chapter 16 discusses three more sorting methods. Two of those three are usually better than even the fastest sort presented in this section, but unfortunately, they are much more difficult to program.

When you sit down to write a program, it's always a good idea to ask yourself if there's anything you do in real life that's analogous to what you want the computer to do. For sorting lists, what often comes to mind is ordering playing-card hands. There seem to be two types of people: those who pick up all the cards at once and sort their hands by first finding the smallest card, then the next smallest, and so on; and those who pick up one card at a time, scan what they have already sorted, and then immediately place the new card in the correct place. (For what it's worth, computer scientists have proved that these two methods take roughly the same amount of time, with the second method usually being a tiny bit faster.) Each of the methods for ordering playing cards translates into a way to sort lists, and each is taken up in turn.

RIPPLE SORT

The sorting method analogous to the first way of sorting cards just described is usually called *ripple sort*. Here's an outline for it:

1. Start with the first entry.
2. Look at the remaining entries one by one. Whenever you find a smaller entry, swap it with the first.
3. Now shrink the list; start with the second entry and look at the remaining entries (3, 4, and so on).
4. Continue this until all items are worked through.

Notice that if, say, the list has 50 entries, you only have to do the fourth step of this outline 48 times. This is because by the time this procedure works its way to the last entry, enough switching has happened that it has to be the largest entry. Here's the procedure. (Like many of the sorts in this chapter, it assumes you've written a SWAP general procedure to interchange the values of two variables, filling in the gap left by the designers of Visual Basic.)

```
Private Sub RippleSort (A$())
  'Local variables NumOfEntries%, NumOfTimes%, I%, J%
  Dim NumOfEntries%, NumOfTImes%, I%, J%

  NumOfEntries% = UBound(A$)
  NumOfTimes% = NumOfEntries% - 1
  For I% = LBound(A$) To NumOfTimes%
    For J% = I% + 1 To NumOfEntries%
      If A$(J%) < A$(I%) Then SWAP A$(J%), A$(I%)
    Next J%
  Next I%
End Sub
```

This procedure assumes the list starts from 1. An even more elegant idea is to make this procedure depend on two more parameters, say Low and High, and use these to establish the bounds on the loops. (That way you can sort all or part of the list.)

FIRST STEPS FOR TESTING SORTS

How do you write a module to test a sort? Well, you need a way of creating random lists of strings. Here's one way. Add the following lines to a Form_Click procedure:

```
Dim B$(100)
Dim I As Integer, RndInt1 As Integer, RndInt2 As Integer

Randomize
For I = 1 To 100
  RndInt1 = Int(26*RND(1)) + 1: RndInt2 = Int(26*Rnd(1)) + 1
  B$(I) = Chr$(RndInt1+ 65) + Chr$ (RndInt2 + 65)
Next I
```

At this point of course, you have only one sort to test, although this method can be used to test any sort. In any case, to test Ripple sort use the following:

```
RippleSort B$()
```

Now print out the list to make sure it's been sorted:

```
For 1 To 100
  Print B$(I);"    ";
Next I
```

INSERTION SORT

The second sorting method, usually called *insertion sort*, is no harder to program. In this sort, at every stage you'll have an already sorted, smaller list. Look through the list, from the first entry to what is currently the last, until you find something smaller than the new entry. Unfortunately, unlike the case of playing cards, you have to move all the entries down by one to make room for the new entry. This leads to a slight *tweak* (computer jargon meaning "a small change that improves performance"). The new version is even easier to program. Instead of moving forward from the start of the list, move backward from the end of the list. Now, each time the comparison fails, move the old entry down by one. If you do this, you'll be moving a "hole" along as you move through the list. When the comparison finally fails, you drop the new entry into the hole. Here's that procedure:

```
Private Sub InsertionSort (A$())
  'LOCAL Variables are NumOfEntries%, I%, J%, Temp$
  Dim NumOfEntries%, I%, J%, Temp$

  NumOfEntries% = UBound(A$)
  For I% = 2 To NumOfEntries%
   Temp$ = A$(I%)
   For J% = I% - 1 To 1 Step -1
     If Temp$ >= A$(J%) Then Exit For
     A$(J% + 1) = A$(J%)
   Next J%
   A$(J% + 1) = Temp$
  Next I%
End Sub
```

As with ripple sort, you might want to make this procedure depend on a Low and High parameter. Notice, however, that starting the For-Next loop at 2 takes care of the special case of the list having one entry. The loop moves entries forward until conditions are ripe for the Exit For statement. This occurs when you have located the position of the hole—in preparation for the statement A$(J%+1) = Temp$, which fills the hole.

Since these methods follow the playing-card analogy closely, they are not hard to program. Moreover, for small lists, they are reasonably fast. Sorting 100 strings by using the ripple sort takes about one-third of a second on a basic 33MHz 486. Unfortunately, sorting 200 entries takes about 1.25 seconds. Although the insertion sort is a little faster than the ripple sort (0.25 seconds for 100 items), both these types of sorts have the unfortunate property that doubling the list quadruples the time. Sorting a list of 13,000 names (by no means a very large list) would take about 1.5 hours, so you can see that these are not the methods to use for lists much longer than 200 or so entries. You need to turn to a faster method. (Now you can see why the binary search is so nice—doubling the list adds only one step.)

The next section shows you one of the very fastest all-purpose sorts.

SHELL SORT

The faster sort discussed in this section, *Shell sort*, was discovered by Donald Shell around 30 years ago. (Three other fast sorts are discussed in Chapter 19.)

Shell sort is unusual because while the procedure is simple—and short—understanding what makes it work is not. This is partially because there is nothing that you do in real life that's analogous to Shell sort and partially because it's a really neat idea. Another problem is that even after you understand why it works, it's unclear why it's so much faster than the previous two methods.

To understand Shell sort, you should ask yourself what are the advantages and disadvantages of the two previous sorting methods. One obvious disadvantage of ripple sort is that most of the time, the comparisons in the various loops are wasted. The disadvantage of insertion sort is that most of the time it moves objects inefficiently. Even when the list is mostly sorted, you still have to move the entries one-by-one to make the hole. The big advantage of ripple sort is that it moves objects efficiently. Once the smallest object gets to the top, it stays there.

In a sense, then, insertion and ripple sorts are opposites. Donald Shell decided to improve insertion sort by moving the keys long distances, as is done in ripple sort. Consider the following list of numbers to sort:

57, 3, 12, 9, 1, 7, 8, 2, 5, 4, 97, 6

Suppose, instead of comparing the first entry to the second, you compare it with the seventh, and instead of comparing the second with the third, you compare it with the eighth. In short, cut up the list into six different lists. Now do an insertion sort on these six small lists. After this, you have six lists, each of which is sorted, while the whole list is probably still not sorted. Merge the smaller lists and break up the result into three new lists (the first with the fourth, sixth, and so on, and the second with the fifth, eighth, and so on). Do an insertion sort on these three smaller lists and merge again. Now the resulting list is very close to being sorted. A final sort finishes the process. (Insertion sort is efficient when it doesn't have much work to do.)

If the numbers are already stored in a list, you never have to break up the list into smaller lists. Instead, you shift your point of view by concentrating on the different sublists. Also, because on the earlier passes the entries moved fairly long distances, when you're down to the final step, not many more moves are needed. Here's a version of Shell sort:

```
Public Sub ShellSort (A$())
  'LOCAL variables are NumOfEntries%, Increm%, J%, Temp$
  Dim NumOfEntries%, Increm%, J%, Temp$
  NumOfEntries% = UBound(A$)
  Increm% = NumOfEntries% \ 2
  Do Until Increm% < 1
    For I% = Increm% + 1 To NumOfEntries%
      Temp$ = A$(I%)
      For J% = I% - Increm% To 1 Step -Increm%
        If Temp$ >= A$(J%) Then Exit For
        A$(J% + Increm%) = A$(J%)
      Next J%
      A$(J% + Increm%) = Temp$
    Next I%
    Increm% = Increm% \ 2
  Loop
End Sub
```

The Do loop gives you the way of dividing the lists into smaller lists. Inside the Do loop, the inner For-Next loop does an insertion sort on the smaller lists. Since each entry on the smaller list differs from the next by the number given in the variable Increm%, the Step command gives you a way of working with the smaller lists.

What's amazing about Shell sort is that it's so much faster than the ripple or insertion sort, although, surprisingly enough, nobody yet knows how much faster it will be in general. (A way to get a first-rate Ph.D. would be to fully analyze Shell sort.) In any case, sorting a list of 3,600 names will take only about five seconds using Shell sort on a basic 33MHz 486.

The speed of Shell sort depends somewhat on the numbers you use to split the list into smaller ones. These are usually called the increments (the 6, 3, and 1 used in the preceding example), and they should be chosen with care. (Because the increments get smaller on each pass, Shell sort is sometimes known as a "diminishing increment" sort.) The numbers used in the example (half the current size of the list) are Shell's original choice. Today we know you can obtain slightly better results with other increments. One of the simpler choices that gives slightly better results is

...3280, 1093 364 121 40 13 4 1

where each number is arrived at by multiplying the preceding number by 3 and adding 1. (You start with the largest increment that's smaller than the size of your list, so a list with 5,000 entries would start with an increment of 3,280.) In any case, no one yet knows the best choice of increments. Try other sequences and see if you get better results.

How do you write a realistic test module for a fast sorting routine? Obviously, you want to create a long list of random strings. This is not very difficult to do, but it can sometimes take longer than the sort. For a list of random four-letter strings for Shell sort, use

```
Dim Test$(1 To 3600)
Dim I%, J%, CNumber
  For I% = 1 To 3600
    For J% = 1 To 4
      Cnumber = Int(26*RND(1))
      Test$(I%) = Test$(I%) + Chr$(CNumber + 65)
    Next J%
  Next I%
```

and call Shell sort. (I wouldn't recommend trying to sort a list of 3,600 names with insertion or ripple sort.) Finally, add a routine to print out parts of the transformed list. If the results are ordered, then you can be satisfied. Once you are, then you might want to add a routine to time the various sorts. (If you devise your own sort or want to test these, you might want to test the sorts on the two "boundary cases" also. For a sorting routine, this is usually thought of when the list is either already ordered or completely in reverse order.)

A COMMON BUT BAD SORT: THE BUBBLE SORT

Finally, you should be aware of (or may already be using) a sort called bubble sort. It's very common in elementary programming books. The idea of bubble sort is the easiest of all: you constantly compare an entry with the one below it. This way, the smallest one "bubbles" to the top. The code for this is almost trivial:

```
Private Sub BubbleSort(A$())
'assume list starts with 1
N = UBound(A$)
For I = 2 To N
 For J = N To I Step -1
  If A$(J-1) > A$(J) Then
    ' need to SWAP A$(J-1), A$(J)
    Temp$ = A$(J-1)
    A$(J-1) = A$(J)
    A$(J) = Temp$
   End If
  Next J
Next I
End Sub
```

The problem is that bubble sort is almost always the slowest sort of all. Since it has few if any redeeming virtues, it should be replaced, at the very least, by an insertion or ripple sort (which are just as easy to program) for small lists and one of the faster sorts, such as Shell sort, for longer lists.

Records (User-Defined Types)

Suppose you want to have a three-dimensional array for 100 employees in a company. The first column is to be for names, the second for salaries, and the third for social security numbers. This common situation can't be programmed in a multidimensional array except by using the variant data type. Some people would call using the variant data type in this situation a kludge. The problem is that variants use more memory and are slower as well. For both speed and memory reasons, you might prefer to set up three parallel lists—one for the names, the second for salaries, and the third for social security numbers (they are strings to include the dashes), as shown here:

```
Dim Names$(100), Salary!(100), SocSec$(100)
```

Having done this, you now would use the same pointer (that is, the row number) to extract information from the three lists.

The way around this extra work is to use a new structure called a record. Records are not part of traditional BASICs, although they are common in programming languages such as C and Pascal. Essentially, a record is a type of "mixed" variable that you create as needed. It usually mixes different kinds of numbers and strings. Visual Basic makes it easy to avoid maintaining parallel structures or using arrays of variants.

Here's the first step: in the Declarations section of a code module, enter

```
Type  VitalInfo
    Name as String
    Salary as Long
    SocialSec as String
End Type
```

This defines the type. From this point on in the program, it's just as good a variable type for variables as single precision, double precision, or variants.

Now, to make (set up) a single variable of "type" VitalInfo, write either

```
Private YourName as VitalInfo
```

or

```
Public HisName As VitalInfo
```

in the Declarations section of any form or module. (YourName would then be private to the form or module and HisName would be global to the project.) You can also write

```
Static MyName As VitalInfo
```

inside a procedure. You can also set up global variables of this type using the Global statement.

Each of these statements sets up a single "mixed" variable. The jargon is to say, "YourName is a record variable of type VitalInfo."

Now you use a dot (period) to isolate the parts of this record:

```
YourName.Name = "Howard"
YourName.Salary = 100000
YourName.SocSecNumber = "036-78-9987"
```

tip: *Many of the Windows API functions require being passed a record of a specific form. The API viewer gives you the structure needed.*

You can make up an array of records. For example:

```
Dim CompanyRecord(1 To 75) as VitalInfo
```

sets up a list capable of holding 75 of these records.

Now imagine you want to design a form to allow inputting the data needed to fill the 75 records. Set up a form-level array called CompanyRecord to hold the 75 records. Next, the form used for this input operation requires three labels to identify the text boxes, three text boxes (control names of Names, Salary, and SSNum), and a command button. If you give the command button the control name (value of Name property) AddButton and add to the Form the form name ofDataForm, you can use the following code to add up to 75 records:

```
Private Sub AddEmpData_Click ()
  Static Count As Integer
  Count = Count + 1
  If Count > 75 Then
     MsgBox("Too Many records")
     Exit Private Sub
  End If
  DataForm.Caption = "Adding data for entry" + Str$(Count)
  CompanyRecord(Count).Name = Names.Text
  CompanyRecord(Count).Salary = Val(Salary.Text)
  CompanyRecord(Count).SocialSec = SSNum.Text
End Sub
```

Note that the caption on the form changes to reflect the number entered. Making Count a static variable and adding 1 before checking ensures that at most 75 entries are allowed. Also note the periods for each component, or element, of the record.

You can even have a component of a record be a record itself. For example, you could make up a RecordOfSalary type to keep track of monthly earnings along with the previous year's salary:

```
Type RecordOfSalary
  SalInJan As Integer
  SalInFeb As Integer
  SalInMar As Integer
  SalInApr As Integer
  SalInMay As Integer
  SalInJun As Integer
  SalInJul As Integer
  SalInAug As Integer
  SalInSep As Integer
  SalInOct As Integer
  SalInNov As Integer
  SalInDec As Integer
  SalInPrevYear As Long
End Type
```

Now you can set up a record of records:

```
Type ExpandedVitalInfo
  Name As String
  Salary As RecordOfSalary
  SocSecNumber As String * 11
End Type
```

Of course, filling out all the information needed for a single record is now that much harder. Filling in the record RecordOfSalary for a single employee requires at least 13 lines of code, so filling in a record of type ExpandedVitalInfo requires at least 15. It also gets a little messy to refer to the information in ExpandedVitalInfo. You thread your way down by using more periods. After using

```
Dim GaryStats As ExpandedVitalInfo
```

to set up a variable of this new type, use a statement like

```
Print GaryStats.Salary.SalInPrevYr
```

to display the information on the previous year's salary.

You can have records as one of the parameters in functions or subprograms. For example, you might write a general procedure to analyze salary data. The first line in the procedure would look like this:

```
Private Sub AnalyzeSalary (X As ExpandedVitalInfo)
```

This procedure allows (and in fact requires) that only variables of type ExpandedVitalInfo be passed to it. Now you can call it at any time by using a line of code like this:

```
AnalyzeSalary(BillStats)
```

This would analyze Bill's salary information. You also can pass individual components of a record whenever they match the type of the parameter.

note: *You can also use arrays in user-defined records. For example:*

```
Type RecordOfSalary
  Salaries(1 To 12) As Integers
  SalInPrevYear As Long
End Type
```

You can then use a loop plus one individual statement to fill a record rather than using 13 statements.

The With Statement

By now navigating through multiple periods has gotten tiring. You will be happy to know that Visual Basic offers a small shortcut. You can use the With statement as a convenient method for quickly getting at the parts of a record. For example,

```
With YourName
  .Name = "Howard"
  .Salary = 100000
  .SocSecNumber = "036-78-9987"
End With
```

lets you avoid some typing. You can even nest With statements if one of the components of a record is itself a record.

```
Dim MyStats As ExpandedVitalInfo
With MyStats
 .Name = "Gary Cornell"
  With .Salary   'notice the period is still needed
   .SalaryInJan = 1000
    SalaryInFeb = 2000
    .
    .
    .
  End With
End With
```

tip: *You can also use the With statement with properties of objects. For example:*

```
With txtBox
  .Height = 2000
  .Width = 2000
  .Text = "This is a text box"
End With
```

Pointer Mimicking

(This section is addressed only to people who are coming from a language that has pointers. If you are not one of these people, you may want to skip this section.)

Well, first off, the quick answer is that there aren't any pointers—so the obvious next question is how to imitate them if you need to create data structures such as linked lists or trees that use them. There is no perfect solution because you will need to go through some contortions to dispose of the memory allocated. (You can easily increase the amount of memory; it's disposing of it that requires contortions.)

This being said, the only way to create analogues to pointers in Visual Basic is to create an array of records and use one or more of the fields in the record to hold the row of the next item. You need to keep on using ReDim Preserve to build up the object and assign the memory. For example, if you wanted to create a binary tree (see Chapter 19 for more on binary trees):

```
type DataInBinaryTree
  Data As String
  LeftChild As Integer   'row where LeftChild is
```

```
  RightChild As Integer 'row where right child is
End Type
```

In this example the two fields LeftChild and RightChild act as pointers to the row containing the child. To build the tree, for example, you start with an array of records of this type of size 1.

```
ReDim Data(1 To 1) As DataInBinaryTree
```

Each time you need to enter the next item you have to:

1. Update the counter of the number of items.
2. Use ReDim Preserve to enlarge the array of records.
3. Fill in the "pointer" rows as needed (use a -1 for a pointer to Null).

note: *The only way to reclaim memory from these imitation pointers is to copy the array of records to a new array of records (or a variant)—after eliminating the entry you want to remove. Then erase the old array. This makes them less than ideal for situations in which you need to reclaim memory.*

Chapter Eleven

Objects

At this point, you are probably pretty comfortable with the basic techniques for manipulating Visual Basic's built-in objects. To go further with Visual Basic, you will need to know more than just how to manipulate its objects by setting properties and applying methods. This chapter will show you new ways of manipulating Visual Basic's built-in objects (and get you started on creating your own). In particular, Visual Basic 4 is the first version of Visual Basic that gives you access to some of the power and so some of the advantages of *object-oriented programming*.

Object-oriented programming (OOP) seems to be the dominant programming paradigm these days, having replaced the *structured* programming techniques that were developed in the early 1970s. If you haven't worked with OOP before, you are probably wondering what all the hoopla is about. This chapter is designed to show you (well, at least to give you a glimpse). Since there's a fair amount of terminology needed to make sense of OOP, the chapter starts with some concepts and definitions. After this, you'll learn the basics of how Visual Basic implements the part of OOP that it supports.

note: *Visual Basic lets you add other objects (such as ones representing Word or Excel) to the toolbox. You can use those objects in ways similar to ordinary controls. See Chapter 18 for more on this.*

Getting Started with Object-Oriented Programming

Let's start with a question that, on the surface, seems to have nothing to do with programming: how did Gateway 2000 become a billion-dollar company faster than any other company in American history? Most people would probably say they made good computers and sold them at rock-bottom prices. But go further—how did they do *that*? Well, a big part of the answer is that they farmed out a lot of the work. They bought components from reputable vendors and then assembled them. They didn't invest any money in designing and building power supplies, disk drives, motherboards, and so on. This made it possible for them to have a good product at a low price.

Ask yourself for a second how this could work. The obvious (and to a large extent, correct) answer is that what they were buying was "prepackaged functionality." For example, when they bought a power supply, they were buying something with certain properties (size, shape, and so on) and a certain functionality (smooth power output, amount of power available, and so on). Object-oriented programming springs from the same idea. Your program is made up of objects with certain properties and functions. You depend on the objects not to interact in undocumented ways with other objects or the code in your project. Whether you build the object or buy it might depend on the state of your wallet or how much time you have free. In either case, as long as the objects satisfy your specifications, you don't much care how the functionality is implemented. In OOP, the way people put it is that what you care about is what the objects *expose*.

So, just as Gateway doesn't care about the internals of a power supply as long as it does what they want, most programmers don't need to care how command buttons are implemented in Visual Basic as long as they do what *they* want. And, as you certainly know by now, on the whole, Visual Basic's objects do what you would expect them to!

The key to being most productive in object-oriented programming is to make your objects as complete as possible and, *as much as possible,* have the other objects and parts of your program tell the objects what to do. OOP jargon describes this by saying that what you do in object-oriented programming is *have clients send messages to objects*. By designing your objects to handle all appropriate messages and manipulate their data internally, you maximize reusability and minimize debugging time.

By now you have seen pretty clear evidence that Visual Basic's built-in objects fit this paradigm well. They are extremely rich in functionality. Of course, occasionally you may need to add your own objects to Visual Basic by either buying them from third-party vendors or writing them yourself. Generally speaking, it is rarely worth reinventing the wheel. If it takes you 40 hours to build a component in C++ and you can buy it for $200, one should really ask: is it worth it? Commercial vendors such as MicroHelp produce quality products that are worth the (usually) small cost. I have always used commercial products in my applications and have been generally happy with the results.

Unfortunately, Visual Basic misses implementing one of the key features of OOP here. Ideally, if you do have to write your own objects, another tenet of OOP would make this easier as well: objects can be built on other objects.

When you do this, the new object starts out by inheriting all the properties and functions of its parent—you can pick and choose whether you want to keep or modify any property or function of the parent. Visual Basic 4 simply doesn't allow this.

Vocabulary of OOP

Traditional structured programming consists of manipulating data. (This is one reason computer programming used to be called data processing.) You manipulate the data in specific ways that are theoretically sure to terminate. (These are usually called *algorithms*.) Now, for the next bit of terminology you have to know: computer scientists talk about *data structures* when they want to single out the arrangements used in your program for the data. All this explains in part why one of the most important computer scientists (he designed Pascal, for example), a Swiss professor named Niklaus Wirth, called his famous book on programming *Algorithms + Data Structures = Programs* (Prentice Hall, 1976). Notice that in Wirth's title the algorithms come first and the data structures come after. This mimics the way programmers worked at that time. First, you decided how to manipulate the data, then you decided what structure to impose on the data in order to make the manipulations easier. OOP puts both algorithms and data structures on the same level. With OOP you work with packages consisting of both data and the functions that manipulate them.

The rest of this section explains the basic terminology of OOP. There's a fair amount of it but it is worth learning for two reasons. The first is that you will need some of this terminology to understand the discussions in this chapter, the second is that knowing this terminology is useful if you move on to a full OOP language such as C++ or Delphi in order to extend Visual Basic.

CLASSES

A *class* is usually described as the template or blueprint from which the object is actually made. The standard way of thinking about classes is to think of them as the cookie cutter and the actual object as the cookie. The "dough" in the form of memory will sometimes need to be allocated as well. Visual Basic is pretty good about hiding this "dough preparation" step from you. You almost never have to worry about creating memory for an object or releasing memory when a program ends under Visual Basic.

When you create an object from a class, you are said to have *created an instance* of the class. For example, all forms in Visual Basic are instances of the Form class, and an individual form in your application is actually a class you can use to create new forms. (See the section on the New keyword a bit later in the chapter.) On the other hand, the controls on the toolbox represent individual classes, but an individual control on a form does not.

ENCAPSULATION

Encapsulation is the key concept in working with objects. Formally, encapsulation is nothing more than combining the data and behavior in one package.

note: *The data in an object is usually called its* instance variables *or* fields, *and the functions and procedures are its methods.*

A key rule in making encapsulation work is that programs should never (well, almost never) access the instance variables (fields) in an object directly. Programs should interact with this data only through the object's methods. (Properties in Visual Basic are designed to give you a way to interact with the instance variables without violating encapsulation.) Encapsulation is the way to give an object its "black box"-like behavior, which is the key to reuse and debugging efficiency.

note: *Visual Basic fully supports encapsulation.*

INHERITANCE

The ability to make classes that descend from other classes is called *inheritance*. The purpose of inheritance is to make building code for specialized tasks easier. The instance variables and methods of the descendent (sometimes called the *subclasses*) start out being the same.

note: *Visual Basic does not support inheritance for creating new subclasses.*

Subclasses will usually use (inherit) the same methods as the parent class. OOP (but not Visual Basic) allows you to define a new method in a subclass but give it the same name. This is called *overriding*. A true object-oriented language such as C++ (and not, alas, Visual Basic) allows you to go beyond simply overriding a method into what is usually called *polymorphism*. The idea behind polymorphism is that while the message may be the same, the *object* determines how to respond. Polymorphism can apply to any method that is inherited from a base class.

note: *Visual Basic does not support polymorphism in any form for the objects you create.*

Polymorphism is helpful when creating new objects from old ones because it makes a programmer's job simpler. When you define a new object based on an existing object, you do not want to rebuild the parent's code in order to take into account that a new object exists. (Imagine some giant case statement in the parent class that just grows and grows!)

The key to making polymorphism work is called *late binding*. This means the compiler doesn't generate the code to call a method at compile time. Instead, every time you use a method with an object, the compiler generates code that lets it calculate which method to call using pointer information built into the object that called it. Methods that allow late binding are called *virtual methods* because they do not exist in the .EXE file but are only potentially there.

note: *We can only hope that the next version of Visual Basic will support class hierarchy and polymorphism. Microsoft has made no announcement on this, and your guess is as good as mine.*

Manipulating Objects Built into Visual Basic

The key to working with objects in Visual Basic is using variables of the special *object* type. For example, when you use the Me keyword to refer to the current object, you are using an object variable.

In general, you declare an object variable with the same Dim, Private, Public, Static, and so on keywords that you've already seen. Thus, you can have local, form-level, or public (global) object variables. Here are some examples:

```
Dim AForm As Form
Dim InfoBox As TextBox
Public AButton As CommandButton
Private MyBar As ScrollBar
```

note: *Microsoft suggests using an "obj" prefix for object variables. For example:*

```
Dim objTheLabel As Label
```

In general, the name used for an object variable of a given control type is the name given in the help file for that control. You can define arrays of object variables in the same way you define an ordinary array:

```
Dim LotsOfTextBoxes(1 To 100) As TextBox
```

note: *You can use variant variables as the type instead of object variables, but this will slow your program down and make it harder to debug.*

When you want to make an object variable refer to a specific object of that type in your project, use the Set keyword. For example, if your project has a form named Form1 and a command button named Command1, your code would look like this:

```
Set AForm = Form1
Set AButton = Command1
```

tip: *The Set command can also be used to simplify lengthy control references.*

Here's an example:

```
Dim Foo As TextBox
Set Foo = frmHelp.txtHelp
```

Now you can write

```
Foo.BackColor
```

instead of

```
frmhelp.txtHelp.BackColor
```

note: *It is important to note that the Set command does not make a copy of the object as a variable assignment would. Instead, the Set command points the object variable to the other object.*

In particular, you cannot use an assignment statement to make an object variable equal to, say, a text box. Trying to use code like this

```
Dim Foo As TextBox
Foo = Text1
```

will give you an error message.

That all the Set keyword does is point your variable to an object can occasionally lead to problems. For example, if you change a property of an object variable that is set to another object, the property of the original object changes as well (much like passing by reference in procedures does).

You can use the Is keyword to test whether two object variables refer to (have been set to) the same object. Suppose AControl and BControl are two control object variables. A line of code such as

```
If AControl Is BControl Then
```

lets you test whether they refer to the same object. (It is a wise precaution to find out whether changing the properties of one variable will also change the properties of the other!)

THE NEW KEYWORD

One case where you can create a new instance of a Visual Basic object at run time is when you use an existing form as the class. The syntax for this is a little different. Assume you have a form named Form1 in your project already. Then the statement

```
Dim AForm As New Form1
```

creates a new instance of Form1. This new instance has the same properties as the original Form1 at the time the code is executed. Use the New keyword only when you want Visual Basic to create a new instance of the original object. For example,

```
Dim AForm As New Form1
Dim BForm As New Form1
AForm.Show
BForm.Show
AForm.Move Left - 199, Top + 100
BForm.Move Left - 399, Top + 200
```

shows two copies of the original Form1. The locations are determined by the value of the Left and Top properties of the original Form1. (We needed to change them to prevent them from stacking one on another because instances inherit all the properties of their parent.)

It would be logical if you could also use the New keyword to create controls at run time; unfortunately, that isn't the way it works. Visual Basic 4 still uses the older (and somewhat clumsier) method of control arrays that you saw in the previous chapter. Only forms in Visual Basic 4 are classes (templates for new objects).

Thus a statement such as

```
Dim Foo As New Text1
```

gives an error message when you try to compile it.

You usually use the New keyword with objects you create yourself. (See the sections "Collections" and "Creating a New Class Module" later in the chapter for more examples of using the New keyword.)

THE NOTHING KEYWORD

Once you use the Set keyword to assign an object to an object variable, you need to release the memory used for the object. You do this by setting the object variable to the keyword Nothing. For example:

```
Dim objFrm As New Form1
   ' code to manipulate the new instance of Form1 would go here
   '
   '
Set objForm = Nothing
```

note: *Since object variables merely point to the object, it is possible for several object variables to refer to the same object. When several object variables refer to the same object, you must set all of them to Nothing in order to release the memory and system resources associated with the object.*

(Memory may be released automatically: this happens, for example, after the last object variable referring to the object goes out of scope. However, relying on this is sloppy. For example, if you set a local object variable inside a procedure, set it to Nothing before the Sub is exited; don't rely on Visual Basic to clean up after you!)

note: *An uninitialized object variable can be thought of as having a current value of Nothing.*

GENERAL OBJECT VARIABLES

There are a few general types of object variables for use when you need to refer to objects of many different types. For example,

```
Dim objFoo As Control
```

gives you a way to refer to any control. Similarly,

```
Dim objGeneral As Object
```

lets you set the variable named objGeneral to *any* Visual Basic object.

tip: *Always use the most specific object variable you can find.*

For example, code with this statement

```
Dim txtFoo As TextBox
Set Foo = Text1
```

will always run faster than

```
Dim Foo As Control
Set Foo = Text1
```

which in turn will always run faster than

```
Dim Foo As Object
Set Foo = Text1
```

Manipulating Object Variables via Code

You have already seen how to manipulate individual objects by setting their properties or applying one of their methods to them. Suppose, however, you want to write a general procedure to manipulate properties of forms or controls or the forms and controls themselves—you simply don't yet have the techniques needed for this. This section explains them.

First off, *properties* of forms and controls can only be passed by value. For example, consider the following simple Sub procedure:

```
Sub ChangeText (ByVal X As String, Y As String)
  Y = X
End Sub
```

If you call it using the following code,

```
Call ChangeText(Form1.Caption, Y$)
```

then the current value of Y$ is the caption for Form1.

tip: *If you set the Tag property of the form or control to contain information otherwise not available at run time, you can write a general procedure using this technique to analyze the Control.Tag property in order to find information about the control that would otherwise not be available at run time.*

On the other hand, you will often want to affect the properties of a form or control by using a general procedure. For this, you have to pass the form or control as a parameter by reference. To do this, declare the argument to the procedure to be one of the object types. (You could use variants too, of course, but this should be avoided unless absolutely necessary because it is slower and also leads to code that is harder to debug.) For example, the following code makes a command button visible if it is invisible:

```
Sub MakeVisible (X As CommandButton)
  If X.Visible = False Then
    X.Visible  = True
  End If
End Sub
```

Notice that the parameter is declared to be an object variable of Command Button type and will be passed by reference (the default behavior for procedures). Otherwise, the code is pretty straightforward. Since X is being passed by reference, Visual Basic knows where in memory the object is located. Since it knows this location, it can change the properties of the object. You access properties of an object variable inside a procedure using the dot notation you have become familiar with. In this case, the code is straightforward: if the button isn't visible (so X.Visible = False), the procedure makes it visible.

tip: *This kind of procedure would usually be in a code module, since you will want to use it for many different buttons.*

As another example, if you often find yourself writing code to center a form on the screen, why not use the following general procedure:

```
Public Sub CenterForm(X As Form)
    X.Move (Screen.Width - X.Width)/2, _
(Screen.Height - X.Height)/2
End Sub
```

Then whenever you are in a procedure attached to a specific form, you can simply write

```
Center Me
```

to center the form on the screen.

Similarly, you can have a Sub or Function procedure that affects a property of a control. For example, a first approximation to a general procedure to change the caption on a control might look like this:

```
Sub ChangeCaption (X As Control, Y As String)
  X.Caption = Y
End Sub
```

Notice that this procedure uses the general Control type. However, suppose you tried to use this procedure in the form of

```
Call ChangeCaption(Text1, "New text")
```

where Text1 was the name of a text box. Then Visual Basic would give you a run-time error because text boxes do not have a Caption property.

The solution for this is to use a variant on the If-Then-Else loop in Visual Basic that allows you to determine what type of control is being manipulated. This takes the following form,

If TypeOf *Control* Is *ControlType* Then

.

.

.

Else

.

.

.

End If

where the *ControlType* parameter is the same as is used in declaring an object variable (Form, Label, TextBox, and so on).

For example, if all you wanted to do was work with both text boxes and all the other controls you wanted to change *did* have Caption properties, you could use

```
Sub ChangeCaptionOrText (X As Control, Y As String)
  If TypeOf X Is TextBox Then
    X.Text = Y
   Else
    X.Caption = Y
   End If
End Sub
```

You cannot use the keyword Not in this type of control structure, so you will often find yourself using an empty If clause. For example, if you wanted to play it safer:

```
Sub ChangeCaption (X As Control, Y As String)
  If TypeOf X Is TextBox Then
```

```
    '  Do Nothing
  Else
    X.Caption = Y
  End If
End Sub
```

Since there is also no version of the Select Case for controls, you may need the If-Then-ElseIf version of this control structure:

```
If TypeOf X Is...Then
  .
  .
ElseIf TypeOf X Is...Then
  .
  .
ElseIf TypeOf X Is...Then
  .
  .
Else
  . .
  .
End If
```

Collections

A Collection object is an object whose parts can be referred to individually as needed, *and* you still can refer to the object as a whole when needed. You have already seen the Printers collection in Chapter 6. Visual Basic also has built-in collections that give you information about all the forms in a project and all the controls on a specific form. They are called Forms and Controls. Just as with the Printers collection, the Count property of the Forms or Controls collection tells you how many forms you have loaded or how many controls are loaded on a specific form.

You can access individual forms or controls by writing, for example, Forms(0), Forms(1), and so on. Unfortunately, although the count starts at 0, Forms(0) is not necessarily the startup form. The order of the Forms( ) collection is unpredictable as is the order of the Controls collection. For example, the following code prints the captions of all the *loaded* forms in your project in the Debug window.

```
Dim I As Integer
For I = 0 To Forms.Count - 1
  Debug.Print Forms(I).Caption
Next I
```

(Since the Count property starts at 0, we go to one less than Forms.Count - 1.)

Although the preceding code works fine, most programmers would use the For-Each structure for iterating through a collection. They feel the For-Each structure makes the code a bit clearer when you need to iterate through all the elements in a collection. A framework for this structure takes the following form,

```
For Each Element In TheCollection

Next
```

as shown in the following rewritten version of the program to print the captions of all the loaded forms in a project:

```
Dim objForm As Form
For Each objForm In Forms
  Debug.Print objForm.Caption
Next
```

An Example of Using the Controls Collection with Set

The Set statement is also useful when working with collections of objects. For example, suppose you need to know a non-enabled control on your form. The following code finds one and assigns it to an object variable named NotEnabledControl:

```
Dim AControl As Control
Dim NotEnabledControl As Control
For Each AControl in Form1.Controls
  If Not(AControl.Enabled) Then
     Set NotEnabledControl = AControl
     Exit For
  End If
Next
```

This code moves through all the controls on a form until it finds one that is not enabled and then sets the AControl object variable to it.

Building Your Own Collections

Occasionally it is useful to build your own collections. The items in a collection (usually called its *members* or *elements)* can be of any type, and you can mix types in a collection if necessary.

Since a collection is an object, you must create it as an instance of a built-in class in Visual Basic. The class you need is called, naturally enough, the Collection class. For example

```
Dim X As New Collection
```

creates a new collection as an instance of the Collections class.

Just as with the Forms, Controls, or Printers collection, the Count property of each collection you create tells you the number of items in a collection. (Collections start out with no elements, so Count is 0.) Each element in a collection can be referred to by its index—just as you saw in the Forms and Controls collections. This means that the following gives you one way of dealing with all the elements in a collection:

```
For I = 1 To NameOfCollection.Count-1
  'work with NameOfCollection(I)
Next I
```

However, it is usually a bit clearer to use the For-Each structure.

Of course, you still don't know how to add or remove elements from a collection. But before moving on to the important Add and Remove methods that do this, you need to learn about one other method for working on a collection.

THE ITEM METHOD

The Item method is the default method for a collection; it is how you refer to (or return) a specific element of a collection. Its syntax is

CollectionObject.Item(index)

The *index* parameter specifies the position of a member of the collection. It is a long integer (you can have *lots* of elements in a collection) and goes to the number of items in the collection. For example

```
MyCollection.Item(1)
```

is the first item in the collection.

caution: *Collections you create start with an index of 1 and go up to the count of the collection. The built-in collections (Forms, Controls, and Printers) start at 0 and go up to the Count -1.*

In general, Visual Basic lets you use a key to access the elements in a collection. This key is set up at the time you add the element to the collection. Using a key rather than an index is often more effective: you can easily associate a useful mnemonic as the key. For example, this means a statement such as

```
Debug.Print Forms(1).Caption
```

is actually the same as:

```
Debug. Print Forms.Item(1).Caption
```

note: *The Item method is the default method for a collection.*

THE ADD METHOD

Once you create the collection by using the New keyword, you use the Add method to add items to it. The trick in using the Add method is to remember you have to set up a variant variable first to hold the information before you use the Add method. For example:

```
Dim Versions As New Collection
Dim Foo As Variant
Foo = "Visual Basic 3.0"
Versions.Add(Foo)
Foo = "Visual Basic 4.0"
Versions.Add(Foo)
```

In general, the Add method has the following syntax (it supports named arguments by the way):

CollectionObject.Add *item as Variant [, key as string][, before As Long] [, after As Long]*

Here are short descriptions of the parts of the Add method:

- *CollectionObject* is any object or object variable that refers to a collection.
- The *item* parameter is required. Since the information will be held in a variant variable, it can be an expression of any type. (As mentioned previously, you can mix types in a collection.)
- The *key* parameter is optional. It must be a string expression, and within the collection it must be unique or you'll get a run-time error. For example:

  ```
  Dim Presidents As New Collection
  Dim Foo As Variant
  Foo = "George Washington"
  Presidents.Add Foo, "Didn't lie"
  Foo = "John Adams"
  Presidents.Add item := Foo, key:= "Proper Bostonian"
  ```

  Now you can access George by:

  ```
  Presidents.Item("Didn't lie")
  ```

  But remember that the match to the string in the key must be perfect. For example, this doesn't work:

  ```
  Presidents.Item("didn't lie")
  ```

- The optional *before* and *after* parameters are usually numeric expressions that evaluate to a (long) integer. The new member is placed right before (right after) the member identified by the before (after) argument. If you use a string expression, it must correspond to one of the keys that was used to add elements to the collection. You can specify before or after positions but not both.

THE REMOVE METHOD

When you need to remove items form a collection, you use the Remove method. It too supports named arguments and its syntax is

CollectionObject.Remove *index*

Here, as you might expect, the *index* parameter is used to specify the element you want removed. If *index* is a numeric expression, it must be a number between 1 and the collection's Count property. If it's a string expression, it must exactly match a key to an element in the collection.

The Object Browser

You've seen how to use the Object Browser (shown in Figure 11-1) to look at the built-in constants in Visual Basic and to navigate among the procedures you have written. The Object Browser can do far more. In particular, it gives you complete access to the classes, objects, and their methods and properties that you can use in your Visual Basic projects.

More precisely, objects that are usable in Visual Basic are usually collected into *object libraries*. For example, there are Visual Basic's object library, the Visual Basic for Applications' object library, Excel's object library, and so on. An object library contains the information that Visual Basic needs to build instances of its objects as well as information on the methods and properties of the object in the library. One of the purposes of the Object Browser is to help you understand the object libraries in your project better.

To bring up the Object Browser shown in Figure 11-1:

- Choose View | Object Browser, press F2, or use the toolbar shortcut (the eighth tool).

To close the Object Browser:

- Click the Close button.

(The Object Browser also closes whenever you choose the Paste button in order to paste the current selection into the active Code window.)

What follows are short descriptions of the parts of the Object Browser.

Figure 11-1
The Object Browser

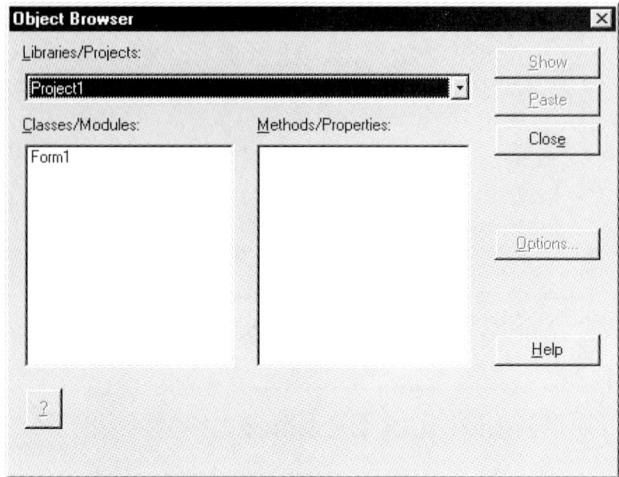

LIBRARIES/PROJECTS DROP-DOWN LIST BOX

This list box displays the libraries available to your project and, as you have seen earlier, it also lists the modules in your project. In general, you can select from available object libraries, including the ones in the current Visual Basic project. Once you choose a library, other parts of the Object Browser let you look at the classes, modules, procedures, methods, and properties of that library.

note: *When you use Tools|References to add another object library to Visual Basic, you will add information about its object library to the Object Browser, and it is automatically listed in this drop-down list box.*

CLASSES/MODULES

As you have already seen in Chapter 9, if you select your own Visual Basic project in the Libraries/Projects box, this box displays modules from your project, including any classes you defined in the current project. You also have already used this box to get at the library of built-in constants in both Visual Basic and Visual Basic for Applications. When you select another object library in the Libraries/Projects list box, the Classes/Modules pane displays the classes available in that library.

METHODS/PROPERTIES

You already saw in Chapter 9 how to use Methods/Properties to display the procedures in the current project. Once you select an object library in the Libraries/Projects list box, the Object Browser gives you a list of the methods and properties for the class that you have selected in the Classes/Modules box.

THE "?" BUTTON

Clicking this button displays the online Help topic for the item selected in the Classes/Modules or Methods/Properties box. In particular, the Object Browser places the syntax for the item you have selected next to this button.

SHOW

Clicking on Show takes you to the code for the selected procedure in the Code window.

PASTE

Clicking on Paste pastes a template of the Visual Basic code needed for the procedure, property, or method directly into your Code window at the current insertion point.

OPTIONS

Clicking on Options displays the Member Options dialog box, as shown here. You can use this box to add help information or comments about any modules, procedures, classes, properties, and methods that you define in your project.

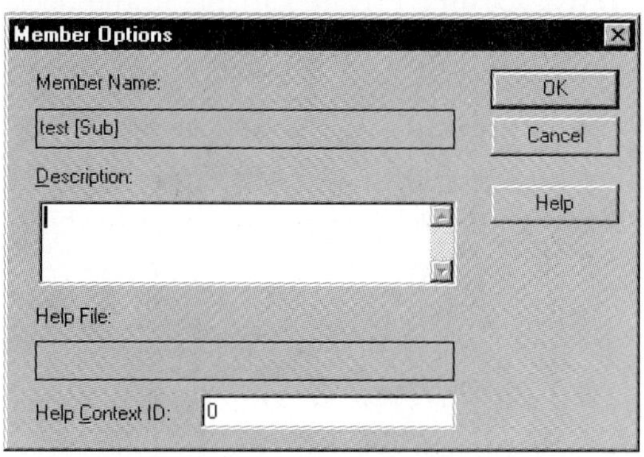

Creating an Object in Visual Basic

You can build objects in two ways in Visual Basic. One is by adding custom properties to an existing form and then using that form as a class (template) for new instances of the form. Each new instance of the form will have the new properties. The second is by using a special type of module called a *class module*. Class modules have the advantage that they can be compiled separately (see Chapter 18) and used by other Windows applications. The disadvantage is that, at present, they can have no visual components associated with them. Classes created out of a form, on the other hand, are obviously visual, but they cannot be compiled separately for use in some other project. (They would have to be added at the design stage whenever they were used.)

Still, in both cases, you use the same ideas for adding properties to these classes (templates). Once you think about it the right way, the terminology used actually makes sense—but at first it can be confusing. First off, what are the most basic things you will want to be able to do with a new property?

- You want to get its current value.
- You want to assign a new value to it.

For the first situation, you use a special type of procedure called a *Property Get* procedure. For the second you use a *Property Let* procedure. (The way I remember the terminology is that a Let statement is the way you make assignments in BASIC.)

For example, suppose you want to add a custom property to a form that will tell you whether a form named frmNeedsToBeCentered is centered and also center it if you set the property to True. Here's what you need to do.

First, set up a Private variable in the declarations section of the form. (It's a Private variable to enforce encapsulation.)

```
Private IsCentered As Boolean
```

Then add the following procedures to the form:

```
Public Property Let Center(X As Boolean)
  IsCentered = X 'used for the current state of the property
  If X then
    Me.Move (Screen.Width - Me.Width)/2, _
Screen.Height - Me.Height)/2
```

```
  End If
End Sub
```

The first line of code uses the Private variable to store the current value of the property. Now you can use a line of code like

```
Me.Center = True
```

to center the form (or any instance of it). From another form or code module, you can use a line of code like:

```
frmNeedsToBeCentered.Center = True
```

Of course, it might also be useful to know whether a form is centered. For this you need to use a Property Get procedure that returns a Boolean:

```
Public Property Get Center() As Boolean
 Center = IsCentered
End Sub
```

This picks up the current value of the IsCentered Private variable that you are using to hold the information about the current value of the property. (Notice that Property Get procedures are a bit like Function procedures: you assign a value to them within the body of the procedure.)

note: *You may be wondering why all this bother? You can certainly use a Public function to determine whether a form is centered or not. The point is that the designers of Visual Basic 4 are trying to give objects as much "black box" behavior as they can. Using a Public function to determine whether a form is centered would partially defeat this. All this being said, in my opinion, given the current limited object orientation of Visual Basic, all Property procedures in a form are really doing is setting the stage for what will be in later versions of Visual Basic!*

In any case, you can use code like this:

```
If Not(frmNeedsToBeCentered.Center) Then MsgBox _
("Why did you move the form?")
```

General Property Procedures

Did you notice how the Property Let and Property Get procedures in the example worked in tandem? The value returned by the Property Get procedure is of the same type as the one used in the assignment for Property Let. In general, the number of arguments for a Property Get is also one less than that of the corresponding Property Let (the last argument being the one that will be changed). A Property Get procedure that you write without a corresponding Property Let procedure gives you a read-only property—since you have no way to change it.

The full syntax for a Property Let procedure template looks like this:

```
[Public | Private][Static] Property Let name [(arglist)]
    [statements]
    [name = expression]
    [Exit Property] ' if need be
End Property
```

- Use Public to make the Property Let procedure accessible to every procedure in every module.
- Use Private to make the Property Let procedure accessible only to other procedures in the module where it is declared.

The other keywords work as they would in any procedure. Use the Static keyword if you need the Property Let procedure's local variables preserved between uses. The Exit Property keywords give you a way to immediately exit from a Property Get procedure, and so on. The name of the Property Let procedure must follow standard variable naming conventions, except that the name can, and will most often, be the same as a Property Get or Property Set procedure in the same module.

The full syntax for a Property Get procedure template looks like this:

```
[Public | Private][Static] Property Get name [(arglist)][As type]
    [statements]
    [name = expression]
    [Exit Property] ' if need be
End Property
```

note: *The name and type of each argument in a Property Get procedure must be the same as the corresponding arguments in the Property Let procedure—if it exists. The type of the value returned by a Property Get procedure must be the same data type as the last argument in the corresponding Property Let procedure if it exists.*

The last type of Property procedure is the Property Set statement. Use this when you need to set a reference to an object instead of just setting a value (for example, when you want to set a printer different than the current one). Here is the syntax:

```
[Public | Private][Static] Property Set name [(arglist)]
    [statements]
    [Exit Property]
    [statements]
End Property
```

Building Your Own Classes

Although you can add custom properties to a form and then use them as templates for new objects, the most common way to build a new class (template) for new objects in Visual Basic is to use a class module. A class module object contains the code for the custom properties (via Property procedures) and methods that objects defined from it will have.

You can then create new instances of the class from any other module or form in your project. (You can even compile class modules for use by other applications as in-process OLE servers—see Chapter 18 for more on this important concept.) A class module cannot have a visible interface of its own. Each class module you create gives you, naturally enough, a single class (template) for building new instances of that class. However, you can have as many class modules in a project as you like (subject only to operating system constraints of course).

As you might expect, once you have a class module, you use the New keyword to create new instances of it. For example, if FirstClass is the name of a class module in your project:

```
Dim AnInstance As New FirstClass
```

you use Property procedures to define the properties of your class and use Public Sub and Public Function procedures for its methods.

Creating a New Class Module

You create a new class module at design time by choosing Insert | Class Module. Each class module can respond to only two events: Initialize and Terminate. They are triggered when someone creates an instance of your class or terminates it. (As you might expect, the Terminate event for a class module is triggered when the class created via the New keyword is set to Nothing. *It does not occur if the application stops because of the End statement.*)

There are three properties for a class module that you set at design time via the Properties window. As you might expect, the Name property determines the name of the class. The other two properties are described next.

PUBLIC

The Public property determines whether other applications can write code to invoke the properties and methods of your class. This property can only be set to True in the Professional and Enterprise editions of Visual Basic.

INSTANCING

If you set the Instancing property to True, then other applications outside your project can declare new instances of your class. (This is appropriate when using a class module in OLE—see Chapter 18.) You must have the Public property set to True to be able to set the Instancing property to True.

An Example: A Deck of Cards Class Module

Start by imagining you want to provide a toolkit for the designers of computer-generated card games. You obviously need an object that takes the place of a deck of cards. Since class modules in Visual Basic can't be visual, you only need to be concerned about the data and methods this deck of cards object must support.

Let's call this class module CardDecks. This object needs to expose individual cards and have methods for shuffling the deck and dealing the cards. (You will use the Initialize event to build up the deck of cards.)

The code for creating this nonvisual object might look like this. First off, start with the Private variables used for the data:

```
Private Deck(0 To 51) As Integer
Private TheCard As String
Private Position As Integer
```

The Deck array will be used to hold the integers that are the internal representation of the cards. The Private TheCard variable will be used for the Property procedures to encapsulate the card. (This will make it easy to change the names of the cards for a different country, for example.)

The Initialize procedure simply fills the array with 52 consecutive integers:

```
Private Sub Class_Initialize()
Dim I As Integer
For I = 0 To 51
  Deck(I) = I
Next I
End Sub
```

Now it's on to the methods. First off, there's got to be a Shuffle method for shuffling the deck. It might look like this:

```
Public Sub Shuffle()
 Dim X As Integer, I As Integer
 Dim Temp As Integer, Place As Integer
 Randomize
  For I = 0 To 5199 '10 times through the deck should be
enough
    Place = I Mod 52
    X = Int(52 * Rnd)
    Temp = Deck(Place)
    Deck(Place) = Deck(X)
    Deck(X) = Temp
  Next I
End Sub
```

Of course, you can easily add an argument to this procedure to control how many "shuffles" are made. If you do, then the method this procedure generates would have an argument:

```
Foo.Shuffle 10
```

Next, give the read-only property that tells you the current card. It simply looks up the current value of the Private ThisCard variable:

```
Public Property Get CurrentCard() As String
  TheCard = CalculateCard(Deck(Position))
  CurrentCard = TheCard
End Property
```

(It is read-only because there is no associated Property Let procedure to change the current card.)

Notice we call a private procedure that converts the integer in the Deck array to the card called TheCard. The DealCard method might look like this:

```
Public Function DealCard() As String
  If Position > 51 Then Err.Raise Number :=vbObjectError + 32144,_
Description := "Only 52 cards in deck!"
  TheCard = CalculateCard(Deck(Position))
  DealCard = TheCard
Position = Position + 1
End Function
```

Finally, here's the private procedure for converting a number in the card array to a string describing the card:

```
Private Function CalculateCard(X As Integer) As String
  Dim Suit As Integer, CardValue As Integer
  Suit = X \ 13
  Select Case Suit
   Case 0
     TheCard = "Clubs"
   Case 1
     TheCard = "Diamonds"
   Case 2
     TheCard = "Hearts"
   Case 3
     TheCard = "Spades"
   End Select

  CardValue = X Mod 13
  Select Case CardValue
   Case 0
    TheCard = "Ace of " + TheCard
   Case 1 To 9
    TheCard = Str$(CardValue + 1) + " of " + TheCard
   Case 10
     TheCard = "Jack of " + TheCard
```

```
    Case 11
      TheCard = "Queen of " + TheCard
    Case 12
      TheCard = "King of " + TheCard
    End Select
CalculateCard = TheCard
End Function
```

Now all you have to do to use this class module is have a line such as

```
Dim MyDeck As New CardDeck
```

before you start working with it. For example, you could test it with the following code:

```
Private Sub Form_Load()
Dim MyDeck As New CardDeck, I As Integer
  MyDeck.Shuffle
  For I = 1 To 20
    MyDeck.DealCard
    MsgBox MyDeck.CurrentCard
  Next I
End Sub
```

Chapter Twelve

The Interface Revisited

To this point the controls you have used have been restricted to the most basic ones. This way you could concentrate on the underlying programming language. Since you have now seen most of the programming language constructs, it is time to return to interface development. This chapter shows you how to use most of the remaining standard controls on the toolbox. (The next chapter shows you how to use the Windows 95-specific and custom controls supplied with the Professional and Enterprise editions.) The controls covered in this chapter let you add check boxes, option (radio) buttons, and list and combo boxes to your Visual Basic projects. In addition, you'll learn how to use timers to have parts of your program spring to life at specified time intervals. You'll also see another method for creating multiple controls on a form at design time. Next, it's on to using the common dialog control: this control lets you add the dialog boxes users expect to see in your projects.

Menus are covered in the second half of this chapter. Think of menu items as specialized controls that you add to your forms. Menu items respond only to the Click event, and unlike all the other controls in Visual Basic, menus are not added to forms by using the toolbox. Instead, you use the Menu Design window, which is available from the Window menu on the main menu bar or via the Menu Designer tool on the toolbar.

This chapter ends with a short general discussion of interface design. In particular, you will learn techniques for keeping the controls on a form in proportion regardless of size or display changes.

The Toolbox Revisited

In Chapter 4 you saw the basic controls for a Visual Basic project: command buttons, image controls, text boxes, and labels. Figure 12-1 shows you the controls covered in this chapter. Following is a brief description of each control. See the appropriate sections following this one for more on the individual controls.

- The icon for the frame control looks like a box with a bit of text (xyz) at the top. This control is mainly used to group other Visual Basic controls. Frames give you a way to visually separate parts of a form from other parts.
- The icon for check boxes gives a good feel for what the control will look like on your form: a box with a cross. When your project is running, check boxes are toggled on and off via mouse clicks or by using the TAB key to move the focus to the control and then pressing the SPACEBAR.
- The icon for option buttons looks like an old-fashioned radio button—hence the other popular name for this control. Unlike check boxes, option buttons work in groups. When the user chooses one button in the group, all the others are turned off. Option buttons are also toggled on and off via mouse clicks or the TAB and SPACEBAR combination.
- Use list boxes when you want to give users a list of items from which they must make a choice. As the icon indicates, list boxes often come with scroll bars, which are automatically added if there are too many items to display for the current size of the list box.

Figure 12-1 Additional controls for a Visual Basic project

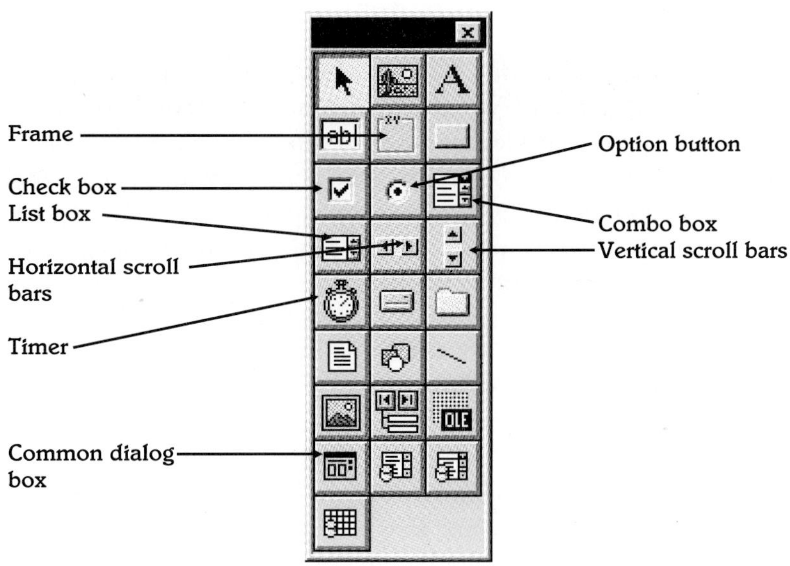

- Combo boxes combine a list box and a text box. The icon indicates this by showing a blank space above the list area. You use this control when you want to give users the option of entering their own choices in addition to those you provide on the list.
- The controls for vertical and horizontal scroll bars give you another way of getting user input. Another possibility is to use them to display how close you are to the beginning or end of a time-consuming process. (Windows 95 developers, with the Professional or Enterprise edition, have a custom control for this. See the next chapter.)
- The icon for timers looks like an old-fashioned alarm clock. This reminds you that this control will wake up at specified time intervals. Unlike all other controls in the standard edition of Visual Basic, timers are always invisible to the user. You can see them only during the design phase of your project.
- By now you've seen lots and lots of common dialog boxes. Whether opening or closing a file, choosing a font, printing a page, or changing the color of a Windows object, there are standard dialog boxes that users expect to see. This control lets you add them to your Visual Basic application.

Frames

You rarely write event procedures for frames. In fact, currently there are only seven events to which frames can respond. (Besides the usual Click and Double-click events, there are the mouse events that tell you whether a control was dragged over or dropped onto the frame. See Chapter 16 for these events.) You usually use frames passively to group images or controls. For example, a frame with image controls is the standard way of creating a toolbar in the standard version of Visual Basic. (See the next chapter for the more direct way using the toolbar control under Windows 95.) The screen in Figure 12-2 is an example of a form with multiple frames used to divide the form functionally.

There are 31 properties for frames, and all of them are common to the controls you are already familiar with. For example, the font properties control how the caption appears, MousePointer controls how the mouse pointer appears, and so on. The only properties you haven't seen for frames are the ones for mouse activities; they're covered in Chapter 16.

Finally, the important point to keep in mind when using a frame is that you usually will draw the frame first. Only after the frame is on the form should you

Figure 12-2
Form with frames

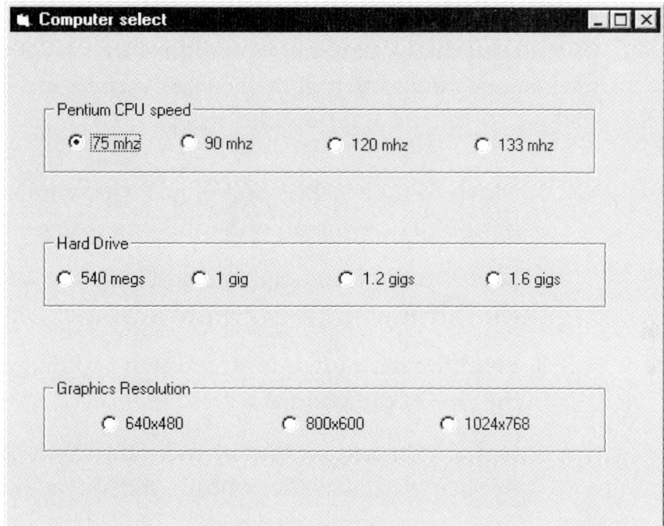

place controls inside it that you want attached to it. In this way, Visual Basic knows the controls are attached to the frame. (Otherwise, Visual Basic will not let the control respond to events that the frame can respond to.) In particular, do not use the Double-click method for creating a control when you want to attach a control to a frame. The Double-click method places the control in the center of the screen, but even if the frame is there, Visual Basic will not attach the control to the frame. Instead, use the method described in the next section or select the control from the toolbox and position the mouse pointer inside the frame before dragging and dropping the control. (See Chapter 4 for more details on this method for creating controls.)

tip: *You can also attach a control directly to a frame or picture box at run time by setting the Container property of that control to the name of the frame or picture box.*

THE STICKY CLICK METHOD FOR CREATING CONTROLS

Visual Basic has one other way to create controls on a form. It is especially useful when working with frames (or picture boxes used as containers). This method is a cross between the Double-click method and the drag-and-drop methods you've seen already. Using the *sticky click method*, you can create multiple copies of the same control but position and size them as you see fit. (Recall that the Double-click method always gives you similarly sized controls, stacked one on another, in the center of the form.) To create controls using the sticky click method, follow these steps:

1. Move to the toolbox and press CTRL while clicking the left mouse button. The control in the toolbox is highlighted.
2. Move to the form or frame and click the left mouse button. The top left corner of the new control is "stuck" at this location.
3. Hold the left mouse button down and drag until you are happy with the size of the control.
4. Release the mouse button and repeat steps 2 and 3 until you have finished placing all the controls of that type on the form or in the frame.

To change to another way of working with the toolbox, go back to the toolbox and click the pointer, or any control other than the one you were working with, using the sticky click method.

Option (Radio) Buttons

Option buttons always work together. When the user chooses one button, all the other buttons in the group are turned off. For this reason, any application that uses more than one group of option buttons on a form must use a frame to separate the groups. (See the section "Frames" earlier in this chapter.) You add option (radio) buttons to a form when you want the user to choose from a finite list of possibilities. For example, the screen in Figure 12-3 shows how a form for a database might look.

The Value property of the option button tells you whether a button was selected by the user. If the Value property is True, the user selected that button; otherwise, its Value property is False.

If you give control names to the option buttons in Figure 12-3 of optMr, optMs, optMrs, and optOther, you could use code like the following to pick up the information:

```
If optMr.Value Then
  Title$="Mr."
ElseIf optMs.Value Then
```

```
  Title$= "Ms."
ElseIf optMrs.Value Then
  Title$= "Mrs."
Else
  Title$=InputBox("Please enter the title you want us to
use.")
End If
```

This code works because of the Boolean (True/False) nature of the Value property. For example, the clause optMs.Value will be True only when the user has chosen the optMs. option button.

Option buttons respond to the Click and Double-click events as well as to the key events. They can also detect whether a button has received or lost the focus. Visual Basic generates the Click event when the user selects the button by clicking with the mouse or moving via the TAB key and pressing SPACEBAR. If you reset the Value property of the option button to True inside code, then you also generate the Click event. This is occasionally useful for demonstration programs. You can also turn on one of the buttons at design time by setting its Value property to True via the Properties window.

The 31 properties for option buttons are a subset of those for command buttons. For example, you can set the Caption property to change how Visual

Figure 12-3 Form for possible database

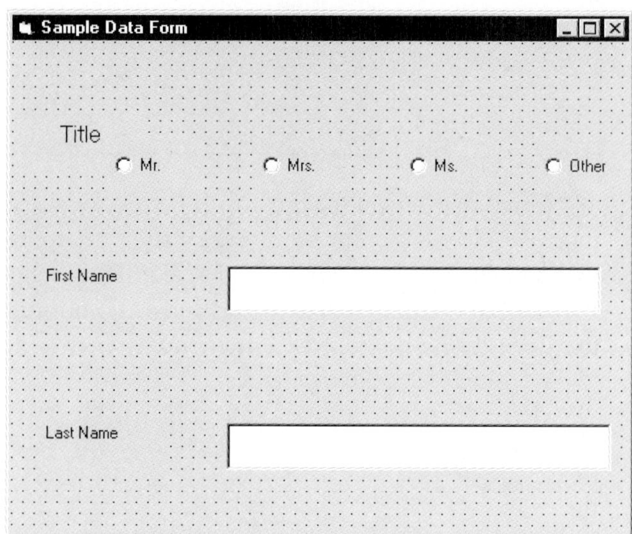

Basic displays the caption. You can also temporarily disable the button by setting the Enabled property to False at design or run time, as you see fit.

Check Boxes

Check boxes differ from option buttons in that, regardless of how many check boxes you place on a form, they can all be turned on and off independently. For this reason, placing check boxes in a frame is necessary only when you think it polishes the appearance of your form.

However, like option buttons, whether a check box is on or off is also determined by its Value property. If the user has selected a check box, the Value property switches to True. It stays True until the user deselects that box. (This is unlike the situation with option buttons, where selecting one of the buttons flips the value of all the others to False.) If you want a check box to be on when the project starts up, either set the Value property of the box to True at design time or set it to True in the Form_Load or Form_Initialize procedure.

As an example of where you might want to use check boxes, consider the following form:

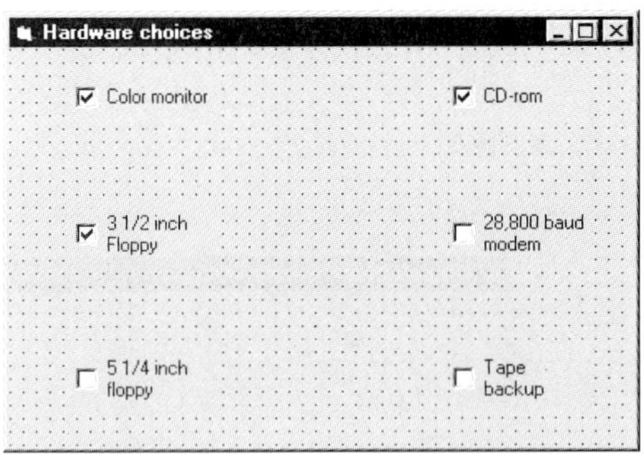

Notice that several of the check boxes are already on by default. (After all, most people want color monitors for their computers.) On the other hand, the user can choose no monitor by deselecting the check box.

You can combine check boxes and radio buttons. A good example of this is the Print dialog box on the File menu:

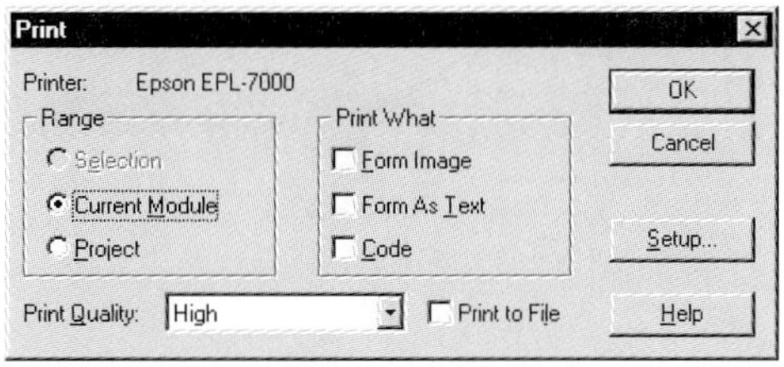

As with option buttons, check boxes will respond to the Click and Double-click events as well as to the key events. They will also detect whether a button has received or lost the focus. As with option buttons, Visual Basic generates the Click event when the user selects the button by clicking with the mouse or moving the focus via the TAB key and pressing SPACEBAR. If you reset the Value property of the button to True inside code, you also generate the Click event.

List and Combo Boxes

Use list boxes when you have a fixed list of choices. For example, suppose you are designing an application to provide information about the presidents of the United States. The form might look like the one in Figure 12-4. Note that (as in this figure) Visual Basic automatically adds vertical scroll bars whenever the list box is too small for all the items it contains.

On the other hand, you might want this application to let the user select a president by number rather than by scrolling through the list. To allow users to input data as well as make choices from a list, use a combo box, as shown in Figure 12-5. Notice that this form has a label near the combo box to identify what the user should type into the input area of the combo box.

There are actually two types of combo boxes, and which one you get depends on the value of the Style property.

- If the value of the Style property is set to the default value of 0, you get a combo box with an arrow. If the user clicks the arrow, he or she will see the list of choices given in the box.
- If the value of the Style property of a combo box is 1, the user sees the combo box with the list already dropped down.

Figure 12-4 List box with presidents' names

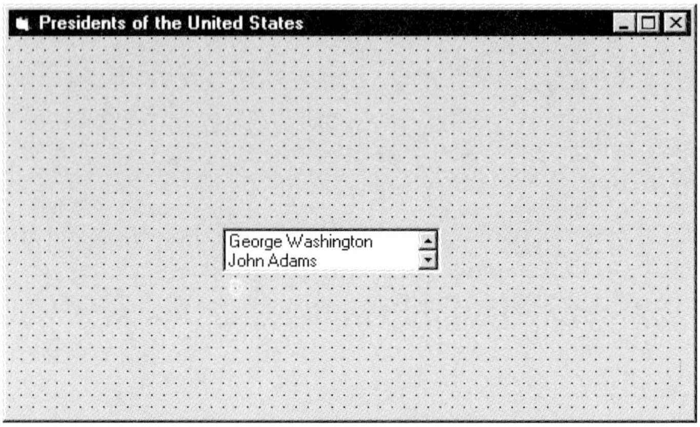

Here are examples of these two types of combo boxes:

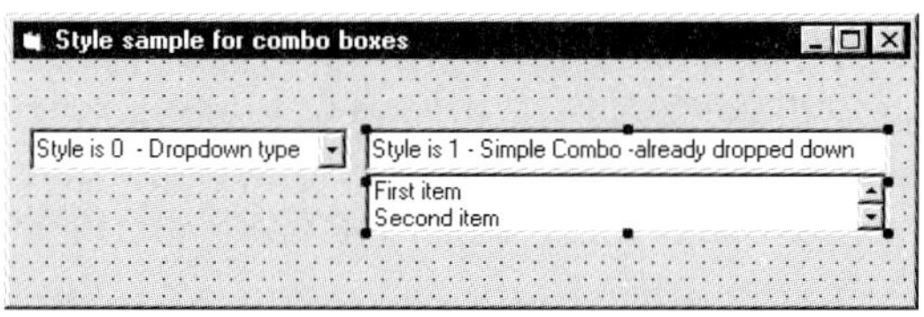

Figure 12-5 Combo box with label for presidents' names

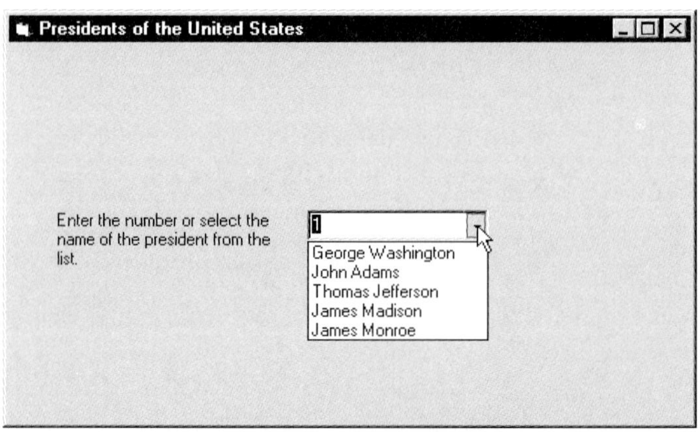

Notice that in both cases, the user still has a text area to enter information. On the other hand, the final possible choice for the Style property for combo boxes, a value of 2, gives you a pull-down list box, as in the following:

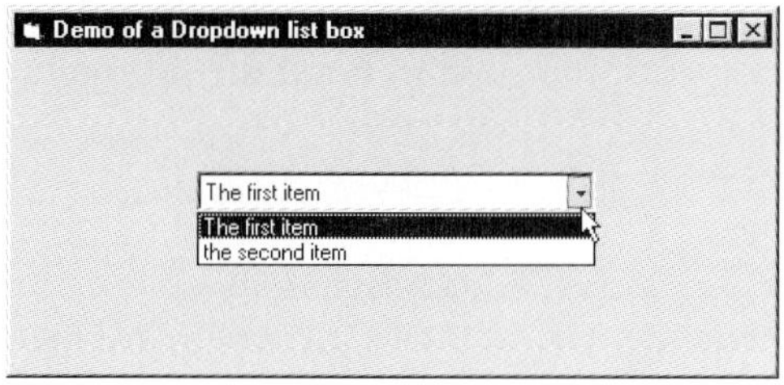

Thus, although you draw a pull-down list box by using the Combo Box icon, once you set the Style property to 2 (either via code or at design time), the text area disappears and what appears on the screen looks like a different version of a list box. On the other hand, the events that a pull-down list box will respond to are those of a combo box and not those of a list box.

Items in a list or combo box can be sorted in ASCII order. This depends on the value of the Sorted property. If you set the Sorted property to True, Visual Basic will order the items in ASCII order. Otherwise, the order of the items depends on the order in which you placed them in the list box. You can set the Sorted property to True at design or run time, as well as switch it back and forth via code as necessary.

MANIPULATING THE ITEMS ON A LIST OR COMBO BOX

You usually add or remove items from a list or combo box while the project is running. (Visual Basic 4, however, unlike earlier versions of Visual Basic, does allow you to populate list and combo boxes at design time. See the next section.) Use the AddItem method to add an item to a list or combo box. The syntax for this method is

ListName.AddItem Item [, *Index*]

ListName is the control name of the list or combo box, and Item is a string or string expression. If the Sorted property is True for the list or combo box, then Item goes where ASCII order places it. If the Sorted property is False, Visual Basic places Item either at the position determined by the *Index* parameter or at the end of the list when you do not specify the index. The *Index* parameter must be an integer or integral expression. An *Index* value of 0 (not 1) means you are at the beginning of the list. The *Index* option has no effect on where the item is added to the list if the Sorted property of the list box is set to True.

If you don't add the initial items to a list or combo box at design time, then the most common place to do so is in the Form_Load or Form_Initialize procedure. For example, if the list or combo box had the control name of Presidents, the code to build the list might start like this:

```
Private Sub Form_Load()
 Presidents.AddItem "George Washington"
 Presidents.AddItem "John Adams"
 Presidents.AddItem "Thomas Jefferson"
 Presidents.AddItem "James Madison"
..
End Sub
```

GW-BASIC and QuickBASIC users should note that there is no direct analogue of the READ/DATA combination to build information into your program. Of course, you can store the information that will go on the list in a file (see Chapter 17) or in a collection (Chapter 11).

You can also remove an item from a list while the program is running. The syntax for the RemoveItem method is

ListName.RemoveItem *Index*

where, as before, *ListName* is the control name for the list or combo box and *Index* is the position where the item was located.

In addition to removing individual items on a list, you can use the Clear method to remove all the items on the list. The syntax is

ListName.Clear

LIST AND COMBO BOX PROPERTIES

Many of the properties of list and combo boxes determine how the information should appear. These properties are the same as those you've already seen. For example, the font properties control how the items appear in the list, and the BackColor and ForeColor properties control what colors are used for the background and foreground, respectively. Similarly, properties such as Height, Left, Top, and Width control the shape and location of the list or combo box. The properties special to list and combo boxes let you get at the information in the box or the item the user has moved to within the box. They also allow you to have multiple columns in a list box.

For example, when a user moves the focus to a list or combo box, he or she can select an item by using the ordinary Windows conventions—the arrow keys, PGUP, PGDN, the END key, and so on. In fact, once the user moves the focus to the list or combo box, he or she can also use the Windows shortcut of pressing a letter key to move to the first item on the list beginning with that letter. The item the user selects is always highlighted. All these details are handled automatically by Visual Basic. The item selected by the user is the value of the Text property of the box.

Following are descriptions of the six list and combo box properties you'll need to work with these controls.

ListIndex The value of the ListIndex property gives the index number of the highlighted item, which is where the user has stopped in the list. If no item was selected, the value of this property is -1. For example, suppose you've stored information about the presidents in a string array named PresidentInfo$, and you need to get at the item in this array containing information about the president that the user has selected from the Presidents list box. A statement such as

```
If ListIndex = -1 Then
  MsgBox "No president selected!"
Else
  Info$ = PresidentInfo$(Presidents.ListIndex + 1)
End If
```

makes the value of the Info$ string variable the information you'll need. The code also assumes you've stored the information about George Washington in the first position in the PresidentInfo$ string array. If you've put the information about Washington in the zero slot, you don't need to add 1 to the value of President.ListIndex to get at this information.

Text The Text property gives the currently selected item stored as a string. (If you need the numeric equivalent, apply the Val function.)

List The List property is a string array that contains all the items on the list. The value of the BoxName.Text property for a list or combo box is the same as that of BoxName.List(ListIndex). In Visual Basic 4, unlike earlier versions of Visual Basic, the List property is available at design time. This gives you another way to initialize the items in the list or combo box. (Choosing the List property in the Properties Window opens up a list box where you can type the items. Place each item on a separate line.)

ListCount The ListCount property gives you the number of items on the list. Since the Index property starts at 0, to analyze the contents of the list using a For-Next loop, write the limits of the loop as

```
For I% = 0 To BoxName.ListCount-1
```

Columns and MultiSelection The Columns property controls the number of columns in a list box. If the value is 0 (the default), you get a normal single-column list box with vertical scrolling. If the value is 1, you get a single-column list box with horizontal scrolling. If the value is greater than 1, you allow (but do not require) multiple columns.

tip: *Multiple columns show up only when the items don't fit into the list box. To force multiple columns, reduce the height of the list box accordingly.*

The MultiSelect property controls whether the user can select more than one item from the list. (Of course, you may have to parse the resulting string assigned to the Text property to determine the individual items selected.) There are three possible values for this property:

Type of Selection	Value	How It Works
No multiselection allowed	0	
Simple multiselection	1	Use ordinary Windows techniques and mouse dragging (SHIFT+arrow keys, CTRL+RIGHT ARROW, and so on) to select more items.
Extended multiselection	2	SHIFT+mouse click extends the selection to include all list items between the current selection and the location of click. Pressing CTRL and clicking the mouse selects or deselects an item in the list.

LIST BOX EVENTS

List boxes respond to 12 events. The KeyUp, KeyDown, and KeyPress events work exactly as before. The mouse events are covered in Chapter 16. List boxes can also tell you whether they've received or lost the focus.

However, the two most important events for list boxes are the Click and Double-click events. An important Windows convention is that clicking on an item selects the item but does not choose the item. This is reserved for double-clicking on the item. In general, therefore, you do not write code for the Click event procedure for a list box but only for the Double-click event procedure.

Another reason not to write code for the Click event procedure unnecessarily is that each time the user moves through the list, Visual Basic generates the Click event. Landing on an item in a list box by using the keyboard is the functional equivalent of clicking on the item. (There is no keyboard equivalent for double-clicking, although you can write your own for a specific list box by using the key events.)

tip: *You might have the Click event update a status bar (see the next chapter) that gives information about the item.*

COMBO BOX EVENTS

Combo boxes respond to many of the same events as list boxes. You can analyze which keys were pressed or whether the box has received or lost the focus.

The first event that is different is the Change event. The Change event occurs only for pull-down combo boxes and simple combo boxes (Style = 0 or 1). Visual Basic does not generate this event if you are using a pull-down list box (Style = 2). Visual Basic generates this event whenever the user enters data in the text area of the combo box or you change the Text property of the combo box from code.

As an example of where you might use this, suppose you've set up the list of presidents using a simple combo box (Style = 0, control Name = Presidents). Again, let's assume the information you want to display about each president is stored in the string array: PresidentsInfo$. As the directions on the screen in Figure 12-5 indicate, you want to allow the user the possibility of entering the number of the president instead of scrolling through the list. Now, suppose someone types a number in the text box. Then you might first try to use the following Change event procedure to give the user the information he or she is looking for:

```
Sub Presidents_Change()
  PresidentNumber% = Val(Presidents.Text)
  If PresidentNumber% < 1 Or PresidentNumber% >42 Then
    MsgBox("Only 42 presidents with Clinton's election!")
  Else
    MsgBox(PresidentsInfo$(PresidentNumber%))
  End If
End Sub
```

The trouble with this is that the Change event procedure is too responsive for this particular task. Visual Basic calls this event procedure every time the user types a character in the text area of the combo box. This means that for all but the first nine presidents, the procedure is called twice. (For example, if the user entered 16, he or she would see information about both Washington and Lincoln!) Also, if the user drops down the list and clicks, text rather than a number fills the text box. A better way to analyze the information is to put this code inside the KeyPress event procedure but check for the user's pressing ENTER. You can do this with the following code:

```
Sub Presidents_KeyPress(KeyAscii As Integer)
  If KeyAscii = vbKeyReturn        'or 13 - the Enter key
 PresidentNumber% = Val(Presidents.Text)
    Select Case PresidentNumber%
      Case 0
       MsgBox("Please enter a number or double-click on an entry.")
      Case Is < 1
       MsgBox("No negative (numbered at least) presidents.")
      Case Is > 42
       MsgBox("Only 42 presidents so far.")
      Case Else
      MsgBox(PresidentsInfo$(PresidentNumber%))
    End Select
  End If
End Sub
```

You can easily modify this procedure to let the user select an item by scrolling through the list and pressing ENTER. (Change the Case 0 clause.)

Since simple combo boxes (Style = 1) recognize the Double-click event, another possibility is to code this in the Double-click event procedure. However, since there is no keyboard equivalent for double-clicking, you still might want to write a KeyPress event procedure to add keyboard equivalents for the user.

Visual Basic calls the DropDown event procedure right after the user clicks the arrow to drop the list box down or presses ALT+DOWN ARROW when the combo box has the focus—before the list drops down. For this reason, this event procedure is mostly used to update a combo box before the list appears. Since you can have a pull-down list only when the Style property is 0 or 2, this event is not invoked for simple combo boxes (Style = 1).

ASSOCIATING NUMBERS TO ITEMS ON LIST OR COMBO BOXES

In the Checkbook Management Program (Chapter 21) we need to associate an account ID number to the account's name. Needing to associate integers to items in a list or combo is so common that a simple method of doing this was added way back in Visual Basic 2.0. Of course, you could create an array to store this information and keep track of this array yourself but you no longer need to do that—at least as long as all you need is a (long) integer associated to the item.

Whenever you create a list or combo box, Visual Basic automatically creates a long integer array called the ItemData array. This array is another property of the box like the List array that you saw previously. And, like any property of a Visual Basic control, you can examine it or modify it.

If you want to add the numeric data to an entry in this ItemData array, you need to know the array index of the item. This is taken care of by the NewIndex property of the box. This property gives you the index of the last item added to the box. (If the Sorted property is True this is particularly useful information.)

At this point you need to write the code to update the ItemData array. The code will always look something like this.

```
List1.AddItem ItemToBeAdded
List1.ItemData(List1.NewIndex) = LongIntegerData
```

(See Chapter 21 for how this might be used in a more realistic situation.)

Scroll Bars

Scroll bars are used to get input or display output when you don't care about the exact value of an object but you do care whether the change is small or large. A good example of using scroll bars to accept input may be found in the

Custom Color dialog box available from the color palette. As you saw in Chapter 3, this dialog box lets you adjust the amount of red, green, or blue for the custom color by moving the scroll bars. Although you can use the Color common dialog box to get this information (see the section "The Color Choice Box" later in this chapter), you may occasionally want to let users adjust the color of a form or picture box by using scroll bars. The upcoming example shows you how to code this.

Vertical scroll bars and horizontal scroll bars work the same way. Scroll bars span a range of values; the scroll box shows where the value is relative to the two extremes. Scroll bars work with nine events and 26 properties. The event that is the key to using scroll bars is the Change event. This is activated whenever the user manipulates the scroll bar.

SCROLL BAR PROPERTIES

Only five of the 26 properties are special to scroll bars. What follows is a short description of those properties.

Min The Min property is an integer that defines the smallest value for a scroll bar. For red, green, or blue color codes, which range from zero to 255, the Min property would be set to zero for a project that sets colors via scroll bars. Since Min takes integer values, the possible settings are from -32,768 to 32,767.

Max The Max property is an integer that defines the largest value for a scroll bar. For the primary color codes, the Max property would be set to 255 for a project that sets the colors via a scroll bar. Since Max also takes integer values, the possible settings are also from -32,768 to 32,767. You can set the Max value to be less than the Min value. This causes the maximum value of the scroll bar to be reached at the left or top of the scroll bar, depending on whether it's a horizontal or vertical scroll bar. Both Max and Min are usually set at design time, but you can change them with code while a project is running.

Value The Value property tells you where the scroll bar is. It is always an integer. The range is determined by the Min property and the Max property. The Value property can be as small as the Min value or as large as the Max value.

SmallChange The setting for SmallChange determines how Visual Basic changes the Value property of the scroll bar in response to a user's clicking one of the scroll arrows. If the user clicks the up scroll arrow, the Value property of the scroll bar increases by the amount of SmallChange until the Value property reaches the value of the Max property. If the user clicks the down scroll arrow, Visual Basic decreases the Value property similarly. The default value of SmallChange is 1, and it can be set to any integer between 1 and 32,767. As with Min and Max, this property is usually set at design time but can be changed in code as well.

LargeChange The setting for LargeChange determines how Visual Basic changes the Value property of the scroll bar in response to a user's clicking between the scroll box and the scroll arrow. The default LargeChange value is also 1 but is usually set to a multiple of the SmallChange value. It too is an integer between 1 and 32,767. As with Min, Max, and SmallChange, this property is usually set at design time but can also be changed at run time.

AN EXAMPLE: ADJUSTING COLOR CODES VIA SCROLL BARS

Suppose you want to begin an application by letting the user adjust the background and foreground colors. The initial form might look like the one in Figure 12-6. Notice that this application has three vertical scroll bars, a picture box, and two radio buttons.

Here is a table describing the important properties of the controls that make up this application:

Control Name	Property	Setting
RedBar	Min	0
	Max	255
	SmallChange	5
	LargeChange	25
VsbGreenBar	Min	0
	Max	255
	SmallChange	5
	LargeChange	25
VsbBlueBar	Min	0
	Max	255
	SmallChange	5
	LargeChange	25

Control Name	Property	Setting
btnBkColor	Caption	BackColor
btnFrColor	Caption	ForeColor

Leave the picture box with the default name of Picture1. Here's an example of the first step in the code you would use for this project:

```
Sub vsbRedBar_Change()
  If btnBkColor.Value Then
    Picture1.BackColor = _
RGB(vsbRedBar.Value,vsbGreenBar.Value,
vsbBlueBar.Value)
  ElseIf btnFrColor.Value Then
    Picture1.ForeColor = _
RGB(vsbRedBar.Value,vsbGreenBar.Value,
vsbBlueBar.Value)
    Picture1.Cls
    Picture1.Print "This is displayed in the current
foreground color."
  End If
End Sub
```

Figure 12-6

Form to adjust color using scroll bars

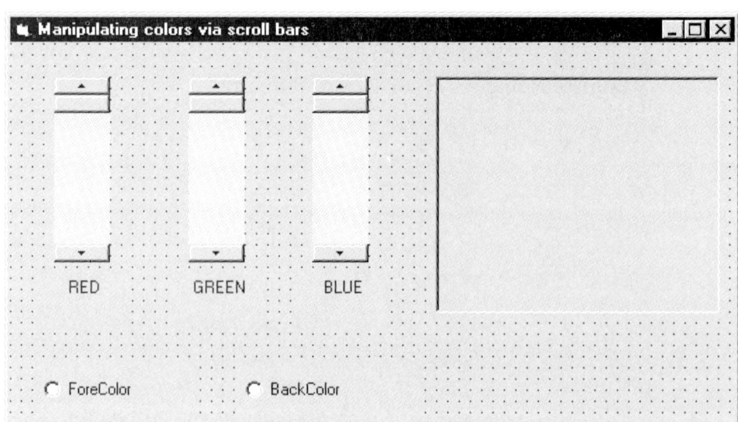

The other Change procedures would work the same way—which should immediately make you think that this is a perfect situation for using a general procedure attached to the form that does it once and for all. Here's the code for the more sophisticated version of this procedure:

```
Sub vsbRedBar_Change()
  ColorChange
End Sub

Sub ColorChange()
 If btnBkColor.Value Then
    Picture1.BackColor = _
RGB(vsbRedBar.Value,vsbGreenBar.Value,
vsbBlueBar.Value)
  ElseIf btnFrColor.Value Then
    Picture1.ForeColor = _
RGB(vsbRedBar.Value,vsbGreenBar.Value,
vsbBlueBar.Value)
    Picture1.Cls
    Picture1.Print "This is displayed in the current
foreground color."
  End If
End Sub
```

Notice that to show the ForeColor change requires displaying some text inside the picture box. Finally, notice that in an actual application, you would probably add a command button called Finished, perhaps, and have a click on that button hide this form, saving the BackColor and ForeColor information as the values of global variables to use for the other forms in your project. You might also combine all this code into a single general procedure that uses a color as the parameter.

Timers

Use a timer control whenever you want something to happen periodically. You might want to have a program that wakes up periodically and checks stock prices. On a more prosaic level, if you want to display a "clock" on a form, you might want to update the clock's display every minute or even every second. Timers are not visible to the user; the icon appears only at design time. For this reason, where you place or how you size the timer control at design time is not important. Although timers are an important tool for Visual Basic programmers, they shouldn't be overused. In fact, Windows restricts all the applications (not just the Visual Basic applications) running at one time to 16 timers.

The screen in Figure 12-7 shows an example of a form at design time with a label and a timer control that you can use to develop a simple clock (see "The Timer Event and Some Sample Uses").

TIMER PROPERTIES

Besides the control name of the timer (the defaults are Timer1, Timer2, and so on), there are two important properties of timer controls: Enabled and Interval.

Enabled Enabled is a Boolean (True/False) property that determines whether the timer should start ticking or not. If you set this to True at design time, the clock starts ticking when the form loads. "Ticking" is meant metaphorically; there's no noise unless you program one. Also, because timer controls are invisible to the user, he or she may well be unaware that a timer has been enabled. For this reason, you may want to notify the user that a timer is working by means of a message box or picture box with a clock icon.

If you set the Enabled property to False at design time, the timer control starts working only when you switch this property to True in code. Similarly, you can disable a timer inside code by setting its Enabled property to False.

Figure 12-7 Form for a simple clock

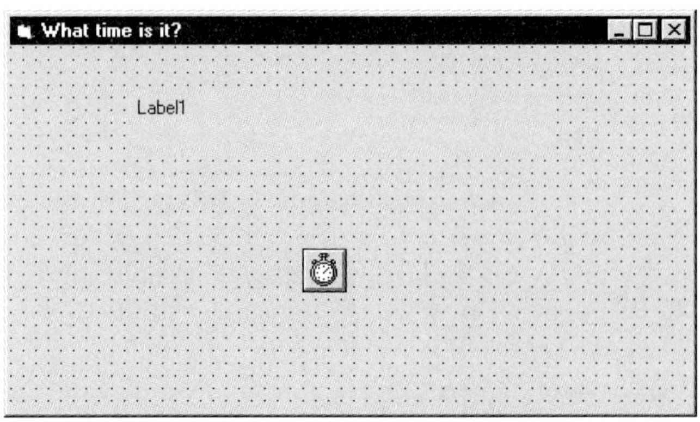

Interval The Interval property determines how much time Visual Basic waits before calling the Timer event procedure (see the next section). The interval is measured in milliseconds, and the theoretical limits are between 1 millisecond and 65,535 milliseconds (a little more than one minute and five seconds). The reason these are only theoretical limits is that the underlying hardware reports the passage of only 18 clock ticks per second. Since this is a little less than 56 milliseconds per clock tick, you can't really use an Interval property any less than 56, and intervals that don't differ by at least this amount may give the same results.

The smaller you set the Interval property, the more CPU time is spent waking up the Timer event procedure. Set the Interval property too small and your system performance may slow to a crawl.

---

note: *An Interval property of zero disables the timer.*

Finally, since the CPU may be doing something else when the interval time elapses, there is no guarantee that Visual Basic will call the Timer event procedure exactly when you want it. (Visual Basic will know when the interval has elapsed; it just may need to finish what it is doing before activating the Timer event.) If the interval has elapsed, Visual Basic will call the Timer event procedure as soon as it is free to do so. The next section explains how to deal with this problem.

THE TIMER EVENT AND SOME SAMPLE USES

Suppose you want to develop a project with a clock that will update itself every second, following the form shown in Figure 12-7. To design the form, follow these steps:

1. Add a label and a timer to a blank form.
2. Set the AutoSize property of the label to True and the FontSize to 18. Set the Interval property of the timer control to 1000 (1000 milliseconds = 1 second).
3. Now write the following code in the Timer event procedure for the Timer1 control:

```
Sub Timer1_Timer()
  Label1.Caption = "The time is " + Format(Now,"Long Time")
End Sub
```

Visual Basic will call this event procedure and update the clock's time roughly every second because the Interval property is 1000. (See Chapter 6 for the Format function.) It would be easy enough to add an option button to let the user switch to an AM/PM display if he or she wanted.

Here is another example. One of the problems with computer screens is that they may be left on too long. This can (especially with cheaper monitors) cause an image to be burned into the screen, its ghostly presence interfering with efficient use of the monitor forever after. Screen-blanking programs work by constantly drawing a different image in a different color. This prevents burn-in. It is trivial to use a timer control to write a screen-blanking program. While commercial programs provide beautiful images, the following project gives you a randomly colored, randomly placed "Press any key to end" message.

For this, start up a new project and add a timer control to it. Next, make the BackColor property black. You can do this either by using the color palette or by directly setting the BackColor property color code to the color code for black (&H0&). Finally, since you want to have this screen take over the whole screen, set the Border property to None (0) and the WindowState property to Maximal (2).

Here's the code for the Timer1_Timer event procedure:

```
Sub Timer1_Timer()
  Dim X As Integer
  Cls
  X = DoEvents()
  CurrentX = Rnd*ScaleWidth
  CurrentY = Rnd*ScaleHeight
  ForeColor = QBColor(16*Rnd)
  Print "Press any key to end!"
End Sub
```

This program first clears the screen. Next, it calculates a random location on the screen and sets the ForeColor randomly using the QBColor function. (See Chapter 15 for more on this function.) Of course, since you are taking a percentage of the screen height and width, this may occasionally not give the program enough room to display the full message. If this bothers you, you can easily add code using the TextHeight and TextWidth methods to make sure the text is always completely on the screen.

Now, having the program end when the user presses a key requires only a simple KeyDown event procedure to unload the form and the QueryUnload event to end.

```
Sub Form_KeyDown(KeyCode As Integer, Shift As Integer)
  Unload Me
End Sub

Private Sub Form_QueryUnload(Cancel As Integer, UnloadMode As _
Integer)
  End
End Sub
```

The KeyDown event is triggered whenever the user presses any key, thus ending the application.

To make this into a practical screen-blanking program, you have to choose a value for the Interval property. A relatively large value such as 1000 (one second) or even 2000 (two seconds) for the Interval property seems to work best.

Next, suppose you want to have a Timer event procedure do something even less frequently than the maximum setting for the Interval property—much more slowly than once a minute. The trick is to add a static variable to the Timer event procedure. For example, suppose you want to have a Timer event procedure wake up only once an hour. Set the Interval property to 60,000 (one minute):

```
Sub Timer1_Timer()
  Static TimerTimes As Integer
  TimerTimes = TimerTimes + 1
  If TimerTimes = 60 Then
    TimerTimes = 0           'reset counter
   'Here's where the once an hour code would go
  Else
    Exit Sub
  End If
End Sub
```

The If clause is activated only when the counter TimerTimes reaches 60. But this happens only when the Timer event procedure has been called 60 times, because TimerTimes is a static variable. Now, put whatever code you want inside the If clause. That code will be processed only once an hour (because you reset TimerTimes back to 0).

Finally, to take into account the possibility that Visual Basic was doing something else exactly when the timer elapsed, you can add code inside the Timer event procedure to check the system clock if you feel this is necessary. (See Chapter 5 for the functions that check the clock.)

Menus

Designing the right kind of menus will make your applications much more user-friendly. Visual Basic lets you build up to six levels of menus. The screen in Figure 12-8 shows you a menu with four of the possible six levels. Menus that contain submenus are usually called *hierarchical menus*. Of course, using too many levels of menus can make the application confusing to the user. Four is almost certainly too many, and two or three levels are the most you will usually see. The user knows that a submenu lurks below a given menu item when he or she sees a ► following the menu item.

Notice in the illustration on the following page that each of the four items in the first level of menus in Figure 12-8 has the ► and so conceals a submenu.

Figure 12-8
Hierarchical menus

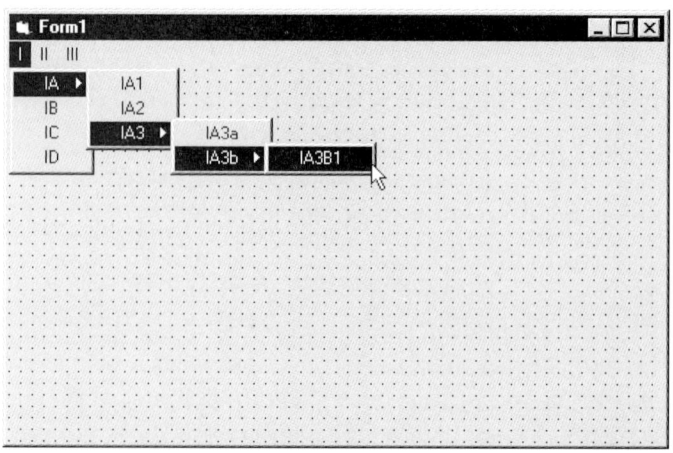

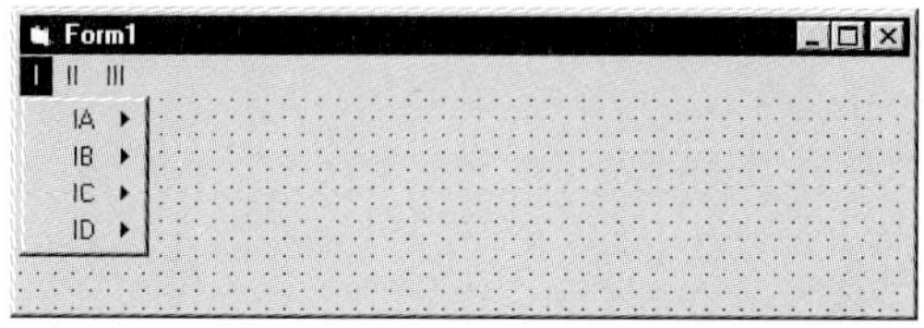

You can open a submenu by using the standard Windows conventions: press ENTER, click the item with the mouse, or press LEFT ARROW.

Menu Designer

You create menus in Visual Basic by using the Menu Design window available by choosing Tools | Menu Designer. (You can also choose the Menu Designer tool from the toolbar, and Menu Designer is one of the options on the shortcut menu when the focus is in the form window.) The Menu Designer is shown in Figure 12-9. What follows is a short description of each of the components of this dialog box.

Caption Text Box What you type in the Caption text box is what the user sees. The caption also shows up in the text area inside the dialog box. Unlike other Visual Basic controls, menu items do not have default captions. ALT+P is

Figure 12-9 Menu Design window

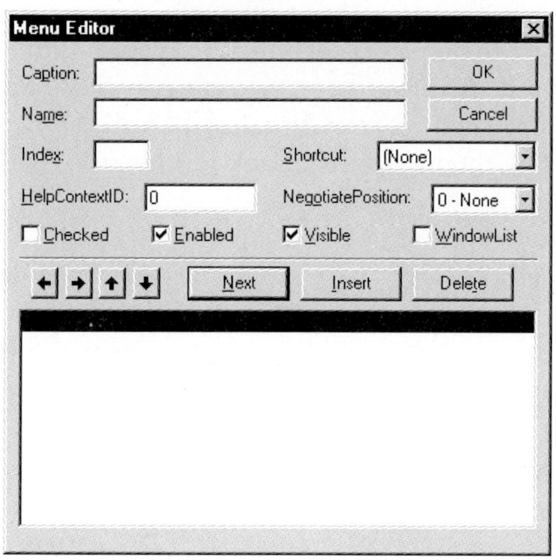

the access key for the Caption text box in the Menu Design window.

tip: *If the Caption property is set to a hyphen (-), a separator bar is used. Separator bars break long menus into groups.*

Name Text Box Each menu item must have a control name. Unless the menu items are part of a control array (see Chapter 10), they must have different control names. What you enter in the Name text box becomes the control name that is used by Visual Basic for the Click event procedure for the menu item. Visual Basic will not let you leave the Menu Design window until you give each menu item a control name. The access key is ALT+M.

OK and Cancel Buttons Click the OK button when you are finished designing the menu. Click the Cancel button if you decide not to build the menu at all. Even after you've finished designing a menu and clicked on the Done button, you can return to the Menu Design window and make changes.

Index Box Use the Index box if you want to make a menu item part of a control array. As you saw in Chapter 10, control arrays let you add new instances of the control at run time. In the case of menu items, this would let you have the menu enlarge or shrink while the program is running. Once you've set a menu item to be part of a control array at run time, you add new menu items with the Load method you saw in Chapter 10. Similarly, you remove menu items from a control array by using the Unload method. It is quite common to leave the Caption property blank for the first menu item in a control array.

Shortcut Box The Shortcut box lets you add accelerator keys to your menu items. Recall that accelerator keys are either function keys or CTRL+key combinations that activate a menu item without the user's needing to open the menu at all. If you click the down arrow to the right of the Shortcut box, a list box drops down with the choices for accelerator keys. You need only click the key you want.

tip: *ALT+F4 is not an available shortcut. If you have an Exit item and want to remind people that ALT+F4 will exit the program, add ALT+F4 as part of the caption to the Exit item. (That ALT+F4 triggers the QueryUnload event and closes the form if not canceled means there is functionality built into any form that has a control box.)*

WindowList Check Box Window lists are used when you have MDI windows. (See the section "MDI Forms" later in this chapter.)

HelpContextId Box This is used when you are working with the Help compiler—available in Visual Basic Professional edition (see the next chapter).

The Checked Check Box The Checked check box determines whether a check mark shows up in front of the menu item. As you'd expect, this box controls the setting of the Checked property of the menu item. The default is off. It is much more common to switch the Checked property to True when a user selects the item while the program is running than to set it at design time.

Enabled Check Box The Enabled check box determines the value of the Enabled property of the menu item. A menu item that is Enabled will respond to the Click event. An item that has been changed to False—either at design time by toggling the box off or at run time via code—shows up grayed.

Visible Check Box The Visible check box determines the value of the Visible property of the menu item. If a menu item is made invisible, all its submenus are also invisible.

Arrow Buttons The arrow buttons work with the current menu items. The menu item you're currently working with is highlighted in the large text window below the arrow buttons. Submenus are indicated by the indentation level in this text window, as you'll see in the next section. The left and right arrow buttons control the indentation level. Clicking on the left arrow button moves the highlighted item in one level; clicking on the right arrow button moves it one indentation level deeper. You cannot indent an item more than one level deeper than the item above it. If you try, Visual Basic will not let you leave the Menu Design window until you fix it.

Clicking on the up arrow button interchanges the highlighted menu item with the item above it; clicking on the down arrow button interchanges the highlighted item with the item below it. The up and down arrows do not change the indentation pattern of an item. See the section "Sample Menu Design Window" for more on using the arrow buttons.

Next Button Clicking the Next button moves you to the next menu item or inserts a new item if you are at the end of the menu. The indentation of the new item starts out the same as the indentation of the previous item. ALT+N is the access key. You can also use the mouse to move among items.

Insert Button Clicking the Insert button inserts a menu item above the currently highlighted menu item. ALT+I is the access key.

Delete Button Clicking the Delete button removes the currently highlighted item. The access key is ALT+T. You cannot use the DEL key to remove menu items.

Sample Menu Design Window

The Menu Design window that led to the hierarchical menu in Figure 12-8 began like the screen in Figure 12-10. Notice that the menu item that is not indented appears on the main menu bar. Menu items that are indented once (preceded by 4 dots) appear as a menu item below the main menu bar. Items indented twice (8 dots) are submenus, items indented 12 dots are sub-submenus, and so on. You can always determine the main menu bar by looking for items that appear flush left in the text window in the Menu Design window.

Working with Menus at Run Time

Suppose you want to write a program that would help people convert between various kinds of units—for example, between inches, centimeters, meters, and feet. A form for this application might look like the one in Figure 12-11. Notice that this form has three items on the menu bar: Target, Source, and Quit. The Menu Design window for this form looks like the one in Figure 12-12.

The control names and captions for the menu items and controls are given in the following table:

Control Name	Caption
txtSource	Source
txtTarget	Target
mnuFromInches	Inches
mnuFromFeet	Feet
mnuFromCentimeters	Centimeters
mnuFromMeters	Meters
mnuToInches	Inches
mnuToFeet	Feet
mnuToCentimeters	Centimeters
mnuToMeters	Meters
Text1	
Label1	
Label2	Source Units
Label3	Target Units

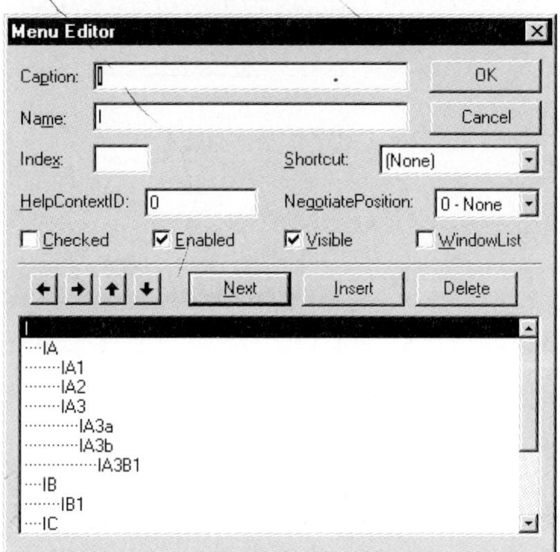

Figure 12-10 Beginning of the Menu Design window for the menus in Figure 12-8

Figure 12-11 Form for conversion program

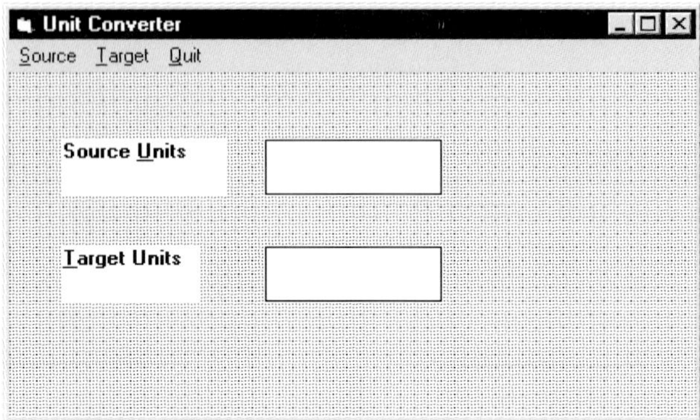

Notice that the Caption properties are the same for the items on the Target and Source menus; only the control names are different. The first label should have the BorderStyle property set to 1 so that it resembles a text box (or use a locked text box).

Figure 12-12 Menu Design window for conversion program

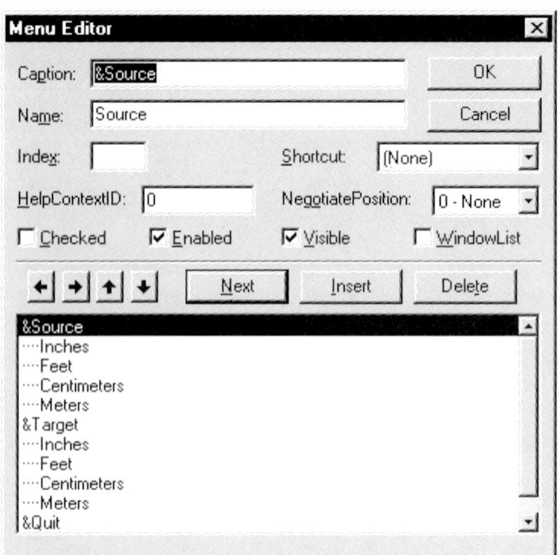

Whenever you write a conversion program, it's easiest to establish one unit as the basic unit and convert all the units using that as an intermediary. For this, set up the form-level variable

```
Dim BasicLength As Single
```

in the Declarations section of the form.

Now, suppose the user clicks the menu item marked Inches in the Source menu. The code should do the following:

- Put a check mark next to the Inches item and remove check marks from all other items.
- Disable the Inches item in the Target menu and enable all the other items.

Here's the code for the Click procedure that implements this outline for one of the menu items. (The others work the same.)

```
Sub mnuFromInches_Click()
  mnuFromInches.Checked = True
  mnuFromFeet.Checked = False
  mnuFromCentimeters.Checked = False
  mnuFromMeters.Checked = False
'change items on Target menu
  mnuToInches.Enabled = False
  mnuToFeet.Enabled = True
  mnuToCentimeters.Enabled = True
  mnuToMeters.Enabled = True
'set the caption for units
  Label2.Caption = "Inches"
End Sub
```

Now suppose the user clicks an item in the Target menu. You need to read the value from the text box, calculate the new value, and display the result in the first label. Suppose, for example, the user clicked the Meters item, indicating he or she wanted to convert from inches to meters. Here's the code that does this, using centimeters as the basic length:

```
Sub mnuToMeters_Click()
  Label3.Caption = "Meters"
  If mnuFromInches.Checked Then
    BasicLength = Val(Text1.Text)*2.54—'2.54 Centimeters/inch
```

```
  ElseIf mnuFromFeet.Checked Then
    BasicLength = Val(Text1.Text)*2.54 *12
  ElseIf mnuFromCentimeters.Checked Then
    BasicLength = Val(Text1.Text)
  End If
  Label1.Caption = Str(BasicLength/100)
End Sub
```

This procedure uses the fact that clicking on an item in the Target menu changes the Checked property to False for all but the unit to be converted. If you add some directions to the Form_Load procedure, you can see the result shown in Figure 12-13.

Common Dialog Boxes

While working with Windows and Visual Basic you've become accustomed to seeing one of the five standard "common" dialog boxes for opening or saving a file, printing, choosing fonts, or setting colors. Common dialog boxes are easy to use in principle but they are somewhat less easy to use in practice. This is because they may require a fair amount of initializing to get them to look exactly the way you want. The online help is essential for working with common dialog boxes. This section can only give you a feeling for how to work with them.

Figure 12-13 Results of running the conversion program

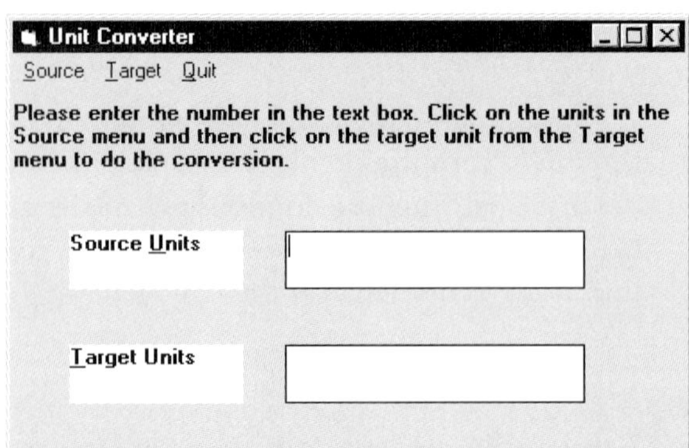

note: *The common dialog boxes take no actions; they accept information only. You will always need to write the code that gets Visual Basic to read off the information entered and then write the code that takes the appropriate actions when the user clicks on OK.*

The common dialog box control is automatically added to the toolbox unless you have changed your AUTOLD*.VBP file to remove it. To use a common dialog box you need to place a common dialog control on the form. Here's a picture of this control:

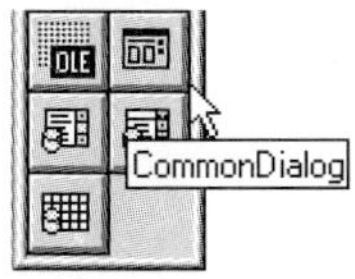

note: *What the common dialog control does is let you get at the routines in the Microsoft Windows dynamic link library COMMDLG.DLL without using API functions. To use this control, the file called COMMDLG.DLL must be in the Microsoft Windows SYSTEM directory. The actual files for the common dialog control are called COMDLG16.OCX for the 16-bit or COMDLG32.OCX for the 32-bit version and these must also, of course, be available.*

You determine which common dialog control pops up by applying one of the following methods to the common dialog control:

Method	Dialog Box
ShowSave	Shows a File Save dialog box
ShowOpen	Shows a File Open dialog box
ShowColor	Shows the color choice dialog box
ShowPrint	Shows the Print dialog box
ShowFont	Brings up the font choice dialog box

(You can also bring up the Windows help engine via a common dialog control. This is done with the ShowHelp method and is discussed in the next chapter.)

A Simple File Viewer Example

As an example of using a common dialog box, let's build a simple bitmap viewer. For this, start up a new project by selecting File|New Project. Add an image control for displaying graphics, and a command button. Use the default names of Image1 and Command1. Next, add a common dialog control. Your screen will look like Figure 12-14.

You now need to set the Filter properties of the common dialog control so that only files with the .BMP extension, which indicates a bitmap, will be shown. Set the Filter property of the common dialog control to Bitmaps|*.bmp. Next, enter the text **Choose bitmap** as the value of the DialogTitle property. (This property controls the title bar of the dialog box.) Since you want to show an Open File dialog box, you use the ShowOpen method, which tells Visual Basic to display the File Open common dialog box. Here's all the code you need to get the most primitive form of the bitmap viewer working:

```
Private Command1_Click()
  CommonDialog1.ShowOpen
  Image1.Picture = LoadPicture(CommonDialog1.FileName)
End Sub
```

That's it. If you run this project, you'll be presented with an ordinary Windows dialog box (with the caption "Choose Bitmap") that will be restricted to displaying only files with the .BMP extension. You can navigate among the directories on your drives by clicking and double-clicking as is usual with any

Figure 12-14 Initial screen for bitmap viewer

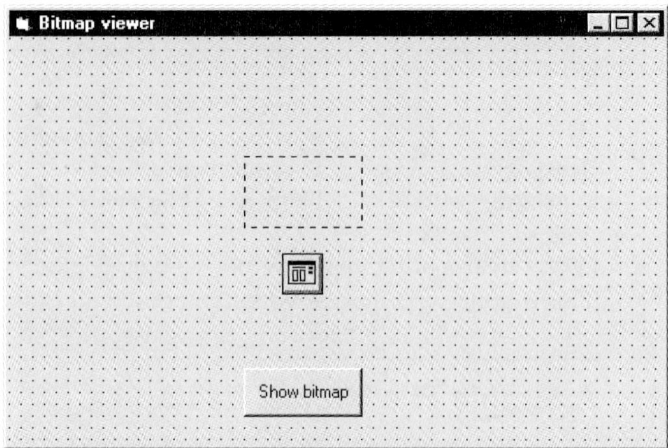

common dialog box in Windows. Find a bitmap, click on OK, and Visual Basic will display the bitmap on the form.

tip: *You'll find a large number of bitmaps in the directories under C:\VB\BITMAPS.*

Of course, this is by no means a bulletproof application: if you select a non-bitmap file, the application will crash. Also, if the user selects the Cancel button, one cannot be sure of what might happen!

Working with Common Dialog Boxes

As you saw in the preceding example, before you pop up a dialog box, you need to initialize the various properties that determine how the common dialog box looks. As with any Visual Basic object, this can be done at run time or design time.

The first problem you encounter when using a common dialog property in real life is to distinguish between the user clicking the OK button (in which case you want to use the information) or clicking the Cancel button (in which case you don't want to do anything). All the common dialog boxes can generate an error if the user clicks the Cancel button. Whether they *will* generate the error depends on the current value of the CancelError property. If you want to trap a user clicking the Cancel button, either set this property to True at design time or use code like:

[*FormName*].*CommonDialogControlName*.CancelError = True

The default is False, so no error is reported when the Cancel button is clicked. On the other hand, it is hard to imagine a use of the common dialog control that would not require trapping this error!

The reason why setting the CancelError property to True and then trapping this error is important is that whether the user clicks OK or Cancel, certain property values of the common dialog control may have been changed. For example, a user may have entered a new filename, changed his or her mind, and clicked the Cancel button. However, the FileName property of the common dialog box would still have changed. Since you only want to use the information when the OK button is clicked, you must have a way to know whether the Cancel button was used to close the dialog box. This is done with an error trap. For example, here's a modification of the image viewer that uses an error trap to detect whether the Cancel button was pressed—in which case you do nothing.

```
Private Command1_Click()
  CommonDialog1.CancelError = True
  On Error GoTo DoNothing
  CommonDialog1.ShowOpen
  Image1.Picture = LoadPicture(CommonDialog1.FileName)
  Exit Sub
DoNothing:
  If Err.Number= cdlCANCEL Then
   'do nothing Cancel button clicked
  Else
   MsgBox Err.Description 'you have a real error to handle
  End If
End Sub
```

MORE ON THE FILE OPEN AND FILE SAVE DIALOG BOXES

Just as the ShowOpen method is used to show an Open dialog box, the ShowSave method is used to display the File Save dialog boxes. Other than that, the properties are essentially the same for both these dialog boxes. For example, you use the CancelError property the same way for both dialog boxes. Similarly, the DialogTitle property lets you set the title bar. In particular, you do not need to use Open and Save as the titles of these boxes if you are using them in other contexts.

Here is a table with descriptions of the most important properties used for these dialog boxes:

Property	What It Does
DefaultExt	Sets the default extension for files shown in the box.
FileName	Gives the name and full path of the file selected.
FileTitle	Gives the filename *without* the path.
Filter	Affects the Type box in the dialog box. You saw an example of this earlier when the example bitmap viewer used a Filter property of Bitmaps|*.bmp. You can have multiple filters by separating them with a pipe symbol (| = CHR$(124). In general, the format is the description string, the pipe symbol, the filter, another pipe symbol, and so on.
FilterIndex	This is used when you set up many filters using the Filter property.
Flags	This property is used to set various possible options on how the box will look or behave (see the next section).
InitDir	Specifies the initial directory.
MaxFileSize	Sets the maximum size of the filename including all the path info.

MORE ON THE FLAGS PROPERTY OF THE FILE DIALOG BOXES

The Flags property is very important in determining the final look and feel of the box. For example, a line of code like

```
CommonDialog1.Flags = cdlOFNAllowMultiselect
```

allows the File name list box to use multiple selections. You can combine more than one flag by adding them together. You read back their current values using bit-masking techniques with the And operator. The following summarizes the most important of the possible flags for the File dialog boxes.

note: *You must set the values of the Flags property before you display the dialog box.*

cdlOFNAllowMultiselect This flag (as you just saw) allows multiselection using the standard Windows techniques of holding down the SHIFT key and using the UP ARROW and DOWN ARROW keys to select the desired files.

note: *If you allow multiselection, the value of the FileName property is a string containing the names of all selected files. Each filename is separated from the next by spaces, so you can use the standard techniques you have already seen for parsing text to identify them.*

cdlOFNCreatePrompt Suppose you are generally going to be working with existing files. This flag lets you give users a warning that they are using a new filename. When you set the Flags property to this constant, Visual Basic pops up a message box that asks the user if he or she wants to create the file when it doesn't already exist, as shown here:

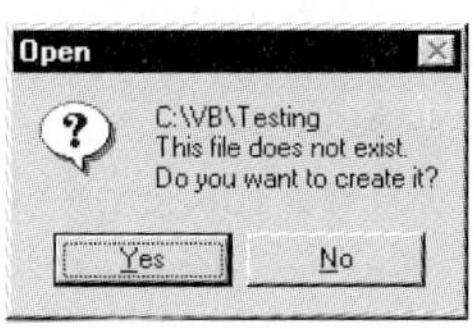

Setting this flag automatically sets the cdlOFNPathMustExist and cdlOFNFileMustExist flags.

cdlOFNExtensionDifferent After the user clicks on OK you can analyze the current value of the Flags property to see if it contains this constant (use the And operator). You may need to do this because you will often need to know if the user is using a nonstandard extension on a file. If you set the Flags property to this value at design time, Visual Basic will let you determine after the user closes the dialog box whether the user has specified a filename with an extension different from the one specified in the DefaultExt property. After the dialog box is closed, you could use code that begins like this:

```
If (CommonDialog1.Flags And cdlOFNExtensionDifferent) = _
dlOFNExtensionDifferent Then 'has a different extension
```

Of course, this flag isn't set if the DefaultExt property is Null, if the extensions match, or if the file has no extension.

cdlOFNFileMustExist If you set this flag, a message box pops up if the user tries to enter a file that doesn't already exist. This flag automatically sets the cdlOFNPathMustExist flag as well.

cdlOFNHideReadOnly, cdlOFNReadOnly The first flag hides the Read Only check box. The second flag makes the Read Only check box checked when the dialog box first appears. (You can also check whether the return value of the Flags property contains this value by bit masking. This lets you check the state of the Read Only check box when the user closes the dialog box.)

cdlOFNNoChangeDir If you don't want the user to be able to change the directory from its initial setting, set this flag.

cdlOFNNoValidate This allows the common dialog box to use invalid characters in the returned filename. (This is useful if you are not actually using the name entered as the filename but only as an identifier.)

cdlOFNOverwritePrompt If you use ShowSave and the file already exists, Visual Basic will pop up a message box asking the user to confirm that he or she wants to overwrite the file.

cdlOFNPathMustExist If you set this flag, the user can't enter an invalid path without generating a warning message box.

cdlOFNShareAware If this flag is set, Windows will ignore sharing violation errors.

cdlOFNHelpButton Makes the dialog box display a Help button.

cdOFNLongNames If you are using Windows 95, this flag controls whether you can use long filenames.

THE COLOR CHOICE BOX

To show the Color dialog box, you use the ShowColor method of the common dialog control. The Flags property also controls how this box appears, and the symbolic constants for this box also begin with "cdl". For example, if

```
CommonDialog1.Flags = cdlCCFullOpen
```

then the entire Color dialog box is displayed. If, on the other hand,

```
CommonDialog1.Flags = cdlCCPreventFullOpen
```

then you will disable the Define Custom Colors section of the dialog box. (The other constants are cdlCCRGBInit, which lets you set the initial color value, and cdlCCHelpButton, which determines whether you see a Help button or not.)

As always, you need to check whether the user clicked the Cancel button before using the value of, for example, CMDialog1.Color to get the color. (This is a long integer for the color selected using the &HRRGGBB& code you have seen before.)

THE FONT CHOICE BOX

You pop up this dialog box by using the ShowFont method of the common dialog control. However, before showing the remaining properties for this box, you'll need to know something about how the Flags property works here. Since you might want to have the font choice box reflect printer fonts only, screen fonts only, or both at once, Visual Basic requires you to set the Flags parameter correctly before it will display the Font dialog box. The symbolic constants used are cdlCFPrinterFonts, cdlCFScreenFonts, and cdlCFBoth. If you don't set the Flags property of the common dialog control to one of these three values and still try to show the Font box, the program generates an error and dies.

There are 15 different Flags property values. As always, you combine them using the Or operator. Here is a table with descriptions of the remaining values for the Flags property.

Flag	What It Does
cdlCFHelpButton	Determines whether the dialog box displays a Help button.
cdlCFEffects	Determines whether you want to allow strikeout, underline, and color effects.
cdlCFApply	Determines whether the dialog box enables the Apply button.
cdlCFANSIOnly	Determines whether the dialog box displays only the fonts that include the Windows character set.
cdlCFNoVectorFonts	Determines whether the dialog box should not display vector-based fonts.
cdlCFNoSimulations	Determines whether the dialog box will not allow graphic device interface (GDI) font simulations.
cdlCFLimitSize	Determines whether the dialog box should show only font sizes between those specified by the Max and Min properties (see the next table).
cdlCFFixedPitchOnly	Determines whether the dialog box should display only fixed-pitch fonts.
cdlCFWYSIWYG	Determines whether the dialog box should show only fonts common to both the screen and printer.
cdlCFForceFontExist	Determines whether a message box pops up if a user selects a font or style that doesn't exist.
cdlCFScalableOnly	Determines whether the dialog box will allow the user to only select scalable fonts, such as TrueType fonts.
cdlCFTTOnly	Specifies that the dialog box should allow the user to select only TrueType fonts.
cdlCFNoFaceSel	This is returned if no font name is selected.
cdlCFNoStyleSel	This is returned if no font style is selected.
cdlCFNoSizeSel	This is returned if no font size is selected.

(As usual, you can determine which flag was returned using bit masking with the And operator.)

Here is a table with descriptions of the most important properties of the Font dialog box:

Property	Use
Color	Only used for color printers.
FontBold, FontItalic, FontStrikeThru, FontUnderline	True/False properties. If the cdlCFEffects flag is set, you can allow the user to choose these properties.
FontName	Sets or returns the font name.
FontSize	Sets or returns the font size.
Max, Min	These affect the point sizes shown in the size box. You need to have the cdlCFLimitSize flag set before you can use these properties.

You read back the value of the various font properties to see what the user wants. For example, the value of CommonDialog1.FontName is the name of the font the user chose. Then have Visual Basic process the code to have the new value go into effect.

THE PRINTER DIALOG BOX

As before, the Flags property controls how the box appears. For example, if the flag parameter is cdlPDAllPages, then the All option button in the Print Range frame is set. In particular this means you will need bit-masking techniques to check out what the user did with the box. Use code like this:

```
If (CMDialog1.Flags And cdlAllPages) = cdlAllPages Then
  'all pages button checked
```

Here is a table with the flags for this dialog box:

Flag	What It Does
cdlPDAllPages	Returns the value or sets the All Pages option button.
cdlPDCollate	Returns the value or sets the Collate check box.
cdlPDDisablePrintToFile	Disables the Print to File check box.
cdlPDHidePrintToFile	Hides the Print to File check box.
cdlPDNoPageNums	Returns the value or sets the Pages option button.
cdlPDNoSelection	Disables the Selection option button.
cdlPDNoWarning	Prevents Visual Basic from issuing a warning message when there is no default printer.

cdlPDPageNums	Returns the value or sets the Pages option button.
cdlPDPrintSetup	Displays the Print Setup dialog box rather than the Print dialog box.
cdlPDPrintToFile	Returns the value or sets the Print to File check box.
cdlPDReturnDC	Returns a device context for the printer selection from the hDC property of the dialog box.
cdlPDReturnDefault	Returns the default printer name.
cdlPDReturnIC	Returns an information context for the printer selection value from the hDC property of the dialog box.
cdlPDSelection	Returns the value or sets the Selection option button.
cdlPDHelpButton	Determines whether the dialog box displays the Help button.
cdlPDUseDevModeCopies	Sets support for multiple copies. (This, of course, depends on whether or not the printer supports multiple copies.)

Here is a table with descriptions of the remaining properties used for these dialog boxes:

Property	Use
Copies	Sets or returns the number of copies the user wants.
FromPage, ToPage	Specifies what pages are wanted.
hDC	This is the device context number. It is used for API function calls.
Max, Min	Specifies the maximum and minimum pages the user can put in the Print Range frame.
PrinterDefault	Set this to True and the user can click the Setup button to change the WIN.INI file.

MDI Forms

MDI stands for *multiple document interface*, which is Microsoft's term for a windowing environment in which one window, usually called the *MDI container* or *MDI parent form*, contains many other windows, usually called *child forms*. For example, you can use an MDI parent form to allow a user to work with two separate windows in the same application. You can have only one MDI parent form to a project and that form must, naturally enough, be the startup form.

note: *Only controls with an alignment property such as the picture box control can be placed on an MDI form.*

To make an MDI parent form, choose the New MDI Form option from the File menu. Next, create the additional forms (usually from the File menu as well). These will be the child forms to your newly created MDI form after you set the form's MDIChild property to True. (You can also turn an existing form into an MDI child form by adjusting this property.) At design time, child forms and the MDI parent form look alike—you can't tell any differences between them.

When you run the project, on the other hand, all the child forms must be explicitly shown (with the Show method) and are displayed within the MDI parent form's boundaries. Moreover, if the child form is minimized, its icon appears inside the MDI parent form, rather than in the Windows desktop. (If you maximize a child form, its caption replaces the caption of the parent form.) Finally, you can neither hide nor disable child forms.

One of the nicest features of Visual Basic's MDI forms is that the menus of the parent form change according to which child form has the focus. This lets you work with specific menus for each child form. What happens is that the menu for the child form that has the focus appears on the menu bar of the MDI parent form—replacing whatever menu was previously there. In particular, the user only sees the menu for the child form when that child form has the focus.

tip: *MDI child forms are good candidates to be generated by using the New method (see Chapter 11). This is because you will often want all the child forms to be essentially the same. (A good example of this is when you use an MDI form to build an editor. If you want to allow multiple editing windows, the New keyword is ideal.)*

The Window Menu and the Arrange Method

Every MDI application should have a Window menu that allows the user to arrange or cascade the child windows—much like Windows itself does. The Window menu should also include a list of the MDI child windows. An example of such a menu is shown here:

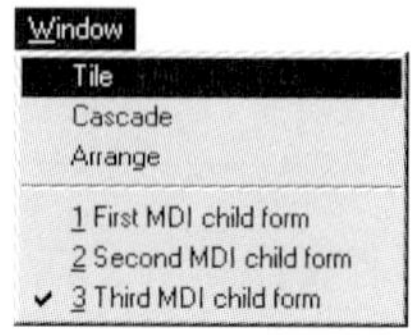

The list of MDI child windows is easy to put on the menu: set the WindowList check box on the Menu Design window to be on. Visual Basic will automatically display the list of the MDI child form captions—and even put a check mark next to the one that most recently had the focus.

To activate the Tile, Cascade, and Arrange items on the Window menu, write code like this:

```
Sub mnuCascadeForms_Click()
  MDIParentForm.Arrange vbCascade
End Sub
```

This uses the vbCascade constant with the Arrange method. The other two constants are vbTileHorizontal and vbArrangeIcons.

More on How Visual Basic Displays Work: ZOrder

When Visual Basic paints the parts of your application, it does so in three layers. The back (bottom) layer is where you draw information directly on the form using the graphical methods that you will see in Chapter 15. The middle layer contains the graphical controls (lines, shapes, picture boxes, and the image control). The top layer contains the nongraphical controls such as command buttons, list boxes, check boxes, and option buttons. Certain controls such as labels have a FontTransparent property that lets information from the layers below shine through.

Within each layer you can control the order in which controls appear. For example, if you use an MDI form, you can control which one is on top after you use the Arrange method. Or, if you overlap two command buttons, you can specify which one appears on top.

You can do this in two ways. At design time you can use the Bring To Front option and Send To Back option from the Edit menu to effect the initial ordering of what's on top. To change it dynamically, while the program is running, you need the ZOrder method. Its syntax is:

[*object*.]ZOrder [*position*]

The *position* parameter can be 0 or 1. If it is 0 or omitted, the *object* named moves to the front. If it is 1, the *object* moves to the back. If you omit the *object* name, the current form moves to the top.

Some Words on Windows Design

This short section cannot substitute for the official Microsoft publication *The Windows Interface Guidelines for Software Design* (ISBN 1-55615-679-0), but perhaps a few words are not out of place.

There's a temptation, especially for experienced DOS programmers, to force Visual Basic programs into a framework that is not Windows-oriented. I have been guilty of this myself on more then one occasion when porting DOS programs to Windows. But this temptation should be resisted. For example, having a sequence of input boxes to get data is very DOS—very linear—and not very Windows. Let the user stay in control; design input forms that the user can access from menus instead. Use DoEvents whenever your application is sitting around idle; don't hog resources. Just because Sub Main lets you write a standard old-fashioned linear program doesn't mean you should. Windows is to some degree multitasking but only if the applications cooperate in not hogging CPU resources.

Make sure you are giving enough feedback to the user. Change the MousePointer to an hourglass when the user is going to have to wait. Don't monkey with what users have grown to expect. Leave control boxes on forms and have ALT+F4 close the form (use the QueryUnload event for the needed cleanup code). Allow users to resize forms and move them around—unless there is some good reason not to do so. Scroll bars are helpful when users are going to have to work through lots of information. Don't crowd your forms with too many buttons; use menus instead. On the other hand, don't make menus too deep. Use custom or common dialog boxes as appropriate.

Make the menus look like what users expect. Programs that handle files should have the standard order in the File menu, with the right captions and the right access keys (where appropriate). Users expect to see a File menu (with an ALT+F shortcut) that will have whatever subset of the following list is appropriate:

New
Open...
Save
Save As...
Print...
Exit

(You may need more items, of course, depending on your application.)

Similarly, the Help menu (ALT+H access key) would usually have at least these three items:

Contents
Search For Help On...
About

The best advice is: When in doubt, look to Visual Basic itself for how to design your menus and forms!

Here's a short table on the actions users expect:

Action	Function
Click left mouse button	Activates a control or selects an item from a list or combo box; in a text box, moves the insertion point
Double-click left mouse button	Performs the action
Click right mouse button	Pops up context-sensitive menus
Drag with left button	Either encloses a specific area or moves an object
Press TAB key	Moves to the next control (watch your tab order!)

Of course, there are lots of keystroke combinations that should work as users expect. The nice thing about Visual Basic is that the objects usually default to the expected response. For example, text boxes recognize the SHIFT+UP ARROW or DOWN ARROW keys to select text.

Making Forms Independent of Resizing and Screen Resolution

As your projects get more complicated, you have probably noticed that your carefully designed forms will easily go astray—whenever the user changes the size of the form. Figures 12-15 and 12-16 show this dramatically. Figure 12-15 was designed with the form in the default size and the command button centered in the bottom of the form. Figure 12-16 is what happens when the user enlarges

Figure 12-15 Form with a command button in default size

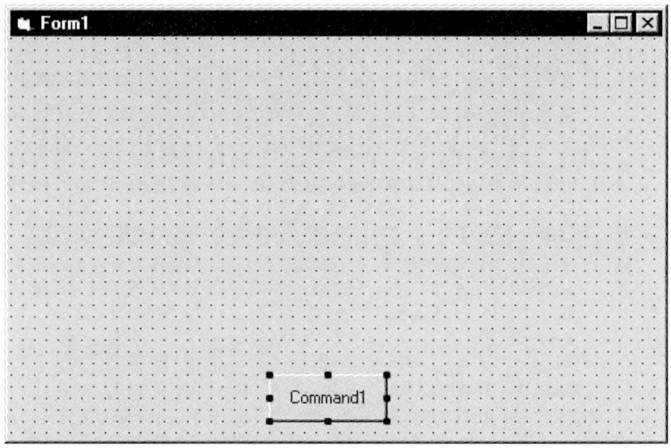

the form to maximal size. (Similar things will happen if you design your screen using a 640 X 480 resolution. They will look strange on a 1024 X 780

Figure 12-16 The form of Figure 12-15 maximized

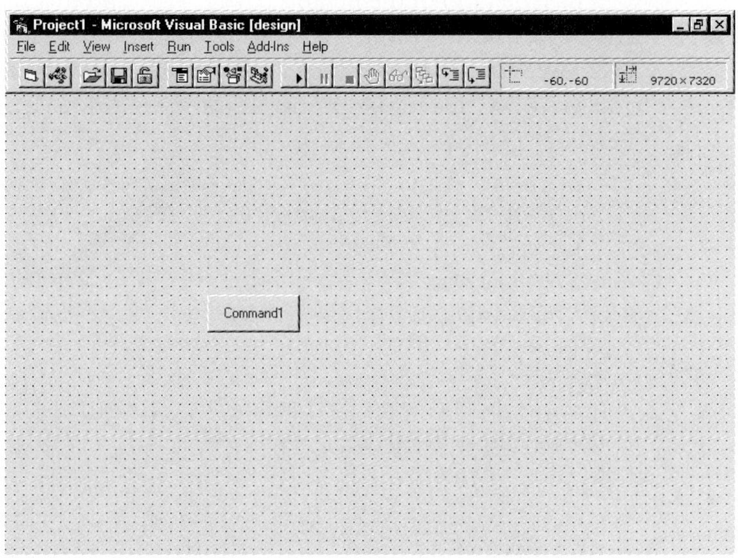

screen—the proportions of the form and controls will change, and if the monitor is too small, they may be far too tiny.)

There are various ways around this problem:

- You can do what many professionals do—buy a custom container control like VideoSoft's VBElastic (see Appendix D) that takes care of the details of adjusting control sizes for size and resolution changes. (If you do a lot of design work, this may be the best choice!)
- You can write the code yourself.

If you choose to write the code yourself, the trick is to get out of the habit of thinking of controls as having a fixed size. Instead, think of them as having certain proportions relative to the form. Let's start with simple examples, the ones used in Figures 12-15 and 12-16. You want to write the code that will guarantee that the command button will always show up centered at the bottom of the form with the same proportions it had when you started out.

Here are the relative dimensions on a VGA form. (Use the ScaleHeight and ScaleWidth properties to get at the dimensions of the interior of the form.)

Object	Height	Width
Command button	495	1215
Form	4140	6690

Thus the ratio of the heights is 495/4140 and that of the widths, 1215/6690. Given this information, you can use the Move method in the Form_Resize event to make sure the command is always centered on the bottom of the form and has the correct proportions. Recall that the Move method has the following syntax:

object.Move *left*, *top*, *width*, *height*

```
Sub Form_Resize()
Dim TheHeight As Single, TheWidth As Single
  TheHeight = (495/4140)*ScaleHeight
  TheWidth = (1215/6690)*ScaleWidth
  Command1.Move ScaleWidth/2 -(TheWidth/2), ScaleHeight -_
  TheHeight, TheWidth, TheHeight
End Sub
```

The key line

```
Command1.Move ScaleWidth/2 -(TheWidth/2), ScaleHeight -_
  TheHeight, TheWidth, TheHeight
```

moves the command button exactly where you want it whenever the size changes.

note: *If you haven't set AutoRedraw to True, you will want to have the Paint event procedure call the Resize event procedure.*

Of course, this is rather cumbersome to do by hand if you have many controls on a form. However, it is not hard to see how to automate this process.

1. Set up a type called ControlProportions in the Declaration section of a code module:

   ```
   Type ControlProportions
   WidthProportions As Single
   HeightProportions as Single
   TopProportions As Single
   LeftProportions as Single
   End Type
   ```

2. Set up a form-level array of these records:

   ```
   Dim ArrayOfProportions() As ControlProportions
   ```

3. In the Form_Load event use the Controls.Count property to redimension the array you are using to hold the proportion information. (Every time you add a control by using a control array, you would have to update the information of course.)
4. Fill the array with the correct values by iterating through the Controls collection to get the proportions of all the controls on the form.
5. Use the information now contained in the ArrayOfProportions in the Form_Resize procedure to resize all the controls on the form whenever the form is resized.

note: *The only thing to be aware of in writing the code is that you want to avoid checking the size of invisible controls such as Timers or CommonDialog controls.*

Here's the complete code for one version that will do this:

```
Dim ArrayProportions() As ControlProportions
Private Sub Form_Load()
  ReDim ArrayProportions(0 To Controls.Count - 1)
  ArrayInitialize
End Sub

Sub ArrayInitialize()
Dim I As Integer
For I = 0 To Controls.Count - 1
'take into account that some controls will be invisible!
If TypeOf Controls(I) Is Timer Then
  'Do nothing
ElseIf TypeOf Controls(I) Is CommonDialog Then
  'Do nothing
Else
  With ArrayProportions(I)
    .WidthProportions = Controls(I).Width / ScaleWidth
    .HeightProportions = Controls(I).Height / ScaleHeight
    .LeftProportions = Controls(I).Left / ScaleWidth
    .TopProportions = Controls(I).Top / ScaleHeight
  End With
End If
Next I
End Sub
'the code for the Form_Resize then looks like this:
Sub Form_Resize()
Dim I As Integer

For I = 0 To Controls.Count - 1
  If TypeOf Controls(I) Is Timer Then
    'Do nothing
  ElseIf TypeOf Controls(I) Is CommonDialog Then
    'Do nothing
  Else
'we will move the controls to where they should be
'resizing them proportionally
    Controls(I).Move ArrayProportions(I).LeftProportions * _
ScaleWidth, _
```

```
ArrayProportions(I).TopProportions * ScaleHeight, _
ArrayProportions(I).WidthProportions * ScaleWidth, _
ArrayProportions(I).HeightProportions * ScaleHeight
  End If
Next I
End Sub
```

You may want to write additional code in the Form_Resize event to prevent the form from getting so small that the controls overlap or are no longer visible. (Yet another reason not to crowd too many controls on a single form.)

DEALING WITH SCREEN RESOLUTION CHANGES

When the screen resolution increases, your forms and controls become smaller relative to the whole screen. (They may also change their proportions.) The methods for adjusting the size of the form are similar to those for adjusting controls—only this time you think of the form as having certain proportions relative to the Screen object. For example, if you add code like the following to the Form_Load, you will always get a centered form that has dimensions half that of the screen—regardless of the screen resolution.

```
Me.Height = Screen.Height / 2
Me.Width = Screen.Width / 2
Me.Top = (Screen.Height / 2) - (Me.Height) / 2
Me.Left = (Screen.Width / 2) - (Me.Left) / 2
```

In general, all you have to do is decide on where and what size you want your forms to be relative to the screen size and code those values into the Form_Load (or Form_Resize if you want to prevent users from changing it).

tip: *If you use this method to initialize a form's size and also want to use the routine from the previous section to resize the controls, you may want to consider initializing the position of the controls before you initialize the array of proportions.*

Chapter Thirteen

Finishing the Interface

This chapter turns to the tools needed to polish the interface. The first section covers the custom controls available only in the Professional or Enterprise edition. (If you are using the standard edition, you still might want to skim this material. After doing so, you will be in a better position to decide whether you need to upgrade.)

note: *Chapter 15 covers the shape and line controls that are supplied with all editions of Visual Basic as well as the graph control supplied with the Professional and Enterprise editions. The file controls supplied with all editions of Visual Basic are covered in Chapter 17.*

The next section takes up the controls available only for 32-bit development under Windows 95 or Windows NT; these controls are available only in the Professional and Enterprise editions of Visual Basic. However, whenever possible, you'll see workarounds for people working with Windows 3.X. (One workaround is checking out whether a third-party control exists that provides the same functionality—see Appendix D for some suggestions.)

Finally, the chapter ends with a brief discussion of methods for adding a help system to your applications. This applies to all editions of Visual Basic although the Help Compiler itself comes only with the higher-end products.

note: *All the controls discussed in this chapter are OCX (OLE-aware) custom controls and, except for the Windows 95 controls, exist in both 16- and 32-bit versions. If you rebuild an existing project that uses the older (VBX) version of one of these controls, Visual Basic will ask if you want to upgrade to the OCX version if you have the Custom Controls box checked on the Advanced page of the Options dialog box.*

Since the reference manual for the custom controls supplied with the Professional and Enterprise editions runs around 500 pages, I can only survey the high points here. If you need to go further than this, you must be willing to consult the online help or the written manual. (I find the online help more accurate and more complete.)

On the other hand, using a custom control, whether it is one supplied with the Professional or Enterprise edition, or one you buy, is no different than using one of the built-in controls or one of the three custom controls supplied with the standard edition of Visual Basic: you set properties via code or the Properties window to get them to look the way you want and use their associated events and methods to get them to behave the way you want. (You saw an example of working with a Windows 95 custom control in the section on using the RichTextBox custom control in Chapter 6.)

tip: *If you need the facilities supported by even one of the custom controls, upgrading to the Professional edition will quickly pay for itself in the time it saves you.*

Custom Controls in the Professional and Enterprise Editions

The non-32-bit custom controls available in the Professional or Enterprise edition are shown in Figure 13-1. Figure 13-2 shows the custom controls for Windows 95 development. Most of the rest of this chapter is taken up with brief discussions (often with an example) of using these controls. (The exceptions are the RichTextBox control, which is described in Chapter 6, and the graph control, which is described in Chapter 15.)

note: *If one of the controls shown in Figure 13-1 or 13-2 does not appear in your toolbox, choose Tools | Custom Controls and then work with the dialog box that pops up in order to add it. Headings for the sections in this chapter correspond to the control names you'll see in the Custom Controls dialog box.*

Sheridan 3-D Custom Controls

For a three-dimensional look to ordinary controls, use the Sheridan 3-D custom controls. These controls are less important in Visual Basic 4 than in earlier versions of Visual Basic because OCX controls on both 16- and 32-bit platforms

Figure 13-1 Custom controls in the Professional and Enterprise editions

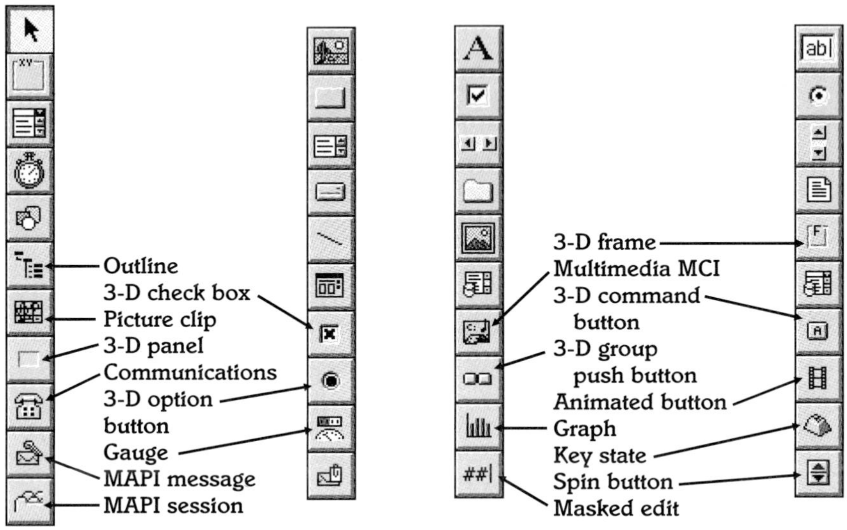

have the Appearance property which allows you to give controls a three-dimensional look. On the other hand, you can use the 3-D custom controls because you prefer their look to that of the Visual Basic versions or because the properties of the Sheridan 3-D controls are enhanced in a way you need.

3-D Check Box This control gives a 3-D version of an ordinary check box.

3-D Command Button This control gives a 3-D version of a command button.

3-D Frame This container control replaces an ordinary frame. It is especially useful for 3-D option buttons.

3-D Group Push Button The 3-D group push buttons are roughly comparable to a group of option buttons. Within each group of buttons (use a 3-D frame for more than one group), clicking one button makes it appear pushed in. This also releases the previously pressed button.

Figure 13-2
Windows 95-specific controls

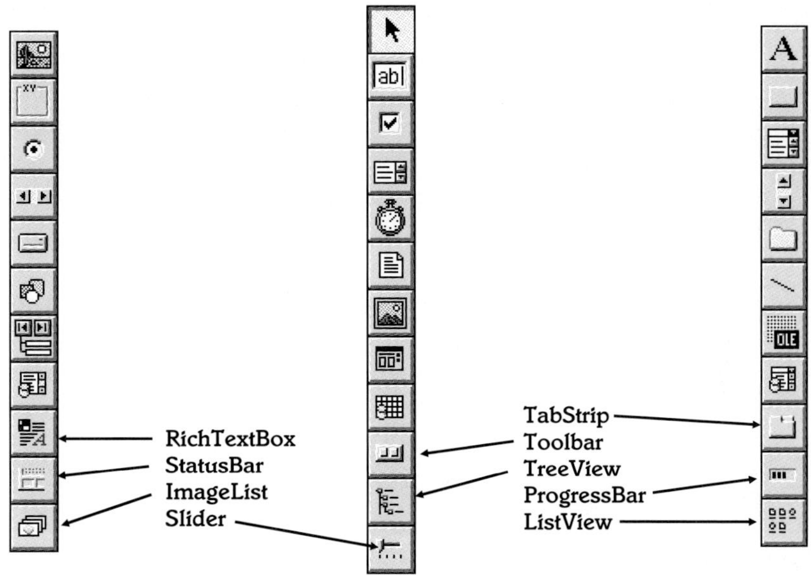

3-D Option Button The 3-D option buttons can replace the standard Visual Basic option (radio) buttons. You use them in groups just as you would ordinary option buttons, but you would normally use a 3-D frame as the container.

3-D Panel The 3-D panel tool combines the properties of a frame with a text box—all in three dimensions, of course.

note: *There are very few differences between using these controls and using their ordinary counterparts. The main differences are in properties, such as the BevelWidth property, that control the three-dimensional look. You can explore the help files for examples on using these controls.*

DesaWare Animated Button Control

You can use animated buttons anywhere you would use a command button (or where you are using a picture box or image control as a command button substitute). They also let you store many bitmaps in one control. This gives you quick access to many bitmap images without tying up scarce Windows resources.

The animation in an animated button works much the way animation does in the movies. You load multiple images in the button and display them sequentially in a way that gives the appearance of animation. In practice, this control can be hard to use if you really want to do animation. You must construct the necessary images for the animation in some way. (There are commercial products that let you do this—morphing software is often a good choice, for example.) On the other hand, animated buttons are perfect for replacing an image control you are using as a command button. This is especially true when you want to display multiple images. Animated buttons will work more quickly and use fewer Windows resources than will updating the image multiple times. Use an animated button and you no longer need to confine yourself to having only a caption, as on ordinary command buttons.

note: *The 3-D group buttons support pictures too, and are a lot easier to program. They are also faster when actually used. Repainting an animated button can be slow.*

Except for the properties pertaining to animation, this animated button control works just like a command button.

Microsoft Comm Control

The communications control is a more limited version of Crescent Software's PDComm control (see Appendix D). This control makes it easy for you to design a communications package customized for your needs providing you don't need extraordinary speed. (It is limited to 19,200 baud at present.)

The various properties of this control let you set the communications port and the settings needed, such as baud rate, number of data bits, or parity. As you would expect, an event-driven language is ideal for dealing with communications. You can program the communications custom control so that it wakes up only when the hardware detects activity at a communications port, for example.

The following table summarizes the key properties of the communications control.

Property	Description
CommEvent	The key property for the communications control. The various values of this property correspond to either events or errors in the communications port. For example, if the value of this property is the constant comEvEOF (= 7), then the traditional End Of File (ASCII character 26) character was received in the buffer.
CommPort	Sets and returns the communications port; use a 1 for COM1, 2 for COM2, and so on.
Settings	Sets and returns the baud rate, parity, data bits, and stop bits. Can be set at design or run time.
PortOpen	Opens and closes a communications port.
Input	Removes characters from the receive buffer.
Output	Writes a string of characters to the transmit buffer.

The only event for the communications control is the OnComm event. This is triggered whenever the value of the CommEvent property changes. Thus, by analyzing the current value of the CommEvent property in the OnComm event, you can have your code take the appropriate actions.

Like many custom controls, the communications control gives you a new way to set its properties. If you add a communications control to your form and go to the Properties window, you will see a new property called (Custom). If you click on this property, you get a dialog box that lets you set the special properties of the custom control. Here's a picture of the Custom dialog box for the communications control:

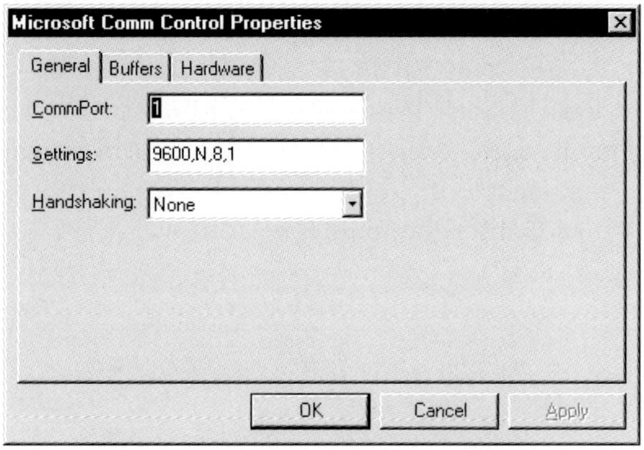

EXAMPLE: USING THE COMMUNICATIONS CONTROL

As a simple example of using the communications control, consider the problem of writing a poller of the COM ports after a button click. (COM1 is used in this example.)

```
Private Sub btnGetData_Click ()
Dim Foo As Integer, TheData As String
    Comm1.CommPort = 1  ' COM1
    '19600 baud, no parity, 8 data, and 1 stop bit.
    'the Communications control can't go faster than 19600
    'baud
    Comm1.Settings = "19600,N,8,1"
    Comm1.InputLen = 0  ' Clear the comm buffer
    Comm1.PortOpen = True
    'Send the Hayes compatible attention signal to the modem.
    Comm1.Output = "AT" + Chr$(13)
Do
    Foo = DoEvents()
    Comm1.InputLen = 0  'clear buffer
    TheData = TheData + Comm1.Input 'TheData will contain
    'the data
Loop Until Comm1.CommEvent = comEvEOF
Comm1.PortOpen = False 'close the port
End Sub
```

MicroHelp Gauge Control

The gauge control lets you add either linear-style gauges or circular (needle) gauges. You can add a custom bitmap or use one of the bitmaps supplied with Visual Basic's Professional and Enterprise editions for this control. Gauges are a dramatic way to replace scroll bars whenever you want to display what percentage of a job is finished. This control is ideal when you want to use an analog instead of digital readout.

tip: *If you make the bitmap for the gauge the value of the Picture property at design time, then like the Picture property of a form, the image gets built into your project—you won't need to save it as a separate file and load it at run time.*

The Style property defines the type of gauge to be displayed. The default setting is 0 (a horizontal bar). The other possible values are 1 for a vertical bar, 2 for a semicircular needle gauge, and 3 for a full needle gauge. When the Style property is one of the bar gauges, the Min, Max, and Value properties determine how the gauge is filled. For example, if Min is 0, Max is 100 (the defaults), and the Value property is 75, then 75 percent of the gauge area will be drawn with the ForeColor, and 25 percent will be drawn with the BackColor.

As shown here, the gauge control, like the communications control, has a custom dialog box for setting its special properties.

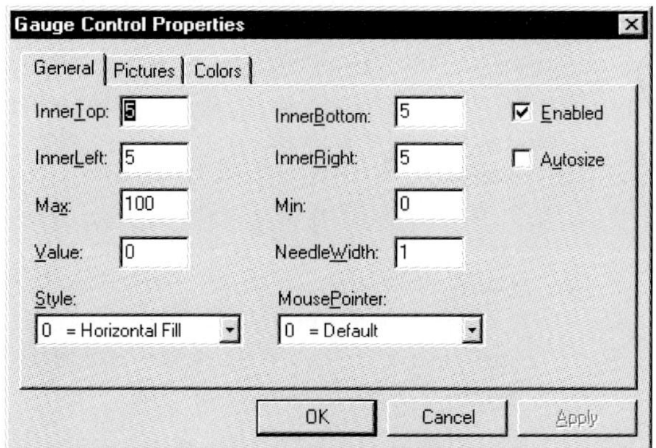

EXAMPLE: USING THE GAUGE CONTROL

As an example of using the gauge control, let's add a gauge control to a form, leave the Max, Min properties at their default values, and change the Needle-Width property to 2. Add four option buttons that are part of a control array so that your form looks like this:

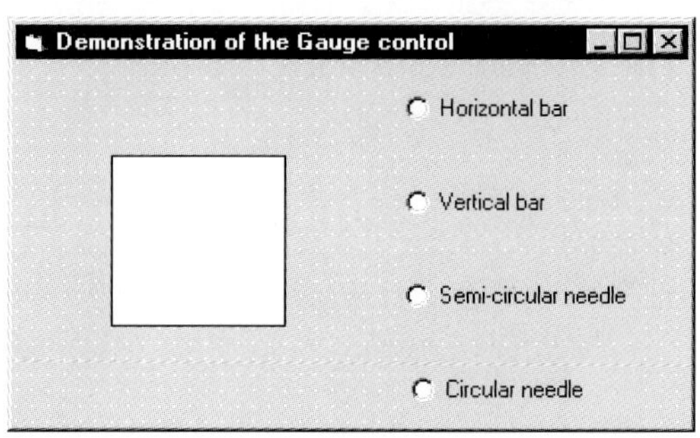

You set the Value property of the gauge control using the Rnd function and use different bitmaps (from the VB\BITMAPS\GAUGE) according to the current style of the gauge. Here's the code:

```
Private Sub Form_Load()
Randomize
Option1(0).Value = True
Option1_Click (0)
End Sub

 Private Sub Option1_Click(Index As Integer)
 Gauge1.Style = Index
 Gauge1.Value = 100 * Rnd 'since we left Max and Min at
                          'defaults
 Select Case Index
   Case 0
     Gauge1.Picture = _
LoadPicture("C:\VB\BITMAPS\GAUGE\HORZ.BMP")
   Case 1
     Gauge1.Picture = _
LoadPicture("C:\VB\BITMAPS\GAUGE\VERT.BMP")
   Case 2
     Gauge1.Picture = _
LoadPicture("C:\VB\BITMAPS\GAUGE\SEMICIRC.BMP")
   Case 3
     Gauge1.Picture =
LoadPicture("C:\VB\BITMAPS\GAUGE\CIRCLOCK.BMP")
 End Select
End Sub
```

MicroHelp Key State Control

The key state control has two purposes:

- To show the user (or to let her or him modify) the state of the CAPS LOCK, NUM LOCK, INS, and SCROLL LOCK keys
- To avoid having to use an API function call to check or modify the state of these keys

EXAMPLE: USING THE KEY STATE CONTROL

Using the key state control is simple. First you set the Style property to determine what the control will affect, as shown in the following table. (Add as many key state controls as you need—generally speaking, you will want to have one control for each state you want to affect.)

Style Setting	What It Affects
0	(Default) Caps Lock
1	Num Lock
2	Insert
3	Scroll Lock

Then all you need to do is manipulate or read off the setting of the Value property associated with the key control. (Use the Change event to detect a change.) Here's a typical way that the key state control would appear on your form:

And here is the code needed to read off what the user does (the code assumes you have changed the control name of the Caps Lock control to be—CapsLock-Control!) .

```
Private Sub CapsLockControl_Change()
 Dim YesNo As Integer
 If CapsLockControl.Value = True Then
    YesNo = MsgBox("You switched on the caps lock key—was
this by mistake?", vbYesNo)
    If YesNo = vbYes Then CapsLockControl.Value = False
 End If
End Sub
```

(Notice that this code will toggle the Caps Lock off, if the user says it was a mistake.)

MAPI Controls

MAPI (which stands for *messaging application program interface*) allows you to work certain electronic mail packages (E-mail), such as Version 3.0 of Microsoft Mail for Windows (or later versions of it). There are two MAPI controls: the first establishes the MAPI session and the second is used to gain access to special features of the E-mail program. MAPI controls are invisible to the user, so you need a command button or image control to establish the MAPI session. MAPI is a specialized topic, and using the MAPI controls is not covered here. Refer to the online help or books on Microsoft Mail for more details.

Microsoft Masked Edit Control

The masked edit control can save you a lot of code work needed to control the input to text boxes. For most purposes, it seems like an ordinary text box. The difference is that you can restrict the characters entered without having to write code in the Key events (see Chapter 7 for discussions of these events). Similarly, you can show certain characters in the control—to give users a visual cue that they should be entering a phone number or a social security number, for example. This control is data-aware. (See Chapter 20 for information on using data-aware controls.)

The most important property when working with the masked edit control is, naturally enough, the Mask property. You can set this property at both design time and run time. This property controls what the user sees and what he or she can enter. For example, if you wanted to allow only a standard U.S. phone number to be entered, you would set the Mask property to:

```
Mask1.Mask = "(###)-###-####"
```

This would result in a masked edit control that looks like this:

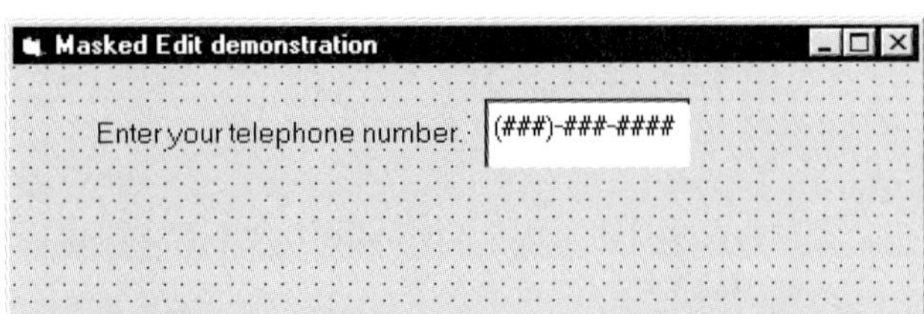

(At design time you would not use the quotes in the Properties window of course.)

In general, the strings for the Mask property work much like format strings in the Format statement (Chapter 6), so, in the preceding example, the # means a digit and the dash (-) appears as a literal on the screen.

The following table summarizes the most common characters used in masks.

Mask Character	Description
#	Allows the user to enter a digit only.
.	Decimal placeholder. Which character the user sees depends on the current Windows settings.
,	Thousands separator. Again, which character the user sees depends on the current Windows settings.
:	Time separator.
/	Date separator.
?	Letter placeholder, for example: a z or A Z.
&	Allows the user to enter a single ANSI character in the ranges 32-126 and 128-255 only.
>	Converts all the characters that follow to uppercase.
<	Converts all the characters that follow to lowercase.
A	Requires that an alphanumeric character be entered.
a	Allows an alphanumeric character to be entered.
9	Allows a digit to be entered.

For example, a mask of "a9" would allow but not require the user to enter two characters. The first can be any alphanumeric character; the second would have to be a digit.

All other symbols are displayed as themselves. (If you want to have one of the special characters show up, precede it with a \. For example, using "\##" as a mask would show up as # followed by a blank where the user can enter a digit.

At design time you can use the following predefined masks:

Mask	Description
empty string ("" in code)	(Default) No mask; makes the Masked Edit box work like a standard text box
##-???-##	Medium date (U.S.)
##-##-##	Short date (U.S.)
##:## ??	Medium time
##:##	Short time

The only unusual event in dealing with input to a Masked Edit box is the ValidationError event. This is triggered whenever a user tries to enter an invalid character. (The Masked Edit box prevents invalid characters from *being* entered—you might just want to know if the user tried.)

Microsoft Multimedia Control

Multimedia devices such as CD-ROM players have become omnipresent on PCs. The idea of combining text, images, and sound on a computer is clearly the wave of the future. The multimedia control lets users initiate what are called *media control interface* (MCI) commands. MCI commands are designed to be device-independent and to control audio-visual peripherals. You use the multimedia device control to tell the multimedia device to start up, move forward, move back, pause, and so on. Since programming the multimedia control is rather specialized, I won't cover it here. If you are interested, check out the Multimedia MCI Sample Application (C:\VB\SAMPLES\MCITEST.VBP) and the online help.

Outline Control

Think of the outline control as a specialized list box that displays the text in a hierarchical manner (for example, the way the drive list box works). Moreover, you can collapse or expand the levels at will. Most of the properties and methods for this control are the same as for list boxes. What follows is a short discussion of the most important of the specialized properties and methods.

Expand Property, Expand Event The Expand property is a True/False property that specifies whether an item is expanded. If the user double-clicks to expand an item, the Expand event is triggered.

Indent Property This is a run-time only property that sets or returns the indentation level for the item specified. The Indent property is an array whose entries correspond to the items in the control.

Style Property This sets or returns the style of graphics and text that appear for each item in the outline control. There are six possibilities, as shown in the following table.

Setting	Style
0	Text only
1	Pictures and text
2	(Default) Plus/minus signs with text
3	Plus/minus signs with pictures and text
4	Tree lines and text
5	Tree lines with pictures and text

PictureType, PictureClosed, PictureOpen, PictureLeaf Properties If you have set the Style property to 1, 3, or 5, use these properties to set or return the type of picture used in the outline control. These properties work together. The PictureType property is an array whose entries correspond to the items in the outline. Each item in the outline control has a PictureType property equal to 0, 1, or 2. A PictureType of 0 refers to the PictureClosed property; 1 refers to the PictureOpen property; 2 refers to the PictureLeaf property. After setting the PictureType property for the current item in the control, you set the appropriate Picture properties to the name of either the bitmap or icon file you want to display.

Microsoft Picture Clip Control

The picture clip control gives you another way to store bitmaps in one control. Just as with animated buttons, this conserves Windows resources and speeds up access to the image. The obvious place to use this control is if you are adding a toolbox of controls to a Visual Basic project for the user to manipulate. Instead of loading each tool as a separate bitmap, you could use a picture clip to build them in all at once. The problem is you need to build up the bitmap that contains the images first.

tip: *One way to build up multiple bitmaps into a single one is to use two copies of Windows Paint running at the same time. Cut and paste the bitmaps from one into the other and repeat the process as often as necessary.*

Because of the difficulty in building up a large bitmap from multiple files that are needed to use the PictureClip control, for Windows 95 development at least, the ListImage control is much easier to use. Nonetheless, the sample picture clip program is quite a lot of fun to watch (C:\VB\SAMPLES\PICCLIP\REDTOP.VBP).

OutRider Spin Button Control

Spin buttons give you yet another way to have users change a counter if you are tired of scroll bars. Spin buttons are especially useful if you want to give users feedback when they are adding to or subtracting from a counter. Once the user moves to one of the arrows in the spin control and clicks, Visual Basic activates one of the two events for this control: SpinUp or SpinDown. The nice feature is that Visual Basic keeps on generating these events until the user releases the mouse button. The Delay property determines how often the SpinUp and SpinDown events are generated. The Orientation property controls whether you have up/down spin arrows or left/right arrows.

EXAMPLE: USING THE SPIN BUTTON CONTROL

Here's an illustration of a typical spin button at work:

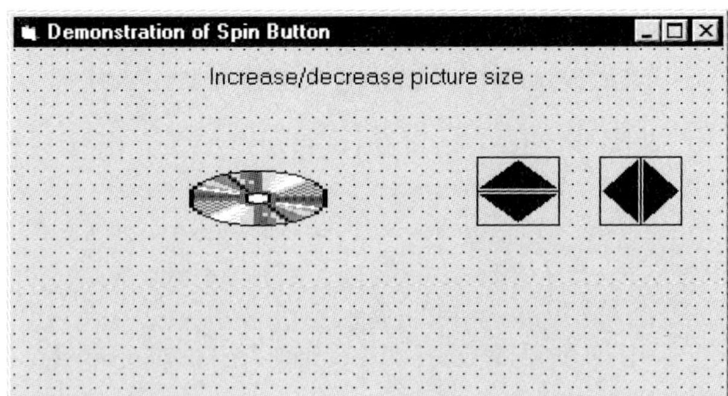

Add an image control with the Stretch property set to True (that way you can see it expand). I used the CDROM01 icon for this example. Here's the code needed to activate this illustration:

```
Option Explicit
Private Sub Form_Load()
  ChangeCaption Label1 'update height width of label
End Sub

Private Sub SpinButton1_SpinDown()
  Image1.Height = Image1.Height - 10 '10 twips at a time
  ChangeCaption Label1
End Sub
Private Sub SpinButton1_SpinUp()
  Image1.Height = Image1.Height + 10
  ChangeCaption Label1
End Sub
Private Sub SpinButton2_SpinDown()
  Image1.Width = Image1.Width - 10
  ChangeCaption Label1
End Sub
Private Sub SpinButton2_SpinUp()
  Image1.Width = Image1.Width + 10
  ChangeCaption Label1
End Sub
Sub ChangeCaption(X As Label)
Dim M$
  M$ = "Click on a button to increase/decrease the size. "
  M$ = M$ + "The current size is " & Str$(Image1.Height) _
  & " by " & Str$(Image1.Width)
X.Caption = M$
End Sub
```

Sheridan Tabbed Dialog Control

The tabbed dialog control lets you add tabbed dialog boxes to your project—like the Tools | Options dialog box in Visual Basic, for example. The way this control works is that it provides a group of tabbed containers for other controls. Here's a picture of the default-sized tab control:

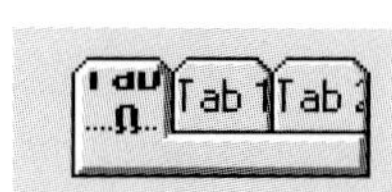

As you can see, the first thing you will want to do is expand the control so that it is a reasonable size for displaying the information you want in each tab!

EXAMPLE: USING THE TABBED DIALOG CONTROL

To work with this control at design time:

- Decide how many tabs you want.
- Decide what controls you want on each tab.

The number of tabs is the value of the Tabs property. (The default value is 3.) If you need more than one row of tabs, set the TabsPerRow Property. Visual Basic then automatically adds the correct number of tabbed pages to your form. Set the Caption property of each tab to be what you want the user to see. (If you want to add a shortcut key, use the ordinary & before the character.) You can also add a picture to the tab via the Picture property. The TabHeight and TabWidth properties control how high and wide the tab appears to the user.

Next, you will want to design the actual tabbed pages. For this, select the tab you want to work with at design time by clicking on the tab. Since each tabbed page acts as a container control, you can add any ordinary control to the page by the usual techniques for working with container controls. (Remember *not* to use the double-click method—see Chapter 12 for more on working with container controls.)

note: *When your project is running, the tabbed dialog box works as the user expects. He or she can navigate by using CTRL+TAB* or via any shortcut key you define using the & in the Caption property.

As with any custom dialog box, you will want to give users both an OK and a Cancel button.

tip: *Make the form that contains a Sheridan tabbed dialog control into a custom dialog box by setting the BorderStyle property of the form appropriately. You may also want to add OK and Cancel buttons on the form* outside *the Sheridan tabbed dialog control.*

Windows 95 Controls

There are nine Windows 95-specific controls. You have seen one of them (the RichTextBox) already. Brief descriptions of how to work with the remaining eight are included in this section. Two of the controls (the StatusBar and Toolbar) give interface features so important that you will see how to mimic much of their functionality using ordinary picture boxes and image controls.

note: *In the Custom Control dialog box most of these controls are grouped under the "Windows Common controls" item (the file is C:\WINDOWS\SYSTEM\COMCTL32.OCX).*

ImageList Control

The ImageList control gives you another way to store a group of images in a single place. You can then use the images in other parts of your application (for example, the images used in a toolbar). The key to working with an ImageList control is ListImage objects (and the ListImages collection), which specify the images stored in the control. (You can think of an ImageList control as a container for a ListImages collection.) The easiest way to work with an ImageList control is via its (Custom) property, which pops up a dialog box that looks like this:

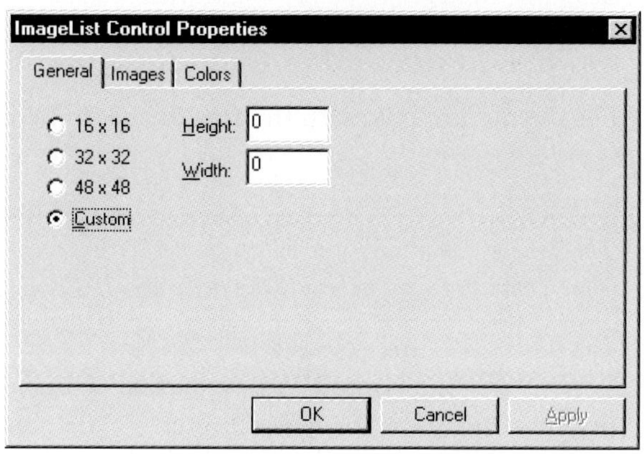

The Images tab on this dialog box gives you a convenient way to add images at design time, as shown here:

(At run time, you can add images using the Add method for the ListImages collection.)

As long as all the images are the same size, the ImageList control can store both bitmaps and icons at the same time. As with all collections (Chapter 11), you can refer to the items (images) stored in the ListImages collection by either an index or a key. For example, suppose you have assigned an Image to ImageList1.ListImages(1), then,

```
Set Picture1.Picture = ImageList1.ListImages(1).Picture ' Set
Picture.
```

fills the picture box with the first image. (The ListImages collection starts at 1.)

note: *The documentation says you must use the Set statement when assigning an image to a Picture object. This seems not to be actually necessary.*

You are not limited to any particular image size, but the total number of images that can be loaded is limited by the amount of available memory.

tip: *The ListImage control need not be used as a passive storage container. The Overlay method creates a composite image from two images.*

ListView Control

The ListView control lets you display items in various ways—essentially the ways you see when working with the Windows 95 Explorer. You can use this control to arrange items into columns (with or without column headings). The items can be accompanied by both icons and text. The View property, as described in the following table, determines what the user sees.

Constant	Value	Description
IvwIcon	0	(Default) Each ListItem object is represented by a full-sized icon and a label.
IvwSmallIcon	1	Each ListItem object is represented by a small icon and a label that appears to the right of the icon. The different items are arranged horizontally.
IvwList	2	Each ListItem object is also represented by a small icon and a text label that appears to the right of the icon. The ListItem objects are vertical on different lines, and the text information is organized into columns.
IvwReport	3	Each ListItem object is displayed with a small icon and a label. The icons and labels appear in columns. (Additional columns are used to display additional text.).

The items displayed in the ListView control are called (naturally enough) ListItem objects. A ListItem object has its own properties that describe the item, the most important of which are shown in the following table.

Property	Description
Icons	Returns or sets the index or key for the icon associated with the ListItem object.
Selected	Tells you (or selects) whether the ListItem was selected.
SmallIcons	Returns or sets the index or key for the small icon associated with the ListItem object.
SubItems	Returns or sets the string representing the data for the subitem associated with a specific ListItem.
Text	As you might expect, this is the text the user sees.

Finally, you can choose to display column headings in the ListView control by setting the value of the True/False HideColumnHeaders property. The actual heading is stored in the ColumnHeader object, and all the column headers are stored in the ColumnHeaders collection.

tip: *You can bind an ImageList control to a ListView control to conserve system resources. To do this, set the Icons and SmallIcons properties of the ListView control to the ImageList control(s). You can also specify the associated ImageList control at design time using the (Custom) property dialog box.*

ProgressBar Control

The ProgressBar is similar to using a vertical bar in the gauge control. It fills in a bar with rectangular chunks. The key properties are described next.

Align Use the Align property to position the control where you want it automatically. The possible values are described in the following table.

Setting	Description
0	(Default) Size and location are arbitrary.
1	Bar is at the top of the form, and it is as wide as the form.
2	Bar is at the bottom of the form, and it is as wide as the form.
3	Bar is left aligned at the edge of the form, and it is as wide as the form.
4	Bar is right aligned at the form, and it is as wide as the form.

Much like a scroll bar, you specify the Min and Max properties to give the range of values the progress bar will show. The Value property specifies the current position within that range.

tip: *To display more chunks, decrease the control's height or increase its width.*

For example, suppose you want to give people a feeling of time passing in some way. Add a timer control, a label, and a progress bar, as shown here:

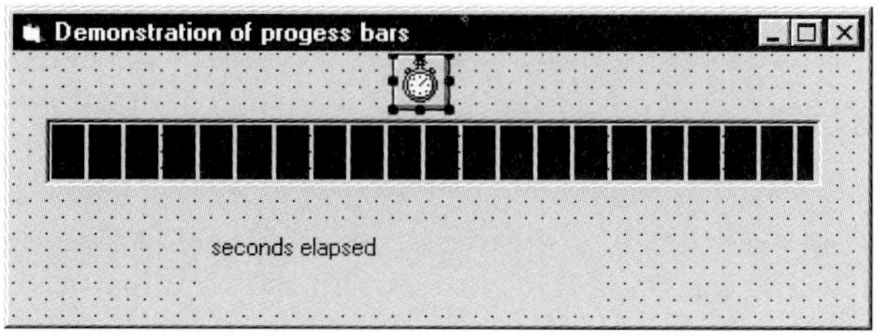

Now set the Min property of the progress bar to 0 and the Max property to 60. Set the Interval property of the timer control to 1000 (one second). Then the following code will show you how the progress bar updates itself (compared to the seconds actually elapsed).

```
Private Sub Timer1_Timer()
 Static Progress As Integer
 Progress = (Progress + 1) Mod 60
 Label1.Caption = Str$(Progress) & " seconds elapsed."
 ProgressBar1.Value = Progress
End Sub
```

Slider Control

The Slider control works similarly to a scroll bar. It is a little box with optional tick marks that contains a slider, as shown here:

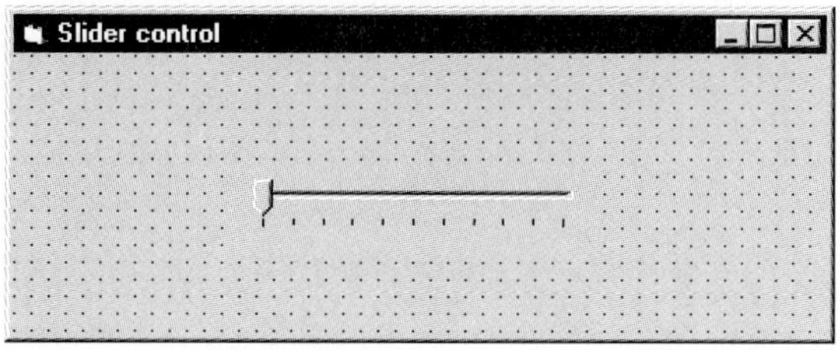

The user can move the slider by dragging it, clicking the mouse to either side of the slider, or using the keyboard. Just as for scroll bars, the key properties are Max, Min, and Value, which determine the largest, smallest, and current values for the slider. The key event is the Scroll event, which is triggered when the user moves the slider on a Slider control, either by clicking on the control or using the keyboard.

StatusBar Control

The StatusBar control gives you a window (usually at the bottom of a form) that you can use to display the status of the application. (For example, word processors such as Microsoft Word use a status bar to tell you where you are on a page, whether you are in insert mode or overstrike mode, and so on.) The Align property governs where the status bar appears. It has the same values as the Align property for a progress bar.

Each status bar can be divided into (at most) 16 panels. At design time you can add the individual panels by using the Panels page in the (Custom) property dialog box, as shown here:

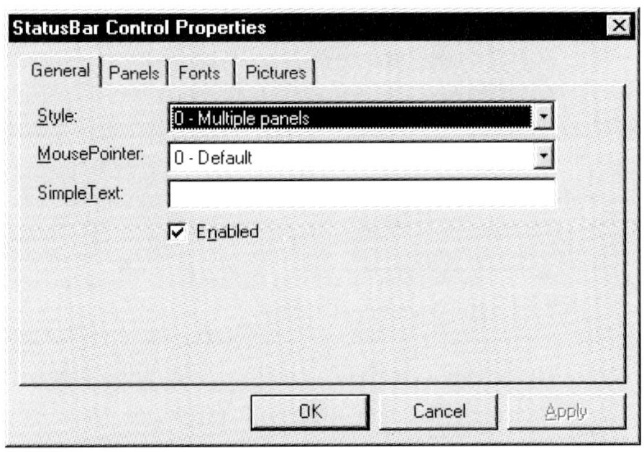

You can add both text and a picture to the panel by working with the dialog box. At run time you will usually use the Add method by first declaring a variable of Panel type and then using the Add method with a syntax that looks like this,

Set PanelObject = *NameOfStatusBar*.Panels.Add([*index*], [*key*], [*text*], [*style*], [*picture*])

where all the parameters are optional. (Since this method does not support named arguments, you need commas for the items you leave out.) The *index* parameter specifies the index where the panel will be added. If you leave it out, the item goes after all the existing panels. (Since you can have at most 16 panels, the index must be between 1 and 16.) The *key* parameter (as in any collection) gives you another way to refer to the items. The *text* parameter is the text for the panel. The *style* property lets you specify how the information appears in the status bar. The values for this parameter are shown in the following table.

Constant	Description
sbrText	(Default) Text and/or a bitmap. Set text with the Text property; set the picture with the LoadPicture method.
sbrCaps	Caps lock. Displays the letters CAPS in bold when CAPS LOCK is pressed and is dimmed otherwise.
sbrNum	Number lock. Displays the letters NUM in bold when the NUM LOCK key is enabled and is dimmed otherwise.
sbrIns	Displays the letters INS in bold when the INS key is enabled and is dimmed otherwise.
sbrScrl	Displays the letters SCRL in bold when SCROLL LOCK is enabled and is dimmed otherwise.
sbrTime	Displays the current time in the current system format.
sbrDate	Displays the current date in the current system format.

Finally, the optional *picture* parameter specifies the bitmap. For example,

```
Private Sub Form_Load()
Dim MyPanel As Panel

StatusBar1.Panels(1).Text = "Default panel exists already"
Set MyPanel = StatusBar1.Panels.Add(, , , sbrTime)
Set MyPanel = StatusBar1.Panels.Add(, ,"Panel demo")
Set MyPanel = StatusBar1.Panels.Add(, , , , LoadPicture _
("C:\VB\ICONS\TRAFFIC\TRFFC01.ICO"))
End Sub
```

would give you a status bar like this:

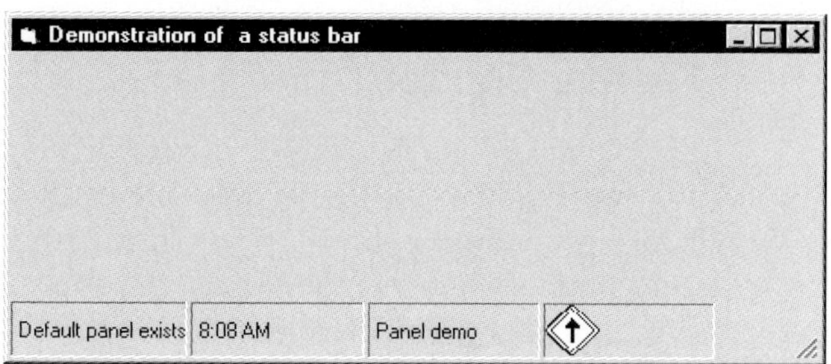

Notice that you need to use an object variable because you want to create the panel as well as refer to its properties. You could have replaced this with two lines of code, by adding the panel first. For example:

```
MyPanel = StatusBar1.Panels.Add
MyPanel = StatusBar1.Panels(2).Text = "Panel demo"
```

The next useful property of the Panel object associated to a status bar is the AutoSize property, which has three possibilities, as described in the following table.

Constant	Description
sbrNoAutoSize	(Default) No automatic resizing occurs.
sbrSpring	When the parent form resizes and there is extra space available, the panel resizes by dividing the available space and growing or shrinking accordingly. (The panel's width is always at least the current value of the status bar's MinWidth property.)
sbrContents	The panel resizes to fit its contents if space is available.

note: *Occasionally you will want a status bar to have only one item. (For example, many programs use this type of status bar to explain a menu item but return to displaying more general status information when the menu bar is closed.) For this, set the Style property to Simple (sbrSimple is the constant to use at run time). Then, use the SimpleText property for the actual text.*

TabStrip Control

A TabStrip control provides another way to give a form the look of a tabbed dialog box. However, since it is not a container, it is not as flexible as the tabbed dialog box that you have already seen, so it isn't covered here.

Toolbar Control

The Toolbar control makes it easy to build toolbars into your Windows 95 projects. Features like ToolTips come essentially for free (see the section on ToolTips coming up shortly). First off, the Align property that you have already seen controls where the toolbar appears. Normally, toolbars appear on the top, so the Align property defaults to 1 (Top).

Next, if you want images to appear in your toolbar, you must first store them in an ImageList control (either at design time or run time). *If you intend to set the images at design time, the associated ImageList control must be on the same form as the toolbar control.* After the images are stored in an ImageList control, you set the ImageList property of the Toolbar control to be the name of the ImageList control. For example, add a Toolbar control and an ImageList control to a blank form at design time using the default names. If you look at the first page of the (Custom) property dialog box, as shown here, you can see that the ImageList drop-down list box will show the ImageList1 control.

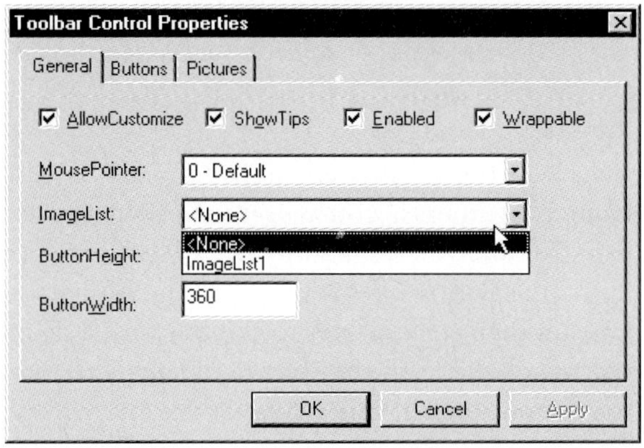

Once you have associated the ImageList control, the next (Buttons) page of this dialog box lets you associate the images stored in the ImageList control to the buttons. You do that by setting the Image text box on this page to the number of the image in the ImageList control. For example, in the example shown here, the second button is associated with the first image stored in the ImageList control.

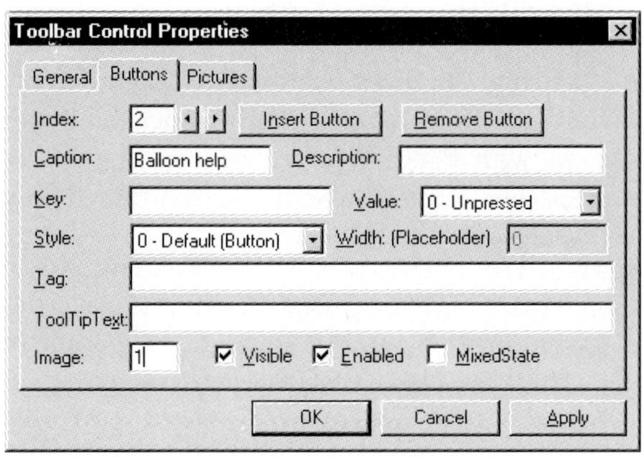

EXAMPLE: WORKING WITH THE TOOLBAR AT RUN TIME

The Toolbar control holds a collection of button objects. At run time you must use the Add and Remove methods to add the buttons. As you might expect, each button has a ButtonClick event that lets you take actions depending on which button is clicked.

The usual way to use the Add object is to declare an object variable to be of Button type. Then the syntax for using the Add method looks like this,

Set *ButtonObject* = *NameOfToolbar*.Buttons.Add([*index*], [*key*], [*caption*], [*style*], [*image*])

where all the parameters are optional. (Since this method does not support named arguments, you will need commas for the items you leave out.) The *index* parameter specifies the index where the button will be added. If you leave it out, the button goes at the end. The *key* parameter (as in any collection) gives you another way to refer to the buttons. The *caption* parameter is the text that will appear beneath the Button object. The *style* property lets you specify how the button appears. The values for this parameter are shown in the following table.

Constant	Description
tbrDefault	(Default) The button is a regular push button.
tbrCheck	The button is a check button.
tbrButtonGroup	The button is part of a button group. This means that the button remains pressed until another button in the group is pressed. Only one button in a group can be pressed at any one time.
tbrSeparator	The button is simply a separator. (It will have a fixed width of eight pixels.)
tbrPlaceholder	The button is a variable width separator.

Finally, the *image* parameter is the index or key that describes which image you want from the previously associated ImageList control.

As with Panel objects, you can first add the button and then describe its properties. For example, if you have added only one button at design time, with a caption of "First button" then,

```
Toolbar1.Buttons.Add
Toolbar1.Buttons(2).Caption = "Second button"
Toolbar1.Buttons.Add
Toolbar1.Buttons(3).Caption = "Third button"
```

gives you a toolbar that looks like this:

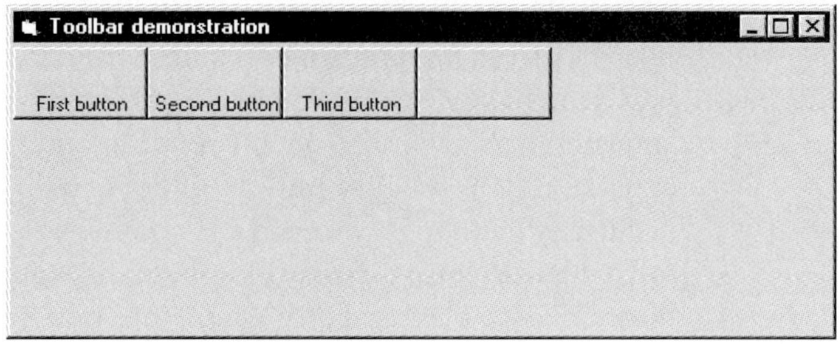

note: *Unless you set the AllowCustomize property to False, then when the user double-clicks on a toolbar at run time, Visual Basic will pop up the Customize Toolbar dialog box, which allows the user to hide, display, or rearrange the toolbar buttons. See the online help for more on run-time customization of toolbars.*

TOOLTIPS

ToolTips can be made to appear automatically as little labels below the tool whenever the mouse moves over the tool and remains there for about one second. To display ToolTips for a Toolbar control, you must:

1. Set the ShowTips property to True.
2. Set the ToolTipText property of each button object to the text you want as your ToolTip.

TreeView Control

The TreeView control works similarly to the outline control. The individual objects are usually called nodes, and the TreeView control has a Nodes collection that holds information about the nodes in the control. The highest node is given by the Root property. For more on the TreeView control, please consult the online help.

Toolbars and Status Bars for 16-bit Windows

Since the Toolbar and StatusBar controls are strictly 32-bit controls, you will need to be creative if you want to have a project that looks the same on both

16- and 32-bit platforms. (One possibility of course is to get a third-party custom control that gives you toolbars and status bars for both platforms.) Anyway, if you don't have a custom control that does this, you will need to add the toolbars and status bars to your 16-bit project in a somewhat ad hoc manner. This section explains the most common way of doing so.

First off, although you can use a frame to put a toolbar or a status bar on a form while doing 16-bit development, most programmers prefer to use picture boxes. This is because placing a picture box on the bottom or top of a form is easy in Visual Basic using the picture box's Align property. The value of the Align property determines where the picture box appears. The Align property has the same five possible values that you have seen for the Windows 95 Toolbar control. Use a 1 (align top) for a toolbar and a 2 (align bottom) for a status bar. Next, decide on the icons you want to use. Assign these icons to the Picture property of the image controls that will be on the toolbar or status bar.

tip: *Make the image controls you use in your toolbar or status bar part of a control array. This makes the necessary code shorter.*

Now, to give the toolbar or status bar a professional look, you should have the Form_Paint event adjust the size and position of the icons inside the picture box whenever the size of the form changes, with code that might look like this. (This code assumes that the image controls have already been loaded with equally sized pictures or icons and that they have AutoSize set to True. It also assumes that you have five image controls in the control array named ToolImage, and the picture box has a control name of ToolBar.)

```
Sub Form_Paint()
  Dim I As Integer, PositionIcon As Integer
  Dim ImageWidth As Integer
  ToolBar.Align = 1
  Toolbar.Height = ToolImage(0).Height
  ImageWidth = Image(0).Width
  For I = 0 To 4
    ToolImage(I).Move ImageWidth*I, 0
  Next I
.
' other code for the Paint event
End Sub
```

What this code does is position the image controls sequentially with no space between them. The width is set before the loop to avoid having to check a property value within the loop. (This is a common way to speed up loops.) You could easily insert gaps between the icons by changing the values used in the Move method. Notice how the code also adjusts the size of the toolbar to be exactly as high as the image controls themselves.

note: *See Chapter 16 for methods to add ToolTips by hand to a project.*

Help Systems

A professional Windows project needs a help system that does what Windows users expect. If your online help doesn't have the look and feel of a Windows help system, users will have to learn too much (and you'll probably be working too hard to teach them). Both the Professional and Enterprise editions come with the Windows help compiler, which lets you build help systems that can be called by the Windows help engine.

note: *Fully explaining all the possible features of Windows help systems would take a book almost the size of this one. This discussion concentrates on how you get a help system to interact with your Visual Basic application—rather than with the mechanics of constructing the help system itself. The Visual Basic Books Online product for both the Professional and Enterprise editions includes full documentation for building help systems.*

Roughly speaking, the way you use the help compiler is simple: you write a text file containing certain formatting codes that the help compiler translates into jumps, pop-up windows, and so on. The text file must be written with a word processor that supports what Microsoft calls RTF (rich text format). Many full-featured word processors support this format.

tip: *There are also several third-party tools that can make writing help files easier. The one I use all the time and highly recommend is "RoboHelp" from BlueSky Software (see Appendix D). If you are building a sophisticated help system, RoboHelp is more than worth the cost. For simpler help systems you might check out the WinHelp Lib of the WINSDK forum on CompuServe for* *shareware tools. WHAT—the "Windows Help Authoring Templates" and WHPE—the "Windows Help Project Editor" are also available on the Microsoft Software Developers CD-ROM and can make building simple help files easier.*

A help system should also feature the customary menu that users see in Windows. (Under Windows 95 you will probably want a multilevel contents screen as well.) The Search item should lead to the list of keywords the user can search through. These keywords will connect to the topics that you write. Various parts of your application (such as Visual Basic itself) should have context-sensitive help. This way users know that if they press F1 (or use the WhatsThisHelp button under Windows 95), they can get help about a specific item on a form.

Writing Help Topics

At the core of your online help system are the help topics you or someone else writes. Ideally, these are short (one or two screen lengths is ideal), self-contained expositions of a single idea. Topics are usually arranged hierarchically. This way users can navigate from general to specific topics when needed. However, within each topic the user should find enough jumps to make navigation possible without having to move through a (possibly) laborious hierarchy.

While topics should ideally be self-contained, complete self-containment is rarely possible. You may need to add pop-up or secondary windows.

- Pop-up windows pop up and give definitions of terms. They are occasionally used for lists of information. Places where the user can pop up a window are indicated by having the text appear with a dotted underline in the window.
- Secondary windows also are used when you need to display information without leaving the current topic. Unlike pop-up windows, secondary windows have their own title bars (and scroll bars, if necessary).

THE NITTY-GRITTY OF A HELP TOPIC

While this discussion does not spend a lot of time on the mechanics of building up the RTF file that will be compiled via the help compiler, it is important to understand the basics.

tip: *If you look at the ICONWRKS.RTF file in the VB\HC directory, you will see a good part of the range of what an RTF help file can be. This file gives the RTF file behind the ICONWRKS sample's help system. (You will find the actual program ICONWRKS.EXE in this directory as well.) By comparing the RTF file with the help screens in ICONWRKS.EXE, you can see how RTF tags translate into features of a help system—and perhaps learn what you need to know about RTF tags—or more likely convince yourself to use a third-party tool.*

I don't actually know anyone who, at the very least, doesn't use a simple macro package for inserting the necessary RTF tags. Using these packages means that you can forget about what identifier means what and rely on a few mouse clicks instead. For example, here is a picture of the RoboHelp toolbar, which gives access to just a small part of its features:

In any case, as mentioned earlier, you'll need to have a word processor that supports Microsoft's RTF (rich text format) in order to actually write the files that will be compiled by the Windows help compiler. (Most of the tools available, such as RoboHelp, are actually add-ons to Microsoft Word, which, of course, fully supports the RTF specification.)

Each topic must be separated from the next by a hard page break. (A *hard page break* is one that you insert manually rather than one calculated by the word processor. This is accomplished by pressing CTRL+ENTER on Microsoft's family of word processors.) Each topic should have a *context string identifier*, a title, and a list of keywords attached to it. The context string is used for jumps, so context strings have to be unique. The keywords are used for the search feature built into the Windows help engine, so many topics can share keywords.

Footnotes using specific identifiers are the key to unleashing the help engine's power. For example, context strings are indicated by placing a footnote with the # footnote identifier. Context strings can use A through Z, numerals, a period, and an underscore. They must be less than 255 characters.

The title of the topic is indicated by a footnote using a dollar sign ($). Titles can be up to 127 characters long and can use any of the Windows characters. Finally, keywords are indicated by the use of a capital K as the footnote identifier. (Keywords are optional, but you can place more than one keyword for a specific topic by separating the keywords with semicolons. Keywords can use any characters in the Windows character set, including spaces, and have a maximum length of 255 characters.)

Look at Figure 13-3. Notice the footnotes, which use the three identifiers mentioned above. Since the # footnote is EDITOR_FILE_MENU, this means that the topic shown in Figure 13-4 corresponds to the context string "EDITOR_FILE_MENU". Similarly, because of the $ footnote, this topic page has the title "File Menu." The keywords for this page are "File Menu," "New," "Open," "Save," "Save As," "Exit," "Viewer," and "Menu." Finally, the + footnote indicates a *browse sequence.* (Browse sequences are optional; they let you specify the order in which users can browse through topics—if you build a Browse button into your help system.) Next, notice the .bmp reference surrounded by braces. These indicate that a bitmap will appear in the corresponding help screen (see Figure 13-4). As Figure 13-3 shows, you can also place bitmaps in a topic page. If you have Word for Windows, you can place the bitmap directly in the file by using the Insert Picture function. (If they're very large, you should include your bitmaps using the "By Reference" method.) Graphics themselves can act as hot spots for jumps. You can place references to bitmaps in your topic files if you do not have Word for Windows.

Next, notice in Figure 13-3 that certain text, such as the term "Status Area," is double-underlined. Double-underlined text indicates a jump. Hidden text placed right after the jump indicates where the jump should go. The syntax is

JumpString CONTEXT_*STRING*

where the context string for where to jump to must be formatted in your word processor as hidden text with no spaces allowed. Similarly, you place a hidden context string following single-underlined text to indicate where the topic page for the pop-up definition will be found for the underlined text.

Figure 13-3 Help file in RTF format

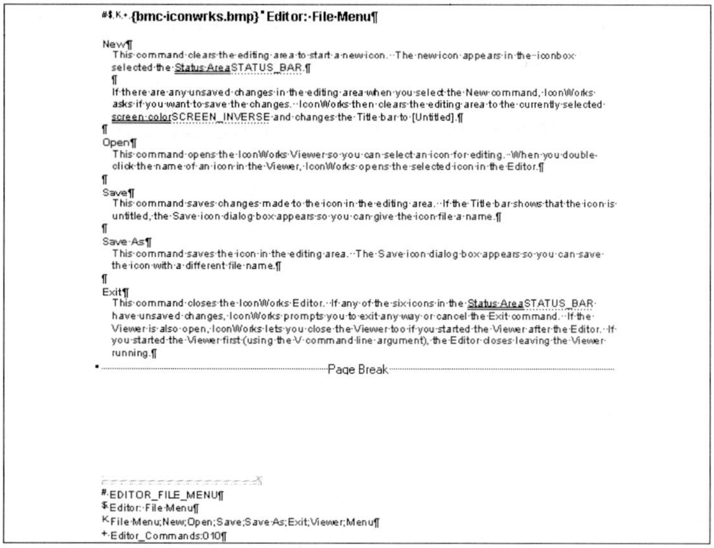

#$K+ {bmc iconwrks.bmp} Editor: File Menu¶

New¶
This command clears the editing area to start a new icon. The new icon appears in the iconbox selected the Status AreaSTATUS_BAR.¶
¶
If there are any unsaved changes in the editing area when you select the New command, IconWorks asks if you want to save the changes. IconWorks then clears the editing area to the currently selected screen colorSCREEN_INVERSE and changes the Title bar to [Untitled].¶
¶
Open¶
This command opens the IconWorks Viewer so you can select an icon for editing. When you double-click the name of an icon in the Viewer, IconWorks opens the selected icon in the Editor.¶
¶
Save¶
This command saves changes made to the icon in the editing area. If the Title bar shows that the icon is untitled, the Save icon dialog box appears so you can give the icon file a name.¶
¶
Save As¶
This command saves the icon in the editing area. The Save icon dialog box appears so you can save the icon with a different file name.¶
¶
Exit¶
This command closes the IconWorks Editor. If any of the six icons in the Status AreaSTATUS_BAR have unsaved changes, IconWorks prompts you to exit any way or cancel the Exit command. If the Viewer is also open, IconWorks lets you close the Viewer too if you started the Viewer after the Editor. If you started the Viewer first (using the V command line argument), the Editor closes leaving the Viewer running.¶

Page Break

EDITOR_FILE_MENU¶
$ Editor: File Menu¶
K File Menu;New;Open;Save;Save As;Exit;Viewer;Menu¶
+ Editor_Commands:010¶

Figure 13-4 How the help topic for Figure 13-3 would appear

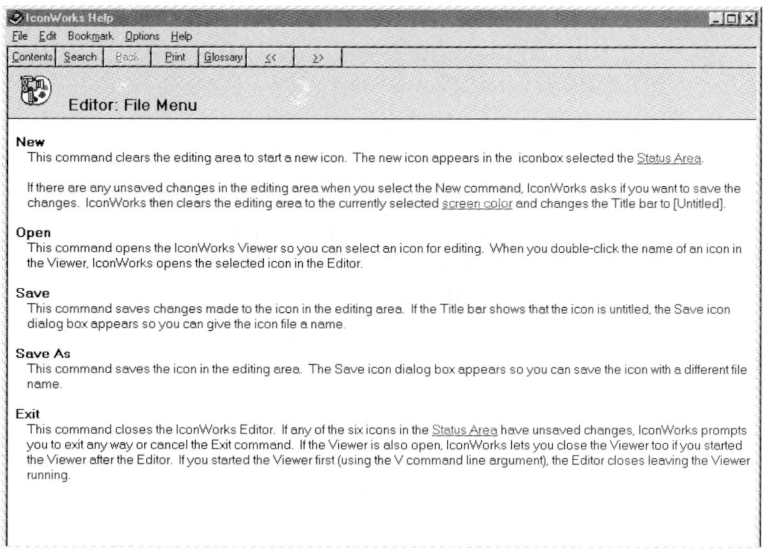

IconWorks Help

File Edit Bookmark Options Help

Contents Search Back Print Glossary << >>

Editor: File Menu

New
This command clears the editing area to start a new icon. The new icon appears in the iconbox selected the Status Area.

If there are any unsaved changes in the editing area when you select the New command, IconWorks asks if you want to save the changes. IconWorks then clears the editing area to the currently selected screen color and changes the Title bar to [Untitled].

Open
This command opens the IconWorks Viewer so you can select an icon for editing. When you double-click the name of an icon in the Viewer, IconWorks opens the selected icon in the Editor.

Save
This command saves changes made to the icon in the editing area. If the Title bar shows that the icon is untitled, the Save icon dialog box appears so you can give the icon file a name.

Save As
This command saves the icon in the editing area. The Save icon dialog box appears so you can save the icon with a different file name.

Exit
This command closes the IconWorks Editor. If any of the six icons in the Status Area have unsaved changes, IconWorks prompts you to exit any way or cancel the Exit command. If the Viewer is also open, IconWorks lets you close the Viewer too if you started the Viewer after the Editor. If you started the Viewer first (using the V command line argument), the Editor closes leaving the Viewer running.

note: *How hidden strings show up depends on your word processor. In Figure 13-3, they show up in all capital letters, for example, as STATUS_BAR.*

Building In Context-Sensitive Help

The help file property is a global property of the App (Application) object. You need to set this property to the name of the help file for the application. To do this at design time:

1. Choose Tools | Options and then click on the Project page.
2. Enter the name of the compiled help file in the HelpFile text box. (Give the full path name if it will not be in the same directory as the application.)

note: *You can also set or read off properties of the App object at run time. Besides the HelpFile property, you will often need the values for the App.ExeName property and App.PathName property.*

Next, let's assume you have written (or someone has given you) a help file that will be compiled and then attached to your project. You will need to coordinate some of the features of the help file with your program before you can actually use context-sensitive help in your project.

- The key as far as the Visual Basic programmer is concerned is setting the HelpContextID of the form or control appropriately. All controls except the line, shape, image, and label controls have a HelpContextID property.
- The key as far as the writer of the help system is concerned is to keep track of the HelpContext ID numbers the programmer assigns to the various elements that will need context-sensitive help.

For example, if the programmer sets the HelpContextID property of the File menu to 5, the writer of the help system must know this. Then, he or she must tell the help compiler how to *map* the HelpContextID property to specific topics (see the next section). In this case, the FILE_MENU topic page has context number 5.

tip: *If you want to assign context-sensitive help to an image control that doesn't have a HelpContextID property, replace it with a picture box that does.*

Building and Compiling the Help Files

The help project file contains the information needed for the help compiler to do its job. The help project file also contains the mapping between context strings and context ID numbers that you will use in your Visual Basic project. (Again, this means that there must be coordination between the information contained in the help project file and the code for your project.)

The help project file must be an ordinary ASCII file. The custom is to use .HPJ as the extension on all help project files. The help compiler changes this to .HLP for the compiled version. The help project file lists all the topic files and can optionally add bitmaps or a map between context strings and context ID numbers. You can also assign two context strings to the same topic by modifying the project file.

To map help context ID numbers to specific topics in order to use context-sensitive help, place the topic after the keyword [MAP], followed by white space (press the SPACEBAR or TAB), followed by the help context numbers. Here's a sample of what you might have in the [MAP] section of a help project file:

```
[MAP]
FILE_MENU     5     ;5 is the context number
        ;Comments follow semicolons
EDIT_MENU     10     ;10 is context number
VIEW_MENU     15     ;15 is context number
```

Now, when you call the Windows help engine (see the next section) with a HelpContextID value of 5, you would get the help screen for the FILE_MENU topic page, set the HelpContextID to 10, call the help engine, get the EDIT_MENU page, and so on.

After you build the help project file, you need only call the help compiler. (The help compiler must be in a directory known to the PATH command, or else you need to specify the full path name when calling it.) For example, under

Windows 95 you might use the Run dialog box available from the Start menu and fill it like this,

C:\VB\HC\HC *NameOfHelpProjectFile*

if you left the help compiler in the default directory for the Professional edition, or

HC *NameOfHelpProjectFile*

if the directory containing the help compiler is in your path.

There is a lot more to the help compiler: You can compile only certain parts of your file at one time, or control the size and shape of the windows in it. You can use a rich supply of macros that Microsoft wrote to extend the power of the help compiler. The documentation is quite detailed, and if you closely study the ICONWRKS.RTF file and refer to the Visual Basic Books Online documentation for the help compiler as needed, you should have all the information you need.

Accessing the Windows Help Engine

You can use the ShowHelp method of the common dialog control to access the Windows help engine. Follow these steps to use this method for the common dialog control:

1. Add a common dialog control to the form where you want to use the Windows help engine.
2. Set the HelpFile and HelpCommand properties of the CommonDialog control to the appropriate constants or values.

For example, if you want to use the ShowHelp method to give context-sensitive help:

1. Set the HelpFile property to the name of the compiled help file.
2. Set the HelpCommand property to cdlHelpContext.
3. Set the HelpContext property to the context ID you want to display at the moment.

4. Finally, use the ShowHelp method to call the Windows help engine.

If you need or want to use the general Windows help engine (for example, to have a "Help on Help" option that would show the Windows "Help on Help" screen), call the WinHelp API function instead. You must add the appropriate declaration to a code module. For the 32-bit Windows help engine, it looks like this:

```
Declare Function WinHelp Lib "user32" Alias "WinHelpA" _
(ByVal hwnd As Long, ByVal lpHelpFile As String, _
ByVal wCommand As Long, ByVal dwData As Long) As Long
```

For the 16-bit engine it looks like this:

```
Declare Function WinHelp Lib "User" (ByVal hWnd As Integer, _
ByVal lpHelpFile As String, ByVal wCommand As Integer, _
dwData As Any) As Integer
```

tip: *Since you need different declarations for each platform, this is a perfect place to use conditional compilation (see Chapter 7).*

The hWnd ("Window's handle") parameter will be the value of the form's hWnd property. The lpHelpFile parameter would be the path name of the help file (if it is not in the same place as the EXE file).

You will also need the following constants, which are used for the wCommand parameter.

```
Global Const HELP_CONTEXT = &H1 'Display topic by id number
Global Const HELP_QUIT = &H2        'Terminate help
Global Const HELP_INDEX = &H3       'Display index
Global Const HELP_HELPONHELP = &H4  'Display help on using
                                    'help
Global Const HELP_SETINDEX = &H5    'Set an alternate Index
Global Const HELP_KEY = &H101       'Display topic for
                                    'keyword in Data
Global Const HELP_MULTIKEY = &H201  'Lookup keyword in
                                    'alternate table
```

For example, to call the general Windows "Help on Help" system, you could use this general procedure:

```
Public Sub DisplayHelp_On_Help(X As Form)
  Dim Foo As Long ' dummy variable
  Foo = WinHelp(X.hWnd,"C:\WINDOWS\HELP\WINDOWS.HLP", _
HELP_HELPONHELP,CLng(0))
End Sub
```

After this, a line of code like this

```
DisplayHelp_On_Help Me
```

would pop up the general Windows help engine.

note: *After you set the hCommand parameter to HELP_CONTEXT, use the dwData parameter for the context string ID number.*

If you use the WinHelp API call to activate the help engine, you will have to call the WinHelp API function again to make sure that the extra help window is closed. (The Windows help engine is a separate Windows application.) This is done as follows (usually in the Form_Unload event). The variables Foo and Bar are "dummy" variables that must be of the right type but don't actually do anything.

```
Sub Form_Unload(Cancel As Integer)
   Dim Foo As Integer, Bar As String  'dummy variables
Foo = WinHelp(Me.hWnd, Bar, Help_Quit, CLng(0))
End
```

What's This Help?

Windows 95 adds a new kind of context-sensitive help that is activated by clicking on the little question mark that appears in the title bar of the form. The mouse cursor changes to a question mark and, when the user moves it over an object and clicks, he or she will expect to see context-sensitive help about that object. As with other context-sensitive help, you must coordinate the project with the MAP section of the help project file in order to use "What's This" help.

note: *If you want to use this method of providing context-sensitive help, you must set the WhatsThisHelp property of the form to True. Also, the WhatsThisHelpID property of the control must be equal to the context ID number (the value of the HelpContextID property).*

There are three ways to provide What's This help in an application. The WhatsThisHelp property must be True for any of these methods to work.

- Place a What's This button in the title bar of the form by setting the WhatsThisButton property of the form to True. If the user clicks on this button, the cursor changes to an arrow with a question mark. Now, whenever the user clicks on a control using the question mark cursor, Windows automatically displays the help topic whose context ID number is given by the WhatsThisHelpID property of the control.
- Call the WhatsThisMode method of the form, whose syntax looks like this:

  FormObject.ShowWhatsThis

- Call the ShowWhatsThis method of a control. The user again sees whatever help topic has a context ID number equal to the WhatsThisHelpID property of the control.

Finally, you can bypass the user completely by using the WhatsThisMode method of the form. Calling this has the same effect as if the user clicked the What's This button in the title bar. (One place you might use this is in a "learn mode" for your project. By using this method you can have users see the help screen whenever they click on a button or menu item.)

Chapter Fourteen

Tools and Techniques for Testing and Debugging

ONCE a program becomes in any way complicated, no matter how carefully you outline your program or how carefully you plan it, it probably won't do what you expect—at first. This is one lesson programmers are forced to painfully relearn over and over again. It seems that no matter how robust you try to make a program, someone, somehow, will find a way to crash it. A realistic goal is not a perfect program, but one that is as bulletproof (or robust) as possible, that even while crashing, tries to save the user's work before fading away. So you might make it your goal to write programs that conform to a sign the author once saw. Slightly paraphrased, it read,

> Our goal is a program
> THAT SPUTTERS OUT AND DOESN'T BLOW UP!

The technical phrase for this is a program that *degrades gracefully*.

So after you write a program, you will need to test it for *bugs*. Once the testing process convinces you that there are bugs lurking, you need to find them and then eradicate them. Visual Basic has many tools to assist with this task, and this chapter will show you how to use them. Before trying to test and debug a program, you should first make a hard copy of the program source code. You might also want a copy of the specifications of the forms in ASCII format (see Chapter 4) so you can quickly check whether the initial properties of a form and its controls match what you expect.

Finally, this chapter gives you techniques for speeding up your programs that do the job but are unlikely to introduce new bugs (trying to over-optimize code is one of the most common sources of programming bugs) and some words on good programming style.

The Debugging Tools and What They Do

You use the Debug menu to gain access to the tools needed for debugging, and most of the tools needed for testing and debugging can be found on the toolbar as well (see Figure 14-1). Usually, the debugging tools are used when the program is temporarily suspended (in *break mode*). The following table lists the debugging tools you can use.

Tool	Keyboard Equivalent	Function
Run/Restart	ALT R, S (F5/SHIFT+F5)	Starts the program anew or restarts it
Break	CTRL+BREAK	Interrupts the program
End		Ends the program
Breakpoint	ALT R, B (F9)	Sets a line before which the program will stop
Instant Watch	ALT T, W (SHIFT+F9)	Checks the value of the expression while the program is in break mode
Calls	ALT T, S (CTRL+L)	Shows how the procedure calls interrelate
Single Step (Step into)	ALT R, I (F8)	Moves through the program one statement at a time
Procedure Step (Step Over)	ALT R, O (SHIFT+F8)	Performs like the single-step tool except procedure and function calls are treated as one step

The first three tools provide the most common way of switching from project design, or design mode, to break mode—where you'll be doing most of your debugging. You can always tell what mode you're in by looking at the title bar.

Figure 14-1 The debugging tools on the toolbar

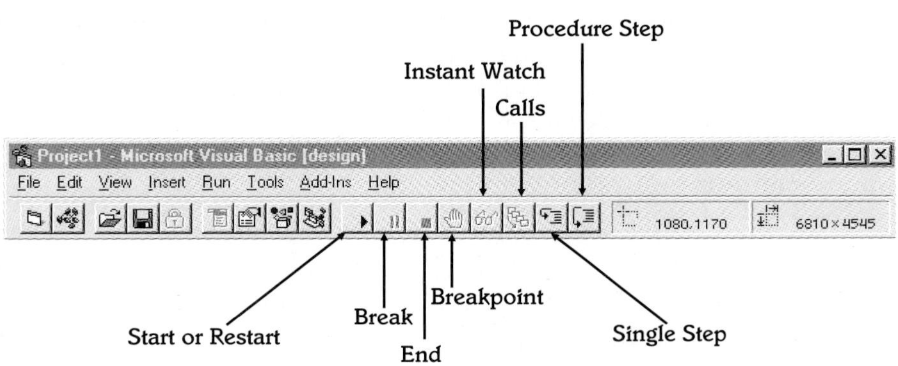

For example, when you stop a program by switching to break mode, the title bar switches to

Testing Programs

Testing programs is the first step in debugging because you cannot correct errors until you determine that errors exist. Some people's idea of testing a program consists of running the program a few times to see what happens, each time using slightly different input. This process can succeed when you have a short program, but it's not effective (or convincing) for a long program or even a short program that is in any way subtle. In any case, even for the simplest programs, the choice of test data (sometimes dignified with the fancy term *the testing suite*) is all-important.

Testing programs is an art, not a science. There's no procedure that always works. If your program is so long and complicated that you can't test all the possibilities, you have to be content with testing the reasonable ones.

The key to testing lies in the word *reasonable,* and the following story explains how subtle this concept can be. A utility company had a complicated but, they thought, carefully checked program to send out bills, follow up bills, and finally, automatically cut off service if no response to a bill was received. One day, the story goes, someone went on vacation and shut off the electricity. The computer sent out a bill for $0.00, which, understandably, wasn't paid. After the requisite number of follow-up requests, the computer finally issued a termination notice saying that if this unfortunate person didn't pay $0.00 by Thursday, his electricity would be cut off.

A frantic call might have succeeded in stopping the shut-off; the story doesn't say. If this story is true, the programmer forgot to test what the program would do if the bill was $0.00. To the programmer, this wasn't a "reasonable" possibility. (All the programmer had to do was change a >= to a > somewhere in the program.)

One moral of this story is that you must always test your programs using the boundary values—the extreme values that mark the limits of the problem, like the $0.00 that the programmer in the story forgot. For example, for sorting routines, a completely ordered or reverse-ordered list is a good test case. In programs that require input, the empty string (or 0) is always a good test case.

Since errors are often caused by bugs, error trapping can help you isolate what portion of a procedure caused the bug. For example, you can add line numbers to your program and then use the Erl statement to find out which half of the program caused the error. Continue this bisection process until you isolate the line that caused the bug. (Of course, Visual Basic ordinarily stops a program at the line that causes an error, but you will often need to insert line numbers to debug a program with an error trap.)

tip: *Having an active error trap (On Error Goto) can prevent your tests from doing their job. You often will need to temporarily disable any active error traps before starting the testing process. For more information on error traps, see Chapter 8.*

note: *Professionals might want to consider buying Microsoft's Test program. This comes with a language related to Visual Basic and lots of tools to make a professional testing procedure go smoother.*

Designing Programs to Make Testing Easier

Long and complicated programs are never easy to test, but writing the programs in certain ways will make your job easier. (These methods also make programming in general easier.) By breaking the program into manageable pieces (giving the program *modularity,* in the jargon), each of which ideally does one task alone, you can make testing your programs much, much easier. After you finish each procedure or function, you can test it thoroughly to see whether it can handle all possible parameters that may be passed to it. Another good principle is to always have a program that runs, regardless of whether all features are yet implemented.

Next, combine all the procedures you've checked and test everything again. In some cases, a procedure or function may need results from a piece not yet written in order to run. In this case, the best technique, often called *stub programming,* substitutes constants, where necessary, for the results of as-yet-unwritten procedures or functions. Define the Sub procedure or Function procedure, but fill it with constants instead of having it do anything. The procedure calls will still work the same, but they receive only the constants from the stubs. You can then change the constants to vary the tests.

Now suppose you have eliminated the obvious syntax errors and can get the program to run—after a fashion. But testing the program has told you that it doesn't work as it's supposed to; it contains bugs that you need to isolate and eradicate. Don't be surprised or dismayed; bugs come with the territory. You have to find them and determine what kind they are.

There are essentially two kinds of bugs: grammatical and logical. An example of a grammatical error is a misspelled variable name, which leads to a default value that ruins the program. Surprisingly enough, they are often the most difficult kind of bug to detect. Probably the best way to avoid such bugs in Visual Basic is to prevent them in the first place by using the Option Explicit command (see Chapter 5), which forces you to declare all variables. Logical bugs are a vast family that encompasses all errors resulting from a misunderstanding of how a program works. This includes procedures that don't communicate properly and internal logic errors inside code.

Another useful tool for understanding how variables are used in your programs is a programmer's tool called a cross-reference (or XREF) program. This program works through the source code of a program and then lists the names of all variables and where they occur. A cross-referencing program is especially useful for detecting the common error of an incorrect variable in an assignment statement. Although using meaningful variable names can help to a certain extent, the mistake of using the variable ThisWeeksSales when you really meant the variable ThisMonthsSales is still easy to make. (The Option Explicit command doesn't help if the wrong variable was already dimensioned.) You'll learn about the tools needed to write an XREF program in Chapter 19. Commercial programs that do far more also are available. See Appendix D for more information on them.

Logical Bugs

To get rid of subtle logical bugs, you have to isolate them—that is, find the part of the program that's causing the problem. If you've followed the modular approach, your task is a lot easier. The pieces are more manageable, so finding the bug means the haystack isn't *too* big.

If you've been testing the program as you develop it, then you should already know in what procedure or function the problem lies. Pinpointing the problematic procedure or function is usually easier if you developed the program, mostly because you start off with a good idea of the logic of the program. If the program is not yours or you've waited until the program is "finished," you can use the following techniques to check the pieces one at a time.

Assume that you've chosen a faulty procedure or function to test. There are only three possibilities:

- What's going in is wrong—what you've fed to the procedure or function is confusing it.
- What's going out is wrong—the procedure or function is sending incorrect information to other parts of the program (for example, it may be causing unplanned side effects).
- Something inside the procedure or function is wrong (for example, it's performing an operation too many times, or it's not clearing the screen at the right time).

In the first two cases, the fault can be traced to any or all of the following: the parameters you send to the procedure or function, what you've assigned to the parameters, or the form-level or global variables modified within the function or procedure.

How do you decide which situation you're dealing with? First, it's hard to imagine a correctly written *short* procedure or function that you can't analyze on a piece of paper to determine what should happen in most cases. Work through the procedure or function by hand, "playing computer" (this means don't make any assumptions other than what the computer would know at that point; don't assume variables have certain values unless you can convince yourself that they do). You now need to check that the functions and procedures are doing what they are supposed to.

The Debug Window

Most versions of BASIC have a way to test program statements, procedures, and functions, and Visual Basic is no exception. Visual Basic uses the Debug window, shown in Figure 14-2.

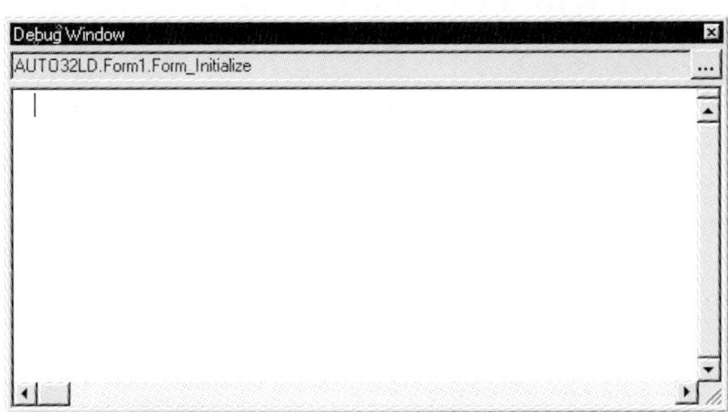

Figure 14-2 The Debug window

note: *The Debug window has its own shortcut menu that contains most of its common operations. Like any shortcut menu, a click on the right (non-primary) mouse button brings it up.*

The main difference with non-Windows versions of BASIC is that you cannot use the Debug window to test programs when you are developing a program. The Debug window pops up only when you run a program and is available for testing when you press CTRL+BREAK (or choose the Break option from the Run menu or toolbar) to interrupt a program.

To bring the Debug window to the foreground, use the View menu or click any part of the Debug window that is visible. The Debug window is moveable or resizeable by ordinary Windows technique. As in QuickBASIC, you can use the Debug window to test statements or to perform quick calculations when you are in break mode. If you type **Print 2 + 2** in the Debug window and press ENTER, Visual Basic quickly responds with a 4. You can use the ordinary Microsoft Window editing commands to modify the contents of a line in the Debug window. You can also cut and paste between lines. Keep in mind, though, that the moment you press ENTER, Visual Basic attempts to process the line.

Lines in the Debug window can use the colon separator and the line continuation character. Because of these restrictions, you can write loops in the Debug window, although they'll look strange. For instance,

```
For I = 10 TO 1 STEP -1:Form1.Text1.Text = STR$(I)+VBcrLf+_
: NEXT I
```

is a perfectly acceptable line of code for the Debug window.

Keep in mind that you can always reexecute any lines that currently appear in the Debug window by moving the cursor anywhere in the line and pressing ENTER. (If you have used the line continuation character, you must move to the last physical line before hitting ENTER.) Use the arrow keys or mouse to move around the Debug window.

More on Debugging in the Debug Window

When you stop a program the Debug window displays the title all the time. Also, the active form or module is highlighted in the title bar of the Debug window, as shown in Figure 14-3. The title bar displays the name of the active form and the name of the procedure (if any) that Visual Basic was processing at the moment program execution was stopped—in this case, the

Figure 14-3 Debug window in break mode

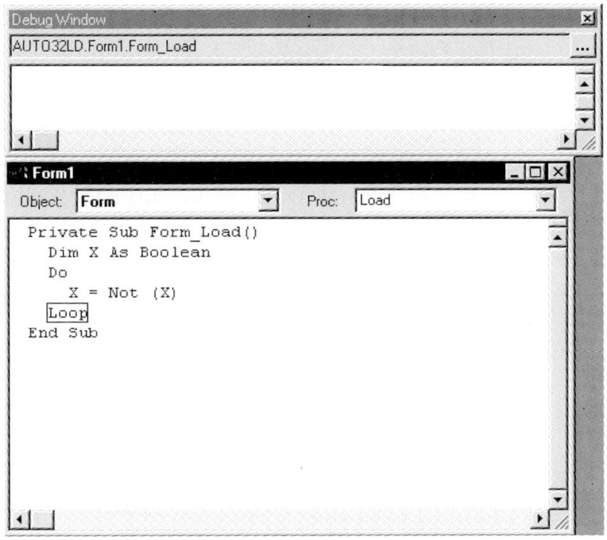

Load procedure for Form1. It also shows the line about to be processed, in a box (which, incidentally, is drawn right on top of any embedded underscores, making them almost invisible).

The Debug window makes it easy to test an isolated procedure or function for its effects on certain values (for example, to see whether the results match with your hand calculations). You can test only procedures and functions that are attached to the form or module shown in the title bar of the Debug window (anything which is in the scope).

Most debugging techniques use the Debug window to examine the current value of variables, but the only variables you can view from the Debug window are

- Variables local to the procedure listed in the title bar
- Form-level variables for the form listed in the title bar
- Global variables

To look at the value of a variable that fits one of these categories, use a simple Print statement inside the Debug window:

Print *NameOfVariable*

You can also add lines of code to your program that print values directly to the Debug window. For this, you use a predefined Visual Basic object called Debug:

Debug.Print *NameOfVariable*

Whenever Visual Basic encounters a Debug.Print statement, it sends the requested information to the Debug window. It does not stop the program. You can then examine it at your leisure. Many programmers like to have these statements identify the variable, as shown here:

```
Debug.Print "The value of X is";X
```

When you are through debugging your program, you'll want to remove all the Debug.Print statements, although theoretically you can leave them in a compiled .EXE file without the user noticing. Finally, you can change the values of variables that are in the current scope by making assignments in the Debug window.

Single Stepping

Often, when you have worked through a program by hand, you will want to have the computer walk through the same example, one line of code at a time. Visual Basic lets you execute one statement in your program at a time—single-stepping—by repeatedly pressing F8 or the single-step tool on the toolbar. (Of course, if Visual Basic is waiting for an event to happen, there won't be any statements to execute.)

When single-stepping is first used, the first executable statement of the program is boxed in the code window (see Figure 14-4). (Usually, the first statement will be in the Form_Initialize or Form_Load procedure if there is no Form_Initialize procedure). Each subsequent press of F8 or the single-step tool executes the boxed statement and boxes the next statement to be executed. As you can imagine, single-stepping through a program is ideal for tracing the logical flow of a program through decision structures and procedures.

Another possibility is to use the Debug window to check the values of constants, variables, or conditions by using Print statements. You also might want to consider having the Debug window and code window simultaneously on the screen. You can do this by resizing and relocating them as needed.

Figure 14-4 Debug window when single-stepping

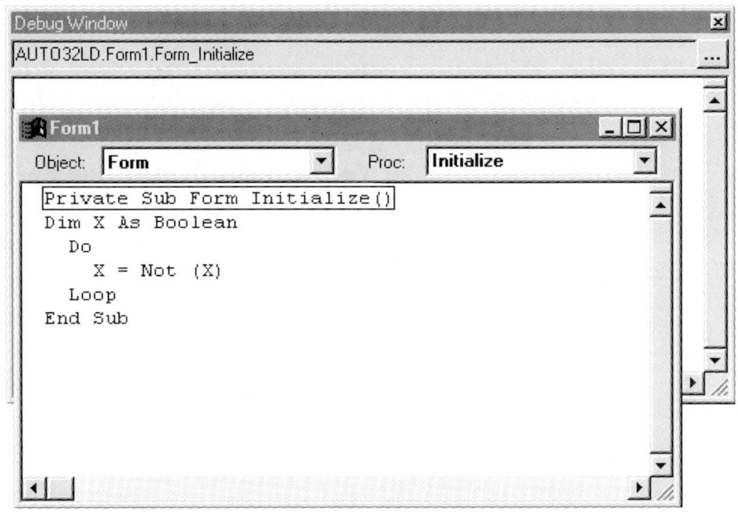

note: *Some programmers like to dispense with the Debug window and use a special form that they have added to their projects for debugging information.*

Whenever a procedure is called during single-stepping, the procedure code fills the code window. After its statements have been highlighted and executed (one at a time), the routine that called it reappears in the code window.

Besides the F8 key or single-step tool from the toolbar, you can also use SHIFT+F8 (or procedure-step tool) to single-step through a program. With this tool, each procedure is processed as if it were a single statement. In many cases, this is preferable to single-stepping through a complex function that you already know works.

Single-stepping through a program will probably take you to the place where you know a problem lurks. Now you want to place a break at that point before continuing the debugging process. This can be done with the Stop statement or, more commonly, by using a *breakpoint,* one of the tools available from the Debug menu or toolbar (see the next section).

Stopping Programs Temporarily

Debug.Print statements help you debug your program by printing values *dynamically*—while the program is running. More often than not, though, you'll need to stop your program temporarily and look at a snapshot of the values of many of the variables. For example, suppose you want to know why a variable seems not to have the value you want. You need to pinpoint the location where the value starts behaving strangely. Just printing the values to the Debug window may not be enough. There are two ways to stop a program temporarily. The least flexible is to use the Stop statement within your code. This method was inherited from GW-BASIC. Stop statements remain in your code until you remove them by hand.

Breakpoints, on the other hand, are toggled off or on by pressing F9 or using the hand-up tool from the toolbar. (You can also select Toggle Breakpoint from the Run menu by pressing ALT R, D). Breakpoints are usually shown in red in your code. When you run the program and Visual Basic encounters a breakpoint, Visual Basic stops the code just before the statement with the breakpoint is executed and enters break mode.

You can set multiple breakpoints. To remove a breakpoint, position the cursor on the breakpoint and press ALT R, B (or press F9). To clear all breakpoints from a program, press ALT R, A (or choose the Clear All Breakpoints option on the Run menu—CTRL+SHIFT+F9 is the shortcut).

Using Breakpoints to Test Programs

Now suppose you want to test a procedure. Put a breakpoint right before the call to the procedure or function you want to test. Once the program stops at the breakpoint, open up the Debug window, if necessary, and write a driver program. A *driver* is a program fragment that calls a function or procedure with specific values. For example, suppose you know that with the parameter

```
Variable1 = 10
```

and the parameter

```
Variable2 = 20
```

the result of a procedure of two parameters is to make a form (a form-level variable named, say, FormLevel1) have the value 97. When you want to test how this procedure or function behaves at a particular place in a program, add the breakpoint at the appropriate point and use the Debug window to enter

```
WhateverYouAreTesting 10, 20
Print "The value of the variable FormLevel1 is: "; FormLevel1
```

See what happens. If the value of the variable FormLevel1 isn't right, then you can begin to suspect that something inside this procedure is wrong. To confirm your suspicions, you'll need to check that no other form-level variable is causing the problem. You can add Print statements inside the Debug window to check this. (Another possibility is to use Watch variables—see the section on these that follows.) Examine the values of the relevant variables, the variables whose values affect the value of the variable FormLevel1. This check may quickly tell you whether something is wrong inside the procedure or function. If the value of the variable FormLevel1 is correct, then determine, again by hand, what happens for some other values. Always remember to try the boundary values (the strange values, like the $0.00 that the programmer in the story forgot). If the values always match your expectations, there's probably nothing wrong with the procedure or function.

Of course, in practice, you have to make sure your driver fragment sends all the information needed by the procedure or function—and that's not likely to be only the values of two variables. Before calling the procedure, you can make all the necessary assignments in the Debug window while the program is stopped.

Assume that you've tested the procedure and know that the problem seems to be coming from outside it. Check each procedure that calls this procedure or function. Apply the same techniques to them: check what goes in and out of these procedures or functions. Of course, good documentation of a routine can help you by specifying the inputs and outputs.

tip: *Use* SHIFT+F8 *or the procedure-step tool on the toolbar to treat a call to a Sub procedure or Function procedure as a single step. This way, you don't have to step through all the lines in all the functions and procedures in your program when you don't need to. Combine this with the Calls option on the Debug menu to see which procedure called the one you are in or to look at the entire chain of procedure calls if need be.*

Also, when you are in break mode you can use the Step To Cursor item on the Run menu to process a group of statements in a procedure. (The shortcut is CTRL+F8.) Just move the cursor to where you want to execute up to and press CTRL+F8.

INSTANT WATCH

In every case, you eventually wind your way down to a procedure or function that just doesn't work. You now know that you have an error internal to a procedure or function. Although the Debug window can be used to examine the values of expressions while single-stepping through a program, using Visual Basic's *Instant Watch* provides a more efficient mechanism.

The Instant Watch item (SHIFT+F9) on the Debug menu lets you look at the value of any variable or expression. For example, you can look at the truth or falsity of an expression (see Figure 14-5). It complements Visual Basic's feature that lets you use the Debug window to look at the value of any variables inside a procedure when a program is stopped within the procedure.

To use Instant Watch,

1. Select the variable or expression you want to watch by moving the cursor to the item or highlighting the expression using SHIFT+arrow key combinations.
2. Choose Instant Watch from the Tools menu (ALT T, W or SHIFT+F9) or the Instant Watch tool.

A dialog box like the one in Figure 14-5 appears.

Figure 14-5
Instant Watch dialog box example

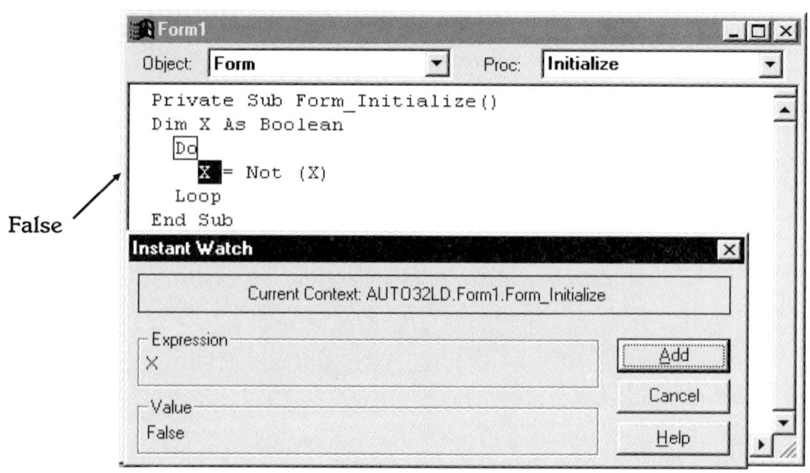

If the value isn't currently available, Visual Basic will tell you. At this point, you can close the box with the ESC key or choose to add this variable as a Watch item.

WATCH ITEMS

Watch items are variables, expressions, or conditions that are displayed in a special part of the Debug window (see Figure 14-6). Notice that the Debug window has split into two parts: the *Watch Pane* (where the watch items are shown) and the *Immediate Pane* (which you use for displaying information or checking code). You use the split bar to enlarge or shrink the panes as needed.

You can choose the watch items you want to examine either before you start the program or while the program is running and you have temporarily stopped it. Any variable, expression, or condition can be entered into the dialog box that pops up when you choose Add Watch from the Debug menu. However, you can watch only global variables or variables attached to the current form or module. When you press ENTER, the item will appear in the Watch Pane of the Debug window with a little pair of eyeglasses as the icon at the far left (see Figure 14-6). As Visual Basic executes the program, the values of the watch items will be updated in the Watch Pane of the Debug window.

To create a watch item, press ALT T, A (the Add Watch option on the Tools menu). A dialog box will appear as shown in Figure 14-7. The expression box

Figure 14-6 Debug window with watch item

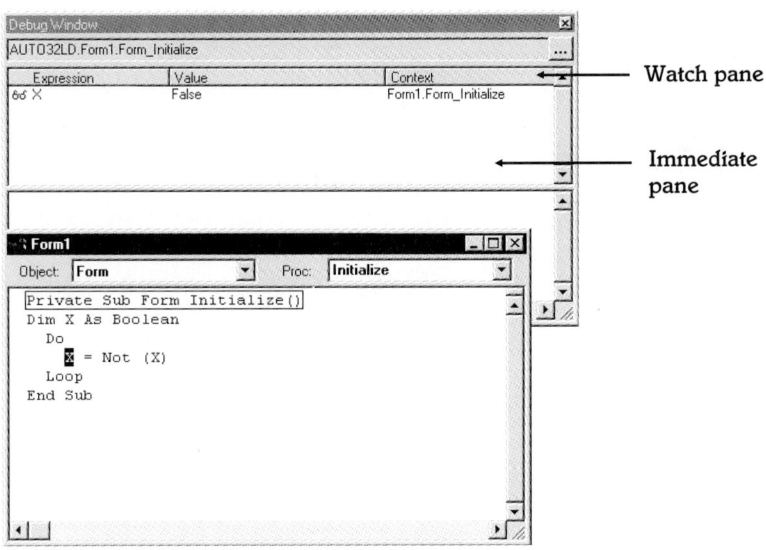

Figure 14-7
Add Watch dialog box

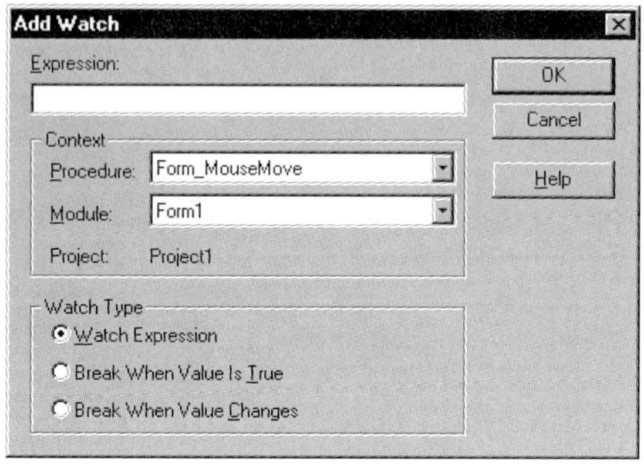

initially uses whatever expression you highlighted. The context option buttons are used to set the scope of the variables in the expression. You can restrict the scope to procedure-level, form-level, module, or global variables. The last option buttons offer two other ways of watching your program, covered in the next section.

To remove an item from the Debug window, press ALT T, E (Edit Watch). This opens up a dialog box that looks like this:

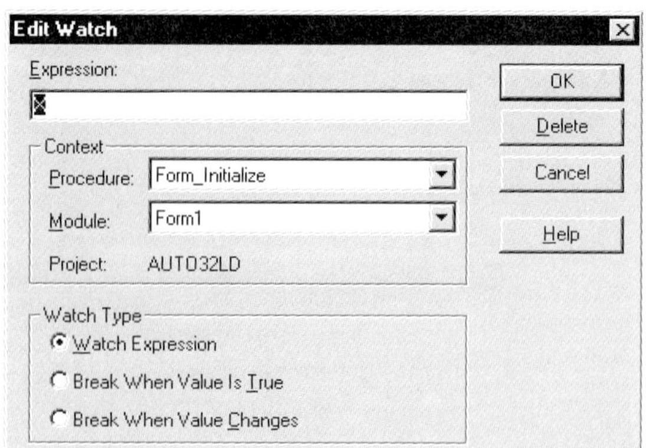

Click on the Delete button. You can also highlight the item in the Watch Pane and press DEL.

tip: *If you have to watch a string variable, use an expression like*

"{" + *NameOfStringVariable* + "}"

Then you can quickly detect whether the string is the empty string, because if it is, all you'll see in the Debug window are the brackets with nothing between them.

WATCHPOINTS

As mentioned above, sometimes the problem with a program appears to be tied to a variable or expression whose value falls outside some anticipated range, yet it is unclear in which line this occurs. In this case, setting a breakpoint at a specific line is not appropriate, and watching the variable and single-stepping may be too time-consuming. What is needed instead is the ability to suspend the program at the line that causes the variable or expression to reach or exceed some value. In Visual Basic, this debugging procedure is referred to as setting a watchpoint and is done from either the Add Watch Item or the Edit Watch dialog box.

If you choose the Break When Value Is True option button, Visual Basic stops the program as soon as the watched expression is True, and it highlights the line after the one that caused the expression to become True. The other option button lets you stop execution when an expression has changed. The icons for these watch items in the Watch pane are a raised hand with an equal sign and a raised hand with a triangle.

SETTING THE NEXT STATEMENT

Set Next Statement (CTRL+F9 is the shortcut) on the Run menu lets you bypass part of a program while you are stepping through it. Sometimes (especially when using the stub programming technique described earlier) you'll want to start a program other than at the beginning of a procedure or function, or you may, while single-stepping, want to skip to another place in a procedure (you can't move to a different procedure). To use this option, you need to be running a program in break mode (usually one you are stepping through). To set this option, while in the code window, move the cursor to the line where you want to restart execution. Press CTRL+F9. When you tell Visual Basic to continue, Visual Basic starts executing at the line you just set. You can move both backwards and forwards within the procedure. You can also modify code at this point in order to test changes. Similarly, you can use the Show Next Statement item to have the cursor move to the line that Visual Basic intends to execute next.

Final Remarks on Debugging

Feeding a procedure or function specific numbers and using the debugging techniques described here are not cure-alls. No technique can help unless you have a good grip on what the procedure or function should do. If you are using an If-Then statement, are you testing for the right quantity? Should a >= be a >? Use watch items to check the value (True or False) of any Boolean relations that seem to be off (it is perfectly legal to enter X=19 as a watch value). Check any loops in the routine; loops are a common source of problems. Are counters initialized correctly (is there an off-by-one error)? Are you testing your indeterminate loops at the top when you should be testing them at the bottom?

AN EXAMPLE: DEBUGGING A BUGGY LOOP

Recall in Chapter 7 we discussed a loop that looks like this:

```
Total = 0
PassNumber = 0
Do
  PassNumber = PassNumber + 1
  Total = Total + .1
Loop Until Total = 1
```

This loop would continue forever. Suppose you put a loop like this in a procedure, forgetting that you should never test single-precision numbers for equality. How can you use debugging techniques to find and then fix this bug?

Whenever you have a loop that is running amok, you'll need to either watch the loop variable, set up a watchpoint involving the loop variable, or both. In this case, you might first watch the value of Total. You would quickly discover that it is growing without bound. Knowing this, you need only set a watchpoint with the expression

PassNumber > 10

Once the program stops, you can examine the value of Total to discover that it isn't quite equal to 1—and that is the root of your problem.

tip: *When a Do loop seems to be running too long, add a temporary counter to the Do loop. Then use the counter in a watchpoint at some (fairly) large value. When the program stops, examine the state of the expression tested in the loop to help determine why your loops are running too long.*

Event-Driven Bugs and Problems

When you debug an event-driven program, you have to be aware of certain problems that could never come up in older programming languages. "Event cascades" are perhaps the most common. These are bugs caused by an infinite sequence of one event procedure calling itself or another event procedure, with no way to break the chain. The most likely time such bugs are introduced is when you make a change in the Change event procedure for a control. The Change procedure is called again, which in turn is called again, and so on—theoretically forever, but in practice you'll get an "Out of Stack Space" error message.

Other special problems occur when you stop a program during a MouseDown or KeyDown event procedure. In both situations, during the debugging process you'll naturally release the mouse button or lift the key that invoked the event procedure. However, when Visual Basic resumes the program, it assumes the mouse button or the key is still down, and so the relevant MouseUp and KeyUp procedures will never be called. The usual solution is to call the MouseUp or KeyUp procedure from the Debug window as needed.

Documentation and Program Style

Although you can remember the logic of a complicated program for a while, you can't remember it forever. Good documentation is the key that can open the lock. Some people include the pseudocode or outline for the program as multiple remark statements. Along with meaningful variable names, this is obviously the best form of documentation. Set up conventions for global, form, or local variables and stick to them. Try to avoid tricky code; if you need to do something extraordinarily clever, make sure it's extensively commented. (Most of the time, you'll find that the clever piece of code wasn't really needed.) Nothing is harder to change six months down the line than "cute" code. Cute code often comes from a misplaced attempt to get a program to run more quickly. While this is sometimes necessary, versions of Visual Basic after 1.0 are usually fast enough for most situations. The author once saw a sign that made this point clearly:

> **Rules for program optimization:**
>
> 1. Don't do it.
> 2. (For expert programmers only) DON'T DO IT!
>
> (Unless performance is unacceptable to the user.)

The point is that when you start thinking of tricks to speed up your programs, you can too easily lose sight of the fundamental issue: making sure your programs run robustly in the first place. In fact, dramatic speedups usually come from shifts in the algorithms in the program, not from little "tweaks." Roughly speaking, an *algorithm* is the method you use to solve a problem. For example, in problems that involve sorting a list, the sort method you choose determines the speed of the sort. As you saw in Chapter 11, choosing the right sorting technique can speed up a program manyfold. This is more than any minor tweak can ever hope to accomplish. Discovering new (and, with luck, faster) algorithms is one of the main tasks of computer scientists and mathematicians.

This is not to say that *after* a program is running robustly, you might not want to consider ways of making it run faster. Making sure that variables are integers whenever possible is an obvious and not dangerous change. Don't use variant variables unless you need their special properties. Any statement using a variant that requires converting it to another type will run slower. For-Next loops with counters that are variants instead of integers may run half as fast; using single-precision counters can slow a loop down 10-fold.

Try the following additional techniques to increase the speed of your program if necessary:

- Preload VBRUN400.DLL when the user starts Windows by putting a compiled Visual Basic program in the Windows Startup group. (This gives the appearance of speed but really doesn't speed up a program.)
- Use dynamic arrays whenever possible and free up the space if it is not needed.

- Unload forms when no longer needed.
- Delete code if it is no longer used in your project.
- Use local variables whenever possible.
- Use a Picture box for graphics rather than another form.
- Write a general-purpose error handler and pass the error code to it instead of having complicated error handlers in every procedure.

Finally, for advanced users:

- Use Dynamic Link Library (DLL) routines in particular API calls when appropriate.

(Obviously it also helps to have as much RAM and as fast a hard disk as possible.)

caution: *Some ways known to make Visual Basic programs run faster (such as using global variables instead of parameters) are usually more dangerous than the speed is worth.*

In any case, it's extremely difficult to modify or debug a program (even one that you, long ago, wrote yourself) that has few or no remark statements, little accompanying documentation, and uninformative variable names. A procedure called MakeMartini(Shaken,ButNotStirred) should be in a program about James Bond (and perhaps not even there), not in a program about trigonometric functions. In addition, since Visual Basic allows long variable names, don't make your programs a morass of variables named X, X13, X17, X39, and so on. If you strive for clarity in your programs rather than worrying about efficiency at first, you'll be a lot better off.

Finally, if a procedure or function works well, remember to save it for reuse in other programs. Complicated programs will often have many procedures and functions. These procedures and functions may often have come up before in a slightly different context. This means that after you design the interface, sometimes all you have to do is modify and connect parts of a thoroughly debugged library of subprograms and functions to the event procedures for the interface. (This is one reason why commercial toolkits for Visual Basic are so useful. The time saved is worth the small cost.)

Chapter Fifteen

An Introduction to Graphics

This chapter introduces you to the techniques needed for building graphics into your Visual Basic applications. It starts with reviewing and extending the information on the Scale method you saw way back in Chapter 3. This is followed by a discussion of how the important AutoRedraw method works. Next, it's on to the Line and Shape controls. These let you easily draw lines and various shapes such as circles and rectangles on your form. (They work best if you have relatively few things to draw.) Then it's on to the graphical methods built into Visual Basic. Using the graphical methods can require writing a fair amount of code, but in return, these methods allow you to control every dot that appears on your screen or prints on your printer. Because Windows is a graphically based environment, the graphics powers of Visual Basic can be astonishing. The screen in Figure 15-1 shows you what a short program from this chapter can do.

The graphics methods in Visual Basic allow you to control each dot (usually called a *pixel* or *picture element*) that appears on the screen. If you take a

Figure 15-1 Rotating squares

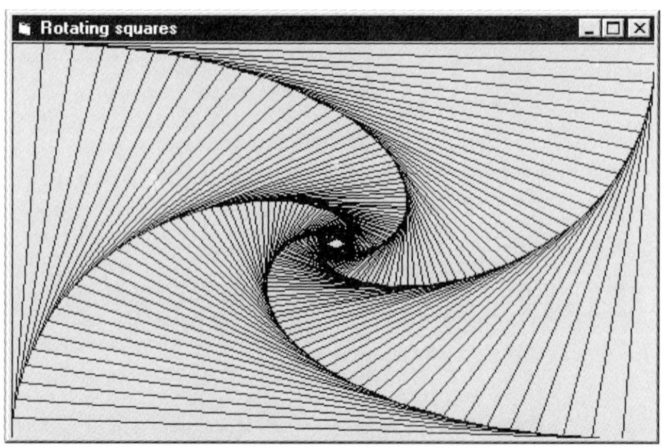

magnifying glass to a monitor, you can see that each character is made up of many of these pixels. In fact, certain combinations of software, hardware, and monitors can divide the screen into more than 1,000,000 dots and theoretically choose from a palette of more than 16,777,216 (256 * 256 * 256) colors for each pixel. And the same graphics statements that work for the screen apply to the Printer object. This lets you control every dot your printer can put out; on a laser printer, this is at least 300 dots per inch.

In addition to drawing pretty pictures, the graphical methods and controls also allow you to embellish your Visual Basic projects, making them more professional. For example, as you'll see in this chapter, lines drawn around controls in special ways can dramatically change the look of your applications.

Computer graphics (especially three-dimensional drawings) is a subject in which mathematics must inevitably rear its head. However, this chapter uses nothing beyond a little trigonometry, and that only in the last few sections. Of course, you can just skip the math and use the programs; the results are pretty spectacular. Figure 15-2 shows an example of what you can do with polar coordinates.

Chapter 19 describes one other technique for creating graphics: using recursion to draw fractals. That chapter includes a short introduction to fractal graphics. Figure 15-3 is an example of what you can draw using those techniques.

You should be aware that in traditional programming languages, graphics are usually distinguished from text. This distinction is much less important with Windows and, therefore, with Visual Basic. With the exception of the various kinds of text boxes and labels, Visual Basic considers essentially everything

Figure 15-2 Polar coordinates demonstration

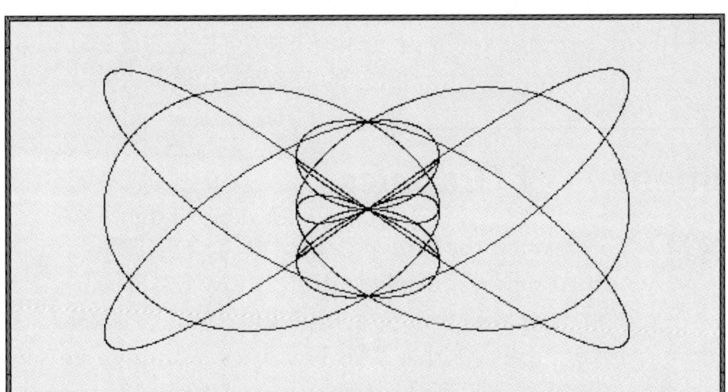

Figure 15-3 Fractal drawing

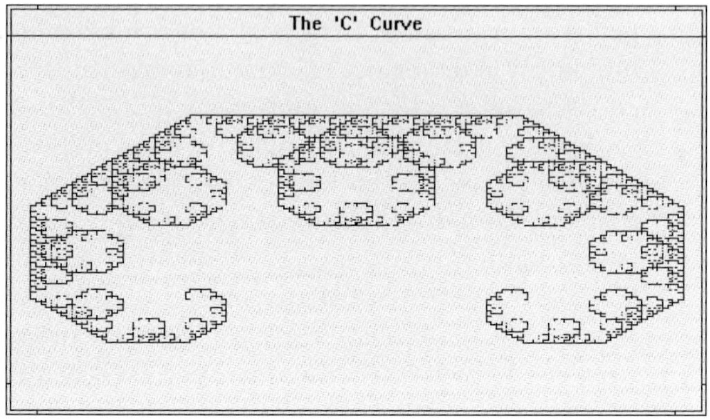

placed on a form to be graphical. This is why forms can display text with such varied fonts and why you are able to use the CurrentX and CurrentY properties to position text accurately on the screen or in a picture box. Nonetheless, the graphics methods themselves work only on forms, picture boxes, and the printer. Since the ZOrder layer for controls (in particular picture boxes and text boxes) is above that of the form, you can often get dramatic special effects by combining the two.

Finally, although this chapter shows you the techniques needed to do presentation-style graphs and charts, the Professional and Enterprise editions have a custom control to do this. If you need to make graphs and charts, you may want to upgrade to this version of Visual Basic rather than reprogram all the tools yourself. The Graph custom control supplied with the Professional and Enterprise editions makes it amazingly simple to build the most complex graphs. The end of this chapter is an introduction to this very important custom control. (Nonetheless, even if you have one of these editions, you may still want to learn the techniques needed for drawing charts and graphs.)

Fundamentals of Graphics

To draw on the screen, Visual Basic tells Windows what to display. Windows in turn tells the display adapter how to display the image. What this means is that what you can do with Visual Basic's graphics statements depends on the driver programs that Windows uses to control the screen and printer. However, using these driver programs is automatic. You do not have to worry about all the possible hardware combinations a user may have. This is different from what

MS-DOS programmers are used to. When graphics is programmed under DOS, part of the program must check what kind of graphics board is installed (or whether any graphics board is installed), and then the program must be adjusted accordingly.

However, nothing comes for free. Windows has to do a lot to manage a graphics environment, and this forces trade-offs. For example, unless you set the AutoRedraw property to True so that Visual Basic saves a copy of the object in memory, you will have to manage the redrawing of graphics yourself. (The jargon says that AutoRedraw controls whether graphics are *persistent* or not.)

note: *Images derived from setting the Picture property of a control or those that come from the Line and Shape controls are always persistent.*

There are slight differences between how the AutoRedraw property being set to True works for forms and picture boxes:

- For a resizable form, Visual Basic saves a copy of the entire screen. Thus, when you enlarge the form, no graphics information is lost. This option requires by far the most memory, but if your graphics do not currently fit on a form, but will when the form is enlarged, choose this option.
- For a picture box, Visual Basic saves an image only as large as the current size of the box. Nothing new will appear even if the box is enlarged later.

Thus, drawing to picture boxes requires less memory than drawing to the form, even if the picture box fills up the form.

A Feature of the AutoRedraw Property

There is one other interesting feature of AutoRedraw: Suppose you change AutoRedraw to False while a program is running. Then you clear the object by using the Cls method. Whatever you drew before you changed the AutoRedraw property will remain, but everything that was drawn after the switch will disappear. This feature can be very useful. To see how it works, start a new project and try the following demonstration program (recall that text is treated as graphics output on a form). For the Form_Load procedure, write

```
Private Sub Form_Load ()
  AutoRedraw = True
  Print "Please click to see a demonstration of AutoRedraw."
  Print "These two lines will stay on the screen after you double click."
End Sub
```

Now, for the Click procedure, add

```
Private Sub Form_Click ()
  AutoRedraw = False          'keeps old stuff
  Cls
  Print: Print: Print      'third line
  Print "But this line will disappear after you double click."
End Sub
```

Finally, the Double_Click procedure is simply:

```
Private Sub Form_DblClick ()
  Cls                       'Clears line from Click() procedure
End Sub
```

The ClipControls Property and the Paint Event

Visual Basic activates the Paint event each time a part of the form is newly exposed. What happens within the Paint event in this case depends on how the ClipControls property is set at design time. If the ClipControls property is set to True (the default) and the AutoRedraw property is False, then Visual Basic repaints the entire object. If ClipControls is set to False, Visual Basic repaints only the newly exposed areas.

The ClipControls property has a few other features worth noting. Setting ClipControls to True also creates what Microsoft calls a *clipping region* around nongraphical controls on the object. This means Visual Basic creates an outline of the form and the controls on it in memory. Because the clipping region is created in memory, setting this property to False can reduce the time needed to paint or repaint the object. The cost is more time needed if the object is graphically complex. Clipping regions exclude the Image, Label, Line, or Shape controls.

tip: *If AutoRedraw is set to True, you can speed up your program by setting ClipControls to False.*

More on the Paint Event

In any case, if AutoRedraw is False, you write the necessary code in the Paint procedure whenever you want to redraw part or all of a form or picture box. Therefore, the least memory-intensive way to handle the problem of graphics disappearing because a user covered a form or picture box, is to redraw the image in the form or picture box in the Paint event procedure. Again this solution involves a trade-off between memory-intensive and CPU-intensive programming activities. Setting AutoRedraw to True uses up memory (if you have it), potentially speeding up the program. Using the Paint event procedure uses up time. You have to choose what's best for the application. At the extremes, the choice is easy: if the amount of drawing to be done is minimal, using the Paint event procedure is better. In any case, Visual Basic calls the Paint procedure for the object only if the AutoRedraw property of the object is set to False.

caution: *Be very careful about including in the Paint event procedure any commands that move or resize the object. If you include such commands, Visual Basic will just call the Paint procedure again, and you'll be stuck in an infinite regression.*

The Refresh Method

You will occasionally need to use the Refresh method when working with graphics. This method applies to both forms and controls. It forces an immediate refresh of the form or control and, as mentioned previously, will let you see an image develop even when AutoRedraw is True. If you use the Refresh method, Visual Basic will also call any Paint event procedure you have written for the object. This method is commonly used in the Form_Resize procedure to redisplay any graphics that are calculated in the Paint event procedure. Also, while Visual Basic handles refreshing the screen during idle time, occasionally you will want to control this process yourself. Whenever Visual Basic processes an *Object*.Refresh statement, it will redraw the object immediately and generate the Paint event, if the object supports this feature.

Saving Pictures

Finally, Visual Basic makes it easy to save the pictures you've drawn to a form or picture box. The SavePicture statement uses the following syntax:

SavePicture *ObjectName.Image, Filename*

The operating system uses the Image property to identify the picture in the form or picture box. If you leave off *ObjectName*, then, as usual, Visual Basic uses the current form. The syntax for this version of the method is

SavePicture *Image, Filename*

If you originally loaded the picture from a file by assigning an image to the Picture property of the form or picture box (see Chapter 16), Visual Basic saves the picture in the same format as the original file. (For example, icon files stay icon files.) Otherwise, Visual Basic saves the picture as a bitmap (.BMP) file.

An Example: Simple Animation

Although Visual Basic has many powerful tools to perform animation (see the sections "Animation and DrawMode" and "The PaintPicture Method" later in this chapter), you now have the tools to simulate one kind: a so-called drunkard's walk (or, more technically, a random walk). All this means is that you imagine an object whose movements you can plot over time. If it seems to move randomly, you have a random walk. To simulate this, start with a form with a single command button, using the default settings. For this program, all you need to do is start a new project and double-click the command button. As you've seen, this puts the button at the default location in the middle of the screen.

The Click event procedure will have the code for moving the button around. However, instead of moving the button a fixed amount, this project will move up and down and left and right randomly 50 times. If you run the program, you'll see that the square will spend most of its time in a narrow range around the center. For this program, pixels (ScaleMode = 3) seem to be the appropriate choice:

```
Private SubCommand1_Click()
  ' moving squares to imitate a random walk
  Dim X As Single, Y As Single
  Dim I As Integer

  Randomize
  Form1.ScaleMode = 3              'pixel scale

  X = Form1.ScaleWidth/2           'start roughly in center
  Y = Form1.ScaleHeight/2
```

```
  For I = 0 To 50
   XMove = 3*Rnd
   YMove = 2*Rnd
   If Rnd < .5 Then
     X = X + XMove
   Else
     X = X - XMove
   End If
   If Rnd < .5 Then
     Y = Y + YMove
   Else Y = Y - YMove
   EndIf
   If X < 0 Or X > ScaleWidth Or Y < 0 Or Y > ScaleHeight Then
    ' DO NOTHING
   Else
     Command1.Move X, Y
   End If
  Next I
End Sub
```

The first two If-Then-Elses give the size of the random motion. The Else clause of the third If-Then-Else actually moves the command button up or down and left or right, depending on whether the random number generator delivers a number less than one-half or not. Later sections of this chapter show you how to add the code needed to give a trace of where the control has been. If you add the commands to change the background color of the command button (see the section "Colors" later in this chapter), the results are usually a quite attractive random pattern.

Screen Scales

The default scale for forms and picture boxes uses twips. The default size for a form on an ordinary 14-inch VGA monitor is roughly 7,485 twips long by 4,425 twips wide. A twip is 1/1440 of an inch when printed, thus creating a form of roughly 5 inches by 3 inches if you use the PrintForm method.

The following table gives you the coordinates in one column and the location of the point in the other for a form of the default size (assuming your form has these dimensions).

Coordinates	Location
(0,0)	Top left corner
(7485,0)	Top right corner
(0,4425)	Bottom left corner
(7485,4425)	Bottom right corner
(3742,2212)	Roughly the center

If two points have the same first coordinate, they're on the same vertical line; if they have the same second coordinate, they're on the same horizontal line.

There are six other possible scales besides the default scale, as well as a totally flexible user-defined scale that you'll see in the next section. These scales are set by changing the ScaleMode property at design or run time, as shown here:

ScaleMode	Units
1	Twips (the default)
2	Points (72 per inch)
3	Pixels (the number of dots as reported by Windows)
4	Characters (units default as 12 points high and 20 points wide)
5	Inches
6	Millimeters
7	Centimeters

Once you set the ScaleMode property, you can read off the size of the *drawing area*, which is the area inside the form (excluding the title bar and borders) or control or the printable area on the paper. This is reported in the current units when you use the ScaleHeight and ScaleWidth properties. Since both ScaleHeight and ScaleWidth report their results using the units selected by ScaleMode, they are very convenient for resetting form-level or global variables in a Resize event procedure. On the other hand, the Height and Width properties of an object are less useful for graphics. This is because these properties give you the area of the object, including the borders and title bar if there are any. In graphics, you usually care more about the dimensions of the drawing area.

tip: *Use form or global variables for the Height and Width properties of the Screen object and recalculate these in the Form_Resize event. Then you can use a percentage of these variables in your code in order to make it easier to have your code independent of the particular monitor and card. An example of this is in Chapter 12.*

Custom Scales

The screen is normally numbered with (0,0) as the top left corner. This is obviously inconvenient for drawing tables, charts, graphs, and other mathematical objects. In most of these situations, you want the coordinates to decrease as you move from top to bottom and increase as you move from left to right. For example, mathematics usually uses an X-Y (Cartesian) system, with X measuring how much across you are from a central point (the origin) and Y measuring how much up or down from the center you are. For example, Figure 15-4 plots a few points on the X-Y plane.

The Scale method sets up new coordinates for forms and picture boxes that you can use in any of the graphics methods. For example,

```
Scale (-320,100) - (320,-100)
```

sets up a new coordinate system with the coordinates of the top left corner being (-320,100) and the bottom right corner being (320,-100). After this method, the four corners are described in a clockwise order, starting from the top left:

(-320,100)
(320,100)
(320,-100)
(-320,-100)

Figure 15-4
X-Y plane with points

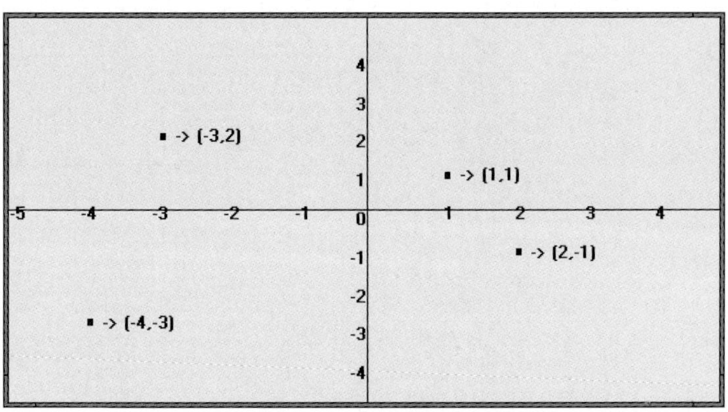

Now 0,0 is roughly in the center of the screen. This placement occurs because whenever Visual Basic processes a Scale method that changes to a custom scale, the program automatically finds the pixel that corresponds to your coordinates (rounding if necessary).

On the other hand, a scale such as

```
Scale (0,0) - (640,199)
```

would give you roughly the same detail as the previous scale, but (0,0) would be the coordinates of the top left corner. (This scale would be useful in converting ordinary GW-BASIC or QuickBASIC SCREEN 2 graphics.)

In general, the Scale method looks like this,

Scale (*LeftX*, *TopY*) - (*RightX*, *BottomY*)

where *LeftX* is a single-precision real number that will represent the smallest X coordinate (leftmost), *TopY* is a single-precision number for the largest Y (top), *RightX* is the right corner, and *BottomY* the bottom edge. For example,

```
Scale (-1E38, 1E38) - (1E38,-1E38)
```

gives you the largest possible scale, which means the smallest amount of detail. Large X and Y changes are needed to light up adjacent pixels.

The statement

```
Scale (-1,1) - (1,-1)
```

gives you a relatively small possible scale. Since a default-sized form will be 268 by 491 pixels, you can get very fine detail. Only tiny (less than 1) changes in X and Y are needed to light up adjacent pixels.

If you use the Scale method with no coordinates, Visual Basic will reset the coordinates back to the default scale of (0,0) for the top left corner and the units being twips.

note: *Some programmers prefer using a custom scale rather than percentages of the Screen.Height (ScaleHeight) and Screen.Width (ScaleWidth) properties in their code.*

ANOTHER WAY TO SET UP CUSTOM SCALES

The Scale method is the simplest way to set up a custom scale. There is one other way that occasionally may be useful. You can specify the coordinates of the top left corner and how Visual Basic should measure the vertical and horizontal scales. You do all this by using combinations of the ScaleLeft, ScaleTop, ScaleWidth, and ScaleHeight properties. For example, after Visual Basic processes

```
Object.ScaleLeft = 1000
Object.ScaleTop = 500
```

then the coordinates of the top left corner of the object are (1000,500). After Visual Basic processes a statement like this one, all graphics methods for drawing within the object are calculated based on these new coordinates for the top left corner. For example, if you made these changes to a form, then to place an object at the top left corner now requires setting its Top property to 500 and its Left property to 1000.

Similarly, if you set the ScaleWidth to 320 and the ScaleHeight to 200, the horizontal units are 1/320 of the graphics area, and the vertical units are 1/200 of the height of the graphics area.

Just as with the Scale method, you can use any single-precision number to reset these four properties. If you use a negative value for ScaleWidth or ScaleHeight, the orientation changes. If ScaleHeight is negative, the coordinates of the top of the object are higher values than those of the bottom. If ScaleWidth is negative, the coordinates of the left side of the object are higher values than those of the right side, as shown in Figure 15-5.

The Line and Shape Controls

You can quickly display simple lines and shapes or print them on a printer with the Line and Shape controls. They are different than most other controls because they do not respond to *any* events: they are for display or printing only. They are also quite sparing of Windows resources.

The Shape control can be used to display rectangles, squares, ovals, or circles. You can also use it to display rounded rectangles and rounded squares. The icon for the Shape control is three overlapping shapes. The Line control can be used to display lines of varying thickness on a form. The icon for the Line control

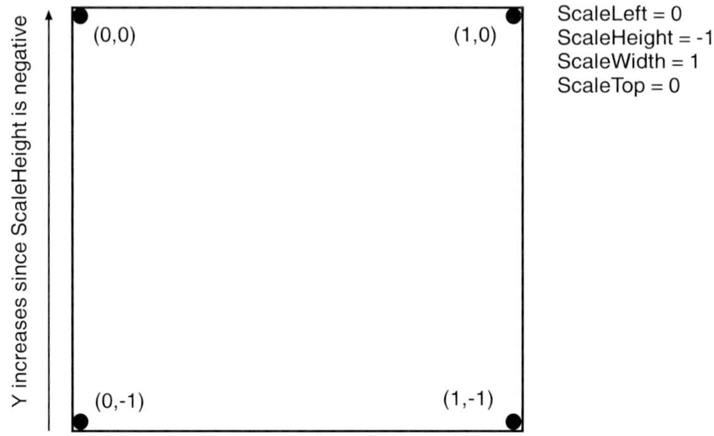

Figure 15-5 ScaleHeight with negative values

on the toolbox is a diagonal line. Figure 15-6 shows the various possibilities for lines and shapes.

The Shape Control

The Shape control has 20 properties. Usually, you change them dynamically with code while the application is running. The most important properties for the Shape control at design time are described in this section.

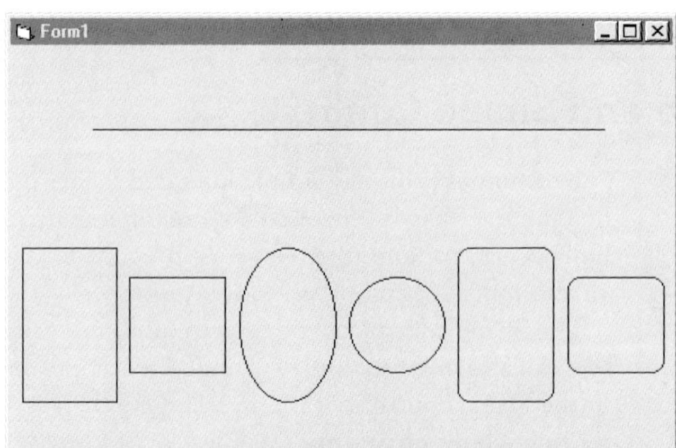

Figure 15-6 Possible Line and Shape controls

Shape The Shape property determines the type of shape you get. There are six possible settings:

Setting of Shape Property	Effect
0	Rectangle (default)
1	Square
2	Oval
3	Circle
4	Rounded rectangle
5	Rounded square

For example, if you add a Shape control in the default size and shape to a form and write the following in the Form_Click procedure, you can see the shapes for yourself.

```
Private Sub Form_Click
  Static I As Integer
  Shape1.Shape = I
  I = I + 1
  I = I Mod 6 'to prevent error
End Sub
```

BackStyle The BackStyle property determines whether the background of the shape is transparent. The default value is 1, which gives you an opaque border; BackColor fills the shape and obscures what is behind it. Set it to 0 (transparent) and you can see through the shape to what is behind it.

BorderWidth The BorderWidth property determines the thickness of the line. It is measured in pixels and can range from 0 to 8192 (rather too large to display on most forms).

BorderStyle Unlike image controls, the BorderStyle property for Shape controls has six possible settings, as shown in the following table. Having no border (BorderStyle = 0) prevents the control from being visible unless you modify the FillStyle and FillColor properties.

Setting of BorderStyle Property	Effect
0	No border
1	Solid (default)
2	Dashed line
3	Dotted line
4	Dash-dot line
5	Dash-dot-dot line

note: *If you set the BorderWidth property to greater than 1, resetting the BorderStyle property has no effect.*

(To see these in effect, add the line Shape1.BorderStyle = I to the previous demonstration program.)

FillColor, FillStyle The FillColor property determines the color used to fill the shape in the manner set by the FillStyle property. You can set the FillColor property in the same way as setting any color property, either directly via a hexadecimal code or by using the color palette.

The FillStyle property has eight possible settings:

Setting for FillStyle Property	Effect
0	Solid
1	Transparent (default)
2	Horizontal line
3	Vertical line
4	Upward diagonal
5	Downward diagonal
6	Cross
7	Diagonal cross

To see the various possibilities at work, modify the previous demonstration program as follows:

```
Private Sub Form_Click
  Static I As Integer
  Shape1.FillStyle = I
  I = I + 1
  I = I Mod 8 'to prevent error
End Sub
```

(This uses rectangles, the default shape. If you want to see the effect of FillStyle on the other shapes, add the appropriate Shape1.Shape statement.)

The Line Control

The Line control has 15 properties. Usually, you change them dynamically with code while the application is running. The most important properties for the Line control at design time are the BorderWidth property and the BorderStyle property. BorderWidth determines the thickness of the line. It is measured in pixels and can range from 0 to 8192 (too large to display on most forms). Like the Shape control, the BorderStyle property of the Line control has six possible settings, but as before, only the last five are really useful.

The most important properties at run time for the Line control are the X1, Y1, X2, Y2 properties. These govern where the edges of the line appear. The X1 property sets (or tells you) the horizontal position of the left end of the line. The Y1 property sets (or tells you) the vertical position of the left-hand corner. The X2 and Y2 properties work similarly for the right end of the line.

note: *These properties use the underlying scale of the container for the line control.*

Graphics via Code

If all you want to do is draw a few shapes on the screen, there is no need to use any of the graphical methods. On the other hand, once you master this material, you'll be able to take complete control of each dot that appears on the screen or that prints on the printer.

Colors

The first step is to decide what colors you want. If you do not specify a color, Visual Basic uses the foreground color of the object for all the graphics methods. There are four ways to specify colors. The first way is directly from the hexadecimal coding (see Chapter 5).

The second way is to use the RGB function. The syntax for this function is

RGB(*AmountOf Red, AmountOfGreen, AmountOf Blue*)

where the amount of color is an integer between 0 (do not blend in that color) to 255 (maximum amount of that color blended in). Strangely enough, this is exactly the opposite order of that used in the &HBBGGRR coding. (This is unfortunate because what this function does is return a long integer corresponding to the codes chosen, although you can still use this function in the Immediate window as another way to find the hex coding for a color.)

If you are comfortable with QuickBASIC and want to use the color scheme from there, use the fourth way, the QBColor function. The syntax for this function is

QBColor(*ColorCode*)

where *ColorCode* is an integer between 0 and 15. The colors this function gives are summarized in the following table:

0	Black	5	Magenta	10	Light green
1	Blue	6	Brown	11	Light cyan
2	Green	7	White	12	Light red
3	Cyan	8	Gray	13	Light magenta
4	Red	9	Light blue	14	Yellow
				15	High-intensity white

For example, you can set up a blank form and try the following demonstration program:

```
Private Sub Form_Click()
    Static CNumber As Integer

    BackColor = QBColor(CNumber)
    CNumber = CNumber + 1
    CNumber = CNumber Mod 16      'recycle after 16 clicks
End Sub
```

Because CNumber is a static variable, each click on the form gives you the next color in the table as the background color.

Pixel Control

Now you know how colors are assigned and can change the scale of your screen as you see fit. How do you turn a pixel on? The syntax for this method is

PSet(*Col, Row*) [, *ColorCode*]

(The Pset method doesn't support named methods.)

Since the color code is optional (as indicated by the square brackets), all you need to do is replace the parameters with the values you want. The value of the first entry determines the column and the second determines the row. After Visual Basic processes this statement, the pixel defined by that point lights up. Obviously, where that point is depends on what scale you've chosen. For example, in the ordinary scale, using the default size for a form. The line

```
PSet(3722,2212)
```

would turn on the center pixel on a standard 14-inch VGA screen, but after a ScaleMode=3 command, this would cause an overflow run-time error.

It is possible to use PSet outside the current limits of the form, but if you exceed the limits on the size of the screen, you'll almost certainly get an overflow run-time error. When you use PSet to turn on a point that is outside the form, Visual Basic records this information but doesn't plot any points. This is where the AutoRedraw property's being set to True can help. Suppose you ask Visual Basic to plot a point that is too large to fit the current size of the form and AutoRedraw is True for the form. Then the information isn't lost; set the WindowState property to 2 (maximized), and the point will show up.

For example, the following simple Form_Click procedure uses PSet to draw a straight line down the center of the screen and a line across the bottom of the screen. Notice that the vertical line goes a little bit beyond the default size of the form.

```
Private Sub Form_Click()
  ' line via PSet with a bit of 'clipping'
  Dim I As Integer
  AutoRedraw = True                   'slows things down a bit

  For I =0 To 5000
   PSet (3742,I)
  Next I
  For I =0 To 7485
    PSet (I, 3500)
  Next I
End Sub
```

Figure 15-7 Line via Pset (parts are hidden)

The second For-Next loop gives you a horizontal line near the bottom of the screen. Figure 15-7 shows what you'll see. However, if you maximize the form, you can see that the graphics information wasn't lost, as shown in Figure 15-8.

Suppose you want to erase every other dot in this line. Although there are many ways to do this, at this point the simplest is to notice that redrawing a

Figure 15-8 Parts revealed from Figure 15-7

point in the background color erases it. For example, you might add another loop that reads

```
For I =0 To 5000 Step 2
 PSet (3742,I), BackColor
Next I
```

You might suppose that this fragment would make Visual Basic erase every other point. However, because of the way Visual Basic rounds off coordinates, this probably won't work on your monitor. In fact, adding this fragment to the previous program will probably accomplish nothing or too much. The coordinates of the points that are erased are so close to the ones that are turned on that either no changes show up or all the points are erased. This is because twips are a much finer scale than the actual screen resolution. For this reason, one possibility is to change the program to work in ScaleMode 3 (pixels) and modify the limits on the For-Next loop accordingly. Another possibility is to use a much larger Step. (Fifty seems to work well.)

tip: *In a situation like this, where you need to know how many twips correspond to a single pixel, turn to Visual Basic's built-in TwipsPerPixelX/TwipsPerPixelY functions. (Since Windows API functions usually require pixels, these functions are often needed in using API graphics calls.)*

You can use the Point method to determine the color code of any point on the screen. This returns a long integer using the &HRRGGBB& code you saw in Chapter 5. The syntax is

object.Point(*x*, *y*)

where *x*, *y* are single-precision values giving the X (left/right) and Y (up/down) axes and vertical (Y-axis) coordinates of the point using the ScaleMode property of the form or picture box.

An Example Program: "Visual Basic A-Sketch"

The following program shows how powerful even a seemingly trivial method like PSet can be when combined with Visual Basic's event-driven nature. Many people find this program appealing because of its similarity to a popular toy called Etch-A-Sketch. This program imitates that toy. For those who aren't familiar with this toy, the idea is that you can control the growth of a line by twisting and turning two knobs that control the up/down and left/right directions. The trick (and what makes the game so appealing) is that the line has to be continuous; you can't break it up. Nonetheless, you can draw what appears to be circles and other complicated shapes by carefully combining twists of the up/down and left/right controls. It obviously isn't nearly as sophisticated as the Paint program supplied with Windows, but it is a lot of fun.

The following program imitates this game by using the KeyDown event procedure to detect the arrow keys. Each time you press UP ARROW, the pixel directly up from where you were turns on. Each time you press LEFT ARROW, the pixel directly to the left is turned on, and so on. If you hold an arrow key down, you can draw multiple pixels in the same direction.

The program needs two forms, one for directions (the startup form) and one for the drawing area. The second form should have AutoRedraw set to True. The initial screen should look like the one in Figure 15-9. The two command buttons have control names: btnDirections and btnStart. The following table summarizes the properties of the command buttons set at design time.

Control	Properties and Settings
First command button	Default: size, shape, color
ControlName = btnDirections	Caption = Directions
Location: left corner	
Second command button	Default: size, shape, color
ControlName = btnStart	Caption = Start!
Location: right corner	

Figure 15-9 Initial screen in Visual Basic A-Sketch

Here are the event procedures and what they do:

Event Procedure	Task
btnDirections_Click	Prints directions on startup form
btnStart_Click	Loads the form for drawing
vbKeyDown	Interprets keystrokes, plots

Here's the btnDirections_Click procedure:

```
Private Sub btnDirections_Click ()
  Print "This program imitates the Etch-A-Sketch (TM) game."
  Print "As you hold down an arrow key a line will grow in";
  Print " that direction starting"
  Print "from the center of the screen. Press the End key ";
  Print "to end while drawing.": Print
  Print "Click on the Start button to start."
End Sub
```

For the btnStart_Click procedure, you load the form that contains the drawing area and hide the directions:

```
Private Sub btnStart_Click ()
  Form2.Show
  Form1.Hide
End Sub
```

Now, the second form needs some form-level variables to contain information about how big the screen is.

```
Dim PixelHeight As Single, PixelWidth As Single
Dim WhereX As Single, WhereY As Single
```

The variables PixelHeight and PixelWidth hold the current size of the form. The program uses these variables to make sure the user doesn't go off the form. WhereX and WhereY give the current position on the screen.

The program sets all these variables as well as the ScaleMode in the Form_Load procedure for the form containing the drawing area.

```
Private Sub Form_Load ()
  AutoRedraw = True
  ScaleMode = 3                         'Pixels
```

```
  PixelHeight = ScaleHeight
  PixelWidth = ScaleWidth
  WhereX = PixelWidth / 2
  WhereY = PixelHeight / 2
End Sub
```

Next, to allow a user to resize the form, the program uses the Resize event procedure. The Resize event procedure is invoked by Visual Basic when the form is first displayed or if the user resizes it. This way you can change the allowable limits for drawing while the program is running.

```
Private Sub Form_Resize()
  PixelHeight = ScaleHeight
  PixelWidth = ScaleWidth
End Sub
```

Note that these methods are needed in both the Resize and Form_Load procedures in order to initialize the WhereX and WhereY variables in the Form_Load procedure. All the work is actually contained in the KeyDown event procedure attached to the second form. To make it easier to read the codes for the KeyDown procedure, this program uses the symbolic constants built into Visual Basic for the various keys.

```
Private Sub Form_KeyDown (KeyCode As Integer, Shift As Integer)
  Dim YesNo%
  Select Case KeyCode
    Case vbKeyLeft
      If WhereX <= 0 Then           'don't go off drawing area
        WhereX = 0                    'but round down may occur
      Else
        WhereX = WhereX - 1          'move left 1
      End If
    Case vbKeyRight
      If WhereX >= PixelWidth Then
        WhereX = PixelWidth
      Else
        WhereX = WhereX + 1            ' right 1
      End If
    Case vbKeyUp                      'up 1
      If WhereY <= 0 Then
        WhereY = 0
      Else
```

```
        WhereY = WhereY - 1
      End If
    Case vbKeyDown
      If WhereY >= PixelHeight Then
        WhereY = PixelHeight
      Else
        WhereY = WhereY + 1
      End If
    Case vbKeyEnd
      YesNo% = MsgBox("Are you sure you want to end?", vbYesNo)
      If YesNo% = vbYes Then End          '6 is Yes button click
    Case Else
      Beep
  End Select
   PSet (WhereX, WhereY)
End Sub
```

The message box uses Yes/No buttons and ends only if the user clicks the Yes button.

Lines and Boxes

Obviously, if you had to draw everything by plotting individual points, graphics programming would be too time-consuming to be practical. In addition to Line and Shape controls, Visual Basic comes with a rich supply of graphics tools, usually called *graphics primitives*, that allow you to plot such geometric figures as lines, boxes, circles, ellipses, and wedges with a single statement.

For example, the following fragment replaces the two For-Next loops in the PSet demonstration with the Line method:

```
Private Sub Form_Click()
  ' line via Line with a bit of 'clipping'
  AutoRedraw = True                    'slows things down a bit
  Line (3742,0) - (3742,5000)
  Line (0,3500) - (7485,3500)
End Sub
```

More generally, the statement

Line (*StartColumn*, *StartRow*) - (*EndCol*, *EndRow*), ColorCode gives you a line connecting the two points with the given coordinates, using the color specified by ColorCode. (The Line method also doesn't support named arguments.)

As another example, the following program gives you a starburst by drawing random lines in random colors from the center of the screen. This program uses a custom scale so that (0,0) is the center of the screen. Since the number of pixels in the default-sized form on a 14-inch monitor is 491 across and 268 down, (-245,134) is the top right corner and (245,-134) is the bottom right corner:

```
Private Sub Form_Click()
  'random lines in random colors
  Dim I As Integer, CCode As Integer
  Dim Col As Single, Row As Single

  Randomize
  Cls
  Scale (-245, 134) - (245, -134)
  For I = 1 To 100
    Col = 245*Rnd
    If Rnd < .5 Then Col = -Col
    Row = 134*Rnd
    If Rnd < .5 Then Row = -Row
    CCode = 15*Rnd
    Line (0, 0) - (Col, Row), QBColor(CCode)
  Next I
End  Sub
```

The body of the For-Next loop calculates a random point and color code on each pass. Another use of Rnd determines whether the coordinates are positive or negative. Next, the Line method tells Visual Basic to draw a line from the center of the screen to that point. The screen in Figure 15-10 is an example of what you get.

Last Point Referenced

Visual Basic keeps track of where it stopped plotting. This location is usually called the *last point referenced (LPR)*, and the values of the CurrentX and CurrentY variables store this information. If you are continuing a line from the last point referenced, Visual Basic allows you to omit the LPR in the Line method.

Figure 15-10
Starburst

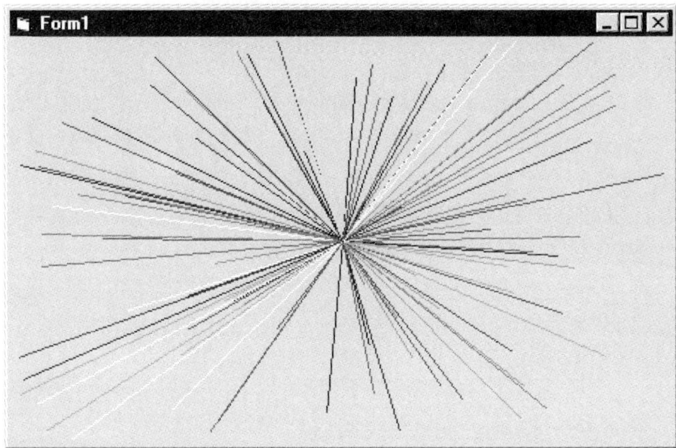

For example,

```
Line - (160, 90)
```

draws a line from the last point referenced to the point with the coordinates (160,90). When you start any graphics mode with a ScaleMode method or a custom scale, the last point referenced has the coordinates (0,0) in that scale. For custom scales, this need not be the top left corner. After a Line method, the last point referenced is the end point of the line (the second coordinate pair).

AN EXAMPLE DRAWING PROGRAM

Suppose you wanted to have a program that would use the mouse to draw lines on the screen. To make it more powerful, you can let a click on the right mouse button start and stop drawing. Surprisingly enough, a program to do this takes one form-level variable and just a few lines of code. You use the MouseDown event to determine whether the right mouse button has been clicked (see the next chapter). If it has, you flip the global flag and reset the CurrentX and CurrentY properties. You do the actual drawing in the MouseMove event.

Here's the code:

```
Dim OKDraw As Boolean ' set as a form level variable
```

```
Private Sub Form_MouseDown(Button As Integer, Shift As _
Integer, X As Single, Y As Single)
  If Button = vbRightButton Then OKDraw = Not (OKDraw)
  CurrentX = X
  CurrentY = Y
End Sub

Private Sub Form_MouseMove(Button As Integer, Shift As _
Integer, X As Single, Y As Single)
  If OKDraw Then Line -(X, Y)
End Sub
```

Relative Coordinates

Up to now you've been using *absolute coordinates*. Each point is associated with a unique row and column. It's occasionally useful to use *relative coordinates*, where each point is defined by how far it is from the last point referenced. For example, if you write

```
PSet(12, 100)
```

which makes (12, 100) the last point referenced, then you can write

```
PSet Step(50, 10)
```

to turn on the point in column 62 (50 + 12) and row 110 (10 + 100). In general, when Visual Basic sees the statement

Step (*X*, *Y*)

in a graphics method, it uses the point whose coordinates are X units to the right or left and Y units up or down from the last point referenced (depending on whether X and Y are positive or negative).

AN EXAMPLE: THE X-Y PLANE

Suppose you need to create an X-Y axis that allows numbers on the axes satisfying the following requirements:

-5<= X, Y <= 5

Here's a fragment that will do this:

```
Scale (-5,5) - (5,-5)
Line (-5,0) - (5,0)                'X Axis
Line (0,5) - (0,-5)                'Y Axis
' Now to label the axes add:
LetterHeight = TextHeight("X")     'How high is a letter
LetterWidth  = TextWidth("X")
CurrentX = -5 + LetterWidth
CurrentY = LetterHeight
Print "X - Axis";
For I = 1 To 6
  CurrentX = LetterWidth
  CurrentY = 5 + (I * LetterHeight)
  Print Mid$("Y Axis", I ,1)
Next I
```

This fragment calculates how high a letter is, using the TextHeight function, before resetting the CurrentX and CurrentY to allow a little space away from the axis. Since the CurrentX remains the same, all the letters are aligned, as shown in Figure 15-11. Finally, you might want to add numbers on the axes. You can do this by using the following fragment:

```
For I = -4 To 4
   CurrentX = I
   CurrentY = -LetterHeight/2
   If I <> 0 Then Print I
Next I
For I = -4 To 4
   CurrentX = -LetterWidth/2
   CurrentY = I-(LetterHeight/2)
   Print I
Next I
```

The result looks like the screen in Figure 15-12.

Figure 15-11
X-Y plane

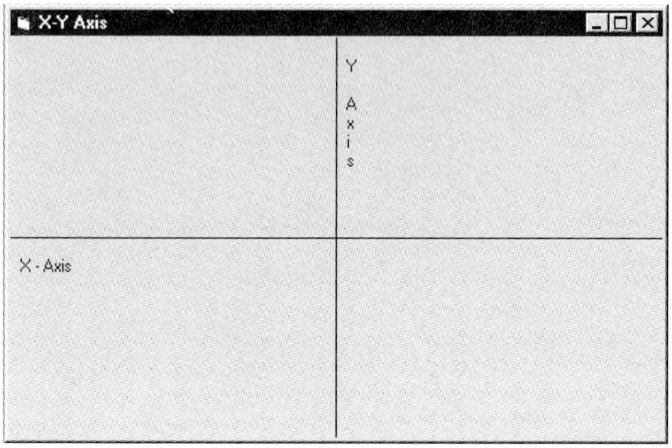

Grid Graphics

Suppose you want to draw a rocket ship, as shown in Figure 15-13. Since you can read off the coordinates from the diagram, it's easy (if a bit tedious) to write the following fragment.

```
Scale (0,0) - (25,20)
Line  (6,20) - (14,20)
Line  - (12,18)
Line  - (12,9)
Line  - (10,6)
Line  - (8,9)
Line  - (8,18)
Line  - (6,20)
```

It's at least theoretically possible to draw almost anything by outlining it using graph paper; just mimic the preceding example. However, as the object becomes more complicated, this method becomes less and less practical. One of the reasons that mathematics is needed for computer graphics is to give formulas for various complicated objects. The formulas then shorten the length of the program because they themselves incorporate an enormous amount of information. This makes it practical to write the program, whereas writing a few thousand PSet statements is not.

Figure 15-12 Labeled X-Y plane

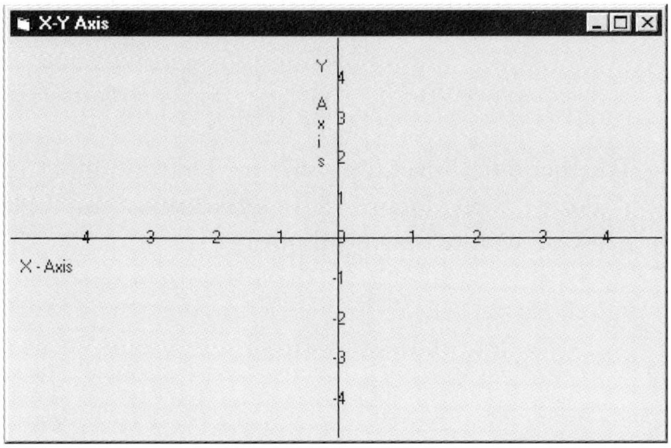

DrawWidth, DrawStyle

When you draw on the printer or the screen by using the PSet or Line method, Visual Basic uses dots that are normally drawn one pixel wide. (This is also true of circles. See the section "Circles, Ellipses, and Pie Charts" later in this chapter.)

Figure 15-13 Rocket ship via grid graphics

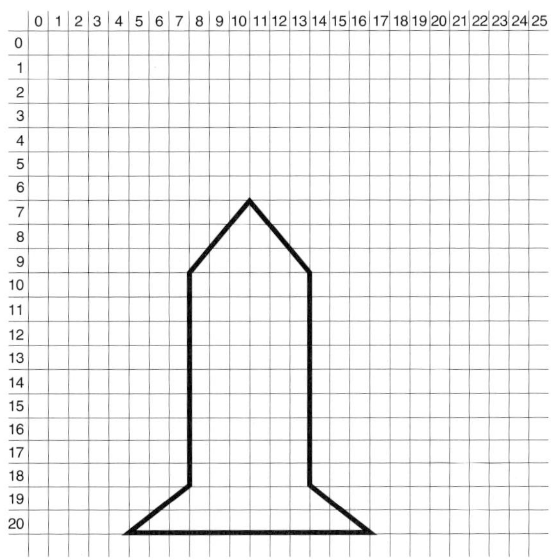

If you need to change the width of points or lines, use the DrawWidth property. The syntax for this method is

Object.DrawWidth = *Size%*

The theoretical maximum size for DrawWidth is 32,767.

For example, Figure 15-14 shows what you'll get if you run the following Click procedure on a blank form:

```
Sub Form_Click()
  ' Demonstrates DrawWidth
  WindowState = 2
  Dim I as Integer

  For I = 1 to 10
    DrawWidth = I      ' Form is default
    Line (0,I*ScaleHeight/12)-(ScaleWidth-15*TextWidth("D"), _
        I*ScaleHeight/12)
    Print " DrawWidth =";I
  Next I
End Sub
```

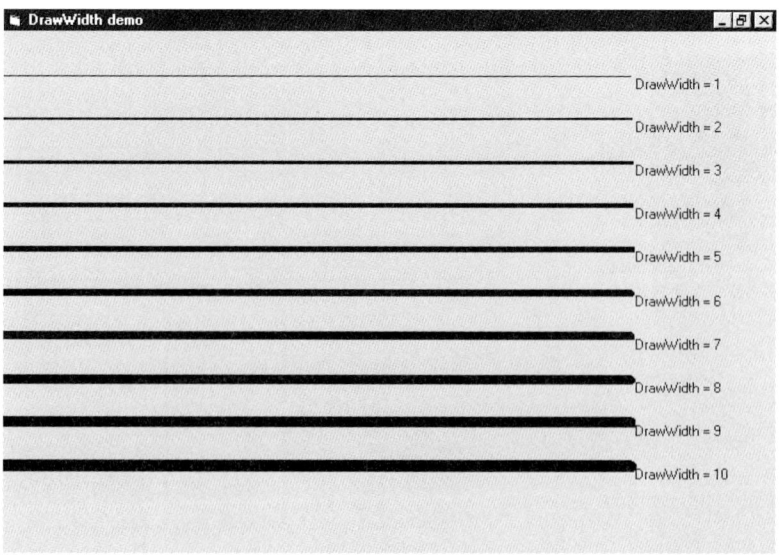

Figure 15-14 DrawWidth demonstration

If you do not want a solid line, all you need to do is change the DrawStyle property. You can see the effect of DrawStyle only when the DrawWidth is 1. There are seven possible settings when DrawWidth is 1:

Setting of DrawStyle Property	Effect
0 (default)	Solid
1	Dashed line
2	Dotted line
3	Dash-dot-dash-dot pattern
4	Dash-dot-dot pattern
5	Transparent
6	Inside solid (see the next section)

Figure 15-15 shows what you get if you run the following demonstration program and then enlarge the screen.

```
Private Sub Form_Click()
  ' Demonstrates DrawStyle
  AutoRedraw = True
  Dim I as Integer
  For I = 1 to 5
    DrawStyle = I
    Line (0,I*ScaleHeight/6) -(ScaleWidth, I*ScaleHeight/6)
    Print "DrawStyle =";I
  Next I
End Sub
```

Boxes

A modification of the Line method lets you draw a rectangle. The statement

Line (*FirstCol, FirstRow*) - (*SecCol, SecRow*), *CCode,* B

Figure 15-15 DrawStyle demonstration

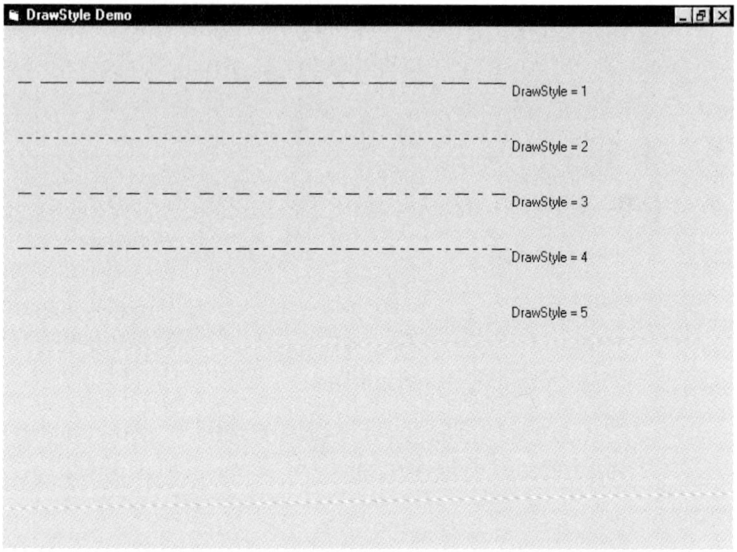

draws a rectangle in the given color code (*CCode*) whose opposite corners are given by *FirstCol*, *FirstRow* and *SecCol*, *SecRow*. For example, the following fragment gives you nested boxes in a scale like QuickBASIC's SCREEN 2:

```
Private Sub Form_Click()
  Dim I As Integer
  Scale (0,0) - (639,199)

  For I = 1 To 65 Step 5
    Line (5*I,I) - (639 - 5*I,199-I), ,B
  Next I
End Sub
```

Notice that this program leaves off the color code but still keeps the comma to separate out the B. Without this comma, Visual Basic would think the B was the name of a variable rather than the Box command. Leave out the comma, and Visual Basic would think you're asking for a line connecting

(5*I, I)-(639-5*I, 199-I)

with color code the current value of B. (Since an uninitialized numeric variable 0 has value 0, you probably get a color code of 0.)

The width of the line defining the boundary of the box is determined by the current value of DrawWidth for the object on which you are drawing. When you have a fairly wide line for the boundary, you can see the effect of using the "inside solid" (DrawStyle = 6). As the following demonstration programs show, using the inside solid line makes for a boundary of the box that is half inside, half outside (see Figures 15-16 and 15-17).

Notice in Figure 15-16 the boundaries of the boxes merge, whereas in Figure 15-17 they don't. This is because the inside solid style puts half the boundary of the box inside itself—so there's less of a common boundary. Here is a program that doesn't use InsideLine:

```
Private Sub Form_Click()
  ' Demonstrates Not Using InsideLine
  WindowState = 2
  DrawWidth = 10
  Line (100,100) - (ScaleWidth/2, ScaleHeight/2), , B
  Line(ScaleWidth/2, ScaleHeight/2) - (ScaleWidth-100,_
ScaleHeight-100), , B
End Sub
```

Figure 15-16 Boxes with normal boundary

Figure 15-17
Boxes with inside/outside boundary

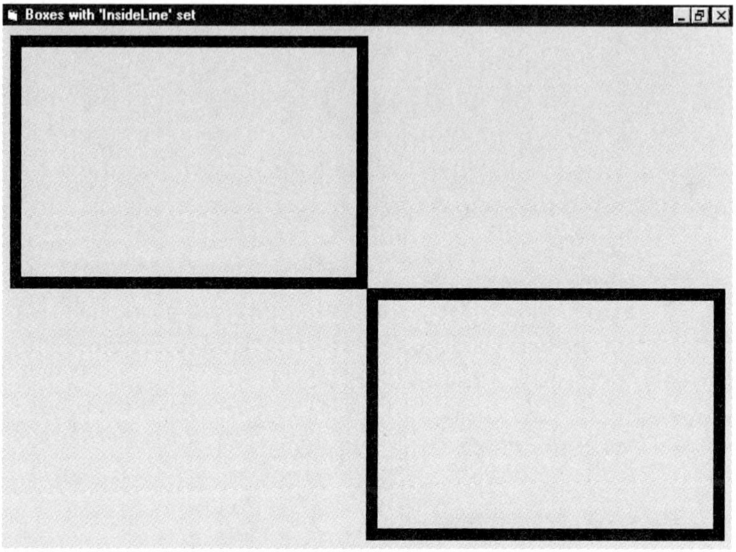

Now, to see InsideLine at work, run

```
Private Sub Form_Click()
  ' Demonstrates  Using InsideLine
  WindowState = 2
  DrawStyle = 6
  DrawWidth = 10
  Line (100, 100) - (ScaleWidth/2, ScaleHeight/2),,B
  Line(ScaleWidth/2, ScaleHeight/2) - (ScaleWidth-100,_
ScaleHeight-100), , B
End Sub
```

FILLED BOXES

You can arrange for the variant on the Line method that gives boxes to fill the box as well. All you need to do is use BF rather than B, and you get a filled box. Therefore,

Line (*FirstCol, FirstRow*) - (*SecCol, SecRow*), *CCode*, BF will yield a solid rectangle whose opposite corners are given by *FirstCol, FirstRow* and *SecCol, SecRow*. For example, change the nested box program so the code looks like this:

```
Dim I As Integer
Scale (0, 0) - (639, 199)
For I = 1 To 64 Step 5
 CCode = QBColor(I Mod 16)
 Line (5*I, I) - (639 - 5*I, 199-I), CCode, BF
Next I
```

You get a rather dramatic nesting of colored frames, as shown with shades in Figure 15-18. This happens for two reasons. The first is that the Mod function lets you cycle through the QuickBASIC color codes in order, and the second is that when Visual Basic draws each smaller rectangle, it overdraws part of the previous one using the new color.

FILLSTYLE, FILLCOLOR

Boxes (and circles—see the next section) are usually empty or solid, but Visual Basic allows you seven different patterns to fill boxes. To do this, you

Figure 15-18 Demonstration of colored boxes

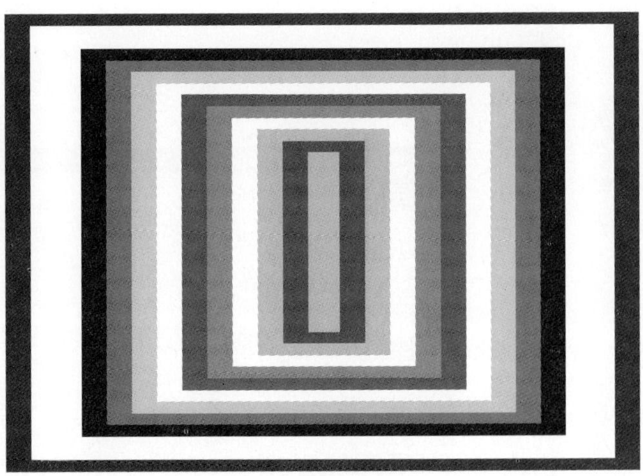

need to change the FillStyle property of the form or picture box. Here are the FillStyle settings:

Setting of FillStyle Property	Effect
0	Solid
1 (default)	Empty
2	Horizontal line
3	Vertical line
4	Upward diagonal
5	Downward diagonal
6	Cross
7	Diagonal cross

The screen in Figure 15-19 shows you the results of the following demonstration program.

```
Private Sub Form_Click()
  ' demonstrates FillStyle
  Dim I%
  Scale (0, 0) - (25, 25)
  For I% = 0 To 7
    FillStyle = I%
    Line (0, 3*I%) - (4, 3*(I%+.8)), , B
    CurrentX = 4.1: CurrentY = 3*I% + .5
    Print "This is FillStyle #";I%
  Next I%
End Sub
```

Figure 15-19 Fill patterns

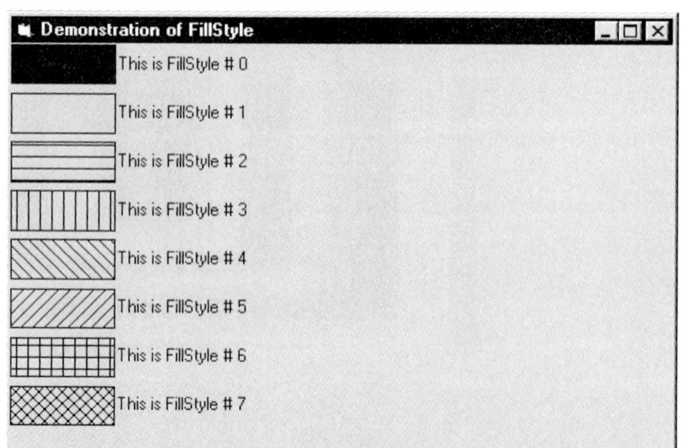

Once you have changed the FillStyle property from its transparent default (FillStyle = 1), you can use the FillColor property to set the color used for FillStyle. This property has the syntax

Object.FillColor = ColorCode

where, as usual, you can set the color code in any of the four ways mentioned previously.

AN EXAMPLE: FRAMING A CONTROL

Windows 3.1 (and now of course Windows 95) are much more visually appealing than Windows 3.0 for many reasons, but some of the little things have turned out to matter the most—one is the way controls look. For example, command buttons give the impression of being pressed when clicked. You can also make your application much more appealing by framing controls in various ways other than simply setting the Appearance property, using the frame control, or changing the BorderStyle property of the control.

To do this, you need to draw different-colored lines of various thicknesses around the control. If the colors you choose contrast with the background color of the form, you can get dramatic effects. Here's a routine that puts a frame around a single control:

```
Sub FrameControl (X As Control, CTop%, CRight%, CBot%, _
CLeft%, WidthOfFrame As Single)

  Dim LeftBoundary As Single
  Dim TopOfControl As Single
  Dim HeightOFControl As Single

  DrawWidth = 1
  FillStyle = 1
  ScaleMode = 1

  LeftBoundary = X.Left
  TopOfControl = X.Top
  HeightOfControl = X.Height
  WidthOfControl = X.Width

  Line (LeftBoundary, TopOfControl -_
WidthOfFrame)-(LeftBoundary_
+ WidthOfControl + WidthOfFrame, TopOfControl),_
```

```
QBColor(CTop%), BF
  Line -(LeftBoundary + WidthOfControl, TopOfControl + _
HeightOfControl + WidthOfFrame), QBColor(CRight%), BF
  Line -(LeftBoundary - WidthOfFrame, TopOfControl + _
HeightOfControl), QBColor(CBot%), BF
  Line -(LeftBoundary, TopOfControl - WidthOfFrame), _
QBColor(CLeft%), BF
End Sub
```

The idea of this routine is simple. You draw four narrow filled boxes around the four sides of the controls. This version of the routine accepts a control, four color codes for the sides, and a width.

If you call this routine three times, first with a thicker width and one set of color codes and then with successively narrower widths and different sets of color codes, the effects become even more dramatic. For example, if the BackColor of the form is light gray, try this routine with a black boundary around the box (QBColor(0)), a thick light gray box, and then thin white lines across the top and left (QBColor(15)) and dark gray across the bottom and right (QBColor(8)). Figure 15-20 was created using the following additional lines of code to surround a metafile that came with the Professional edition.

```
Call FrameControl(Picture1, 0, 0, 0, 0, 100)
Call FrameControl(Picture1, 7, 7, 7, 7, 75)
Call FrameControl(Picture1, 15, 8, 8, 15, 25)
```

Figure 15-20 Demonstration of special effects from framing controls

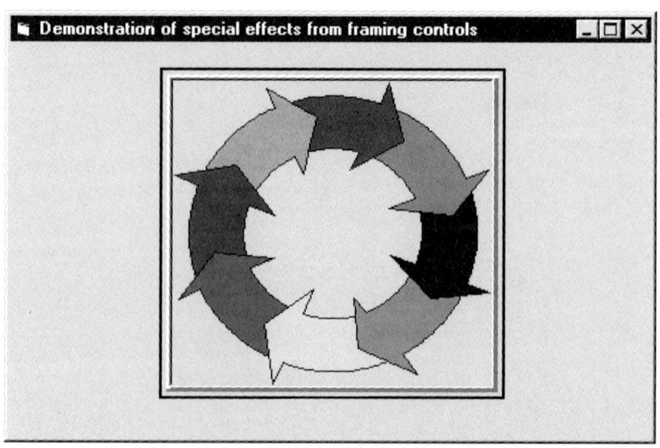

There are many other possibilities. Try reversing the white and gray lines; try leaving out the outer black lines. Experiment!

tip: *For a routine that can frame many controls at once, replace the Control parameter in the above routine by four additional parameters that come from the leftmost control, the top control, the bottom control, and the rightmost control. Use these in place of the information provided by the control in the routine above. One way to obtain these parameters is to set up an array of the controls you want to frame. Next, write a routine to find out this information by passing the array to the routine and analyzing the position properties of the controls in the array.*

(The Professional and Enterprise editions come with various 3-D controls—no work is needed except setting their various Bevel properties in order to get a nice effect.)

Animation and DrawMode

The main problem with animation in Visual Basic is in redrawing what was there before the moving object obscured it. Redrawing the whole screen would take too long. Drawing the line in the background color wouldn't work because this would erase what was there before.

The key to successful animation is to use the analog for drawing of the Xor operator that you saw in Chapter 8. Recall that when you use this logical operator twice, it brings you back to where you started. When you set the DrawMode property to 7 for a form or picture box, then drawing a line restores the background exactly as it was before. The most dramatic way to see this is to run the following demonstration program, which combines the starburst demonstration given earlier with a box that moves randomly each time you click the form:

```
Sub StarBurst()
  'random lines in random colors
  Dim I As Integer, CCode As Integer
  Dim Col As Single, Row As Single
  WindowState = 2
  Randomize

  Scale (-245,134) - (245,-134)
  For I = 1 To 100
    Col = 245*Rnd
```

```
    If Rnd < .5 Then Col = -Col
    Row = 134*Rnd
    If Rnd < .5 Then Row = -Row
    CCode = 15*Rnd
    Line (0,0) - (Col, Row) , QBColor(CCode)
  Next I
End  Sub
```

A Form_Resize procedure can simply call the StartBurst routine. Now, for the Form_Click procedure, try the following with the DrawMode line commented out and then with the line being executable:

```
Private Sub Form_Click()
  Static Col, Row As Single
  Static CCode As Integer
  DrawMode = 7

  'This line erases the box and restores the background
  Line (0, 0) - (Col, Row), QBColor(CCode), BF
  'These lines move the box randomly
  Col = 100*Rnd
  If Rnd < .5 Then Col = -Col
  Row = 50*Rnd
  If Rnd < .5 Then Row = -Row
  CCode = 15*Rnd
  Line (0, 0) - (Col, Row), QBColor(CCode), BF
End Sub
```

(Use the Run menu or the CTRL+BREAK combination to stop the demonstration.)

There are 15 other possible settings for DrawMode. In all cases, Visual Basic compares the color code for each pixel in the object that it is in the process of drawing with the color code of the pixel that was already there. This is done at the bit level by converting the color code to a bit pattern. For example, the DrawMode value of 7 that you've just seen applies the Xor operator to the color codes. A DrawMode property of 6 draws the new object by applying the Not operator to the color code of the original object. With a DrawMode of 4, Visual Basic applies the Not operator to the color code of the foreground and uses that code for drawing. You can find a complete list of the 16 possible settings for DrawMode in the online help, but 4, 6, and 7 are the most common values.

To see this at work, use the starburst fragment in the Form_Paint procedure and add the following Form_Click procedure:

```
Private Sub Form_Click()
  DrawWidth = 10
  DrawMode = 4
  Line (-245, 134) - (245, -134)
  DrawMode = 6
  Line (245, 134) - (-245, -134)
End Sub
```

Circles, Ellipses, and Pie Charts

Normally, to describe a circle in Visual Basic, you give its center and radius. The following fragment draws a circle of radius .5 units starting at the center of the screen:

```
Scale (-1,1) - (1,-1)
Circle (0,0), .5
```

The last point referenced (*CurrentX, CurrentY*) after a Circle method is always the center of the circle. You can also add a color code to the Circle method. For example,

```
Circle (0,0), .5 , CCode
```

would draw a circle of radius .5 in the color code indicated here by the variable CCode. The following demonstration program shows off the Circle method, which produces the nested circles shown in Figure 15-21.

```
Private Sub Form_Click()
  Dim I As Single, CCode As Single
  WindowState = 2

  ' nested circles
  Scale (-1,1) - (1,-1)
  For I = .1 To .7 Step .05
    CCode = 16*Rnd
    Circle (0,0), I, CCode
  Next I
End  Sub
```

Figure 15-21 Circle demonstration

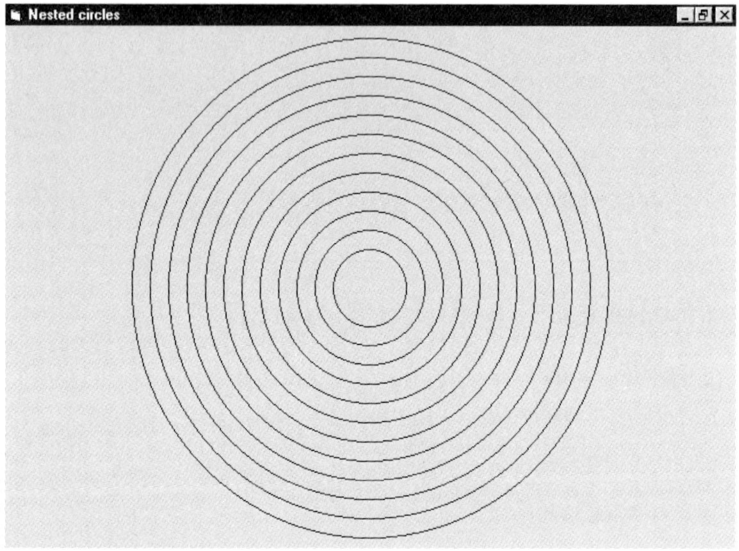

You may be wondering what exactly the radius is. Is it measured in column units or row units, or is the measure the same in both the horizontal and vertical directions, as a mathematical radius would be? It turns out that the Circle method usually counts pixels by columns (horizontal units) to determine the radius. If you use the same horizontal units as vertical units, then the only problems will come from the aspect ratio of the screen (the aspect ratio is the ratio between the height and width of your screen). Usually Windows takes care of any aspect ratio problems automatically. In fact, the major screen resolutions (640 X 480, 800 X 600, 1024 X 768) all have the same ratio. It's in the EGA area that you might have problems. You can take care of any aspect ratio problems with a variant on the Circle method, which will be discussed shortly.

You may have seen pie charts used to display data. Visual Basic sets up a pie chart with a modification of the Circle method. First, some terminology: a *sector* is a pie-shaped region of a circle, and an *arc* is the outer boundary of a sector, as shown in Figure 15-22.

To draw a sector or an arc, you have to tell Visual Basic at which angle to start and at which angle to finish. You do this using radian measure, which you may have learned about in school. (It is also used in the trigonometric functions in Visual Basic.) Radian measure isn't very difficult. It measures angles by what percentage of the circumference of a circle of radius 1 that the radian measure would give. For example, all the way around a circle of radius 1 is 2π units. It

Figure 15-22

A sector and an arc

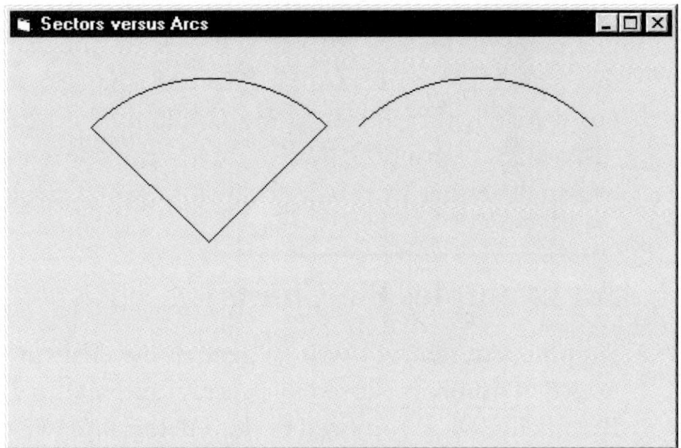

is also 360 degrees, so 360 degrees is equal to 2π radians. One-half of a circle of radius 1 is 180 degrees and is p units. Therefore, 180 degrees is π radians. Similarly, one-quarter of a circle (90 degrees) is 2π radians, and so on. To go from degrees to radians, multiply by $\pi/180$; to go back, multiply by $180/\pi$. (Since π is roughly 3.14159, 360 degrees is roughly 6.28 radians.) In any case, the statement

Circle (*XRad, YRad), Radius, CCode, StartAngle, EndAngle*

draws an arc of the circle starting at the angle given in radians by StartAngle and ending with EndAngle. (The Circle method does not, unfortunately, support named arguments.) To get a sector, use negative signs. Therefore, assuming you've set up Scale as (-1, 1) - (1, -1) and have set up a global variable called Pie = 3.14159 (or better yet, set Pie = 4*Atn(1) as a global variable), then the screen in Figure 15-22 may be obtained from the following code:

```
Scale (-1, 1) - (1, -1)
Circle (-.4, 0), .5, , -Pie/4, -3*Pie/4
' above line gives you the sector in Figure 15-22. And:
Circle (.4, 0), .5, , Pie/4, 3*Pie/4
' gives you the arc.
```

There are a few peculiarities of these methods that you should be aware of. The first is that although mathematics allows negative angles, Visual Basic does not. The negative sign only serves to indicate, "Draw a sector rather than an arc." The second peculiarity is that if you want your arc to start with a vertical line pointed due east (that is, 0 degrees = 0 radians), you shouldn't use -0 for the StartAngle or EndAngle. Instead, use -2 *π (= -6.28 . . .). The final peculiarity is that angles in the Circle method can only have values between -2π (-6.28 . . .) and 2π (6.28 . . .). (In the current version of Visual Basic, using 8*Atn (1) rather than 6.28 for 2*π seems to result in an error message.)

An Example: Pie Charts

Suppose you want to write a general pie chart program. This program takes a bunch of numbers (stored in an array) and sets up a pie chart using the numbers. Essentially, what you need to do is determine what percentage of the total each positive number is and set up an arc using that percentage. This should be a general procedure that is sent an array as a parameter:

```
Sub MakePie( A() As Single )
  ' This procedure takes an array of positive single
precision entries and
  ' creates a pie chart using proportions determined by the
  ' array.

  ' LOCAL variables: I,First,Last,Total,StartAngle,EndAngle
  ' Global variable is assumed to be TwoPie
  ' TwoPie should be 6.28 and not 8*Atn(1)

  Dim I As Integer, First As Integer, Last As Integer
  Dim Total As Single, StartAngle As Single
  Dim EndAngle As Single, LastAngle As Single

  First = LBound(A,1)
  Last = UBound(A,1)
  Total = 0
  For I = First To Last
    Total = Total + A(I)
  Next I
  Scale (-1,1) - (1,-1)
  StartAngle = -TwoPie
  For I = First To Last
    EndAngle = ((A(I)/Total)*TwoPie) + StartAngle
    Circle (0,0),.5, , StartAngle,EndAngle
    StartAngle = EndAngle
```

```
  Next I
End Sub
```

The key to this program is the statement determining the EndAngle. This statement determines what fraction of the total a particular entry is. Multiplying by TwoPie (roughly 2 * 3.14159) gives you the radian equivalent. Since the StartAngle is -2 *p, adding this angle gives you the necessary negative number for the size of the sector starting due east and going counterclockwise.

You can add other parameters to control the size of the circle used and the scale used. You could also change the procedure to pass an array of strings that you could use to label the sectors.

How can you test this procedure? Simply create some random arrays of random sizes with random positive entries and call the procedure.

This is only a sample of the kind of business-related graphics you can produce with Visual Basic. It would be very easy to modify this program to produce bar charts if that was what you needed. However, if you are constantly using presentation-style graphs, you should consider getting the Visual Basic Professional edition. This product has almost all the graphing capabilities you'd ever want available via a custom control (including 3-D bar and pie charts). The basics of using this control are described at the end of this chapter.

Ellipses and the Aspect Ratio

You convert the Circle drawing method to an Ellipse drawing command by adding one more option. This also lets you override Visual Basic's default settings if you need to adjust the aspect ratio for your monitor. The syntax for this method is

Circle [*Step*] (*XCenter, YCenter), radius, , , , aspect*

The four commas must be there even if you are not using the color code and angle options that you saw earlier. (Step is optional, of course.) This version of the Circle method lets you change the default ratio of columns to rows. (It's really an Ellipse command.)

If the aspect parameter is less than 1, the radius is taken in the column direction and the ellipse is stretched in the horizontal direction. If the aspect parameter is greater than 1, the radius is taken in the row direction and the ellipse is stretched in the vertical direction. The following program demonstrates this:

```
Private Sub Form_Click()
  Scale (-2,2) -(2,-2)
  Static I As Single

  Cls
  Circle (0, 0), .5, , , , I+ .1
  CurrentX = -2: CurrentY = 2
  Print "This is aspect ratio";Format$(I+.1,"#.#");
  Print ". Click to see the next size ellipse"
  I = I + .1
End Sub
```

As the aspect ratio gets larger, the ellipse gets closer and closer to a vertical line.

Curves

This is where the math starts. The first of the following sections uses the X-Y plane (Cartesian plane) and therefore a tiny bit of analytic geometry. The next section uses polar coordinates, and the last section uses some trigonometry.

The Scale method makes graphing any mathematical function trivial. The only problems come in deciding the maximum and minimum values to use for the Scale statement, which often takes calculus. However, as before, Visual Basic will clip any figure that is off the axis, so no problems result from setting the wrong scale, unless you are way out of line. In this case, you'll have to trap the overflow error that may result. You could have the error trap call a Resize procedure that would rescale the drawing area to allow the new information to be used. This might require recalculating all the points already drawn, however.

For example, here's a fragment that draws a cosine graph, as shown in Figure 15-23:

```
Dim I As Single, TwoPie As Single
TwoPie = 8*Atn(1)
Scale (-TwoPie, 1) - (TwoPie, -1)

For I = -TwoPie To TwoPie Step .01
  PSet (I, Cos(I))
Next I
```

Figure 15-23
Cosine graph

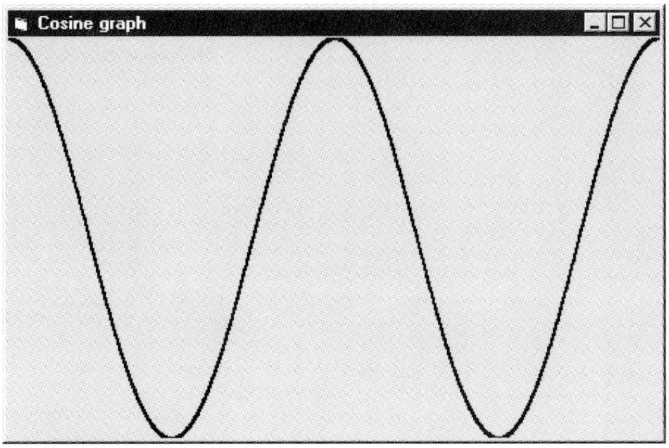

You saw earlier in this chapter how to put in the axes and mark them. If you want to experiment with other functions, you'll need to change the scale accordingly.

Pictures Without Too Many Formulas

Now that you know about the Scale method, you can get to some serious picture drawing. The first method you'll see depends on the following simple idea. Imagine two points in the plane (say, with a tortoise at one and a hare at the other) chasing each other. As the second point (the hare) moves, draw the line connecting the first point's (the tortoise's) old position to the new position of the second point. Now move the tortoise down this line a little bit (say, 10 percent of the way). Continue the process. The screen shown in Figure 15-24 is what you get after a few stages if the second point (the hare) moves directly down five units and the first always moves 10 percent of the way.

To implement this idea, you need a formula that calculates the new coordinate. Suppose first that you want the point halfway down on the line connecting, say, 50,100 to 100,200. It's pretty obvious that it has to be 75,150. Suppose, though, you wanted a point that was only 10 percent of the way along this line. This turns out to be 55,110 (since, in a sense, you have 50 X units to move and 100 Y units to move). In general, the formula to move T% of the way on a line connecting *X1*, *Y1* to *X2*, *Y2* is

```
(1-T ) * X1 + T * X2
```

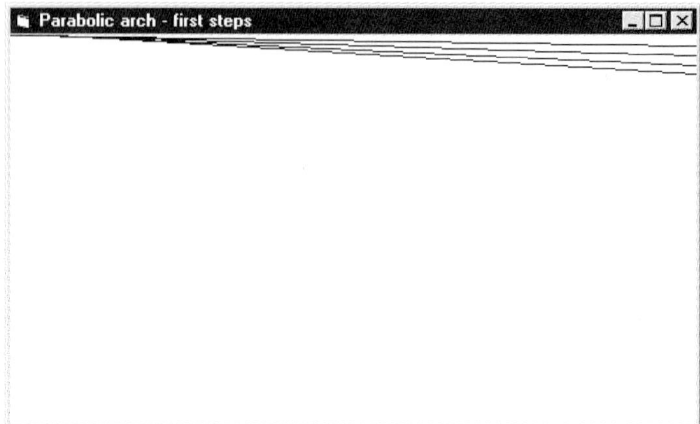

Figure 15-24 First steps in tortoises and hares

for the new X coordinate and

(1-T) * Y1 + T * Y2

for the new Y coordinate. Here, *T* is the percentage moved, expressed as a decimal. (Some people like to think of this as a weighing formula.) Here is the listing that implements this method, and the result is shown in Figure 15-25.

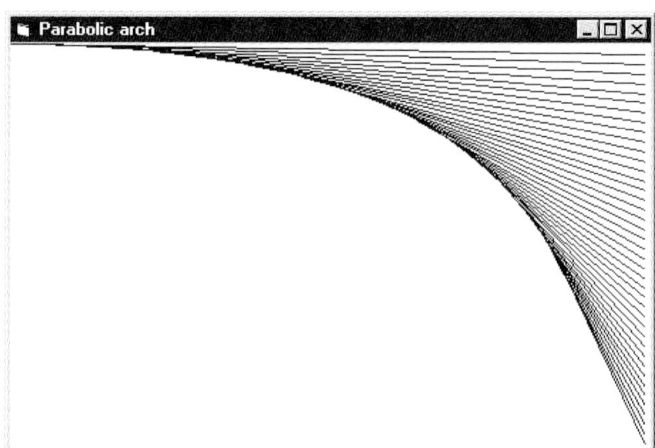

Figure 15-25 Parabolic arch

```
Private Sub Form_Click()
  ' parabolic arch by tortoise and hare
  Dim PerCent As Single, X1 As Single, X2 As Single
  Dim Y1 As Single, Y2 As Single

  Scale (-300, 100)-(300, -100)
  PerCent = .1
  X1 = -300: X2 = 300
  Y1 = 100: Y2 = 100
  Do Until Y2 < -100
    Y2 = Y2 - 5                        'down five units
    Line (X1, Y1)-(X2, Y2)             'connect the points
    X1 = (1 - PerCent) * X1 + (PerCent * X2)    'move down line
    Y1 = (1 - PerCent) * Y1 + (PerCent * Y2)
  Loop
End Sub
```

Although this is not a bad start, you don't really begin getting results until you add more animals (points). Imagine that four animals start at the corners of a square. The first animal chases the second, the second chases the third, the third the fourth, and the fourth chases the first. The screen in Figure 15-26 shows you what you get after only four moves. Obviously, what is happening is that each square is both rotating and shrinking. If you continue this process, then you get what was shown in Figure 15-1. Before you can work through the program, though, you'll need one more formula: the *distance formula* for

Figure 15-26

First steps in rotating squares

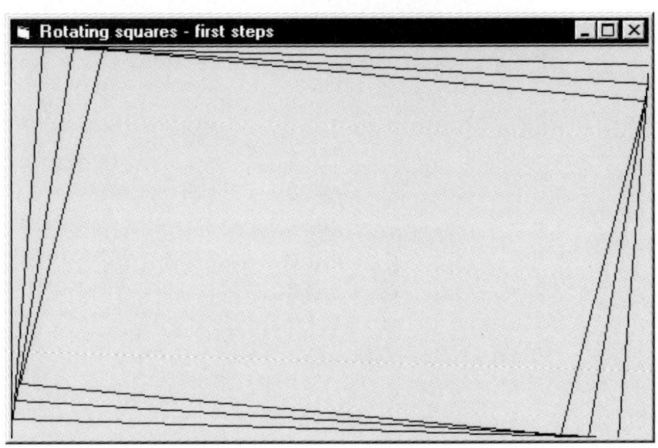

points in the plane. This says that the distance between two points, *X1, Y1* and *X2, Y2*, in the plane is

Sqr((*X2* – *X1*)^2 + (*Y2* – *Y1*)^2)

where Sqr is the square root function. In Visual Basic, you'll want to make a function out of it:

```
Function Dist(X1, Y1, X2, Y2) As Single
   Dim A As Single, B As Single

   A = (X2 - X1)*(X2 - X1)
   B = (Y2 - Y1)*(Y2 - Y1)
   Dist = Sqr(A + B)
End Function
```

The purpose of the distance function is to tell the program when to stop—to know when the animals are "close enough." Next, you need a MoveIt procedure for the chase:

```
Sub MoveIt (A, B, T)
  A = (1 - T) * A + T * B
End Sub
```

Here's the Form_Click( ) procedure that does all the work:

```
Private Sub Form_Click()
  Dim T As Single, X1 As Single, Y1 As Single
  Dim X2 As Single, Y2 As Single, X3 As Single
  Dim Y3 As Single, X4 As Single, Y4 As Single

  Scale (-320, 200)-(320, -200)
  T = .05                            'Percentage moved if 5%
  X1 = -320: Y1 = 200
  X2 = 320: Y2 = 200
  X3 = 320: Y3 = -200
  X4 = -320: Y4 = -200
  Do Until Dist(X1, Y1, X2, Y2) < 10
    Line (X1, Y1)-(X2, Y2)
    Line -(X3, Y3)
    Line -(X4, Y4)
    Line -(X1, Y1)
```

```
    MoveIt X1, X2, T
    MoveIt Y1, Y2, T
    MoveIt X2, X3, T
    MoveIt Y2, Y3, T
    MoveIt X3, X4, T
    MoveIt Y3, Y4, T
    MoveIt X4, X1, T
    MoveIt Y4, Y1, T
  Loop
End Sub
```

The Do loop ends when the points get close enough—less than ten units from each other. Notice that you can't use the Box command because the square is rotated.

The block of repeated calls to the MoveIt function finds the new coordinates for each of the four points. By adding more parameters, you could have made the MoveIt subprogram make the changes one point at a time instead of one coordinate at a time.

If you imagine the animals are moving independently along curves, then the kinds of pictures produced can be even more dramatic. The screen in Figure 15-26 shows one of the simplest ones. In this picture, you should imagine that one point is constantly moving around a circle around the origin while the other point chases it by moving along the line of sight. To write a program to do this or to construct one whose results are even more dramatic (chases along more complicated curves), you'll need formulas for the curves. That's the subject of the next section. That section shows you how to write the program that will draw what you see in Figure 15-27.

Figure 15-27 Circle chase

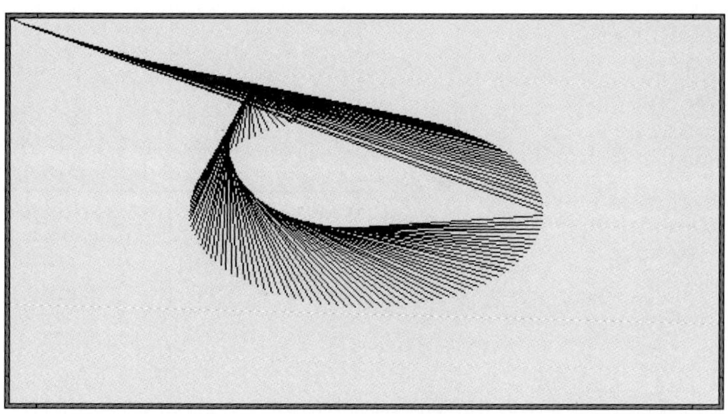

Polar Coordinates

Most complicated mathematical curves are more easily described by using polar coordinates. With polar coordinates, you describe the position of a point by saying how far it is from the origin and what angle a line connecting the origin to it makes with the positive X axis. Figure 15-28 shows this.

To go from polar coordinates to X-Y coordinates, use the formulas

```
X=R * Cos(Angle)
```

and

```
Y=R * Sin(Angle)
```

where *Angle* is the angle indicated in Figure 15-28. (These formulas come from dropping a perpendicular to the X axis and making a right triangle.)

To go from X-Y coordinates to polar coordinates, use

$$R = \sqrt{X^2 + Y^2} \text{ (in Visual Basic, Sqr(X*X + Y*Y))}$$

and the angle is Atn(Y/X) (unless X is zero).

The point of polar coordinates for computer graphics is that the equation of a curve may have a much simpler formula than in rectangular (X-Y) coordinates.

Figure 15-28 Polar coordinates

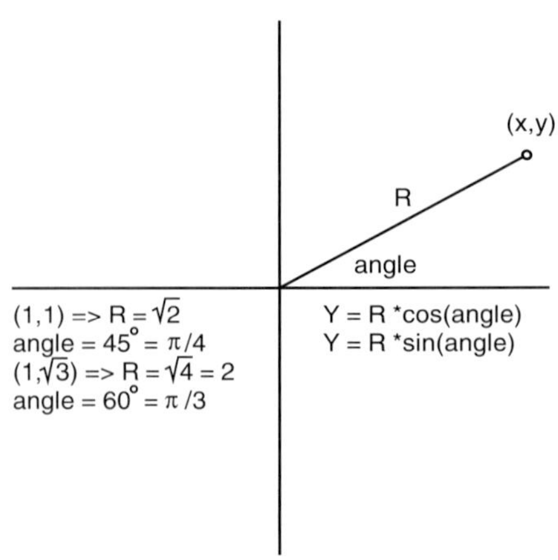

For example, the equation of a circle of radius .5 around the origin is simply R 20=.5 (instead of $X^2+Y^2 = 25$). This means the expressions

```
R * Cos(Theta)

R * Sin(Theta)
```

where the angle Theta runs from zero to 2π radians are the X and Y coordinates of a circle in polar coordinates.

Here's the program that runs a chase around a circle, as was shown in Figure 15-27:

```
Private Sub Form_Click ()
  Dim X1 As Single, Y1 As Single, X2 As Single
  Dim Y2 As Single, TwoPie As Single, I As Single

  Scale (-1, 1) - (1, -1)
  X1 = -1
  Y1 = 1
  TwoPie = 8 * Atn(1)
  For I = 0 To TwoPie Step .05
    X2 = .5 * Cos(I)
    Y2 = .5 * Sin(I)
    Line (X1, Y1)-(X2, Y2)
    X1 = (.95 * X1) + (.05 * X2)
    Y1 = (.95 * Y1) + (.05 * Y2)
  Next I
End Sub
```

Polar coordinates let you draw much more complicated figures. For example, you can easily draw objects like a four-leaf clover, as shown in Figure 15-29. The formula for the four-leaf clover curve is

```
Cos(2*Angle)
```

as the angle runs from zero to 2π (0° to 360°). (The rectangular X-Y version is very messy.) Combine this formula with the conversion formulas for X and Y given previously, and you have the following simple fragment that draws a four-leaf clover:

```
Private Sub Form_Click ()
  Dim X As Single, Y As Single
  Dim TwoPie As Single, I As Single, R As Single

  TwoPie = 8 * Atn(1)
  Scale (-2, 2) - (2, -2)
  For I = 0 To TwoPie Step .01
    R = Cos(2 * I)
    X = R * Cos(I)
    Y = R * Sin(I)
    PSet (X, Y)
  Next I
End Sub
```

Don't be surprised if this takes a bit of time. After all, it requires a few thousand sine and cosine computations.

Combine this with a chase and you get something like what is shown in Figure 15-30. (You can easily modify the "circle chase" program given previously to draw this.)

Of course, you have to know the formula for whatever object you're trying to draw. Over the years, people have collected this information, and you can

Figure 15-29 Four-leaf clover

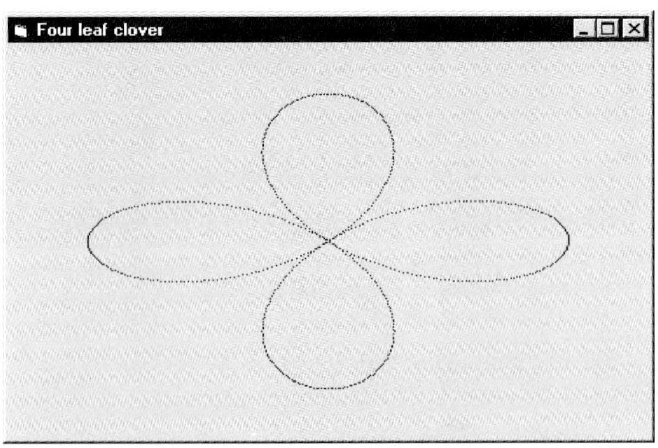

find books with massive lists of figures and their polar equations. Here's a short list of some of the more common ones:

Polar Equation	Figure
R = PositiveNumber	Circle of that radius
R = 1 + Sin(2*z)	Infinity symbol on angle
R = 1 + Cos(z)	Cardioid (heart-shaped)
R = 1 + 2*Cos(z)	Limacon (Write a program to find out what this is!)
R = Sin(n*z)	Petaled rose—number of leaves depends on n>2
R = z/c	Spiral
R =1 + 2*Cos(2*z)	Loop-the-loop
R = Sec(z) + Tan(z)	Strophoid (z <> 0,90,180...)
R = Sec(z) + 1	Conchoid
R^2 = Cos(2*z)	Lemniscate
x = Cos(z)^3	Astroid
y = Sin(t)^3	Also an astroid
x = 3*Cos(z)-Cos(3*z)	Nephroid
y = 3*Sin(z)-Sin(3*z)	Also a nephroid

It's easy to modify the four-leaf clover program to draw any one of these objects.

Figure 15-30 Four-leaf clover chase

The PaintPicture Method

One problem with earlier versions of Visual Basic was that there was no quick way within the program to paint a picture at a specific place on a form or picture box. (You had to use the BitBlt API call.) Visual Basic 4 has added a version of this API call directly to its language. This new method is called *PaintPicture*. It has many uses—for example, it lets you do simple animation quite effectively solely within Visual Basic.

The simplest version of the syntax for PaintPicture looks like this:

object.PaintPicture picture, *x1*, *y1*, *width*, *height*

The object can refer to any form, picture box, or the printer. (If you leave it out, Visual Basic assumes you mean the form.) The picture parameter gives the source of the graphic to be drawn. (For example, it could be the Picture property of a picture box.) Finally, the x1 and y1 parameters give the coordinates of the top left corner where you want the picture to appear (using the scale of the object parameter).

To see the PaintPicture method at work, add a picture box with the default size and width to the form. Assign the Picture property of the picture box to any of the bitmaps that come with Visual Basic (look in the subdirectories of the BITMAPS directory under the VB directory). Now try the following code:

```
Private Sub Form_Click()
  Dim I As Integer, J As Integer
  Dim NumberOfCols As Integer, NumberOfRows As Integer
  Picture1.Visible = False
  NumberOfRows = Form1.ScaleHeight / Picture1.Height
  NumberOfCols = Form1.ScaleWidth / Picture1.Width
  For I = 1 To NumberOfRows
    For J = 1 To NumberOfCols
       Form1.PaintPicture Picture1.Picture, (J - 1) *
Picture1.Width, (I - 1)*_ Picture1.Height, Picture1.Width
    Next J
  Next I
End Sub
```

What this code first does is figure out the number of copies of the picture you can place on the form. For example, if the picture box is 400 twips high and the form is 4400 twips high, you can have 11 rows. (A similar calculation is made for the columns.) Next, comes the crucial line,

```
Form1.PaintPicture Picture1.Picture, (J - 1) *
Picture1.Width, (I - 1)*
Picture1.Height, Picture1.Width
```

which paints multiple copies of the picture on the form.

By the way, if you add the following code to the Form_Resize procedure, you can see the effects of this code for forms of varying sizes:

```
Private Sub Form_Resize()
  Form_Click
End Sub
```

Finally, the full version of PaintPicture has the following syntax (it doesn't use named parameters, unfortunately):

```
object.PaintPicture picture, x1, y1, width1, height1, x2, y2, _
width2, height2,
opcode
```

The first three parameters you have already seen—they are all required. All the remaining parameters are optional. However, if you want to use an optional argument, you must specify all the optional arguments that would appear before it. (No empty commas allowed!)

The optional width1 and height1 parameters are single-precision values that let you set the width and height of the resulting picture. The optional x2 and y2 parameters let you specify single-precision values that give the left/right (x) and up/down (y) coordinates of a clipping region within the original picture. The optional width2 and height2 parameters are single-precision values that give the coordinates of a clipping region within the original picture.

The optional opcode parameter is a long integer that is used only with bitmaps. This parameter will affect how the picture blends with whatever image was at the location. Its uses are highly specialized, so please refer to the online help for the BitBlt API function call in WIN32API.TXT if you think you need to use this. (It uses the same values as the dwRop parameter in the BitBlt function.)

tip: *You can flip a bitmap horizontally or vertically by using negative values for the destination height (height1) or the destination width (width1).*

The Graph Control

If you have the Professional edition and need to draw graphs, most of the work is done for you—it's all built into the Graph custom control. (Since it is a custom control, you'll need to add it to the toolbox by the methods described in Chapter 2. The files are called GRAPH16.OCX and GRAPH32.OCX for the 16- and 32-bit versions, respectively.)

This section gives you the basic events, properties, and methods of this extremely powerful control. (Since the reference for the Graph control takes up 75 pages, only the high points are touched on here!)

tip: *The Graph control supplied with Visual Basic Professional edition is a less powerful version of the one produced by Pinnacle Publishing (1-206-251-1900). If you find yourself needing more graph types or things like curve fitting, check out the full version.*

The Graph control lets you construct 11 types of graphs. They are listed here, with examples of the most common ones.

Two- and three-dimensional pie charts (either exploded or not):

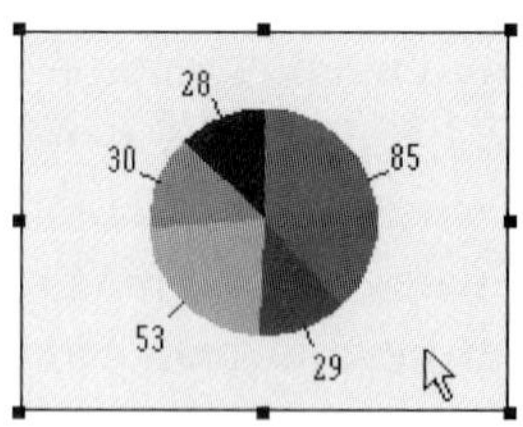

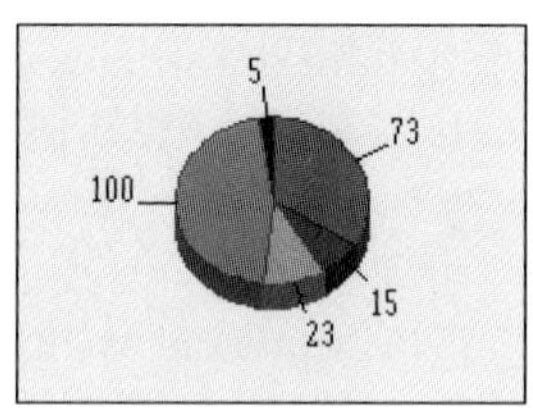

Two- and three-dimensional bar charts:

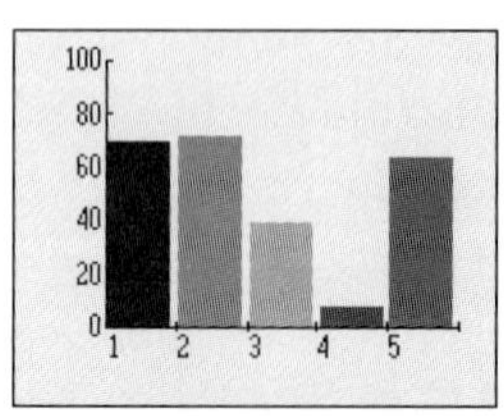

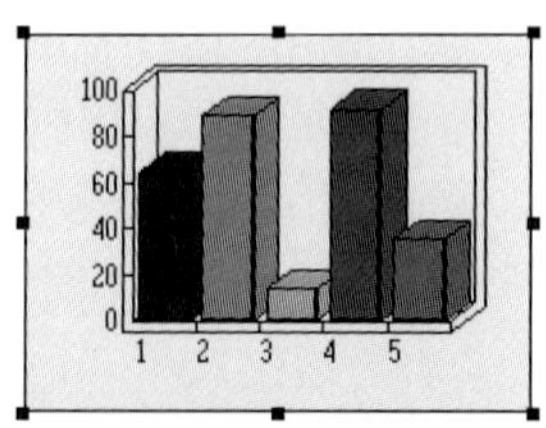

Line charts:

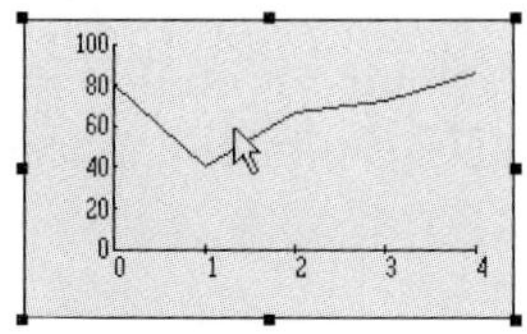

Log/line charts:

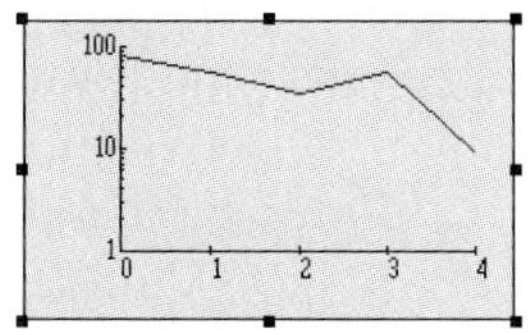

Area charts:

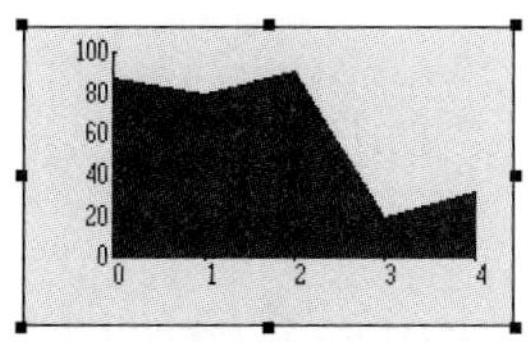

Scatter charts:

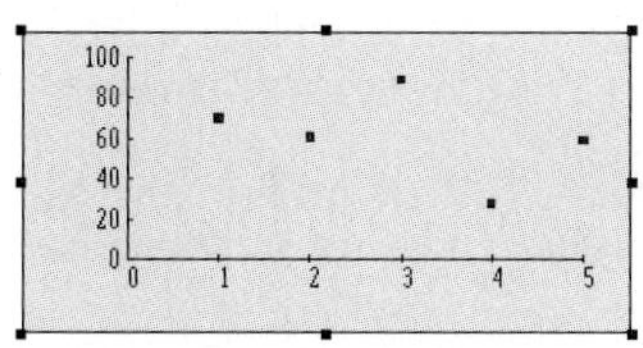

There are also high-low close charts, Gantt charts, and polar charts (for more specialized uses, such as stock market plotting).

Although you design the graphs when you're building your project, you're not restricted to that. In fact, the graphing facility that the Graph control adds to Visual Basic is so useful because you can easily write code that allows the user to do the following while the project is running:

- Change or add to the data used for the graph. Given new data, the Graph control will redraw the graph automatically.
- Rescale the graph, change labels, or switch to a new kind of graph that displays the data from a different point of view.

- Send either a bitmap or Windows metafile version of the graph to the printer.
- Use the clipboard (DDE or OLE—see Chapter 18) to incorporate graphs into other Windows applications, such as word processors and desktop publishers.

You release all of these features by changing the values of the 71 (!) properties associated with the Graph control. (The Custom property dialog box is *very* helpful in dealing with the graph control's properties.) The property that determines the type of graph is called the GraphType property. For example, suppose you started with a two-dimensional bar chart at design time. Now you want to switch to a three-dimensional bar chart while the program is running. All you need to do is have Visual Basic process the following line of code:

```
Graph1.GraphStyle=gphBAR3D
```

This uses a symbolic constant supplied with the control. (To see all the constants use the Object Browser to look at the GraphLib Library.)

Using the Graph Control

When you add a Graph control to your form, Visual Basic automatically adds five random points for data and draws a bar chart accordingly. This lets you see the effect of the changes you make to the properties at design time. (Add a Graph control and then try the various settings of the GraphStyle property to see what I mean.) Essentially all the properties of the Graph control can be set at design time—and their effects can be seen immediately.

The key to using the Graph control for your data is the GraphData property. To add the data at design time:

1. Set the NumPoints property to the number of values you will be entering.
2. Set the AutoInc property to 1 (on).
3. Type each number into the value column for this property and press ENTER. The data is automatically added to the graph.

The graph will be updated as you enter the data. In particular, it will be rescaled as needed. (If you change the GraphStyle property at design time, you will see the effects immediately.)

At run time the easiest way to proceed is

1. Set the AutoInc property to 1 (on).
2. Set the NumPoints property to the number of points you want to plot.
3. Set the DataReset property to 1. (This tells the Graph control to use the new data.)
4. Use as many statements as you need of the form

```
GraphControlName.GraphData = Value
```

5. Set the DrawMode property to 2 ("draw") to actually draw the graph.

For example, the following Sub program takes the values stored in an array of single-precision numbers and then graphs them in a Graph control whose name would be passed as a parameter as well.

```
Sub GraphIt( A() As Single, Foo As Graph)
  Dim I As Integer
  Foo.DataReset = 1
  Foo.AutoInc = 1
  Foo.NumPoints = UBound(A) - LBound(A)

  For I = LBound(A) To UBound(A)
    Foo.GraphData = A(I)
  Next I
  Foo.DrawMode = 2
End Sub
```

Brief descriptions of the most important properties of the Graph control follow—there are no methods or events that will not be familiar to you. (If you need more information, please consult the Custom Control reference supplied with the Professional edition.) Before describing the properties, you'll need to know some terminology. An *array property* for the Graph control is a property that takes a group of data. The GraphData property that you have seen is an example of an array property. (Unfortunately, none of the array properties will take an actual array—you will always have to program a loop as in the above example.) A *data set* is the information that will be displayed in the graph.

AutoInc The AutoInc Property should generally be on (setting = 1). It allows you to set the properties of the points without having to increment the ThisPoint counter property that controls which point is currently being set. When the NumSets property (which controls the number of distinct types of data you are graphing) is greater than 1, the AutoInc property tells the control to go through all the points in the first data set and then move on to the first point in the next data set.

BottomTitle The BottomTitle property gives the string to go at the bottom of the graph, parallel to the horizontal axis. (This has no effect on pie charts.)

ColorData The ColorData property lets you set the colors for each of the data sets on the graph. For pie charts and bar graphs with only one data set (NumSets = 1), use it to specify a color for each point. The ColorData property is an array property so that you can set it sequentially for each point (or each data set).

DataReset You saw the DataReset property at work in the example above. In general, you use this property to remove any information stored in a particular array property of the graph control. This lets you start anew. The syntax is

[*FormName.*]Graph.DataReset[= *setting%*]

The effects of the various settings are described in the following table.

Setting	Property It Resets
0	(Default) None
1	GraphData
2	ColorData
3	ExtraData
4	LabelText
5	LegendText
6	PatternData
7	SymbolData
8	XPosData
9	All Data

For example, the statement

```
Graph1.DataReset = 9
```

resets all data sets to be blank.

DrawMode The DrawMode property defines how the graph should be drawn. (In the example program, you saw how a setting of DrawMode = 2 was necessary to actually draw the graph.)

The following table shows the various effects of the DrawMode property.

DrawMode Setting	Effect
0	The graph will not appear. When you want the graph to appear, set DrawMode to 2.
1	The graph remains blank, but the caption and background color are changed to reflect the Caption and Background properties.
2	(Default) At design time, this redraws your graph every time you change a property. At run time, setting DrawMode to 2 redraws the graph.
3	After a brief pause, the graph appears complete—instead of being built in stages.
4	Copies the image of the graph to the clipboard in either bitmap or metafile format. If DrawMode is set to 3 (Blit), it is in bitmap format; otherwise, it is in metafile format.
5	Prints a copy of the graph. (See the PrintStyle property.)
6	Writes an image of the graph as either a bitmap (.BMP when DrawMode = 3) or metafile (.WMF). You must first set the ImageFile property to be the name for the file.

ExtraData The ExtraData property lets you explode pie charts (0 for not exploded, 1 for exploded) or specify the color of a three-dimensional bar chart. (When used with three-dimensional bar charts, it is an array property, so you can set the colors of the individual bars.)

GraphCaption The GraphCaption property gives the caption of the graph.

GraphData As you have seen, the GraphData property sets the data to be graphed. Where the data is placed on the graph is determined by the current setting of the ThisPoint and ThisSet properties.

GraphStyle The GraphStyle property determines the characteristics of the graph. The effect depends on what kind of graph you are working with (the current value of the GraphType setting).

GraphTitle The GraphTitle property lets you give a title to the graph (up to 80 characters are allowed).

GraphType The GraphType property specifies the type of graph, as shown in the following table.

GraphType Setting	Effect
0	None
1	2-D pie
2	3-D pie
3	(Default) 2-D bar
4	3-D bar
5	Gantt
6	Line
7	Log/line
8	Area
9	Scatter
10	Polar
11	High-low close

ImageFile The ImageFile property lets you set a file name where you want the current graph stored (when DrawMode is set to 6). The appropriate extension (.BMP or .WMF) is added automatically. If you don't specify the path, Visual Basic uses the current directory.

LabelEvery The LabelEvery property works with the LabelText array property and determines how often labels are displayed on the X axis. The limits are from 1 to 1000. (If you set LabelEvery to 1, you get a label for every element in the LabelText array.)

Labels The Labels property determines whether labels are displayed along the graph's X and Y axes. For pie charts, this property determines whether labels are displayed at all. The possible settings are 0 for no labels, 1 for both, 2 for X axis only, and 3 for Y axis only.

LabelText The LabelText property is an array property that gives the labels. You enter the text (up to 80 characters) sequentially. (If you don't set any text for the LabelText property, the Graph control uses the value of the ThisPoint property for the labels of all graphs except pie charts. For pie charts, if no LabelText is specified, the Graph control shows the size of the slices.

LeftTitle The LeftTitle property gives the text (also up to 80 characters) to place at the left of the vertical axis.

LegendText The LegendText property is an array property that gives the legend for the graph. It too is limited to 80 characters per item.

NumPoints You have seen this important property in the example. The NumPoints property specifies the number of points to use for each data set. (You can plot up to 3,800 points.)

NumSets The NumSets property allows you to have more than one data set on the same graph. (For example, you might want to have both Microsoft's sales per year and the number of PCs sold in order to see the correlation.)

PrintStyle If you are lucky enough to have a color printer, the PrintStyle property lets you determine how the graph is printed when the DrawMode property is 5. The following table lists the PrintStyle property settings for the Graph control.

PrintStyle Setting	Effect
0	(Default) Monochrome
1	Color
2	Monochrome with border
3	Color with border

QuickData The QuickData property is often used in conjunction with the Grid control (see Chapter 10). It gives you (or takes) a string of numerals that are separated by tab characters (just like the Clip property of a grid) and either places it in the GraphData or takes it from the GraphData property. It separates each point by a tab character (Chr$(9)) and each data set by a carriage return/line feed combination. For example,

```
Grid1.Clip = Graph1.QuickData
```

fills the currently selected region of a grid with the data from the graph. (You have to make sure the number of rows selected is at least the value of the NumSets property and the number of columns is at least the value of the NumPoints property.)

RandomData The RandomData property is used mostly at design time. It gives you random data to check whether your graph fits your design goals.

ThisPoint The ThisPoint property sets or returns the current point number in the data set. (You can use this property to modify a specific data set value manually, for example, so that a particular data point can be changed.)

ThisSet As with the ThisPoint property, the ThisSet property controls (or returns) which data set you are working with. (It is obviously only relevant when the NumSets property is greater than 1.)

Ticks The Ticks property determines whether axis ticks are displayed. The following table summarizes the various settings.

Ticks Setting	Effect
0	(Default) No tick marks
1	Both X and Y tick marks
2	X tick marks only
3	Y tick marks only

TickEvery The TickEvery property determines the interval between tick marks on the X axis if the Ticks property is set to 1 or 2. The possible range is 1 to 1000.

YAxisTicks The YAxisTicks property specifies the number of ticks on the Y axis of your graph. (It is only relevant if the setting of the Ticks property is 1 or 3.) You can use up to 100 tick marks.

Chapter Sixteen

Monitoring Mouse Activity

WINDOWS, and therefore Visual Basic, constantly monitors what the user is doing with the mouse. Up to this point, all you have used are the Click and Double-Click events. These detect whether the user clicked the mouse once or twice in a form or control. This chapter shows you how to obtain and use more subtle information. Was a mouse button pressed? Which button was it? Is the mouse pointer over a control? Did the user release a button, and if so, which one? Did the user move the mouse out of one form and into another? Exactly where inside the form is the mouse? Visual Basic can detect all these events. Of course, as with all Visual Basic operations, you must write the event procedures that determine how Visual Basic will respond to the event. For example, if you want to pop up a menu after a right mouse click, you'll need to write the necessary lines of code.

note: *To allow the possibility of context-sensitive pop-up menus, all controls in Visual Basic 4 are now mouse-sensitive.*

Finally, just as designing a Visual Basic application involves dragging controls around a blank form, Visual Basic lets you write applications that let the user do things by moving controls around via dragging and dropping. The last section of this chapter shows you how.

The Mouse Event Procedures

There are three fundamental mouse event procedures:

Name	Event That Caused It
MouseDown	User clicks one of the mouse buttons
MouseUp	User releases a mouse button
MouseMove	User moves the mouse pointer to the control or to a blank area of the form

In many ways, these procedures are analogous to the KeyUp, KeyDown event procedures that you saw in Chapter 8. For example, as with those event procedures, Visual Basic lets you use bit masking to determine if the user was holding down the SHIFT, ALT, or CTRL key at the same time he or she pressed or released a mouse button.

Only forms and picture boxes return where the mouse pointer is in terms of their internal scales. For the other controls, it's necessary to calculate this information by using the scale of the surrounding container—a method that may or may not be practical.

Controls recognize a mouse event only when the mouse pointer is inside the control; the underlying form recognizes the mouse event in all other cases. However, if a mouse button is pressed *and held* while the mouse pointer is inside a control or form, that object *captures the mouse*. This means that no other Visual Basic object can react to mouse events until the user releases the mouse button, regardless of where the user moves the mouse.

All mouse event procedures take the same form and use the same parameters:

Object_MouseEvent(*Button* As Integer, *Shift* As Integer, *X* As Single, *Y* As Single)

If the object was part of a control array, then, as usual, there is an optional first *Index* parameter:

*ObjectIn*ControlArray_*MouseEvent*(*Index* As Integer, *Button* As Integer, *Shift* As Integer, *X* As Single, *Y* As Single)

As the next sections show, bit masking lets you use the *Button* argument to determine which mouse button was pressed. Similarly, you can find out if the user was holding down any combination with the SHIFT, CTRL, or ALT key by bit masking, using the *Shift* parameter. Finally, *X* and *Y* give you the information you need to determine the position of the mouse pointer, using the internal coordinates of the container object.

The MouseUp/MouseDown Events

To see the event procedure given in this section at work, start up a new project. Double-click to open the Code window and move to the MouseDown event procedure. Now enter the following:

```
Private Sub Form_MouseDown(Button As Integer, Shift As _
Integer, X As Single, Y As Single)
  Circle (X,Y), 75
End Sub
```

This simple event procedure uses the positioning information passed by *X* and *Y*. Each time you click a mouse button, a small circle is centered exactly where you clicked—namely, at CurrentX = X and CurrentY = Y, of size 75 twips. If you add a MouseUp event procedure that looks like

```
Private Sub Form_MouseUp(Button As Integer, Shift As Integer, _
X As Single, Y As Single)
  Dim CCode As Integer
  Randomize
  CCode = Int(15*Rnd)
  FillStyle = 0
  FillColor = QBColor(CCode)
  Circle (X,Y), 75
End Sub
```

then each time you release the same button, Visual Basic fills the circle with a random color. On the other hand, even though you may have two or even three mouse buttons, Visual Basic will not generate another MouseDown event until you release the original mouse button. This prevents you from making some circles filled and others empty when using these two procedures.

Suppose, however, you wanted to make some circles filled and some empty. One way to do this is to use the added information given by the *Button* argument. For example, suppose the user has a two-button mouse. You can easily write code so that if the user presses the right mouse button, he or she gets a filled circle, and otherwise all he or she gets is a colored circular outline. The *Button* argument uses the lowest three bits of the value of the integer, as shown here:

Button	Constant	Value of Button Argument
Left	vbLeftButton	1
Right	vbRightButton	2
Middle	vbMiddleButton	4

Visual Basic will tell you about only one button for the MouseUp/MouseDown combination. You cannot detect if both the left and right buttons are down simultaneously, for example. Thus you can rewrite the MouseUp event procedure to allow both filled and empty circles using the left/right buttons:

```
Private Sub Form_MouseUp(Button As Integer, Shift As Integer, _
X As Single, Y As Single)
  Dim CCode As Integer
  Randomize
  CCode = Int(15*Rnd)
  Select Case Button
    Case 1, 4
      Circle (X,Y), 75, QBColor(CCode)
      FillColor = &HFFFFFF&
    Case 2
      FillStyle = 0
      FillColor = QBColor(CCode)
      Circle (X,Y), 75
   End Select
End Sub
```

If you want a pop-up menu in response to a right mouse click, use a line of code like this:

If Button = vbRightButton Then Me.PopUpMenu *MenuName*

(See Chapter 12 for more on pop-up menus.)

You can also let the user combine the keyboard with a mouse. For example, you can have the SHIFT+right mouse button combination drop down a special menu. This uses the *Shift* argument in the MouseUp or MouseDown event procedure. Here's a table of the possible values for the lower three bits of the *Shift* parameter:

Action	Constant	Bit Set and Value
SHIFT key down	vbShiftMask	Bit 0: Value = 1
CTRL key down	vbCtrlMask	Bit 1: Value = 2
ALT key down	vbAltMask	Bit 2: Value = 4
SHIFT+CTRL keys down		Bit 0 and 1: Value = 3 (vbShiftMask + vbCtrlMask)
SHIFT+ALT keys down		Bit 0 and 2: Value = 5
CTRL+ALT keys down		Bit 1 and 2: Value = 6
SHIFT+CTRL+ALT keys down		Bits 0, 1, and 2: Value = 7

At the present time, most people seem to be writing code for the SHIFT key by using a Select Case statement, as follows,

```
Select Case Shift
  Case 1
   Print "You pressed the Shift key."
  Case 2 vbShiftMask
   Print "You pressed the Ctrl key."
  Case 3 vbShiftMask
   Print "You pressed the Shift + Ctrl keys."
  Case 4 vbAltMask
   Print "You pressed the Alt key."
```

and so on.

Microsoft discourages this practice because they reserve the possibility of using the higher order bits for something else. It's preferable then to use the And operator to isolate the first three bits before proceeding. As you saw with the KeyUp event procedure in Chapter 7, you can do this as follows:

```
Bits = Shift And 7
Select Case Bits
  Case 1 'or vbShiftMask
    Print "You pressed the Shift key."
  Case 2
    Print "You pressed the Ctrl key."
  Case 3
    Print "You pressed the Shift + Ctrl keys."
  Case 4
    Print "You pressed the Alt key."
```

By Anding with 7 (binary pattern = 111), you eliminate any information that may eventually be contained in the higher order bits, letting the program concentrate on the information contained in the lowest three bits. You might also want to apply the same preventative against future problems for the *Button* argument.

The MouseUp/MouseDown event procedures work similarly for picture boxes, the only difference being that, as you've seen, you must use the control name of the picture box (and the index if the picture box is part of a control array), as shown here:

Private Sub *CntrlName*_MouseDown(*Button* As Integer, *Shift* As Integer, _
X As Single, *Y* As Single)

note: *Microsoft Windows 95 uses the convention that the right mouse button pops up a context-sensitive menu.*

THE MOUSEMOVE EVENT

Visual Basic calls the MouseMove event procedure whenever the user moves the mouse. This is the most powerful of the mouse event procedures because, unlike the MouseUp/MouseDown event pair, you can use it to analyze completely the state of the mouse buttons. For this event procedure, the *Button* argument tells you whether some, all, or none of the mouse buttons are down.

You should not get into the habit of thinking that the MouseMove event is generated continuously as the mouse pointer moves across objects. In fact, a combination of the user's software and hardware determines how often the MouseMove event is generated. To see the MouseMove event at work, start a new project and enter the following MouseMove event procedure:

```
Private Sub Form_MouseMove(Button As Integer, Shift As _
Integer, X As Single, Y As Single)
  DrawWidth = 3
  PSet (X,Y)
End Sub
```

Now run the project and move your mouse around the form at different speeds. Figure 16-1 shows an example of what is obtained as you decrease your speed, moving from left to right in a vaguely rectangular motion. As you can see, the dots are more tightly packed when you move the mouse slowly than

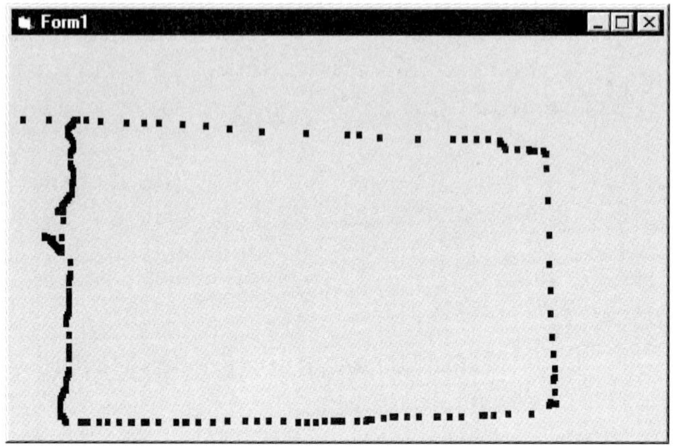

Figure 16-1 Demonstration of MouseMove response time

when you move it rapidly. This happens because Visual Basic relies on the underlying operating system to report mouse events, and such events are generated frequently but not continuously. Because the MouseMove event procedure is *not* called continuously, the dots are relatively sparse when the mouse is moved rapidly.

Nonetheless, since the MouseMove event procedure will be called relatively frequently, any code inside this event procedure will be executed often. For this reason, you will want to tighten the code inside the MouseMove event procedure as much as possible or provide a flag to prevent repetitive processing. For example, use integer variables for counters and do not recompute the value of variables inside this procedure unless the new value depends on the parameters for the event. Always remember that accessing object properties is *much* slower than using a variable.

As mentioned in the previous section, the MouseMove event uses the three lower bits of the value of the *Button* parameter to tell you the complete state of the mouse buttons, as shown here:

Button	Value	Constant
Left button	1	vbLeftButton
Right button	2	vbRightButton
Middle button	4	vbMiddleButton
Left + right	3	vbLeftButton + vbRightButton
Left + middle	5	vbLeftButton + vbMiddleButton
Right + middle	6	vbRightButton + vbMiddleButton
All three	7	

Of course, if you don't have a three-button mouse, the third bit will always be zero. As with the *Shift* parameter in the MouseUp/MouseDown event procedures, you are safest masking out all but the lowest three bits before using this information:

```
Bits = Shift And 7
Select Case Bits
  Case    vbLeftButton
    Print "The left mouse button is down."
  Case    vbRightButton
    Print "The right mouse button is down."
  Case    vbLeftButton + vbRightButton
    Print  "The left and right mouse buttons are down."
  Case    vbMiddleButton
    Print  "The middle mouse button is down."
```

tip: *Use the MouseMove event to add tool tips to your toolbars. All you have to do is have an invisible label with the correct caption become visible in the correct location. When the mouse moves off the tool, make the label invisible in the MouseMove event of all the other controls and of the form itself.*

Dragging and Dropping Operations

To move a control as you are designing the interface in your Visual Basic project, you hold down a mouse button (the left one) and then move the mouse pointer to where you want the control to end up. A gray outline of the control moves with the mouse pointer. When you are happy with the location, you release the mouse button. The Microsoft Windows documentation calls moving an object with the mouse button depressed *dragging* and calls the release of the mouse button *dropping*. Visual Basic makes it easy to program this potential behavior into your projects. You can even drag and drop from one form to another if your project uses multiple forms.

Controls permit two types of dragging. These correspond to two different values of the DragMode property. The default is to not allow you to drag controls around except under special circumstances. (As always, you'll need to write the code for these special circumstances; see the next section.) This is called *manual dragging,* and the DragMode property will have the value zero. Changing the value of this property to 1, *automatic,* means that the user may drag the control around the project. Regardless of the setting for the DragMode property, the control will actually move only if you write the code using the Move method to reposition it, as shown in the next example.

For this example, start up a new project and add a single command button to it. Set the DragMode property of that command button to 1 (automatic). The event that recognizes dragging and dropping operations is called the DragDrop event, and it is associated with the control or form where the "drop" occurs. Thus, if you want to drag a control to a new location on a form, you write code for the form's DragDrop event procedure. For example, to allow dragging and dropping to move the single command button around the form in this example, use the following:

```
Private Sub Form_DragDrop(Source As Control, X As Single, Y _
As Single)
  Source.Move X, Y
End Sub
```

Since the type of the *Source* parameter is a control, you can refer to its properties and methods by using the dot notation, as in the preceding example. If you need to know more information about what type of control is being dragged before applying a method or setting a property, use the If TypeOf Control Is... statement you saw in Chapter 8.

If you run this example, you will notice that the object remains visible in its original location while the gray outline moves. You cannot use the DragDrop event to make a control invisible while the dragging/dropping operation takes place. This is because this event procedure is called only after the user drops the object. In fact, the DragDrop event need not move the control at all. You often use this event to allow the user just to initiate some action. This is especially common when dragging from one form to another. The reason is that the only way a similar control can appear on a new form in Visual Basic is if you created it on another to place an invisible control of the same type on the new form at design time, to make the control part of a control array, or to use the new keyword to make a new instance of the form.

If you want to change the gray outline that Visual Basic uses during a drag operation, you can change it. The easiest way to do this is to set the DragIcon property of the control at design time. To do this, select the DragIcon property from the Properties box. Now click the three dots to the left of the Settings box. This opens up the Load Icon dialog box for choosing icons. You can also assign the drag icon or icon property of one object to another. For example:

FirstControl.DragIcon = *SecondControl*.DragIcon

The final possibility is to use the LoadPicture function. For example:

Control.DragIcon=LoadPicture("C\VB\ICONS\MISC\CLOCK01.ICO")

If you design a custom icon, a common practice is to reverse the colors for the drag icon.

The following table summarizes the events, methods, and properties used for dragging and dropping:

Item	Description
DragMode property	Allows automatic dragging (value = 1) or manual dragging (value = 0)
DragIcon property	Set this to change from the gray rectangle to a custom icon when dragging
DragDrop event	Associated with the target of the operation; generated when the source is dropped on the target control
DragOver event	Associated with any control the source control passes over during dragging
Drag Method	Starts or stops dragging when DragMode is set to manual

MANUAL DRAGGING

If you have left the value of the DragMode property at its default value of zero, then you must use the Drag method to allow dragging of the control. The syntax for this method is

Control.Drag *TypeOfAction*

The *TypeOfAction* is an integer value from zero to 2, as shown here:

Control.Drag 0	Cancel dragging
Control.Drag 1	Begin dragging
Control.Drag 2	Drop the control

If you omit the *TypeOfAction* argument, the method has the same effect as the statement Control.Drag 1. That is, Visual Basic initiates the dragging operation for the control.

One way to use the flexibility this method gives you is to allow expert users to drag and drop controls but make the default so that users cannot do this. For example, use the CTRL+MouseDown combination to allow dragging to take place. You can do this by beginning the MouseDown event procedure with the following:

```
Private Sub CntrlName_MouseDown(Button As Integer, Shift As _
Integer, X As Single, Y As Single)
  If (Shift And 7) = 2 Then  'or vbCtrlMask
    CntrlName.DragMode = 1
.
.
End Sub
```

THE DRAGOVER EVENT

All Visual Basic objects except menus and timers will detect if a control is passing over them. You can use the DragOver event to allow even greater flexibility for your projects. This event lets you monitor the path a control takes while being dragged. You might consider changing the background color of the control being passed over. The event procedure template for forms is

```
Private Sub Form_DragOver(Source As Control, X As Single, Y _
As Single, State As Integer)
.
.
End Sub
```

For controls, this event procedure template takes the form

```
Private Sub CtrlName_DragOver([Index As Integer,]Source As _
Control, X As Single, Y As Single, State As Integer)
.
.
End Sub
```

As usual, the optional *Index* parameter is used if the control is part of a control array. The *Source* is the control being dragged, but the event procedure is associated with the control being passed over. The *X* and *Y* parameters give you the CurrentX and CurrentY values in terms of the scale of the object being passed over for forms and picture boxes and the underlying form for all other controls. The *State* parameter has three possible values:

Value of State Parameter	Description
0	Source is now inside target
1	Source is just left of target
2	Source moved inside target

tip: *You will want to test for the type of control using the If Type Of statement.*

AN EXAMPLE: DELETING FILES VIA DRAG/DROP

The idea of letting the user drag an icon of a file to another icon representing a disposal unit has been around as long as graphical user interfaces. Apple's Macintosh uses a simple trash can; the Next computer uses a black hole. Since Apple has caused problems for those who use a simple trash can for this type of application, this example presents a slightly different form. The Trash03 icon supplied with Visual Basic seems appropriate.

Figure 16-2 shows an example of what the screen might look like. As you can see, the files are represented by labeled icons. The project in this section allows the user to drag one of the icons representing a file into the disposal unit, at which point (after a warning, of course) the file is deleted from the disk. Since you haven't yet seen the file-handling controls from the toolbox (Chapter 17), this project is

Figure 16-2 Form for drag and drop demo

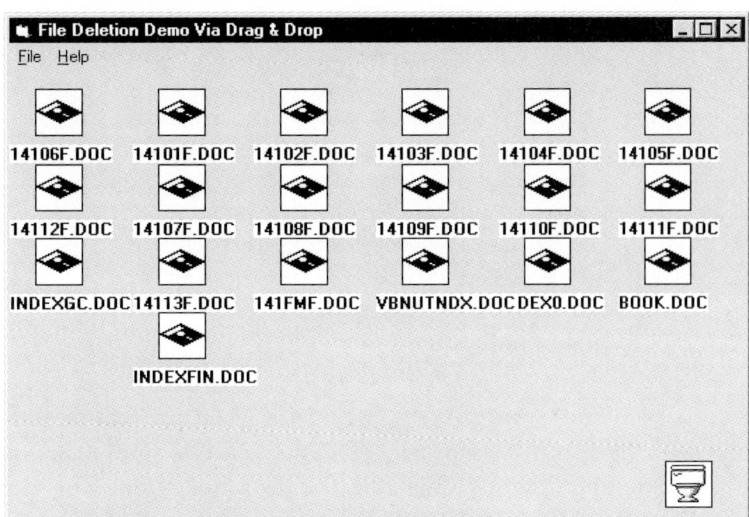

a little less user friendly than it could be. Nonetheless, it demonstrates the techniques needed for handling dragging and dropping in one of its most common contexts.

To follow this discussion, start up a new project with two forms. Add a picture box (or image control) in the lower-right corner of the startup form. Set the picture property of this control to the icon found in the TRASH03.ICO file. This file may be found in the Computer subdirectory of the Icon library. Set the AutoSize property to True if you use a picture box (or set the Stretch property to False if you choose an image control).

Next, set up two control arrays: an array of labels with the control name of FileName and an array of image controls named Files. Set the DragMode property of the image control to 1 (Automatic). Make both the label and the image control invisible at run time by setting the Visible property to False. As usual, all subsequent elements in these control arrays will inherit these properties.

Most of the work in this project is in the following simple DragDrop event procedure:

```
Private Sub Garbage_DragDrop (Source As Control, X As _
Single, Y As
Single)
  'local variables
  Dim Msg As String
  Dim ControlIndex As Integer, YesNo As Integer
  ControlIndex = Source.Index
  Form1.FileName(ControlIndex).Visible = False
  Form1.Files(ControlIndex).Visible = False
  Msg = "Do you really want to delete " +
Form1.FileName(ControlIndex).Caption
  YesNo = MsgBox(Msg, vbYesNo, "Confirmation Box")
  If YesNo = vbYes Then
    Kill (Form1.FileName(ControlIndex).Caption)
    Unload Form1.Files(ControlIndex)
    Unload Form1.FileName(ControlIndex)
  Else
    Form1.FileName(ControlIndex).Visible = True
    Form1.Files(ControlIndex).Visible = True
  End If
End Sub
```

The ControlIndex line in this event procedure finds out the index array of the control being dragged. The next two lines make the picture box and label temporarily invisible after the drop operation. The ControlIndex variable lets Visual Basic extract the caption (which will be the name of the file) from the label. The message box has type = vbYesNo (4) so it's a Yes/No message box. The title is Confirmation Box. The Kill command deletes a file from a disk. (You'll learn more about this command in Chapter 17.) Once the program deletes the file, the program unloads the label and picture box from the control array. If the user has made a mistake, this code makes the original picture box and label visible again.

Next, you need a general procedure called Directions that will give the user the information needed for this application. This will print on a form that will be used as a custom dialog box (BorderStyle = 3).

```
Sub Directions ()
  Form1.Hide
  Form2.Show
  Form2.Cls
  Form2.Print "This program illustrates dragging and dropping
mouse operations."
  Form2.Print "The user gives a file spec inside the message
box and a form"
  Form2.Print "appears with icons labelled by all the files
with that file specification."
  Form2.Print "The user can drag the icon to be 'flushed' away
i.e. deleted."
End Sub
```

The program displays this information on the second form in this project. It gives you a screen like the one shown in Figure 16-3. Notice that we have changed the BorderStyle property to 3 ("Fixed Dialog"). You probably want to set Auto Redraw to True as well.

The click procedure for the OK button on our dialog box is:

```
Private Sub btnOK_Click ()
  Me.Hide
  Form1.Show
End Sub
```

The Form_Load procedure for the initial form needs to load the directions form and call the general procedure that gives the directions. It looks like this:

```
Private Sub Form_Load ()
  Load Form2
  Directions
End Sub
```

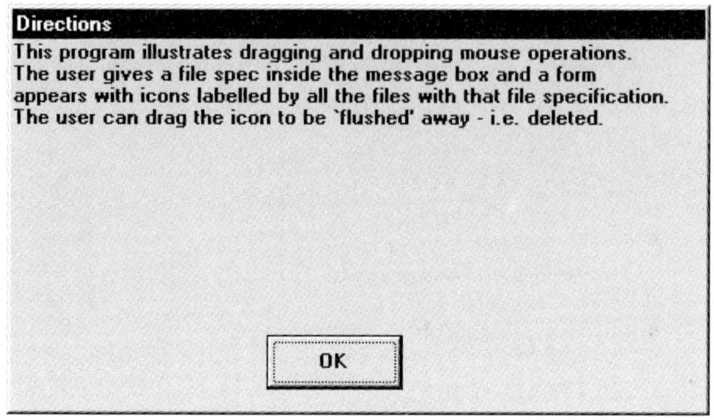

Figure 16-3 Information screen for drag and drop demo

The File menu on the startup form has two items:

New File Spec
Exit

Clicking the New File Spec menu item will let the user examine a new directory or drive. Clicking this menu item will call a general procedure called GetFile that reads the names of the files from the disk.

Now the question is how to deal with a new file specification. The first time the user uses this application, Visual Basic loads a certain number of elements in the two control arrays. The program needs to change the information contained in the captions. These captions contain the names of the files to delete. There are various ways of changing the information. The easiest is to unload the form and then reload it. This automatically clears out the old information contained in the control array. It also avoids any error messages that might result from loading the same element of a control array twice. Then the procedure can reload new members of the control arrays that represent the files.

One other way you might consider is a bit more complicated to code. However, it will often be somewhat faster when the program runs. To use this method, load the two control arrays only once. Then set up a string array that reads the file information from the disk using the Dir$ command. Finally, assign the entries in this array to the Caption property of the labels. The code for this is more complicated as you must read the disk information twice to redimension the arrays appropriately.

Regarding the menu item, since the "N" is underlined, the user can press N as a shortcut to activate this item. Once the menu is open, the control name for this menu item is set to be mnuNewFileSpec. The Click event procedure for this control is

```
Private Sub mnuNewFileSpec_Click ()
  Unload Form1
  Load Form1
  GetFile
End Sub
```

The Unload Form1 line clears out the old elements of the control array. The GetFile general procedure looks like this:

```
Public Sub GetFile ()
  'local variables
  Dim FileSpec As String

  Form2.Hide
  FileSpec = InputBox$("File specification?")
  If FileSpec = "" Then
    Directions
  Else
    Form1.Show
    DisplayFiles (FileSpec)
  End If
End Sub
```

As you can see, the details of displaying the files on the startup form are contained in a general procedure with one string parameter called *DisplayFiles*. This procedure allows up to 30 files. It looks like this:

```
Public Sub DisplayFiles (FileSpec As String)
  'local variables
  Dim NameOfFile As String
  Dim ControlIndex As Integer

  Form1.Show
  Form1.Width = 8000              'slightly larger for 30 files
  Form1.Height = 5500
  Form1.Garbage.Move 7000, 4200  'move the garbage can icon
```

```
  NameOfFile = Dir$(FileSpec)
  If NameOfFile = "" Then
    MsgBox "No Files found with that file specification!"
  End If
  ControlIndex = ControlIndex + 1      'start with index = 1
  Do While NameOfFile <> ""
    Load Form1.Files(ControlIndex)
    Load Form1.FileName(ControlIndex)
    Column = (ControlIndex Mod 6)
    Row = (ControlIndex - 1) \6
    Form1.Files(ControlIndex).Move (1300 * Column) + 275, _
800 * Row + 200                               'to allow for menu
    Form1.FileName(ControlIndex).Move 1300 * Column, 800 * _
(Row + 1)
    Form1.Files(ControlIndex).Visible = True
    Form1.FileName(ControlIndex).Visible = True
    Form1.FileName(ControlIndex).Caption = NameOfFile
    ControlIndex = ControlIndex + 1
    If ControlIndex > 30 Then
      MsgBox ("Too many files!")
      Exit Do
    End If
    NameOfFile = Dir$
  Loop
End Sub
```

The Do loop does the work of spacing the picture boxes and labels. The spacing was determined by experimenting with different values. As with all new elements in a control array, they remain invisible until you set the Visible property to True.

Clicking the menu item marked Help calls the Directions general procedure:

```
Sub Help_Click ()
  Directions
End Sub
```

To finish the program, you need only associate the simplest of event procedures with the Quit menu items on the form and add a query Unload event to end the program.

```
Sub mnuQuit_Click ()
  Unload Form2
  Unload Me
End Sub

Sub Form_Query Unload (Cancel As Integer, UnloadMode As _
Integer)
  End
End Sub
```

Chapter Seventeen

Working with Files

This chapter shows you how to handle disks and disk files within Visual Basic. You'll also see how to work with the executable version of a Visual Basic project. In particular, you'll see a technique for adding licensing screens to your completed applications (much like Microsoft itself does—you see to whom the copy is licensed whenever Visual Basic starts up).

The first section explains the Visual Basic commands that let you rename files, change the logged drive, or switch directories. Then you'll see the commands that make handling disk files easier. For example, you can copy files within a Visual Basic program with a single command. Next you'll see how to use the file system controls on the toolbox. Finally, there's an extensive introduction to file handling in Visual Basic, including a discussion on how to keep file information confidential by encrypting the information in the files.

Although Visual Basic 4 contains many features for handling databases (see Chapter 20), the ability to set up and work with files directly remains very important. Random-access files are still useful for setting up certain kinds of databases, and binary file techniques are needed to work with files stored in non-ASCII format and to add licensing screens. In addition, these techniques are important when you need to write your own file conversion routines.

caution: *(For Visual Basic 3 users especially) The techniques for handling binary files have changed. You may need to change the source code of any projects built using binary files in order to have them run correctly under the 32-bit version of Visual Basic 4. (See the section on binary files for the techniques that are now needed.)*

Finally, use the common dialog boxes that you saw in Chapter 11 when manipulating files for other users. Windows users expect to see these boxes when working with the files!

File Commands

Visual Basic has six commands under Windows 3.1 that interact directly with the underlying operating system, mimicking the usual operating system commands that handle files and drives on your machine. You already saw one of the commands in Chapter 13, the Kill command, which lets you delete a file. Table 17-1 summarizes these commands.

You use these commands by following them with a string or string variable. For example,

```
MkDir "TESTDIR"
```

would add a subdirectory called TESTDIR to the current directory. The line

```
MkDir "C:\TESTDIR"
```

would add the subdirectory to the root directory of the C drive.

The commands that handle files also accept the normal file-handling wildcards. For example,

```
Kill "*.*"
```

deletes all the files in the current directory (not to be used casually!). As Table 17-1 indicates, the Name command can actually do a bit more than the old

Command	Function
ChDrive	Changes the logged drive for the underlying operating system
ChDir	Changes the default directory
MkDir	Makes a new directory
RmDir	Removes a directory
Name	Changes the name of a file or moves a file from one directory to another
Kill	Deletes a file from a disk

Table 17-1
Visual Basic's File-Handling Commands

DOS REN command; it can move files from one directory in the current drive to another. To do this, give the full path name. For example,

```
Name "C:\VB\TEST.BAS" As "C:\EXAMPLES\TEST.BAS"
```

moves the TEST.BAS file from the VB directory to one named EXAMPLES.

In addition, the CurDir function returns a string that gives the path for the current drive. You can also specify a drive:

CurDir$ (*Drive*)

The first character of *Drive* determines the drive. When used in this form, the function now gives the path for the specified drive. (You can also use the CurDir function, which returns a variant rather than a string.)

As with any function that uses disk drives, you can generate a run-time error if the underlying operating system cannot perform the requested function. See the section "Making a File Program Robust: Error Trapping" later in this chapter for more on dealing with these types of errors.

Example: How to Reset the Logged Drive

Programs for other users that change the logged drive or path will often need to reset the drive to where it was when the program started. (It's the neighborly thing to do.) The original logged drive and path information are often stored in global variables in the Form_Load procedure of the startup form. If there is a chance that the Form_Load will be called more than once, you'll need to modify the obvious code. Here's an example of the modifications needed:

```
Sub Form_Load ()
  'Global variables OldDrive$ and OldPath$
  Static AlreadyLoadedOnce As Boolean
  If Not (AlreadyLoadedOnce) Then
    OldDrive$ = Left(CurDir, 2) 'get current drive
    OldPath$ = CurDir    'and path so can reset at end
    AlreadyLoadedOnce = True
    'other code you want to use once goes here
    'Examples are copyright notices and such
  End If
End Sub
```

The Shell Function

Although a few file-handling utility-type programs are built into Visual Basic commands—usually with slightly different names, such as Kill for Del—most are not. Experienced users can move to the Windows 95 desktop and use the Explorer or the Start button to format disks, copy multiple files, or run another program. On the other hand, inexperienced users might not be comfortable doing this. For this reason you may want to build in the ability to start other programs from your Visual Basic programs.

You can use the Shell function to run any .COM, .EXE, .BAT, or .PIF file from a Visual Basic program. For example, you can call the FORMAT.COM program under Windows 95 with a line like this:

```
X = Shell "C:\WINDOWS\COMMAND\FORMAT.COM A:"
```

(The value returned by the Shell function is now only useful under the 16-bit version of Visual Basic under Windows 3.X.)

In general, Windows 95 must know where the file you are running is located. It can know this if the file you are shelling to is located in a directory in the path or in the current directory. If you give the full path name of the application, then you can use files not in these directories.

When Visual Basic shells to a program, it generates a new iconized window and gives it the focus. In many situations this is not ideal. For example, the user has to actually press ENTER for formatting to occur. You can change this behavior with the general form of the Shell function, as follows:

Shell(*Pathname, WindowStyle*)

Here, *Pathname* contains the full path name of the stand-alone program (or batch file) that you want to execute along with any information needed by the program, and WindowStyle sets the type of window the program runs in. The possible values for WindowStyle are as follows:

Symbolic Constant	Value	Type of Window
vbHide	0	Window is hidden but has the focus
vbNormalFocus	1	Normal with the focus
vbMinimizedFocus	2	Iconized with the focus
vbMaximizedFocus	3	Maximized with the focus
VbMaximizedNotFocus	4	Normal without the focus
vbMinimizedNoFocus	6	Iconized without the focus

note: *The Shell function takes named arguments, so you can use it in the form:*

Shell PathName:= , Windowstyle:=

Use the Shell function with care, especially while you're developing the program within Visual Basic. Ideally, you should have enough memory to keep Windows, Visual Basic, all programs currently running, and the program to which you are "shelling" all simultaneously in memory. Otherwise, you have to rely on Windows to manage the memory for you by swapping to disk, and things will slow down dramatically.

The integer returned by the Shell function identifies the task identification number of the started program (or 0 if the program wasn't successfully started). This information was extremely useful in earlier versions of Visual Basic—it is less useful now. You used to be able to use this value along with the Windows 3.1 GetModuleUsage API call in order to make sure the program you have shelled to finishes before the next Visual Basic statement executes. This no longer works under Windows NT or the 32-bit version of Visual Basic.

tip: *There is still a way to do this—see Appendix D.*

Command-Line Information

Most professional programs allow users to type in additional information when they invoke the program. This extra information is usually called *command-line information*. For example, when you use

```
COPY A:*.* B:
```

the command-line information is the string "A:*.* B:". The internal operating system program COPY uses this information to know what to do. Visual Basic makes it easy to read this information. When you run any program from the Run box on the Start button and use the line,

FileExeName info1 info2 info3...

then the value of the reserved variant variable Command is the string whose value is "*info1 info2...*". Since you have already seen in Chapters 7 and 8 how to write a program that parses a string, you now know how to analyze the command-line information by breaking the string Command into its component parts.

Obviously, you need a way to create sample pieces of command-line information while developing the program; otherwise, you wouldn't have any test data with which to debug the program. Choose Tools | Options and then go to the Advanced page on the Options dialog box. This gives you the page shown here:

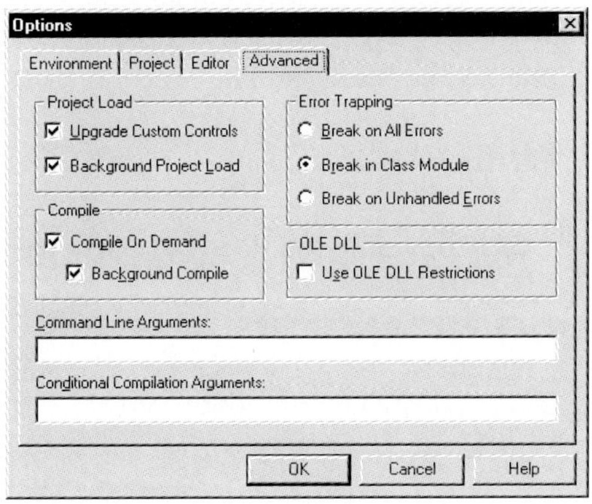

In the Command Line Arguments box, enter the string that you want to be used in the Command command within the program.

You can also pass command-line information to Visual Basic itself when Visual Basic starts up. For this, start Visual Basic from the Run box on the Start menu and use the form:

VB /CMD *CommandLineInfo*

Now, anything after the /CMD switch is sent to Visual Basic as command-line information.

tip: *Command is not a variable but a function and so should be made the value of a variable before extensive manipulation such as parsing.*

File-Handling Functions

Certain tasks are so common that the designers of Visual Basic decided to add them to the language itself rather than make you use Windows API calls or shell to one of the utility programs. There are four of these functions: FileCopy, FileDateTime, GetAttr, and SetAttr.

THE FILECOPY FUNCTION

The FileCopy function copies a file from the source path to another path. It does not use SHELL to activate the underlying operating system copy routine or call the File Manager. This function takes named arguments, and its syntax is

FileCopy *source, destination*

The FileCopy function does not allow wildcards.

THE FILEDATETIME FUNCTION

The FileDateTime function returns the date and time a file was created or last modified. The syntax is

FileDateTime (*pathname*)

THE GETATTR FUNCTION

The GetAttr function returns an integer. Using masking techniques to get at the individual bits, you can determine how the various attributes are set. The syntax for this function is

GetAttr (*pathname*) As Integer

Table 17-2 summarizes these values as symbolic constants.
For example, if

GetAttr(*FileName*) = vbReadOnly + vbHidden

then the file is hidden and read-only. (You can also use: GetAttr(*FileName*) = 3 since vbReadOnly + vbHidden = 3.)

Attribute	Constant	Value
Normal	vbNormal	0
ReadOnly	vbReadOnly	1
Hidden	vbHidden	2
System	vbSystem	4
Volume	vbVolume	8
Directory	vbDirectory	16
Archive	vbArchive	32

Table 17-2
Attribute Constants

tip: *You can use this masking technique with the Dir function to find files that match both a file specification and a file attribute. The syntax for this version is*

Dir(*pathname, attributes*)

where you add together the various symbolic constants (or their values) in order to specify the types of files to be looked for. For example,

```
Dir("C:\" , vbHidden+vbSystem+vbReadOnly)
```

would find files in the root directory that were simultaneously hidden, read-only, and of system type.

THE SETATTR FUNCTION

The SetAttr function sets attribute information for files. Using the same bit values given in Table 17-2, you can change the various attributes. The syntax for this function is

SetAttr *Pathname, attributes*

You can use the same symbolic constants shown in Table 17-2 for the GetAttr function. For example,

SetAttr *FileName$*, vbHidden+ vbReadOnly

would hide the file and set it as read-only.

tip: *Use the SetAttr function to hide files that you don't want casual users to know about. For example, putting an encrypted password in a hidden file and then examining that file is a common (and reasonably secure) method of making sure that a program is being used by the right person. (See the section "Adding Licensing Screens" later in this chapter.)*

File System Controls

The file system controls in Visual Basic allow users to select a new drive, see the hierarchical directory structure of a disk, or see the names of the files in a given directory. As with all Visual Basic controls, you need to write code to take full advantage of the power of the file system controls. In addition, if you want to tell the underlying operating system to change drives or directories as the result of a mouse click by a user, you need to write code using the commands listed in Table 17-1. The file system controls complement the common dialog boxes you saw in Chapter 12.

Figure 17-1 shows a version of the toolbox with the file system controls marked. Your toolbox may vary. The file system controls are designed to work together. Your code checks what the user has done to the drive list box and passes this information on to the directory list box. The changes in the directory list box are passed on to the file list box. (See the section "Tying All the File Controls Together" a little later in this chapter.)

Figure 17-1
File system controls in the toolbox

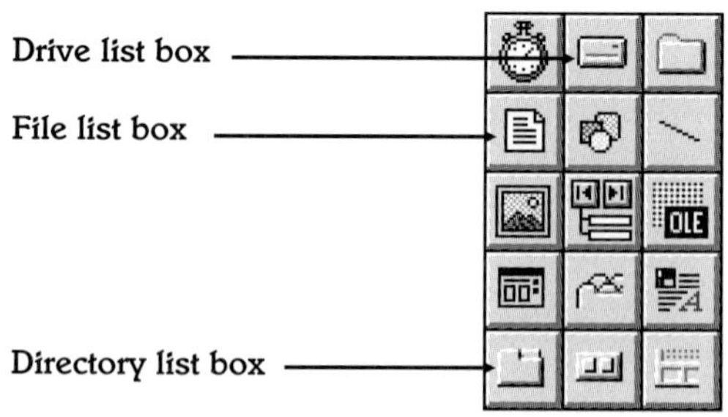

File List Boxes

A file list box defaults to displaying the files in the current directory. (Microsoft's suggested prefix for the Name property is "fil".) As with any list box, you can control the position, size, color, and font characteristics at design time or via code. Most of the properties of a file list box are identical to those of ordinary list boxes. For example, as with all list boxes, when the number of items can't fit the current size of the control, Visual Basic automatically adds vertical scroll bars. This lets the user move through the list of files using the scroll bars. You can set the size, position, or font properties of file list boxes via the Properties window or via code, as needed. Similarly, file list boxes can respond to all the events that list boxes can detect. For example, you can write event procedures for a keypress or a mouse movement. One point is worth remembering, though: the Windows convention is that double-clicking a file, not single-clicking, chooses the file. This is especially important when using a file list box because using an arrow key to move through a file list box would call any Click procedure that you have written. (Recall that arrow movements are functionally equivalent to a single mouse click for a list box.)

It is quite common to use the List, ListCount, and ListIndex properties to analyze the information contained in a file list box rather than using the Dir command. For example, suppose the file list box has the default name of File1 and you have already set up a string array for the information contained in the box. Then a fragment such as

```
For I% = 0 To File1.ListCount -1
  FileNames$(I%) = File1.List(I%)
Next I%
```

fills a string array with the information contained in the file list box named File1. If you need to find out the name of the file that a user selects, you can use File1.List(ListIndex) or the FileName property which, when read, has the same function.

You can have a file list box display only files that are read-only (good for novice users) or those that have the Archive bit turned on or off (that is, to indicate whether or not the files have been backed up since the last change). There are five Boolean properties (True, False) that control what type of files are shown in a file list box: Archive, Hidden, Normal, ReadOnly, and System. The default setting is True for Archive, Normal, and ReadOnly and False for Hidden and System.

As an example of this, consider the code to activate the form shown in Figure 17-2, which has a single file list box and five check boxes to specify the type of files the file list box shows. For example, if the file list box is named File1 and one of the check boxes is named ShowHidden, a line of code like

```
File1.Hidden = ShowHidden.Value
```

would tell the file list box to display (or not display) hidden files, depending on whether or not the box was checked.

PATTERN AND PATH

The most important properties for file list boxes are Pattern and Path. The Pattern property determines which files are displayed in the file list box. The Pattern property accepts the ordinary file wildcards—the * (match any) and the ? (match a single character). The default pattern is set to *.* to display all files. (Of course, the Pattern property works with the attribute properties discussed earlier before Visual Basic displays the files.) When you change the Pattern property, Visual Basic looks to see if you have written a PatternChange event procedure for the file list box and, if so, activates it.

Figure 17-2 Form with a single file box and five check boxes for file properties

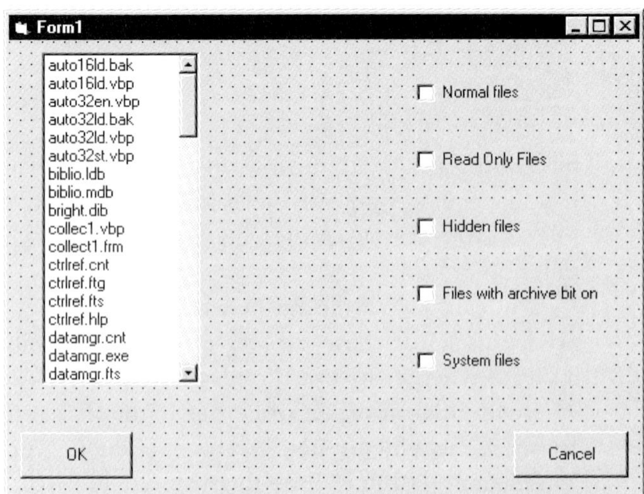

tip: *Multiple patterns can be used; just separate them with semicolons.*

The Path property sets or returns the current path for the file list box, but not for the underlying operating system. To tell the underlying operating system to change the current path from Visual Basic, you need the ChDir command. On the other hand, you may just need to accumulate this information for use by your program without disturbing the default path. When you change the Path property, Visual Basic looks to see whether you have written a PathChange event procedure for the file list box and, if so, activates it.

Changing the FileName property activates the PathChange event or the PatternChange event (or both), depending on how you change the FileName property. For example, suppose you are in the C:\ root directory. Setting

```
File1.Filename ="C:\WINDOWS\COMMAND\*.COM"
```

activates both the PathChange and PatternChange events.

Directory List Boxes

A directory list box displays the directory structure of the current drive. (Microsoft's naming convention is to use a "dir" prefix for the Name property.) The current directory shows up as an open file folder. Subdirectories of the current directory are shown as closed folders, and directories above the current directory are shown as nonshaded open folders.

note: *When the user clicks on an item or moves through the list, that item is highlighted. When he or she double-clicks, Visual Basic automatically updates the directory list box.*

The List property for a directory list box works a little differently than it does for file list boxes. While subdirectories of the current directory are numbered from zero to ListCount-1, Visual Basic uses negative indexes for the current directory and its parent and grandparent directories. For example, -1 is the index for the current directory, -2 for its parent directory, and so on. Unfortunately, you cannot use the LBound function to determine the number of directories above a given directory; you must either count the number of backslashes in the Path property or move backward through the items in the directory list box.

As an example of how powerful the file system controls can be when they begin to work together, put a directory list box and a file list box together on a new project, as shown in Figure 17-3. Now suppose you want a change by the user in a directory list box named dirBox to tell Visual Basic to update the file list box immediately. All you have to do is enter one line of code in the Change event procedure:

```
Sub dirBox_Change()
  File1.Path = dirBox.Path
End Sub
```

This is all it takes to update the file list box whenever a user changes the current directory. To activate this event procedure, the user must double-click a new directory in the Dir1 list box.

note: *Directory list boxes do not recognize the DoubleClick event; instead they call the Change procedure in response to a double-click and reassign the Path property.*

Again, Visual Basic cannot use a single click to activate the Change event because then users could not use the arrow keys to move through the list box.

Figure 17-3

Project with a directory list box and file list box

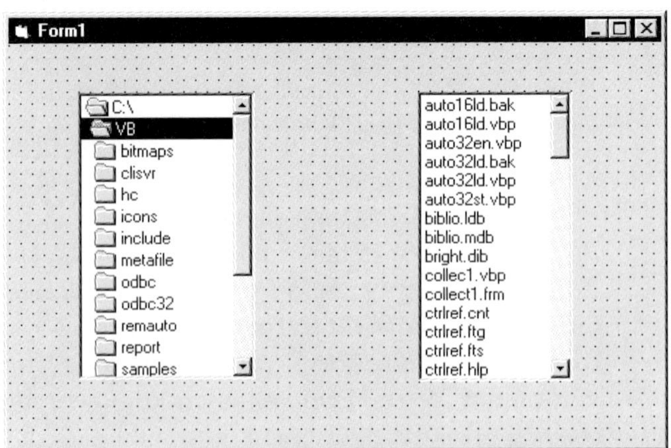

If you want users to be able to press ENTER to update the file list box as well, use the directory list box's KeyPress event procedure as follows:

```
Sub dirBox_KeyPress(KeyAscii As Integer)
  If KeyAscii = 13 Then     'Or vbKeyReturn
    dirBox.Path = dirBox.List(dirBox.ListIndex)
  End If
End Sub
```

You can also write a procedure that calls the previous event procedure when the user presses ENTER.

Again, this procedure doesn't change the Path property directly because doing so is superfluous. Visual Basic calls the Change event procedure for a directory list box whenever you change the value of the Path property.

Finally, it's important to keep in mind that while the meaning of the Path property for file list boxes and directory list boxes is similar, it is not identical. For directory list boxes, the Path property specifies which directory was selected; for file list boxes, the Path property specifies where to look for files to display.

Drive List Boxes

Unlike file and directory list boxes, drive list boxes are pull-down boxes. (Microsoft's naming convention suggests "drv" as the prefix for the Name property.) Drive list boxes begin by displaying the current drive, and then when the user clicks on the arrow, Visual Basic pulls down a list of all valid drives.

The key property for a drive list box is the Drive property, which can be used to return or reset the current drive. For example, to synchronize a drive list box with a directory list box, all you need is code that looks like this:

```
Sub drvBox_Change()
  dirBox.Path = drvBox.Drive
End Sub
```

On the other hand, if you also want to change the logged drive that the underlying operating system is using, write

```
Sub drvBox_Change()
  dirBox.Path = drvBox.Drive
  ChDrive drvBox.Drive
End Sub
```

Tying All the File Controls Together

When you have all three file system controls on a form, you have to communicate the changes among the controls in order to have Visual Basic show what the user wants to see. For example, if the user selects a new drive, Visual Basic activates the Change event procedure for the drive box. Then the following occurs:

1. The Change event procedure for the drive box assigns the Drive property to the directory box's Path property.
2. This changes the display in the directory list box by triggering the Change event procedure for the directory list box.
3. Inside the Change event procedure, you assign the Path property to the file list box's Path property. This updates the File list box.

It is easy to add a text box for a file pattern (assign the box to the file list box's Pattern property) and check boxes that allow the user to choose what type of files to view in the file list box. Including all this information gives you something that looks like the usual Microsoft Windows file control box that you saw in Chapter 12. Occasionally you will need the extra flexibility that using file controls provides.

caution: *Often you will combine the path name obtained from the Path property with the file name taken from the FileName property to get the full path name of a file. Unfortunately, if you are in the root directory, there is a "\" at the end of the path name property that would lead to two backslashes in a row if you naively combined the two properties. Instead, use code such as the following:*

```
If Right(File1.Path, 1) <> "\" Then
  NameOfFile = File1.Path + "\" + File1.FileName
Else
  NameOfFile = File1.Path + File1.FileName
End If
```

Sequential Files

Sequential files are analogous in Visual Basic to recording information on a cassette tape. The analogy is a particularly useful one to keep in mind. For example, the operations on sequential files that are analogous to easy tasks for a cassette recorder, such as recording an album on a blank tape, will be easy. Those analogous to more difficult tasks, such as splicing tapes together or making a change within a tape, will be more difficult.

To avoid unnecessary work, use a sequential file only when you know that you will

- Rarely make changes within the file
- Massage (process) the information the file contains from start to finish, without needing to constantly jump around
- Add to the file at the end of the file

It's not that you can't make changes within the file, jump around when processing information, or add to the file other than at the end; it's just that these procedures are a bit painful.

Here's a table of some common operations on a cassette tape and the analogous operations on a sequential text file called TEST in the currently active directory:

Operation	Visual Basic Equivalent
Rewind the tape, put the machine in playback mode, and pause	Open "TEST" For Input as #1
Rewind the tape, put the machine in record mode, and pause	Open "TEST" For Output as #1
Push Stop	Close #1

Each time Visual Basic sees the Open command, it gets ready to send information into or take information out of the file. (The jargon is that it "sets up a channel" to communicate with the file.) What follows the Open command is the name of the file you are working with. The filename must be a string variable or enclosed in quotation marks, and unless it is in the current directory, you need to provide enough information to identify its path. (The value of a string variable must be a legal filename.) Under Windows 95, of course, what constitutes a legal filename is much improved over the earlier versions of Windows. You can use up to 255 characters, and spaces are allowed. (You still can't use a \, ?, :, *, <, >, or |, however.)

On the other hand, if you want your files to be completely compatible with machines not running Windows 95 or Windows NT, you should follow the rules for filenames that DOS imposes:

- The filename can be at most eight characters with an optional three-character extension following the period.
- The characters you can use are

  A - Z 0 - 9 ( ) { } @ # $ % & ! - _ ' / ~

- Lowercase letters are automatically converted to uppercase.

note: *Only the 32-bit version of Visual Basic supports long filenames.*

In any case, you also need a file identifier. This is a number between 1 and 255 preceded by the # sign that you will use to identify the file. Although you can't change this number until you close the file, the next time you need the file you can open it with a different ID number. The number of possible files you can have open at once is limited by operating system constraints. (You can raise this, for example, by modifying your CONFIG.SYS file under Windows 3.X.)

When Visual Basic processes an Open command, it also reserves a file buffer in the computer's memory. Without a buffer, each piece of information sent to (or from) the disk would be recorded (or played back) separately. Since mechanical operations such as writing to a disk are much slower than writing to RAM, this would waste a lot of time. Instead, when a file buffer fills up, Visual Basic tells the underlying operating system to activate the appropriate drive, and a whole packet of information is sent in a continuous stream to the disk. The number of buffers can also be changed from your CONFIG.SYS file.

The Close command usually empties the buffer and tells the underlying operating system to update the FAT (file allocation table). But because of Windows' own buffering techniques, this may not happen precisely when Visual Basic processes the Close command. For this reason, a sudden power outage when you have a file open almost inevitably leads to lost information and occasionally even to a corrupted disk. (The SCANDISK command is often necessary when this happens.)

tip: *The Reset command, unlike the Close command, seems to force the underlying operating system to flush the buffers. Use this command in critical situations to make it more likely that the underlying operating system file buffer is flushed.*

The Print command sends information to a form. A slight modification, Print #, provides one way to send information to a file. Here is an example of a fragment that sends one piece of information to a file named TEST:

```
' Writing to a file
Open "TEST" For Output As #1
Print #1, "TESTING, 1 2 3"
Close #1
```

After the usual Remark statement, the first executable statement tells Visual Basic that you are going to set up a file named TEST having file identifier #1.

caution: *If a file in the current directory already exists with the name TEST, it is erased by this statement. Opening a file for sequential output starts a new file; the contents of a previous file with the same name are lost.*

Next comes the statement that actually sends the information to the file. The comma is necessary, but what follows the comma can be anything that might occur in an ordinary Print statement. And what appears in the file is the exact image of what would have occurred on the screen. For example, the file does not contain quotation marks. More precisely, the file will contain the word TESTING, followed by a comma, followed by a space, followed by the numeral 1, followed by another space, followed by the numeral 2, followed by a space, followed by the numeral 3, and then, although you may not have thought of it, the characters that define a carriage return/line feed combination—a CHR$(13) (carriage return) and a CHR$(10) (line feed).

It is extremely important that you keep in mind that the Print # command works exactly like the Print command. By now you know of the automatic carriage return/line feed combination that follows an ordinary Print statement. More precisely, if the line read

```
Print #1, "TESTING, 1 2 3";
```

then the file would contain two fewer characters. The CHR$(13) and CHR$(10) would no longer be there because the semicolon (just as for an ordinary Print statement) suppresses the carriage return/line feed combination.

This is important because the cardinal rule of file handling is that you must know the exact structure of a file if you want to be able to efficiently reuse the information it contains.

As a third example, suppose you change the line to read

```
Print #1, "TESTING",1,2,3
```

Now the file contains many spaces (occurrences of CHR$(32)) that were not there before. To see why this must be true, just recall that a comma in a Print statement moves the cursor to the next print zone by inserting spaces. Use a comma in a Print # statement, and the same spaces are placed in your file.

Finally, the Close command (followed by a file identifier) *flushes,* or moves, whatever is in the appropriate file buffer to the disk. The Close command without a file ID flushes all open buffers—that is, it closes all open files.

Instead of using FileLen, once a file is open you can use the Visual Basic command LOF( ) (Length Of File) to learn how large the file is. To use this command, place the appropriate file identifier number within the parentheses. To see this command at work (and to confirm what was said earlier about the sizes of the various versions of the TEST file), try the following Click procedure in a new project:

```
Sub Form_Click()
' a file tester
' demonstrates the 'exact' image property of Print #
  Open "Test1" For Output As #1
  Open "Test2" For Output As #2
  Open "Test3" For Output As #3
  Print #1,"TESTING, 1,2,3"
  Print #2,"TESTING, 1,2,3";
  Print #3,"TESTING",1,2,3
  Print LOF(1)
  Print LOF(2)
  Print LOF(3)
  Close
End Sub
```

If you run this program, you'll see

```
16
14
47
```

As you can see, the first file does contain 2 more characters than the second (to account for the carriage return/line feed combination). And the third contains far more than the 14 characters in the phrase "TESTING, 1 2 3". The extra characters, as you'll soon see, are indeed spaces (CHR$(32)).

Reading Back Information from a File

To read information back from a file, you must open the file for Input using its name (again, the full path name if it's not in the currently active directory) and give it a file identifier that is not currently being used within the program. (It doesn't have to be the same identifier that it was set up with originally.) The easiest way to find an unused file identifier is with the command FreeFile. The value of FreeFile is always the next unused file ID number. Therefore, you merely need a statement like

```
FileNumber% = FreeFile
```

at the appropriate point in your program, followed by:

Open *FileName* For Input As #FileNumber%.

caution: *Never use Open* FileName *For Input as #FreeFile.*

Next, you choose a variant on the PC-BASIC Input command to retrieve the information. For example, suppose you want to read back the file TEST1. This contains the word TESTING, followed by a comma, followed by the numbers. It ends with the carriage return/line feed combination. For those who know some form of PC-BASIC, to choose how to read this information back from this file, pretend for a second that you were going to enter this information into the computer via the keyboard in the older version of BASIC. You could not write INPUT A$ because that would pick up only the word TESTING. (The INPUT command would read information only up to the first comma.) So you would likely use LINE INPUT A$ because the LINE INPUT command from ordinary BASIC disregards any spaces or commas that may have been typed; it accepts all the information typed until ENTER is pressed. (The carriage return/line feed combination corresponds to the ENTER key.) In general, you use the Line Input # statement to read information in a sequential file one line at a time. Here is a fragment that reads back and displays the contents of the file named TEST1:

```
' Reading back a file
Open "TEST1"  For Input As #1
Line Input #1, A$
Print A$
Close #1
```

As an alternative you could use

```
Open "TEST1" For Input As #1
Input #1, A$, B$, C$, D$
Print A$; " "; B$; " "; C$; " "; D$
Close #1
```

or

```
Open "TEST1" For Input As #1
Input #1, A$, B, C, D
Print A$; B; C; D
Close #1
```

both of which seem clumsier and in any case yield slightly different results. For example, the last program has recovered the numbers as numbers (values of numeric variables) rather than as strings of numerals (part of a larger string). On the other hand, if you have stored numbers in a file, this is often the method to choose to retrieve them.

If you know how many entries there are in a file, a For-Next loop is often the easiest way to read the information back. For example, suppose you're a teacher with a class of 25 students. You know the currently active disk contains a file called CLASS that stores the information about the class in the following form:

Student's Name (first last)
First Exam Grade
Second Exam Grade — 25 times
Third Exam Grade
Fourth Exam Grade

Two useful terms that recur often in file handling are *fields* and *records*. Think of this file as being made up of 25 records and each record as consisting of 5 fields. Usually, a program that manipulates this file will read back the information by records—that is, 5 fields at a time. And each field can be picked up by a single Input # rather than needing the Line Input command. The similarity with user-defined records (see Chapter 11) is not a coincidence. You'll often find yourself filling in the components of a record from a file.

note: *Field is actually now a keyword. It is used for the new data access features of Visual Basic. It is an object type that's part of a recordset—see Chapter 20.*

Knowing the exact format of this file means you can easily write a procedure that will retrieve this information. First set up a record type:

```
Type StudentRecord
   Name As String
   FirstExam As Integer
   SecondExam As Integer
   ThirdExam As Integer
   FourthExam As Integer
End Type
```

Now make up an array of StudentRecords as a global variable,

```
Global StudentGrades() As StudentRecord
```

and then use the following general procedure:

```
Sub RetrieveGrade()
  Dim FileNum As Integer, I As Integer
  ReDim StudentGrades(1 To 25)
  FileNum = FreeFile
  Open "GRADES" For Input As #FileNum
  For I = 1 To 25
   Input #FileNum, StudentGrades(I).Name
   Input #FileNum, StudentGrades(I).FirstExam
   Input #FileNum, StudentGrades(I).SecondExam
   Input #FileNum, StudentGrades(I).ThirdExam
   Input #FileNum, StudentGrades(I).FourthExam
  Next I
```

```
  Close FileNum
End Sub
```

Now each row of the array StudentGrades contains a record with the name and grades of a student. You could easily incorporate this type of general Sub procedure into a program that analyzes the grades or places the information on a grid.

This file has a simple structure because the cardinal rule remains: You can't do anything with a file until you bring into memory the information you need from it.

The more complicated the structure of the file, the harder it is to work with. If you can keep the structure of your files simple, then filling up an array is often the method of choice. The reason is that once the information contained in the file is stored, massaging it is easy, usually requiring only a few For-Next loops to run through the array.

For example, suppose you want to write a procedure that can return the average and number absent on each exam. As always when dealing with an array of records, you could choose to store this information in two parallel arrays or in one string array. In this case, if you chose to store this information in an array of strings rather than in the array of records given earlier, you could write a Sub that would take a parameter for the exam number, as in the following listing:

```
Sub AnalysisOfExams(ExamNumber As Integer)
  Dim NumAbsent As Integer, Total As Integer, I As Integer
  ' StudentGrades() is a global string array
  NumAbsent = 0
  Total = 0
  For I = 1 To 25
    If StudentGrades(I, ExamNumber) = "absent" Then
     NumAbsent = NumAbsent + 1
    Else
     Total = Total + Val(StudentGrades(I, ExamNumber))
    End If
  Next I
  Print "The number absent was"; NumAbsent
  Print "The class average was"; Total/(25 - NumAbsent)
End Sub
```

This procedure is straightforward. The parameter tells the procedure what exam number (column of the array) to look at, and the For-Next loop runs through each row. (The Val command is needed because the exam grades are stored in a string array.)

Adding to an Existing File

The GRADE file contains each student's name followed by a list of his or her grades. This is a bit unnatural. A different, more natural kind of file structure would occur if the teacher entered everything in steps: first the student's name and then, after a while, the results of the first exam, and so on. To write a program to do this, you need a command that lets you add information to the end of an already existing file. The statement Open *FileName* For Append As *File#* causes three things to occur at once:

- Visual Basic opens the file (if the file doesn't exist, it creates it) and sets up the appropriate buffer.
- Visual Basic locates the end of the file on the disk.
- Visual Basic prepares to output to the file at its end.

caution: *Recall that if you open an existing file for Output, you erase it. Only by using the Append command can you add to an existing file.*

If you are writing this type of program for yourself, then for a single class's records, you might want to update this file, using a short fragment that reads the students' names and stores them in an array before appending:

```
Dim I As Integer
ReDim StudentNames$(25)
Open "StudentGrades" For Input As # 1
For I = 1 To 25
 Input #1, StudentNames$(I)
Next I
Close #1
Open "StudentGrades" For Append As #1
For I = 1 To 25
 M$ = "The grade for " + StudentNames$(I) + " is ?"
 StudentGrade$ = InputBox$(M$)
 Print #1, StudentGrade$
Next I
Close
```

This fragment assumes the file was already created and contains the names of the students. The point of the Close command is that to change a sequential file's status from reading to writing, it must first be closed. Once the file is closed, the Append command lets you add to it.

You will probably find yourself writing lots of these "quick and dirty" programs as you become more familiar with file-handling techniques. Although they're never very robust, they do get the job done. (You need special techniques to make file-handling programs robust; see "Making a File Program Robust: Error Trapping" later in this chapter.)

Suppose, however, you are teaching five classes, each with a different number of students. Then the "quick and dirty" approach is not worthwhile. It's possible to get the classes mixed up, leading to an error message or even to losing a student's grades. To prevent this kind of mishap, write a header to all your files. Use this header to put standard information about the file at the beginning of the file. You can then use this information to build a grid to allow data entry.

To write a usable grade book program, you can use the first few entries in the file for the name of the class, the semester, the number of exams, and the number of students. This kind of information isn't likely to change. (If you want to change it, see the section "Binary Files" later in this chapter.) Also, this has the added advantage that you can use this information to set up the bounds on the loops that will read and process the information contained in the file. The following table shows you the properties of the form that let the user fill in this header information inside various text boxes:

Type of Object	Control (Form) Name	Caption (Text)
Form	frmHeader	General Information
Label	Label1	File Name
Label	Label2	Class Name
Text box	txtNameOfFile	
Text box	txtNameOfClass	
Text box	txtNumberOfExams	
Text box	txtNumberOfStudents	
Command button	cmdSetUp	Set Up File

Now you can have the following general procedure that sets up a grade book on a disk in the currently active directory. (This procedure assumes you've checked that the filename is acceptable already, and it does not contain the error trap that is needed for any serious file-handling program.)

```
Sub cmdSetUp_Click()
' local variables
Dim ExamNum As Integer, StuNum As Integer, FileNum As Integer

FileNum = FreeFile
Open txtNameOfFile.Text For Output As #FileNum
 Print #FileNum,txtNameOfClass.Text
 Print #FileNum, Val(txtNumberOfExams.Text)
 Print #FileNum, Val(txtNumberOfStudents.Text)
Close #FileNum
End Sub
```

General Sequential Files

Although For-Next loops are a convenient way to read back information contained in a file, obviously there are times when they are not practical. There may be too much information in the file, or you don't know what limits to use. You need a way to implement the following outline:

```
While there's information left in the file
  Get next piece of INFO
  Process it
Loop
```

To do this, you need a way to test when you're at the end of a file. The statement in Visual Basic that lets you do this is mnemonic: it's called EOF( ) (End Of File), where the parentheses hold the file ID number. A quite general program to read back the information contained in a file set up with Print # statements looks like this:

```
FileNum = FreeFile
Open FileName$ For Input As #FileNum
Do Until EOF(FileNum)
   Line Input #FileNum, A$
  ' process line - this would probably be a procedure call or
  ' function call
Loop
Close #FileNum
```

You use a loop with the test at the top to take into account the unlikely possibility that the file exists but doesn't contain any information—that is, it was opened for output but nothing was actually sent to the file. This fragment is a more or less direct translation of the outline. It picks up a line of data (that is, all the data up to a carriage return/line feed pair), and it continues doing this until it gets to the end of the file.

Use this kind of fragment to write a simple print formatter for text files. All you need to know is that you can enter each line (that is, that the lines are not too long or too short); then add the lines to the current value of a string variable. When you're done, make the lines the Text property of a multiline text box with vertical scroll bars.

tip: *Remember, it's much faster in Visual Basic to create the string first and assign the Text property when you're finished retrieving the information than to change the Text property itself repeatedly.*

By the way, a lot of people use the Do While form of these loops. They prefer

```
Do While Not EOF(1)/Loop
```

or

```
While Not EOF(1)/WEnd
```

Since all three forms are equivalent, which one you choose is a matter of taste.

READING BACK CHARACTERS

One common use of the EOF statement is to read back the information contained in a file character-by-character. The analogy to keep in mind if you know PC-BASIC is that you read a file as if it were the keyboard. The command that picks individual characters from the keyboard is Input$. In Visual Basic, you pick up individual characters from a file with the statement

StringVariableName = Input$(*NumberOfChars, File Id*)

where the first entry holds the number of characters and the second holds the file ID. Therefore,

```
SixChar$ = Input$(6,#2)
```

picks up six characters from a file opened for input with file ID #2 and assigns it to a string variable named SixChar$.

Here is a fragment that reads the contents of a text file named FileName$ character-by-character and prints both the ASCII code and the character on the same line:

```
' A 'semi' master text file reader
FileNum = FreeFile
Open FileName$ For Input As #FileNum
Do Until EOF(FileNum)
 A$ = Input$(1,#FileNum)
 Print  A$, ASC(A$)
Loop
Close FileNum
```

If you use this program on the files TEST1, TEST2, and TEST3 created earlier, you can easily check that the spaces and carriage return/line feed combinations the Print # sends to a file (as stated earlier) are, in fact, there.

Although the Input$(,) statement lets you examine the structure of many text files character-by-character, it shouldn't be overused. For example, it's usually much slower than using the Line Input # or even the Input # function. (If you read many characters at once, Input$ speeds up considerably.) Moreover, it's possible for files created by word processors or programs not to be readable by this method. This is because Visual Basic stops reading the file when it encounters a CTRL+Z combination (CHR$(26)), the traditional end-of-file character. (Some files created by programs use CHR$(26)s internally for purposes other than to indicate the end of the file.) You can see this by trying to use the previous program to read back the file created with the following fragment:

```
'demonstrates Ctrl+Z (=^Z=CHR$(26)) as EOF
Dim FileNum As Integer, I As Integer
FileNum = FreeFile
Open "TEST" For Output As #FileNum
Print #FileNum, CHR$(26)
For I = 1 To 10
  Print #FileNum, "The previous program can't ever read this"
Next I
Close #FileNum
```

tip: *Placing a CHR$(26) at the beginning of your file is a simple yet effective way to keep casual snoopers out of your files.*

Since it can be very important to massage non-ASCII files (such as spreadsheet files), Visual Basic has another method of reading back files that, among its other powers, gets around this CTRL+Z problem. (See the section "Binary Files" later in this chapter.)

In any case, even if a file can be read with the Input$ function, it's usually better to think of a file as being made up of fields, possibly grouped into records. Each field is separated from the next by a delimiter—that is, a comma or carriage return/line feed combination. The delimiter is what lets you use a single Input # to pick up the field. This is much faster than doing it character-by-character. (For example, you might use it to load a list or combo box.)

Sending Special Characters to a Sequential File

Since you send information to a file as if it were the screen, you again have to solve the following problems:

- How do you send special characters (such as quotation marks) to the screen?
- How do you nicely format a file?

Visual Basic uses the Write # statement, separated by commas and with quotes around strings, to send items to a file. For example,

```
Write #3, "Testing 1,2,3"
```

sends everything (including the quotes and the commas) to the output (or append) file with ID #3. This is similar to (and, of course, less cumbersome than) writing

```
Print #3, Chr$(34);
Print #3, "Testing";
Print #3, Chr$(34)
Print #3, "1, 2, 3";
```

(Note the three semicolons to prevent inadvertent carriage return/line feed combinations.)

As long as you send individual pieces of information to a file, the Print # and Write # commands can be used interchangeably. For example,

```
Print #FileNum, "Hello"
```

and

```
Write #FileNum, "Hello"
```

both put a single piece of information into a file. In either case, you can read back the information by using the Input # command. (Although the files won't be the same size, the Write command adds two quotation marks (Chr$(34)) to the file.) It's only when you send more than one piece of information at a time that the differences really emerge. For example, to send three numbers to a file using

```
Print #FileNum, 1, 2, 3
```

sends a rather large number of superfluous spaces. The command

```
Write #FileNum, 1,2,3
```

sends the appropriate commas to the file, saving space and making it easier to read back the information. It's equivalent to the cumbersome

```
Print #FileNum, 1; ","; 2; ","; 3
```

Simply put, use Write # together with Input #, and use Print # with Line Input #.

Making Changes Inside a Sequential File

The information inside a sequential file is packed tight and is hard to change, but that doesn't mean you can't do it. If the changes you're making don't alter the size of the file, then the methods described in the "Binary Files" section of this chapter are your best bet. This section explains some other ways that do not use these techniques.

The Open FileName For Append As #FileNum command lets you add information to the end of a sequential file. Suppose you now want to add information to the beginning of a file. Proceed as follows:

1. Open a temporary file for output.
2. Use Print # or Write # to place the new information in the temporary file.
3. Close the temporary file.
4. Append the information from the original file onto the end of the temporary file. Two techniques are available to perform this task:
   - The first technique involves reopening the temporary file For Append. The original file is then opened for input, and information is read from the original file and appended to the temporary file. Finally, the temporary file is closed again.
   - The second technique is much faster when the original file is large. Visual Basic's Shell command is used to execute the underlying operating system's COPY command. The underlying operating system command

     COPY *file1+file2*

     appends the file named *file2* onto the file named *file1*. Thus, the Shell command would take the form

     Shell "COPY *TempFileName+OriginalFileName*"

     or:

     Shell "COPY" + *TempFileName$* +"+" + *OriginalFileName$*
5. Delete the original file using the Kill command.
6. Rename the temporary file to the original file's name by using the Name command.

Suppose the information does not go right at the beginning of the file, or you want to remove or replace information already in the file. To do this, imagine what you might do if you were to make these modifications on a cassette tape. First, you'd record the words to be added on a separate tape with a little bit of leader, which means you'd leave some blank tape so you can cut and paste. Then you'd find where on the tape the new information is to go and splice (or cut) the tapes.

For example, suppose you want to change all occurrences of the word "QuickBASIC" in a file to "Visual Basic" (or, more generally, to write your own search and replace function). Follow these steps:

1. Read the information in the file into a temporary file, stopping whenever you get to the string "QuickBASIC".
2. Write "Visual Basic" into the temporary file.
3. Move past the occurrence of the word "QuickBASIC" and continue repeating steps 1 and 2 until you reach the end of the file.
4. Now kill the original file and rename the temporary file with the original file's name.

Because you have to read the information back character-by-character, a program that implements this outline can run for a long time if done in this naive manner. Binary techniques can work much faster. (See the section on "Binary Files" for more on this.)

On the other hand, the program will run more quickly (and is also simpler to program) if you know that each occurrence of the string you're searching for is in a separate field. If this is true, you can use a loop that in pseudocode is

```
OPEN Original File
OPEN Temp File
INPUT Field from Original File
DO UNTIL EOF(Original File)
 If field <>"QuickBASIC" THEN
  WRITE It To Temp File
 ELSE
  WRITE "Visual Basic" to Temp File
 END IF
 INPUT nextfield
LOOP
KILL Original File
ReNAME Temp File as Original File
```

Finally, if you knew that each field contained the words you were searching for but weren't necessary equal to it, you could input the field and then write a little procedure to search through the field after it is in memory.

The RichTextBox Control and File Handling

If you are working with Windows 95 and have the Professional or Enterprise edition of Visual Basic, you can use some properties of the RichTextBox control to make it easy to send its contents to a file (or conversely, to display the contents of a file inside of one). Here are short descriptions of the properties and methods of the RichTextBox control that can be used in file handling.

LOADFILE METHOD

The LoadFile method loads an .RTF file or text file into a RichTextBox control at one gulp. The syntax is

NameOfRichTextBox.LoadFile(*pathname*, *filetype*)

where *pathname* is a string expression defining the path and filename of the file you want to load into the control. The optional *filetype* parameter controls whether the file is loaded as an .RTF file. (The default is that it is, but you can use a value of 0 or the symbolic constant rtfRTF.) Use the value 1 (or the constant rtfText) to load a text file.

note: *The LoadFile method replaces whatever was in the control with the contents of the file.*

SAVEFILE METHOD

The SaveFile method saves the contents of a RichTextBox control to a file in one swoop. The syntax is similar to that of LoadFile:

NameOfRichTextBox.SaveFile(*pathname*, *filetype*)

note: *You can use ordinary file-handling techniques for working with a RichTextBox control. For example:*

```
Open "FOO.RTF" For Input As 1
RichTextBox1.TextRTF = Input(LOF(1), 1)
```

Making a File Program Robust: Error Trapping

Usually, when you're testing a program, you don't care if you get a run-time error and your program crashes. However, when an open file is around, then after a crash, strange things may get written into your files, or information you need may never get there. Even if you've thoroughly debugged the program, someone may try to send information to a full disk or try to access a file that doesn't exist. To solve these problems, you must stop the program when, for example, it faces a full disk. The command that activates error trapping, as you saw in Chapter 8, is

```
On Error GoTo ...
```

where the three dots are for the label (line number) that defines the error trap. (Recall that labels must be unique across a module or form.)

Now you need to transfer control to a part of the procedure that identifies the problem and, if possible, fixes it. If the error can be corrected, you can use the Resume statement to pick up where you left off. However, you can't correct an error if you don't know why it happened. Table 17-3 gives the error codes most common to file-handling programs and their likely causes. You would use this information as outlined in Chapter 9. For example, place the following statement somewhere in the program before the error can occur:

```
On Error GoTo DiskErrorHandler
```

Now add code to your event procedure like the fragment given here:

```
DiskErrorHandler:
Select Case Err.Number
    Case 53
     M$ = "Your file was not found. Please check on the "
     M$ = M$ + "spelling or call your operator for assistance."
    Case 57
     M$ = "Possibly big problems on your hardware. You should "
     M$ = M$ + "call your operator for assistance."
    Case 61
     M$ = "The disk is full. Please replace with a slightly less "
     M$ = M$ + "used model." 'could Shell to FORMAT.COM here
    Case 71
     M$ = "I think the drive door is open - please check."
```

```
    Case 72
     M$ = "Possibly big problems on your hard disk. You"
     M$ = M$ + " definitely should call for help."
    Case Else
     M$ = "Please tell the operator (= program author?) that"
     M$ = M$ & " error number " & Err.Number & " occurred. "
  End Select
  M$ = M$ + vbCrLf + vbCrLf + "If the error has been corrected click
on"
  M$ = M$ + " retry, otherwise click on cancel."
  WhatToDo% = MsgBox(M$, vbRetryCancel)      'retry/cancel message box
  If WhatToDo% = vbRetry Then Resume Else End
```

Code	Message
52	Bad filename or number (Remember to use FreeFile correctly.)
53	File not found (This probably indicates a typo.)
54	Bad file mode (The code uses two types of file handling—without closing the file in between.)
55	File already open (You obviously can't open a file that is already open unless you use a different identification number.)
57	Device I/O error (Big problems! Your hardware is acting up. I/O stands for input/output, but check the disk drive anyway.)
58	File already exists
59	Bad record length
61	Disk full (There's not enough room to do what you want.)
62	Input past end of file (You put the test for EOF in the wrong place.)
63	Bad record number
64	Bad file name (You didn't follow the naming conventions for a filename.)
67	Too many files at the same time
68	Device unavailable
70	Permission denied (The disk you're writing to has the write-protect notch covered or the file is write protected.)
71	Disk not ready (The door is open, or where's the floppy?)
72	Disk media error (Time to throw out the floppy or start thinking about the state of your hard disk.)
74	Can't rename files across different drives
75	Path/File access error
76	Path not found (Probably a typo—you asked to open a file that doesn't exist.)

Table 17-3
Common File-Handling Errors

The idea of this error trap is simple—the Select Case statement is ideal for handling the many possibilities. Each Case tries to give some indication of where the problem is and, if possible, how to correct it. If you reach the Case Else, the error number has to be reported. In any case, the final block gives you the option of continuing or not, using a Retry/Cancel message box (Type = 5).

note: *Only the most common errors are covered here—and, as mentioned in Chapter 9, you might want to consider a centralized message error handler that takes the error number property of the Err object.*

Error trapping isn't a cure-all. Obviously, very little can be done about a hard disk crash. On the other hand, if you can "shell" to the FORMAT command, then not having a formatted (empty) floppy around is not a crisis for the novice user. (Experienced Windows users can always use Windows' multitasking possibilities to leave the program in order to format a disk.)

Adding a complete DiskCheck fragment to your file-handling programs is the only way to make them robust. You can merge the same module containing this kind of error trap into all your serious file-handling programs, using the Load Text option in the File menu or the clipboard.

On the other hand, as mentioned in Chapter 9, probably the simplest and cleanest way to put error trapping in your program is to write a function in a code module that analyzes the error code and gives the user the necessary feedback. A global function can do the work once the program passes the error code to it as a parameter. In any case, writing a serious file-handling program without an error trap is an awful idea.

Random-Access Files

Suppose you are tired of having to search through entire cassettes for certain songs. To avoid this, you decide to put songs that you want instant access to on individual cassettes. The advantages of doing this are obvious, but there are disadvantages as well. First, to gain more or less instant access to an individual song, you're going to waste a considerable amount of blank tape on each cassette. If, to prevent this, you decide to create a standard-sized tape—one that holds, say, four minutes—you're sure to have at least a couple of songs that run more than four minutes. It's clear that no matter what you do, you'll either waste space or have a few songs that won't fit. Also, if you single out too many songs for separate tapes, you increase the number of cassettes you have to store.

If you have hundreds of tapes, each containing an individual song, then you're almost back where you started. It can't possibly be easy to find an individual song if you have to search through a hundred tapes. At this point you would probably choose to alphabetize the tapes by some key feature (such as singer or title), set up an index, or both.

Random-access files are stored on a disk in such a way that they have much the same advantages and disadvantages as the song collector's tapes. You gain instant access to individual pieces of information, but only at some cost. You must standardize the packets of information involved, which means that some things may not fit or that space is not efficiently used, and if the file grows too big—with too many pieces of information—you'll have to set up another file to index the first.

note: *The data-handling features of Visual Basic make random-access files somewhat less important. But the amount of overhead involved with using data access sometimes makes setting up your own random-access files the right choice. This is especially true for small files.*

When setting up a sequential file, it's occasionally useful to think of a group of fields as forming a single record. For example, in the grade book program, grouping the fields by fives gave a logical and convenient way to read back the information. It's worth stressing that this particular grouping was not intrinsic to the file—it's only the way the program looks at the file. The only intrinsic divisions within a sequential file are those created by the delimiters (commas or carriage return/line feed combinations). When you read back information, you read it field by field, with the delimiters acting as barriers.

In a random-access file, however, the notion of a record is built in. A *random-access file* is a special disk file arranged by records. This lets you immediately move to the 15th record without having to pass through the 14th before it, which saves a considerable amount of time.

When you first set up a random-access file, you specify the maximum length for each record. When you enter data for an individual record, you can, of course, put in less information than this preset limit, but you can never put in more. So just like the song collector, you might need to prepare for the worst possible situation.

The command that sets up a random-access file is analogous to the one for opening a sequential file. For example,

```
Open "SAMPLE.RND" As #5 Len = 100
```

opens a random-access file called SAMPLE.RND on the current directory with a file ID of 5, and each record can hold 100 characters. Note that, unlike the situation for sequential files, you don't have to specify whether you're opening the file for input, output, or appending. As you'll soon see, this distinction is taken care of in the commands that manipulate a random-access file; an open random-access file can be read from and written to essentially simultaneously. You can have any mixture of random-access and sequential files open at the same time. The only restrictions are set by the underlying operating system (the FILES command in your CONFIG.SYS file). To prevent confusion between file types, many programmers use an extension like .RND for all random-access files, as in the preceding example.

Similarly, you close a file opened for random access by using the Close command followed by the file ID number. As before, the Close command alone closes all open files, regardless of whether they were opened for sequential or random access. This is especially useful because a sophisticated program for random files often has many files open simultaneously—both sequential and random.

Suppose you want to write a random-access file that would keep track of someone's library. You start by designing the form. You decide on five categories—AUTHOR, TITLE, SUBJECT, PUBLISHER, and MISCELLANEOUS, and after looking over your library, you decide on the following limits for the categories:

Category	Size
AUTHOR	20
TITLE	30
SUBJECT	15
PUBLISHER	20
MISCELLANEOUS	13

Therefore, the total for each record is 98. A random-access file to fit this form is set up (via FileNum = FreeFile, as always):

```
Open "MYLIB.RND" As FileNum Len = 98
```

Just as each file has an ID number, each record within a random-access file has a record number. A single random-access file can hold from 1 to 16,777,216 records. Moreover, you don't have to fill the records in order. As you'll see, you can place information in the 15th record without ever having touched the first 14. The disadvantage of doing this, however, is that Visual Basic would automatically set aside enough space for the first 14 records on the disk, even if nothing is in them.

The word "record" has been used frequently in this chapter. This is no coincidence. One of the main reasons QuickBASIC and then Visual Basic implemented record types was to simplify working with random-access files. First, set up a user-defined type (record):

```
Type Bookinfo
  Author As String*20
  Title As String*30
  Subject As String*15
  Publisher As String*20
  Miscellaneous As String*13
End Type
```

You must use fixed-length strings in order to work within the limitations of a random-access file because of the record length.

Next, suppose ExampleOfBook has been previously dimensioned as being of type Bookinfo. Then the command

```
Get FileNum, 10, ExampleOfBook
```

would transfer the contents of the 10th record from the random-access file into the record variable ExampleOfBook, automatically filling in the correct components of ExampleOfBook.

The command

```
Put FileNum, 37, ExampleOfBook
```

would send the components of ExampleOfBook to the 37th record of file #FileNum.

This method of sending information to a random-access file is unique to QuickBASIC and Visual Basic, and it's a valuable improvement over the older PC-BASIC. Visual Basic does not allow you to use the older (and much clumsier) method, which requires what are called field variables.

The record types you create determine the size of the random-access file. Since records can hold numbers as well as text, it's a bit messy to compute the length of a record variable of a given record type. (Remember that an integer takes 2 bytes, a long integer 4, and so on.) Visual Basic makes it simple, however, because the Len command not only gives the length of a string, it gives you the length of a record as well. Take any variable of the given type—for example,

```
Dim ExampleOfRecord As ThisType
LenOfRecord = Len(ExampleOfRecord)
```

and use this to set the length for the Open command used to create the random-access file.

Headers and Indexes for Random-Access Files

If you have the information you want to transfer to a newly created random-access file stored in an array of records, you can use a loop to send the information there. The loop counter determines where to put the record. Usually, however, you set up a variable whose value is the number of the next record you want to read from or write to.

Similarly, you can read back all the information in a random-access file by using the EOF flag after making the dimensions of the array records sufficiently large:

```
Dim I As Integer
Do Until EOF(FileNum)
 I = I + 1
 Get FileNum, I, Records(I)
Loop
```

There are many problems with doing this. For one, you're unlikely to want all the information contained in the file at once, and it may not fit, anyway—suppose you have 1,000,000 records. Also, go back to square one: how do you even know what length to use to open the random-access file? While there are many ways to determine this, a common practice is to set up another file that contains this (and other) vital information about the random-access file. At the very least, this sequential file will contain information about the sizes and types of the fields, possibly names for the fields, and the number of records stored to date. In fact, it may even contain an index of certain keys and the numbers of the records that contain those keys.

Indexes are vital to a random-access file. Many database managers are nothing more than elaborate programs to manage random-access files. Their speed depends on how the program finds the record containing keyed information.

This can only be done effectively through indexes. (The alternative is to examine the relevant component of each record one by one.)

An index can be as simple as a sequential file containing a list of keys followed by a record number, or it can be a more elaborately ordered one.

note: *Given the database-handling features of Visual Basic, you are unlikely to go to the trouble of creating a random-access file if it needs an elaborate index. If you do need an index for a random-access file, then a good choice for the index are binary trees (Chapter 19). Other possibilities are to Quicksort (Chapter 19) or Shell sort (Chapter 11) the keys once you've read this information into memory. In all cases, however, you're likely to read the index into an array or arrays.*

Binary Files

Binary files are not a new type of file but a new way of manipulating any kind of file. Binary file techniques let you read or change any byte of a file. They are extraordinarily powerful tools but, like any powerful tool, they must be used with care.

caution: *(For Visual Basic and QuickBasic programmers especially) Binary file-handling techniques have changed from Visual Basic 3, so be sure to read the next few sections carefully. Depending on what you are doing, you may have to change your code in order to make it work with the 32-bit version of Visual Basic.*

Among other features, binary file techniques do not care about any embedded EOFs (CTRL+Z = Chr$(26)) that the file may have. (Recall that it was impossible to read back the file created earlier in the chapter using sequential file techniques because of the CTRL+Z sequences in the file.)

The command

Open *FileName* For Binary As # *FileNum*

sets up a file to be read with these new techniques. And, just as with random-access files, you can now both read and write to the file.

Now, as long as you are reading back information you are sure was stored as strings, then the easiest way to pick up the information from a text file open in binary file mode is with the Input$(,) function you saw earlier. Because of the automatic conversions that the 32-bit version of Visual Basic makes between Unicode and ANSI strings, this will work transparently for you. (Visual Basic automatically converts ANSI strings to Unicode when data is read back to your application, and back to ANSI when strings are written back to a file.)

The first slot of the Input$ function still holds the number of characters and the second the file ID number. For example, the following listing gives a module that prints the contents of any file, regardless of any embedded control characters:

```
Sub PrintAFile(A$)
' example of binary input
Dim I As Integer, FileNum As Integer, Char$
FileNum = FreeFile            ' get free file i.d.
Open A$ For Binary As #FileNum

For I = 1 To LOF(FileNum)
 Char$ = Input$(1,#FileNum)
 Print Char$;
Next I
Close #FileNum
End Sub
```

More often than not, however, you'll want to modify this module by adding some filtering lines—for example, to make it strip out the control characters or those with ASCII codes greater than 127. Once you strip such a file, it can be displayed with the underlying operating system TYPE command or more easily sent by a modem.

For example, suppose you are confronted with converting a program from the archaic (but at the time very popular) WordStar word processing program. It turns out this program normally stores a file in such a way that if you try to import this as a text file, you will have trouble reading the file. Stated simply, here's what WordStar does:

- It uses certain control codes inside the file (such as CTRL+B for bold).
- Each word-wrapped line ends with CHR$(141)+CHR$(10). Note that 141 = 13 + 128. Thus, 141 corresponds to a carriage return with the high-order bit set. Also, the first letter of each word in a word-wrapped line may have its high-order bit set.
- WordStar uses the carriage return/line feed combination (CHR$(13)+CHR$(10)) for hard returns. This means that someone has pressed ENTER rather than that the program performed word wrapping.

It's easy to modify the procedure given earlier to strip out all formatting (control) codes and then convert characters with their high-order bits set. (For those who do use WordStar, the procedure will not strip out dot commands; the changes needed for that are left to you.) Here's how to modify the procedure:

```
Sub WordStarStripper (A$)
  Dim FileNum As Integer, I As Integer
  Dim Char$

' Example Of Binary Input for a text file!
  FileNum = Freefile                        ' get free file i.d.
  Open A$ For Binary As #FileNum
  For I = 1 To LOF(FileNum)
    Char$ = Input$(1, #FileNum)
    ' strip high-order bit, if any
    If Asc(Char$) > 127 Then
      CharCode = Asc(Char$)
      Char$ = Chr$(CharCode - 128)
    End If
    ' Ignore All Control Codes Except Line Feed
    If Char$ >= Chr$(32) Then
      Print Char$
    Elseif Char$ = Chr$(10) Then
      'Issue A Chr$(13) And A Chr$(10)
      Print
    End If
  Next I
End Sub
```

Of course, in a more general program, you'd probably want to do something more than print the character.

note: *This program reads the information one byte at a time. This is often inefficient. Consider reading in the information in larger chunks as described in the following tip.*

tip: *On my system, the optimum setting seems to be 4096 character chunks. Read in chunks this size and then analyze the characters in the string after they've picked up the information contained in the file.*

Using Binary Access in More General (Non-Text) Situations

The big change (and one that will break a lot of previous code, unfortunately!) is that in the 32-bit version of Visual Basic, you can not use the Input$(,) for picking up individual bytes from a non-text file such as a TIF or JPG file. Instead, you must use the Get statement with an array of bytes. (Arrays of bytes will also work in the 16-bit version of Visual Basic, so you might as well use it all the time.) The problem is that because of Unicode, a character no longer takes up a single byte. Thus, because of Unicode, the procedure is a lot more cumbersome than it was in earlier versions of Visual Basic. (In general, in a Unicode 2-byte encoding for an ordinary ANSI string, the first byte will be the ANSI code; the second is used only for the language. Visual Basic is smart enough to recognize text files where the characters take up only one byte. This is why it doesn't automatically pick up two bytes for each use of Input$(1,).)

The first step is easy:

- Get the bytes out of the file into a byte array using the Get function. The syntax is

  Get *file#, position,* ByteArray

The number of characters this statement picks up is equal to the size of the byte array given as the last parameter. The second parameter is needed because Visual Basic maintains a file pointer within a file opened for binary access. Each time you pick up a byte, the file pointer moves one position farther within the file.

Here's an example of how to use Get for a small enough binary file to fit in memory:

```
Sub BinaryPickUp (A$)
  Dim FileNum As Integer, I As Integer
' Example Of Binary Input for a general file!
  FileNum = Freefile                   ' get free file i.d.
  Open A$ For Binary As #FileNum
  Redim ArrayOfBytes(1 To LOF(FileNum) As Byte
  Get #FileNum,1, ArrayOfBytes
```

(Theoretically this would let you store up to 2^31 characters—but I suspect memory constraints would prevent this in the vast bulk of machines.)

Once you have the bytes in memory, you will have to decide how you want to manipulate the raw byte information. One possibility is that you can leave the bytes in the array and then work with them using ordinary array handling techniques. Another possibility is to:

- Assign the byte array to a string. (This will not do any translations.)
- Use the appropriate B character function, as given in Table 17-4, to work with the byte string. (B character functions work similarly to their ordinary namesakes that you saw in Chapter 9—except that they work with byte strings.)

THE SEEK COMMAND

The Seek command is a fast forward command and a rewind command combined into one. More precisely,

Seek *filenum, position number*

moves the file pointer for the file with *filenum* directly to the byte in that position. Any Input$ would start picking up characters from this location.

Seek has another use. Seek(*filenum*) tells you the position number for the last byte read for either a binary or sequential file. You can also use the Seek function with random-access files. Now it will return the record number of the next record.

THE PUT COMMAND

To place information within a file opened for binary access, use a modification of the Put command. For example,

```
Put #1, 100, ByteArray()
```

Function	Purpose
AscB	Returns the value given by the first byte in a string of binary data
InStrB	Finds the first occurrence of a byte in a binary string
MidB	Returns the specified number of bytes from a binary string
LeftB, RightB	Takes the specified number of bytes from the left or right end of a binary string
ChrB	Takes a byte and returns a binary string with that byte

Table 17-4
Binary Array Equivalents of the String Functions

would place the contents of the byte array directly into the file with file ID #1 starting at the 100th byte. The number of characters sent to this file is, of course, given by the size of the byte array. The Put command overwrites whatever was there. If you leave a space for the byte position but don't specify it in the Put command, like this:

```
Put #1, , ByteArray()
```

then the information is placed wherever the file pointer is currently located.

note: *You can also use Put with string variables by replacing the ByteArray with a string variable. However, to avoid problems that come from mixing bytes and strings in the same file when doing binary access, you are best off doing this only for text files. Also, if you choose to do this, you should initialize a string to be the correct size using the Space$ command.*

Final Remarks on Binary File Handling

Now that you know the commands for working on the byte level for a file, you're in a position to write any file utility you like. (If you need to massage the output of an application program, you will need to know the internal format of the program.)

For example, the features of the Seek command make it easy to write a function to search through a text file for a string and replace it as well (see the next section). To find a string, read the file back in chunks. Use the Instr function to search for the string inside the chunk. If the string is found, exit the function and report success. If the string is not found in a specific chunk, reset the Seek pointer back by one less than the length of the string searched for and repeat until the file is processed. (You have to reset the file pointer back to allow for the string being only partially digested by the Input$ command.)

If you want to allow for replacement, combine the above technique with a temporary file, as you saw in the section "Making Changes Inside a Sequential File." If the replacement string is exactly the same size, you can use the Put command instead of a temporary file.

For example, the following procedure takes any text file and replaces all occurrences of one string inside of it by another. It adjusts the size of the replacement string by padding or truncating to match the original string.

note: *If you want to modify this program to work with any binary file, replace the Input$ command by the appropriate Get command with a binary array and the various string functions by their "B" equivalent as shown in Table 17-4.*

Here's the procedure:

```
Const ChunkSize = 4096

Sub ChangeFile(FName$, IdString$, NString$)
  Dim PosString As Integer, WhereString As Integer
  Dim FileNumber As Integer, A$, NewString$
  Dim AString As String*ChunkSize

  FileNumber = FreeFile
  PosString = 1
  WhereString = 0
  AString = Space$(ChunkSize)

  'Make sure strings have same size
  If Len(IdString$) > Len(NString$) Then
    NewString$ = NString$ + Space$(Len(IdString$) - Len(NString$))
  Else
    NewString$ = Left$(NString$, Len(IdString$))
  End If

  Open FName$ For Binary As FileNumber
  If LOF(FileNumber) < ChunkSize Then
      A$ = Space$(LOF(FileNumber))
      Get #FileNumber, 1, A$
      WhereString = InStr(1, A$, IdString$)
  Else
    Get #FileNumber, 1, AString
    WhereString = InStr(1, AString, IdString$)
  End If

  If WhereString <> 0 Then
    Put #FileNumber, WhereString, NewString$
  End If
  PosString = ChunkSize + PosString - Len(IdString$)

  Do Until EOF(FileNumber) Or PosString > LOF(FileNumber)
    If PosString + ChunkSize > LOF(FileNumber) Then
      A$ = Space$(LOF(FileNumber) - PosString)
```

```
      Get #FileNumber, PosString, A$
      WhereString = InStr(FileNumber, A$, IdString$)
    Else
      Get #FileNumber, PosString, AString
      WhereString = InStr(FileNumber, AString, IdString$)
    End If
    If WhereString <> Then
      Put #FileNumber, PosString + WhereString - 1, NewString$
    End If
     PosString = ChunkSize + PosString - Len(IdString$)
  Loop
  Close
End Sub

Problems:
  ' error trap goes here
End Sub
```

This procedure is fairly subtle, so let's go over it carefully. First, it sets up a constant for the size of each chunk. As mentioned earlier, 4096 seems to give the best performance on my machines, but your experience may vary.

Next come the declarations for the various counters used in this program. In particular, there is a fixed-length string equal in size to the chunk size. Since binary file techniques for text files require that the strings replaced be exactly the same size, the first If-Then-Else takes care of this by setting up a correctly sized local variable NewString$ to hold the replacement string.

The procedure then starts picking up pieces of the file. Because you are reading the file in chunks you have to be careful not to go past the boundaries of the file. You use a temporary value A$ in case the file is smaller than the size of the chunks. Because Get only reads as many characters as are currently stored in the file, you need to initialize A$ properly. (Remember that we are assuming the file contains only ordinary ASCII/ANSII strings.)

Next, you use the Instr command to search for the IdString$. If you find it, you put the NewString in its place. Next comes the Loop that looks through the rest of the file. This allows you to do multiple replacements. At each step you have to adjust the pointer back slightly because of the possibility that you have picked up part of the target string in a chunk. Notice as well that the chunk size again requires you to monitor the remaining characters in the file inside the loop. Finally, this procedure indicates where the error trap would go, although to save space one hasn't been included.

note: *You can easily modify this procedure to change it into a function that returns True or False depending on whether the string is found or not. You can also modify this to allow changes in individual bytes in a file by using a byte array instead of the string for picking up the data.*

Sharing Files

As more files are available only off networks, it becomes more important to prevent someone from inadvertently working with a file while you are working with it. Visual Basic's file handling functions can easily be adapted to a networking environment by using the keywords described in the following table.

Keyword	Function
Lock	Prevents access to all or part of an open file
Unlock	Allows access to a file previously locked

You can use these functions after you have opened the file, in which case the syntax takes the form

Lock [#]*filenumber*[, *WhatToLock*]

for the Lock command and

Unlock [#]*filenumber*[, *WhatToUnlock*]

for the Unlock command. Both commands use the file number with which the program opened the file. The *WhatToLock* (*WhatToUnlock*) parameter specifies what portion of the file to lock or unlock. You use it by giving the Start and End values where they denote the first record (for random access files) or first byte (for binary access). For example,

```
Open "foo" For Binary As #1
Lock #1, 1 To 100
```

locks the first 100 bytes of the file FOO. If you leave off the optional parameter, then Lock locks the whole file. (For sequential files, Lock and Unlock affect the entire file, regardless of the range specified by the *WhatToLock* parameter.)

caution: *Be sure to remove all locks with the corresponding Unlock statement before closing a file or quitting your program. (The arguments must match exactly.) Not doing this may foul up the files from that point on!*

General Form of the Open Command

You can also control file sharing at the time you open the file using the most general form of the Open statement. Its full syntax looks like this:

Open *pathname* [For *mode*] [Access *access*] [lock] As [#] *filenumber* [Len=*reclength*]

What follows are short descriptions of the syntax elements.

PATHNAME

This string expression specifies the filename. It may include both directory and drive information.

MODE

This keyword specifies the file mode you have already seen: Append, Binary, Input, Output, or Random.

ACCESS

You specify what operations are permitted on the open file with *access*. There are three: Read, Write, and Read Write. You use one as in the following example:

```
Open filename For Binary Access Read As #1
```

This will let you read the file but not make any changes to it.

LOCK

This parameter specifies the operations permitted on the open file by other processes (unlike the Access parameter, which controls how your program can access the file). There are four possibilities: Shared, Lock Read, Lock Write, and Lock Read Write, as described in the following table:

Keyword	Description
Shared	Other processes can both read and write to the file even while your program is working with it.
Lock Read	No other program can open the file to read it while your program is working with it.
Lock Write	No other program can open the file to write it while your program is working with it.
Lock Read Write	No other programs can work with the file at all while you are working with it.

The following example lets you read the file but nobody else:

```
Open filename For Binary Access Read Lock Read As #1
```

FILENUMBER

A valid file number must be in the range 1 to 511, inclusive. (As you have seen, it's best to use the FreeFile function to find the next available file number.)

RECLENGTH

This is an integer from 1 to 32,767. For files opened for random access, this number gives the record length. For sequential files, this value is the number of characters buffered by the operating system.

note: *In binary, input, and random file modes, you can open a file using a different file number without first closing the file. For sequential append and output, you must close a file before you can use it.*

Adding Licensing Strings

If you are going to distribute your program, you'll probably want to add a startup licensing screen. This section describes one simple technique for doing this completely in Visual Basic.

tip: *In prior versions of Visual Basic, you used to be able to modify a global variable in the .EXE file directly; this no longer seems to work in Visual Basic 4.*

This technique ultimately depends on using binary file techniques to carefully examine and make some subtle changes in a file. The routine in the previous section is a general purpose procedure for doing this for text files.

First, though, you'll need to use information derived from the App object. This is a very useful Visual Basic object for this situation because it can tell you the full path name of the Application (App.Path) or the root name of the .EXE file (App.EXEName), as well as the Help file associated with the application, the Title, or whether another copy of it is running at the present time.

Now that you have the procedure to make changes inside any text file and the necessary properties of the App object, you can move on to my favorite of the techniques for adding licensing screens. By far the easiest way to do this is to have the Form_Initialize (or Sub_Main) look for a hidden file in the same directory as the application. Install this hidden file at the same time as the program. During the installation procedure, open this hidden file and modify a string so as to give the licensee's name. (If you also want to encrypt this information inside the file, see the end of the chapter.) You can use the Path property of the App object to determine the directory to examine. If you can't find the required information inside the hidden file, or can't find the hidden file, do not permit the program to proceed.

To modify the hidden file, you can use a Form_Initialize procedure in the installation program that uses the ChangeFile program you saw earlier. The procedure might look something like this.

```
Form_Initialize ()
On Error GoTo Problems
  Dim InstallTries As Integer, Install$, Person$

  Person$ = ""
  Do Until Person$ <> "" Or InstallTries > 2
    Person$ = InputBox$("Please enter your name.")
    InstallTries = InstallTries + 1
  Loop
  If InstallTries > 3 Then
    MsgBox "Installation Failure - no name supplied "
    End
  End If
  User$ = "Program licensed by " + Person$
IdString$ = "This program has not been licensed to anybody. "
Call ChangeFile(HiddenFileName$, IdString$, Person$)
```

This program assumes you would supply the hidden file name as the value of the HiddenFileName$ variable and that the IdString$ to search for (and change) is, "This program has not been licensed to anybody."

Once you modify the hidden file, the Form_Load of the .EXE file can use the function variation on the ChangeFile mentioned in the previous section to ensure that the string "This program has not been licensed to anybody" no longer occurs.

Keeping File Information Secret

Since a simple utility program using binary file techniques can read back the information contained in any file, the data contained in your files is readily available to anyone with a compatible computer, a little programming skill, and a copy of your disk. In the next few sections you'll see how to encode a file so that only people having the right key can easily read your file. These methods work very well with the hidden file technique just described for handling licensing screens. Of course, the methods here aren't perfect, but considering how easy they are to implement, they are surprisingly secure.

First, a little history. All the earliest ciphers that we know about use simple substitutions. For example, Julius Caesar kept his messages secret by taking each letter in the message and replacing it with the one three letters further on; the letter A is replaced by D, B by E, and so on, until you get to the letters after X. Since X is the 24th letter of the alphabet, you have to wrap around to the beginning of the alphabet, and X becomes A, Y becomes B, and Z becomes C. Here is a normal alphabet and below it a complete Caesar alphabet:

ABCDEFGHIJKLMNOPQRSTUVWXYZ
DEFGHIJKLMNOPQRSTUVWXYZABC

(Actually, in Caesar's time, the alphabet had fewer letters—23 instead of 26. For example, U and V developed out of V around a thousand years ago, and J came around 500 years after that.) For example, the sentence, "Can you read this" becomes

FDQ BRX UHDG WKLV

Shift ciphers go back further than Caesar; one occurs in the Bible. In Jeremiah 25-26, the prophet conceals his prophecy by changing the name of Babylon using a cipher that splits the Hebrew alphabet in half and replaces the first letter with the middle letter, the second by the middle + 1, and so on.

Here is a general procedure that shifts any character by any number of characters, wrapping around if necessary.

```
Sub CaesarShift(A$, Shift%)
  Dim CharNum As Integer
  CharNum = (Asc(A$) + Shift%) Mod(256)
  A$ = Chr$(CharNum)
End Sub
```

It wouldn't be hard to incorporate this procedure into a file encrypter; just pass the contents of the file to the procedure character-by-character. The trouble is that a shift cipher is easy to break; you can even do it by hand. Look at the coded message and run back down the alphabet by steps, shifting the letters back step by step. After, at most, 25 steps, you're done. Here's what you get at each step in the example:

FDQ	BRX	UHDG	WKLV
ECP	AQW	TGCF	VJKU
DBO	ZPV	SFBE	UIJT
CAN	YOU	READ	THIS

Note that it's better to work with the whole message than with individual words because occasionally English words (*clear text*) show up by mistake. For example, the word "HTQI" backs up to the word "FROG" on the second try and to the word "COLD" on the fifth.

Decoding a Caesar cipher, simple as it is, stresses the usefulness of the computer and its limitations. It can do the drudgery, but you have to recognize when to stop. For the more complicated ciphers described in what follows, this division of labor is essential.

More Complicated Ciphers

Since a shift cipher provides virtually no security, the next step is to change the letters in a more random manner. Write down the alphabet, and below it, write all the letters in some arbitrary order:

ABCDEFGHIJKLMNOPQRSTUVWXYZ
QAZXSWEDCVFRBGTYHNUJMIKOPL

Now, every time you see an A in your original message, replace it with a Q, replace each B with an A, each C with a Z, and so on. This cipher can't be broken by the techniques used for shift ciphers, but it's extremely hard to remember the random alphabet used for the code. Around 1600, in an attempt to combine the virtues of this method with the ease of shift codes, people began to use a *keyword cipher*. The idea is to replace the letters of the alphabet with the letters in the key phrase, using the order in which they occur there. For example, suppose the key is THE RAY GUN ZAPPED ME QUICKLY. Now look at the following:

ABCDEFGHIJKLMNOPQRSTUVWXYZ
THERAYGUNZPDMQICKLBFJOSVWX

What this does is take the individual letters from the key phrase, avoiding duplicates as needed, and place them below the normal alphabet. Since the phrase contains only 18 different letters, the unused letters go at the end. To encipher a message using this code, replace the letters in the original message with the ones directly below them—A with T, B with H, and so on.

Here's one possible outline for a procedure that takes a key phrase and creates the code:

```
Get keyphrase
  Run through each letter in keyphrase
  Check if already used
     if not used:
     store in next place in 'cipher' list
     mark that letter as used
  Until no more letters are in the keyphrase
Now store unused letters from normal alphabet into key
```

However, this outline turns out to be not quite the best way of proceeding. For example, suppose you want to decipher a message enciphered this way. Say you see an A in the coded message; then, because an A is below an E in the alphabets just given, the original letter must have been an E.

To set up the two lists to be used for encoding and decoding, start with two ordinary alphabets. Now, since T replaces A, you swap the A in the first alphabet with the T in the second. Next, you swap the B and the H. How can you tell if a letter is already used? Just look at that letter's position in the second alphabet. If the letter is still in its original position, that letter has not been used. When you are done with the letters in the key phrase, any remaining letters should be swapped out of the first alphabet into the second one.

To actually write this program, set up two lists. To make life easier, use two global arrays of integers dimensioned to run from 65 to 90 (the ASCII codes for A to Z):

```
Global Dim EncodeAlph() As Integer, DecodeAlph() As Integer
```

Now call an Initialize procedure from the Form_Load procedure:

```
Sub Initialize( )
  Dim I As Integer
  Redim EncodeAlph(65 To 90) As Integer
  Redim DecodeAlph(65 To 90) As Integer
  For I = 65 To 90
   EncodeAlph(I) = I
   DecodeAlph(I) = I
  Next I
End Sub
```

Now you can write the Sub that creates both lists by translating the preceding outline. To do this, you need to keep track of where you are in the original alphabet because that determines where the letter will go. Suppose you call this variable PosOfLet. Each time you use a letter from the key, swap the letter determined by this position number with its counterpart in the other alphabet, determined from the key, and increase PosOfLet by one. The tricky part comes when you've used up all the letters in the key. Then you have to decide where to put the letters remaining from the first alphabet. The problem occurs because there is no convenient pointer to the unused letters in the second alphabet. To take care of this, set the letters you use to the negative of their ASCII values. For example, if X, Y, and Z were the only letters not used in the key, then they would be the only ones that were still positive in the Decode alphabet.

```
Sub Makelists (Key$)
  'Uses Global Variables EncodeAlph(), DecodeAlph()
  'Local Variables
  Dim LenKey As Integer, PosOfLetUsed As Integer
  Dim I As Integer, A As Integer
  Dim A1$

  LenKey = Len(Key$)
```

```
  PosOfLetUsed = 65                    'start with Asc("A")

  For I = 1 To LenKey
   A1$ = Mid$(Key$, I, 1): A$ = UCase$(A1$)
   Select Case A$
    Case "A" To "Z"
      A = Asc(A$)
      If DecodeAlph(A) = A Then         'Character Not Yet_
Used
        EncodeAlph(PosOfLetUsed) = A
        DecodeAlph(A) = -PosOfLetUsed    'Swap The_
Encode/Decode
                                         'And Flag A Used Char
        PosOfLetUsed = PosOfLetUsed + 1
      End If
    Case Else
      ' Not A Letter - Of Course You Can
      ' Do Something With These Too
    End Select
  Next I
  ' Now Throw In Unused Letters
  ' This Loop Should End If You've Used Up All 26 Letters Or
  ' You Can't Find Any New Letters To Swap
  For I = 65 To 90                  ' Start Looking In Second Alph
                                    ' Here.
    If DecodeAlph(I) = I Then
       EncodeAlph(PosOfLetUsed) = I
       DecodeAlph(I) = -PosOfLetUsed   'Swap The Encode /_
Decode
       PosOfLetUsed = PosOfLetUsed + 1
    End If
  Next I
End Sub
```

Now encoding or decoding a letter is almost a trivial task. Suppose you want to encode a C (ASCII code 67). You just look at the value of Encode(67) to find the ASCII value for the coded version. Similarly (and this is the nice part), to decode a C, you just have to look at the absolute value of the entry in Decode(67). Thus, you can pass the appropriate array as a parameter and use the following listing:

```
Sub EncodeDecode(A(),X$)
  Dim X1 As Integer
```

```
  X1 = Asc (UCase$(X$))
  X$ = Chr$(Abs(A(X1)))
End Sub
```

A More Secure Cipher

Having spent all of the previous section on a fairly subtle program to create a keyword cipher, you might expect it to be secure—or at least difficult to break. (It does work quickly, though.) Unfortunately, any substitution cipher can be broken, given enough text. In fact, assuming the encoded text was originally written in standard, everyday English, it's pretty easy to find the encoding algorithm if you have, say, a thousand words of encoded text. The key to breaking a substitution code is that letters do not exist in isolation. The letter E is almost certainly the most common letter, T is likely to be the next most common, and A is likely to be third highest. Over the years, cryptographers have examined thousands of pages of texts to determine the frequency of letters in standard English. The problem with a simple substitution cipher is that if you always replace a letter with the same symbol, someone can break it by using frequency analysis.

One way to avoid this method of breaking a code is to change the substitution. Instead of always replacing, say, an E with the letter T, use a T" the first time and a Z the next. This way, each time an E occurs, it is replaced with another letter. This method is called a *multi-alphabet substitution cipher.* It's much more difficult to break this cipher, but it's also much more difficult to set up. After all, you have to devise a way of getting these multiple alphabets.

However, you can use the built-in random number generator in Visual Basic to generate the alphabets. Recall that the command

```
X = Rnd       'or X = Rnd(1)
```

gives you a different random number between zero and 1. However—and this is the key to breaking the cipher—given enough data, a professional cryptographer (or a good amateur) can find out the next number in the sequence. Cryptographers would say the random number generator in Visual Basic isn't "cryptographically secure." Finding (and then proving that you have) a cryptographically secure random number generator is probably the most important problem in cryptography.

The idea for the cipher that follows is that you scale this number and use it to determine the "Caesar shift." Now, instead of using the same shift for the next letter, use the random number generator to get a different shift for each letter. Each time you encode a letter, it's transformed differently.

Unfortunately, this method won't quite work. Since the patterns don't obviously repeat (that's what is meant by random), there isn't any reasonable method of decoding the message. You would never know what to shift back by. You have to modify this approach slightly. The first idea that might come to mind is that the Rnd function, when given a negative number as an argument, is supposed to give a repeatable sequence. Thus, if you precede all other uses of Rnd with a statement of the form

Randomize *Seed*

where *Seed* is a negative number, then Visual Basic is always supposed to give you the same sequence of random numbers. Each seed is *supposed* to yield a different, repeatable sequence of random numbers. *Unfortunately, because of a bug in the current version of Visual Basic, this feature won't work as it is supposed to.* You need to modify the procedure slightly. To get a repeatable sequence of random numbers, you must have Visual Basic process the following statement before generating the next random number in the sequence:

Rnd(*the negative number*)

To use random Caesar shifts, you need only ask the user for a key—say, a four-digit positive number. Use this to reseed the random number generator:

```
X = Rnd(-Key)
```

Now you can generate a list of shifts, one for each character in the file:

```
NextShift = Int(256 * Rnd)
```

Use these shifts just as in a Caesar cipher—call this shift generator for each letter in the message.

Now the question is how to decode. The whole point of repeatability is that if you process the command

```
X = Rnd(-Key)
```

again, then when you generate Caesar shifts, you get the same series of numbers as you did before. As before, if you know what the original shift was, you can reverse it just as easily.

However, rather than using this procedure as presented, you can use a more elegant and faster approach. Recall from the bit twiddling section of Chapter 8 that the Xor operator has a convenient property: If

```
B = A Xor Shift
```

and you enter

```
C = B Xor Shift
```

again, then the value of C is the same as the original value of A. Thus, by Xoring twice, you get back to where you started. Thus, you can use the same procedure to both encode and decode. Here's the procedure to do that:

```
Sub EncodeDecode (FileName$, KeyValue)
  ' local variables:
  Dim FileNum As Integer, X As Single, I As Integer
  Dim CharNum As Integer, RandomInteger As Integer

  Dim SingleChar As String * 1        'for use in GET and PUT

  X = Rnd(-KeyValue)
  FileNum = FreeFile
  Open FileName$ For Binary As #FileNum
    For I = 1 To LOF(FileNum)
    Get #FileNum, I, SingleChar
    CharNum = Asc(SingleChar)
    RandomInteger = Int(256 * Rnd)
    CharNum = CharNum Xor RandomInteger 'this is it
    SingleChar = Chr$(CharNum)
    Put #FileNum, I, SingleChar
  Next I
  Close FileNum
End Sub
```

As mentioned before, you will find that the program works faster if you read the information from the file in larger (4096-character) chunks. You can also choose the improved version of the random number generator presented in Chapter 9 to make this approach even more secure. Finally, you should be aware that a quick but insecure way to encrypt a file is to Xor the contents of the file with a single password.

Chapter Eighteen

Communicating with Other Windows Applications

THE various versions of Windows can *multitask,* or run several applications at once. (How effective this will be depends on how the applications were written; for example, 16-bit applications must cooperate by releasing the CPU for multitasking to work.) As you'll soon see, Visual Basic lets you take advantage of Windows' multitasking powers by writing code that activates any Windows application or that sends commands directly to the active application from a Visual Basic project.

Multitasking becomes even more powerful if the various applications can work with each other. Suppose you could write a Visual Basic program that monitors what a spreadsheet, such as Excel or Lotus 1-2-3 for Windows, is doing. This would make it possible to use Visual Basic to add a feature that isn't built into the spreadsheet. For example, you might want to notify the user if a crucial quantity has changed or reached a target. Perhaps you want to write a program that analyzes a document being written in a Windows word processor such as Word for Windows in real time, notifying the user when he or she has written a certain number of words. All this and more are possible through *dynamic data exchange* (DDE for short) and *object linking and embedding* (OLE for short), both of which are surveyed in this chapter.

DDE may seem mysterious at first, but if you think of it as an automated use of the Windows clipboard, the mystery should disappear. The first section of this chapter covers the clipboard. If you haven't spent much time using the clipboard, you'll see that it is much more than a passive place to store objects for cutting and pasting. Essentially, what your Visual Basic program does in DDE is tell the other application what to put into or take out of the clipboard.

note: *Although you must use a registered clipboard format, DDE doesn't use the clipboard the way an ordinary cut-and-paste operation does. Any data already there doesn't get overwritten, and you can have multiple simultaneous DDE conversations.*

OLE is potentially an even more powerful way to have Windows applications communicate. OLE lets you build your own integrated Windows applications using Visual Basic as the "glue" to bind the disparate applications.

note: *While OLE 2.0 support may one day be common in Windows applications, right now very few applications support it fully. (Even Microsoft Office only gives you access to part of OLE's power.) Nonetheless, OLE is an essential part of a product receiving Windows 95 certification, and so more and more Windows 95 applications will work with OLE.*

Finally, because of the currently limited availability of fully OLE-compliant applications, the section on OLE 2 in this chapter is more a survey of what you will be able to do with it someday than what you can do with it now. In particular, this book gives only the simplest example of OLE Automation, which is the ability of one application to actually program another application. Using Visual Basic to build OLE servers is also only briefly surveyed here.

The Clipboard

The Windows clipboard lets you exchange both graphics and text between Windows applications and is often used for cut-and-paste operations inside a specific Windows application. In particular, Visual Basic uses the clipboard for its cut-and-paste editing feature, and you can use the clipboard together with the properties given in the section "Selecting Text in Visual Basic" to implement similar features into your projects.

The clipboard can hold only one piece of the same kind of data at a time. If you send new information of the same format to the clipboard, you wipe out what was there before. (You can use the Clipboard Viewer program supplied with Windows to examine the current contents of the clipboard.)

Sometimes, however, you will want to make sure that the clipboard is completely free before working with it. To do this, add a line of code inside your project that looks like this:

```
Clipboard.Clear
```

As you might expect, this applies the Clear method to the predefined Clipboard object. If you need to send text to and from the clipboard, use the two additional methods described next.

Clipboard.SetText The SetText method is normally used in the following form:

Clipboard.SetText *StringData*

This sends the string information contained in the variable or string expression *StringData* to the clipboard, wiping out whatever text was there.

Clipboard.GetText The Clipboard.GetText method takes a copy of the text currently stored in the clipboard. Because the text contents of the clipboard remain intact until you explicitly clear the clipboard or send new text to it, you can do multiple pasting operations.

You use this method like a function. The general form is

Destination = Clipboard.GetText( )

Selecting Text in Visual Basic

When you use any kind of text box or a combo box on a Visual Basic form, users can select text following the usual Windows convention: press SHIFT and use an arrow key, PGUP, or PGDN. Sending selected text to other Windows applications is quite common. Moreover, you will often want to add cut-and-paste editing functions that work with selected text to your project, especially for multiline text boxes. To do this within Visual Basic, you refer to selected text by three properties, two of which have long integer values and the third of which is a string.

SelStart The SelStart long integer gives you the place where the selected text starts. If the value is 0, the user has started selecting text from the beginning of the text or combo box. If the value is equal to the length of the text string—Len(Text1.Text), for example—the user wants the code to start working after all the text that's currently in the box. You can specify where selected text starts (for example, in a demonstration program) by setting the value of this property from code. For example, for a text box named Text1, a line of code like

```
Text1.SelStart = Len(Text1.Text)/2
```

starts the selected text in midstream.

SelLength SelLength gives you the number of characters the user has selected. If SelLength equals 0, no text was selected. If SelLength is equal to the length of the text string, all the characters in the control were selected. To highlight the first half of the contents of a text box, you would use code like this:

```
Text1.SelStart = 0
Text1.SelLength = Len(Text1.Text)/2
```

SelText SelText is the actual string the user has selected. If the user hasn't selected any text, this is the empty (null) string. If you add the following line of code to the fragment just given,

```
FirstHalfOfText$ = Text1.SelText
```

then the value of the string variable FirstHalfOfText$ is the selected string.

If you assign a new string value to the SelText property, Visual Basic replaces the selected string with the new value. To allow users to copy selected text, combine these properties with the SetText method. For a menu item named Copy and a text box named Text1, all you need to do is use

```
Private Sub Copy_Click()
  Clipboard.SetText Text1.SelText
End Sub
```

To change this to a procedure that cuts out the selected text, use the following code:

```
Private Sub Cut_Click()
  Clipboard.SetText Text1.SelText
  Text1.SelText = ""
End Sub
```

By adding the line that resets the value of SelText to the empty string, you have cut the selected text out of the text box.

For example, to implement a Paste_Click procedure at the place where the user has set the insertion point inside a text box named Text1, use the following code:

```
Private Sub Paste_Click()
  Text1.Text = Clipboard.GetText()
End Sub
```

Notice that if the user hasn't selected any text, this acts as an insertion method. Otherwise, it replaces the selected text.

Clipboard Formats and Graphics Transfers

To retrieve graphical images from the clipboard, Visual Basic must know what type of image is stored there. Similarly, to transfer images to the clipboard, the program must tell the clipboard what type of graphics it is sending. The following table summarizes this information. The first column of the table gives the name of the predefined constants.

Symbolic Constant	Value	Format
vbCFLink	&HBF00	DDE conversation information
vbCFText	1	Text (.TXT)
vbCFBitmap	2	Ordinary bitmap (.BMP)
vbCFMetafile	3	Windows metafile (.WMF)
vbCFDIB	8	Device-independent bitmap (.DIB)
vbCFPalette	9	Color palette

You ask the clipboard what type of image it is currently storing by using the GetFormat method. The syntax for this method is

Clipboard.GetFormat(*Format%*)

where *Format%* is one of the values given in the previous table. This method returns True if the image in the clipboard has the right format, for example:

```
If Clipboard.GetFormat(2) Then MsgBox "Clipboard has a bitmap"
```

To retrieve an image from the clipboard, you use the GetData method. The syntax for this method looks like this,

Clipboard.GetData(*Format%*)

where *Format%* has the value 2, 3, 8, or the appropriate symbolic constant, as in the preceding table. (Remember, you use the GetText method to retrieve text data from the clipboard.)

Clipboard Example Program

As an example of how to use the clipboard methods, start a new project and add a picture box and a multilevel text box with vertical scroll bars and four command buttons. The screen in Figure 18-1 shows you what the form might look like. Suppose you give the command buttons the following control names: TextCopy, TextGet, PictureCopy, and PictureGet. Then the code that activates the Click procedures for these four buttons looks like this:

```
Private Sub btnTextCopy_Click ()
  If Text1.Text = "" Then
    MsgBox ("No text to copy.")
  Else
    Clipboard.Clear
    Clipboard.SetText Text1.Text
  End If
End Sub
```

This code checks the contents of the Text1 text box. If there is nothing there, it tells Visual Basic to inform the user. Otherwise, it clears the clipboard and sends the text contained in the box to the clipboard. (Strictly speaking, the Clear

Figure 18-1 Clipboard example program

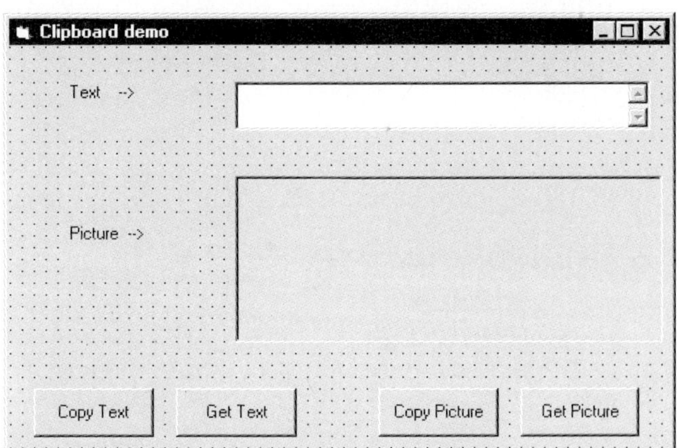

method isn't needed except in unusual circumstances; sending new text to the clipboard wipes out whatever text was there.)

To retrieve text from the clipboard, you first have to make sure the clipboard contains text. The If clause in the following procedure does this, using the GetFormat statement:

```
Private Sub btnTextGet_Click ()
  If Clipboard.GetFormat(vbCfText) Then
    Text1.Text = Clipboard.GetText()
  Else
    MsgBox ("No text in Clipboard")
  End If
End Sub
```

Retrieving a graphical image requires checking the format by using GetFormat and then modifying the parameter for the GetData method accordingly. Here's the procedure:

```
Private Sub btnPictureGet_Click ()
  If Clipboard.GetFormat(vbCfText) Then
    MsgBox ("Only text in Clipboard")
  ElseIf Clipboard.GetFormat(vbCfBitmap) Then
    Picture1.Picture = Clipboard.GetData(vbCfBitmap)
  ElseIf Clipboard.GetFormat(vbCfMetafile) Then
    Picture1.Picture = Clipboard.GetData(vbCfMetafile)
  ElseIf Clipboard.GetFormat(vbCfDIB) Then
    Picture1.Picture = Clipboard.GetData(vbCfDIB)
  Else
    MsgBox "No recognizable picture in Clipboard"
  End If
End Sub
```

To copy images from the picture box to the clipboard as a bitmap, use

```
Private Sub btnPictureCopy_Click ()
  ' As BITMAP
  Clipboard.Clear
  Clipboard.SetData Picture1.Picture, 2
End Sub
```

Finally, you might want to consider using menus rather than command buttons. The control names can remain the same. The Menu Design window would look like the screen shown in Figure 18-2.

Activating Windows Applications

Not all Windows applications can engage in dynamic data exchange. However, you can always send to the active Windows applications any keystrokes you want via Visual Basic. You can even have a Visual Basic project send keystrokes to itself—the obvious key to a self-running demo.

The AppActivate statement moves the focus to another project currently running on the Windows desktop; it does not start a program, nor does it change whether the application is minimized or maximized. The syntax for this statement (it takes named arguments) is

AppActivate *title*[, *wait*]

The *title* argument is a string expression that matches the one in the title bar of the application you want to activate. It is not case-sensitive. The *wait*

Figure 18-2

Menu Design window for the clipboard example

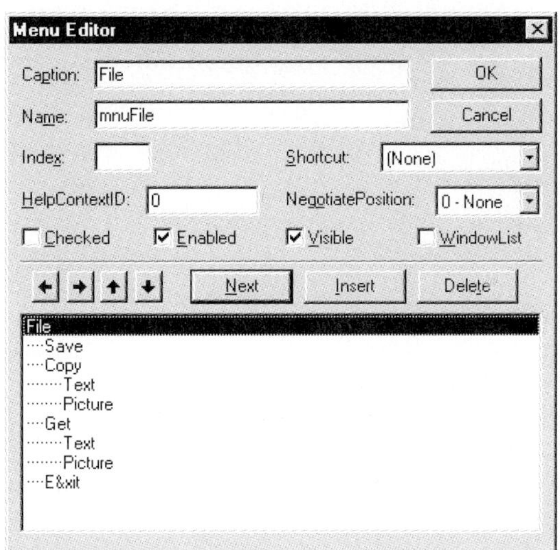

parameter is either True or False. Usually you will leave it at the default value of False. (If you set it to True, then whichever application is doing the calling waits until it has the focus before it activates the new application.)

If the title parameter doesn't make a match with the whole title bar of an active application, Windows looks for any application whose title string begins with that title and activates it—you cannot control which one gets activated in this case. For example, AppActivate "Exploring" will usually start an instance of the Windows Explorer even though its title bar might be something weird like "Exploring - HardDisk1_(C:)."

Sending Keystrokes to an Application

Once you've activated another Windows application by using AppActivate, you use the SendKeys statement to send keystrokes to the active window. SendKeys cannot send keystrokes to a non-Windows application that happens to be running under Windows in a virtual DOS window. If no other window is active, the keystrokes go to the Visual Basic project itself. (This is useful in testing programs and self-running demos.) The syntax for this statement (it takes named arguments) is

SendKeys *string*[, *wait*]

If the *wait* Boolean expression is True (nonzero), Visual Basic will not continue processing code until the other application processes the keystrokes contained in *string*. If the expression is False (0, the default), Visual Basic continues with the procedure immediately after it sends the keystrokes to the other application. The *wait* parameter matters only when you are sending keystrokes to applications other than your Visual Basic application itself. If you send keystrokes to your Visual Basic application and you need to wait for those keys to be processed, use the DoEvents function (see Chapter 5).

The value of the *string* parameter is the keystrokes you want to send. For keyboard characters, use the characters. For example,

```
SendKeys "Foo is not Bar", False
```

sends the keystrokes "F", "o", "o", and so on, to the active application, exactly as if the user had typed them on the screen. Since the *wait* parameter is False, Visual Basic does not wait for these keystrokes to be processed by the active application.

The only exceptions to sending keystrokes are the plus sign (+), caret (^), percent sign (%), brackets ([ ]), tilde (~), parentheses (( )), and braces ({ }). As you'll soon see, these have special uses in the SendKeys statement. If you need to send these keys, enclose them in braces. For example, to send "2+2" to the active application, use this:

```
SendKeys "2{+}2"
```

You'll often need to send control key combinations, function keys, and so on, in addition to the ordinary alphanumeric keys (A to Z, 0 to 9). To send a function key, use F1 for the first function key, F2 for the second, and so on. For other keys, such as BACKSPACE, use the following codes:

BACKSPACE	{BACKSPACE} or {BS} or {BKSP}
BREAK	{BREAK}
CAPS LOCK	{CAPSLOCK}
CLEAR	{CLEAR}
DEL	{DELETE} or {DEL}
DOWN ARROW	{DOWN}
END	{END}
ENTER	{ENTER} or ~
ESC	{ESCAPE} or {ESC}
HELP	{HELP}
HOME	{HOME}
INS	{INSERT}
LEFT ARROW	{LEFT}
NUM LOCK	{NUMLOCK}
PGDN	{PGDN}
PGUP	{PGUP}
PRTSCRN	{PRTSC}
RIGHT ARROW	{RIGHT}
SCROLL LOCK	{SCROLLLOCK}
TAB	{TAB}
UP ARROW	{UP}

For combinations of the SHIFT, CTRL, and ALT keys, use the codes just given, but place one or more of these codes first:

Key	Code
SHIFT	+
CTRL	^
ALT	%

To indicate that one (or all) of the SHIFT, CTRL, and ALT keys should be used with a key combination,, enclose the keys in parentheses. For example, to hold down CTRL while pressing A and then B (that is, what this book would symbolize as CTRL+A+B), use "^(AB)". The string "^AB" would give you the three keystrokes individually.

You can also send repeated keys more easily by using the string in the form *Keystrokes$ Number%*. There must be a space between the keystrokes and the number. For example, SendKeys "UP 10" sends ten presses of the UP ARROW to the active application.

As an example of putting all this together, the following fragment activates the Windows Explorer and maximizes the window in which it is running by sending the keystrokes needed to open the control box and then choosing the Maximize item on its control box menu:

```
AppActivate "Exploring"
SendKeys "% {Down 4}{Enter}", -1
```

The SendKeys statement sends the ALT key followed by a press of the SPACEBAR (because the quotes enclose a space). These keystrokes open the control menu. The next strokes move you to the Maximize menu item and choose that item.

note: *This technique (using cursor keys instead of the accelerator letters) also works in the international version of Visual Basic where the words on a menu may differ.*

As another example, if your current Visual Basic application is active, and a text box has the focus, you can send an "Undo" command to the text box via SendKeys:

```
SendKeys("^Z")
```

(In fact, this will send an Undo command to any application that follows standard Windows conventions.)

Dynamic Data Exchange (DDE)

The way DDE works is that one Windows application (called the *client*) tells another Windows application (called the *server*) that it wants information. (Technically, a DDE conversation is between two *windows*, and from the point of view of Microsoft Windows, it turns out that most controls are windows—as, of course, are forms themselves.) This is called setting up a DDE conversation or DDE link. For Visual Basic, only forms can be DDE servers, but text boxes, picture boxes, or labels can be DDE clients. Although technically only forms can be servers, the controls on the form will probably be providing the information via their properties, so this isn't usually much of a problem. Information generally flows from the server to the client, although the client can, if necessary, send information back to the server.

Windows allows an application to engage in many DDE conversations at the same time. An application can even play the role of server and client simultaneously. For example, your Visual Basic project can send information to Word for Windows while receiving it from Excel. However, only one piece of information may be sent at any one time.

You must know the name of the application you want to talk to. If an application supports DDE, the DDE name will be given in the documentation. For example, as far as DDE is concerned, the name for Word for Windows is "WinWord." The DDE name for Excel is still "Excel." The DDE name for any Visual Basic form acting as a DDE server is the name you choose when you make it into an executable file. If you are running the project within the Visual Basic development environment, the DDE name is the name of the project without any extension.

Next, you need to know the *topic* of the DDE conversation. Usually this is a specific filename. For example, Excel recognizes a full filename (a path name) ending in .XLS or .XLC as a suitable topic. Finally, you need to know what you are currently talking about. This is called the *item* of the DDE conversation. For example, if Excel is the DDE server, the item for a DDE conversation could be a cell or range of cells. If Visual Basic is the DDE server, the control name of a picture box, text box, or label can be the item for a DDE conversation.

note: *The one exception to this rule is the System topic. This allows a program to find out information about the application as a whole (for instance, what data formats it supports, what the other valid* *topics are, and so on). The System topic also allows you access to DDEExecute commands, which typically run macros (or, in the case of Visual Basic, become parameters to subroutines).*

You can have three kinds of DDE conversations (links). A *hot link* means that the server sends the data contained in the item specified for the DDE conversation whenever it changes in the server application. Hot links occur in real time. A *cold link* means that the client must explicitly request updates. A *notification link* is one in which the server tells the client that data has changed, but the destination is only changed after a LinkRequest method is processed (see the further discussion of LinkRequest a bit later in the chapter).

Creating DDE Links at Design Time

This section uses Microsoft Excel for the examples. If you do not have Excel, you should still be able to follow the discussion. All you need to know is that spreadsheets like Excel are organized into rows and columns and that Excel, like Visual Basic itself, has a Copy menu on its main menu bar with similar items.

For the following discussion, start a new project and add a text box and label to it. Next, start Excel (or imagine that you are starting it). To set up a client link with Excel as the DDE server and the contents of the first row and column as the item for this DDE conversation, do the following:

1. Move to the Excel window and highlight (select) the contents of the cell in the first row and first column.
2. From the Edit menu in Excel, choose the Copy command.
3. Move to the Visual Basic window and select the text box by moving the mouse and clicking.
4. From the Edit menu in Visual Basic, choose Paste Link. (If you followed steps 1 through 3, this should be enabled.)

Now you can test whether the link was successfully made. For this, move back to the Excel window and type something in the cell in the first row and first column. Whatever you type should instantaneously appear in the text box in the Visual Basic window, because links made at design time are hot links. In addition, every time the DDE server updates the information for a Visual Basic control acting as the DDE client, Visual Basic generates the Change event. This lets you act on the information in real time as well.

note: *Excel 5.0 fully supports OLE, and you would actually be more likely to use OLE than DDE for dealing with Excel 5.0. (See the discussion of OLE objects later in the chapter for some examples of using OLE with Excel.)*

When you switch from designing a Visual Basic project to running it within the development environment, Visual Basic must break the DDE link. Many applications will automatically attempt to reestablish the DDE link, but you may find that server links, especially, need to be established by code.

This link is permanent. If you save the project, Visual Basic preserves the information about the link as the value of certain properties. You'll see these properties in the next section. In particular, try the following for the DDE link that you set up previously:

1. Close Excel and save the Visual Basic project.
2. Start a new project temporarily.
3. Open the Visual Basic project with the DDE link.

As you will see, Visual Basic will always attempt to start the application that was the server for a DDE conversation set up at design time.

You can also make a Visual Basic form the server at design time (although ultimately the contents of a control provide the data) by essentially interchanging the roles of Visual Basic and Excel in the previous outline. For example, to have the contents of a text box sent automatically to the cell in the first row and first column of an Excel spreadsheet, follow these steps:

1. In the Visual Basic project, select the text box.
2. From the Edit menu in Visual Basic, choose the Copy command.
3. Move to the Excel window and select the cell in the first column and first row.
4. From the Edit menu in Excel, choose Paste Link.

As before, this link is permanent, but this time Excel will tell Windows to try to start the Visual Basic project when you load this spreadsheet into Excel.

DDE Properties

As you might expect, DDE conversations—at least as far as Visual Basic is concerned—are determined by the value of certain properties. Manipulating the values of these properties via code will make your DDE conversations far more flexible than DDE links made at design time can ever be.

LinkTopic The value of the LinkTopic property always takes the form

ServerName | Topic

The name of the application is separated from the topic by the pipe symbol (|, found above the backslash on most keyboards; it is ASCII code 124). For example, for the default Excel worksheet SHEET1.XLS found in the \EXCEL directory, this property takes the form

```
Excel|C:\EXCEL\SHEET1.XLS
```

You can set the value of this property for any text box, picture box, or label.

If a Visual Basic form is acting as the server, the LinkTopic property for the form determines which DDE requests the form will respond to. For example, suppose the name of the Visual Basic project is IaServer and you set the LinkTopic property of a form in that project to AskForInfo. Then any DDE client application that asks for a conversation named

IaServer | AskForInfo

will link up with the project named IaServer. Moreover, if this project were made into an .EXE file that Windows had access to, then Windows would try to start it. Any controls on the form whose link property was AskForInfo could be items for this DDE link.

If you change the LinkTopic property at design time or run time, all conversations on that topic are ended. This lets client applications switch topics.

LinkItem The LinkItem property identifies what data is actually going to be passed from server to client. For example, if Excel was the server, the item can be R1C1—the contents of the cell in the first row and first column. The syntax for this property is

[*FormName.*]*ControlName.LinkItem* = *Item$*

You only set the *LinkItem* for the client control, so *ControlName* in the previous syntax statement must identify a text box, picture box, or label. *Item$* is the string expression that identifies the item the server should send, such as R1C1.

If the DDE server determines what kind of item to send, the value of the LinkItem property is set to the string "DDE_LINK" for the first link, "DDE_LINK2" for the second, and so on. These generic LinkItems are used if the application doesn't have a way to name items systematically, as Excel does by rows and columns. Visual Basic uses the control name of the control for the DDE item.

LinkMode Setting the LinkTopic and LinkItem properties is not enough to activate a DDE link; you must also change the LinkMode property to Hot (a value of 1) or Cold (a value of 2). The default value of this property is None (0). Once you change the LinkMode property to a nonzero value, Visual Basic tries to establish the link using whatever topic you specified as the value of the LinkTopic properties.

Any time you change the value of LinkMode, Visual Basic ends the link. The standard programming practice is to set LinkMode to 0 (None) before you fiddle with the LinkTopic or LinkItem properties.

LinkTimeOut The LinkTimeOut property specifies how long Visual Basic will try to establish the link. The default value is five seconds. However, the LinkTimeOut property uses tenths of seconds; so to double the time to ten seconds, for example, change the value of this property to 100 (instead of the default value of 50). (Some applications are slower to respond than others.)

DDE Events

There are four link events. Like any Visual Basic events, you can write code to respond to these events as you see fit. The four events are described here.

LinkOpen Visual Basic generates the LinkOpen event when a DDE link succeeds. One common use of this event procedure is to generate a message telling the user that the link is open, for example:

```
Private Sub Picture1_LinkOpen(Cancel As Integer)
  M$ = "DDE link made with" + Picture1.LinkTopic
  M$ = M$ + " concerning "+ Picture1.LinkItem
  MsgBox M$
End Sub
```

If you change the value of the Cancel parameter to a nonzero value (True) in the course of a LinkOpen event procedure, Visual Basic will not immediately cancel the link.

LinkClose The template for the LinkClose event procedure starts out like

Private Sub *FormName*_LinkClose( )

for forms, or

Private Sub *ControlName*_LinkClose([*Index As Integer*])

for controls. As always, the optional index parameter identifies an element of a control array. Visual Basic calls this event procedure when the DDE link ends.

LinkExecute The LinkExecute event procedure is used only when the DDE client wants the DDE server to do something. This event is generated when the DDE client sends a command to the server (see the upcoming section "DDE Methods"). The template for this event procedure starts out like this:

Private Sub Form_LinkExecute(*CommandString As String*, *Cancel As Integer*)

The syntax for the command string depends completely on the application you are talking to. You must consult the documentation provided with that application to see what to say.

LinkError Visual Basic calls the LinkError event procedure whenever something goes wrong in a DDE conversation. The syntax for this event procedure template starts out like this for forms

```
Private Sub Form_LinkError(LinkErr As Integer)
```

and like this for controls:

```
Private Sub ControlName_LinkError(LinkErr As Integer)
```

There are 12 possible error codes. Visual Basic will supply these as the value of the LinkErr parameter. The following table gives these codes:

LinkErr Value	Reason
1	The other application requested data in the wrong format.
2	The other application tried to get data before a link was established.
3	The other application tried to send data before a link was established.
4	The other application tried to change an item before establishing a link.
5	The other application tried to poke data (see the LinkPoke method in the next section) before a link was established.
6	After you cut links by changing LinkMode to 0 (None), the other application tried to continue the conversation.
7	Too many DDE links for Windows to handle.
8	Text too long to send via DDE.
9	Client specified wrong control array index.
10	Unexpected DDE message.
11	Too little memory for DDE.
12	The server tried to switch roles and become the client.

The LinkError event is not generated for ordinary run-time errors, such as your project accepting a value of 0 from a server and then trying to divide by 0. You handle these errors by using an ordinary error trap (see Chapter 8). Roughly speaking, Visual Basic generates the LinkError event only when no code is running—for example, when a client tries unsuccessfully to send data automatically because of a previously established hot link.

LinkNotify This event occurs only when the LinkMode property is set to 3 (Notify). This is used when the server has changed the source and needs to tell the client that. Use the LinkRequest method to actually get the new data.

DDE Methods

There are four DDE methods you can use with Visual Basic controls that are acting as clients for a DDE link.

LinkExecute Use the LinkExecute method to send a command to the DDE server. The syntax for this method is

ControlName.LinkExecute *CommandString$*

where, as with the LinkExecute event procedure, the form of the command string depends on what the server application will accept.

LinkPoke The LinkPoke method is the only way for a DDE client to send data to the server. You can use this method to transfer the contents of any DDE client control on your Visual Basic project to the server. The syntax for this method takes the form:

ControlName.LinkPoke

If the client control is a text box, Visual Basic sends the string that is the value of the Text property. For a label, it's the value of the Caption property. For a picture box, it's the value of the Picture property.

LinkRequest You use the LinkRequest method to request the DDE server to send information to the control. This method is needed only if you've set the value of LinkMode to 2 (Cold). (Recall that for hot links, the server sends updates automatically.) The syntax for this method takes the form

ControlName.LinkRequest

LinkSend The LinkSend method is used when you have a form acting as a DDE server and want to send the contents of a picture box. Although hot links normally work automatically, the designers of Visual Basic felt that resending the contents of a picture box every time even one pixel is changed would cut down performance too much. For this reason, you must use the LinkSend method to tell the DDE client that the contents of a picture box have changed. (For example, you could use this method after you make a significant change to the image stored in a picture box.) The syntax for this method takes the form

```
PictureBoxControlName.LinkSend
```

The picture box must be a control on the form that is the DDE server.

OLE 2

OLE, which originally stood for *object linking and embedding,* is a technology that complements and extends dynamic data exchange. (Now it's just another one of those acronyms that has passed into simply meaning—itself.) OLE goes beyond DDE in that, instead of information being merely transferred, information passed with OLE is presented in the same way it would appear in the originating application. Spreadsheets appear as spreadsheets, word-processed documents as they would in the word processor, and so on. When you add an OLE container control to your Visual Basic project, you give the user a bridge to another Windows application, and what they see *will look to them like that other application.*

When working with OLE, first and foremost come the *objects.* This is the data supplied by the Windows applications that support OLE—for example, an Excel worksheet (or, more likely, part of an Excel worksheet). You use Object variables (Chapter 11) for dealing with OLE objects, and you normally use the Variant data type when communicating information to these objects.

To understand *linking,* imagine that you are part of the group working on this book. Besides the author, there are a technical editor, a copyeditor, a proofreader, and others involved. The most efficient method for your group to work would be to maintain a single copy of the document and have each person involved be able to link to it and make changes. *There should still be only one copy of the document involved* (on a central server); that way your group doesn't have to worry about important changes being missed. (In the jargon, it allows work in a parallel rather than a serial way.) With a linked object, the data stays in the application that created it. Think of linking as attaching a chain to preexisting data—like any chained objects, you can effect changes by jerking on the chain. Technically, linking inserts a placeholder into the Visual Basic application, and an image of the data is stored in the OLE 2 control.

The idea of the *embedding* part of OLE is that you create documents that integrate various Windows applications under one roof. Embedding in OLE 2 allows the custom control to maintain the data in the object inside itself. When Visual Basic activates the OLE 2 control, control switches back to the application that created the data, and you can use that application's power to modify the data in place.

One of the main ideas behind the introduction of OLE was that Microsoft wanted to get users away from thinking of applications as being paramount. Instead you think of the document itself as central. For example, suppose you are preparing a complicated report that uses spreadsheet data and a graphics package. You want parts of the document to be under the control of the word processor and parts to be under the control of the spreadsheet. In OLE 2, the other application temporarily takes over to work with the data embedded in the control. When you embed an object in an OLE client control, then no other application can access the data (as opposed to linking it where they can). Moreover, the application that created the embedded data is automatically started up whenever the user works with the embedded data.

You can also use the newest part of OLE called *OLE Automation*, which allows you to take control of other applications. For example, from Visual Basic you can control Excel by using *its* version of Visual Basic, or you can control Word using *its* WordBasic. In fact your own Visual Basic applications can be controlled by other applications. (Although we don't spend much time on it here, Visual Basic can create OLE servers, which in turn can be driven by applications that support OLE Automation.)

Using OLE

When you add an OLE 2 client control to your Visual Basic projects, you create what Microsoft calls an *OLE compound document.* (In fact, the moment you add a client control, Visual Basic pops up a dialog box asking you for the name of the application it should hook into. See the next section for more on this dialog box.) The OLE client control comes with all versions of Visual Basic—it is one of the three custom controls supplied with the standard edition of Visual Basic. The icon is usually at the bottom of the toolbox and has a grid and an "OLE 2" in a box inside of it.

As with DDE, your Visual Basic project can be the client (or *container*) application that receives the information or the server (*source*) application that sends it out. In most cases with OLE, your Visual Basic project receives the information and serves as the client. In any case, the OLE control supplied with Visual Basic is an OLE client control and does not allow a Visual Basic application to become an OLE server (although Visual Basic 4, unlike early versions of Visual Basic, does allow this: you just need to use code or a custom control in order to create an OLE server).

Creating OLE Objects

As mentioned earlier, an OLE object is any data the OLE control can work with. It can be a single graph, a range of cells in a spreadsheet, a whole spreadsheet, or part or all of a word-processed document. An application that supports OLE will have an *object library* that it can *expose*. (Expose is jargon for "here are the things you can work with. You can work with them in the following ways.") Before moving on with OLE, there is one phrase that will frequently recur, that is, the *OLE class*. This is the application that produces the OLE object. Any application that supports OLE has a unique OLE class name. For example, "WordDocument" or "ExcelWorksheet." (Class names can be case-sensitive.) You can get a list of the class names available by clicking on the ellipsis for the Class property in the Properties window.

There are four ways you can create OLE objects. The simplest is

- Embed or link the object within an OLE container control. This enables you to change objects on the form at run time and create linked objects.

Descriptions of the more sophisticated methods follow.

CREATING OLE OBJECTS VIA THE TOOLBOX

To add an OLE object to the toolbox:

1. Choose Tools|Custom Controls.
2. Check off the box in the dialog box that pops up.

For example, you can add an Excel Worksheet object to the toolbox by filling in the dialog box as shown here:

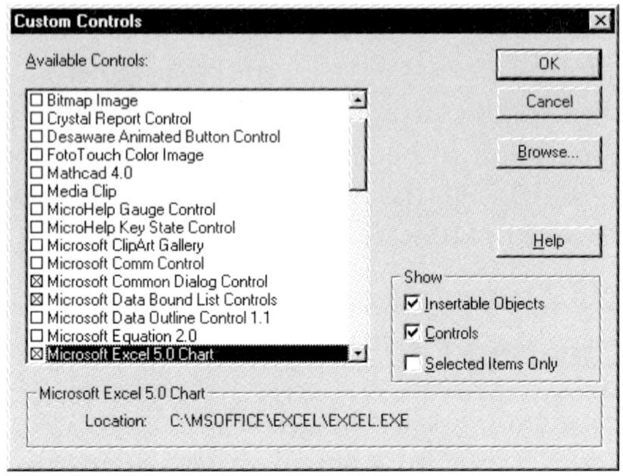

Now, when you use this tool to draw the object directly on a form, you automatically embed the object in your application. Figure 18-3 is a picture of what your form looks like if you embed an Excel object this way. (Notice the Excel object in the toolbox in Figure 18-3.)

OBJECTS VIA THE TOOLS|REFERENCES ITEM

The most modern OLE-compliant applications are available from the dialog box that pops up when you choose Tools|References. These object libraries are particularly nice because they contain definitions of all the objects, methods,

Figure 18-3

An Excel embedded object

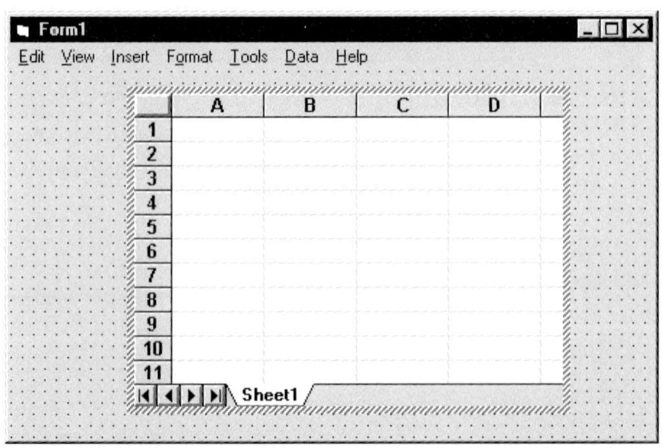

and properties the object supplies. Moreover, help is usually available for the syntax of the needed commands from the Object Browser. For example, if you add the Excel object library to Visual Basic this way and then use the Object Browser to study this library, you can see at a glance what the syntax is. Figure 18-4 is an example of this.

tip: *You can add Visual Basic's IDE via Tools | References. This is the key to writing add-ins.*

Once you have set a reference to the object library via the Tools | References dialog box, you can use the CreateObject function with a previously declared object variable to create the object in code. Here's an example of the code for an Excel worksheet:

```
Dim objExcel As Object
Set objExcel = CreateObject("EXCEL.SHEET")
```

These two lines of code create an object variable (named objExcel in this case). This object variable can be used to control Excel. (See the section on OLE Automation a little later in the chapter.)

Figure 18-4 Using the Object Browser to study the Excel object library

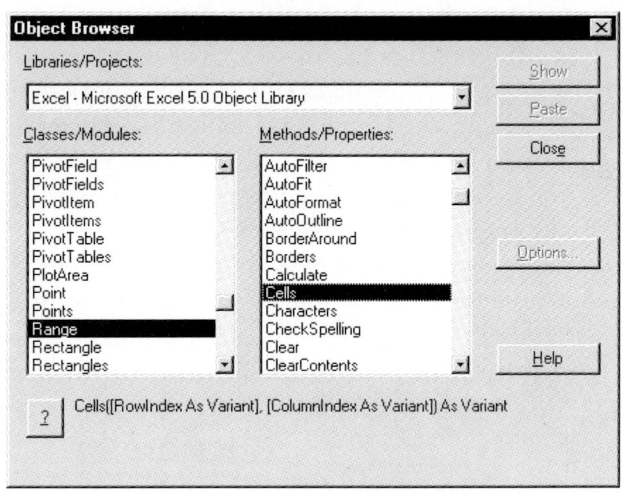

caution: *Always set the object variable to Nothing when you are finished with it. (Otherwise the memory and resources it takes up will not be freed.)*

CREATING OBJECTS WHEN THE OBJECT DOES NOT SUPPLY AN OBJECT LIBRARY

An object library is not supplied for some objects such as Word 6.0, which, although they are OLE-aware, do not yet have all the behavior the user would like. In particular, applications that do not expose an object library make you dig out their objects, methods, and properties from their documentation (or in some cases, from a cry on the Internet). For this situation you must still first use the CreateObject function to refer to the object. Here's an example:

```
Dim objWordBasic As Object
Set objWordBasic = CreateObject("Word.Basic")
```

(Remember to set the object variables to Nothing in this case as well.)

Using OLE 2 at Design Time

Compared to OLE 1.0, creating links or embeddings with OLE 2 at design time is easy. Essentially, you need only work with the dialog boxes that will be described in this section.

If you have added an OLE 2 client control to a form, you immediately get a dialog box like Figure 18-5. (The more applications you have, the more items will appear.) This gives you the names of all the Windows applications you can hook into. As Figure 18-5 indicates, you can have the object show up as an icon or with the data visible in the OLE 2 control. The two radio buttons on the far left determine whether you will work with an existing file created by the application (a linked object) or want the other application to create one anew (an embedded object). If you choose to link the control by choosing the Create from File option, the dialog box changes to Figure 18-6. You can click on the Browse button to open a dialog box that lets you pick the file. When you have done that check the Link box in Figure 18-6.

Figure 18-5

Insert Object dialog box

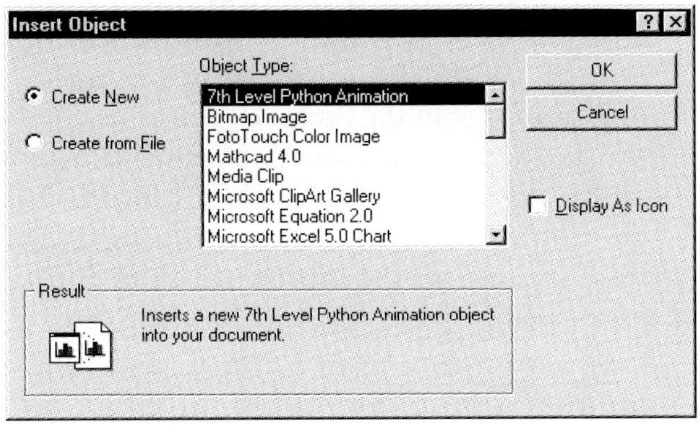

Note: *You can click on Cancel if you want to set the OLE properties via code. You do not need to use this dialog box in order to work with OLE. In fact, if you create an executable file with an OLE connection made at design time, the file will be much larger than if you create the connection at run time with code.*

Figure 18-6

Insert dialog box for Create from File

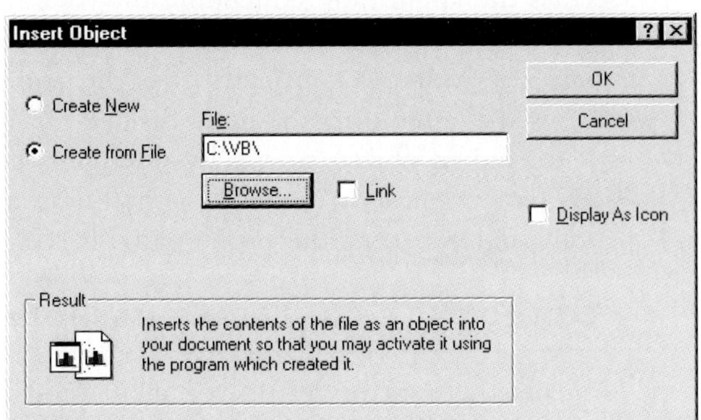

Paste Special

Sometimes you want to create linked or embedded objects by using information stored in the Windows clipboard to determine the SourceDoc and SourceItem properties. To do this, you first need to copy the data from the application to the clipboard by using the Copy command in the application. You then need to use the Paste Special dialog box, which is available at design time by clicking the right mouse button when the focus is in the OLE control and choosing Paste Special from the pop-up menu that results. This dialog box automatically examines the contents of the clipboard to determine the needed OLE properties.

OLE Properties

As you might expect, the dialog box only makes it simpler to set the properties of the OLE control. You can always change them via the Properties window or code (and, of course, you will have to do this to enable OLE at run time).

For example, the Icon/Display Data choice in Figure 18-6 actually sets the DisplayType property. The SizeMode property allows you to change how the control looks at run time. If the value is 0 (vbOLESizeClip), then the control clips the data displayed at run time. If you want to stretch the image to fit the current size of the OLE control, set the value of this property to 1 (vbOLE-SizeStretch). Finally, you can have the control automatically resize itself by setting the property to a value of 2 (vbOLESizeAutoSize).

The dialog box that pops up is also setting the crucial Class property, which specifies the application containing the data. The OLETypeAction property determines what type of object you have created. Is it linked, embedded, or either? The SourceDoc property gives the name of the linked object or the file to be used as a template for an embedded object. The SourceItem property is used for linked objects to specify what portion of the linked document the Visual Basic application can work with. (For example, a spreadsheet range might be indicated by setting this property to "R1C1:R1C10.")

COMMON OLE CONTAINER METHODS

Finally, there are the very important methods that apply to the OLE container control, which specifies exactly what should be done to the OLE object. Do you want to update the object, create it, delete it, save the information in the object to a file, retrieve it from a file, and so on? The syntax is always

```
OLEControlName.CreateEmbed
```

What follows is a short discussion of the methods.

CreateEmbed This creates an embedded OLE object. To do this, you must first set (via the OLE dialog box or code) both the Class and OleTypeAllowed properties. Recall that the OleTypeAllowed property is 1 for Embedded or 2 for Either, and the Class property determines the type of OLE object. (Class names are available from the OLE dialog box or the Properties window.) When you create a new embedded OLE object, the application must either be active (use AppActivate) or in the system's path.

CreateLink This creates a linked OLE object from an existing file. To do this, first set the OleTypeAllowed and SourceDoc properties. In this case the OleTypeAllowed is 0 (linked) or 2 (either).

The SourceDoc property gives the name of the file for the linked object. If you want to restrict yourself to working with a portion of the linked object, set the SourceItem property as well.

Just as with embedding a document, the application must either be active or in the path.

Copy This sends all the data and linking properties of the object to the Windows clipboard. Both embedded and linked information can be copied to the clipboard.

Paste This copies data from the clipboard to an OLE control. You'll need to check the PasteOK property of the control.

Update This is a very important action because it pulls the current data from the application and gives you a view of it in the OLE control.

DoVerb This activates an OLE object. To use this action, you will need to set the Verb parameter of this method, which specifies what operation you want performed.

note: *If you set the AutoActivate property of the control to double-click (value = 2), the OLE control will automatically activate the current object when the user double-clicks in the control. If the application supports "In Place Activation," then you can arrange it so that the application is activated whenever the OLE control gets the focus (set AutoActivate to 1).*

Close This is used only for embedded objects, since it closes the OLE object and cancels the connection with the application that controlled the object.

Delete Use this if you want to delete the object. OLE objects are automatically deleted when a form is closed.

SaveToFile If the OLE object is embedded, this method is vital. Because the OLE control data is maintained by the OLE control, it will be lost unless you save it by tying together the necessary code with setting the SaveToFile method to this value.

ReadFromFile If you use the SaveToFile method just discussed, this method reloads an OLE object from the data file created using the SaveToFile method. The code needed for this action is similar to that for saving data, except, of course, this time you'll be reading the data back.

InsertObjDlg This pops up the same Insert Object dialog box that Visual Basic uses when you put an OLE control on a form. At run time, use this method to allow the user a friendly way to create a linked or embedded object.

PasteSpecialDlg This displays the Paste Special dialog box. At run time, you display this dialog box to allow the user to paste an object from the clipboard.

FetchVerbs This gets the list of verbs supported by the application.

SaveToOLE1File Use this if you need backward compatibility with the earlier version of OLE.

OLE Automation

Visual Basic is extendable—that's one of its greatest strengths. However, you may not want to spend your time creating custom controls or DLLs that duplicate functionality found in other applications such as Excel or Word. The key to tapping other (OLE-compliant) applications is OLE Automation. You can use Visual Basic to write programs that let you manipulate the data and the objects in these applications.

Some objects that support OLE Automation also support linking and embedding. If an object in an OLE container control supports OLE Automation, then you can access its properties and methods using the Object property. If you draw the object directly on a form or create it in code, you can directly access the properties and methods of the object. A full discussion of OLE Automation is beyond the scope of this section. If what you read here whets your appetite, refer to your Visual Basic manuals for more information.

Using OLE Automation

As you have seen earlier, you can create a reference to objects in code if you can set a reference to the object with the New keyword, CreateObject, or GetObject from outside the OLE server that created it. Microsoft Excel's and Word's Application objects are examples of these types of objects. Some subsidiary objects, such as a cell in Excel, can only be accessed by a method of a higher level object.

For example, go to Tools | References and then select the Excel object library in order to make Visual Basic aware of Excel's objects. Now add a text box to a form. Then use the following OLE Automation code to fill a bunch of cells in the second column of an Excel worksheet with consecutive values, sum them, and then place the sum into a text box in Visual Basic:

```
Private Sub Form_Click()
  Dim objExcel As Object
  Set objExcel = CreateObject("EXCEL.SHEET")
  objExcel.Application.Visible = True
  For I = 1 To 10
    objExcel.Cells(I, 2).Value = I
  Next I
  objExcel.Cells(11, 2).Formula = "=sum(B1:B10)"
  Text1.Text = objExcel.Cells(11, 2)
  objExcel.Application.Quit
```

```
  Set objExcel = Nothing
End Sub
```

A few points worth noting:

1. OLE Automation requires being familiar with the object you want to program. The syntax is always going to be tricky.
2. Even on a Pentium 90 with 16 megabytes of RAM (the fastest machine available to the author), this simple code took a bit of time (roughly .6 of a second).
3. Point 2 shows that although OLE may be a great technology, incredibly fast it ain't. You should think long and hard before using OLE Automation in an application that is destined to run on anything less than state-of-the-art machinery. (You can use Windows API calls to detect the kind of hardware a user has. The amount of RAM seems to be even more important than the speed of the CPU. Don't try to use OLE Automation with 4 megabytes of RAM; think hard before using it when you have 8. OLE will start getting usable when you have 16 megs of RAM, but 32 megs (!) seems to be the "sweet spot.")

USING OLE AUTOMATION WITH WORD

Using OLE Automation with applications such as Word, which don't let you use Tools | References to add their object library to the Browser, will almost always be a pain. The documentation for the application will be essential—and even that may not be enough. For example, consider the simple problem of trying to use Word's spelling checker on the contents of a text box via OLE Automation. The only way this can be done currently is to:

- Copy the contents of the text box into a new document in Word
- Start Word's spelling checker

So far so good. By searching through Word's documentation, I managed to find the commands to do this. Next, I had to figure out how to copy the spell-checked text back into Visual Basic. A problem arose when I tried to implement this: Word doesn't seem to have any way to copy the information back into Visual Basic. After some fooling around, I decided to copy the information to the clipboard (which Word does support). Then I was able to copy the information from the clipboard back into the text box.

Next I found that Word sends back an (undocumented) error when it has finished spell checking a document. So I had to trap that error to get the program to run. After *a lot* of trial and error the following program seems to do the job:

```
Option Explicit

Private Sub Command1_Click()
On Error GoTo Continue
Dim WordLanguage As Object
Set WordLanguage = CreateObject("Word.Basic")

Form1.WindowState = 1
With WordLanguage
  .FileNewDefault
  .Insert Text1.Text
  .StartOfDocument
  .ToolsSpelling
End With

Continue:
  If Err.Number = 51 Then
   With WordLanguage
     .EditSelectAll
     .EditCopy
     .FileClose 2
   End With
   Set WordLanguage = Nothing
  Else
    WordLanguage.FileClose 2
    Set WordLanguage = Nothing
    MsgBox Str$(Err.Number) + Err.Description
  End If
 Form1.WindowState = 0
 Text2.Text = Clipboard.GetText()
End Sub
```

The moral of this section is that if you want to use the current version of Word, you may be better off using the OLE custom control rather than OLE Automation.

OLE Servers

The ability to create OLE servers is a new feature in the 32-bit versions of both the Professional and Enterprise editions of Visual Basic 4. As you have seen in the preceding sections, OLE servers are applications that expose their object's properties and methods to other applications. There are two types of OLE servers you can create. The first is usually called an *out-of-process OLE server*. This is an executable file that runs in its own process and therefore has its own memory space reserved for it by the operating system. An *in-process OLE server* is a DLL (dynamic link library) that runs in the space of the OLE client that calls it (and therefore the operating system allocates memory in the calling process's memory space).

note: *To create an out-of-process OLE server, you follow steps similar to those used to create any Visual Basic executable application, except that you choose the OLE Server option on the Project page in the Tools | Options dialog box.*

Creating an Out-Of-Process OLE Server

Here are the steps needed to create an out-of-process OLE server:

1. Add a code module and create a Sub Main( ).
2. Add a class module for the class you want to define.
3. Create Public properties and methods for the class.
4. Add code to the class's Initialize and Terminate event procedures.

Now you need to set the Project options for your OLE server to ensure that it functions properly.

Choose Tools | Options and then select the Project page.

1. Set the Startup Form to Sub Main. (Using a Sub Main will allow your application to run and not have to display a visible interface.)
2. Set the Project Name edit field. The Project Name is part of the fully qualified class name used to create objects exposed by your application.

3. Choose the OLE Server option for StartMode. (Normally OLE servers stop running when no applications are requesting their objects. This means if you do not have StartMode set to OLE Server, your application would start and immediately stop. The StartMode option takes care of this problem by keeping your application running until you can test it.)

The last important setting you need to work with on this page is the Application description. This edit field identifies your OLE server in the References dialog boxes of other applications.

note: *StartMode is a design-time-only setting to help you debug your OLE server. StartMode has no effect when you make an executable file.*

To actually create the code:

1. Insert a code module and create a Sub Main procedure.
2. Place any initialization code, if needed, in this procedure.
3. Insert a class module and, in the Properties window, set the Name property.
4. Set the Public property to True to expose the class to other applications.
5. Set the property Instancing to Creatable MultiUse. (This allows an OLE client to create multiple instances of your class.)

Now that you have exposed an object, you need to give your OLE clients something to use. The Public variables and Property procedures in the class will be the properties that your OLE clients see. To expose methods, you must create Public Sub and Public Function procedures. For example, the following line in a class module's declarations section

```
Public Name As String
```

exposes the variable Name as a property that another application can read and write. Creating a read-only property requires a Property Get procedure.

```
Private Name As String
Property Get NameOfClass () As String
  NameOfClass = Name
End Property
```

The Property NameOfClass will now be read-only to other applications.

The following code exposes a method called SquareIt in the OLE server:

```
Public Sub SquareIt (Foo as Long)
  Foo = Foo *Foo
End Sub
```

The last step in creating an OLE server is to place any needed startup or cleanup code in the Initialize and Terminate event procedures.

Of course, you will want to test your OLE server, and Visual Basic 4 makes this easy by actually allowing you to run multiple instances of Visual Basic. The first instance of Visual Basic will contain a running version of your OLE server. The second instance can contain an application that will test your OLE server. Once the second instance of Visual Basic—the one with the test application—is loaded, use Tools|References to add a reference to the new OLE server. Now, you are ready to add code in your test form to call the properties and methods of the object you exposed in the OLE server's class module.

Once you fully test the code for your OLE server, you are ready to make the final executable. An out-of-process OLE server executable is created the same way as any Visual Basic executable, by using the Make EXE File choice from the File menu.

You will also need to register the OLE server in Windows' registry. Registering the OLE server on your machine is done automatically by Visual Basic. To register the OLE server on another machine, simply execute the OLE server with the command-line parameter of /REGSERVER. For example, if your out-of-process OLE server is called MYOLE.EXE, you would use the line

```
MyOLe.EXE /REGSERVER
```

from the Run box on the Start menu.

The /REGSERVER command-line parameter will automatically register the OLE server on that machine and then immediately terminate the OLE server. It is advisable to use the Visual Basic Setup Wizard to distribute your

OLE server (see Appendix A). The Setup Wizard creates disk images or a network installation that automatically handles many of the complicated configuration needs for a Visual Basic 4 application.

Creating an In-Process OLE Server

An in-process OLE server is a DLL (dynamic link library) that another application can access using OLE Automation. This means that other Visual Basic applications can access the in-process DLL, but so can applications such as Excel that support OLE Automation.

Most of the steps you used to create the code for an out-of-process OLE server are the same: the Public procedures are the methods, you can use Property Get and Property Let procedures to work with the properties of the object, and so on. At compile time though, you choose File | Make OLE DLL File rather than the Make EXE File option.

note: *Please see the chapter "In-Process OLE Servers" in the Visual Basic Professional edition manual for more on the details (and pitfalls) of creating in-process OLE servers.*

(The tricky points in what you can and can't do arise because an in-process OLE server runs in the same process—and so the same memory area—as the calling OLE client.)

note: *Visual Basic's Enterprise edition also allows you to create remote OLE Automation servers. This moves the OLE server off the workstations and onto the network servers.*

Chapter Nineteen

Recursion

RECURSION is a general method of solving problems by reducing them to simpler problems of a similar type. For the experienced programmer, thinking recursively presents a unique perspective on certain problems, often leading to particularly elegant solutions and, therefore, equally elegant programs. In Visual Basic, you usually use recursion in general procedures to make event procedures or the whole project run more smoothly or quickly. For example, this chapter shows you how to use recursion to build three very fast sorting routines. Among them is what most programmers regard as the best general-purpose sort—it's called, naturally enough, Quicksort.

This chapter also shows you how recursion makes it easy to construct efficient indexes and so build a cross-reference program to make your programming jobs easier. This chapter also has a section that introduces you to recursive graphics, called *fractals*. The screen in Figure 19-1 shows an example of the Koch Snowflake. This is just one of the figures that can be drawn using the programs in this section.

Figure 19-1 A fractal drawing

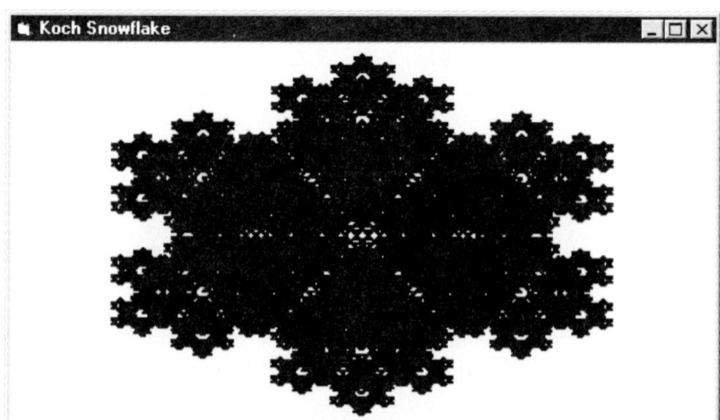

Like many powerful tools, recursion can be overused. At the end of this chapter, you will find a short section on when not to use recursion.

If you are an experienced GW-BASIC programmer, you may be wondering why you haven't used recursion before. In fact, recursion is not supported in GW-BASIC, and in spite of its power, recursion is too often slighted in books on languages like QuickBASIC and Visual Basic that do support it. This is sometimes because recursion is thought of as too sophisticated for BASIC, but modern BASICs (like Visual Basic) are essentially as powerful as languages like Pascal and C, where recursion is commonly used. Another reason is that recursion is sometimes thought of as a mysterious, even mystical, process, but this reputation is undeserved. See, for example, the Pulitzer prize-winning book, *Gödel, Escher, Bach,* by Douglas Hofstadter (New York: Basic Books, 1979). It's a book some people swear by and others swear at.

Getting Started with Recursion

Before this chapter shows you how to program recursive procedures and functions, let's look at some typical examples of recursive problem solving. Discovering a recursive solution to at least one problem seems innate—at least with children. Have you ever met a three-year-old who didn't intuitively know how to solve the following problem with the solution given here:

PROBLEM:	How do I deal with my parents?
SOLUTION:	Deal with father first, then deal with mother (or vice versa).

This method of solving a problem is, naturally enough, called *divide and conquer,* and it clearly has a long history.

For a more serious example of divide and conquer, consider the following old problem: You have 7 balls and a balance scale. One ball is heavier than the other 6. Find the heaviest ball in just two weighings. To solve this, first try a simpler case—3 balls. Notice that if you try to balance 2 balls, there are only two possibilities:

- They balance (in which case the remaining ball is the heaviest).
- They don't balance (in which case the heaviest one is obvious).

Now, to do the 7-ball problem, divide the balls into two groups of 3 with 1 left over. If they balance, then, as before, the heaviest one is the one left over. If they don't balance, then whichever side is heavier is also obvious. This reduces the problem to the previous case. (Similarly, you can do 15 balls in three weighings, 31 in four, and so forth.)

As a final example of divide and conquer, here's an outline of a recursive method for sorting (called merge sort) that you'll see soon. Merge sort follows this outline:

```
To SORT a LIST
  If a list has one entry stop
Otherwise:
  SORT(the first half)
  SORT(the second half)
  Combine (merge) the two halves
```

As long as the operation of combining the two takes substantially less time than the sorting process, you have a viable method of sorting. As you'll soon see, it does take less time.

Finally, any operation on a directory that is supposed to work similarly on subdirectories will need recursion when the operation is programmed. For example, when you use

XCOPY *.* *NewPath* /S

to copy files in all subdirectories to a new place, you are using recursion. The XCOPY routine constantly calls itself on lower and lower subdirectories until it finishes.

A recursive solution to a problem will always follow this outline:

```
Solve recursively (problem)
     If the problem is trivial, do the obvious
     Simplify the problem
   Solve recursively (simpler problem)
     (Possibly) combine the solution to the simpler problem(s)
     into a solution of the original problem
```

A recursive procedure constantly calls itself, each time in a simpler situation, until it gets to the trivial case, at which point it stops. (There's also indirect recursion, where a function or procedure calls itself via an intermediary. For example, function A calls function B, which in turn calls function C, which calls function A, and so on.)

Recursive Functions

You know a function can call another function. (These are called nested function calls.) Recursion occurs when a function eventually calls itself. Before looking at an example of a recursive program in Visual Basic, stop and think for a second what Visual Basic must do when one function calls another. Obviously, Visual Basic has to communicate the current value or location of all the parameter variables to the new function. To do this, Visual Basic places the locations of the variables (or the location of a copy of the values, if you are passing by value) to a reserved area in its memory called the *stack*. Now suppose this second function needs the results from a third function. This requires yet another storing of the locations of variables, and so on. However, this process can take place regardless of the nature of the other functions. It is this that makes recursion possible.

Here's an example. The factorial of a positive integer is the product of the numbers from 1 up to the integer and the custom is to use the ! to symbolize it. For example:

```
2! = 2*1              (=2)
3! = 3*2*1            (=6)
4! = 4*3*2*1          (=4*3! = 24)
5! = 5*4!
```

As you can see, the factorial of an integer can be written using the factorial of the previous integer and a multiplication. Using this idea, here's a recursive definition of the factorial:

```
Function Factorial (N As Integer) As Long
 If N <= 1 Then
  Factorial = 1                        'factorial not usually
 Else                                  'defined for N<0
  Factorial = N * Factorial(N - 1)     'note the call to
 End If                                'itself in a simpler
End Function                           'situation
```

Suppose you now write Print Factorial(4). Then Visual Basic does the following:

1. It calls the function with N = 4. The first statement processed is the If-Then test. Since the If clause is false, it processes the Else clause.

2. This says compute 4*Factorial(3).

3. It tries to compute Factorial(3). And so it now has to start building up its stack. The stack will hold partial results—those obtained to date. Think of what gets pushed onto the stack as a little card containing the status, location, and values of all the variables as well as what is still left "up in the air." In this case, the card would say

   3. Need to compute 4 * (an as yet unknown number = Factorial(3))

4. Now Visual Basic repeats the process, calling the factorial function with a variable now having the value 3. And so another card gets pushed onto the stack:

   2. Need to compute 3 * (an as yet unknown number = Factorial(2))

5. Repeat the process again so the stack contains three cards:

   1. Need to compute 2 * (an as yet unknown number = Factorial(1))

Now Visual Basic does one final call, with the variable N having the value 1, and sets up a fourth card. But at this point the process can stop—the top card no longer contains an unknown quantity. By the first clause, Factorial(1) is 1, so Visual Basic can start "popping the stack." The results of the top card (the number 1) feed into the second card. Now Visual Basic can figure out what the second card stands for (the number 2), and so Visual Basic can pop the stack one more time and feed the information accumulated to the third card (the number 6). Finally, Visual Basic feeds the results to the bottom card and comes out with 24 = 4!. Since the stack is empty, this is the answer. Figure 19-2 shows you one way of imagining the stack.

The explanation of the process, of course, takes much longer than the actual solution via Visual Basic. Visual Basic keeps track of the partial results of any recursive operation via its stack. You don't need to be aware of the stack—most of the time. The only time you do worry about the stack is when it "overflows" and your program crashes or behaves erratically. The disastrous error message you'll see is number 28, "Out of stack space." Unfortunately, unlike in QuickBASIC or Visual Basic for DOS, where you can enlarge the stack, you have to rely on Windows to handle the stack; there is no way to enlarge the stack from within a Visual Basic program. This is not usually a problem, however, as the stack has more than enough for normal needs. (The number of recursive calls you can make varies with how much information the stack needs to keep track of. With minimal use of the stack in each call you can get around 450 recursive calls in the 16-bit version of Visual Basic. The limit in the 32-bit version is many thousands. Heavy use of the stack, where many variables are being passed, could cut this down by a factor of 2.)

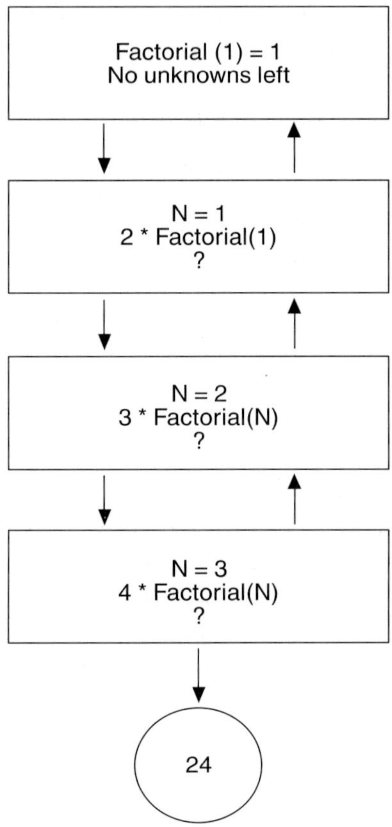

Figure 19-2 Picture of the stack

There are many other examples of recursive functions. For example, the Fibonacci numbers are defined as follows:

- The first Fibonacci number is 1 (in symbols, Fib(1) = 1).
- The second Fibonacci number is also 1 (in symbols, Fib(2) = 1).
- From that point on, the next Fibonacci number is the sum of the two preceding ones (in symbols, Fib(n) = Fib(n–1) + Fib(n–2)).

For example:

$$\text{Fib}(3) = \text{Fib}(2) + \text{Fib}(1) \quad (= 1 + 1 = 2)$$
$$\text{Fib}(4) = \text{Fib}(3) + \text{Fib}(2) \quad (= 2 + 1 = 3)$$
$$\text{Fib}(5) = \text{Fib}(4) + \text{Fib}(3) \quad (= 3 + 2 = 5)$$

and so on. The recursive definition of the Fibonacci numbers is almost simple:

```
Function Fib (N As Integer) As Integer
 If N <= 2 Then
   Fib = 1              'Making negative Fibonacci numbers = 1
 Else
   Fib = Fib(N - 1) + Fib(N - 2)
 End If
End Function
```

Note the pattern. The simple case is taken care of first. This is followed by reducing the calculation to a simpler case. Finally, the results of the simpler case or cases are combined to finish the definition. (Also, the Fibonacci numbers were arbitrarily defined at negative N to be 1.)

However elegant this may seem, it turns out to be an incredibly inefficient way to calculate these numbers. See the section "When Not to Use Recursion" later in this chapter for more on this.

As a final example of a recursive function, consider the calculation of the greatest common divisor (GCD) of two numbers. (For those who have forgotten their high school mathematics, this is defined as the largest number that divides both of them. It's used when you need to add fractions.) Therefore,

- GCD(4,6) = 2 (because 2 is the largest number that divides both 4 and 6)
- GCD(12,7) = 1 (because no integer greater than 1 divides them both; 1 is the largest "common divisor")

Around 2,000 years ago, Euclid gave the following method of computing the GCD of two integers, *a* and *b*:

If *b* divides *a*, then the GCD is *b*. Otherwise,
GCD(*a*,*b*) = GCD(*b*, a Mod *b*)

note: *This is usually called the Euclidean algorithm. Algorithms are what programming is ultimately about. More precisely, an algorithm is a method of solving a problem that is both precise (no* *ambiguity allowed) and finite (the method must not go on forever). In the case of the Euclidean algorithm, since the Mod operation shrinks the integer each time, the process must stop.*

Recall that the Mod function gives the remainder you get by dividing *b* into *a*; it's obviously less than *b*. If a Mod *b* is zero, then *b* divides *a*. Here is this recursive outline translated into a Visual Basic function:

```
Function GCD (P As Long, Q As Long) As Long
  If Q Mod P = 0 Then
    GCD = P
  Else
    GCD = GCD(Q, P Mod Q)
  End If
End Function
```

Here, the pattern is a trivial case followed by a reduction to a simpler case, with no need to combine results. (Since the Mod function is not restricted to long integers, it's easy enough to change the function to work with short integers as well. The advantage of this is that you can use the preceding code for both kinds of integers by converting the integer to a long integer before calling the function.)

Simple Recursive Procedures

Just as you can have recursive functions, you can have, through the magic of the stack, recursive procedures. A good example of this is a rewritten version of the binary search method for looking through an ordered list:

If list has length one
  then check directly (the simple case)
Else
  look at the middle of the list
If middle entry is too big then
  search the first half
Else
  search the second half

Note that this outline for a recursive solution is quite close to one's intuitive notion of how to search an ordered list. Here is this outline translated to a procedure:

```
Sub RecursiveBinSearch (X$, A$(), Low as Integer, High as _
Integer)
'LOCAL variable is: Middle
 Dim Middle As Integer
   If Low >= High Then     'If list is empty or has 1 item
     If A$(Low) = X$ Then
       MsgBox ("Target found at entry" + Str$(Low))
     Else MsgBox ("Target not found!")
     End If
     Exit Sub
   End If

 Middle = (Low + High) \ 2
 If A$(Middle) = X$ Then
     MsgBox ("Target found at entry" + Str$(Middle))
     Exit Sub
  Else If A$(Middle) > X$ Then
     RecursiveBinSearch X$, A$(), Low, Middle - 1
  Else
     RecursiveBinSearch X$, A$(), Middle, High
 End If
End Sub
```

To test this you can use the same techniques as for testing the nonrecursive binary search mentioned in Chapter 9.

Whenever you're trying to understand a recursive program, it's a good idea to think about what is on the stack and what happens when the stack is finally popped. In this case, each "card" on the stack contains

- The address of the array
- The current values (actually the addresses) of the variables Low and High and the location of a new copy of the local variable Middle

Knowing what is on the stack is also essential when you are debugging a recursive procedure. After all, watching the variables on the stack is useless if you don't know what values they're supposed to have.

An Example—The Tower of Hanoi

By now you may be thinking that recursion is just a fancy way of avoiding loops. There's some truth to this (see the last section of this chapter), but there are many problems for which it would be hard to find the loop equivalent. Perhaps the most famous example of this is the "Tower of Hanoi" problem. (As the quote that follows indicates, it was originally called the "Tower of Brahma.") Here's the problem, extracted from *Mathematical Recreations and Essays* by W. W. Rouse Ball and H. S. M. Coxeter (New York: Dover, 1987):

> In the great temple at Benares, says he, beneath the dome which marks the center of the world, rests a brass plate in which are fixed three diamond needles, each a cubit high and as thick as the body of a bee. On one of these needles, at the creation, God placed sixty-four discs of pure gold, the largest disc resting on the brass plate, and the others getting smaller and smaller up to the top one. This is the Tower of Brahma. Day and night unceasingly the priests transfer the discs from one diamond needle to another according to the fixed and immutable laws of Brahma, which require that the priest on duty must not move more than one disc at a time and that he must place this disc on a needle so that there is no smaller disc below it. When the sixty-four discs shall have been thus transferred from the needle on which at the creation God placed them to one of the other needles, tower, temple and Brahmins alike will crumble into dust, and with a thunderclap the world will vanish.

(There's also a famous Arthur C. Clarke story on a similar theme.)

The idea, then, is to transfer the disks one at a time, taking care to never put a larger disk on a smaller one. The explanation that follows continues to use 64 disks, but solving this problem with this many disks would take the priests (or a super computer, for that matter) more time than scientists say the universe has been around or is likely to be around. For *n* disks, the solution takes 2^*n* – 1 steps; for 64 disks, this has 19 digits (approximately 1.844674E+19, according to Visual Basic). The graphically based solution found in the next section limits you to 15 disks, and that many disks take about 15 minutes to solve the problem on a 386.

To solve this problem recursively, you need to decide on the "trivial" case—the one that the recursion stops on. Obviously, when the tower is down to 1 disk (height 1), you can just move that disk. Next, you have to find a way to simplify the problem while retaining the same form (and making sure that this process does eventually lead to the trivial case). The key is to note that the bottom disk is irrelevant when you move the first 63 disks from the first tower to any other tower. Since it's larger than any disk, you can just as well regard a peg with it alone as being empty when it comes to moving disks around. Next, note that you can change the destination temporarily if this helps to simplify the problem. Given all this, here's an outline of a solution to the Tower of Hanoi:

Move the top 63 disks to tower 3 using tower 2 (a simpler case)
Move the bottom disk to its destination (tower 2)
Move the top 62 disks to tower 1 using tower 2
(Of course, to move 62 disks is a problem of smaller size. And just as before, the bottom disk will be irrelevant.)

Here is procedure code that implements this outline. This procedure only gives directions for a solution:

```
Sub SolveTowerOfHanoi (Height As Integer, FromTower As
Integer, ToTower As Integer, UsingTower As Integer)

  If Height = 1 Then
   Print "Move a disk from tower #"; FromTower; "to tower#";
ToTower
  Else
   SolveTowerOfHanoi Height - 1, FromTower, UsingTower,ToTower
   Print "Move a disk from tower #"; FromTower; "to tower
#";ToTower
   SolveTowerOfHanoi Height - 1, UsingTower, ToTower,FromTower
 End If
End Sub
```

If you've set up a global variable called NumberOfDisks, then to actually see the directions for solving the problem, all you have to do is write

```
SolveTowerOfHanoi NumberOfDisks, 1, 2, 3
```

As mentioned in the outline, the key to this solution is the switch in the destinations between the two procedure calls:

```
SolveTowerOfHanoi Height-1,FromTower,UsingTower,ToTower
```

and

```
SolveTowerOfHanoi Height-1,UsingTower,ToTower,FromTower
```

If this is confusing, try analyzing the stack for the simple case of three disks by "playing computer." Work through this case using the outline and the procedure. Next, get a printout of the steps by changing the Print statements to Printer.Print statements. Finally, compare your hand solution to the solution that Visual Basic will print out using the preceding program.

A VISUAL VERSION OF THE TOWERS

While the preceding section gives the directions for solving the problem, it would be much more interesting to have Visual Basic move disks around. The initial screen might look like the one in Figure 19-3.

If you use two forms, you can use the second form for directions and the first for the solution. To follow this discussion, you need to start up a new project and add another form. The second form will need to have the Caption property set to Directions but otherwise needs no special treatment. The directions form would just tell the user about the problem and ask him or her to click a command button to start the project. To get to the screen in Figure 19-3, the first form should have the following properties:

Property	Setting
Caption	Tower of Hanoi/Brahma
BorderStyle	Fixed single (=1)
ControlBox	False
MaxButton	False
MinButton	False
Auto Redraw	True

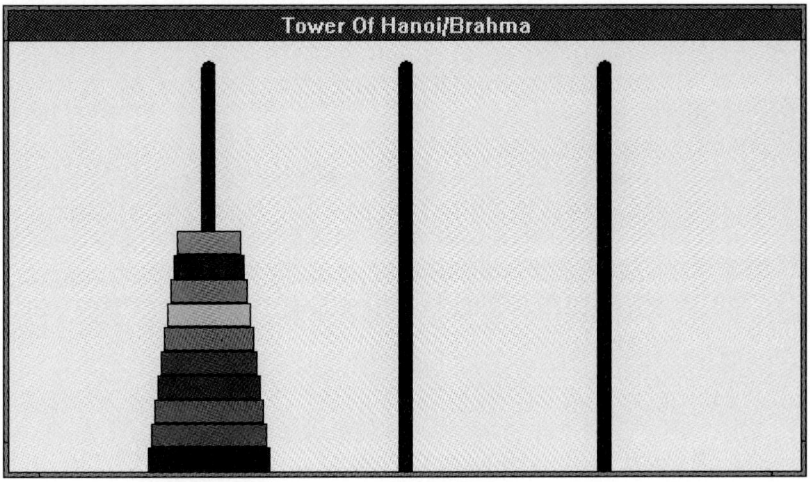

Figure 19-3 Initial screen for Tower of Hanoi/Brahma

Next, add a text box called Disk and set the Index property to zero for this control, thus setting up a control array. Change the Height property to 285 to make the text boxes flatter and make the Text property the empty string. Now, the code to initialize the first form in order to get the screen in Figure 19-3 uses the following in a code module:

```
Sub Init ()
 Dim I As Integer

 HowWide = Form1.ScaleWidth       'global variable
 HowHigh = Form1.ScaleHeight      'ditto
   Form1.Show
   Form1.Cls
   DrawWidth = 9
   For I = 1 To 3
     Line ((I / 4) * HowWide, HowHigh)-((I / 4) *
HowWide,ScaleTop - 250)      'on one line
   Next I
   M$ = InputBox$("Number of disks - 15 or less?")
   NumberOfDisks = Val(M$)
   Do Until NumberOfDisks > 0 And NumberOfDisks < 16
     M$ = InputBox$("Number of disks - 15 or less?")
     NumberOfDisks = Val(M$)
   Loop

 ReDim DiskInfo(NumberOfDisks, 3)
 ' Put Picture boxes

 For I = 1 To NumberOfDisks
 DiskInfo(I, 1) = NumberOfDisks + 1 - I
 Disk(I).Move (HowWide / 4) - 600 + 30 * I, HowHigh - (285 *_
I),
 1200 - (65 * I), 285
 Disk(I).BackColor = QBColor(I)
 Disk(I).Visible = -1                'TRUE
 Form1.Refresh
 Next I
 DiskInfo(0, 1) = NumberOfDisks
 DiskInfo(0, 2) = 0
 DiskInfo(0, 3) = 0
End Sub
```

The DiskInfo global array will hold the information as to which disks are on which towers. The zeroth position holds the number of disks. Because of the previous For-Next loop, DiskInfo(1,1) holds the number of the bottom disk, DiskInfo(2,1) the number of the second disk, and so on. The Move method is used to stack the disks in the right place.

As the initialization routine showed, you'll need the following global variables in a code module:

```
Global DiskInfo() As Integer
Global HowWide, HowHigh As Single
Global NumberOfDisks As Integer
```

The Form_Load procedure hides the original text box (disk), sets the AutoRedraw property to True, and loads 15 new disks (text boxes) but keeps them invisible. When Visual Basic finishes loading the text boxes (disks), you call a procedure to display the second form with directions:

```
Private Sub Form_Load ()
  Disk(0).Visible = 0 : AutoRedraw = True
  For I% = 1 To 15
    Load Disk(I%)
  Next I%
  GiveDirections          'should give the directions
End Sub
```

The Directions form tells the user to click the first form to start the process.

The procedure to actually solve the puzzle replaces the Print statements by a call to a procedure that will move the disks around using the information contained in the DiskInfo( ) array:

```
Sub SolveTowerOfHanoi (Disks As Integer, FromTower As Integer,
ToTower As Integer, UsingTower As Integer)

If Disks = 1 Then
   MoveADisk FromTower, ToTower
Else
   SolveTowerOfHanoi (Disks - 1), FromTower, UsingTower, _
ToTower
   MoveADisk FromTower, ToTower
   SolveTowerOfHanoi (Disks - 1), UsingTower, ToTower, _
FromTower
```

```
End If
End Sub
```

Now the key MoveADisk procedure replaces the simple Print statement in the solution from the previous section:

```
Sub MoveADisk (FromTower As Integer, ToTower As Integer)
  DiskNumber = DiskInfo(0, FromTower)
  DiskIndex = DiskInfo(DiskNumber, FromTower)
  DiskInfo(DiskNumber, FromTower) = 0
  DiskInfo(0, FromTower) = DiskInfo(0, FromTower) -1
  DiskInfo(0, ToTower) = DiskInfo(0, ToTower) +1
  DiskNumber = DiskInfo(0, ToTower)
  If DiskNumber > NumberOfDisks Then
    Exit Sub
  Else
    DiskInfo(DiskNumber, ToTower) = DiskIndex
  End If

  NewLeft = (HowWide * ToTower / 4) - Disk(NumberOfDisks + 1 -
  DiskIndex).Width / 2
  NewTop = HowHigh - (DiskNumber * 285)
  Disk(NumberOfDisks + 1 - DiskIndex).Move NewLeft, NewTop
  Form1.Refresh
  End Sub
```

The click procedure that starts the process is now pretty simple:

```
Private Sub Form_Click ()
  Init
  Form1.Enabled = 0  'no user input needed
  SolveTowerOfHanoi NumberOfDisks, 1, 2, 3
End Sub
```

Recursive Sorts

In Chapter 9, you saw three useful methods for sorting: insertion, ripple, and Shell sorts. Insertion and ripple sorts are good for short lists, and Shell sort is good for moderately sized lists. The sorts you'll see in this section are among the fastest known; they are often the sorts of choice for very large lists.

Merge Sort

The first sort, called merge sort, has the easiest outline. You saw it in the first section of this chapter:

```
To SORT a LIST
  If a list has one entry stop
Otherwise:
  SORT(the first half)
  SORT(the second half)
  Combine (merge) the two
```

Once you write the merge procedure, the procedure to sort a list is easy. Here's the sort procedure:

```
Sub MergeSort (A$(), Start As Integer, Finish As Integer)

 'LOCAL  Variable is Middle
  Dim Middle As Integer

  If Start < Finish Then
    Middle = (Start + Finish) 2
    MergeSort A$(), Start, Middle
    MergeSort A$(), Middle + 1, Finish
    Merge A$(), Start, Middle, Finish
  End If
End Sub
```

This procedure keeps on splitting the list. When it gets to *n* lists of size one, the merge procedure combines them into *n*/2 ordered lists of size two, *n*/4 ordered lists of size four, *n*/8 ordered lists of size eight, and so on. (At this point, the details have been swept under the rug by moving them to the as-yet-unwritten merge procedure.)

Merging two ordered files (or ordered parts of the same file) is intuitively obvious but a bit tricky to program. What you have to do is set up a temporary array and work your way slowly through the lists, filling up the temporary array with the appropriate entry from one of the two lists. When you're done, you have to write the temporary array back to the original array.

Here's the Merge procedure:

```
Sub Merge (A$(), Start As Integer, Middle As Integer, Finish
As Integer)
  'local variables are:
  'Temp$(),Begin1,End1,Begin2,End2,TempLocation,I

  ReDim Temp$(Start To Finish)
  Dim  Begin1 As Integer,End1 As Integer,Begin2 As Integer
  Dim  End2 As Integer,TempLocation As Integer,I As Integer
  Begin1 = Start
  End1 = Middle
  Begin2 = End1 + 1
  End2 = Finish
  TempLocation = Start
  Do While Begin1 <= End1 And Begin2 <= End2
    If A$(Begin1) <= A$(Begin2) Then
      Temp$(TempLocation) = A$(Begin1)
      TempLocation = TempLocation + 1
      Begin1 = Begin1 + 1
    Else
      Temp$(TempLocation) = A$(Begin2)
      TempLocation = TempLocation + 1
      Begin2 = Begin2 + 1
    End If
  Loop
  If Begin1 <= End1 Then
     For I = Begin1 To End1
      Temp$(TempLocation) = A$(I)
      TempLocation = TempLocation + 1
     Next I
  ElseIf Begin2 <= End2 Then
     For I = Begin2 To End2
      Temp$(TempLocation) = A$(I)
      TempLocation = TempLocation + 1
     Next I
  End If

  For I = Start To Finish
   A$(I) = Temp$(I)
  Next I
End Sub
```

The Do loop runs through the list that is passed to the procedure. It systematically compares entries in the two parts of the list and moves the smaller one to the temporary list. After every move, it shifts a pointer (TempLocation) that moves one step forward within the temporary list. Similarly, it moves a pointer within a given sublist (either Begin1 or Begin2) whenever it does a swap. The loop constantly checks the status of these pointers to avoid going past the boundaries of the individual sublists.

You get to the If statement following the Do loop when one of the sublists is "used up." This block copies the remainder of the other list to the temporary array.

The final For-Next loop copies the temporary array back to the original array. Without this, the recursion would fail.

Although merge sort is theoretically one of the fastest sorts, in practice the simple formulation just given is not very fast for small or moderate-sized lists. A list of 300 random four-letter strings takes about the same amount of time for insertion sort and merge sort (approximately three-fourths of a second), and both are far slower than Shell sort, which takes only about one second for this problem on a 33MHz 386. However, unlike insertion sort, doubling the size of the list no longer quadruples the time; it slightly more than doubles it. Therefore, even this simple formulation of merge sort will be much faster than insertion sort for a list of 600 items. (The rounded time for insertion sort is 2.5 seconds and for merge sort is 1.75 seconds. Shell sort still remains much faster; it takes about 0.5 second.)

One problem is that copying the temporary array back to the original list takes too much time. You can speed the program up considerably by replacing the arrays with variant variables (see Chapter 10).

The procedure also spends too much time (and stack space) on the trivial cases of lists of sizes one and two. You can dramatically speed up merge sort (and save a lot of stack space) by modifying what the procedure regards as the "trivial case." For example, suppose you directly sort all lists of length one or two by swapping entries as needed. Change the original procedure to read like the following:

```
Sub MergeSort(A$(),Start As Integer,Finish As Integer)
  'local variables
  Dim Middle As Integer

  If  Finish - Start <= 1 Then
   If A$(Finish) < A$(Start) Then
    'SWAP A$(Finish),A$(Start)
     Temp$ = A$(Finish)
     A$(Finish) = A$(Start)
     A$(Start) = Temp$
    End If
```

```
   Else
     Middle = (Start + Finish) \ 2
       MergeSort A$(),Start,Middle
       MergeSort A$(),Middle+1,Finish
       Merge A$(),Start,Middle,Finish
  End If
End Sub
```

Now you are directly swapping the entries when the lists are tiny. The savings are dramatic. For 1,000 random four-letter combinations, which take 8 seconds for insertion sort and approximately 2.9 seconds for the original version of merge sort, this tweaked version of merge sort takes approximately 2.25 seconds—around a 20 percent improvement. (Shell sort is still the fastest; it takes approximately 0.6 second.)

Slightly more savings result from modifying the "trivial case" even further. Recall that insertion (or ripple) sort is very fast for small lists (say, lists of size 64 or less). Modify insertion sort's procedure to allow a start and a finish location within the array. Then modify the procedure for the merge sort by rewriting the fundamental procedure, as in the following:

```
Sub MergeSort (A$(), Start As Integer, Finish As Integer)
  If Finish - Start <= 7 Then
    InsertionSort A$(),Start,Finish
  Else
    Middle = (Start + Finish)
    MergeSort A$(),Start,Middle
    MergeSort A$(),Middle+1,Finish
    Merge A$(),Start,Middle,Finish
  End If
End Sub
```

In any case, all these tweaks preserve the essential advantage of the original merge sort—doubling the list still only slightly more than doubles the time needed. Unfortunately, all the versions of merge sort do have one big disadvantage, and ironically this disadvantage shows up only for the very large lists on which merge sort should shine: you need twice as much space as is needed for Shell sort because of the temporary array or variant used in the merge procedure. This means that you're likely to run out of space for very large lists. It turns out that merge sort is of more theoretical than practical interest in most situations, but see the section "Making Sorts Stable" for these exceptional situations.

Quicksort

As many people have remarked, finding a better general-purpose sort is the "better mousetrap" of computer science. Unfortunately, the best general-purpose sort currently known, usually called Quicksort, unlike the various modifications of merge sort, is not guaranteed to work quickly. In very unlikely situations, it can be the slowest sort of all.

If the merge sort is a "divide-and-conquer" recursion, then Quicksort can be thought of as a "conquer-by-dividing" recursion. To understand this, consider this list of numbers:

5,12,4,9,17,21,19,41,39

The number 17 is in an enviable place: all the numbers to the left of it are smaller than it and all the numbers to the right of it are greater than it. This means that 17 is in the correct position for when this list is sorted. It *partitions* the list and will not have to be moved by any sort. The idea of Quicksort is to create these "splitters" artificially, on smaller and smaller lists. Here's the basic outline:

1. Take the middle entry of a list.
2. By swapping elements within the list, make this element into a splitter. (Note that this element may need to move, and this is obviously the most difficult part to program.)
3. Divide the list into two at the splitter and repeat steps 1 and 2.
4. Continue until both the lists created by making a splitter have a size of at most one.

The following code translates this outline into a procedure.

```
Sub QuickSort (A$(), Start As Integer, Finish As Integer)
  'Local variable PosOfSplitter
  Dim PosOfSplitter As Integer

  If finish > Start Then
     Partition A$(), Start, Finish, PosOfSplitter
     QuickSort A$(), Start, PosOfSplitter - 1
     QuickSort A$(), PosOfSplitter + 1, Finish
  End If
End Sub
```

Now you need to write the procedure that forces the splitter. This procedure is subtle and makes Quicksort harder to program than merge sort. Luckily, there are many ways to do this. The one shown here is inspired by insertion sort. You move the splitter "out of the way" first. Next, you start from the left end of the list and look for any entries that are smaller than the splitter. Whenever you find one, you move it, keeping track of how many elements you've moved. When you get to the end of the list, this marker will tell you where to put back the splitter. Here is that procedure. (It assumes you've written a Swap procedure to interchange two elements in the array, fixing the gap in Visual Basic.)

```
Sub Partition (A$(), Start As Integer, Finish As Integer,
 LocOfSplitter As Integer)
' LOCAL variables are: SplitPos,NewStart,I,Splitter$
Dim SplitPos As Integer, NewStart As Integer
Dim I As Integer, Splitter$

  SplitPos = (start + finish) \ 2
  Splitter$ = A$(SplitPos)
  SWAP A$(SplitPos), A$(start)          'get it out of the way
  LeftPos = start                       'needs to be written!
     For I = start + 1 To finish
       If A$(i) < Splitter$ Then
         LeftPos = LeftPos + 1
         SWAP A$(LeftPos), A$(i)
       End If
     Next i
  SWAP A$(start), A$(LeftPos)       ' LeftPos marks the hole
  LocOfSplitter = LeftPos           ' This gets passed
End Sub                             'to the original procedure
```

Quicksort is usually quite fast. (It will actually be a bit faster to write the Swap routine inside the module instead of using another procedure.) For example, sorting a list of 2,000 random four-letter strings takes approximately 2 seconds on a 33MHz 486—roughly on a par with Shell sort. Quicksort is usually faster than Shell sort for larger lists.

However, how fast Quicksort works depends completely on how much the splitter splits; the ideal is when it splits the list in two. If each time you sort the smaller list, the element you are trying to make into a splitter is the smallest (or largest) in the list, then in one of the recursive calls, too little work is done, and in the other, too much is done. This makes Quicksort slow down; for all practical purposes, it becomes a complicated version of insertion sort. If this unfortunate situation should come to pass, you may end up waiting a long time to sort a list of 2,000 entries. Luckily, this worst case is quite unlikely, but it can happen.

To prevent this situation, computer scientists offer some suggestions. The first is that you use an insertion or ripple sort for small lists, much like the tweaked version of the merge sort. (This appears to work best when you use insertion sort or ripple sort on lists of size eight or smaller.) Using an insertion or ripple sort for small lists speeds up the program by around 10 percent. It also saves stack space.

Second, and most important, to eliminate the chance of the worst case happening, don't use the middle element as the potential splitter. One idea is to use the random number generator to find a "random" element on the list. Change the lines

```
SplitPos = (Start + Finish) \ 2
Splitter$ = A$(SplitPos)
```

to

```
SplitPos = Start + Int((Finish -Start+1)*Rnd)
```

Doing this makes it almost inconceivable that you'll end up with the worst case. The problem is that using the random number generator takes time. While it makes the worst case almost inconceivable, it does appear to slow down the average case around 25 percent. On the other hand, if you use this idea in the tweaked version described earlier, the deterioration is much less. This combination seems to cause only a 10 percent reduction, and it's still faster than the original version of Quicksort. Far fewer calls to the random number generator are necessary because Visual Basic is not dealing recursively with small lists. (This is the author's favorite version of Quicksort.)

Another possibility that many people prefer is to keep on using insertion or ripple sort for small lists but, instead of calling the random number generator to find a candidate for the splitter, use the median of the start of the list, the middle term, and the end of the list. The code for finding the median of three items is simple (and doesn't take very much time).

Making Sorts Stable

Finally, why so many sorts? One reason for presenting them is that they illustrate programming techniques so well, but there's a more serious reason. Although Quicksort and Shell sort are fast, they do have one disadvantage that insertion, ripple, and merge sorts do not have. They are not *stable.* To understand what stability means, suppose you have a list of names and addresses that is already ordered alphabetically by name. Suppose now that you want to re-sort the list by city and state. Obviously, you want the list to be ordered alphabetically by name within each state. Unfortunately, if you use Quicksort or Shell sort, the alphabetical order of the names will disappear. With merge sort, you can preserve the old order within the new.

There is one other way to deal with the problem of making your sorts stable. You can set up an integer array and fill the entries with consecutive integers. These entries serve as pointers to the items in the list you want to re-sort. Next, sort the pointer array using the entries in the original list, but leave the original list intact. This solution requires a lot more programming to print the list in the new order because you have to check both lists at the end. In addition, this solution adds to the space requirement since you need to maintain two arrays instead of one, but it can be faster if you need to move many large entries in an array around.

Binary Trees

In many cases, you don't really need to sort a list; rather, you sort the list so you can easily search through the list later (using a binary search). Or suppose you have a person entering random names and you want to be able to prevent duplicates. If the list were ordered, this would be easy, but a new entry requires re-sorting the list. (If you choose this option, use insertion sort; it's obviously the best way to insert a new item.) Finally, you may know that at some point in the future you'll frequently need to search through the list, possibly ordering the list as well. Stopping and re-sorting the list each time the user enters a new name is obviously not the method of choice if the final ordering happens in the far future.

It should come as no surprise that programmers have long searched for methods of accepting information for a list so you can still search through the list as quickly as through an ordered list (that is, as fast as a binary search) and, at some future time, sort it quickly as well. And all this should take place without having to stop and constantly re-sort.

Of course, you can't expect to get something for nothing. The methods that programmers invented require more sophisticated programs and use a lot more space. Moreover, unless you use very sophisticated methods (which are not described here), the method given here works only if the names are entered in a "random" order. If someone applies these methods when entering an ordered list, the results will be disastrously slow.

To understand this method, called binary trees, first suppose you have a list of names:

Mary, Susan, Gary, Karen, Ted, Saul, David, Fran, Harry, Hal

Start by putting the first name at the center of the top of a piece of paper:

Mary

Since the name Susan comes in the alphabet after Mary, draw an arrow pointing to the right. (It's sometimes called an "after" or "right" arrow.):

Gary comes before Mary, so draw a left arrow (a "before" arrow):

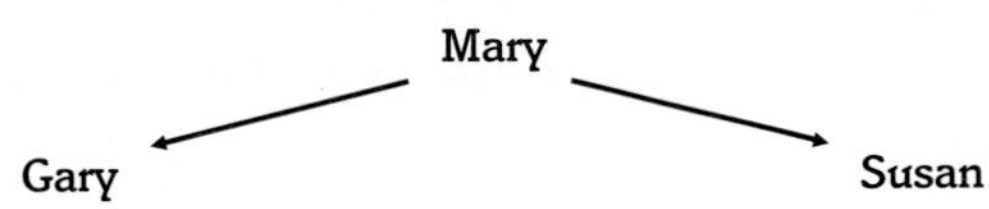

Karen comes before Mary but after Gary, so the picture looks like this:

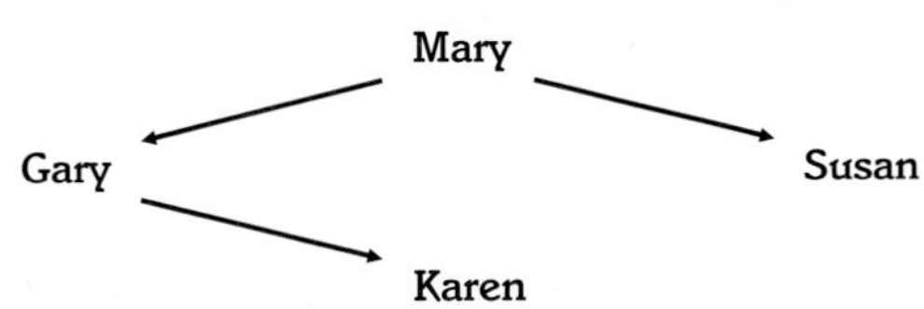

Ted comes after Mary and after Susan, so the picture now looks like this:

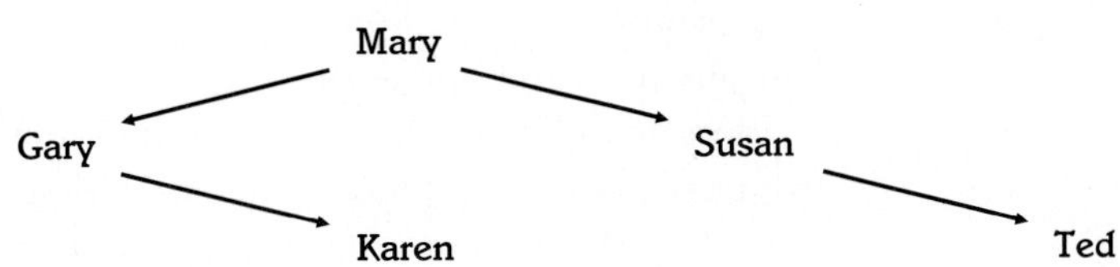

The idea is that when you insert a new name, follow the "branches" in the right order. Saul comes after Mary and before Susan. At the next step, the picture looks like this:

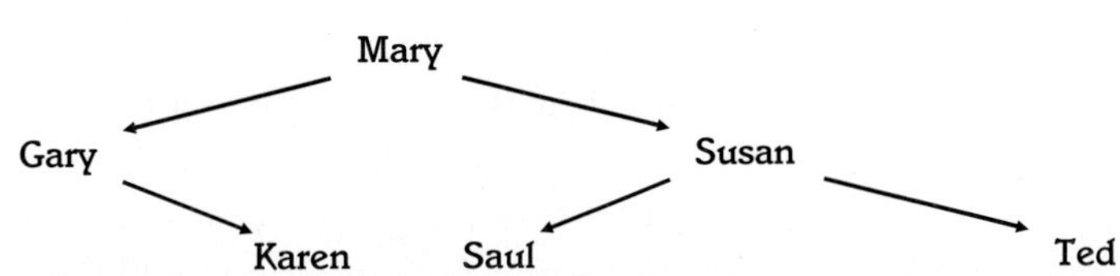

Finally, the picture looks like this:

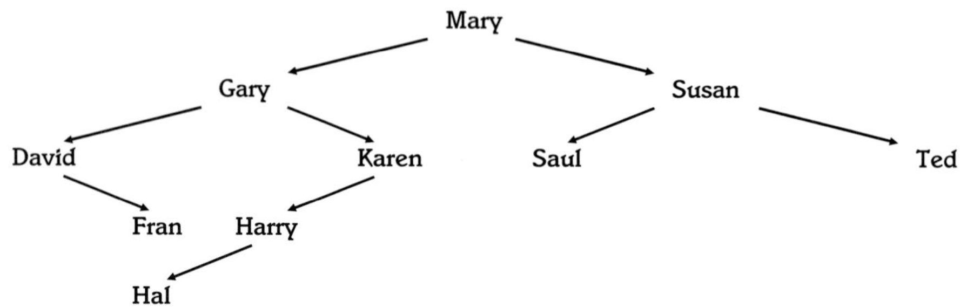

Naturally enough, programmers call the resulting diagram a *binary tree*—"binary" because there are never more than two branches, and "tree" because the picture supposedly resembles an upside-down tree.

It's a good idea to learn some of the terminology computer scientists use to describe binary trees. For example, they say that each of the names forms (or sits in) a *node* on the binary tree. The top node is called the *root* of the tree. The node directly above (that points to) a node is called the *parent* of that node. For example, Karen is the parent node for Harry, and Gary is the parent node for David and Karen. Every parent in a tree can have either no children, a younger (left) child, an older (right) child, or both. A node that has no children is said to be a *leaf.*

When you enter names and form a binary tree by following the procedure just given, you are said to have *loaded* the tree. Adding a new name to a loaded tree is fairly quick, almost as fast as just sticking the name at the end of an ordinary list. Although now, instead of merely sticking it at the end, you follow the correct branch of the tree until you can go no farther. At that point, stick the new name where the hole is. Note that searching a tree and loading a tree are basically the same operation.

Note as well that a binary tree is inherently a recursive object. After all, start from any node at all; then all the nodes that are attached to it form a binary tree as well, with the first node as the new root (usually called a *subtree*). The left child of a parent gives you the left subtree, and the right child of a parent gives you the right subtree. It is this recursive property that makes most of the operations on a binary tree simple.

A recursive version of loading a tree will be a procedure that depends on the contents of the current position in the tree as well as the subtree. An outline in something close to pseudocode might look like this:

```
Procedure LoadATree(Tree,NodeInTree,ThingToAdd)
  If the current node is empty, add the word there
```

```
Else
  If the word precedes the contents of the node
  LoadATree(Left Tree, LeftChild, ThingToAdd)
  Else
  LoadATree(Right Tree, RightChild, ThingToAdd)
```

To write a program that implements this, you have to decide how you're going to represent the arrows and the holes. This is usually called the *data structure*. The ideal situation would be to use a three-column array. Each row on the array would use the first column for the contents of the node, the second column for the row the left child is on, and the third column for the row the right child is pointing to.

The trouble with this is that if you use a string array, you can't use numbers for the entries in the second and third columns (the rows of the children). If you use an array of variants you will build in a fair amount of additional overhead.

Instead, you might turn to a list of records as follows:

```
Type ContentsOfTree
  NodeContents As String
  RowOfLftChil As Integer
  RowOfRtChild As Integer
End Type
```

In the example, the 10×3 array would look like this (using –1 if there's nothing to point to):

Row Number (= node number)	Contents of Node	Row "Before" Arrow Points To	Row "After" Arrow Points To
1	Mary	3	2
2	Susan	6	5
3	Gary	7	4
4	Karen	9	–1
5	Ted	–1	–1
6	Saul	–1	–1
7	David	–1	8
8	Fran	–1	–1
9	Harry	10	–1
10	Hal	–1	–1

For example, the third row of the array of records that will represent the tree would contain three entries—one in each column:

"Gary" 7 4

Note that the first column has the entries in the order in which they were entered. It's the other two columns that give you the extra information needed to quickly search through the tree.

The method used here employs the idea of parallel lists (discussed in Chapter 9), which save space. Ultimately, which method you use is a matter of taste.

The first list will hold the contents of the nodes. It will be a string array, with a two-column integer array for the pointers to the left and right children.

Here is the procedure to load a tree:

```
Sub LoadATree (Nodes$(), Arrows%(), Item$, CurrentPos%)
  ' LOCAL variables are: Items%,WhereToGo%,Direction$
  Dim Items%, WhereToGo As Integer, Direction$
  Items% = Val(nodes$(0))
  If Items% = 0 Then
    Nodes$(0) = "1"
    Nodes$(1) = Item$
    Arrows%(1, 0) = -1
    Arrows%(1, 1) = -1
    Exit Sub
  End If
  If Item$ < Nodes$(CurrentPos%) Then
    WhereToGo% = Arrows%(CurrentPos%, 0)
    Direction$ = "left"
  Else
    WhereToGo% = Arrows%(CurrentPos%, 1)
    Direction$ = "right"
  End If
  If WhereToGo% = -1 Then
    Items% = Items% + 1
    Nodes$(Items%) = Item$
    Arrows%(Items%, 0) = -1
    Arrows%(Items%, 1) = -1
    Nodes$(0) = Str$(Items%)
  ' Now change pointers on parent node
    Select Case Direction$
      Case "left"
        Arrows%(CurrentPos%, 0) = Items%
      Case "right"
        Arrows%(CurrentPos%, 1) = Items%
     End Select
  Else
      LoadATree Nodes$(), Arrows%(), Item$, WhereToGo%
```

```
  End If
End Sub
```

As mentioned earlier, the contents of the nodes are stored in a string array indicated by the parameter array Nodes$, with Nodes$(0) being the string equivalent of the number of items. The arrows are stored in an array Arrows% (,). The parameter Item$ is for the item to be loaded, and the parameter CurrentPos% is used to indicate where you are in the tree. (To load the tree, call this procedure with CurrentPos% = 1.)

You need a special case when you're setting up the tree. Note that the zeroth position of the nodes is used to keep track of the number of items in the first If statement. This is necessary for two reasons. The first is that you have to know in which row of the array you'll add the next entry. The second is that when using this procedure, you have to have previously dimensioned the arrays. A robust program would constantly monitor this number.

The final If gives you a way out of the recursion. When the arrow is pointing to a hole, it's time to place the entry. The Else starts the recursion.

Of course, in a more serious example you would have to use a ReDim Preserve command to add more room as needed. In any case, to print out the table in the current form for debugging purposes, you can use something like this:

```
Sub PrintaTree (Nodes$(), arrows%())
  ' LOCAL variable is NumberOfItems
  Cls
  Print "Row          Contents     Row 'before'       Row _
'after'"
  Print "Number       of Node      arrow points       arrow _
points"
  Print "(= node                   to                 to"
  Print "number)"
  Print : Print
  NumberOfItems = Val(Nodes$(0))
  For I = 1 To NumberOfItems
   Print I, Nodes$(I), arrows%(I, 0), arrows%(I, 1)
  Next I
End Sub
```

Another possibility for debugging is to replace the Print statement with Printer.Print statements. Modifying the LoadATree to SearchATree is simple and is left to you. In any case, you should be aware that the efficiency of SearchATree depends on the shape of the tree.

The best situation (usually called a complete or balanced tree) is when the tree is as "bushy" as possible:

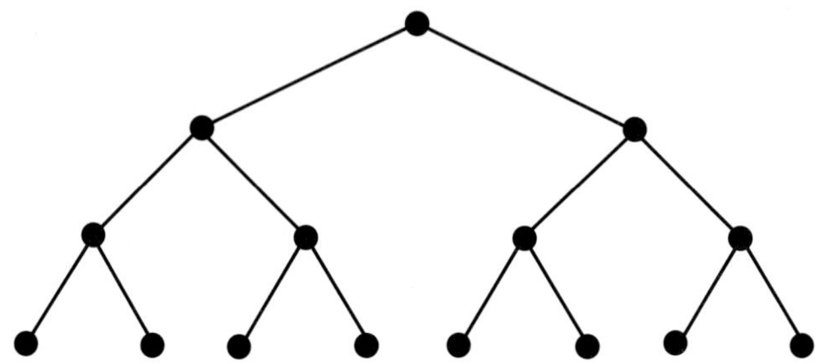

In this case, it works as fast as an ordinary binary search. The worst case is when someone gives you an ordered list, in which case the tree is unbalanced and is as narrow as possible:

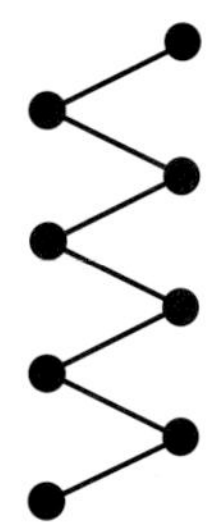

With an unbalanced tree, if you use SearchATree, you'll end up searching the list one item at a time.

When users enter data randomly, then most of the time they'll be very close to the balanced tree and very far from an unbalanced tree. This is why one technique for rebalancing a tree consists merely in pulling out entries from the array that defines the tree at random and rebuilding the tree randomly. This requires adjusting all the pointers again as you rebuild the tree.

Tree Sort

One of the nicest features of trees is that you can sort the items in the tree quite quickly—about as quickly as for the Quicksort. To do this, you have to traverse (move through) nodes cleverly. (It's usually called *inorder traversal.*) Here is an outline of how this is done:

1. Go left as far as you can. Print the node.

2. Print the parent of the node from step 1.
3. From the parent, if you can, go right and repeat step 1. If you can't go right, move up to the grandparent from step 1 and repeat step 3.

This outline obviously describes a recursive procedure. The following listing shows you one version:

```
Sub TreeSort (Nodes$(), Arrows%(), CurrentPos%)
  'LOCAL variable is: WhereToGo%
  Dim WhereToGo%
  If Arrows%(CurrentPos%, 0) <> -1 Then
    WhereToGo% = Arrows%(CurrentPos%, 0)
      TreeSort Nodes$(), Arrows%(), WhereToGo%
  End If
  Print Nodes$(CurrentPos%)
  If Arrows%(CurrentPos%, 1) <> -1 Then
    WhereToGo% = Arrows%(CurrentPos%, 1)
      TreeSort Nodes$(), Arrows%(), WhereToGo%
  End If
End Sub
```

To use this in the preceding example, call

```
TreeSort Nodes$(), Arrows%(), 1
```

The only problem with using this method to sort a list is that, just as when you use SearchATree, its efficiency completely depends on the shape of the tree. The closer the tree is to being balanced (maximum bushiness), the more quickly this works. On the other hand, if the tree degenerates because the names entered were already ordered, then TreeSort does as well. Consult an advanced book like R. Sedgwick's *Algorithms* (Reading, MA: Addison-Wesley, 1990) to learn how to make sure your trees stay balanced. Doing so requires careful monitoring of the shape of the tree and making some rather complicated switches, and you may prefer to use the random method mentioned in the previous section.

Trees do have one other problem, especially when you're using arrays to represent the contents of the nodes and the pointers: it's quite painful to delete a node. (In fact, it's almost never worth the trouble to try to reclaim the space.) Probably the best method to delete a node is to follow the outline given here. (The details are left to you.)

1. If the node has no children, simply delete it by zeroing out the contents.

2. If the node has one child, attach the parent of the node to be deleted to the lone child by changing the pointers.
3. If the node to be deleted has two children, go to its left child and then as far right as possible. This is the entry that alphabetically comes right in front of the entry being deleted. Swap it with the entry to be deleted.

In spite of the occasional problems they cause, binary trees are an extremely useful technique. Most of the time they are the best way to build an index. As you saw in Chapter 14, an efficient index program is the key to writing an XREF program to cross reference your programs (which, if you stop to think about it, is exactly the same problem as writing any other kind of index).

Fractals

This section depends on an understanding of recursion and trigonometry. Benoit Mandelbrot of IBM, who coined the term "fractal" and is doing much to show how useful the idea is, begins his book *The Fractal Geometry of Nature* (San Francisco, CA: W. H. Freeman, 1982) with the following:

> Why is geometry often described as "cold" and "dry"? One reason lies in its inability to describe the shape of a cloud, a mountain, a coastline, or a tree. Clouds are not spheres, mountains are not cones, coastlines are not circles, and bark is not smooth, nor does lightning travel in a straight line.

A little bit later he goes on to say that these objects are most often "identical at all scales." This is the simplest way to understand fractals; they are objects that, no matter how powerful the magnifying glass, remain essentially the same. The large-scale structure is repeated ad infinitum in the small structure. One of Mandelbrot's standard examples is a coastline: from an airplane, from afoot, or using a magnifying glass, you get the same pattern on an ever-smaller scale. A pseudocode description of a general fractal is

```
Draw the object in the large
Replace pieces of the large object with smaller versions of itself
```

This is obviously a description of a recursive process. Before you get to any of the classic fractals, look at Figure 19-4. As you can see, this figure consists of squares, the corners of which are replaced by still smaller squares. The pseudocode for this program might be something like:

Figure 19-4 Beginning of recursive squares

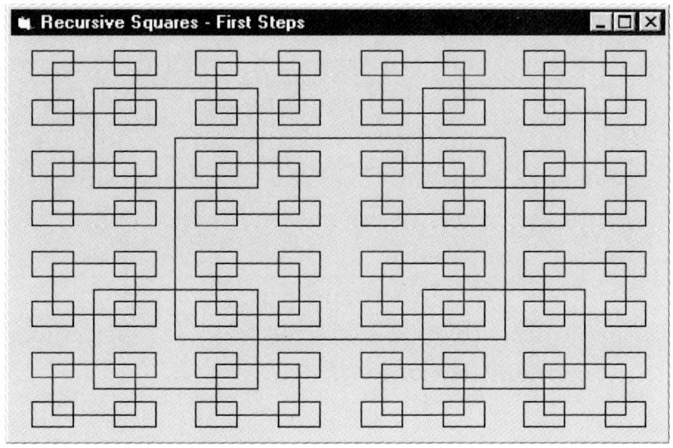

Sub Draw A Square
  At each corner of the square
  Draw a square of smaller size,
    Draw a square unless the squares are already too small
End Sub

Here's a Form_Click procedure that implements this outline:

```
Sub Form_Click()
  ' recursive squares
  Scale (-2000, 2000)-(2000, -2000)
  Square -1000, 1000, 2000
End Sub

Sub Square (x, y, Size)
  'To end recursion
  If Size < 50 Then Exit Sub
  Line (x, y)-(x + Size, y - Size), , B   'Draws the large
                                          'square

    Square x - Size / 4, y + Size / 4, Size / 2   'Recursive
                                                  'call
    Square x + Size - Size / 4, y + Size / 4, Size / 2
    Square x - Size / 4, y - Size + Size / 4, Size / 2
    Square x + Size - Size / 4, y - Size + Size / 4, Size / 2
End Sub
```

On each recursion, there are four new corners. Each one is moved one-quarter of the size of the previous one in or out from the previous one and is half as big.

Figure 19-5 is a screen dump of the start of one of the first fractals to be discovered. It's the beginning of a fractal called the Koch Snowflake that you saw in Figure 19-1. As you can see, this consists of a star repeated on an ever-smaller scale. The key to programming this is to notice that if you start from the center of the star of, say, size eight, then each vertex has a one-, two-, or four-unit shift in the X or Y level.

Once you understand this, then writing the program only requires setting up an array that, on each call, holds the current values for the 12 vertexes. Here's a fragment that does this:

```
Sub Koch (Xpos, Ypos, size)
' The Koch Snowflake
 'local variables are X(),Y(),shift,i,colnum
 ReDim x(12), y(12)
 Dim shift As Single, I As Integer
  If size < 4 Then Exit Sub
  shift = size / 8
  x(1) = Xpos: y(1) = Ypos + 4 * shift
  x(2) = Xpos + shift: y(2) = Ypos + 2 * shift
  x(3) = Xpos + 3 * shift: y(3) = y(2)
  x(4) = Xpos + 2 * shift: y(4) = Ypos
  x(5) = x(3): y(5) = Ypos - 2 * shift
  x(6) = x(2): y(6) = y(5)
  x(7) = Xpos: y(7) = Ypos - 4 * shift
  x(8) = Xpos - shift: y(8) = y(5)
  x(9) = Xpos - 3 * shift: y(9) = y(5)
  x(10) = Xpos - 2 * shift: y(10) = Ypos
  x(11) = x(9): y(11) = y(2)
  x(12) = x(8): y(12) = y(2)
  Line (x(1), y(1))-(x(5), y(5))
  Line -(x(9), y(9))
  Line -(x(1), y(1))
  Line (x(3), y(3))-(x(7), y(7))
  Line -(x(11), y(11))
  Line -(x(3), y(3))
    Koch Xpos, Ypos, 2 * shift
    For I = 1 To 12
        Koch x(i), y(i), 3 * shift
    Next I
End Sub
```

Figure 19-5 Start of the Koch Snowflake

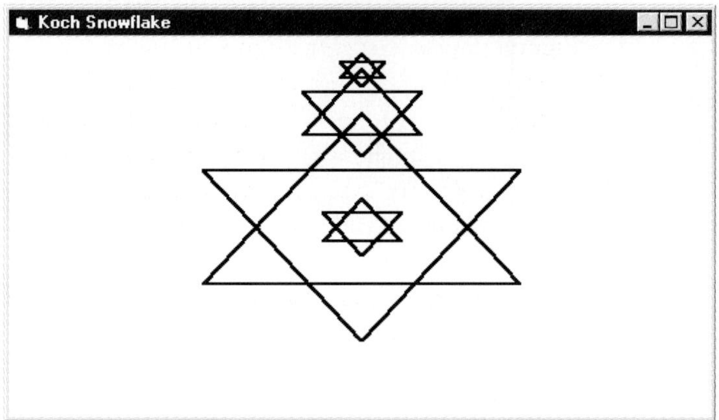

If you have a color monitor, you might want to experiment by adding color to the routine by changing the ForeColor property. The results can be fascinating.

To actually use this procedure, you need to put this fragment in the event procedure that will start the process:

```
Scale (-100,100) -(100,-100)
Koch 0, 0, 120
```

Other Fractal Curves

To better understand the fractal curves described in this section, observe that there's another way to think of the Koch Snowflake. What you're doing is replacing each straight line segment with a line segment that looks like this:

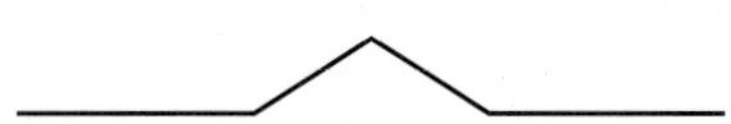

This idea of continually replacing a straight line with a "bent" line is the key to the next two curves. In the first, usually called a C-curve, you replace each straight line with a bend, like this:

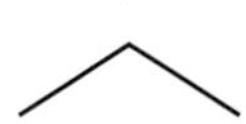

This eventually gives you a figure that looks like the one in Figure 19-6. You can modify the C-curve for the next fractal, called the Dragon curve, by putting

Figure 19-6
The C-curve

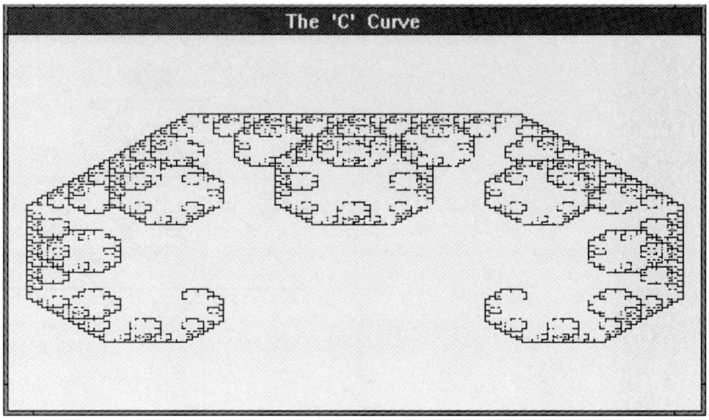

the bends on opposite sides. The replacement parts alternately go out and in. The screen in Figure 19-7 shows a picture of what you get. The pseudocode for both these programs is the same:

```
Sub DrawAFractal with MakeABend
  If the line isn't too small
  Replace the line with the bent one.
    Sub for the smaller line
End Sub
```

Figure 19-7
The Dragon curve

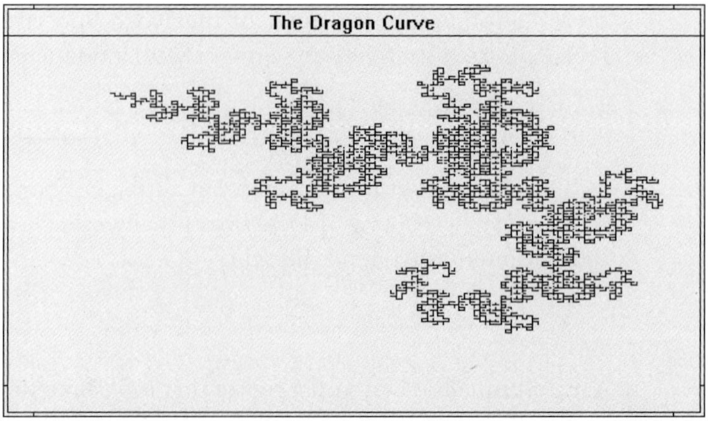

Figure 19-8 The trigonometry of finding a new point

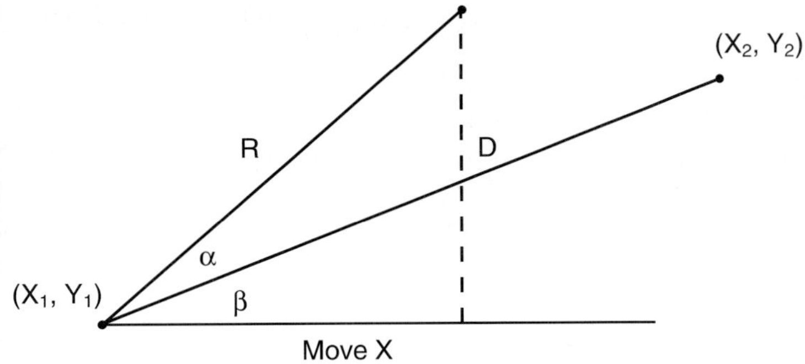

$$\begin{aligned}\text{Move X} &= R\cos(\alpha+\beta)\\ &= R[\cos(\alpha)\cos(\beta)-\sin(\alpha)\sin(\beta)]\\ &= R[\cos(\alpha)\frac{(X_2-X_1)}{D}-\sin(\alpha)\frac{(Y_2-Y_1)}{D}]\\ &= \frac{R}{D}[\cos(\alpha)(X_2-X_1)-\sin(\alpha)(Y_2-Y_1)]\end{aligned}$$

The only point remaining is to describe, mathematically, "making a bend." This is where trigonometry comes in. What you need is a formula that, given a line connecting any two points and angle, finds the coordinates of the new point that gives the bent line. Look at Figure 19-8. Notice that if the angle is 45 degrees, as it is in the C- and Dragon curves, then the size of the spike is

COS(45°)*D= (SQR(2)/2)*D

because the triangle is a 45°-45°-90° right triangle. Using this, the keys to a program for the C-curve are the following MoveX and MoveY functions:

```
Function MoveX (X1!, Y1!, X2!, Y2!) As Single
  ' local variables: Angle(in radians),D,XShift,YShift
  Dim Angle As Single, D As Single
  Dim XShift As Single, YShift As Single
  Angle = Radians(45)
  D = Dist(X1!, Y1!, X2!, Y2!)
  R = (SQR(2) / 2) * D
  XShift = Cos(Angle) * (X2! - X1!)
  YShift = Sin(Angle) * (Y2! - Y1!)
MoveX = R / D * (XShift - YShift)
End Function
```

```
Function MoveY (X1!, Y1!, X2!, Y2!) As Single
  ' local variables: Angle(in radians),D,XShift,YShift
  Dim Angle As Single, D As Single
  Dim XShift As Single, YShift As Single
  Angle = Radians(45)
  D = Dist(X1!, Y1!, X2!, Y2!)
  R = (SQR(2) / 2) * D
  XShift = Sin(Angle) * (X2! - X1!)
  YShift = Cos(Angle) * (Y2! - Y1!)

  MoveY = (R / D) * (XShift + YShift)
End Function
```

Before you can get to the main recursive procedure, you need the distance function and a function to convert to radian measure:

```
Function Dist (X1!, Y1!, X2!, Y2!) As Single
  ' finds the distance between points
  ' local variables are: x,y
  Dim X As Single, Y As Single
  X = (X2! - X1!) * (X2! - X1!)
  Y = (Y2! - Y1!) * (Y2! - Y1!)
  Dist = SQR(X + Y)
End Function

Function Radians! (X!)
  ' converts degrees to radians
  ' Needs global variable PI = 4*Atn(1)
  Radians! = X! * PI / 180
End Function
```

Next, you have the main (recursive) Sub:

```
Sub Curve (X1!, Y1!, X2!, Y2!)
  Dim DistPt As Single, NX1 As Single, NY1 As Single
  DistPt = Dist(X1!, Y1!, X2!, Y2!)
  If DistPt < 10 Then
    Exit Sub
  End If
  NX1 = X1 + MoveX(X1!, Y1!, X2!, Y2!)       'find the coord _
for
  NY1 = Y1 + MoveY(X1!, Y1!, X2!, Y2!)       'the spike
  ' If these are in a module replace Line with FormName.Line
```

```
    Line (X1!, Y1!)-(X2!, Y2!), BackColor   'erase previous _
line
    Line (X1!, Y1!)-(NX1, NY1)              'make the spike
    Line -(X2!, Y2!)
  Curve X1!, Y1!, NX1, NY1                  'now recurse on _
the
  Curve NX1, NY1, X2!, Y2!                  'spikes
End Sub
```

Here's the rest of the program for the C-curve. First, as commented in the Radians function, you need a form-level variable, Pi, for the value of π. Then all you have to do is set Pi = 4*Atn(1) in the Form_Load procedure and do the following:

```
Private Sub Form_Click()
  Dim X1!, X2!, Y1!, Y2!
  Scale (-500, 500)-(500, -500)
  X1! = -250: Y1! = -200
  X2! = 250: Y2! = -200
  Curve X1!, Y1!, X2!, Y2!
End Sub
```

The nice thing about these kinds of fractals is that all you ever have to do is change the MoveX and MoveY functions. For the Dragon curve, you need to modify them so they alternate sides each time—a perfect situation for static variables. For example, here's what you need to do to modify the MoveX function—the MoveY function is similar and left to you.

```
Function MoveX (X1!, Y1!, X2!, Y2!) As Single
  ' modified mover for Dragon curve
  ' local variables: Angle(in radians),D,XShift,YShift
  Dim D As Single, XShift As Single, YShift As Single
  Static J As Integer
  J = J + 1
  Angle = Radians!(45)
  If J Mod 2 = 0 Then Angle = -Angle:J=0  'alternate on each
                                          'call!
  D = Dist(X1!, Y1!, X2!, Y2!)
  R = (SQR(2) / 2) * D
  XShift = Cos(Angle) * (X2! - X1!)
  YShift = Sin(Angle) * (Y2! - Y1!)
  MoveX = R / D * (XShift - YShift)
End Function
```

Figure 19-9
A fractal landscape

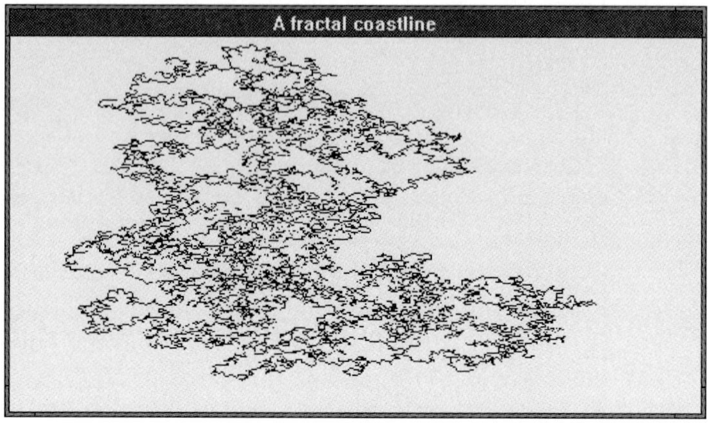

The screen in Figure 19-9 shows the result of a program to draw a model of a landscape. Modification of this program can give extremely realistic three-dimensional pictures. Even clicking twice gives a more three-dimensional effect, as you can also see in Figure 19-9. (For example, fractal techniques were used to create the Genesis sequence in the Star Trek movie *The Wrath of Khan*.) The only difference between this and the two preceding curves is that this time the angle is to be random, as is the size of each "spike." To do this, you have to change the Move functions by incorporating a random factor for the angle (instead of 45 degrees) and for the size of the spike (instead of Cos(45°*D). For example, the following listing does this for MoveX.

```
Function MoveX (X1!, Y1!, X2!, Y2!) As Single
  ' local variables: Angle(in radians),D,XShift,YShift
  Dim Angle As Single, D As Single, R As Single
  Dim XShift As Single, YShift As Single
  Angle = Radians!(15 + 60 * Rnd)
  If Rnd(1) > .5 Then Angle = -Angle
  D = Dist(X1!, Y1!, X2!, Y2!)
  R = (.15 + (.6 * RND(1))) * D
  XShift = Cos(Angle) * (X2! - X1!)
  YShift = Sin(Angle) * (Y2! - Y1!)
  MoveX = (R / D) * (XShift - YShift)
End Function
```

Finally, instead of one call that acts recursively on a single line, this time you'll build the shoreline out of three recursive calls to three lines that form a triangle. The following fragment will do this:

```
Scale (-500!, 500!)-(500!, -500!)
X1! = -250: Y1! = 200
X2! = 250: Y2! = 200
Curve X1!, Y1!, X2!, Y2!
Curve X2!, Y2!, 0, -Y2!
Curve 0, -Y2!, X1!, Y1!
```

When Not to Use Recursion

Many of the example programs given in this chapter could have been solved by iteration (writing a loop). To quote Niklaus Wirth, the inventor of Pascal, from his book, *Algorithms + Data Structures = Programs* (Englewood Cliffs, NJ: Prentice Hall, 1976), "...the lesson to be drawn is to avoid the use of recursion when there is an *obvious* solution by iteration" [italics in original].

The reason is that although a recursive procedure is often shorter to write, it almost inevitably takes longer and uses much more memory to run. (You may counter that memory is cheap, but no matter what you do in Visual Basic, the stack is limited to what Visual Basic provides.)

In fact, as Wirth and others have pointed out, what should be the standard examples of when not to use recursion are also the examples most commonly given of recursion: the factorial and the Fibonacci numbers. (They're used as they were in this chapter because they illustrate the techniques well.)

Both the factorial and Fibonacci numbers can be computed more easily and quickly (and using much less memory) by using loops. The factorial is obvious, the Fibonacci numbers only slightly less so. You need to keep track of the previous two Fibonacci numbers, as in the following listing:

```
Function Fib% (n as Integer)
' LOCAL variables are: I,First,Sec,CurrentFib
Dim First As Integer, Sec As Integer
Dim I As Integer, CurrentFib As Integer
  If N <= 1 Then
   Fib% = N
```

```
    Exit Function
   Else
     First = 0
     Sec = 1
      For I = 2 To N
       CurrentFib = First + Sec
       First = Sec
       Sec = CurrentFib
      Next I
    Fib% = CurrentFib
   End If
End Function
```

Although you can use the Timer command to demonstrate the difference between the two versions, a more graphic demonstration is obtained by drawing a diagram of how much wasted effort there is in the recursive version of Fibonacci, as shown in Figure 19-10.

Note that to compute Fib(5) recursively, a program has to compute Fib(3) twice, Fib(2) three times, and get to the trivial case eight times. It never saves the information it so laboriously computes—it just recomputes it constantly.

Figure 19-10

Calls needed for recursive Fib

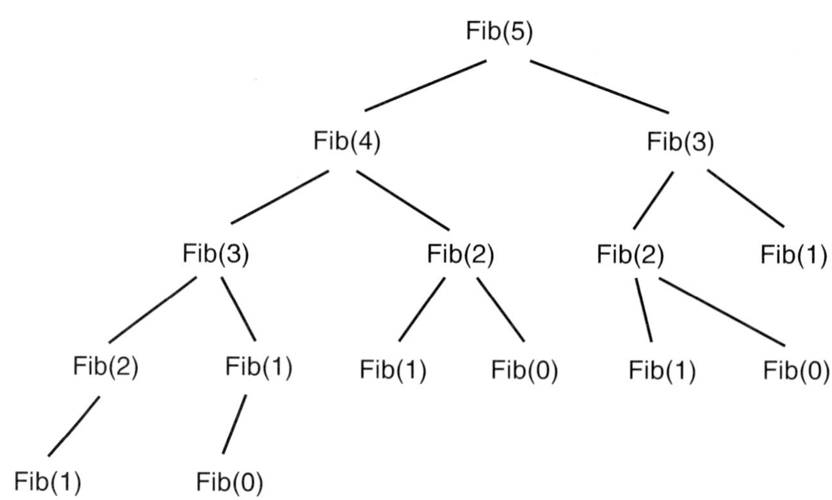

Another example of where you can replace recursion is in the LoadATree and SearchATree procedures. Since the recursive call happens only at the end (when a hole has not yet been detected), you can rewrite that part of the procedure in, for example, LoadATree, as follows:

```
Do Until WhereToGo% = -1
 If Item$  < Nodes$(CurrentPos%) Then
   WhereToGo% = Arrows%(CurrentPos%,0)
   Direction$ = "left"
 Else
   WhereToGo% = Arrows%(CurrentPos%,1)
   Direction$ = "right"
 End If
Loop
```

The reason it's easy to change the original version to a nonrecursive, iterative version is that LoadATree is a *tail recursive program*. This means that when you make the recursive call, nothing is left to be done on the stack; it doesn't need to remember anything. Any tail recursive program can be changed to a loop controlled by the trivial case, exactly as was done earlier. On the other hand, TreeSort is not tail recursive because the stack contains many requests to "Print a node."

One other point that may be of interest to you is that you can theoretically translate any recursive procedure, tail recursive or not, into an iterative version. The trouble is that you do it by setting up a stack and keeping track of everything—work that is best done by the compiler.

note: *The one time you will need to do this is when your programs consistently run out of stack space. You would then use an array to imitate the stack in the recursive process.*

Chapter Twenty

A Survey of Database Features

This chapter introduces you to the database features in Visual Basic. It starts with an introduction to modern database development using both the sample database and the Data Manager application supplied with Visual Basic. After this introduction, you'll see how to use the Data Manager to build your own simple databases.

note: *If you have the Enterprise edition of Visual Basic, you will have even more power at your disposal—the Enterprise edition features of Visual Basic are not covered in this book.*

Next, you'll see how Visual Basic can work with an existing database through the data control. Finally, you'll see how to use Visual Basic code to move beyond the simplest database manipulations built into the data control.

Keep in mind that this chapter can only be an introduction, because you will quickly discover that if you want to do any serious work with databases using Visual Basic, you will both need and want the extra power that database programming will give you. And you will then discover just as quickly that you must consult more specialized books. Database programming, whether done from Visual Basic or from a full-fledged database manager such as Microsoft Access, is not trivial. (It is worth noting that while Microsoft Access includes much of the power of Visual Basic, and vice versa, they work best together.) It would take a book at least three times as large as this one to explain any substantial part of the database programming power available to you with Visual Basic.

tip: *The VisData sample supplied with the Professional and Enterprise editions of Visual Basic is a superb example of the database development you can do with the higher-end versions of Visual Basic. Running this project will whet your appetite for what Visual Basic can do, and studying the code in this sample (after you read the appropriate sections of the* Programmer's Guide *and this chapter!)—will teach you a lot.*

Some General Words on Modern Databases

Before you start working with data access, it is a good idea to get a feel for what modern databases are all about. Without getting too technical, this section explains what is usually called "the relational model" for a database. This is the model used by Visual Basic, Microsoft Access, and many other programmable PC databases such as FoxPro.

Let's return to the simpler databases before getting into the more sophisticated relational model of a database. A rolodex is a good analog for this kind of simpler database, called a *flat file* database. This is merely an indexed set of "cards" and can easily be created using the techniques you saw in Chapter 17. Random-access files are ideal in building such databases because they are easy to set up and manipulate and don't require massive resources. Notice that in these databases the data exists in a set form. Indices are added as a way of quickly getting to specific records, but they are not essential—especially for small sets of data.

The trouble with using only (indexed) random-access files for all database applications is that they are too limited. Suppose, for example, you are running a business. This business maintains a list of customers in one indexed system and a list of bills in another. Someone's address changes; ideally you would want the address to change in both places automatically. This is impossible without a lot of work, as long as data for each situation is kept in separate databases.

More sophisticated databases, like the ones you can begin to build with the Data Manager (and build completely with Microsoft Access or the data access power of Visual Basic's Professional and Enterprise editions), don't fit the indexed card model. This makes it easy to avoid the update problem mentioned in the previous paragraph. They have many other advantages as well, although the extra power comes at a cost. The extra cost usually will be the need for more powerful computers and more code.

There really is no convenient way to describe the underlying structure of the databases that you can build using the Access engine supplied with Visual Basic—that is, what actually lies on the user's hard disk. In fact, for now, think of a database as a large amount of data that exists in no fixed form; it is merely "out there" in some sort of nebulous glob. However, the data is controlled by an oracle with great powers. These powers let the oracle bring order out of chaos.

For example, suppose the database is all computer books published (or even all books published!). You want to ask this oracle a specific question about computer books. There are a lot of computer books out there, many covering the same subject with the same title (as authors well know). There are also a lot of authors out there (as publishers well know). So there is a lot of information out there. The oracle, being very powerful and with lots of storage space, has all possible information about computer books stored away in some form or other—the authors, the titles, the page counts, the publishers, and lots more. The information kept by the oracle could be used in many ways. You might need all books by a specific author, all books with a specific string in the title, all books by a specific publisher, or all books that satisfy the three conditions.

Now, imagine that you ask the oracle a question such as, "Present me with all books published by Osborne/McGraw-Hill in 1994. Show me the title, the author, and the page count." The oracle works through all its data and then presents you with a gridlike arrangement of the books satisfying the question you just asked. Notice that you neither know nor care how the oracle does this—how the information is actually stored and processed. You are satisfied with a grid that you can easily manipulate.

Next, notice that a random-access file really can't handle this type of situation. If you had a single record associated to each author, you would simply have no way of knowing how many fields to add to allow for all of the books by one author. He or she may continue to write and write. Of course, you could have a separate record for each book, but this forces a lot of duplication—the vital statistics of the author would need to be repeated each time, for example.

However, if the data is simply out there in some vague formless mass, the oracle can use lots of internal bookkeeping tricks to avoid redundancies, to compact the data, to search through the data, and so on.

In modern database terminology, the questions you ask are called *queries* and the grid you are presented with is either a *table* or a *view*. The difference between a table and a view is that a table is built into the database structure, and a view is a way of looking at information that might span many tables. The oracle (in Visual Basic it's the Microsoft Access "Jet" engine) will respond to different queries with different tables (views), although there is still only one (potentially huge) database out there.

The usual language for asking queries of a relational database is called *SQL* (usually pronounced "es que el," "seekel," or "sequel"), which stands for *structured query language*. SQL is built into Visual Basic's Professional and Enterprise editions, and a subset is built into the standard edition.

Now, in real life, oracles don't exist and data can't be nebulous. So, as you'll see in the next section, data is essentially stored in overlapping tables (grids) that are joined together as needed by the database engine. The columns of these tables are called *fields* and the rows are called *records*.

When you make a query, the Access engine either sends you a subset of one of the tables that already exists or temporarily creates a new grid (view) in memory by combining data from all the tables it has already stored. Since the grid is made up of a set of records extracted from the database, the object on Visual Basic is called, naturally enough, a RecordSet.

note: *Microsoft does not follow standard relational database terminology completely. Instead of the term "view," they use the term "dynaset" if the grid is updatable and "snapshot" if it is not. This book uses the term "view" if we are not specifying whether the table is updatable, and Microsoft's terms if we are distinguishing between the table being updatable or not.*

The Data Manager

The Data Manager is the only way to build a database in the standard edition of Visual Basic. It is available as an option from the Add-Ins menu in all the editions of Visual Basic, but it is really a separate application (DATAMGR.EXE) that can be run independently of Visual Basic. (The Data Manager is written completely in Visual Basic and its compiled form is 281,000 or so bytes, which means it is only a few thousand lines of code.)

The main screen of the Data Manager looks like Figure 20-1.

The Data Manager lets you look at the structure of an existing Microsoft Access format. (This is usually called Jet format because Microsoft named the database tool the "Jet Engine.") The Data Manager can also build a new database in Jet format. Jet format databases usually have the extension .MDB for the filename.

tip: *The Data Manager has been changed in Visual Basic 4 to let you use only Jet (Access) .MDB formats. You can no longer use it to deal directly with other database formats. The VisData sample in the Professional and Enterprise versions of Visual Basic can help if you need this ability.*

The Data Manager can also add information to Jet databases and delete information from an existing Jet database.

Figure 20-1 Main screen of the Data Manager

note: *The Data Manager has its own (fairly extensive) Help system. For more details on the Data Manager than are given here, please consult its on-line help.*

Using the Data Manager to Examine Existing Databases

As a way to get more comfortable with data access, let's use the Data Manager to examine the BIBLIO.MDB database that is supplied with Visual Basic. Open the File menu in the Data Manager and choose Open Database. This brings up the Open Database dialog box. The BIBLIO.MDB database is usually stored in the same directory as Visual Basic. Open this database by double-clicking the name and you'll see a screen like this:

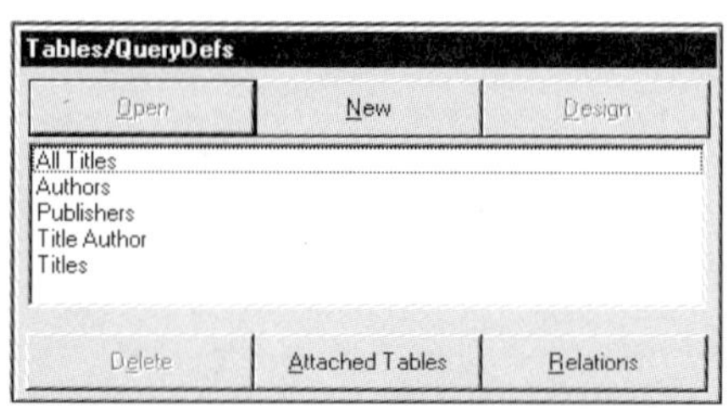

Notice that there are five tables in this database: one for All Titles, one for Authors, one for Publishers, one for Title Author, and one for Titles. Notice as well that these names do not fit normal DOS filename conventions. (Since the Jet (Access) engine stores all the information in the database file, the parts of the database do not need to follow ordinary DOS naming conventions. This is different from many earlier database managers such as dBASE III.)

Highlight the Authors table and click Design. Your screen will look like this:

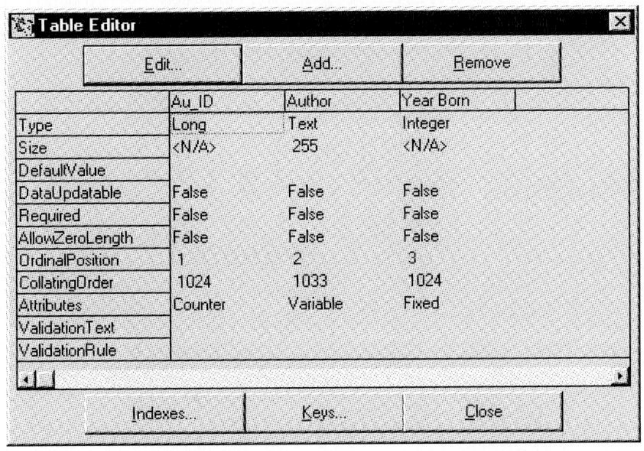

Notice that the Authors table has only three fields. The first field seems strange: it is a long integer called Au_ID, which stands for Author ID. This field exists because of the requirement that every table have at least one field (or combination of fields) that is unique. In this case the author's name alone would not satisfy this requirement. Next, notice that the Author field is a text field and can hold up to 255 characters. Then notice that the Year Born field is an integer field.

Turn your attention to the button marked Indexes. Click the Indexes button, and the Indexes dialog is displayed, as shown here:

Select PrimaryKey from the list box and then click Edit to display the Edit Index dialog shown here:

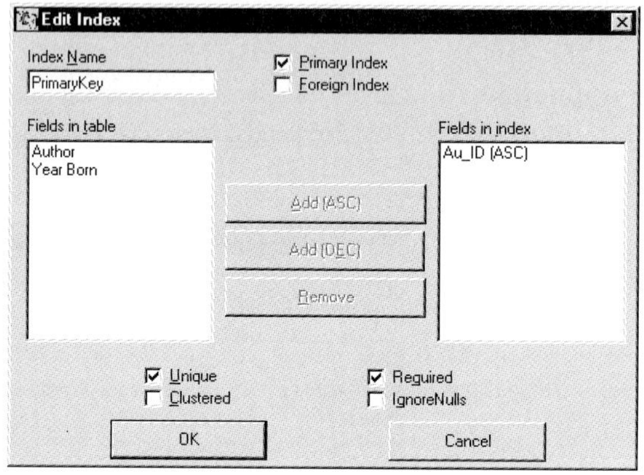

Notice that the field Au_ID(ASC) is shown as a "unique, primary index" (because these are the only boxes checked). The words "unique, primary index" mean that the Au_ID number is unique and that the Access engine should use this field to determine whether someone is trying to enter duplicate data. Therefore, the Jet engine will allow you to enter the same author twice but will demand a different author ID number each time. (It turns out that in this database, author IDs are merely arbitrary integers that correspond to the order in which the title was entered.)

Notice that this particular table is *not* indexed on the authors' names at present. Setting up another index is worthwhile if you will need to search through the data using criteria derived from that index. For example, adding Authors as an index would certainly be worth considering in a more realistic database about books. You almost certainly would like to look for specific authors. This kind of index is allowable because index entries with the Access engine need not be unique. That way you can index on the Author field even though one author may have written many books. Obviously, multiple indexes speed searching through the data. The cost is more overhead, just as it is with random-access files. You can index a field by clicking on it, then clicking on the Add (ASC) for ascending order or Add (DEC) for descending order.

Whenever two tables share a common field, you can easily program them to be joined. The Data Manager lets you do this by working the Relationships dialog box that pops up when you click on the Relations button in the main screen. (The Professional and Enterprise editions of Visual Basic or Microsoft

Access let you do this using code.) After two tables are joined, a change in one affects the common fields in the other (and usually vice versa).

An example of this is when a table of customer records has a unique customer ID as the primary key, but another table in the same database for orders by customers has the customer ID as a field. Obviously, since a customer may order more than once, the second table could not possibly have the customer ID number as a primary key field. In the second table the customer ID number would be an ordinary (but possibly index) field. This is called a *many to one relationship* and is the hallmark of relational databases. Notice that you would want changes in, say, the ordering database to affect changes in the account database. These two tables would be joined using the customer name and/or the customer ID.

Adding Information to a Database

Suppose you want to add to this database Tom Sheldon's *Windows 3.1 Made Easy* (ISBN 0-07-881725-0, published by Osborne/McGraw-Hill). Information in a relational database is not added globally but must be added to specific tables.

To add data to a table, you have to open the table. If any of the tables are still open in design mode, close them. Return to the main screen of the BIBLIO.MDB database, select Authors, and click on Open. You are taken to a screen that looks like Figure 20-2. Click where the pointer is (at the >> symbol). This takes you to the last record. From that you can determine the next unused author ID. Add the information requested in Figure 20-2. When you are satisfied, click on the Update button or move to another record by clicking on any one of the arrow keys.

tip: *Any movement using one of the arrow keys will add the information you entered in the Add dialog box. You must click on the Cancel button to cancel the entry.*

The Data Manager is not programmed to make it easy to reuse data entered in one table in another. This could be added as a feature via code in data applications you write with Visual Basic. (You would need to save the information for reuse as it is entered.) In our case, if you wanted to enter this book into the only other table that would be appropriate—the Titles table—you would need to reenter whatever data is duplicated between the tables. You

Figure 20-2 Working with the Data Manager

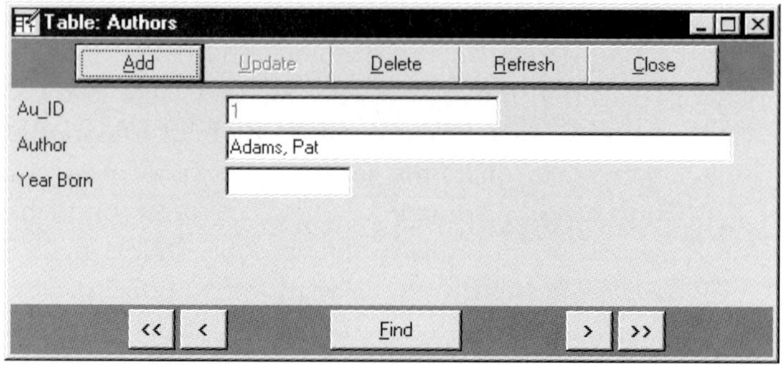

would also need to look up the publisher ID for McGraw-Hill, which you could get by using the arrow keys at the bottom of the add/record screen to move through the list of records. (As indicated in Figure 20-2, the forward pointing arrow moves forward one record at a time, the backward pointing arrow moves back. The double arrows move to the beginning or end of the table, respectively.)

The Find button in the Data Manager has a great deal of power to search for records in an open table. You can use pattern matching to look for records with specific fields, for example, by popping up the Find dialog box shown here,

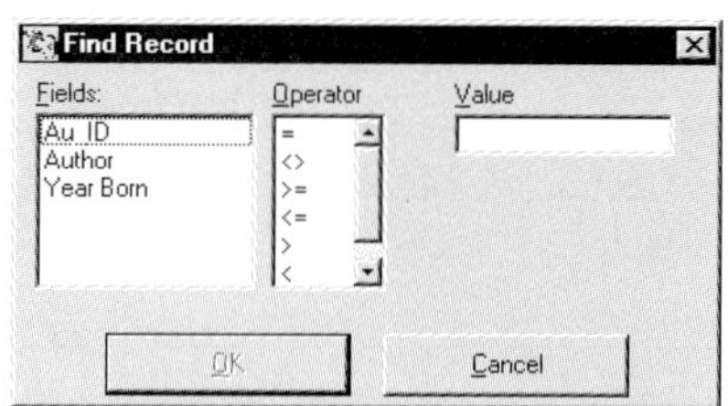

and filling it. For example, you could fill it in as shown here to find all authors born after 1952:

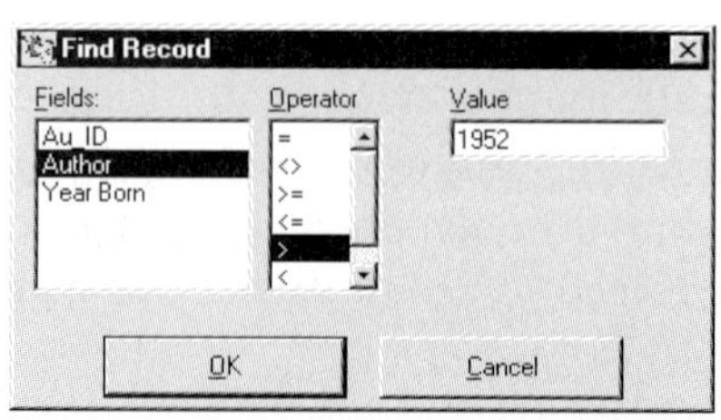

(What would happen is the Data Manager would search through the BIBLIO.MDB database and isolate only those authors born after 1952.)

Using the Data Manager to Create New Databases

Now let's suppose that you want to build a new database from scratch. Open the File menu in the Data Manager and click on New. Your screen looks like this:

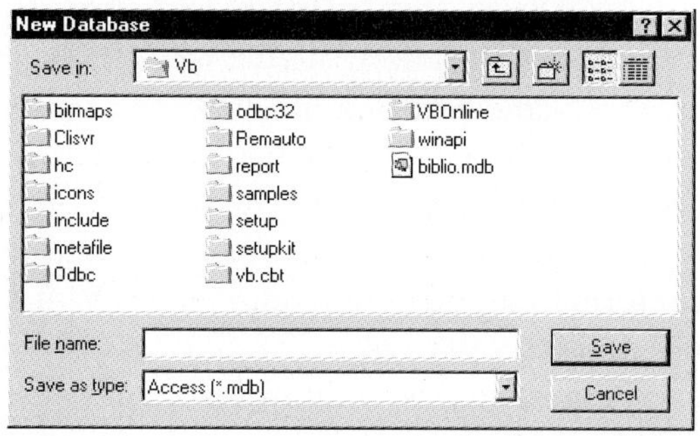

Say you want to create a database for information about cities in the United States. You set the filename to CITY.MDB and press ENTER. Your screen now looks like this:

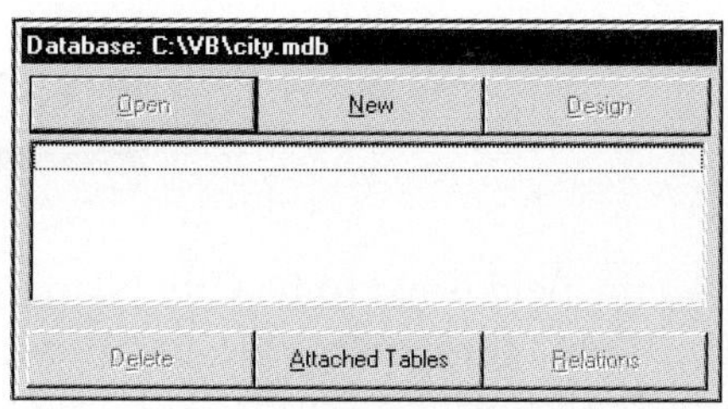

As it turns out, the oracle may be all powerful but in reality you will have to build the framework for all the tables used by your database unless you get the Professional or Enterprise edition of Visual Basic. With the higher-end products, you can define the structure of tables via code. This is often much easier. (On the other hand, even in the standard edition, with a little bit of code, you can arrange it so that you don't have to reenter duplicate data.)

When you click on New, a dialog box that lets you build the structure of your database pops up, as shown here:

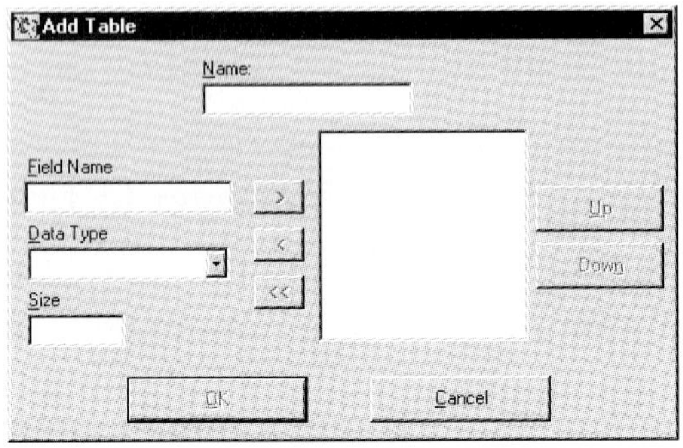

The Name text box is where you will name the table. Let's call this one City_Info. In general, the name for a table in a database need only follow the ordinary Visual Basic conventions for object names. (Of course, if you intend to use the database with another type of database manager, you would have to conform to both sets of requirements: Visual Basic's and those of the other data manager.)

The next step is to fill in the names of the various fields. You do this one field at a time. For each field you need to choose the data type of the information contained in the field. You can do this by dropping down the Data Type combo box, as shown here:

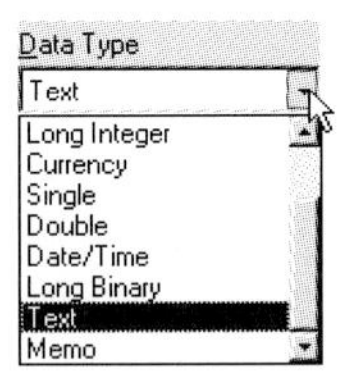

Set the field name to be City Name, and then move to the text box for field type. If you click on the down arrow, you see a list of the possible types for fields. In this case you want to choose text and a size of, say, 25. Then click on the arrow button to add it to the table. Similarly, set up another text field named State with room for 25 characters. Finally, add a long integer field called Population. When you are done, your screen will look like this:

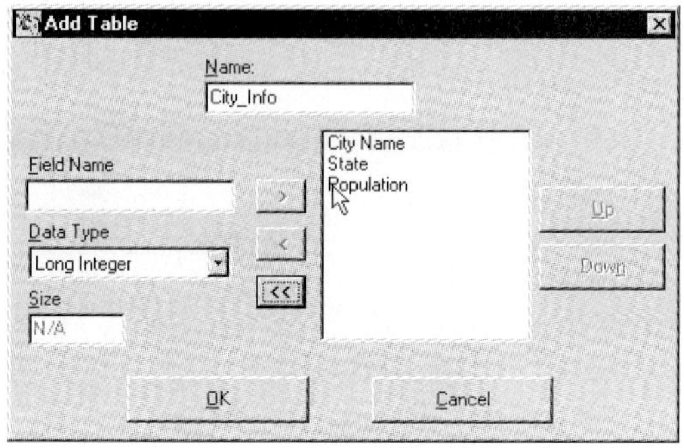

note: *Besides text and numbers, fields can accept binary input (for pictures, for example), Boolean (for True/False, Yes/No type data), and what are called Memo fields for large amounts of text that will be stored as comments.*

When you are done, click on OK. You are then taken to a screen that looks like Figure 20-3. You need to add at least one index for this table. (Each table

Figure 20-3 Defining a table screen

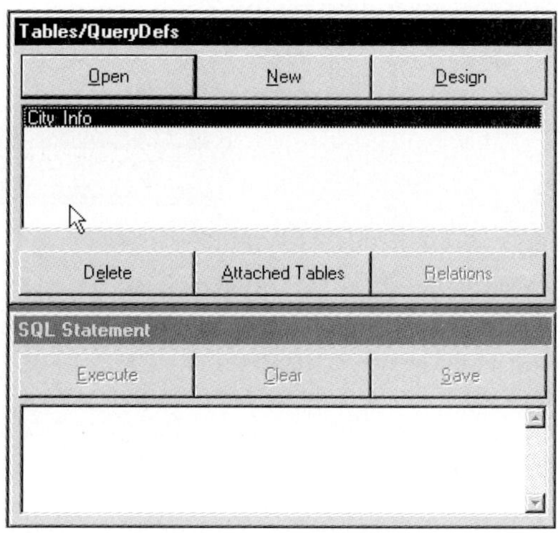

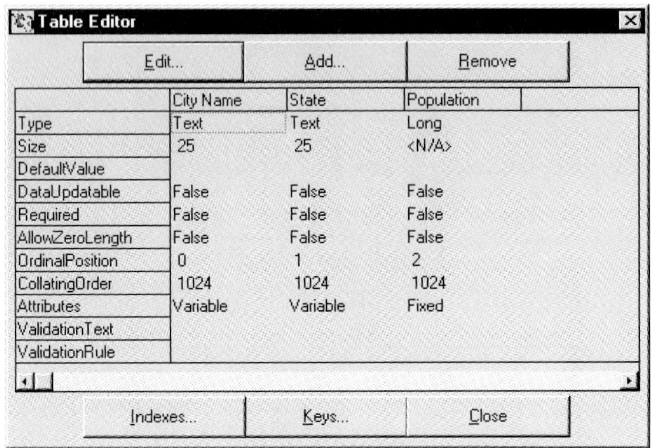

Figure 20-4 The Design screen in the Data Manager

in the database can have one or more indexes, and you can index any text or numeric field.) For this, select the table and then click on Design. This takes you to a screen like Figure 20-4.

Click on the Indexes button. You are taken to a screen that looks like this:

Click the Add button. You are taken to the Add Index dialog box shown here:

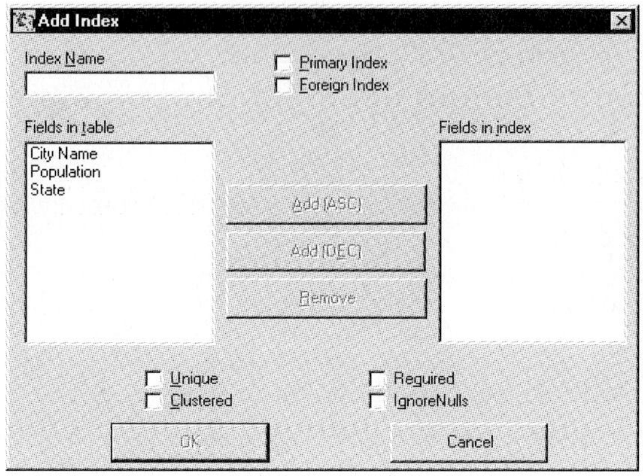

Type the name of the index and make the City Name the Primary Index (don't check off Unique because two cities can have the same name). Click on the Required check box because you want to require a city name in order to add this information to the table. Finally, click on the Add (Asc) button to tell the Data Manager you want this information sorted in ascending order, and then click on OK.

After you click on Close twice to go back to the main screen, you are now done with this particular table. In a similar way, construct another table called City History with two fields, one called City Name and the other one called Date Founded. Index this table on the Date Founded integer field.

You are ready to add data to the two tables. Make sure the table is selected, and click on Open to start adding the data. Your screen will look like this:

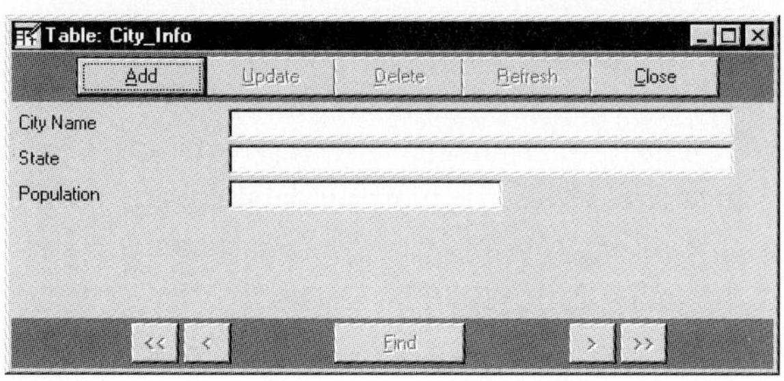

Now you have to fill each table with data. You'll soon see how to do this programmatically, but for now use the information in the following table to fill in the two tables.

City Name	State	Population	Date Founded
Detroit	MI	1027974	1701
Atlanta	GA	394017	1837
Boston	MA	574283	1630

note: *Because you are using the Data Manager to fill in the information, you cannot use any shortcuts that arise because the two tables share a common field. Only code will let you do this.*

When you fill in each field of the table and click on the Update button (or the right pointing arrow) you are said to have added a record to the table. When you have finished entering all the data you want, click on the Close database command from the File menu after closing all subsidiary windows. Click on the Refresh button if you make a mistake entering the data.

Other Operations You Can Do with the Data Manager

Besides editing indexes and creating databases, the Data Manager allows you to add records to tables and delete records. For example, to delete a record:

1. Move to the record you want using the arrow buttons.
2. Click the Delete button.

The Data Manager also lets you add new fields to an existing table in the database. Open the existing database and then click the Design button. You can also join two tables in the same database by working with the Relationships dialog box shown here:

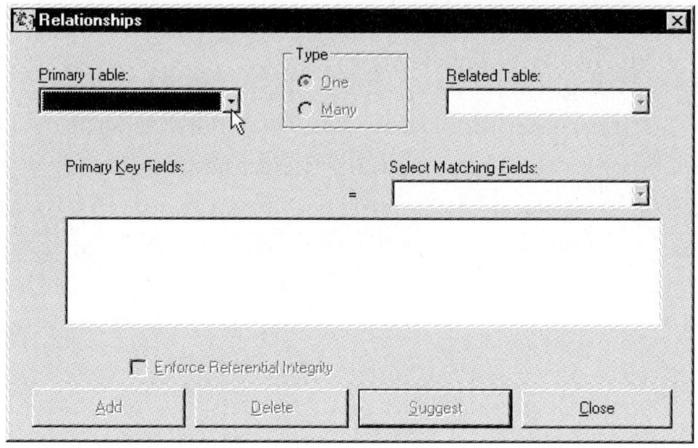

(The point of joined fields is to allow changes in one table to be reflected in the other instantly.)

You can even encrypt a database created with the Data Manager. Finally, as you delete and add records, your databases will seem to grow very quickly. For this reason you may want to use the Compact Database option on the File menu periodically.

caution: *Although you can use the same name for both the original database and its compacted version, you are better off using a new name and, after the compacting is over, deleting the original and renaming the compacted version. If you use the same name, you run the risk of losing both versions if anything goes wrong.*

tip: *The Repair DataBase option on the File menu of the Data Manager can sometimes repair databases that are corrupted because of buffer problems (such as a power failure). There are no guarantees, however.*

Using the Data Control

Roughly speaking, here's how the data control works: By setting properties of the data control, you hook the data control to a specific database and a table in it. (Code lets you query the database in order to create a dynaset or a snapshot.) You then add controls to a form that will display the data.

The data control itself displays no data. Think of the data control as only conducting the flow of information back and forth between your project and the database. You use ordinary Visual Basic controls to display the data.

Controls that can work with the data control to access data are said to be *data-aware,* and the process of tying a data-aware control to a data control is called *binding* the data-aware control. Among Visual Basic standard controls, the only intrinsically data-aware controls are text boxes, labels, check boxes, image controls, list boxes, combo boxes, OLE Client, and picture boxes. Among the custom controls, DBGrids, Masked edit, 3-D Panel, and 3-D check boxes are also data-aware. Data-aware controls must be on the same form as the data control, but they need not be visible in order to pick up the information. Once these controls pick up the information sent to them by the data control, the information will be stored as values of properties of the controls.

Seeing the Data Control at Work

If you look at the toolbox, the data control looks a little bit like a VCR control panel. When you work with a data control on a form, you need to stretch it out in order to see the caption and the buttons for moving through the database table. If you stretch out the data control, it looks like this:

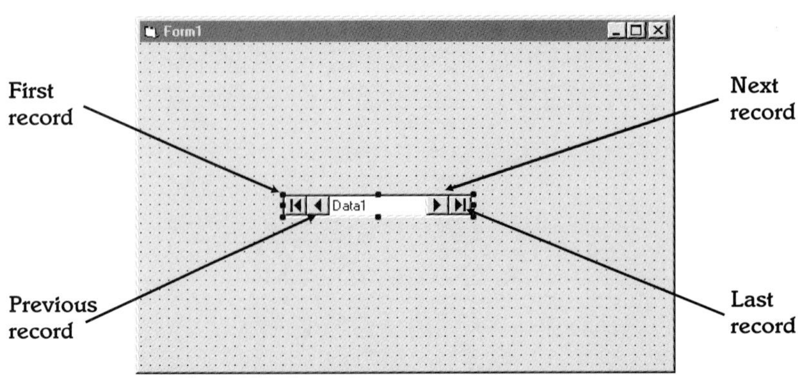

As noted in the illustration, the arrows that look like VCR buttons move to the beginning of the table, back one record, forward one record, and to the end of the table. Each time you press one of these arrow keys, the bound controls are automatically updated. You do not have to write any code for this to take place.

You can have many data controls in a single project, each of which can be connected to a different database or a different table in the same database (or with code to a query about a database and so to a dynaset or snapshot). The properties that control this are easiest to set at design time but can be set (or reset) at run time as well.

The DataBaseName property of the data control determines which database the data control will (try to) connect to. If you go to the Properties window and click the ellipses for the DataBaseName property of the data control, you are presented with a common dialog box to select the database. Notice that you can use the Type list box on the left to change the kind of extensions that are shown. The default is to show only .MDB extensions. For example, if you double-click on the BIBLIO.MDB file, you will attach this database to the data control.

Next, you need to set the RecordSource property to the specific table or query in the database. For example, using the BIBLIO.MDB database, you have the choices shown here:

(In general, if Visual Basic can find the database determined by the DataBaseName property, it will list the tables and queries in the database when you click the down arrow for the RecordSource property.)

note: *You can also set the RecordSource property to an SQL query and so get a view from your database. Please see the section on SQL later in this chapter for how to do this.*

Now you need to add the data-aware controls to the form and bind them to the data control. Choose the kind of control that best suits the information to be picked up. Use a Picture or Image control if it is a graphical image, or a check box if it is a Boolean. You could use a label if you don't want someone to be able to update it, or a text box if you do. (If you want to get tabular information, use the data bound grid control described shortly.)

The DataSource property must be set to the name of the data control for each data-aware control. (You will want to have added the data control before you set the DataSource property.) Only after you set the DataSource property to the name of the data control can the data-aware control display data from the database.

Next, you have to tell the newly data-aware control what column of the RecordSource to bind the information to. This is done by setting the DataField property of the data-aware control to the column name. If Visual Basic can access the database at design time, then clicking on the down arrow for the DataField property will give you a list of the columns in the RecordSource that are connected by the DataSource property.

For example, the following table summarizes the properties you would need to set up controls to accept all the data available in the Authors table in the BIBLIO.MDB database.

Control	Needed Properties	Settings
Data1	DataBaseName	C:\VB\BIBLIO.MDB
	RecordSource	Authors
Text1	DataSource	Data1
	DataField	Author
Text2	DataSource	Data1
	DataField	Au_ID

The nice thing is that once you have set this up, the user can do simple lookups merely by clicking the arrow keys on the data control. The data control automatically gets the needed information from the database and passes it on to the bound controls.

note: *Each click of one of the buttons changes the current record. (Think of the current record as being the row that Visual Basic is currently looking at.)*

caution: *If data is changed in a bound control and you click an arrow key in the data control to move to a new record, Visual Basic will update the database with this new information. (See the section on "Monitoring Changes to the Database" for more on how to work with this.)*

OTHER PROPERTIES COMMONLY SET AT DESIGN TIME

Four other properties of the data control that you will commonly set at design time (although you are just as likely to reset them as needed at run time) are Connect, Exclusive, ReadOnly, and RecordSet. Here are short descriptions of them.

Connect This property specifies the type of database. You do not need to set this property if you are working with a database in Microsoft Access format. The Connect value is usually the name of the data file type (the program)—for example, FoxPro 2.5.

Exclusive Set this True/False property to True and no one else will be able to gain access to the database until you relinquish it by closing the database. The default is False. (Set it to True and you eliminate the need to run SHARE.EXE.)

note: *It is possible to change the Exclusive property at run time, but you will have to close and reopen the database in order for it to take effect.*

ReadOnly This True/False property is set to True when you want to be able to look at the database but don't want to affect it in any way. One common way to use this property is to set it at design time to True and change it to False only in response to a password at run time. (See the Refresh method in the section, "Other Useful Methods and Events for the Data Control" for more on this property.)

RecordSet This property is used if you create a RecordSet via code or another data control. You need to make sure the DataField property of the bound data control matches the fields in the RecordSet.

AN EXAMPLE: USING THE DATA BOUND GRID TO VIEW THE BIBLIO.MDB DATABASE

One of the gaps in Visual Basic 3 was the lack of a data bound grid control. After all, nothing is more natural than wanting to fill the contents of a grid with the contents of a database table. Visual Basic 4 fills this gap by adding a version of Apex's data bound grid custom control. (You may need to choose Tools|Custom Controls if this custom control is not part of your toolbox already.) Here's what the data bound grid control looks like:

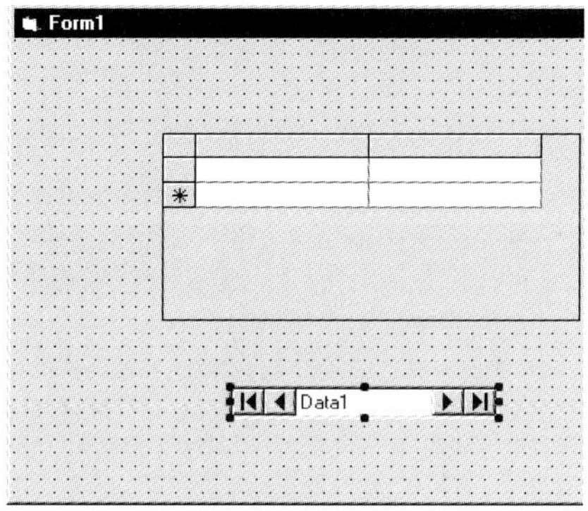

When you use the data bound grid, it starts out with only one row and column. However, once you set the DataSource property, the data bound grid automatically adjusts the number of columns and caption to reflect the number of columns and name of the table (RecordSet). For example, to see the information in BIBLIO.MDB via the data bound grid, do the following:

1. Add a data control and set its DataBaseName property to BIBLIO.MDB and the RecordSource property to Authors.
2. Add a data bound grid control and set its DataSource property to be the Data1 data control.
3. Position and enlarge the two controls so that your screen looks like Figure 20-5.
4. Now if you run the program, you will see the data in the BIBLIO.MDB Authors table fill the data bound grid without doing any programming whatsoever, as shown in Figure 20-6!

Figure 20-5
Form with data bound grid

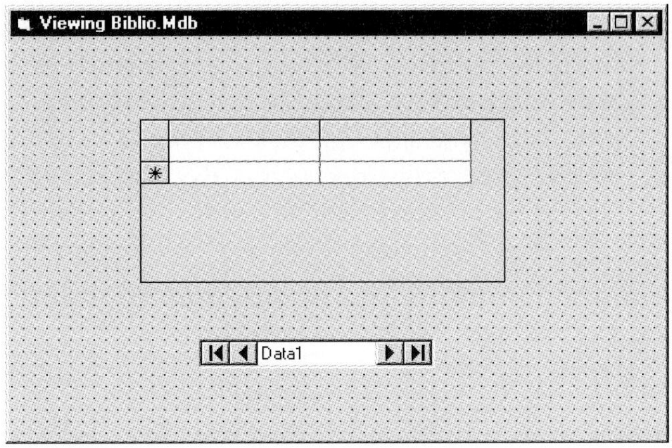

Figure 20-6
BIBLIO.MDB database viewed via data bound grid

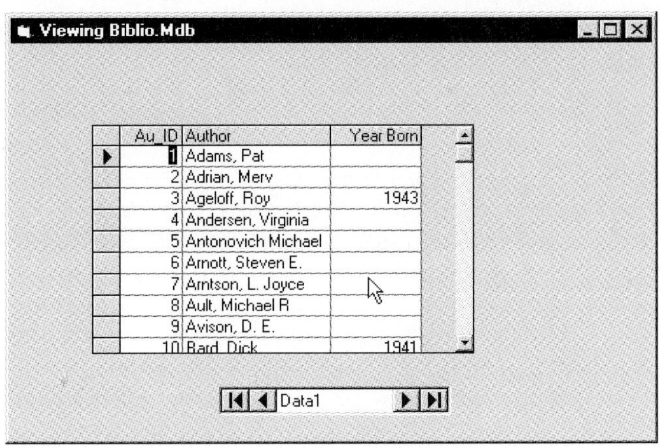

Programming with the Data Control

Although you can do many things with the data control without code, only code lets you take full advantage of its powers. However, for the data control in particular, there is no need to go overboard on setting properties at run time. This is because although the data control properties *can* be set at run time, it is easiest to set properties such as RecordSource, DataSource, and DataField at design time when dialog boxes will pop up with the needed information.

To give you an idea of what code for working with the data control will look like, suppose you want to check whether you can update the RecordSet. This is done with code that looks like this:

```
If Data1.RecordSet.Updatable Then
    'RecordSet will be updatable  by  the  user
Else
    'RecordSet is viewable only
End If
```

As you can see, code for working with a data control looks only slightly different from code for working with any Visual Basic object. The difference is that you are actually using a property of the RecordSet object associated with the data control rather than a property of the data control.

Similarly, to determine whether you are at the first or last record, you need to use the BOF (beginning of file) and EOF (end of file) properties of the RecordSet. The code might look like this:

```
If Data1.RecordSet.BOF
If Data1.RecordSet.EOF
```

note: *In most cases you will be working with properties of the RecordSet object associated with the data control rather than with properties of the data control itself.*

In particular, the standard edition of Visual Basic does not allow you to create the necessary database objects independently of the data control. The Professional and Enterprise editions of Visual Basic do allow database objects to be created independently. Think of the RecordSet object as pointing to the underlying table, dynaset, or snapshot that is created by the data control.

Every click on a button of the data control at run time has a corresponding method. The following table summarizes this correspondence for a data control named DATA1 using the current recordset. (All of these methods change the current record.)

Control Action	Data1.Method
Click the |◄	Data1.RecordSet.MoveFirst
Click the ◄	Data1.RecordSet.MovePrevious
Click the ►|	Data1.RecordSet.MoveLast
Click the ►	Data1.RecordSet.MoveNext

The Field Object

The most important object associated with the RecordSet object is the Field object. Think of this as giving you the name and properties of a single column in the grid. By reading or resetting the value of this object you can analyze or update information in the current record of the database. For example, the following line of code might be used to print the name of the author in the current record:

```
Print Data1.RecordSet.Fields("Author")
```

tip: *The default property of the RecordSet object is the Field property. This means you could also use the following line of code:*

```
Print Data1.RecordSet("Author")
```

The following table summarizes the most common properties of the Field object. (Check the online help for more information.) To understand this table, you might want to imagine you are at a specific row (the current record) in the database. Also, keep in mind that the Field object refers to a specific column.

Property	What It Tells You
Attributes	What characteristics the field has; for example, is it updatable?
Size	How large the field can be.
Type	What type of data is contained in the field.
Value	What is actually in the row and column.

You can analyze other properties of the data control, recordset, or Field object to analyze the database's structural properties. This lets you find out lots of information about the database or recordset. Please see the section entitled "Database Objects" in this chapter for more information.

Other Useful Methods and Events for the Data Control

This section discusses most other methods that you will need to go beyond what the data control can do on its own.

Refresh The Refresh method, when applied to a data control, opens a database. If you have changed either the DataBaseName, ReadOnly, Exclusive, or Connect properties, you must have Visual Basic process a line of code containing this method. The syntax looks like this:

DataControlName.Refresh

The Refresh method also resets the current record back to the first record (row) in the table or view.

AddNew The Access engine maintains a buffer (called the *copy buffer*) where it keeps pending data that it will be writing to the database. The AddNew method clears the copy buffer and moves the current record to the end. (Think of this as potentially adding a new row to the grid.)

Since the copy buffer is empty, you will be able to send new information to the table (and so to the database). The syntax is

DataControlName.RecordSet.AddNew

The AddNew method doesn't actually add the information to the database. This is the function of the Update method discussed next.

tip: *Always make the default that users must confirm that they want the data added (you can let them change this default, of course). Since the AddNew method lets you clear out the information in the copy buffer without actually copying it, use this method if the user doesn't confirm the update operation.*

Update This method actually sends the contents of the copy buffer to the table or dynaset. (You cannot use Update on a snapshot, of course.) The syntax is

DataControlName.RecordSet.Update

Suppose you have a table attached to the Data1 control and want to add a record. You have an Author and a Title field only in this table. The code to add this record might look like this:

```
Data1.RecordSet.AddNew
Data1.RecordSet.Fields("Author") = "Homer"
Data1.RecordSet.Fields("Title") = "Iliad"
Data1.RecordSet.Update
```

If the Update is unsuccessful, Visual Basic generates a trappable error.

note: *Any method that moves the current record will cause an automatic update. If the data control is available, then pressing any of the arrow buttons will do this.*

UpdateControls Suppose the current record sent data to the bound control and someone changed this data. Since the current record is still current, there ought to be a quick way to have Visual Basic, for instance, refresh the data without needing to actually move forward and backward. This is exactly what the UpdateControls method does.

tip: *Use the UpdateControls method to reset the contents of bound controls to their original values when the user clicks on a Cancel button. (**Always** provide some method of canceling a database transaction.)*

Edit Visual Basic always maintains a pointer into the current table or dynaset. The Edit method copies the current record into the copy buffer for editing. (Just moving to the record doesn't do this.) If the database or recordset is read-only or the current record is not updatable, then trying to use this method gives a trappable error.

Suppose you have a table attached to the Data1 control and want to edit the Author field in the current record. Suppose the procedure to allow changes to a specific field (via a custom dialog box, for example) is called ChangeField. Then code to use this method might look like this:

```
Data1.RecordSet.Edit
AuthorName = Data1.RecordSet.Fields("Author")
Call ChangeField(AuthorName)
Data1.RecordSet.Fields("Author") = AuthorName
Data1.RecordSet.Update
```

This code assumes the procedure displays the old name and then, since you are passing by reference (see Chapter 10), you can use the same variable to pass on the new information.

UpdateRecord If you want to quickly save the contents of the bound controls to the current record, use this method. It is exactly the same as using the Edit method, moving to a different record, and clearing the copy buffer with the Update method, except that this is a little more dangerous because UpdateRecord does not activate the Validate event (see the section of this chapter "Monitoring Changes to the Database").

Delete This method deletes the current record in the RecordSet. If the RecordSet is read-only, then Visual Basic returns a trappable error. This method deletes one record at a time. The syntax is

DataControlName.RecordSet.Delete

After you delete a record, you must move the record pointer away from the deleted record by a Move method (MoveNext, MoveFirst, and so on). For example, the following code will delete all the records in a table:

```
Data1.RecordSet.MoveFirst
Do While Not Data1.RecordSet.EOF
  Data1.RecordSet.Delete
  Data1.RecordSet.MoveNext
Loop
```

note: *The preceding code is probably overkill. You can use SQL statements to delete all records that satisfy specific criteria.*

Closing a Recordset or Database

If you need to close an open database object attached to a data control or close the specific recordset currently attached to the control, use the following syntax:

ObjectName.Close

The object named can be any open database, recordset, workspace, dynaset, snapshot, or Table object.

You must use the Update method (if there are changes to the database pending) before you use the Close method. This must be done on all open recordset objects before you close the database itself. If you are using the Professional or Enterprise edition and leave a procedure that created a recordset or database object, then, after the database is closed:

- All pending transactions are rolled back.
- Any pending changes to the database are lost.

In particular, any unsaved changes are lost.

AN EXAMPLE: CYCLING THROUGH A TABLE

You now have enough of the methods and properties of the data control to write many useful routines. A good example of tying together all the methods and properties that you have seen is a slide-show routine—a program that cycles through all the records in a table without user intervention. The Timer control makes it easy to do this—just set the Interval property to the space between slides that you desire. Every time the Timer wakes up, the program moves to the next record. The data control automatically updates the information to bound control.

The example here starts by binding a data control to three labels (you don't want the user updating things in a slide show). The form might look like Figure 20-7.

Let's suppose you have bound the labels to the data control and the data control to the right database. A click on the command button refreshes the database and then activates the Timer control. Here's the code for this:

Figure 20-7
Form for slide show

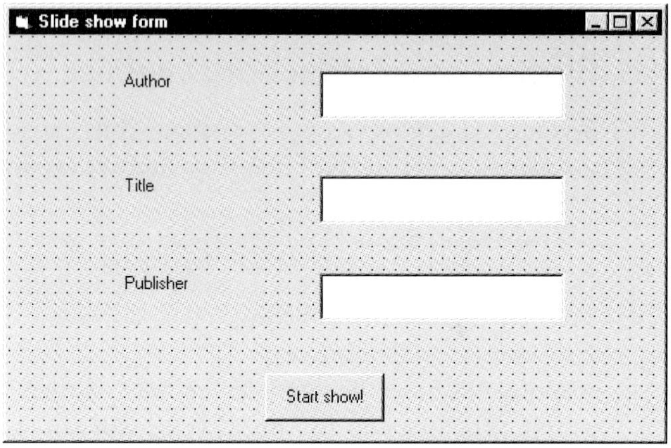


```
Private Sub btnStartShow_Click ()
  Data1.Recordset.Refresh
  Timer1.Enabled
End Sub
```

The code inside the Timer event is

```
Private Sub Timer1.Timer ()
  If Not Data1.RecordSet.EOF Then Data1.RecordSet.MoveNext
End Sub
```

tip: *If you use a database that contains graphical images, adding a bound picture box to a form and using the preceding code gives you an easy and efficient method of creating true automatic slide-show demonstrations.*

Setting Properties via Code

Setting the various startup properties of the data control is easier at design time, but this is not always possible. You may not know the name of the database, for example.

Here is an example of the code needed to connect to a FoxPro database at run time:

```
Data1.DataBase = "C:\FOXPRO\DATA\Business"
Data1.Exclusive = True
Data1.ReadOnly = False
Data1.Connect = "FoxPro 2.6"
```

One property you haven't seen yet that you will often need to set is the Options property. This is discussed next.

OPTIONS

This property is often set in the Form_Load and reset whenever you access a new table. Here is a short description of this important property.

Options is an integer parameter that controls what the user can do with the RecordSet. For example, you can deny other users the ability to write or read from the tables that are the sources of the data contained in the table you created. The reason for this parameter is that you must have the ability to control what is happening to the source of your information if, for example, you are going to change it. (Imagine the problems if everyone is changing the same data at the same time!)

The values for this parameter can be found in the Visual Basic Help file. There are nine possible options. You can combine the options by adding the relevant constants together. The following table summarizes what will happen if you set a specific option.

Data Constant	Effect
dbDenyWrite	Prohibits users from writing to the source tables.
dbDenyRead	Prohibits users from reading from the source tables.
dbReadOnly	Determines whether users can write to the dynaset created (and so to the tables in the database).
dbAppendOnly	Only allows additions to the recordset.
dbInconsistent	A change in one field can affect many rows.
dbConsistent	(Default) A change in one field can affect only one row.
dbSQLPassThrough	When using data controls with an SQL statement in the RecordSource property, sends the SQL statement to an ODBC database, such as an SQL Server or Oracle database, for processing.
dbForwardOnly	The RecordSet is a forward-only scrolling. The only move method allowed is MoveNext. This option cannot be used on RecordSet objects manipulated with the data control.
dbSeeChanges	Generates a trappable error if another user is changing data you are editing.

PUTTING BOOKMARKS IN A TABLE

Generally you should not think of a table as being made up of records in a fixed order, because the order can change depending on what index you are using. Nonetheless, there are times when you will want to tag a specific record for quick access at a later time. This is done using the BookMark property of the RecordSet. The idea is that when you are at the record you want to tag, have Visual Basic process code that looks like this:

```
Dim ABookMark As Variant
ABookMark = Data1.RecordSet.BookMark
```

Now, if you need to get to that record quickly, have Visual Basic process a line of code that looks like this:

```
Data1.RecordSet.BookMark = ABookMark
```

Once the preceding line of code is processed, the record specified by the bookmark immediately becomes the current record.

tip: *One common use for a bookmark is to monitor the record that was last modified. You can do this with a line of code that looks like this:*

```
Data1.RecordSet.BookMark = Data1.RecordSet.LastModified
```

Monitoring Changes to the Database

It is important to be sure that you really want to change the database before having Visual Basic go off and do it. Visual Basic gives you two ways of changing your mind. The first is the Validate event, which Visual Basic generates whenever the current record is going to change—for example, by a MoveFirst method or before it processes the Update, Delete, or Close method. The syntax for this event procedure is as follows:

Sub *DataControlName*_Validate ([Index As Integer,] *Action* As Integer, *Save* As Integer)

caution: *Do not put any method in the Validate event that changes the current record. The result would be an infinite event cascade.*

The only data-access methods you can put into this event are UpdateRecord and UpdateControls, because neither one generates the Validate event. This gives you a way of updating the database or bound controls in this event procedure.

As always, the optional Index parameter is used if the data control is part of a control array. The Action parameter is sent by Visual Basic to the event procedure and tells what actually caused the Validate event to be generated. Here is a list of the possible values using the symbolic constants built into Visual Basic:

Constant	Cause of Validate Event
vbDataActionCancel	Cancel the operation when the Sub exits.
vbDataActionMoveFirst	The MoveFirst method.
vbDataActionMovePrevious	The MovePrevious method.
vbDataActionMoveNext	The MoveNext method.
vbDataActionMoveLast	The MoveLast method.
vbDataActionAddNew	The AddNew method.
vbDataActionUpdate	The Update method.
vbDataActionDelete	The Delete method.
vbDataActionFind	The Find method.
vbDataActionBookMark	The Bookmark property was set.
vbDataActionClose	The Close method.
vbDataActionUnload	The form is about to be unloaded.

If you change the Action parameter to

vbDataActionCancel

then Visual Basic will cancel the operation after it leaves the Sub procedure. In addition, if you change the Action parameter to one of the other values, then Visual Basic will actually perform that operation instead of the original operation when the procedure is over. For example, if the Validate event procedure was caused by a MoveFirstMethod and in the course of the Sub procedure you have a line like,

```
Action =vbDataActionMoveLast
```

then Visual Basic will actually move the current record to the end of the table. You can only use this possibility if the actions are compatible. For example, you cannot change a MoveFirst action parameter to a vbDataActionUnload parameter without an error.

The Save parameter is either True or False. If any information in the bound data-aware controls has been changed, this parameter is True. This gives you a way of analyzing the information contained in the bound control before updating the database. To determine which data-aware controls were changed, use the DataChanged property of the control. This will be True if the contents of the control were changed and False otherwise.

tip: *To make it easier to determine which controls were changed, set up an array for the data-aware controls on the form in the Form_Load event. That way you can use a loop to run through all the data-aware controls, checking the DataChanged property of each.*

Transaction Control

Even if you allow a change to be made to a database, the changes made by Visual Basic need not be irrevocable. You have the ability to keep track of any changes you have made and cancel them if necessary, provided, of course, that the database is sophisticated enough to handle this—Microsoft Access databases certainly can. Consult the documentation of your database to see if it supports *transaction processing,* as this capability is usually called.

Technically, a *transaction* in database terminology is a sequence of alterations made to a table in the database. What you need to do is tell Visual Basic to store all the transactions it is making so that it can undo them. This is done using the BeginTrans statement discussed next.

BeginTrans This statement tells Visual Basic to start logging the changes for possible cancellation later on. Once Visual Basic processes this statement, it must process one of the two statements described next in order to continue working with the database.

note: *It is possible to nest transactions. This way you can undo small portions of the changes without undoing them all. You can have up to five transaction logs going at the same time.*

CommitTrans This statement tells Visual Basic to go ahead and make the changes. If you are nesting transactions, then this closes the innermost transaction log. However, no changes would be made to the actual database until Visual Basic closes all transaction logs.

RollBack This is the statement you need to undo all the changes made once transaction logging (by processing a BeginTrans statement) has started. If you are nesting transactions, this statement closes the innermost log.

Structured Query Language (SQL) Basics

There are many whole books on using SQL; this section can only give you a feel for it. The idea of SQL, though, is very simple. The language consists of English-like statements designed to select records from tables according to criteria that you give. As you'll soon see, SQL statements can be used at run time to set the RecordSource property of a data control. This lets you create dynasets and snapshots associated with a data control programmatically, using only the standard edition of Visual Basic. (A snapshot would be created if the ReadOnly property were also set to True.)

Most commonly, SQL criteria use the SQL keyword SELECT followed by one of these keywords: WHERE, SELECT, FROM, HAVING, GROUP BY, or ORDER BY. (By convention, SQL statements are written in all caps, although this is not necessary.) For example, suppose you wanted to work with a table named Publishers in a database named BOWKER.MDB. This table has four fields: Name, Address, State, and Phone Number.

If a data control (named Data1, for example) had its DataBase property set to BOWKER.MDB, then you could use the following statement (called an *SQL query*) to create a dynaset that consists only of the names contained in the Publishers table.

```
Data1.RecordSource = "SELECT [Name] FROM Publishers"
```

The FROM statement is required in every SQL SELECT statement. The FROM clause tells Visual Basic which table(s) or query(s) to examine to find the data.

caution: *After any query you must use the Refresh method to actually get the records you want from the database.*

More on SELECT Statements

The SELECT statement usually occurs first in an SQL statement. It is almost inevitably followed by the field names. You can have multiple field names by using a comma between them:

```
Data1.RecordSource = "SELECT [Name], [State] FROM Publishers
```

(Strictly speaking, the brackets around field names are only necessary if the field names have spaces in them. Most people use them all the time because it makes it easier to read the SQL statement.)

When you use a FROM clause to select data from more than one table or query simultaneously, you run the risk of having the same field name occur in two different places. In this case you use a variant on the dot notation that you've already seen for Visual Basic properties to specify which field. For example, if you had a database containing customer IDs (field name CuID) in both the Address table and the Orders table and wanted to extract this information from the Address table only, you would use

```
Data1.RecordSource = "SELECT [Addresses.CuID] FROM ...
```

Finally, you can use an asterisk (*) to say you want all fields from the table.

```
Data1.RecordSource = "SELECT * FROM Publishers"
```

Now suppose you wanted to create a dynaset with even more restrictions—for example, the list of publishers located in New York. This can be done by adding a Where clause to the previous SQL query. It would look like this:

```
Data1.RecordSource = "SELECT [Name] FROM Publishers Where _
State = 'NY'"
```

Notice the single quotes inside the SQL statement. This is how you identify a string inside an SQL statement (which is itself a string).

note: *SQL statements must occur on a single line or be a single string.*

The Where clause can use pattern matching using the Like operator:

```
Data1.RecordSource = "SELECT [Name] FROM Publishers Where _
State Like 'New*'"
```

This statement builds a grid consisting of all publishers' names from states beginning with the word "New" (New Hampshire, New Jersey, New Mexico, and New York).

Finding Records Using SQL

You can use the four Find methods combined with an SQL statement to examine the contents of a current recordset attached to a data control. These functions are FindFirst to find the first record, FindLast to find the last record, FindNext to find the next record, and FindPrevious to find the previous record. Here's an example of what this syntax looks like:

DataControlName.RecordSet.FindFirst SQL criterion

note: *The standard edition requires you to use this syntax. Only the Professional and Enterprise editions allow you to dimension objects as recordsets that exist independently of the data control.*

The SQL criterion for the Find method is what would follow the Where clause in an SQL SELECT statement. For example:

Data1.RecordSet.FindFirst "*State* = *'CA'*"

(Use the NoMatch property of the recordset object to determine whether a match was found.)

Modifying a Table's Data Through SQL

To this point you have only seen SQL statements that look through the tables in a database and extract information from them. It is also possible to write *action queries* that actually change data that matches the conditions given in an SQL statement. For example, suppose you have a store with a table named Items and fields named Current Price and Placed On Shelf. You want to reduce the current price of all items that have not sold since January 1, 1995 by 10 percent. This is the kind of situation for which action queries are ideal. Using an action query is much faster than examining each record to see if it matches the necessary condition. The SQL keywords you need to perform an action query like this are UPDATE and SET combined with the Execute method of the DataBase object. UPDATE tells the Access engine that changes should be made, and the SET keyword tells it which field should be changed and how. The Execute property actually carries out the change (although you could be running a transaction control to buffer this change for possible cancellation, of course).

Here's what the action query for this situation might look like:

```
ActionQuery$ = "UPDATE [Items] "
ActionQuery$ = ActionQuery$ + "SET [Current Price] = _
[Current Price]*.9
ActionQuery$ = ActionQuery$ + " WHERE [Placed On Shelf] < _
1995"
Data1.Database.Execute ActionQuery$
```

Similarly, you can change several fields at the same time by separating them with commas. There are many other SQL keywords you can use in an action query. Probably the most important besides UPDATE is DELETE, which allows the query to delete those records that satisfy certain criteria.

tip: *SQL comes with built-in functions for taking averages, finding maximums and minimums in a field, and a lot more. Consult the online help or a book on SQL for more about what you can do with action queries.*

Database Objects

When Visual Basic works with a database, it does so through the creation of special Visual Basic objects and collections associated with the database. You have already seen the RecordSet object. Analyzing properties of these objects and collections can give you much finer information about the database you are working with. For example, every Visual Basic collection has the Count property associated with it. You can use the Count property to find out how many tables there are in the database or how many fields there are in a table. You can then write a loop to analyze this information. What follows is a short discussion of the other important Visual Basic objects and collections.

note: *Visual Basic's Professional and Enterprise editions let you create your own objects for working with databases. You are no longer restricted to using only the ones that Visual Basic supplies. In particular, data access need no longer be tied to the data control. For example, in the Professional and Enterprise editions you can use a statement like*

```
Dim Foo As Database
Dim Bar As Dynaset
```

and then use the Set operator to tie these object variables to a database or SQL query:

```
Set Foo = OpenDatabase ("C:\VB\BIBLIO.MDB")
```

The DataBase Object You can analyze properties of this object to find out what you can do with the object. For example, to store the name of the database, you can use

```
NameDBase$ = Data1.Database.Name
```

Similarly, to find out if the database supports transaction control, you can use

```
TransacFlag% = Data1.Database.Transactions
```

Or to find out if the database is updatable (before trying to update a record), you can use

```
UpdateFlag% = Data1.DataBase.Updatable
```

There are a couple of other properties, such as CollatingOrder, which are less important—consult the online help for information on them.

The TableDef Object and TableDefs Collection Think of a TableDef object as giving the framework of the grid that stores the table. You can use the

DateCreated property of a Table object to find out when it was created and the LastUpdated property to find out when it was last changed.

The TableDefs collection, on the other hand, is a property of the Database object and collects all the TableDef objects in the database into a single group.

For example, to print the name of all the tables in the database and when they were last updated, use

```
For I = 0 To Data1.Database.TableDefs.Count - 1
  Print Data1.Database.TableDefs(I).Name
  Print Data1.Database.TableDefs(I).LastUpdated
Next I
```

The Field Object and the Fields Collection You have already seen the Field object associated with a RecordSet. Field objects are also associated with each TableDef object. (In practice there really isn't that much difference if all you are doing is checking the names of the fields. The main difference is that the Value property of a Field object is only available when a table is bound to a data control, thus creating a RecordSet.)

The Fields collection is the set of all Fields associated with a given TableDef. For example, you can nest the previous loop together with another loop to analyze the fields belonging to all the TableDefs in the database:

```
For I = 0 To Data1.Database.TableDefs.Count - 1
  Print Data1.Database.TableDefs(I).Name
  For J = 0 To Data1.Database.TableDefs(I).Fields.Count - 1
     Print Data1.Database.TableDefs(I).Fields(J).Name
     Print Data1.Database.TableDefs(I).Fields(J).Type
     Print Data1.Database.TableDefs(I).Fields(J).Size
     Print Data1.Database.TableDefs(I).Fields(J).Attributes
   Next J
Next I
```

The Index Object and the Indexes Collection A table may have many indexes or it may not be indexed at all. The Name property of the Index object tells you the name used by the database for this object. The Indexes collection is all the indexes for a specific table. Using loops similar to ones you have seen in the previous section, you can map out the Index collection as well.

Chapter Twenty-One

A Checkbook Management Program

THE purpose of this chapter is to take you through the design and implementation of a professional-quality checkbook management program. The program is supposed to be user-friendly. Therefore, it showcases many of the techniques and tools available in Visual Basic.

The length of the program notwithstanding, there are few, if any, techniques in this program that you haven't seen already (although I occasionally point out other ways to do the same task that may involve new ideas). This means that, although this program is far longer than any other program in this book, none of the pieces that make it up will be surprising or difficult. However, many people do find the jump from small, one-objective programs, to more sophisticated programs with multiple objectives, daunting. This chapter should make the transition easier.

Nothing in this book better demonstrates the power of Visual Basic than this chapter. That roughly one-third of the features you would want in a user-friendly checkbook program can be written by designing eight forms and using only 1,000 or so lines of code clearly shows the power of Visual Basic to improve the productivity of programmers. It is easy to imagine an entire finance program, along the lines of those that have generated tens of millions of dollars of sales, being written in only a few weeks using Visual Basic! (In fact, many parts of the best-selling Quicken program are written in Visual Basic.)

note: *If you don't want to enter all the code by hand, the optional companion disk includes it. The disk also includes additional versions of this program that add features or use different programming techniques. (See the end of the introduction to this book for the order form.)*

Finally, this chapter is organized somewhat differently from the other chapters. The design of the forms and the ideas behind some of the code are explained early on. Then individual sections list the entire code for each form together with a table for the controls on the form. The end of the chapter is a short section on how to convert the program to one using class modules if that is to your taste.

note: *To save space, the code in this chapter has most of the error-trapping code removed. You can easily put the error-trapping code back in—it's the same as the one that is attached to the startup (Finance) form (see the listing in the section "Code for the Finance Form" later in this chapter). Similarly, there is not enough space to list the values of the various properties for the controls; you can use the figures and common sense as your guides for setting these. (For example, it is assumed that you will set the Cancel property to True for a button named btnCancel and the Default property to True for a button named btnOK.)*

Designing the Program

Although there are many commercial home finance programs available, they have added so many bells and whistles that the original purpose of keeping track of your checks and reporting amounts spent by various categories has become obscured. The program in this chapter is designed to be a user-friendly checkbook program. It keeps track of deposits and expenditures and reports totals by categories. It would be easy enough to add a reconciliation feature to the program (the grid control is ideal for this). It is not included because this would have roughly doubled the length of the program.

Imagine for a moment that your boss came in and said: "I want you to write a friendly checkbook management program for me." Like many bosses (i.e., your favorite Dilbert cartoon), he or she has some vague idea for this in mind, but this is a far cry from having enough information for a programmer to proceed (although programmers often regard "ability to read boss's mind" as an unstated job requirement—again, see Dilbert). You start questioning him or her: "Do you want to handle multiple accounts? What kind of information should the program keep track of?" and so on.

After some give-and-take, you find out that the general design goals suggest the program should have the following features:

- Must run under both Windows 3.X and Windows 95.
- Ability to handle multiple accounts, with the account names the same as the ones used by the bank.
- Ability to categorize each check as well as specify tax-deductible status.

- Ability to categorize the source of each deposit.
- The account's statistics should be available to the user at all times when working with an account.

The report facility should be able to:

- Report on either checks or deposits.
- Specify the dates to be included.
- Include, exclude, or ignore tax status.
- Pick one specific category or all categories for totals.
- Send reports to the screen, printer—or both.

Now, as a programmer, you realize that some of these goals will be easier to achieve than others. (And quite often what your boss thinks of as hard may turn out to be easy and, unfortunately, vice versa.) For example, getting a program to run under both Windows 3.X and Windows 95 means either not using any Windows 95-specific controls or maintaining two versions of the forms. (Conditional compilation applies only to code and not to forms.)

Getting reports done is a standard programming task. The information will be stored in files and read back and processed as need be. On the other hand, some of these requirements may require some thought and therefore be harder to achieve than your boss thought. Similarly, the second requirement means that account names should not be restricted to the ordinary DOS file conventions of eight characters plus a three-character extension. However, because of the first requirement that it run under both Windows 3.X and Windows 95, this in turn means that you have to figure out some way to keep track of the account name other than the obvious step of making it the name of a file.

Since these two decisions will affect the whole program, you think about it first. You decide that plain vanilla Visual Basic suffices. (For example, you could use picture boxes with image controls instead of the Windows 95 toolbar control if you choose to have a toolbar.) As for the filename problem, after some thought, you decide to use a common programming trick to set up the accounts. Internally, the accounts are numbered ACCT1, ACCT2, and so on. You'll maintain a separate sequential file in the current directory (called, say, ACCOUNTS) that allows the program to translate these internal filenames (derived from the ID number strings "1", "2", and so on) to what the user sees. Associated to each account are three files, one for the account statistics, one for the checks, and one for the deposits. Internally, as far as the program is concerned, they are called ACCT1.DAT, ACCT1.CHK, and ACCT1.DEP. The value of the global variable AccountId$ is the digit string that identifies the account. For "ACCT1.DAT" this would be a "1". Finally, you can assume the boss means that the categories should be available to all accounts in the current directory, and you will store this information in files called INCATS for deposits and EXPCATS for checks.

tip: *Files like these that contain information useful only to a program are best left with the ReadOnly attribute set when the program ends. Another possibility is to hide the files when the program ends.*

The User Interface

At this point, the design process moves on to the user interface. All you were told was, "Make it friendly." After some thought you decide you need:

- A main menu-driven form
- A form to change the directory (a common dialog box doesn't quite fit)
- A form for choosing from existing accounts or creating a new account
- A form for working with new or existing accounts that lets you modify (or set up) account data
- A form to record checks (make this look like a check)
- A form to record deposits (make this look like a deposit form)
- A form to specify the kinds of reports
- A form to display the reports

Since you (like the author) hate toolbars and you weren't specifically told to include them, you decide to forgo the trouble of adding them.

note: *In this, as in most cases, toolbar items just correspond to menu items anyway. Adding them is simply a matter of calling the Click event of the menu control from the Click event of the image control.*

Then comes the question of how to give the user the information about the current state of the account. After many iterations, it seems that what best fits the Windows look and feel is to attach a status bar to the main form, the deposit form, and the check writing form. This status bar would be the same in all cases. As with any status bar, the easiest choice is to use a picture box with the Align property equal to 1. Labels attached to the picture box can display the necessary information.

The Startup Form and the Set Directory Form

The startup form is the form that users see when they start the program. The Name is set to frmFinance and caption properties for this form are set to Finance. It fills up roughly 80 percent of the screen at the start. It should be menu-driven and follow the Windows convention of having a File menu with an Exit option plus menus for the other operations. For simplicity the form is designed in the location you want it to appear, although users can move it. They aren't allowed to maximize this form, however. We added a Windows metafile as the value of the form's Picture property to jazz things up.

To ensure that the account statistics will always fit on the form, users are not allowed to shrink the form smaller than the minimum size needed to display the picture box used for this information. Figure 21-1 shows the initial screen and Figure 21-2 shows you the Menu Design window for this form.

The Form_Load procedure, as is very common, calls a procedure to position the form nicely. This general procedure that centers any form is sent the Me object variable, so the Center procedure knows which form to work on. Next comes the call to the procedure that initializes everything. Finally come the calls to the procedures that update the status bars (picture boxes) on the three forms where they appear.

The Initialize procedure is actually located in the GENERAL.BAS module and what it does is use a static integer variable (AlreadyLoadedOnce) to determine whether it has been called once already. The first time the Initialize procedure is called, it displays a copyright notice; subsequent times are flagged so no notice appears. The Initialize procedure first clears out the list and combo boxes for both expenses and income categories before reloading. The filenames for these categories are hard-wired by name into the program and so are not associated to the individual accounts but rather to individual directories. However, you can easily make the changes needed to attach categories to specific accounts rather than to all accounts stored in the directory if you choose

Figure 21-1
Startup form with menus

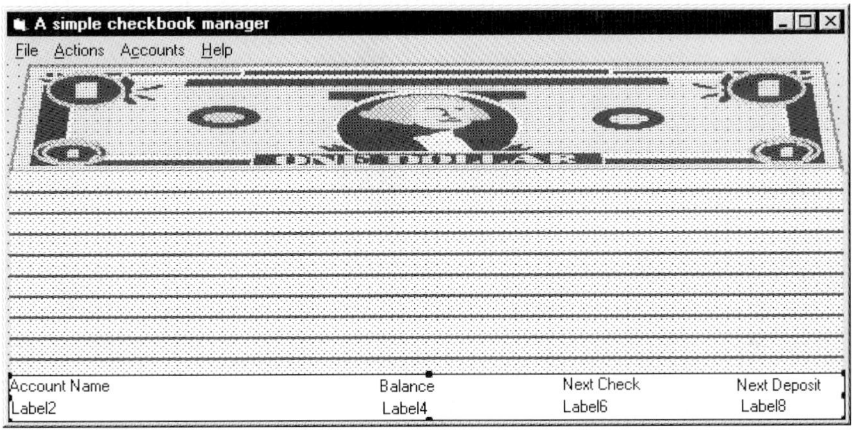

to do so. If no account exists, a new one is created with the default name of Account 1, with ID string "1". If accounts exist, then the account name and

Figure 21-2
Menu Design window for the startup form

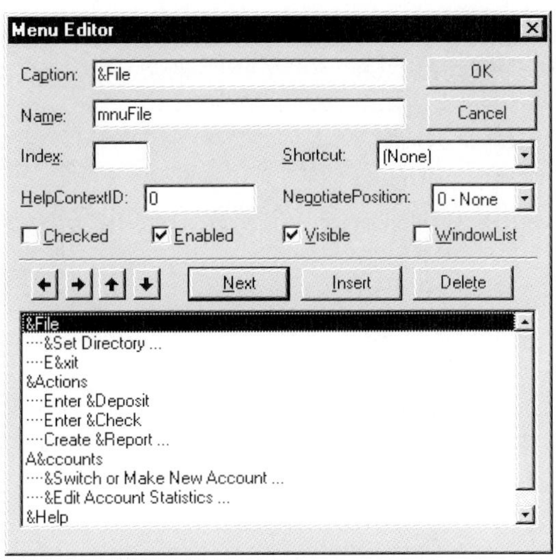

other necessary information is loaded into the combo box displayed on the EStats ("**E**dit **Stat**istic**s**") form. Finally, notice that this procedure (like any procedure handling files or other devices) has an error trap. The error trap sends the error number to a (global) function for processing.

Notice that the global variables in the general procedures begin with a lowercase "g." This is a quite common programming practice and makes it easier to identify these important (but nonetheless potentially bug-breeding) objects.

The code for all the Click procedures attached to each of the menu items is pretty straightforward. The Set Directory Click procedure shows the form to choose the directory. Notice in Figure 21-3 that three labels, a drive, a directory list box, and two command buttons have been placed on this form. This form will usually be invisible, but if the user decides to switch to another directory from the File menu—see Figures 21-1 and 21-2—you will make it appear again.

The Exit procedure ends the program after writing the data to the appropriate file. This is done using the value of the global variable gAccountId$ that internally tracks the account and attaches the .DAT suffix and ACCT prefix to give the filename. You also save the last account accessed so that will be the default account next time in a (tiny) sequential file called LASTACCT.

Figure 21-3

Form for setting a directory

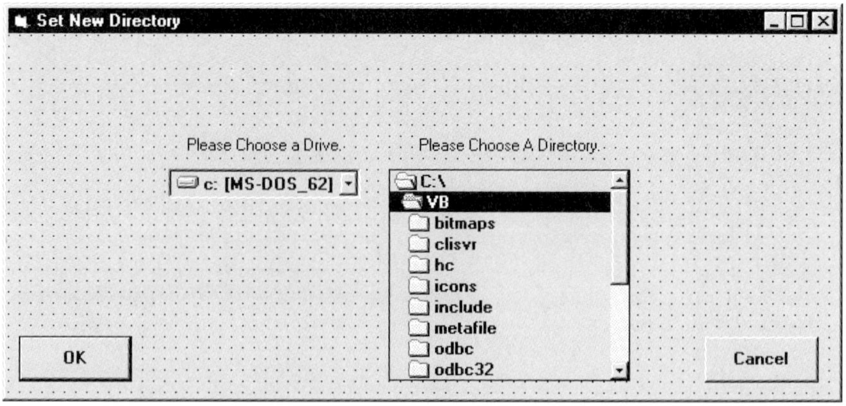

note: *Under Windows 95 this would likely be done by writing the information to the Registry using the DeleteSettings, GetSetting, GetAllSettings, and SaveSetting functions. See the section in the online help on "Additional Information on VBA Registry Functions."*

The directory will then change back to what it was before the program started. (This is a good programming practice—and in any case, it's not neighborly to leave the logged drive changed.) Each of the other menu items when clicked shows the appropriate form and initializes the various objects on the form. The btnCheck_Click procedure that a user activates if he or she wants to write a check resets the values of all the text boxes to be blank except that it adds the current check number (using the value of the global variable gNextChk) to the Number text box and uses a general procedure to update the picture box on the Checks form with the current account statistics.

The two most interesting procedures left in this form are the QueryUnload procedure and the Form_Resize procedure. The QueryUnload procedure is very important to give the Finance form the proper Windows behavior of shutting down in response to the ALT+F4 combination. You need to unload all the remaining forms in order to end the program properly. The Form_Resize procedure is there to ensure that the user cannot make the form too small to display the account statistics. The user can minimize the form but, as long as it is not iconized, the form must (by the design goals) be large enough to display the account information.

The Picture Box Used for Account Statistics Forms

You use what is essentially the same picture box on every form where it needs to show up. Using the same names for all the labels makes it easy to update the picture box by passing the name of the form to a general procedure. There are eight labels in this picture box. Four are used for identification and the other four will be used to show the data.

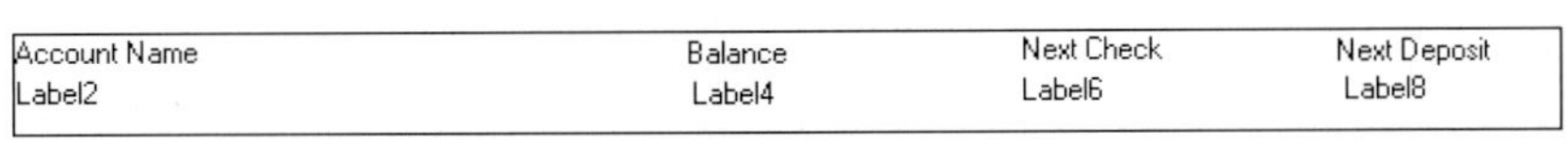

The general code that updates this picture box on every form is simple because the same control names were used on each picture box.

As with all forms in this project, the complete code attached to the form is given in a separate section without a break save for a table that gives the controls.

When you do examine the code notice the error-trapping routine in each procedure that works with files. (You need a different label in each routine because labels must be unique across a module.)

The Accounts Form

When you open the Accounts item on the main menu bar you are presented with two choices. If you choose the first item, Switch or Make New Accounts, then you'll see the form shown in Figure 21-4. As the figure shows, this form is a (modal) dialog box superimposed on the main screen. If the user now chooses the Create a New Account option, as shown in Figure 21-4, then, after some internal bookkeeping to create a new ID string for the account, the form shown in Figure 21-5 appears. This also happens if the user chooses Edit Account Statistics. For more on this form, please see the next section.

The list box shows all the currently assigned account names, with the first item used to create a new account. All user account names are trimmed to have length 50 (the value of the global constant gMaxAcctNameLen—this can easily be changed). The ID string is kept as the value of the ItemData property for the particular entry in the list box.

When the user clicks the OK button (or double-clicks an item), the Click procedure is called. This procedure first saves the current account information and closes the file that handles that account.

Figure 21-4 Form for working with an account

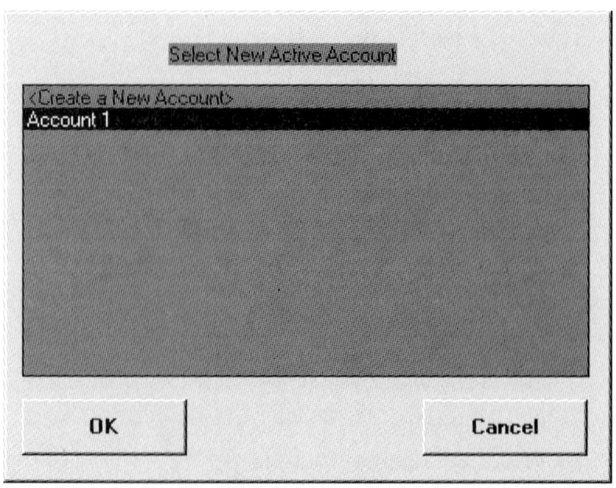

The procedure then checks the name via a call to the ChangeName procedure. This assigns the account name to its internal account ID string and, finally, updates the sequential file that contains the user's version of the account name as well.

note: *This program does not hide these files or change the read attribute. It is best to add any code that modifies file attributes after most of the testing and development of your project is finished.*

Since the Form_Load procedure for the startup (Finance) form clears the old information in the list box and then loads the account information stored in the current directory into the list box on this form, the whole procedure is completely transparent to the user. This Form_Load procedure also loads the data for the account that was last used. Or, if this is the first time the user has used the program in the current directory, it sets up an account with the default name of Account 1 and pops the user in the EStats form (see the next section). The user can, of course, click the Accounts main menu item and choose the Switch or Make New Accounts item to choose another account or add a new account.

There are two interesting procedures attached to this form. The GetNextId procedure is simple: it looks at the master account file (ACCOUNTS) and finds out how many accounts exist in order to create the next ID number string.

When the user clicks the OK button, the btnOK_Click procedure is activated. This procedure records the current account statistics using the internal ID string given by the variable AccountId$. Then it checks whether the user clicked on the New Account menu item. He or she is then asked to confirm the choice. If confirmed, this procedure generates a new ID string using the CreateAccountId Sub procedure. Otherwise, the program finds the account ID by looking at the value of the ItemData property of the current entry in the list box.

The EStats (Edit Statistics) Form

This form (shown in Figure 21-5) is accessed from the Accounts item on the main menu bar by choosing the Edit Account Statistics item. Also, if the user starts the program before any accounts exist or wants to create a new account, he or she will be sent to this form with a default name of Account 1 showing in the first text box. Whether working with a new or existing account, this form lets users enter a new balance, the next check number, or the next deposit number in the appropriate text boxes.

Figure 21-5
EStats form

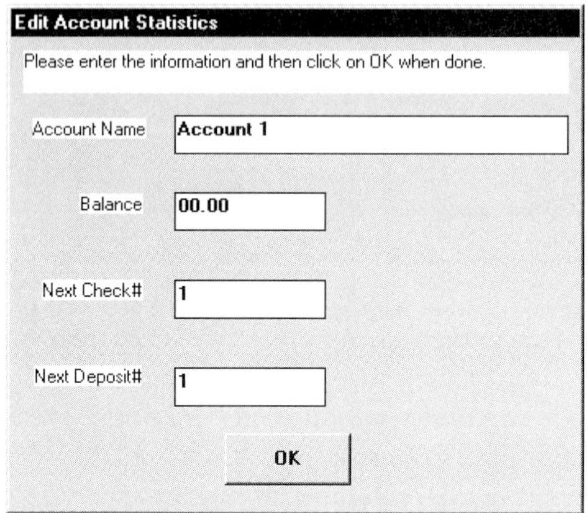

Once the user enters a name, changes the account statistics, and clicks the OK button, the btnOK_Click procedure checks whether the name is already in use. If it is, it pops the user back in the form after a message box pops up telling the user to choose a new name. On the other hand, if the name entered in the first text box hasn't changed or if it has, but the user hasn't tried to create a new account by choosing that option from the appropriate menu, then the program allows this by rewriting the ACCOUNTS file with the new information. Otherwise, the program uses the ID string created in the Accounts form and adds that account name and ID string to the list box and the Accounts file.

The Forms for Entering Checks and Deposits

Figures 21-6 and 21-7 show the forms for entering checks and entering deposits. As you can see in these figures, a frame is used to visually set off the deposit and check from the combo box listing categories or the command buttons that actually activate the event procedures. Both of these forms have a default Cancel button—so the user can press ESC to go back to the main screen (the Finance form). They also have the title bar elements removed. After all they are, in a way, custom dialog boxes.

Figure 21-6 Form for entering checks

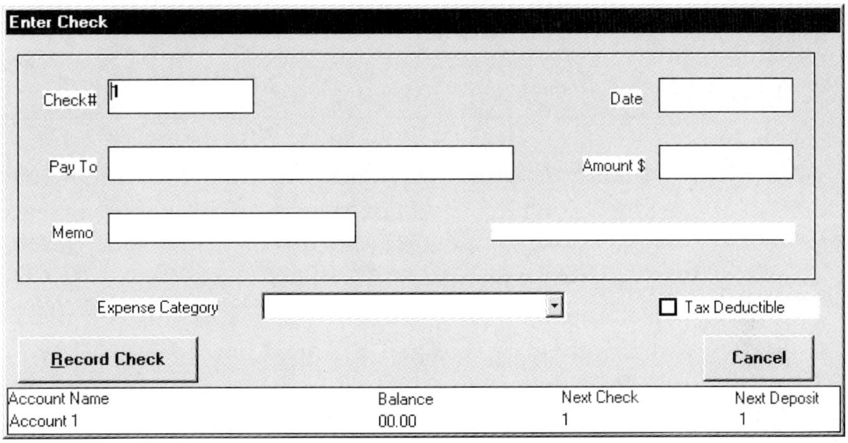

As an example of user friendliness that is easy to add using Visual Basic, you can have the current date show up if the user moves the focus away from the

Figure 21-7 Form for entering deposits

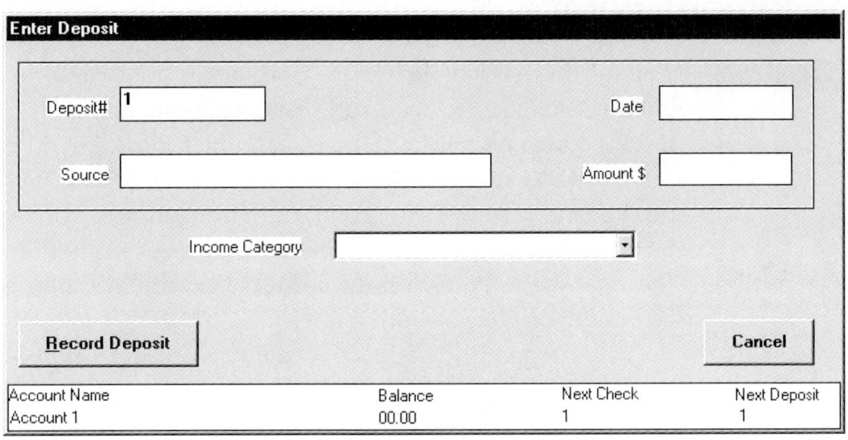

date box without entering a date. This requires only two lines of code in the LostFocus event procedure.

note: *The code for the date assumes that if nothing but blanks is entered, the user wants the current date.*

Both these forms use a similar Function procedure to validate the data entered before writing it to disk. For example, if the user hasn't entered a numeric string for the value, he or she is notified. The string is not restricted to only digits and commas—although you saw the techniques for this additional method of bulletproofing a program in Chapter 9. Just as you use a general function to validate the date, you use a general function to validate values. Whenever a check is written or a deposit is made, the sequential file (identified by the AccountName$ ID string) is immediately updated—but because of Windows buffering it is still possible that data may be lost if there is a system crash.

tip: *Remember the Reset command to flush file buffers in critical situations.*

note: *It would be easy to add a grid control to the deposit form to allow multiple deposits at one time.*

The Reports Form

Most of the hard work in this program is contained in the procedures and functions attached to the form that gives reports. The form (shown in Figure 21-8) is quite complicated. It has six framed areas. As you can see in this figure, some of these are for visual effects, but three are absolutely necessary because they contain independent groups of option buttons. For example, the frame on the top left corner asks users whether they want a report on checks or deposits. The one in the bottom right corner asks whether the report is to go to the screen, the printer, or both.

To understand how the procedures work, let's suppose the user specifies dates, picks a specific category, and wants to know what checks were written in that category during those dates. The user makes the appropriate choices of option buttons, chooses the category from the list box, and clicks the Generate Report command button.

Figure 21-8 Reports form

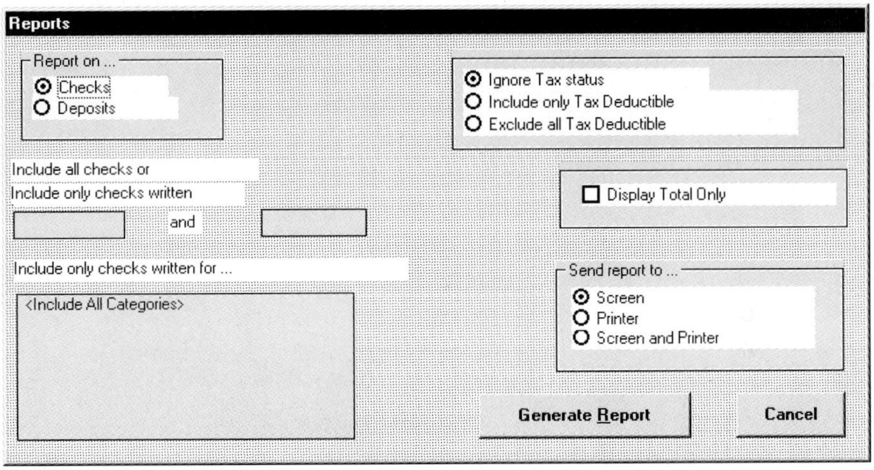

The GenReport_Click procedure first calls the ReportsOptionsOK function to check whether the user's request is acceptable. Because this function passes the key variable DoAll by reference, it can modify this to be True or False depending on whether the first (all categories) or a specific category (any of the others given in the list box) was selected. The function also checks the start and stop dates to see if they are valid. If no date is selected, the values are set to #1/1/100# and #1/1/2100#, respectively. This effectively gives all checks (well, actually those written before the year 2100).

So, suppose the user chooses a single category and specific dates. The key DoAll variable is set to False in the ReportsOptionsOK function. Next, notice that the Do Loop inside the Click procedure is tested at the bottom. This ensures that you always pass through it at least once. However, if the key DoAll variable is False, then you pass through it *only* once. Otherwise, the Do Loop continues until you run out of categories.

What happens inside this loop? You display the title of the report by calling a procedure for it. Next, you identify the category to be analyzed by the line. This procedure then calls a ReportOnOneCategory Sub procedure that analyzes the data contained in the sequential file for either the checks or deposits in the account using this category to identify the acceptable data.

Figure 21-9
Results form

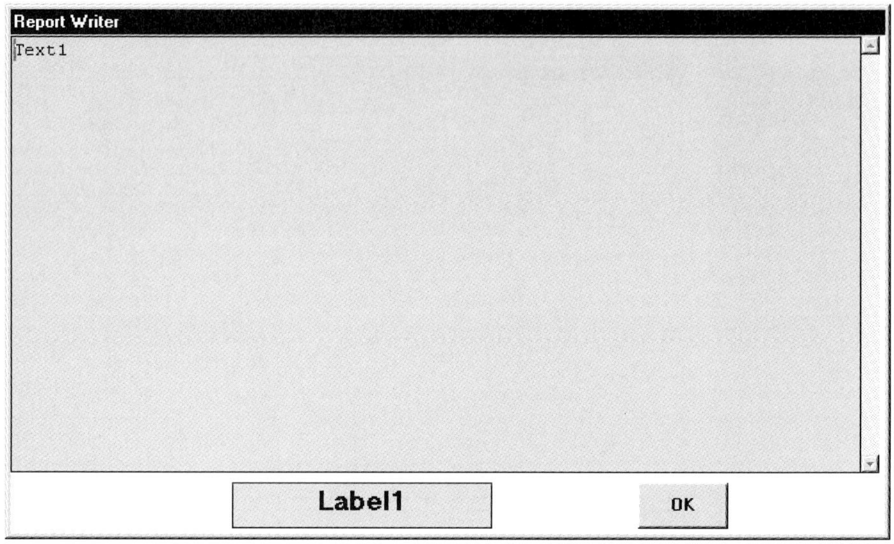

The Results Form

As Figure 21-9 shows, the Results form is a fairly simple project. It consists of a large multiline text box with vertical scroll bars. (I thought hard about using the grid, but decided I liked the look of text boxes better—they remind me of the first version of Quicken.) A label identifying the type of report and a command button to go back to the main form are also needed. To allow the user to use the arrow keys as well as the scroll bars to move through the text box, you use the KeyPress event procedure to filter out all the ordinary typewriter keys. To make it align better, I switched the font to Courier—a non-proportionally spaced font.

The General Code for the Program

The CONSTANT.BAS file contains the global variables and constants. Here it is:

```
'global variables and constants
Public gAccountName$, gAccountId$
Public gCurrentDrive$, gCurrentPath$
```

```
Public gOldDrive$, gOldPath$
Public gBalance As Currency
Public gNextChk As Integer, gNextDep As Integer
Public Const MaxAcctNameLen = 50
```

As you can see, this sets up nine global variables, each with the "g" prefix identifier. These are used to identify the original path and drive, the current path and drive, the account name, an ID number (actually a string of digits) used by the program to identify the account being worked with, the current balance, the number of the next check, and the number of the next deposit. Since this sort of information really needs to be available to the whole program, making them global variables in a code module is the obvious way to proceed. The MaxAcctNameLen constant restricts the names of the accounts to 50 characters.

The General Procedures Module

You have already seen the general procedures used to initialize the program, update the stats picture box, and center a form. You need a few other Sub procedures and Function procedures that are accessible to the entire program. As is common with big programs, one of the Function procedures is used for analyzing errors.

Since adding a category to the various combo and list boxes is such a common operation, it is a good idea to make a general Sub procedure out of this. Making all the combo boxes have the same control name (cboCategory) simplifies the code a little bit. You don't need to pass the name of the combo box—passing the form name is enough.

In the AddCat procedure given below, the loop runs through the items in the combo box on the form being worked with and checks whether the category is included. (By using the UCase$ function, case is ignored.) If the category doesn't exist, the user is given the option of adding the category by means of a message box. The program then appends the category to the sequential file named by the CatFile$ string variable and the item is added to the combo box as well. The code to load the list of categories uses the Clear method first to reset the box before actually loading the information.

The CreateAccount procedure that creates an account sets up a sequential file called ACCOUNTS in the current directory. (The user can change the current directory from the File menu on the startup form.) This file contains the user's name for the account (his or her name, the business name, and so on) and the ID number string that is passed to this procedure. This procedure also creates the basic data file, list of checks, and list of deposits (.DAT, .CHK, .DEP). This way the code that opens an account by reading in the needed information looks for the file named ACCOUNTS in the current directory in order to read back this information. The EditStats procedure resets the display in the Edit Statistics (EStats) form.

The function that checks whether a date or number is valid uses the IsDate and IsNumeric functions, which work with variants. These functions pass either True or False back to the calling procedure.

Finally, there's the error handler. This function analyzes the error number sent to it and gives the user some feedback. This is a pretty bare-bones version, and you could easily make it much more elaborate. (I would probably not change file attributes in an error handler. If the program ends abnormally, the designer should see the state it is in. One exception sometimes worth making is using the Reset command to flush buffers.)

THE COMPLETE GENPROC.BAS CODE

```
Option Explicit
Sub AddCat(NewItem$, frm As Form, CatFile$)
  'local variables:
  Dim I As Integer

  'check to see if category is already listed
  For I = 0 To frm.cboCategory.ListCount
    If Trim(UCase(frm.cboCategory.List(I))) = _
Trim(UCase(NewItem$)) Then
      Exit For
    End If
  Next I
  'if category not listed, confirm and add to list and file
  If I = frm.cboCategory.ListCount + 1 Then
    I = MsgBox("Add new category " + NewItem$ + _
  " to list?", vbOKCancel)
    If I = vbOK Then
      frm.cboCategory.AddItem NewItem$
      Open CatFile$ For Append As #1
      Write #1, NewItem$
      Close #1
    Else
      NewItem$ = ""
      frm.cboCategory.Text = ""
    End If
```

```
  End If
End Sub

Sub Center(frm As Form)
  frm.Move (Screen.Width - frm.Width) / 2, (Screen.Height - _
frm.Height) / 2
End Sub

Sub CreateAccount(Id$)
  'add account name and id to ACCOUNTS file
  Open "ACCOUNTS" For Append As #1
  gAccountName$ = "Account " + Id$
  gAccountId$ = Id$
  Write #1, gAccountName$, gAccountId$
  Close #1
  'create ACCT#.DAT, ACCT#.CHK, and ACCT#.DEP
  Open "ACCT" + gAccountId$ + ".DAT" For Output As #1
  gBalance = 0
  gNextChk = 1
  gNextDep = 1
  Write #1, gBalance, gNextChk, gNextDep
  Close #1
  Open "ACCT" + gAccountId$ + ".CHK" For Output As #1
  Close #1
  Open "ACCT" + gAccountId$ + ".DEP" For Output As #1
  Close #1
  'mark new account as the last account accessed
  Open "LASTACCT" For Output As 1
  Write #1, gAccountName$, gAccountId$
  Close #1
  'add account name (and id) to AccountNames list
  frmAccounts.lstAccountNames.AddItem gAccountName$ _
+ Space$(MaxAcctNameLen - Len(gAccountName$))
  frmAccounts.lstAccountNames.ItemData _
  (frmAccounts.lstAccountNames.NewIndex) = Val(gAccountId$)
  EditStats
End Sub

Sub EditStats()
  frmEStats.txtAcctName.Text = gAccountName$
  frmEStats.txtAcctBalance.Text = Format(gBalance, "00.00")
  frmEStats.txtAcctNextChk.Text = Format(gNextChk, "0")
  frmEStats.txtAcctNextDep.Text = Format(gNextDep, "0")
  frmEStats.Show 1
```

```
End Sub

Sub Initialize()
  Dim ErrorNumber As Integer, M$
  On Error GoTo Problems0
  Static AlreadyLoadedOnce As Integer
  If Not (AlreadyLoadedOnce) Then
    gOldDrive$ = Left(CurDir$, 2) 'get current drive
    gOldPath$ = CurDir$           'and path so can reset at end
    AlreadyLoadedOnce = True
    M$ = "This program is copyright 1995 by Gary Cornell."
    MsgBox M$
  End If

    Call OpenAccount
    Call LoadCatLists
    frmFinance.Show
    UpDateStats frmFinance
    UpDateStats frmChecks
    UpDateStats frmDeposits

    Exit Sub
Problems0:
   ErrorNumber = Err.Number
   If ProcessErrorOK(ErrorNumber) Then
     Resume
   Else
    M$ = "Please report error " & Err.Description
    MsgBox M$
    Unload frmFinance
   End If
End Sub

Sub LoadCatLists()
  'load list of expense categories
  'by looking for a file in the current directory
  'set from the initial form
  Dim ErrorNumber As Integer
  Dim catname$, M$
  frmChecks.cboCategory.Clear
  frmDeposits.cboCategory.Clear
  On Error GoTo Problems1
  If Dir$("EXPCATS") = "EXPCATS" Then
    Open "EXPCATS" For Input As #1
```

```
    Do While Not EOF(1)
      Input #1, catname$
      frmChecks.cboCategory.AddItem catname$
    Loop
    Close #1
  End If
  'load list of income categories
  If Dir$("INCCATS") = "INCCATS" Then
    Open "INCCATS" For Input As 1
    Do While Not EOF(1)
      Input #1, catname$
      frmDeposits.cboCategory.AddItem catname$
    Loop
    Close #1
  End If

Exit Sub
Problems1:

 ErrorNumber = Err.Number
    If ProcessErrorOK(ErrorNumber) Then
     Resume
   Else
    M$ = "Please report error " & Err.Description
    MsgBox M$
    Unload frmFinance
   End If
End Sub

Sub OpenAccount()
  Dim ErrorNumber As Integer, M$
  On Error GoTo Problems3
  If Not (Dir$("ACCOUNTS") = "ACCOUNTS") Then
    'setup initial account files the first time program is run
    Call CreateAccount("1")
  Else
    frmAccounts.lstAccountNames.Clear
    'load list of account names into Accounts combo box
    Open "ACCOUNTS" For Input As #1
    Do While Not EOF(1)
      Input #1, gAccountName$, gAccountId$

      frmAccounts.lstAccountNames.AddItem gAccountName$ + _
Space$(MaxAcctNameLen - Len(gAccountName$))
```

```
  frmAccounts.lstAccountNames.ItemData _
  (frmAccounts.lstAccountNames.NewIndex) = Val(gAccountId$)
    Loop
    Close #1
    'open last account accessed as the default account
    Open "LASTACCT" For Input As #1
    Input #1, gAccountName$, gAccountId$
    Close #1
    Open "ACCT" + gAccountId$ + ".DAT" For Input As #1
    Input #1, gBalance, gNextChk, gNextDep
    Close #1
  End If
  'add an entry for the user to select when a new account is
to be created
  frmAccounts.lstAccountNames.AddItem "<Create a New Account>"
  'make the first account created the default when switching
accounts the first time
  frmAccounts.lstAccountNames.ListIndex = 1
Exit Sub
Problems3:
 ErrorNumber = Err.Number
  If ProcessErrorOK(ErrorNumber) Then
     Resume
   Else
    M$ = "Please report error " & Err.Description
    MsgBox M$
    Unload frmFinance
   End If
End Sub

Function ProcessErrorOK(A As Integer) As Boolean
 Dim Msg$, MsgType As Integer, ErrorResponse As Integer
 Select Case A
  Case 57
   Msg$ = "I/O error."
   MsgType = vbRetryCancel  '5
  Case 61
    Msg$ = "Disk full"
    MsgType = vbRetryCancel
  Case 68   'Device unavailable
   Msg$ = "Can't use that device now - check drive."
   MsgType = vbRetryCancel
  Case 71
```

```
    Msg$ = "Disk Not ready."
    MsgType = vbRetryCancel
   Case 482
    Msg$ = "Printer error."
    MsgType = vbRetryCancel
  End Select

  ErrorResponse = MsgBox(Msg$, MsgType, "Errors")

  Select Case ErrorResponse
   Case vbOK, vbYes '1, 4
    ProcessErrorOK = True
   Case Else
    Msg$ = "Please report error number" + Str$(A) + " to your
  operator"
    Msg$ = Msg$ + vbCrLf + "am shutting down now."
    Close
    Unload Finance
   End Select
End Function

Sub UpDateStats(X As Form)
  X.lblAcctName.Caption = gAccountName$
  X.lblAcctBalance.Caption = Format(gBalance, "0,0.00")
  X.lblAcctNextChk.Caption = Format(gNextChk, "0")
  X.lblAcctNextDep.Caption = Format(gNextDep, "0")
End Sub

Function ValidDate(D$) As Boolean
  'local variables:
  Dim Hold As Variant
  Hold = D$
  ValidDate = IsDate(Hold)
End Function

Function ValidNumber(D$) As Boolean
  'local variables:
  Dim Hold As Variant
  Hold = D$
  ValidNumber = IsNumeric(Hold)
End Function
```

Code for the Finance Form

The following table gives the controls, followed by their names, followed by the caption or text property if appropriate. Controls inside frames follow the frame in this table, making it easier to match the controls with those in Figure 21-1.

Control Type	Name	Caption (or Text) Property Value
Form	frmFinance	Financial Data
PictureBox	Picture1	
Label	lblAcctNextDep	Label8
Label	Label1	Next Deposit
Label	lblAcctNextChk	Label6
Label	Label3	Next Check
Label	lblAcctBalance	Label4
Label	Label5	Balance
Label	lblAcctName	Label2
Label	Label7	Account Name
Menu	mnuFile	&File
Menu	mnuSetDir	&Set Directory ...
Menu	mnuExit	&Exit
Menu	mnuActions	&Actions
Menu	mnuDeposit	Enter &Deposit
Menu	mnuCheck	Enter &Check
Menu	mnuReport	Create &Report ...
Menu	mnuAccts	&Accounts
Menu	mnuSwitch	&Switch or Make New Account ...
Menu	mnuEditStats	&Edit Account Statistics ...
Menu	mnuHelp	&Help

Here's the complete code attached to this form:

```
Option Explicit
Private Sub mnuCheck_Click()
  frmChecks.txtNumber.Text = Format(gNextChk, "0")
  frmChecks.txtCrtDate.Text = ""
  frmChecks.txtPayto.Text = ""
  frmChecks.txtAmount.Text = ""
  frmChecks.txtMemo.Text = ""
  frmChecks.cboCategory.Text = ""
  frmChecks.chkTax.Value = False
  frmFinance.Hide
  UpDateStats frmChecks
```

```
  frmChecks.Show 1
  frmFinance.Show
End Sub

Private Sub mnuDeposit_Click()
  frmDeposits.txtNumber.Text = Format(gNextDep, "0")
  frmDeposits.txtCrtDate.Text = ""
  frmDeposits.txtSource.Text = ""
  frmDeposits.txtAmount.Text = ""
  frmDeposits.cboCategory.Text = ""
  frmFinance.Hide
  UpDateStats frmDeposits
  frmDeposits.Show 1
  frmFinance.Show
End Sub

Private Sub mnuEditStats_Click()
  frmFinance.Hide
  Call EditStats
End Sub

Private Sub mnuExit_Click()
  Dim ErrorNumber As Integer, M$
  On Error GoTo Problems5
  'record final stats on account
  Open "ACCT" + gAccountId$ + ".DAT" For Output As #1
  Write #1, gBalance, gNextChk, gNextDep
  Close #1
  'record last account accessed so it can be the default
account next time
  Open "LASTACCT" For Output As #1
  Write #1, gAccountName$, gAccountId$
  Close #1
  'clear screen and exit

  frmFinance.Hide
  Cls
  ChDrive gOldDrive$
  ChDir gOldPath$
  'here's a good place to change the attributes or hide the
files

  Unload Me
```

```
Problems5:
  ErrorNumber = Err.Number
 If ProcessErrorOK(ErrorNumber) Then
    Resume
 Else
  M$ = "Please report error # " + Err.Description
  MsgBox M$
  Unload Me
 End If
End Sub

Private Sub Form_Load()
  Center Me
  Initialize
  Call UpDateStats(Me)
  Call UpDateStats(frmChecks)
  Call UpDateStats(frmDeposits)
  SetFocus
End Sub

Private Sub Form_QueryUnload(Cancel As Integer, UnloadMode As _
Integer)
  Unload frmAccounts
  Unload frmChecks
  Unload frmDeposits
  Unload frmEStats
  Unload frmReports
  Unload frmResults
  Unload frmSetDir
  Unload Me
  ChDrive gOldDrive$
  ChDir gOldPath$
  End
End Sub

Private Sub Form_ReSize()
  If WindowState <> 1 And Width < 9000 Then
    Width = 9000  'large enough for stats to show
    Center Me
  End If
End Sub

Private Sub mnuHelp_Click()
```

```
 MsgBox ("Help feature not implimented yet.")
End Sub

Private Sub mnuReport_Click()
  frmReports.txtDate1.Text = ""
  frmReports.txtDate2.Text = ""
  'frmReports.lstCategory.ListIndex = -1
  frmFinance.Hide
  frmReports.Show 1
 End Sub

Private Sub mnuSetDir_Click()
  gCurrentDrive$ = Left(CurDir$, 1)
  gCurrentPath$ = CurDir$

  frmFinance.Hide
  frmSetDir.Show
End Sub

Private Sub mnuSwitch_Click()
  'of course where you position and size things is up to you
  frmFinance.Hide
  frmAccounts.Show 1
  frmFinance.Show
End Sub
```

Code for the SetDir Form

As before, the table gives the controls, followed by their names, followed by the caption or text property if appropriate. This makes it easier to match Figure 21-3.

Control Type	Name	Caption (or Text) Property Value
Form	frmSetDir	Set New Directory
CommandButton	btnOk	OK
CommandButton	btnCancel	Cancel
DirListBox	Dir1	
DriveListBox	Drive1	
Label	lblDirection	
Label	Label2	Please Choose A Directory
Label	Label1	Please Choose a Drive

Here's the complete code attached to this form:

```
Option Explicit
Private Sub btnCancel_Click()
  frmSetDir.Hide
  frmFinance.Show
  Drive1.Drive = gCurrentDrive$
  Dir1.Path = gCurrentPath$
End Sub

Private Sub Drive1_Change()
  Dim ErrorNumber As Integer, M$
  On Error GoTo Problems4
  Dir1.Path = Drive1.Drive
  Exit Sub

Problems4:
  ErrorNumber = Err.Number
  If ProcessErrorbtnOK(ErrorNumber) Then
    Resume
  Else
   M$ = "Please report error " & Errpr.Description
   MsgBox M$
   Unload frmFinance
  End If
End Sub

Private Sub Form_Load()
  Dim C$
  Center Me
  C$ = "To change where the program looks for files, change "
  C$ = C$ + "the drive if necessary and then highlight the "
  C$ = C$ + "directory. (Double click on a directory to move "
  C$ = C$ + "to its subdirectories.) When you have "
  C$ = C$ + "highlighted the correct (sub)directory, "
  C$ = C$ + "click on OK for the changes to go into effect. "
  C$ = C$ + "You can always click on Cancel (or press Esc) "
  C$ = C$ + "to use the current path with no changes."
  lblDirection.Caption = C$
End Sub

Private Sub btnOK_Click()
  'This changes the logged drive and directory
  'and hides all the controls used to work with directories
```

```
and drives
  Dim ErrorNumber As Integer
  On Error GoTo Problems2
  ChDrive Drive1.Drive
  ChDir Dir1.Path
  frmSetDir.Hide
  frmFinance.Show
  Initialize
  Exit Sub

Problems2:
  ErrorNumber = Err
  If ProcessErrorOK(ErrorNumber) Then
    Resume
  Else
    MsgBox Err.Description & "closing program"
    Unload frmFinance
  End If
End Sub
```

Code for the Accounts Form

As before, the table gives the controls, followed by their names, followed by the caption or text property if appropriate. This makes it easier to match Figure 21-4.

Control Type	Name	Caption (or Text) Property Value
Form	frmAccounts	
ListBox	lstAccountNames	
CommandButton	btnOk	OK
CommandButton	btnCancel	Cancel
Label	Label1	Select New Active Account

Here's the complete code attached to this form:

```
Option Explicit

Private Sub lstAccountNames_DblClick()
   btnOK_Click
End Sub

Private Sub btnCancel_Click()
```

```
  frmAccounts.Hide
End Sub

Private Sub Form_Load()
  Center Me
End Sub

Private Sub GetNextId(Id$)
  'This routine opens the list of accounts to find out the
  'next valid id number - valid accounts are numbered
  'consecutively and stored in a file called 'ACCOUNTS'

  'local variables
  Dim NextId As Integer, N$

  NextId = 1
  Open "ACCOUNTS" For Input As #1
  Do While Not EOF(1)
    Input #1, N$, Id$
    If Val(Id$) >= NextId Then NextId = Val(Id$) + 1
  Loop
  Close #1
  Id$ = Format(NextId, "#")
End Sub

Private Sub btnOK_Click()
  'This routine opens up a file with the account info
  'the file ideas are of the form ACCT1.DAT ACCT2.DAT etc
  'the global variable gAccountId$ provides the "1" "2" etc

  'local variables:
  Dim Id$, Index As Integer

  'record stats on current account
  Open "ACCT" + gAccountId$ + ".DAT" For Output As #1
  Write #1, gBalance, gNextChk, gNextDep
  Close #1

  'These lines of code check for the < that is the
  'first few characters on the <Create New Account> item in
  'the list box. This shows the user wants to
  'define a new account. Of course, if someone enters
  ' an account name with these leading characters the program
bombs
```

```
  'you can easily add the code to check for this

  Index = lstAccountNames.ListIndex
  If Left(lstAccountNames.List(Index), 7) = "<Create" Then
    'user has asked to create a new account
    If MsgBox("Please confirm: Create a New Account", _
vbYesNo) <> vbYes Then
      Exit Sub
    End If
    frmAccounts.Hide
    Call GetNextId(Id$)
    Call CreateAccount(Id$)
  Else
    'switch to new account
    frmAccounts.Hide
    gAccountName$ = Trim(Left(lstAccountNames.List(Index), _
MaxAcctNameLen))
    gAccountId$ = Trim(Str$(lstAccountNames.ItemData(Index)))
    Open "ACCT" + gAccountId$ + ".DAT" For Input As #1
    Input #1, gBalance, gNextChk, gNextDep
    Close #1
  End If
  Call UpDateStats(frmFinance)
  Call UpDateStats(frmChecks)
  Call UpDateStats(frmDeposits)
End Sub
```

Code for the EStats Form

Here's the table that gives the controls, followed by their names, followed by the caption or text property if appropriate. This makes it easier to match Figure 21-5.

Control Type	Name	Caption (or Text) Property Value
Form	frmEStats	Edit Account Statistics
TextBox	txtAcctName	
TextBox	txtAcctBalance	
TextBox	txtAcctNextChk	
CommandButton	btnOK	
TextBox	txtAcctNextDep	
Label	Label5	Please enter the information and then click on OK when done

Control Type	Name	Caption (or Text) Property Value
Label	Label2	Balance
Label	Label3	Next Check#
Label	Label4	Next Deposit#
Label	Label1	Account Name

Here's the complete code attached to this form:

```
Option Explicit
Private Sub btnCancel_Click()
  txtAcctName.SetFocus
  frmEStats.Hide
End Sub

Private Sub ChangeName(NewName$)
  'local variables:
  Dim N$, Id$, I As Integer

  Open "ACCOUNTS" For Input As #1
  Open "_t_e_m_p" For Output As #2
  Do While Not EOF(1)
    Input #1, N$, Id$
    If Id$ = gAccountId$ Then N$ = NewName$
    Write #2, N$, Id$
  Loop
  Close #1, #2
  Kill "ACCOUNTS"
  Name "_t_e_m_p" As "ACCOUNTS"
  For I = 0 To frmAccounts.lstAccountNames.ListCount - 1
    If frmAccounts.lstAccountNames.ItemData(I) = _
Val(gAccountId$) Then
      frmAccounts.lstAccountNames.List(I) = NewName$ + _
Space$(MaxAcctNameLen - Len(NewName$))
      frmAccounts.lstAccountNames.ItemData(I) = _
Val(gAccountId$)
      Exit For
    End If
  Next I
End Sub

Private Sub Form_Load()
  Center Me
End Sub
```

```
Private Function NotGoodName(A$) As Boolean
  Dim I As Integer
    For I = 0 To frmAccounts.lstAccountNames.ListCount - 1
      If Trim(frmAccounts.lstAccountNames.List(I)) = A$ Then
        MsgBox ("Name already in use. Choose another name.")
        NotGoodName = True
        Exit Function
      End If
    Next I
  NotGoodName = False
End Function

Private Sub btnOK_Click()
  'local variables:
  Dim NewName$, D$
  NewName$ = Trim(Left(txtAcctName.Text, MaxAcctNameLen))
  If NewName$ <> gAccountName$ Then
    'adjust the account name in the ACCOUNTS file & _
AccountNames list
    If NotGoodName(NewName$) Then Exit Sub
    Call ChangeName(NewName$)
    gAccountName$ = NewName$
  End If
  D$ = txtAcctBalance.Text
  If Not ValidNumber(D$) Then
    MsgBox ("Please enter a valid balance")
    txtAcctBalance.Text = ""
    txtAcctBalance.SetFocus
    Exit Sub
  Else
   gBalance = Val(txtAcctBalance.Text)
  End If
  gNextChk = Val(txtAcctNextChk.Text)
  gNextDep = Val(txtAcctNextDep.Text)
  Call UpDateStats(frmFinance)
  Call UpDateStats(frmDeposits)
  Call UpDateStats(frmChecks)
  frmEStats.Hide
  frmFinance.Show
End Sub
```

Code for the Checks Form

Here's the table that gives the controls, followed by their names, followed by the caption or text property if appropriate. (Notice that the picture box containing the account statistics is identical to the one on the Finance form.) The Checks form is shown in Figure 21-6.

Control Type	Name	Caption (or Text) Property Value
Form	frmChecks	Enter Check
PictureBox	Picture1	
Label	lblAcctNextDep	Label8
Label	lblTitle4	Next Deposit
Label	lblAcctNextChk	Label6
Label	lblTitle3	Next Check
Label	lblAcctBalance	Label4
Label	lblTitle2	Balance
Label	lblAcctName	Label2
Label	lblTitle1	Account Name
CheckBox	chkTax	Tax Deductible
ComboBox	cboCategory	Category
Frame	Frame1	
TextBox	txtNumber	
TextBox	txtCrtDate	
TextBox	txtPayTo	
TextBox	txtAmount	
TextBox	txtMemo	
Label	Label1	Check#
Label	Label2	Date
Label	Label3	Pay To
Label	Label4	Amount $
Label	Label5	Memo __________________
CommandButton	btnRecord	Record Check
CommandButton	btnCancel	Cancel
Label	Label7	Expense Category

Here's the complete code attached to this form:

```
Option Explicit
Private Sub btnCancel_Click()
  txtNumber.SetFocus
  frmChecks.Hide
End Sub
```

```
Private Function CheckDataOk(ExpCat$) As Boolean
  'local variables:
  Dim D$

  'verify that all needed check information has been given
  'some people would prefer not to use the Exit
  'function in this code.
  'you can do that by carrying the flag through
  CheckDataOk = False
  If Val(txtNumber.Text) = 0 Then
    MsgBox "Check Number must be indicated"
    txtNumber.SetFocus
    txtNumber.Text = ""
    Exit Function
  End If
  D$ = txtCrtDate.Text
  'Use ValidDate is a function that use the IsDate to check
  If Not ValidDate(D$) Then
    MsgBox "A valid date must be given"
    txtCrtDate.SetFocus
    txtCrtDate.Text = ""
    Exit Function
  End If
  If Len(txtPayto.Text) = 0 Then
    MsgBox "A Payee must be indicated"
    txtPayto.SetFocus
    Exit Function
  End If
  D$ = txtAmount.Text
  If Val(D$) = 0 Or Not ValidNumber(D$) Then
    MsgBox "An amount must be indicated"
    txtAmount.Text = ""
    txtAmount.SetFocus
    Exit Function
  End If
  If Len(ExpCat$) = 0 Then
    MsgBox "An expense category must be chosen"
    cboCategory.SetFocus
    Exit Function
  End If
  CheckDataOk = True
End Function
```

```
Private Sub CrtDate_LostFocus()
  'this shows how easy it is to add a user friendly feature
in VB
  'if the user tabs away from the date box we place the
current date there
  D$ = Trim(txtCrtDate.Text)
  If Len(D$) = 0 Then
    txtCrtDate.Text = Format(Date, "MM-DD-YY")
  End If
End Sub

Private Sub Form_Load()
  Center Me
  Call UpDateStats(Me)
End Sub

Private Sub btnRecord_Click()
  'This routine records the info in a file
  'because of buffering the program should be
  'ended from the file menu and not by ctrl+break - else the
data may not be writtten
  'local variables:
  Dim ExpCat$, CNumber As Integer, CAmount As Currency

  'if a new expense category is given, add it to the list
  ExpCat$ = Trim(cboCategory.Text)
  If Len(ExpCat$) <> 0 Then
    'routine to check for new catagory
    Call AddCat(ExpCat$, frmChecks, "EXPCATS")
  Else
    ExpCat$ = cboCategory.List(cboCategory.ListIndex)
  End If
  If CheckDataOk(ExpCat$) Then
    'record new check and update account statistics
    Open "ACCT" + gAccountId$ + ".CHK" For Append As #1
    CNumber = Val(txtNumber.Text)
    CAmount = Val(txtAmount.Text)
    Write #1, CNumber, CVDate(txtCrtDate.Text), _
txtPayto.Text, CAmount, _
  txtMemo.Text, ExpCat$, chkTax.Value
    Close #1
    gBalance = gBalance - CAmount
    gNextChk = gNextChk + 1
    Call UpDateStats(Me)
```

```
      Call UpDateStats(frmFinance)
      Call UpDateStats(frmChecks)
      frmChecks.txtNumber.SetFocus
      frmChecks.Hide
    End If
  End Sub
```

Code for the Deposits Form

Here's the table; use it to make it easier to match Figure 21-7.

Control Type	Name	Caption (or Text) Property Value
Form	frmDeposits	Enter Deposit
PictureBox	Picture1	
Label	lblAcctNextDep	Label8
Label	lblTitle4	Next Deposit
Label	lblAcctNextChk	Label6
Label	lblTitle3	Next Check
Label	lblAcctBalance	Label4
Label	lblTitle2	Balance
Label	lblAcctName	Label2
Label	lblTitle1	Account Name
ComboBox	cboCategory	
Frame	Frame1	
TextBox	txtNumber	
TextBox	txtCrtDate	
TextBox	txtSource	
TextBox	txtAmount	
Label	Label1	Deposit#
Label	Label2	Date
Label	Label3	Source
Label	Label4	Amount $
CommandButton	btnRecord	&Record Deposit
CommandButton	btnCancel	Cancel
Label	Label7	Income Category

Here's the complete code attached to this form:

```
Option Explicit
Private Sub btnCancel_Click()
  txtNumber.SetFocus
```

```
  frmDeposits.Hide
End Sub

Private Sub txtCrtDate_LostFocus()
  Dim D$
  D$ = Trim(txtCrtDate.Text)
  If Len(D$) = 0 Then
    txtCrtDate.Text = Format(Date, "MM-DD-YY")
  End If
End Sub

Private Function DepositDataOk(IncCat$) As Boolean
  'local variables:
  Dim D$

  'verify that all needed information has been given
  DepositDataOk = False
  D$ = txtNumber.Text
  If Val(D$) = 0 Or Not ValidNumber(D$) Then
    MsgBox "Deposit Number must be indicated"
    txtNumber.SetFocus
    txtNumber.Text = ""
    Exit Function
  End If
  If Len(txtSource.Text) = 0 Then
    MsgBox "A Source must be indicated"
    txtSource.SetFocus
    Exit Function
  End If
  If Len(IncCat$) = 0 Then
    MsgBox "An income category must be chosen"
    cboCategory.SetFocus
    Exit Function
  End If
  D$ = txtAmount.Text
  If Val(D$) = 0 Or Not ValidNumber(D$) Then
    MsgBox "An amount must be indicated"
    txtAmount.Text = ""
    txtAmount.SetFocus
    Exit Function
  End If
  D$ = txtCrtDate.Text
  If Not ValidDate(D$) Then
    MsgBox "A valid date must be given"
```

```
    txtCrtDate.SetFocus
    txtCrtDate.Text = ""
    Exit Function
  Else
    txtCrtDate.Text = Format(D$, "MM-DD-YY")
  End If

  DepositDataOk = True
End Function

Private Sub Form_Load()
  Center Me
  Call UpDateStats(Me)
End Sub

Private Sub btnRecord_Click()
  'local variables:
  Dim IncCat$, DNumber As Integer, DAmount As Currency

  'if a new income category is given, add it to the list
  IncCat$ = Trim(cboCategory.Text)
  If Len(IncCat$) <> 0 Then
    Call AddCat(IncCat$, frmDeposits, "INCCATS")
  Else
    IncCat$ = cboCategory.List(cboCategory.ListIndex)
  End If
  If DepositDataOk(IncCat$) Then
    'record new deposit and update account statistics
    Open "ACCT" + gAccountId$ + ".DEP" For Append As #1
    DNumber = Val(txtNumber.Text)
    DAmount = Val(txtAmount.Text)
    Write #1, DNumber, CVDate(txtCrtDate.Text), _
txtSource.Text, DAmount, IncCat$
    Close #1
    gBalance = gBalance + DAmount
    gNextDep = gNextDep + 1
    Call UpDateStats(Me)
    Call UpDateStats(frmFinance)
    Call UpDateStats(frmChecks)
    frmDeposits.txtNumber.SetFocus
    frmDeposits.Hide
  End If
End Sub
```

Code for the Reports Form

In this table, controls attached to frames follow the frame. This makes it easier to match Figure 21-8.

Control Type	Name	Caption (or Text) Property Value
Form	Reports	Reports
ListBox	lstCategory	
Frame	Frame3	Send report to ...
OptionButton	btnOnScreen	Screen
OptionButton	btnOnPrinter	Printer
OptionButton	btnOnBoth	Screen and Printer
TextBox	txtDate1	
TextBox	txtDate2	
Frame	Frame1	Report on ...
OptionButton	btnCheckReport	Checks
OptionButton	btnDepositReport	Deposits
CommandButton	btnGenReport	Generate &Report
Frame	Frame2	
CheckBox	chkTotalOnly	Display Total Only
CommandButton	btnCancel	Cancel
Frame	Frame4	
OptionButton	btnIgnoreTax	Ignore Tax status
OptionButton	btnTaxOnly	Include only Tax Deductible
OptionButton	btnNonTaxOnly	Exclude all Tax Deductible
Label	labCat	Include only checks written for ...
Label	lblDate	only checks written between ...
Label	Label6	and
Label	lblRepTotal	
Label	Label7	Include all checks or

Here's the complete code attached to this form:

```
Option Explicit
Private Sub btnCancel_Click()
  frmReports.optCheckReport.Value = True
  frmReports.Hide
  frmFinance.Show
End Sub

Private Sub optCheckReport_Click()
  'local variables:
```

```
  Dim I As Integer
  frmReports.lstCategory.Clear
  frmReports.lstCategory.AddItem " <Include All Categories>"
  For I = 0 To frmChecks.cboCategory.ListCount - 1
    frmReports.lstCategory.AddItem _
frmChecks.cboCategory.List(I)
  Next I
  lblAll.Caption = "Include all checks or"
  lblCat.Caption = "Include only checks written for ..."
  lblDate.Caption = "Include only checks written between"
  optIgnoreTax.Enabled = True
  optTaxOnly.Enabled = True
  optNonTaxOnly.Enabled = True
End Sub

Private Sub optDepositReport_Click()
  'local variables:
  Dim I As Integer

  frmReports.lstCategory.Clear
  frmReports.lstCategory.AddItem " <Include All Categories>"
  For I = 0 To frmDeposits.cboCategory.ListCount - 1
    frmReports.lstCategory.AddItem _
frmDeposits.cboCategory.List(I)
  Next I
  lblAll.Caption = "Include all deposits or"
  lblCat.Caption = "Include only deposits written for ..."
  lblDate.Caption = "Include only deposits written between"
  optIgnoreTax.Enabled = False
  optTaxOnly.Enabled = False
  optNonTaxOnly.Enabled = False
End Sub

Private Sub Form_ReSize()
  Center Me
  optCheckReport.Value = True
  Call optCheckReport_Click
End Sub

Private Sub btnGenReport_Click()
  'local variables:
  Dim Total As Currency, SubTotal As Currency
  Dim DoAll As Boolean, Index As Integer
  Dim StartDate As Date, StopDate As Date
```

```
  Dim TaxVal As Integer, SearchCat As String

  frmReports.lblRepTotal.Visible = False
  If ReportOptionsOk(DoAll, Index, StartDate, StopDate, _
 TaxVal) Then
    Call TitleReport(StartDate, StopDate)
    Total = 0
    Do
      SearchCat = Trim(frmReports.lstCategory.List(Index))
      SubTotal = 0
      Call ReportOnOneCategory(SearchCat, SubTotal, _
 StartDate, StopDate, TaxVal)
      Call ReportSubTotal(SearchCat, SubTotal)
      Index = Index + 1
      Total = Total + SubTotal
    Loop Until (Not DoAll) Or (Index > _
 frmReports.lstCategory.ListCount - 1)
    frmReports.optCheckReport.SetFocus
    Call ReportTotal(Total)
  End If
End Sub

Private Sub ReportOnOneCategory(SearchCat As String, SubTotal _
As Currency, StartDate As Date, StopDate As Date, TaxVal As _
Integer)
  'local variables:
  Dim Amount As Currency, Memo$, ItemCat$, Tax As Integer
  Dim UCat$, Who$, Number As Integer, ItemDate
  Dim N$, D$, W$, A$  'spacing characters
  'allocate space for items appearing in each line of report
  N$ = Space$(10)
  D$ = Space$(15)
  W$ = Space$(20)
  A$ = Space$(15)
  UCat$ = UCase(Trim(SearchCat)) 'make upper case and trim
  'open appropriate database
  If optCheckReport.Value Then
    Open "ACCT" + gAccountId$ + ".CHK" For Input As #1
  Else
    Open "ACCT" + gAccountId$ + ".DEP" For Input As #1
  End If
  Do While Not EOF(1)
    If optCheckReport.Value Then
      Input #1, Number, ItemDate, Who$, Amount, Memo$, _
```

```
    ItemCat$, Tax
    Else
      Input #1, Number, ItemDate, Who$, Amount, ItemCat$
    End If
    'only process items which meet search criteria
    If (UCase(Trim(ItemCat$)) = UCat$) And (ItemDate >= _
StartDate) _
  And (ItemDate <= StopDate) And (TaxVal = 99 Or TaxVal = _
Tax) Then
      SubTotal = SubTotal + Amount
      If chkTotalOnly.Value = False Then
        RSet N$ = Str$(Number)
        RSet D$ = ItemDate
        RSet W$ = Who$
        RSet A$ = Format(Amount, "0,0.00")
        If optOnScreen.Value Or optOnBoth.Value Then
          frmResults.txtInfo.Text = frmResults.txtInfo.Text + _
vbCrLf + N$ + Space$(3) + D$ + Space$(3) + A$ + Space$(3) + W$
        End If
        If optOnPrinter.Value Or optOnBoth.Value Then
          Printer.Font.Name = "Courier"
          Printer.Print N$ + Space$(3) + D$ + Space$(3) + A$ _
 + Space$(3) + W$
        End If
      End If
    End If
  Loop
  Close #1
End Sub

Private Function ReportOptionsOk(DoAll As Boolean, Index As _
Integer, StartDate As Date, StopDate As Date, TaxVal As _
Integer) As Integer
  'local variables:
  Dim D$

  ReportOptionsOk = False
  If frmReports.lstCategory.ListIndex = 0 Then
    DoAll = True
    Index = 1
  ElseIf frmReports.lstCategory.ListIndex > 0 Then
    DoAll = False
    Index = frmReports.lstCategory.ListIndex
  Else
```

```
    MsgBox "Category must be selected"
    Exit Function
  End If
  D$ = frmReports.txtDate1.Text
  If Len(Trim(D$)) = 0 Then
    StartDate = #1/1/100#
  ElseIf ValidDate(D$) Then
    StartDate = CVDate(D$)
  Else
    MsgBox "Starting date is not a valid date"
    Exit Function
  End If
  D$ = frmReports.txtDate2.Text
  If Len(Trim(D$)) = 0 Then
    StopDate = #1/1/2100#
  ElseIf ValidDate(D$) Then
    StopDate = CVDate(D$)
  Else
    MsgBox "Ending date is not a valid date"
    Exit Function
  End If
  If optCheckReport.Value Then
    If optIgnoreTax.Value Then
      TaxVal = 99
    ElseIf optTaxOnly.Value Then
      TaxVal = 1
    ElseIf optNonTaxOnly.Value Then
      TaxVal = 0
    End If
  Else
    TaxVal = 99
  End If
  ReportOptionsOk = True
End Function

Private Sub ReportSubTotal(SearchCat As String, SubTotal As _
Currency)
  If optOnPrinter.Value Or optOnBoth.Value Then
    Printer.Font.Name = "Courier"
    Printer.Print
    Printer.Print "Subtotal for " + SearchCat + ": " + _
Format(SubTotal, "$0,0.00")
    Printer.Print
    Printer.Print
```

```
  End If
  If optOnScreen.Value Or optOnBoth.Value Then
    frmResults.txtInfo.Text = frmResults.txtInfo.Text + vbCrLf
    frmResults.txtInfo.Text = frmResults.txtInfo.Text + vbCrLf
    + "Subtotal for " + SearchCat + ": " + Format _
    (SubTotal, "$0,0.00")
    frmResults.txtInfo.Text = frmResults.txtInfo.Text + vbCrLf
    frmResults.txtInfo.Text = frmResults.txtInfo.Text + vbCrLf
  End If
End Sub

Private Sub ReportTotal(Total As Currency)
  If optOnPrinter.Value Or optOnBoth.Value Then
    Printer.Font.Name = "Courier"
    Printer.Print
    Printer.Print "Total: " + Format(Total, "$0,0.00")
    Printer.NewPage   'form feed
  End If
  If optOnScreen.Value Or optOnBoth.Value Then
    frmResults.lblRepTotal.Caption = "Total: " + _
Format(Total, "$0,0.00")
  End If
  frmFinance.Hide
  frmReports.Hide
  If optOnPrinter Then
    ' Printing only should probably do an error trap
  Else
    frmResults.Show 1
  End If
End Sub

Private Sub TitleReport(StartDate As Date, StopDate As Date)
  Dim ReportTitle As String, Header As String
  Dim SDate, EDate

  SDate = Format(StartDate, "MM-DD-YY")
  EDate = Format(StopDate, "MM-DD-YY")
    Header = Space$(4) + "Number" + Space$(14) + _
   "Date" + Space$(12) + "Amount"
    If optCheckReport.Value Then
       ReportTitle = "Report on checks "
       Header = Header + Space$(16) + "Paid to" + _
     vbCrLf + String$(75, "=")
    Else
```

```
        ReportTitle = "Report on deposits "
        Header = Header + Space$(14) + "Received from" + _
vbCrLf + _
String$(75, "=")
    End If
    If chkTotalOnly.Value Then
      Header = ""
    End If
   If StartDate <> #1/1/100# And StopDate = #1/1/2100# Then
    ReportTitle = ReportTitle + "written on or after " & _
StartDate
  ElseIf StartDate = #1/1/100# And StopDate <> #1/1/2100# Then
    ReportTitle = ReportTitle & "written on or before " & _
StopDate
  ElseIf StartDate <> #1/1/100# And StopDate <> #1/1/2100# _
Then
    ReportTitle = ReportTitle & "written between " & _
StartDate & " and " & StopDate
  End If
  If optOnPrinter.Value Or optOnBoth.Value Then
    Printer.Font.Name = "Courier"
    Printer.Print ReportTitle
    Printer.Print
    Printer.Print Header
  End If
  If optOnScreen.Value Or optOnBoth.Value Then
    frmResults.Caption = ReportTitle
    frmResults.txtInfo.Text = Header + vbCrLf
  End If
End Sub
```

Code for the Results Form

Finally, here's the table, followed by the code, for the last form (Figure 21-9).

Control Type	Name	Caption (or Text) Property Value
Form	frmResults	Report Writer
CommandButton	btnOK	OK
TextBox	txtInfo	Text1
Label	lblRepTotal	Label1

```
Option Explicit
Private Sub Form_Resize()
 Center Me
 If Height < 4 * btnOK.Height Then Height = 4 * btnOK.Height
 If Width < 3 * lblRepTotal.Width Then Width = 3 * _
lblRepTotal.Width
 txtInfo.Width = ScaleWidth
 txtInfo.Height = ScaleHeight - (1.5 * btnOK.Height)
 btnOK.Move 2 * ScaleWidth / 3, txtInfo.Height + 0.25 * _
btnOK.Height
 lblRepTotal.Move ScaleWidth / 4, txtInfo.Height + 0.25 * _
btnOK.Height
End Sub

Private Sub txtInfo_KeyPress(KeyAscii As Integer)
  KeyAscii = 0
End Sub

Private Sub btnOK_Click()
  frmResults.Hide
  frmFinance.Show
End Sub
```

How to "Objectify" This Program

The version of the checkbook program presented here will run under most versions of Visual Basic—it is coded to be as plain vanilla as possible. If you want to rewrite this program using class modules, it is a little tedious but conceptually not very hard. It will, however, be somewhat longer (about 25 percent) in terms of lines of code.

Essentially, all you have to do is set up a class module for the account information. Each new account will be a new instance of the class. Then, each piece of data needed by the various forms will become a read/write or read-only property of the class module. For example, the class module will expose a read/write Balance property that you use to find the current balance of the current account. Similarly, each account will need methods that let you write the information, such as account balance and current check number to a disk and methods for reading the information back again.

note: *The optional companion disk has a version of the checkbook program that uses class modules. See the order form in the front of the book.*

Appendix A

Distributing Your Application:

The Setup Wizard

This appendix covers the basics of how to distribute a Visual Basic executable—in most cases, the Setup Wizard makes this a snap. (In special situations you'll need to go in and work with the setup kit directly; see Chapter 30 of the *Programmer's Guide* for the situations not covered here.) However, before covering the Setup Wizard, you'll need to know a bit more about what a Visual Basic .EXE file needs to run. (The short answer is a lot.)

What a Visual Basic Executable Needs to Run

First off, you need the appropriate VBRUN DLL:

VB40016.DLL for 16-bit Visual Basic 4 applications (around 1MB)

VB40032.DLL for 32-bit Visual Basic 4 applications (around 700K)

Then you need the custom control file for each custom control in your applications. These files are relatively small—most often much less than 100K each. The problems come (as you will see) when you start adding OLE controls or OLE objects and database controls. The OLE support files are big—it is easy to imagine the files needed to install a Visual Basic executable on a system requiring two disks, or even more. (This is especially true for 16-bit Visual Basic 4 applications that use OLE, since the OLE DLLs are not part of the operating system.)

When someone runs an executable file that contains a custom control, the .OCX file (or .VBX file for 16-bit applications) for the custom control must be in the system's path or in the same directory as the .EXE file. The Setup Wizard automatically puts the files in the appropriate place. (If the appropriate .OCX or .VBX file can't be found, the Visual Basic run-time DLL generates the error message "File Not Found" and dies.)

note: *Microsoft recommends that your installation procedure copy all required .OCX files into the user's Microsoft Windows \SYSTEM subdirectory. The program the Setup Wizard creates does this automatically.*

Whether you install a third-party OLE custom control or use the Professional or Enterprise edition, OLE custom controls are automatically registered in the system registry. The License section of the system registry determines which controls you can use at design time.

caution: *It is a violation of the copyright laws and your license agreement to copy and distribute any information from the License section of your system registry.*

note: *The VB.LIC file used in previous versions of Visual Basic is not used for OLE custom controls. (You still need to have it if you are using any of the older VBX controls in a 16-bit application.)*

The Setup Wizard

There are two Setup Wizards available (assuming you have used the default names for the directories in your Visual Basic installation):

- C\VB\SETUPKIT\KITFIL32\SETUPWIZ.EXE for 32-bit Visual Basic applications
- C\VB\SETUPKIT\KITFILES\SETUPWIZ.EXE for 16-bit Visual Basic applications

Both Setup Wizards are stand-alone Windows applications written in Visual Basic. The earlier versions of the Setup Wizard had trouble running while Visual Basic was running. Under Windows 95, I haven't had any trouble running them simultaneously (memory seems to be the biggest bottleneck). (The Setup Wizard may start up a copy of Visual Basic in order to build the executable in any case.) However, you must *not* be working on the project that you want to build the setup disks for. Finish it, save all the files it uses, and either close Visual Basic or start up a new project before using the Setup Wizard.

The Visual Basic installation process adds the Setup Wizards as program items in the various Visual Basic program groups. (They are available, for example, off the submenus of the Start menu.)

note: *This appendix uses screens from the 32-bit Setup Wizard—those for the 16-bit Wizard are essentially the same.*

When you start the Setup Wizard, you are taken to the initial setup screen, which looks likes Figure A-1.

Let's go over the items in the main screen. First, there is a Help button that takes you to the (short) online help file and an Exit button to close the wizard. The Next button that takes you forward and the Back button that takes you to the previous step are currently disabled, as is the Finish button. Here are descriptions of the other items.

Project File The project file is the name of the .VBP file. You can click on the Browse button to the left of the text box to open a standard dialog box that lets you search for the .MAK file.

Figure A-1
Initial screen for the Setup Wizard

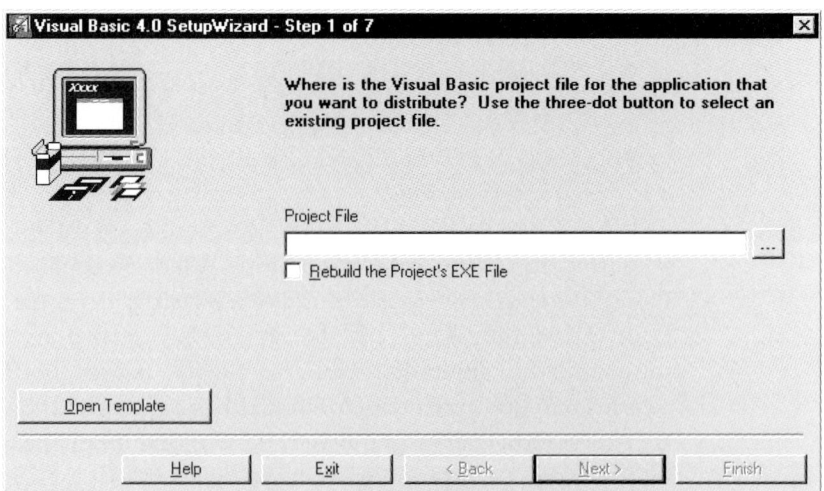

Rebuild the Project's EXE File Files you distribute are stand-alone executable. If you need to re-create a stand-alone product, set this check box to be on. The wizard will automatically rebuild the .EXE file if it doesn't find one.

Open Template This is used to create a template for future uses of the wizard. If you habitually use certain files in your applications, you can include them by clicking on this button and working with the dialog box that appears. This button is available at all times, so you can add frequently used options at any time.

Using the Wizard

For illustration purposes, let's suppose you want to distribute three different applications—the sample checkbook program from Chapter 21, one of the sample data access applications, and the OLE automation sample. (Data access and OLE applications require the most care and cause the largest pain in using the Setup Wizard.)

Let's start with the plain vanilla checkbook project. Once you enter the name and location of the finance .VBP file and click on the Next button (which is now enabled), after a short delay while the files are processed, you are taken to the Step 3 screen of the wizard shown in Figure A-2. (Screen 2 of the Setup Wizard is reserved for data access objects—see the section "Database Setup Problems" at the end of this appendix.)

This screen is where you tell the wizard where you want the files stored and on what type of disk. In Figure A-2, I am storing the files in the A: drive on a 1.4MB floppy. Click on the Next button and you are taken to Figure A-3. This screen is where you would add any necessary OLE server information (see "OLE Automation Setup Problems" later in this appendix).

Since the plain vanilla checkbook program doesn't use any OLE information, click on the Next button, which takes you to Figure A-4. (The Step 5 screen is only for projects containing OLE objects; again, see the section later in this appendix for more on OLE setup.) This screen lets you choose how the application will be used. In this case the checkbook program is supposed to be a stand-alone application—as indicated in Figure A-4.

If you now click on the Next button, you are taken to the final screen shown in Figure A-5. This screen tries to indicate what files you need for your executable. Generally speaking, it is not a good idea to remove any of these file dependencies unless you are absolutely sure that you don't need the file (or that

Figure A-2 Third screen in the Setup Wizard

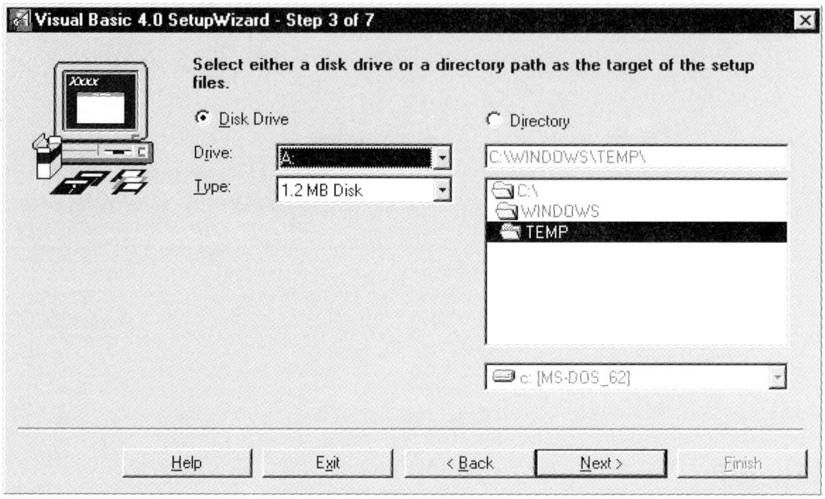

Figure A-3 The wizard's OLE server screen information

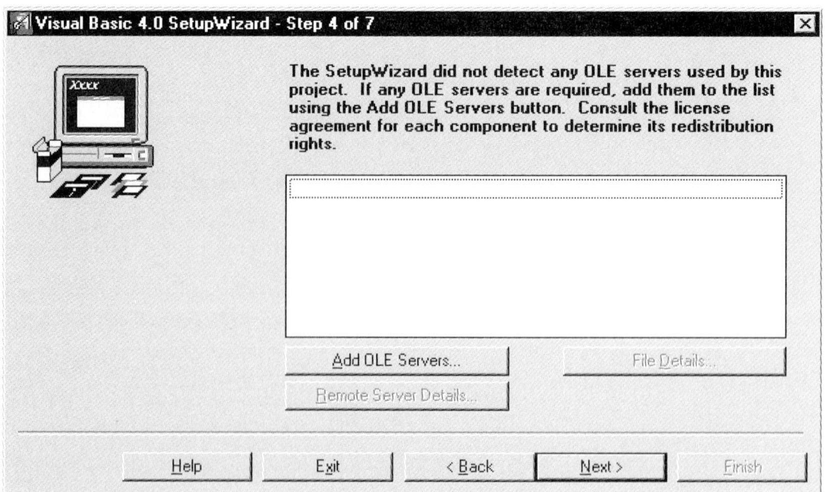

Figure A-4
Step 6 of the wizard

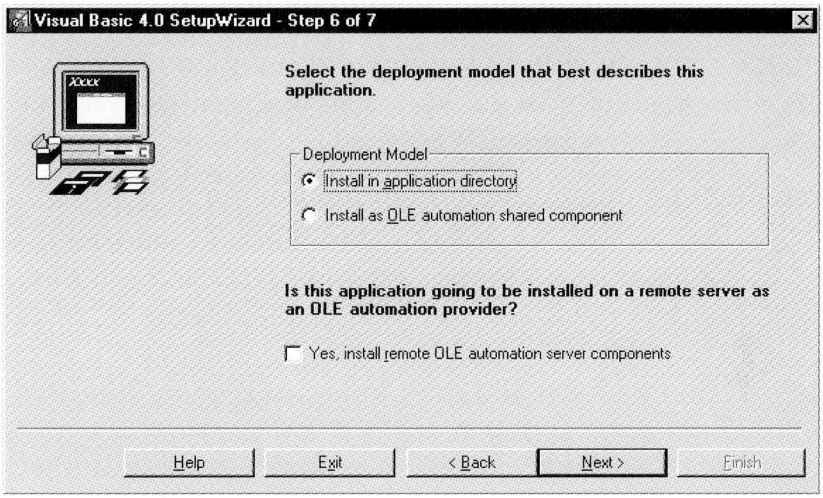

Figure A-5
Dependency screen in the Setup Wizard

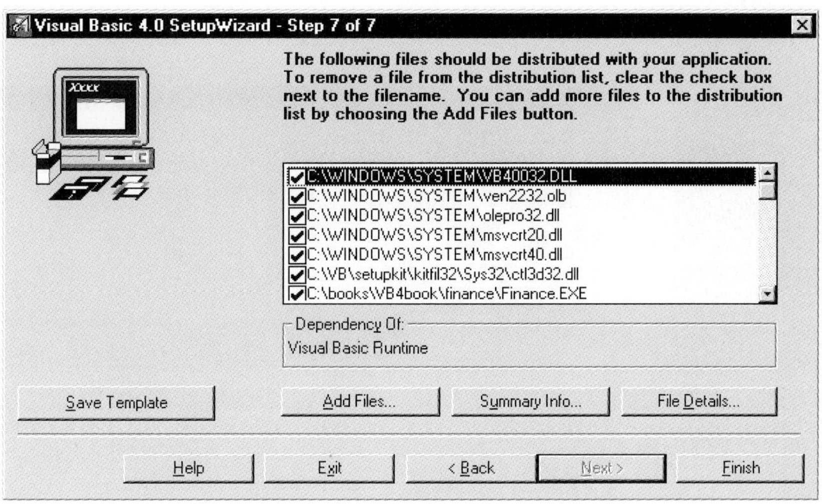

all the machines that will use the applications have these files already installed). For example, it is hard to know whether you are using any functions from the Visual Basic for Applications library (using the Object Browser is one way to check).

If you now click on the Finish button, the wizard pops up screens that indicate what it is doing (compressing the files, calculating the files it needs to copy, and so on). When it is done, if you asked that the application be distributed on floppies, the wizard pops up a message box asking for blank formatted disks. Feed them in, and you will have the disks needed for installing your application. Finally, when the Setup Wizard finishes copying the necessary (compressed) files, you will see the final screen shown in Figure A-6.

note: *Users can now install your application simply by placing the first distribution disk into a drive and running from Windows the SETUP.EXE program that is contained on it. The Setup program that the wizard created follows all the standard Windows conventions. Users can change the installation directory, they are told how the installation is progressing via progress bars, and they will be told when to insert the additional disks. (It will also allow uninstallation via the Add/Remove feature of Windows 95.)*

(The size of the distribution files is striking: counting the space for the Setup program, the disk needed 1100K for the simple checkbook program.)

Figure A-6

Final screen in the Setup Wizard

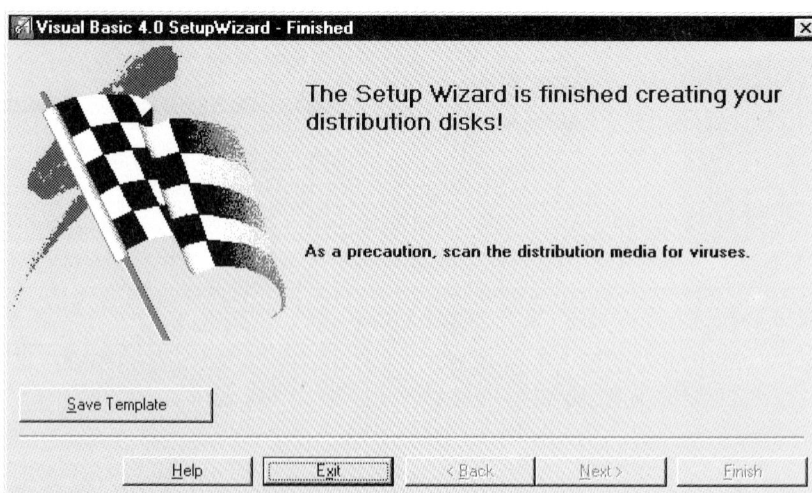

OLE Automation Setup Problems

As an example of what you will run across, suppose you try to install the OLE automation sample (the VB\SAMPLES\OLEAUTO\GEOFACTS.VBP project). After I clicked on the Next button in the initial screen, I saw a message box that looks like this:

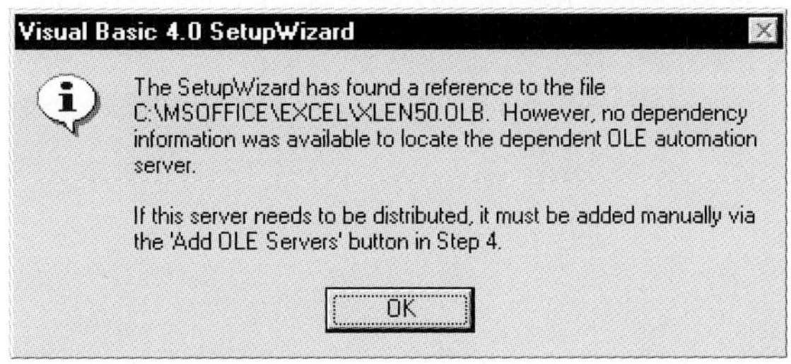

This is pretty typical of what happens if you are using OLE automation—you probably should copy this information down so you can add it manually in the Step 4 screen of the Wizard shown in Figure A-3 (if it is really needed). You can click on the Add OLE Servers button in Figure A-3 to open a dialog box that will make it easier to find the file. (The message box gives you the location.) Unfortunately, the Setup Wizard sometimes gets confused about what it needs to install and register when it comes to OLE automation applications and, for example, it doesn't really need this file on any machine that has Excel installed. (And you could not use Excel in an OLE automation application unless the user already had a copy of Excel, so the whole question is moot!)

Database Setup Problems

The main problem you will encounter in setting up a database is the potential size of any application. For example, let's suppose you want to distribute the moderately sophisticated VISDATA sample application supplied with the Professional or Enterprise edition. Since this uses data access extensively, you will see the Data Access screen in the Setup Wizard shown in Figure A-7. For the sake of illustration, let's suppose you want to allow data access via all the possible data access engines. So you check off all the boxes in the screen shown in Figure A-7. Adding this much functionality combined with the files needed for the VISDATA application itself means that the Setup Wizard has to process 44 files and will need five 1.4MB disks for the eventual Setup program.

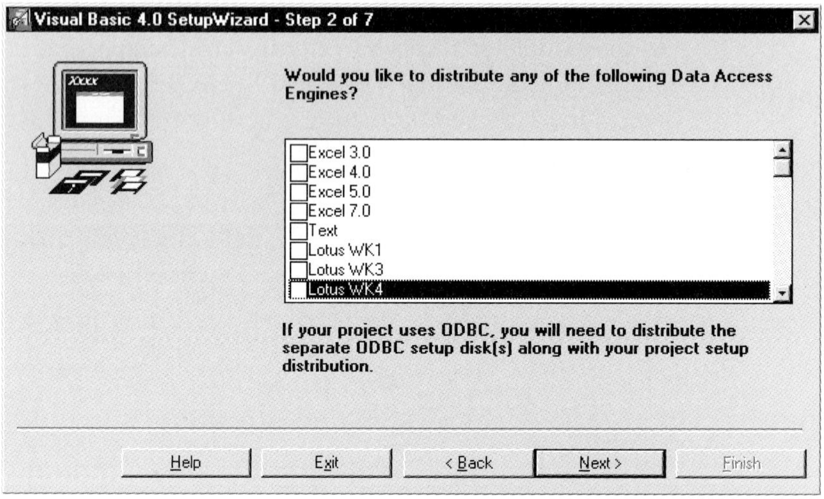

Figure A-7

Screen for adding data access in the Setup Wizard

Appendix B

Microsoft's Top 25 Visual Basic Technical Support Questions

THE following frequently asked questions apply to Microsoft Visual Basic for Windows, version 4.0 (and in some cases, as noted, to earlier versions of Visual Basic as well). They are not listed in order of importance, because the information was collected from several Microsoft sources.

note: *We asked Microsoft for permission to include their answers to the most frequently asked questions about Visual Basic. They most graciously agreed to provide this information. We decided to include this information because, although technical support from Microsoft is free, it is often time-consuming to get through and may turn out to be not free after all (half-hour toll calls during business hours can add up). We are providing this information essentially unchanged except for a few footnotes and some formatting and minor editorial changes.*

Can I get help without paying Microsoft support charges?

You have a number of options to receive assistance from Microsoft as well as other developers. They include telephone support, CompuServe, Internet, and Microsoft Solution Providers.

note: *Even with the paid support options, if Microsoft can confirm that the problem you are having with their product is a bug or defect in the Microsoft product, they will refund any support charges for telephone or Electronic Service Requests (available with support contracts).*

Microsoft's Standard lines offer 30-day no-charge support. The 30-day no-charge support period begins with your first call to Microsoft Product Support Services. This line is available from 6 A.M. to 6 P.M., Pacific time, Monday through Friday, excluding holidays. The number is (206) 646-5105.

Microsoft technical support and programming assistance from other Visual Basic developers is available in the MSBASIC forum on CompuServe. This is a Microsoft-moderated forum; *not* a direct one-on-one support route to Microsoft. Microsoft does not charge for this forum, though you will be billed by CompuServe for connect time and forum access time.[1]

For more information, please call CompuServe at (800) 848-8990 and ask for the CompuServe Information Manager software disk. The software disk provides an option that enables you to set up your own CompuServe account.

The Microsoft Developer Knowledge Base (GO MDKB) is a tremendous resource for dealing with Microsoft products. Developer Support Engineers at Microsoft create solutions and explain problems or techniques that come up in the course of using Microsoft products. These discussions are written up into articles and placed into the Knowledge Base (KB), which is periodically updated on various electronic services. The Visual Basic Knowledge Base (VBKB_FT.EXE) is a downloadable subset of the KB, which contains articles relevant to Visual Basic. It contains a full text search engine to help you locate the information you want. This file is available in the Microsoft Software Library (MSL).[2]

caution: *VBKB_FT.EXE is over 4 megabytes in compressed form; it will take a while to download.*

You can download either VBKB.EXE or VBKB_FT.EXE (both are self-extracting files) from the MSL on the following services:

- **CompuServe**

  GO MSL
  Search for and download VBKB.EXE

  or

  Search for and download VBKB_FT.EXE

- **Microsoft Download Service (MSDL)**

  Dial (206) 936-6735 to connect to MSDL
  Download VBKB.EXE or VBKB_FT.EXE

1 The Microsoft network is another good service.
2 Editor's note: If you subscribe to the Develop Cds, you get the entire Knowledge Base already.

- **Internet (anonymous FTP)**

  ftp ftp.microsoft.com
  Change to the \softlib\mslfiles directory
  Get VBKB.EXE

  or

  Get VBKB_FT.EXE

note: *Look at the Frequently Asked Questions (FAQ) list. This file is one of several FAQs made available to the public by Microsoft Developer Support. Its goal is to answer only the most commonly asked questions as succinctly as possible. These FAQs are divided by technical areas in Visual Basic. Even if you're a long-time MSBASIC user, these FAQs will be useful, if only to steer beginners to the quick answers.*

Other potential sources of Visual Basic information include ftp.microsoft.com, where you can look in the following directories:

- /softlib/mslfiles
- /msdn
- /msdn/vbtech
- /devtools/lang/vb/public

On CompuServe:

- GO MSIC - The Microsoft Sales Information Center forum. The MSIC forum on CompuServe is the place for customers to:

  Ask any pre-sales questions about MS products [Section 1]

  Register their MS products [Section 2]

  Download info on MS products [Libraries]

  Check out job opportunities at MS [Lib 17]

  Get a reseller referral [Section 1]

  Ask a question of the International Sales group [Section 5]

  Check out MS press releases [Library 7: Press Releases]

Microsoft has three services for customers on the Internet:

- www.microsoft.com—World-Wide-Web server
- gopher.microsoft.com—Gopher server
- ftp.microsoft.com—FTP server

All three servers are registered in the Internet's Domain Name Service (DNS), so customers merely have to reference any of the servers by name:

- ftp ftp.microsoft.com
- In mosaic connect to: http://www.microsoft.com
- In gopher connect to: gopher.microsoft.com, port 70, type 1

Will the 16-bit and 32-bit versions of Visual Basic 4.0 run on Windows 95?

The 16-bit version of Visual Basic for Windows, version 4.0[3] will run on Windows, Windows for Workgroups, Windows NT, and Windows 95. Under Windows NT and Windows 95, it is handled as any other 16-bit application. The 32-bit version will only run on Windows 95 and Windows NT version 3.51 or greater. On Windows NT, your application will run in a 16-bit environment provided by the Windows On Windows (WOW) layer, which allows Windows NT to run 16-bit applications in a protected environment.

Why can't I load a Visual BasicX control in the 32-bit version of Visual Basic?

Visual Basic 4.0 includes OLE Controls (.OCX) that are upgrades to the Visual BasicX custom controls that shipped in previous versions. Automatic conversion is provided to replace the Visual BasicX references in projects with references to OLE Controls. Visual Basic 4.0 will ship with OLE equivalents of all of the controls shipped in Visual Basic 3.0, in addition to several brand

3 Supplied only with the Professional and Enterprise editions.

new OLE Controls in both 16- and 32-bit versions. Visual Basic will continue to support Visual BasicXs in the 16-bit version only.

How can I write an application for 16-bit and 32-bit systems at the same time?

Microsoft has taken a number of steps to assure source code compatibility between 16-bit and 32-bit applications:

- All Visual Basic-provided language is portable.
- All custom controls have identical object models.
- Basic file I/O enables files to be shared by applications running on different platforms.

Visual Basic 4.0, Professional Edition, includes both 16-bit and 32-bit versions of Visual Basic.EXE. Using a single source code tree, you can create 16-bit applications that run on Microsoft Windows 3.X, 32-bit applications that run on Microsoft Windows NT 3.X (Intel), and 32-bit Windows 95-based applications. By taking advantage of the new conditional compilation switches in Visual Basic 4.0, you can quickly recompile the same source code to target and exploit the capabilities of different Windows platforms. Conditional compilation switches allow you to target different platforms or languages easily using a single source code tree and a simple recompile.

Visual Basic provides both the language and command-line support for conditionally compiling declarations and procedural code into an application. Both the Project Options dialog box and the Visual Basic 4.0 command line allow the setting of constants that are subsequently used in evaluating #If...#Else...#End If structures. For instance, you can specify "Win16=1" in the Conditional Compilation Arguments field of the Project Options dialog box, thereby selectively compiling Windows 3.1 declarations and other constants in an application:

```
#If Win16=1 Then 'Use Win16 calls
  Declare Function GetWindow Lib "User" (ByVal hWnd As _
     Integer, ByVal wCmd As Integer) As Integer
   #ANSI=True
#Else      'Use Win32 calls
```

```
  Declare Function GetWindow Lib "User32" (ByVal hWnd As _
Long, ByVal wCmd As Integer) As Long
  #ANSI=False
#End If
```

Can a Visual Basic 4.0 32-bit application run on Win32s?

No. Win32s is a subsystem of DLLs that extends the Windows 3.1 16-bit operating system by translating 32-bit calls to the underlying 16-bit operating system. Programs written with 32-bit Visual Basic running on Windows 3.1 with Win32s would generally run slower (due to the extra memory and overhead of the translation layer) than the same program created with 16-bit Visual Basic. Instead of using the more limited Win32s features, Microsoft chose to have the 32-bit version exploit the more advanced 32-bit features available only on Windows 95 and Windows NT.

Can I create DLL files with Visual Basic 4.0?

Visual Basic 4.0 includes an option to make OLE DLL files. These files behave similarly to standard DLLs except that they use OLE as an interface to the objects described by the DLL.

With Visual Basic 4.0, you can create reusable business objects that can be shared across applications. Rather than having to create DLLs using a C compiler or other language, you can now easily create reusable objects entirely within Visual Basic. These OLE components accomplish the reusability of DLLs and are easier to reuse because they are essentially self-documenting.

At design time you can browse the components with the Object Browser and examine what methods and properties the OLE objects expose. Similarly to the way Visual BasicX vendors encapsulated their expertise into controls, Visual Basic programmers can now rapidly package their business rules, commonly used code libraries, as well as any legacy code into reusable, programmable objects. Once created, these libraries of reusable objects, complete with custom properties and methods, can be used by any application that supports OLE Automation.

A few examples of applications that can reuse these objects are Visual Basic 4.0 (which can both use and create OLE objects), Microsoft Excel 5.0, Microsoft Access 2.0, and Microsoft Project. Future versions of Microsoft SQL Server,

Microsoft FoxPro, Microsoft Word For Windows, and Windows will take advantage of these objects as well.

Does this mean that I can use a Visual Basic-created DLL from other languages?

Yes, you can use the OLE DLLs from other languages (such as Microsoft Visual C++), but you do not declare the functions in the DLL as you would a Windows DLL function. Instead you access the functions via the OLE interface.

Will Visual Basic 4.0 exist for other platforms?

Visual Basic 4.0 incorporates the portable Visual Basic, Applications Edition language engine. Microsoft Excel 5.0 was recently released for the Macintosh and along with it the Visual Basic for applications component of Microsoft Excel, so the language engine is there. There are no commitments for a version of Visual Basic for the Macintosh or for MS-DOS, but consideration for one is based strictly on a good business case.

Preliminary discussions have occurred concerning all other major architectures that support Windows NT, and although no commitments have been made, this is certainly a possibility for the future.

The 16-bit version of Visual Basic 4.0 will run on any machine that can run Windows NT. Windows NT includes a Windows On Windows (WOW) emulation layer, which can run 16-bit applications.

Why are there references to Macintosh in the documentation and on-line help?

Visual Basic 4.0 does not run on the Macintosh. The Visual Basic, Applications Edition Help references are included to ease the transition between Visual Basic 4.0 and Visual Basic, Applications Edition in Excel 5.0 for the Macintosh. The references in the documentation to the Macintosh are references *only* available in the Visual Basic, Applications Edition currently found in Excel 5.0 for the Macintosh.

Does the 32-bit version of Visual Basic provide statements and functions for multitasking?

Currently Visual Basic 4.0 does not support threads on Windows NT 3.5 or Windows 95. Our research indicates that the main reasons Visual Basic programmers would want to use threads in a Visual Basic application would be for asynchronous database queries, printing, or file I/O operations. Microsoft is expecting providers of data sourcing OLE Controls to provide the former, and will consider the latter for future versions.

Does Visual Basic 4.0 use the new controls of Windows 95?

Visual Basic does use the new Windows 95 controls, but since these are 32-bit controls for a 32-bit operating system, they are only available in the 32-bit version of Visual Basic.

Do I need to change my Visual Basic 3.0 applications to compile with the 32-bit version of Visual Basic 4.0? What about under the 16-bit version?

There are two significant changes that need to be addressed in order to recompile a Visual Basic 3.0 application to the 32-bit version of Visual Basic 4.0.

First, if API calls are being used by the application, you must change your API calls to the appropriate target environment. Sixteen-bit Windows and 32-bit Windows provide APIs with similar functions but different Declare statements (to take into account the size of the data types). Visual Basic 3.0 typically uses the 16-bit Declarations. The 32-bit version of Visual Basic 4.0 *must* use the 32-bit API declarations. Rather than simply replace the existing API calls, Visual Basic 4.0's conditional compilation feature can be put to good use here to target both 16- and 32-bit platforms from a single source code tree.

Second, the 32-bit version of Visual Basic 4.0 makes use of the newer OLE Control architecture exclusively. Visual BasicXs are not supported for the 32-bit version. This is not a problem for older Visual BasicX controls that were shipped with previous versions of Visual Basic. All of these controls have OLE Control counterparts (in Visual Basic 4.0, these files all end in .OCX). You will be prompted to upgrade these controls the first time you load your project into Visual Basic 4.0. However, you will need to acquire OLE Control upgrades to any third-party controls that you use in your applications. While Microsoft has made the technology available for control developers to easily port their existing Visual BasicX controls to the new OLE Control technology (the Visual Basic Control Migration Pack - CMP), there is no guarantee that all of the available Visual BasicX controls will be available as OLE Controls. Contact the control vendor for upgrade information.

The 'Basic Language' code of both the 16-bit version of Visual Basic 4.0 and the 32-bit versions of Visual Basic are fully compatible.[4] Creating a 32-bit application that runs on either Windows NT 3.5 or Windows 95 from a Visual Basic 3.0 (or 16-bit Visual Basic 4.0) application is a simple matter of loading an existing 16-bit Visual Basic application into the 32-bit version of Visual Basic and choosing the Make EXE command from the File menu.

Do I need to change my Visual Basic 3.0 application to compile with the 16-bit version of Visual Basic 4.0?

No. To run a Visual Basic 3.0 application with the 16-bit version of Visual Basic, load the source code into the 16-bit version of Visual Basic 4.0 running under Microsoft Windows 3.X, Windows NT 3.51, or Windows 95, and make an .EXE file.

When I load an existing application into Visual Basic 4.0, it says it's going to "upgrade" my controls. Is it actually changing my controls, and should I back them up?

No. Your controls are fine. Visual Basic 4.0 contains newer, backward-compatible controls that replace controls shipped with previous versions of Visual Basic. Your project's .MAK file will be updated to use these newer controls if you answer Yes. Microsoft recommends using the latest controls so you can take advantage of any new features that have been implemented.

4 Editor's note: This is technically true because the code will compile, but to obtain the same functionality, some changes may be needed. For example, code that uses binary files may have to change because of Unicode—see Chapter 17 for more information about this.

Why are the distributables so large?

Visual Basic 4.0 uses the OLE Control architecture on a scale unmatched by any other in the industry. This means that until the OLE Control architecture becomes the industry standard and part of the Windows operating system, Visual Basic programs have to include the supporting files that enable this powerful new technology. It is expected that as the OLE model becomes integrated at the operating system level, this requirement will fall away and the size of the distributables will drop dramatically.

I am having problems connecting to my database using open database connectivity (ODBC) and Microsoft Visual Basic for Windows. What am I doing wrong?

If not set up correctly, the following four areas can contribute to problems in connecting to a database server when using ODBC and Visual Basic:

- .INI file settings must be correct.
- Correct DLLs must be in the right place.
- Server information needed to connect to a server correctly must be available.
- Information must also meet the needs of Microsoft and Sybase SQL Servers.

The following sections describe these four areas, giving possible errors and problems that can arise.

.INI File Settings

There are two .INI files (ODBCINST.INI and ODBC.INI) that must reside in the Windows directory and must contain correct information about the installed ODBC drivers and servers.

ODBCINST.INI contains the ODBC driver information needed to register new servers using the RegisterDataBase( ) statement in Visual Basic. Here is an example of an .INI file for the SQL Server driver that ships with Visual Basic:

```
[ODBC Drivers]
SQL Server=Installed

[SQL Server]
Driver=C:\WINDOWS\SYSTEM\sqlsrvr.dll
Setup=C:\WINDOWS\SYSTEM\sqlsetup.dll
```

The [ODBC Drivers] section tells the driver manager the names of the installed drivers. The [SQL Server] section tells the ODBC driver manager the names of the DLLs to use to access data from a server set up as a SQL Server. The order of the two sections and their entries is arbitrary.

ODBC.INI contains the data for each installed driver. The driver manager uses this information to determine which DLL to use to access data from a particular database backend. Here is an example of a file containing three data sources, all using the SQL Server driver:

```
[ODBC Data Sources]
MySQL=SQL Server
CorpSQL=SQL Server

[MySQL]
Driver=C:\WINDOWS\SYSTEM\sqlsrvr.dll
Description=SQL Server on server MySQL
OemToAnsi=No
Network=dbnmp3
Address=\\mysql\pipe\sql\query

[CorpSQL]
Driver=C:\WINDOWS\SYSTEM\sqlsrvr.dll
Description=SQL Server on server CorpSQL
OemToAnsi=No
Network=dbnmp3
Address=\\corpsql\pipe\sql\query
```

The first section tells the driver manager which sections appearing below it define the data source. As you can see, each entry has a value (in this case, SQL Server) that matches a value from the ODBCINST.INI file.

If the information on a data source is incorrect or missing, you may get the following error:

> ODBC - SQLConnect failure 'IM002[Microsoft][ODBC DLL] Data source not found and no default driver specified'

If the DLL listed on the Driver=... line cannot be found or is corrupt, the following error may occur:

ODBC - SQLConnect failure 'IM003[Microsoft][ODBC DLL] Driver specified by data source could not be loaded'

ODBC and Driver DLLs

The following DLLs must be on the path or in the Windows system directory in order for the ODBC to be accessible from Visual Basic:

ODBC.DLL - driver manager
ODBCINST.DLL - driver setup manager
VBDB400.DLL - Visual Basic programming layer

If VBDB400.DLL is missing or corrupt, you see the following error in Visual Basic when you try to run the application:

ODBC Objects require VBDB400.DLL

If either the ODBC.DLL or ODBCINST.DLL file is missing or corrupt, you see the following error in Visual Basic when you try to run the application:

Cannot Find ODBC.DLL, File not Found

The SQL Server driver requires the following files:

SQLSRVR.DLL - actual driver
SQLSETUP.DLL - driver setup routines
DBNMP3.DLL - named pipe routines needed by SQL Server

If the SQLSRVR.DLL is missing or corrupt, you see the following error when calling the OpenDataBase( ) function with a SQL Server data source:

ODBC - SQLConnect failure 'IM003[Microsoft][ODBC DLL] Driver specified by data source could not be loaded'

If the SQLSETUP.DLL is missing or corrupt, you see the following error when calling the RegisterDataBase( ) statement with SQL Server as the driver name:

> The configuration DLL (C:\WINDOWS\SYSTEM\SQLSETUP.DLL) for the ODBC SQL Server driver could not be loaded.

Server Information Needed to Connect to a Data Source

Certain information is needed to connect to a data source using the OpenDataBase() function. This information can be obtained from the server administrator in the case of SQL Server. The following is an example of a call to the OpenDataBase( ) function to connect to a SQL Server called CorpSQL as a user named Guest with password set to taco:

```
Dim db As DataBase
Set db = OpenDataBase( "corpsql", False, False, _
"UID=guest;PWD=taco")
```

If any of this information is missing, an ODBC dialog box appears to give the user a chance to supply the needed data. If the information is incorrect, the following error occurs:

> ODBC - SQLConnect failure '28000
> [Microsoft] [ODBC SQL Server Driver]
> [SQL Server] Login failed'

Information Specific to Microsoft and Sybase SQL Servers

For Microsoft and Sybase SQL Servers, you need to add stored procedures to the server itself by running a batch file of SQL statements to make a Microsoft or Sybase SQL Server ODBC-aware. In other words, before you can run a Visual Basic ODBC application using the SQL Server driver, you must first update the ODBC catalog of stored procedures. These procedures are provided in the INSTCAT.SQL file. The system administrator for the SQL Server should install the procedures by using the SQL Server Interactive SQL (ISQL) utility.

If the INSTCAT.SQL file is not processed on the server, the following error occurs:

ODBC - SQL Connect Failure
"08001" [Microsoft ODBC SQL Server Driver]
'unable to connect to data source 'number: 606'

To install the catalog stored procedures by using the INSTCAT.SQL file, run INSTCAT.SQL from the command line using ISQL. Do not use the SAF utility provided with SQL Server. Microsoft SAF for MS-DOS and OS/2 is limited to 511 lines of code in a SQL script, and INSTCAT.SQL contains more than 511 lines of code.

Run ISQL from the OS/2 command line using the following syntax. Enter the two lines as a single line, and do not include the angle braces (<>).

```
ISQL /U <sa login name> /n /P <password> /S <F128QL server name
/I <drive: \path\INSTCAT.SQL> /o <drive:\path\output file name>
```

The parameters in the preceding command line are as follows:

/U	Login name for the system administrator.
/n	Eliminates line numbering and prompting for user input.
/P	Password used for the system administrator. This switch is case sensitive.
/S	Name of the server to set up.
/i	Provides the drive and fully qualified path for the location of INSTCAT.SQL.
/o	Provides ISQL with an output file destination for results, including error listings.

Here's an example (shown here on two lines but actually entered on one):

```
ISQL /U sa /n /P squeeze /S BLUEDWARF /I C: \SQL\INSTCAT.SQL /o
 C: \SQL OUTPUT>TXT
```

How do I scroll a form when Visual Basic forms are limited to screen size?

This information applies to all editions of Microsoft Visual Basic for Windows, version 4.0.

Summary

A Visual Basic form cannot be sized larger than the screen. This article explains how to scroll the contents of a form to enlarge the usable area. The sample program given here works by scrolling a picture box control that is larger than the form and contains attached controls. When the picture box scrolls, all the attached controls scroll together.

Step-by-Step Example

1. Start a new project in Visual Basic. Form1 is created by default.
2. Add a horizontal scroll bar control and a vertical scroll bar control to Form1. (The size doesn't matter because the program automatically sizes the scroll bars in the Form Resize event code.)
3. Add a picture box control to Form1. Draw a text box control inside the upper-left corner of the picture box such that when the picture box moves, the text box moves with it. Select the Text1 box and press the F4 key to display the Properties window. Set the Text1 Index property to 0, which is required at design time to make an array of text controls. (You can also enhance this sample program by placing more controls into the picture box. When the picture box scrolls, all the controls scroll.)
4. Add the following code to the Form Load event:

```
Sub Form_Load ()
   ' Make the picture box bigger than the form:
   Picture1.Move 0, 0, 1.4 * ScaleWidth, 1.2 * ScaleHeight
   ' Place some sample controls in the picture box:
   Dim i As Integer
   For i = 1 To 20
      Load Text1(i)
      Text1(i).Visible = True
      Text1(i).Left = i * Picture1.Height / 20
      Text1(i).Top = Text1(i).Left
   Next
End Sub
```

5. Add the following code to the Form Resize event:

```
Sub Form_Resize ()
      ' Position the scroll bars:
      hscroll1.Left = 0
      vscroll1.Top = 0
      If Picture1.Width > scalewidth Then
         hscroll1.Top = ScaleHeight - hscroll1.Height
      Else
         hscroll1.Top = ScaleHeight
      End If
      If Picture1.Height > hscroll1.Top Then
         vscroll1.Left = scalewidth - vscroll1.Width
         If Picture1.Width > vscroll1.Left Then
            hscroll1.Top = ScaleHeight - hscroll1.Height
         End If
      Else
         vscroll1.Left = scalewidth
      End If
      hscroll1.Width = scalewidth
      vscroll1.Height = hscroll1.Top

      ' Set the scroll bar ranges
      hscroll1.Max = Picture1.Width - vscroll1.Left
      vscroll1.Max = Picture1.Height - hscroll1.Top
      hscroll1.SmallChange = Abs(hscroll1.Max \ 16) + 1
      hscroll1.LargeChange = Abs(hscroll1.Max \ 4) + 1
      vscroll1.SmallChange = Abs(vscroll1.Max \ 16) + 1
      vscroll1.LargeChange = Abs(vscroll1.Max \ 4) + 1
      hscroll1.ZOrder 0
      vscroll1.ZOrder 0
End Sub
```

6. Add the following code to the HScroll1 Change event:

```
Sub HScroll1_Change ()
   Picture1.Left = -HScroll1.Value
End Sub
```

7. Add the following code to the VScroll1 Change event:

```
Sub VScroll1_Change ()
   Picture1.Top = -VScroll1.Value
End Sub
```

8. Start the program (or press the F5 key). Click the scroll bars to scroll the form. Close the form to end the program.

How do I create a floating toolbar in Visual Basic?

The information in this article applies to all editions of Visual Basic for Windows after version 1.0.

Summary

This article contains code and instructions that show you how to create a floating toolbar in Visual Basic. A toolbar is a modeless dialog box owned by a parent window but not confined to the area of the parent. This article combines methods that are described in more detail in the following articles in the Microsoft Knowledge Base: ARTICLE-ID: Q114775 TITLE : How to Create a Modeless Dialog or Form in Visual Basic and ARTICLE-ID: Q114593 TITLE: How to Move a Form that Has No Titlebar or Caption.

Creating a Floating Toolbar

Instead of offering this article in a number of steps, the usual format has been modified to make it easier for you to create and use this Visual Basic application. Therefore, the three files you need (TOOLBAR.BAS, TOOLBAR.FRM, and PARENT.FRM) are listed below, so you can easily copy them into a text editor and save them as separate files. Instructions for how to use the files are embedded in the files as comments.

```
' Place the following code in a single text file called TOOLBAR.BAS
'
' NOTE: After copying this into a file in a text editor, modify each
' Declare statement so that each one uses only one, single line.

Option Explicit

Type POINTAPI
    X As Integer
    Y As Integer
End Type
```

```
Type ConvertPOINTAPI
     xy As Long
End Type

Declare Function Sendmessage Lib "User" (ByVal hwnd As Integer,
    ByVal wMsg As Integer, ByVal wParam As Integer,
    ByVal lParam As Any) As Long
Declare Sub GetCursorPos Lib "User" (lpPoint As POINTAPI)
Declare Function GetSysColor Lib "User" (ByVal nIndex As Integer) As Long
Declare Function SetWindowWord Lib "User" (ByVal hwnd As Integer,
    ByVal Index As Integer, ByVal wNewWord As Integer) As Integer
Declare Function BitBlt Lib "GDI" (ByVal hDestDC%, ByVal X%, ByVal Y%,
    ByVal nWidth%, ByVal nHeight%, ByVal hSrcDC%, ByVal XSrc%, ByVal Ysrc%,
    ByVal dwRop&) As Integer

Global Const WM_LBUTTONUP = &H202
Global Const WM_SYSCOMMAND = &H112
Global Const MOUSE_MOVE = &HF012

Global Const COLOR_APPWORKSPACE = 12
Global Const COLOR_ACTIVECAPTION = 2
Global Const COLOR_CAPTIONTEXT = 9
Global Const COLOR_GRAYTEXT = 17

Global Const DSTINVERT = &H550009     ' (DWORD) dest = (NOT dest)

Global Const GWW_HWNDPARENT = (-8)

Global ToolbarLoaded As Integer
' The following is a text dump of the TOOLBAR form. It includes the form
' and control description as well as necessary Function and Sub procedures.
' Save the code in a single TEXT file called TOOLBAR.FRM and you will
' be able to load it as a form in Visual Basic.
'
' NOTE: To make the code fit in this article, some of the statements are
' shown in multiple lines. Be sure to modify the lines in the text editor
' to ensure that all lines of code exist as one, single line of code
' in the file. Otherwise, you will receive errors when loading the form in
' Visual Basic.
'
' Also, this program loads some bitmaps from your Visual Basic directory.
' It assumes Visual Basic is installed in C:\VB.  If this is incorrect
' search for all the LoadPicture commands and change the path.
```

```
VERSION 2.00
Begin Form Toolbar
   ClientHeight    =   2160
   ClientLeft      =   1692
   ClientTop       =   1464
   ClientWidth     =   2928
   ControlBox      =   0   'False
   Height          =   2580
   KeyPreview      =   -1  'True
   Left            =   1644
   LinkTopic       =   "Form1"
   MaxButton       =   0   'False
   MinButton       =   0   'False
   ScaleHeight     =   180
   ScaleMode       =   3  'Pixel
   ScaleWidth      =   244
   Top             =   1092
   Width           =   3024
   Begin PictureBox Picture1
      Height          =   780
      Left            =   0
      ScaleHeight     =   756
      ScaleWidth      =   636
      TabIndex        =   1
      Top             =   0
      Width           =   660
   End
   Begin Image Image3
      Height          =   612
      Index           =   0
      Left            =   600
      Top             =   1320
      Width           =   972
   End
   Begin Image Image2
      Height          =   852
      Index           =   0
      Left            =   1680
      Top             =   480
      Width           =   852
   End
   Begin Image Image1
      Height          =   612
      Index           =   0
```

```
        Left              =   720
        Top               =   600
        Width             =   852
    End
    Begin Label Label1
        BackColor         =   &H00FFFFFF&
        Caption           =   "Label1"
        Height            =   372
        Left              =   720
        TabIndex          =   0
        Top               =   0
        Width             =   1332
    End
End
Option Explicit

Dim MDown As Integer
Dim InvertedImage As Integer
Dim OriginalParenthWnd As Integer
Dim MinHeight As Long
Dim MinWidth As Long

Sub Form_Activate ()

    If Not MDown Then parent.SetFocus

End Sub

Sub Form_Load ()

    ToolbarLoaded = True

    Me.ScaleMode = 3   ' Pixels
    picture1.ScaleMode = 3
    picture1.AutoSize = True

    ' Load the picture
    picture1.Picture = LoadPicture("C:\VB\BITMAPS\OUTLINE\MINUS.BMP")

    ' NOTE: You can load the MINUS.BMP bitmap into paintbrush and
    ' change its background color from white to gray. To do this,
    ' load the bitmap into paintbrush, and click the light gray in
    ' the color palette. Then select the paint roller icon, and
    ' click the area between the hyphen and the border to fill
```

```
' the area with light gray. Save it as MINUS2.BMP. If you do this,
' use the following statement to load the picture box:
' picture1.Picture = LoadPicture("C:\VB\BITMAPS\OUTLINE\MINUS2.BMP")

' Get the user's system color for the active window caption:
label1.BackColor = GetSysColor(COLOR_ACTIVECAPTION)

' Position picturebox and label:
picture1.Left = -1                    ' Use -1 to put the controls
picture1.Top = -1                     ' border behind the edge of
label1.Top = -1                       ' the form.

' Overlap edge of label with picture:
label1.Left = picture1.Left + picture1.Width - 1
label1.Height = picture1.Height

' Load and locate the image controls:
Call InitToolbox

' The guesswork on height and width could be replaced with a call to
' the GetSystemMetrics Windows API function to get the border width of
' the form. Change the following two lines to one, single line:
Me.Height =
    (picture1.Height + image1(0).Height + 12) * screen.TwipsPerPixelY
' Change the following two lines to one, single line:
Me.Width =
    (image3(0).Left + image3(0).Width + 10) * screen.TwipsPerPixelX

MinHeight = Me.Height
MinWidth = Me.Width

' Set up the label:
label1.Alignment = 2                  ' Centered
label1.BorderStyle = 1                ' Single
label1.Caption = "Toolbar"

' Choose a small font or whatever looks best on your system:
label1.FontName = "Small Fonts"
label1.FontSize = 6
label1.FontBold = False
' Use active caption color for label's caption:
label1.ForeColor = GetSysColor(COLOR_CAPTIONTEXT)
```

```
   ' Color the background of the form to the MDI client area color:
   Me.BackColor = GetSysColor(COLOR_APPWORKSPACE)

   ' Set parent for the toolbar to display on top:
   OriginalParenthWnd = SetWindowWord(Me.hWnd, GWW_HWNDPARENT, parent.hWnd)

End Sub

Sub Form_Resize ()

   ' Check minimums for resize:
   If Me.Width < MinWidth Then Me.Width = MinWidth
   If Me.Height < MinHeight Then Me.Height = MinHeight

   ' Change size of label:
   label1.Width = Me.ScaleWidth - label1.Left + 1

End Sub

Sub Form_Unload (Cancel As Integer)
   Dim ret As Integer

   ' Return the original parent handle:
   ret = SetWindowWord(Me.hWnd, GWW_HWNDPARENT, OriginalParenthWnd)

   ' Clear the global flag:
   ToolbarLoaded = False

End Sub

Sub Image1_Click (Index As Integer)

   Clipboard.SetText parent.Text1.SelText
   parent.Text1.SelText = ""

End Sub

' Change the following two lines to one, single line:
Sub Image1_MouseDown (Index As Integer, Button As Integer,
   Shift As Integer, X As Single, Y As Single)

   If Button And 1 Then
      MDown = True
      image1(0).Picture = image1(2).Picture  ' Down
```

```
    End If

End Sub

' Change the following two lines to one, single line:
Sub Image1_MouseMove (Index As Integer, Button As Integer,
    Shift As Integer, X As Single, Y As Single)

    If Button And 1 Then                      ' Left button down
        X = X \ screen.TwipsPerPixelX      ' x and y are in twips
        Y = Y \ screen.TwipsPerPixelY      ' Convert to pixels

        ' Change the following two lines to one, single line:
        If (X < 0) Or (X > image1(0).Width) Or (Y < 0) Or
            (Y > image1(0).Height) Then

            image1(0).Picture = image1(1).Picture   ' Up
        Else
            image1(0).Picture = image1(2).Picture   ' Down
        End If
    End If

End Sub

' Change the following two lines to one, single line:
Sub Image1_MouseUp (Index As Integer, Button As Integer, Shift As Integer,
    X As Single, Y As Single)

    If Button And 1 Then
        image1(0).Picture = image1(1).Picture   ' Up
        MDown = False
        parent.SetFocus
    End If

End Sub

Sub Image2_Click (Index As Integer)

    ' Code for copy here:
    Clipboard.SetText parent.Text1.SelText

End Sub

' Change the following two lines to one, single line:
```

```
Sub Image2_MouseDown (Index As Integer, Button As Integer,
    Shift As Integer, X As Single, Y As Single)

    If Button And 1 Then
        MDown = True
        image2(0).Picture = image2(2).Picture   ' Down
    End If

End Sub

' Change the following two lines to one, single line:
Sub Image2_MouseMove (Index As Integer, Button As Integer,
    Shift As Integer, X As Single, Y As Single)

    If Button And 1 Then          ' Left button down
        X = X \ screen.TwipsPerPixelX
        Y = Y \ screen.TwipsPerPixelY

        ' Change the following two lines to one, single line:
        If (X < 0) Or (X > image2(0).Width) Or (Y < 0) Or
            (Y > image2(0).Height) Then
            image2(0).Picture = image2(1).Picture   'up
        Else
            image2(0).Picture = image2(2).Picture   'down
        End If
    End If

End Sub

' Change the following two lines to one, single line:
Sub Image2_MouseUp (Index As Integer, Button As Integer, Shift As Integer,
    X As Single, Y As Single)

   If Button And 1 Then
      MDown = False
      image2(0).Picture = image2(1).Picture  ' Up
      parent.SetFocus
   End If

End Sub

Sub Image3_Click (Index As Integer)

   ' Code for paste here
```

```
    parent.Text1.SelText = Clipboard.GetText()

End Sub

' Change the following two lines to one, single line:
Sub Image3_MouseDown (Index As Integer, Button As Integer,
    Shift As Integer, X As Single, Y As Single)

    If Button And 1 Then
        MDown = True
        image3(0).Picture = image3(2).Picture   ' Down
    End If

End Sub

' Change the following two lines to one, single line:
Sub Image3_MouseMove (Index As Integer, Button As Integer,
    Shift As Integer, X As Single, Y As Single)

    If Button And 1 Then                     ' Left button down
        X = X \ screen.TwipsPerPixelX    ' Convert to pixels
        Y = Y \ screen.TwipsPerPixelY

        ' Change the following two lines to one, single line:
        If (X < 0) Or (X > image3(0).Width) Or (Y < 0) Or
            (Y > image3(0).Height) Then

            image3(0).Picture = image3(1).Picture   'up
        Else
            image3(0).Picture = image3(2).Picture   'down
        End If
    End If

End Sub

' Change the following two lines to one, single line:
Sub Image3_MouseUp (Index As Integer, Button As Integer, Shift As Integer,
    X As Single, Y As Single)

    If Button And 1 Then
        MDown = False
        image3(0).Picture = image3(1).Picture   'up
        parent.SetFocus
    End If
```

```
End Sub

Sub InitToolbox ()
    ' This procedure initializes the toolbox with three controls.
    ' Most of this could be done at design time.

    ' Load extra image control arrays
    Load image1(1)
    Load image1(2)
    Load image2(1)
    Load image2(2)
    Load image3(1)
    Load image3(2)

    ' Load the bitmaps - CHANGE PATHS AS NEEDED!!!!!
    image1(1).Picture = LoadPicture("c:\vb\bitmaps\toolbar3\cut-up.bmp")
    image1(2).Picture = LoadPicture("c:\vb\bitmaps\toolbar3\cut-mds.bmp")
    image2(1).Picture = LoadPicture("c:\vb\bitmaps\toolbar3\copy-up.bmp")
    image2(2).Picture = LoadPicture("c:\vb\bitmaps\toolbar3\copy-mds.bmp")
    image3(1).Picture = LoadPicture("c:\vb\bitmaps\toolbar3\pste-up.bmp")
    image3(2).Picture = LoadPicture("c:\vb\bitmaps\toolbar3\pste-mds.bmp")

    image1(0).Picture = image1(1).Picture
    image2(0).Picture = image2(1).Picture
    image3(0).Picture = image3(1).Picture

    ' Position image controls:
    image1(0).Left = 2
    image2(0).Left = image1(0).Left + image1(0).Width + 1
    image3(0).Left = image2(0).Left + image2(0).Width + 1
    image1(0).Top = label1.Height + 1
    image2(0).Top = image1(0).Top
    image3(0).Top = image1(0).Top

End Sub

' Change the following two lines to one, single line:
Sub Label1_MouseDown (Button As Integer, Shift As Integer, X As Single,
    Y As Single)

    Dim mpos As POINTAPI
    Dim p As ConvertPOINTAPI
    Dim ret As Integer
```

```
    Call GetCursorPos(mpos)   ' Get the current position of the cursor
    LSet p = mpos                ' and convert it for API calls.

    ' Send buttonup to finish the impending buttondown. This line of
    ' code does invoke the Label1_MouseUp() event, so be careful what
    ' code you place there:
    ret = Sendmessage(Me.hWnd, WM_LBUTTONUP, 0, p.xy)

   ' Tell the form someone is clicking the window caption:
   ret = Sendmessage(Me.hWnd, WM_SYSCOMMAND, MOUSE_MOVE, p.xy)
   parent.SetFocus

End Sub

Sub Picture1_MouseDown (Button As Integer, Shift As Integer, X As Single,
                        Y As Single)
Dim ret As Integer

If Button And 1 Then      'if left button pressed
    MDown = True          'set flag and invert bitmap
    ret = BitBlt(picture1.hDC, 0, 0, picture1.ScaleWidth,
              picture1.ScaleHeight, picture1.hDC, 0, 0, DSTINVERT)
    InvertedImage = True  'set flag for inverted bitmap
End If

End Sub

' Change the following two lines to one, single line:
Sub Picture1_MouseMove (Button As Integer, Shift As Integer, X As Single,
   Y As Single)

   Dim ret As Integer   ' Hold return value of BitBlt

   If MDown Then
      ' If left button is down, locate where mouse is:
      ' Change the following two lines to one, single line:
      If (X < picture1.ScaleLeft) Or (X >= picture1.ScaleWidth) Or
         (Y < picture1.ScaleTop) Or (Y >= picture1.ScaleHeight) Then

         ' Outside picturebox, make sure image is normal:
         If InvertedImage Then
            picture1.Refresh
            InvertedImage = False
```

```
            End If
        Else
            ' Inside picturebox, make sure image is inverted:
            If Not InvertedImage Then
                ' Change the following two lines to one, single line:
                ret = BitBlt(picture1.hDC, 0, 0, picture1.ScaleWidth,
                    picture1.ScaleHeight, picture1.hDC, 0, 0, DSTINVERT)
                InvertedImage = True
            End If
        End If
    End If

End Sub

' Change the following two lines to one, single line:
Sub Picture1_MouseUp (Button As Integer, Shift As Integer, X As Single,
    Y As Single)

    If (Button And 1) Then           ' If left mouse
        MDown = False                  ' Clear flag
        picture1.Refresh              ' Refresh image
        If InvertedImage Then         ' If over image
            InvertedImage = False     ' Clear flag
            Me.Hide                   ' Hide toolbar - faster loading next time
        End If
    End If
    parent.SetFocus

End Sub
```

The following is a text dump of the PARENT form. It includes the form and control description as well as necessary Function and Sub procedures. Save the code in a single TEXT file called PARENT.FRM, and you will be able to load it as a form in Visual Basic.

```
VERSION 2.00
Begin Form Parent
   Caption         =   "Form2"
   ClientHeight    =   2724
   ClientLeft      =   1320
   ClientTop       =   1608
```

```
    ClientWidth     =   3816
    Height          =   3144
    Left            =   1272
    LinkTopic       =   "Form2"
    ScaleHeight     =   2724
    ScaleWidth      =   3816
    Top             =   1236
    Width           =   3912
    Begin CommandButton Command1
        Caption         =   "Show Toolbar"
        Height          =   372
        Left            =   840
        TabIndex        =   1
        Top             =   2160
        Width           =   1932
    End
    Begin TextBox Text1
        Height          =   1932
        HideSelection   =   0   'False
        Left            =   240
        MultiLine       =   -1  'True
        TabIndex        =   0
        Text            =   "Text1"
        Top             =   120
        Width           =   3252
    End
End

Sub Command1_Click ()
    Toolbar.Show
End Sub

Sub Form_Load ()
    Me.Caption = "Toolbar Sample"
End Sub

Sub Form_QueryUnload (Cancel As Integer, UnloadMode As Integer)
    If ToolbarLoaded Then
        Unload Toolbar
    End If
End Sub
```

HOW TO CREATE AND RUN THE PROGRAM

1. Start a new project in Visual Basic. Form1 is created by default.
2. From the File menu, choose Remove File to remove Form1.
3. From the File menu, choose Add File, and add TOOLBAR.BAS.
4. Repeat step 3 to add TOOLBAR.FRM and PARENT.FRM to the project.
5. From the Options menu, choose Project, and set Start Up Form to Parent.
6. Run the application.

The example allows the user to choose three clipboard operations (cut, copy, and paste) from the toolbar. These operations are available by default in a standard Visual Basic text box control but were chosen to demonstrate the functionality of the floating toolbar.

How do I create a modeless dialog box or form in Visual Basic?

The information in this article applies to all editions of Visual Basic after version 2.0.

Summary

This article contains information on how to create a modeless dialog box or form in Visual Basic. An example of a modeless dialog box is the toolbar in Microsoft Excel version 5.0 and Word version 6.0. A modeless form always displays on top of the parent form but is not bounded by the parent form, nor does it stay on top of all other applications as does SetWindowPos and HWND_TOPMOST.

For additional information on SetWindowPos, please see the following article in the Microsoft Knowledge Base: ARTICLE-ID: Q84251 TITLE: How to Create a Topmost or Floating Window in Visual Basic.

The Windows API SetWindowWord( ) is used with the value GWW_HWNDPARENT to change the parent of the form that you want to be a modeless dialog box. SetWindowWord( ) returns the original parent's window handle that you need to restore when the form is unloaded to avoid a General Protection Fault.

Step-by-Step Example

1. Start a new project in Visual Basic. Form1 is created by default.
2. Add a second form (Form2) to the project.
3. Add the following code to the Form_Load event for Form1:

```
Sub Form_Load()
   Form2.Show      'display the child form
   Form1.Caption = "Parent"
   Form2.Caption = "Child"
End Sub
```

4. Add the following declarations to the general section of Form2:

```
' Enter the following Declare statement as one, single line:
Declare Function SetWindowWord Lib "User" (ByVal hwnd As Integer,
   ByVal Index As Integer, ByVal wNewWord As Integer) As Integer
Const GWW_HWNDPARENT = (-8)
Dim OriginalParenthWnd As Integer
```

5. Add the following code to the Form_Load event of Form2:

```
Sub Form_Load()
 ' Set parent for the toolbar to display on top of:
 OriginalParenthWnd = SetWindowWord(Me.hWnd, GWW_HWNDPARENT, Form1.hWnd)
 Me.Width = Form1.Width \ 3      ' Scale child form
 Me.Height = Form1.Height \ 3
End Sub
```

6. Add the following code to the Form_Unload event of Form2:

```
Sub Form_Unload()
  Dim ret As Integer
  ' Return the original parent handle to avoid a GP Fault
  ret = SetWindowWord(Me.hWnd, GWW_HWNDPARENT, _
OriginalParenthWnd)
End Sub
```

7. Press the F5 key to run the program. The child form is displayed as a modeless dialog box of the parent form.

How do I bind data controls across multiple forms in Visual Basic 4.0?

The information in this article applies to all versions of Microsoft Visual Basic for Windows, version 4.0.

Summary

The information in this article shows you how to bind two Data Controls on separate forms and have the bound controls updated to scroll through the same recordset.

note: *With Microsoft Visual Basic version 4.0, you can now assign or set the RecordSet property of a Data Control to any other recordset, including an existing Dynaset, Snapshot, or Table object. In addition, you can update the bound fields of the Data Control to reflect changes in the recordset. This allows all bound fields on all open forms to scroll through the same recordset.*

Step-by-Step Example

1. In Visual Basic, start a new project (ALT, F, N). Form1 is created by default.
2. Add a data control (Data1) and two text boxes (text1 and text2) to Form1.

3. Using the following table as a guide, set the properties of the controls on Form1:

Control	Property	Value
Data1	DatabaseName	BIBLIO.MDB
Data1	RecordSource	Titles
Text1	DataSource	Data1
Text1	DataField	Title
Text2	DataSource	Data1
Text2	DataField	Year Published

4. Add the following code to the Load( ) event of Form1:

```
Sub Form1_Load()
        Data1.Refresh  ' Data control must be refreshed before showing
                       ' form2.
        Form2.Show     ' Load second form that refers to data control on
                       ' this form.
    End Sub
```

5. Add a second form to the project (ALT, I, F). Form2 is created by default. Add a data control (Data1) and two text boxes (Text1 and Text2) to Form2.

6. Using the following table as a guide, set the properties of the controls on Form2:

Control	Property	Value
Text1	DataSource	Data1
Text2	DataSource	Data1

7. Add the following code to the Form_Load event of Form2:

```
Sub Form_Load ()
    Text1.DataField = "Subject"    ' Assign the bound field values.
    Text2.DataField = "Comments"
    Set Data1.Recordset = Form1.Data1.Recordset   ' This is the key.
End Sub
```

8. Press the F5 key to run the program. The two forms should display on the screen. When you click either Data Control to scroll through the recordset, the bound fields on both forms will scroll at the same time.

What are the differences between exclamation mark (!) and dot (.) syntax?

The information in this article applies to all editions of Microsoft Visual Basic for Windows, version 4.0.

Summary

In Visual Basic 4.0, the exclamation mark (!) syntax is for collection lookup, and the dot (.) syntax is for properties and methods. However, a control can be accessed as a property, and Visual Basic has a Controls collection on a form. Because the Controls collection is the default property of a form, you can access a control from a form by using the exclamation mark (!) syntax.

More Information

To obtain direct access to the Ctrl1 property on the form, type this:

```
Form1.Ctrl1.Text = "Hello"
```

This line:

```
Form1!Ctrl1.Text = "Hello"
```

translates into this code:

```
Form1.Controls.Item("Ctrl1").Text = "Hello"
```

Visual Basic for Applications has a specific optimization for forms that allows the compiler to translate this syntax:

```
Form1!Ctrl1.Text = "Hello"
```

into this code:

```
Form1.Ctrl1.Text = "Hello"
```

Therefore the performance of the two statements should be identical. Note that this optimization is specific to controls on Visual Basic 4.0 forms. It will not work with any other collection.

caution: *This optimization may not occur in future versions of Visual Basic forms.*

note: *Although the documentation in version 3.0 states that the FormName.Control syntax might be replaced in future versions by the FormName!Control syntax, the possibility of this really happening is unlikely. The FormName!Control syntax is slightly slower, so for performance reasons the dot syntax will remain.*

The following steps will reproduce this behavior in Visual Basic 4.0:

1. Create a new project and add a command button to Form1.
2. Double-click Form1 to edit the Form_Load event and type:

```
Form1!Command1.Caption = "Test"
Form1.Command1.Caption = "It Works!"
```

3. Run the project, and notice how both methods work.

How do I determine whether Visual Basic 4.0 App was launched as an OLE server?

The information in this article applies to all editions of Microsoft Visual Basic for Windows, version 4.0.

Summary

This article describes how to use the StartMode property of the Visual Basic App object to determine whether an application started as a stand-alone project or as an OLE Automation object application.

More Information

If the StartMode property has a value of vbSModeStandalone (or 0), it means that the application started as a stand-alone project. That is, the user started the .EXE from File Manager or by double-clicking the icon from Program Manager. If the StartMode property has a value of vbSModeAutomation (or 1), it means that the application started as an OLE Automation object application. That is, the .EXE started because an OLE Automation client called CreateObject. These constants are listed in the Visual Basic object library in the Object Browser. At design time, you can debug an application as if it were started as an OLE Automation object application. To do this, set StartMode in the Project Options dialog box to 1 (vbSModeAutomation) by selecting the OLEServer option button. But a project's actual StartMode setting is determined by how that application is started at run time, not by its nominal setting in the Project Options dialog box when you create an executable (.EXE) file. When StartMode is set to 1 and there are no public classes in the project, you must use the End statement or choose End from the Run menu or toolbar to end the application. If you choose Close from the Control menu, the form closes but the project is still running.

Step-by-Step Example

1. Start a new project in Visual Basic. Form1 is created by default.
2. Add a new Module to the project by choosing Module from the Insert menu. Module1 is created by default.
3. Copy the following code and paste it into the General Declarations portion of Module1:

```
Public Sub main()
   If App.StartMode = vbSModeStandalone Then
      MsgBox "Application being started as a stand alone EXE!"
   Else
      MsgBox "Application being started as an OLE Automation server!"
   End If
End Sub
```

4. In the Project Options dialog box (choose Options from the Tools menu and then select the Project tab), choose Sub Main as the startup form and choose OLEServer as the start mode.
5. Press the F5 key to run the program. A message box will tell you that the application was started as an OLE Automation server.

How do I determine when a shelled 32-bit process has terminated?

The information in this article applies to all 32-bit versions of Microsoft Visual Basic for Windows, version 4.0.

Summary

Executing the Shell( ) function in a Visual Basic for Windows program starts another executable program asynchronously and returns control to the Visual Basic application. This shelled program continues to run independently of your application until the user closes it. However, if your Visual Basic application needs to wait for the shelled process to terminate, you could use the Windows API to poll the status of the application, but this is not a very efficient process. This article shows by example how to use a better process. There is a completely different process that would be used to accomplish the same thing from a 16-bit application. For additional information on the 16-bit implementation, please see the following question.

More Information

The Win32 API has integrated functionality that enables your application to wait until a shelled process has completed. To use these functions, you need a handle to the shelled process. To accomplish this, you use the CreateProcess( ) function instead of the Shell( ) function to begin your shelled program.

- **Creating the Shelled Process** In a 32-bit application, you need to create an addressable process. To do this, use the CreateProcess( ) function to start your shelled application. The CreateProcess( ) function gives your program the process handle of the shelled process via one of its passed parameters.

- **Waiting for the Shelled Process to Terminate** Having used CreateProcess( ) to get a process handle, you can pass that handle to the WaitForSingleObject( ) function. This causes your Visual Basic application to suspend execution until the shelled process terminates.

Step-by-Step Example

The steps given here build a Visual Basic for Windows program that uses the CreateProcess( ) function to execute the Windows Notepad (NOTEPAD.EXE) application. This code shows by example how to use the Windows API CreateProcess( ) and WaitForSingleObject( ) functions to wait until a shelled process terminates before resuming execution. The syntax of the CreateProcess( ) function is extremely complicated, so in the example code, it is encapsulated into a function called ExecCmd( ). ExecCmd( ) takes one parameter, the command line of the application to execute.

1. Start a new project in Visual Basic. Form1 is created by default.
2. Add the following code to the General Declarations section of Form1:

```
Private Type STARTUPINFO
   cb As Long
   lpReserved As String
   lpDesktop As String
   lpTitle As String
   dwX As Long
   dwY As Long
   dwXSize As Long
   dwYSize As Long
   dwXCountChars As Long
   dwYCountChars As Long
   dwFillAttribute As Long
   dwFlags As Long
   wShowWindow As Integer
   cbReserved2 As Integer
   lpReserved2 As Long
   hStdInput As Long
   hStdOutput As Long
   hStdError As Long
End Type
Private Type PROCESS_INFORMATION
   hProcess As Long
```

```
    hThread As Long
    dwProcessID As Long
    dwThreadID As Long
End Type
Private Declare Function WaitForSingleObject Lib "kernel32" (ByVal _
    hHandle As Long, ByVal dwMilliseconds As Long) As Long
Private Declare Function CreateProcessA Lib "kernel32" (ByVal _
    lpApplicationName As Long, ByVal lpCommandLine As String, ByVal _
    lpProcessAttributes As Long, ByVal lpThreadAttributes As Long, _
    ByVal bInheritHandles As Long, ByVal dwCreationFlags As Long, _
    ByVal lpEnvironment As Long, ByVal lpCurrentDirectory As Long, _
    lpStartupInfo As STARTUPINFO, lpProcessInformation As _
    PROCESS_INFORMATION) As Long
Private Declare Function CloseHandle Lib "kernel32" (ByVal _
    hObject As Long) As Long
Private Const NORMAL_PRIORITY_CLASS = &H20&
Private Const INFINITE = -1&
Public Sub ExecCmd(cmdline$)
    Dim proc As PROCESS_INFORMATION
    Dim start As STARTUPINFO
    ' Initialize the STARTUPINFO structure:
    start.cb = Len(start)
    ' Start the shelled application:
    ret& = CreateProcessA(0&, cmdline$, 0&, 0&, 1&, _
        NORMAL_PRIORITY_CLASS, 0&, 0&, start, proc)
    ' Wait for the shelled application to finish:
    ret& = WaitForSingleObject(proc.hProcess, INFINITE)
    ret& = CloseHandle(proc.hProcess)
End Sub
```

3. Add the following code to the Form_Click( ) event procedure of Form1:

```
Sub Form_Click ()
   ExecCmd "notepad.exe"
   MsgBox "Process Finished"
End Sub
```

4. Press the F5 key to run the application.

5. Using the mouse, click the Form1 window. At this point the Notepad application is shelled.

note: *The MsgBox statement following the ExecCmd( ) subroutine is not executed because the WaitForSingleObject( ) function prevents it. The message box does not appear until Notepad is closed when the user chooses Exit from Notepad's File menu (ALT F, X).*

How do I determine when a shelled 16-bit process has terminated?

Executing the shell function in the 16-bit version of a Visual Basic 4.0 program asynchronously starts another executable program and returns control to the Visual Basic application. The shelled program continues to run indefinitely until the user closes it, not when your Visual Basic program terminates. However, your program can wait until the shelled program has finished by polling the return value of the Windows API function GetModuleUsage. The following text describes the method and provides a code example.

Using the Windows API function GetModuleUsage, your program can monitor the status of a shelled process. The return value from the Shell function can be used to call GetModuleUsage continuously within a loop to poll whether or not the shelled program has finished executing. If the Shell( ) function is successful, the return value is the instance handle for the shelled program. This instance handle can be passed to GetModuleUsage, to determine the reference count for the module. When GetModuleUsage returns a value of 0 or less, the application has finished its execution.

Regardless of the WindowStyle used to shell the program, this algorithm works correctly. In addition, this method does work under the following situations:

- Shelling to Windows programs
- Shelling to MS-DOS programs
- Shelling to applications that do not display a window

Here are the steps necessary to build a 16-bit Visual Basic 4.0 program that uses the Shell( ) function to execute the Windows Notepad accessory. The program is an example of how to use the Windows API function Get-ModuleUsage to wait until a shelled process has terminated before resuming execution.

1. Run the 16-bit version of Visual Basic 4.0 under Windows 3.X. Form1 is created by default.
2. Add the following code to the General Declarations section of Form1:

```
Declare Function GetModuleUsage% Lib "Kernel" (ByVal hModule%)
```

3. Add the following code to the Form_Click event procedure of Form1:

```
Sub Form_Click ()
 x% = Shell("notepad.exe") ' Modify path as needed.
 While GetModuleUsage(x%) > 0 ' Has Shelled program finished?
 z% = DoEvents()  ' If not, yield to Windows.
 Wend
 MsgBox "Shelled application just terminated", 64
End Sub
```

4. From the Run menu, select Start (ALT R, S) to run the program.
5. With the mouse, click on Form1. The Notepad application is shelled.

The MsgBox statement following the Shell( ) function is not executed, as it would normally be without the While loop above it. The message box does not appear until Notepad is closed by choosing Exit from its File menu (ALT F, X).

How do I launch a Win32 application from Visual Basic?

The information in this article applies to all editions of Microsoft Visual Basic for Windows, version 4.0.

Summary

A Windows application can consist of more than one process, and a process can consist of more than one thread. The Microsoft Win32 API supports multitasking, which creates the effect of simultaneous execution of multiple processes and threads. This article describes processes and threads, and explains how to create and use them with a step-by-step example.

More Information

A process is a program that is loaded into memory and prepared for execution. Each process has a private virtual address space. A process consists of the code, data, and other system resources such as files, pipes, and synchronization objects that are accessible to the threads of the process. Each process is started with a single thread, but additional, independently executing threads can be created. A thread can execute any part of the program's code, including a part executed by another thread. Threads are the basic entity to which the operating system allocates CPU time. Each thread maintains a set of structures for saving its context while waiting to be scheduled for processing time. The context includes the thread's set of machine registers, the kernel stack, a thread environment block, and a user stack in the address space of the thread's process. All threads of a process share the virtual address space and can access the global variables and system resources of the process. A multitasking operating system divides the available CPU time among the threads that need it.

In Windows, the Win32 API is designed for preemptive multitasking; this means that the system allocates small slices of CPU time among the competing threads. The currently executing thread is suspended when its time slice elapses, allowing another thread to run. When the system switches from one thread to another, it saves the context of the suspended thread and restores the saved context of the next thread in the queue. Because each time slice is small (approximately 20 milliseconds), it appears that multiple threads are executing at the same time. This is actually the case on multiprocessor systems where the executable threads are distributed among the available processors. On a single processor system, however, using multiple threads does not result in more instructions being executed. In fact, the system can slow down if it is forced to keep track of too many threads.

How to Launch Win32 Applications from Visual Basic

There are two ways to launch another Win32 application from a Microsoft Visual Basic 4.0 application:

- Use the Visual Basic shell command. This spawns a new process and returns its process ID.

However, to be able to do anything useful, a process handle is required, which can be obtained by a subsequent call to the OpenProcess Win32 API function.

- Use the CreateProcess Win32 API function that creates both a process object and a main thread object.

In this case both the process and the initial thread are assigned a 32-bit identifier that remains valid until the respective object (process or thread) terminates. The 32-bit identifier can be used to identify the object uniquely within the system. The new process and new thread handles are also created with full access rights. All four values are returned in the PROCESS_INFORMATION structure that is passed by reference to CreateProcess. The process handle returned by either of the two methods can then be used with other Win32 APIs, such as TerminateProcess, to manipulate the newly launched application. It is important to understand that at creation time, the system gives each object an initial usage count of one. Then, just before CreateProcess returns, the function opens both the process and the thread object and places the process-relative handles for each in the hProcess and hThread members of the PROCESS_INFORMATION structure. When CreateProcess opens these objects, the usage count for each increments to two. This means that before the Windows NT Executive can free the process object, the process must terminate (decrementing the usage count to one), and the parent process must call CloseHandle (decrementing the usage count to zero). To free the thread object, the thread must terminate and the parent process must close the handle to the thread object.

caution: *It is very important to close these handles. Failure to do so can result in a system memory leak because some Windows NT Executive objects are never destroyed.*

Similar considerations are required when obtaining a process handle with OpenProcess. In this case too, the usage count is incremented by one, and unless the handle is closed, the process object will remain in memory even when the process itself has terminated.

Step-by-Step Example

1. Start a new project in Visual Basic. Form1 is created by default.
2. Add the following code to the General Declarations section of Form1:

```
Private Type PROCESS_INFORMATION
   hProcess As Long
```

```
    hThread As Long
    dwProcessId As Long
    dwThreadId As Long
End Type
Private Type STARTUPINFO
    cb As Long
    lpReserved As String
    lpDesktop As String
    lpTitle As String
    dwX As Long
    dwY As Long
    dwXSize As Long
    dwYSize As Long
    dwXCountChars As Long
    dwYCountChars As Long
    dwFillAttribute As Long
    dwFlags As Long
    wShowWindow As Integer
    cbReserved2 As Integer
    lpReserved2 As Long
    hStdInput As Long
    hStdOutput As Long
    hStdError As Long
End Type
Private Declare Function CreateProcess Lib "kernel32" Alias _
    "CreateProcessA" (ByVal lpApplicationName As String, ByVal _
    lpCommandLine As String, lpProcessAttributes As Any, _
    lpThreadAttributes As Any, ByVal bInheritHandles As Long, _
    ByVal dwCreationFlags As Long, lpEnvironment As Any, ByVal _
    lpCurrentDirectory As String, lpStartupInfo As STARTUPINFO,_
    lpProcessInformation As PROCESS_INFORMATION) As Long
Private Declare Function OpenProcess Lib "kernel32.dll" (ByVal _
    dwAccess As Long, ByVal fInherit As Integer, ByVal hObject _
    As Long) As Long
Private Declare Function TerminateProcess Lib "kernel32" (ByVal _
    hProcess As Long, ByVal uExitCode As Long) As Long
Private Declare Function CloseHandle Lib "kernel32" (ByVal _
    hObject As Long) As Long
Const SYNCHRONIZE = 1048576
Const NORMAL_PRIORITY_CLASS = &H20&
```

3. Add the following code to the Form1_Click event:

```
Dim pInfo As PROCESS_INFORMATION
Dim sInfo As STARTUPINFO
Dim sNull As String
sInfo.cb = Len(sInfo)
success& = CreateProcess(sNull, "Calc.exe", ByVal 0&, ByVal 0&, _
   1&, NORMAL_PRIORITY_CLASS, ByVal 0&, sNull, sInfo, pInfo)
' ProcessID& = Shell("Calc.exe", vbNormalFocus)
' ProcessHandle& = OpenProcess(SYNCHRONIZE, True, ProcessID&)
MsgBox "Calculator has been launched!"
ret& = TerminateProcess(pInfo.hProcess, 0&)
ret& = CloseHandle(pInfo.hThread)
ret& = CloseHandle(pInfo.hProcess)
' ret& = TerminateProcess(ProcessHandle&, 0&)
' ret& = CloseHandle(ProcessHandle&)
' ret& = CloseHandle(ProcessHandle&)
MsgBox "Calculator has terminated!"
```

4. Press the F5 key to run the program. Click Form1. The Windows Calculator program launches, and a message tells you so. When you click the OK button on the MsgBox, the Calculator program terminates, and another message tells you so.

note: *To see how this method works using the Shell and OpenProcess method, change the commented code into executed code and change the rest of the code into comments except for the two MsgBox statements.*

How do I create and use a minimal OLE Automation server?

The information in this article applies to all versions of Microsoft Visual Basic for Windows, version 4.0.

Summary

Visual Basic 4.0 introduces the powerful new ability to create OLE Automation servers. This article shows you, step by step, how to create a minimal OLE Automation server and use it from a minimal OLE Client. This article does not exercise the full functionality of OLE servers. It is intended to help you write your first OLE Automation server.

Step-by-Step Example

PHASE ONE—CREATE THE SERVER

1. Start a new project in Visual Basic. Form1 is created by default.
2. From the File menu, choose Remove File to remove Form1.
3. From the Insert menu, add a Module (Module1) and a Class Module (Class1) to your project.
4. Type the following code in the General Declarations section of Module1:

```
Sub Main ()
```

note: *End Sub will be added automatically for you.*

5. Add the following code to the General Declarations section of Class1:

```
Public MyString As String
Public Function MyFunction() As String
   MyFunction = "You never know what you're gonna get."
End Function
```

6. Add the following code to the Class_Initialize event of Class1:

```
Public Sub Class_Initialize()
   MyString = "Life is like a box of chocolates."
End Sub
```

7. In the Properties window for Class1, set the following properties:

Property	Value
Instancing	2 - Creatable MultiUse
Public	True

8. From the Tools menu, choose Options. In the StartMode group of the Project tab, choose OLEServer. You now have a complete (though limited) OLE Automation server. You can choose Make EXE to make an .EXE file that you can run later, or you can choose Make DLL to make an in-process OLE server. Now you're ready to automate your server.
9. Start the program by choosing Start from the Run menu or by pressing the F5 key.
10. Minimize Visual Basic.

PHASE TWO—CREATE A CLIENT TO ACCESS THE SERVER

1. Start a second copy of Visual Basic. A new project (Project1) with a default form (Form1) is created.
2. Add the following code to the appropriate events of Form1:

```
' In the General Declarations section:
Private MyObj As Object
Private Sub Form_Load ()
   Set MyObj = CreateObject("Project1.Class1")
End Sub
Private Sub Form_Click()
   Print MyObj.MyString
   Print MyObj.MyFunction
End Sub
Private Sub Form_Unload ()
   Set MyObj = Nothing
End Sub
```

3. Start the program by choosing Start from the Run menu or by pressing the F5 key.
4. Click Form1. You'll see this output:

```
Life is like a box of chocolates.
You never know what you're gonna get.
```

When Form1 loads, it instantiates one copy of your OLE Automation server. On the click, it makes two OLE calls, one to retrieve the value of the MyString public variable and one to invoke the MyFunction public function. When

Form1 unloads, it destroys its created instance of the OLE Automation server. If this is the last instance in memory, the server process is removed from memory as well.

How do I optimize OLE calls in Visual Basic 4.0?

The information in this article applies to all editions of Microsoft Visual Basic for Windows, version 4.0.

Summary

Because Visual Basic 4.0 makes extensive use of OLE, the correct use of object references can be crucial to the performance of a Visual Basic application. This article suggests some optimizations that can be included at design time.

More Information

note: *First, you should read Chapter 26, "Optimizing Your Application for Size and Speed," in the Visual Basic Programmer's Guide. This chapter lays out in detail many of the most useful size and speed optimizations.*

- **Use the Most Specific Object Available** In Visual Basic, accessing any object model typically requires the repeated use of the Object.Property syntax. This chain of references can get quite long:

  DBEngine.Workspaces(0).Databases(0).RecordSet.Fields(0).Name

  Each dot (.) in this sequence represents an OLE lookup that is required in order for Visual Basic to access the next element. If you put a statement like this into a loop, it can generate a large number of needless lookups:

```
' Assume Fields.Count = 10
For I% = 0 To DBEngine.WorkSpaces(0).Database._
   RecordSet.Fields.Count - 1
      ' Five dots.
      Print DBEngine.WorkSpaces(0).Database.RecordSet.Fields(I%).Name
```

```
        ' Five Dots.
Next
' This loop generates OLE calls for each dot (.)
' in the Print statement
' on each iteration of the loop.
```

By using the most specific object type available, you can reduce the overhead of this same loop significantly, as in this example:

```
Dim X As Fields
Dim F As Field
' Object binding takes place at compile time.
Set X = DBEngine.WorkSpaces(0).Database.RecordSet.Fields(0)
' Four dots, executed only once.
For Each F In X
   Print F.Name
   ' One OLE call.
Next
```

- **Take Advantage of With Statement Blocks to Reduce Repeat References** To set multiple properties of a single object, you can use With...EndWith to reduce the number of times the chain of references is invoked to set your properties. In this case, you don't even need a temporary object of the object type defined. This set of assignments

```
DBEngine.WorkSpaces(0).Database.RecordSet.Fields(0).Name = "NYSE"
DBEngine.WorkSpaces(0).Database.RecordSet.Fields(0).Required = True
DBEngine.WorkSpaces(0).Database.RecordSet.Fields(0).Size = 10
DBEngine.WorkSpaces(0).Database.RecordSet.Fields(0).Type = dbText
DBEngine.WorkSpaces(0).Database.RecordSet.Fields(0).Value = "MSFT"
```

can be optimized by reducing the dot references using the With statement:

```
With DBEngine.WorkSpaces(0).Database.RecordSet.Fields(0)
   .Name = "NYSE"
   .Required = True
   .Size = 10
   .Type = dbText
   .Value = "MSFT"
End With
```

This reduces the number of OLE object lookups that must be done to execute the assignments.

- **Minimize Cross-Process OLE Calls** OLE Automation calls to objects within your program are always faster than cross-process calls (for example, Visual Basic for Windows automating Microsoft Excel). If processing can be done within your program, it may be faster than calling another application. If you do cross-process OLE Automation, an object that is hard-typed (Dim X As Specific Type) rather than "As Object" can cut the overhead significantly because only one cross-process call is needed. Follow the preceding suggestions about using With statements and specific objects.
- **Use In-Process Instead of Out-of-Process OLE Servers** In-process OLE servers (OLE servers created using the Make DLL menu option) are significantly faster than out-of-process OLE servers (OLE servers created using the Make EXE menu option).
- **Use Server-Side Macros to Reduce Cross-Process Calls** Macro functions created on the server side (for example, a WordBasic macro created in Word and called from Visual Basic) require only a single cross-process call but can perform multiple operations. This speeds up the total execution time.

How do I register OLE Controls?

The information in this article applies to all editions of Microsoft Visual Basic for Windows, version 4.0.

Summary

OLE Controls (.OCX files) are OLE servers, so they must be listed in the registry. Visual Basic 4.0 applications require an installation process to ensure that the necessary items are properly registered. During the setup process, if an OLE Control is needed and not registered, Visual Basic uses the autoregistration facility to automatically register an OLE Control by searching along the normal DLL search path for a file with the OLE Control name. This is done both in the design environment and for built executables. If the OLE Control is properly registered by other means, it need not be on the DLL search path. If

Visual Basic 4.0 does not reside on a computer, any Visual Basic 4.0 application targeted to be run on that computer must be installed through the setup process. It cannot simply be copied.

More Information

The DLL search path for 16-bit Windows is

1. The current directory.
2. The Windows directory.
3. The Windows system directory.
4. The directory containing the executable file for the current task.
5. The directories listed in the PATH environment variable.
6. The list of directories mapped in a network.

Under 32-bit Windows, the DLL search path is:

1. The directory from which the application loaded.
2. The current directory.
3. The 32-bit Windows system directory.
4. The 16-bit Windows system directory.
5. The Windows directory.
6. The directories that are listed in the PATH environment variable.

How do I create scrollable viewports in Visual Basic?

The information in this article applies to all editions of Microsoft Visual Basic for Windows from version 2.0 on.

Summary

You can create scrollable viewports in Visual Basic by using standard Basic calls. The viewports can include bitmaps, graphics, or other controls.

More Information

To create a scrollable picture with clipping, you must have two picture controls. The first picture control is called the stationary parent picture control. Within the parent picture control, you need to create a movable child picture control. It is the child picture control that will be moved within the parent picture control. Moving the child picture within the parent picture control creates the clipping effect. During run time when you move the child picture, it will be clipped by the boundaries of the parent picture. To create these two picture controls, do the following:

1. Choose the picture box control from the Toolbox window in Visual Basic.
2. Draw a picture on the form. This is the parent picture.
3. Again choose the picture box control from the Toolbox window.

Draw the second picture on top of and within the boundaries of the first picture control. This is the child picture.

1. Optional: If you want the viewport to resize when the user changes the form size, then add the following code to the form's resize event:

```
Sub Form_Resize ()
   ' When the form size is changed, the Picture1 dimensions are changed
   ' to match.
   Picture1.Height = form1.Height
   Picture1.Width = form1.Width
   ' Re-Initializes picture positions & scroll bars.
   Picture1.Move 0, 0, Scalewidth - Vscroll1.Width, scaleheight -
Hscroll1.Height
   Picture2.Move 0, 0
   Hscroll1.Top = Picture1.Height
   Hscroll1.Left = 0
   Hscroll1.Width = Picture1.Width
   Vscroll1.Top = 0
   Vscroll1.Left = Picture1.Width
   Vscroll1.Height = Picture1.Height
   Hscroll1.Max = Picture2.Width - Picture1.Width
   Vscroll1.Max = Picture2.Height - Picture1.Height
   ' Checks to see if scroll bars  are needed
```

```
        VScroll1.Visible = (Picture1.Height < Picture2.Height)
        HScroll1.Visible = (Picture1.Width < Picture2.Width)
    End Sub
```

The sample application given here shows how to create a scrollable bitmap within a viewport. Perform the sequence just shown to create a parent/child picture control. Add a horizontal scroll bar and a vertical scroll bar to the form. Make sure that the path to your bitmap is correct. Several of the properties are set during run time, which could have been set during design time as well. Moving the thumb of the two scroll bars will move the child picture within the parent picture. The handle (upper-left corner of the picture) to the child picture will be located either at (0,0) of the parent picture or to the left and/or right of the parent picture. Because the clipping region is that of the parent picture, the child picture will appear to move across the parent picture viewport.

Add the following code to the appropriate event procedures:

```
Sub Form_Load ()
   Const PIXEL = 3
   Add the following constant only in Visual Basic 1.0:
   '  Const TRUE = -1
   Const NONE = 0
   ' Set design properties, included here for simplicity.
   Form1.ScaleMode = PIXEL
   Picture1.ScaleMode = PIXEL
   ' AutoSize is set to TRUE so that the boundaries of
   ' Picture2 are expanded to the size of the actual bitmap.
   Picture2.AutoSize = TRUE
   ' Get rid of annoying borders.
   Picture1.BorderStyle = NONE
   Picture2.BorderStyle = NONE
   ' Load the picture that you want to display.
   Picture2.Picture = LoadPicture("c:\win\party.bmp")
   ' Initialize location of both pictures.
   Picture1.Move 0, 0, ScaleWidth - VScroll1.Width,_
   ScaleHeight - HScroll1.Height
   Picture2.Move 0, 0
   ' Position the horizontal scroll bar.
   HScroll1.Top = Picture1.Height
   HScroll1.Left = 0
   HScroll1.Width = Picture1.Width
   ' Position the vertical scroll bar.
   VScroll1.Top = 0
   VScroll1.Left = Picture1.Width
```

```
    VScroll1.Height = Picture1.Height
    ' Set the Max value for the scroll bars.
    HScroll1.Max = Picture2.Width - Picture1.Width
    VScroll1.Max = Picture2.Height - Picture1.Height
    ' Determine if child picture will fill up screen.
    ' If so, then there is no need to use scroll bars.
    VScroll1.Visible = (Picture1.Height < Picture2.Height)
    HScroll1.Visible = (Picture1.Width < Picture2.Width)
End Sub
Sub HScroll1_Change ()
   ' Picture2.Left is set to the negative of the value because
   ' as you scroll the scroll bar to the right, the display
   ' should move to the Left, showing more of the right
   ' of the display, and vice versa when scrolling to the
   ' left.
    Picture2.Left = -HScroll1.Value
End Sub
Sub VScroll1_Change ()
   ' Picture2.Top is set to the negative of the value because
   ' as you scroll the scroll bar down, the display
   ' should move up, showing more of the bottom
   ' of the display, and vice versa when scrolling up.
   Picture2.Top = -VScroll1.Value

End Sub
```

How can I get Windows 95 Logo certification for my application?

The *official* set of technical criteria for the Windows 95 Logo is published and maintained by the Microsoft Windows Logo Department. These criteria will be updated from time to time as needed to clarify frequent questions on the interpretation of these criteria. The most up-to-date version of these criteria will be kept on the WinNews forums on CompuServe, America OnLine, Genie, ftp.microsoft.com, Prodigy, and available by Phone-Fax service at (206) 635-2222 as Doc #136. Logo questions may be e-mailed to

winlogo@microsoft.com

Appendix C

Visual Basic on the Internet

SINCE the previous edition of this book, the Internet has grown tremendously—and so, of course, has the amount of information you can find there about Visual Basic. There are four USENET newsgroups devoted to Visual Basic:

- comp.lang.basic.visual.3rdparty
- comp.lang.basic.visual.announce
- comp.lang.basic.visual.database
- comp.lang.basic.visual.misc

These USENET groups allow you to post questions that literally tens of thousands of people look at. Chances are that someone, somewhere will have an answer to your question. However, before posting a USENET question, it is important that you become familiar with the "FAQ" (Frequently Asked Questions) about that topic. (People who ask questions when the answer can be found in the FAQ will often get dismissed as being a "clueless newbie" and may have less luck with future queries.)

With the kind permission of Jan Haugland (jan.haugland@uib.no), the current maintainer of the Visual Basic FAQ, we have included answers to the questions that seem most relevant to the readers of this book. We have made only minor formatting changes. (Although we couldn't resist an occasional editorial comment or cross-reference.) We have given a list of all the questions that are currently in the FAQ.

note: *See question A2 for where to find the full FAQ, and see Appendix B for Microsoft's description of its Internet resources. Question B4 of the FAQ (reproduced here) is also relevant.*

What follows are the FAQ questions as numbered in the Aug 22 FAQ. We place a [###] after the questions whose answers we do not reproduce here. (Editorial comments are in italics.)

A. Preface

1. About this document
2. Where to get the VB/Win FAQ
3. Kudos & comments

B. General Visual Basic Questions

1. Does VB/Win make standalone .EXE files?
2. What is the current version of Visual Basic for Windows? [###] *(Version 4 of course!)*
3. Where can I get updated VB and other Microsoft files?
4. Help! I am lost on ftp.microsoft.com, what do I do?
5. Where can I get good up-to-date information about VB? *(Well, other than this book :-))*
6. Are there any WWW pages for VB?
7. Are there any examples of commercial applications built using Visual Basic?
8. What are the limits of VB? [###] *(See Appendix D of the Programmer's Guide that comes with VB4 for the current limitations.)*

C. Common Visual Basic Programming Questions

1. What's the difference between MODAL and MODELESS forms? [###] *(See Chapter 5.)*
2. When/why should I use Option Explicit? [###] *(Always, in the author's opinion.)*

3. Why does everybody say I should save in TEXT not BINARY? [###] *(Doesn't apply to VB4.)*
4. Is the Variant type slower than using other variable types? [###] *(See Chapters 5 and 7.)*
5. How do I make a text box not beep but do something else when I hit the ENTER key?
6. How do I implement an incremental search in list/dir/combo/file boxes? [###] *(This is a fairly sophisticated use of the Send Message API call.)*
7. How do I get the TAB key to be treated like a normal character?
8. How do I make an animated icon for my program? [###]
9. What is passing by reference? [###] *(See Chapter 8.)*
10. Why do I get a "file not found" error on the IIF function when I distribute by program? [###]
11. Is there any way to pass a variable to a form apart from using global variables?
12. How should dates be implemented so they work with other language and country formats?
13. Can a VB application be an OLE server? [###] (*Much changed in VB4—see Chapter 18.)*
14. How do I dial a phone number without using the MSCOMM VBX?
15. I have [several] megabytes of memory. Why do I get an "out of memory" error? [###] *(Much less likely to happen in VB4 under Windows 95.)*
16. How do I mimic a toggle button? [###]
17. How do I get my application on top?
18. Is there a way to break long lines in VB code? [###] *(There is one now in VB4—the _ (underscore).)*
19. How do I remove/change the picture property of a control at design time? [###] *(The bug was fixed in VB4.)*
20. Is a [foo] VBX/DLL available as shareware/freeware? [###]

21. How do I make my applications screen-resolution independent? [###] *(See Chapter 12.)*
22. How do I do Peek and Poke and other low-level stuff? [###] *(This is especially dangerous under Windows 95.)*
23. Why doesn't "my string" & Chr$(13) do what I want?
24. How do I prevent multiple instances of my program from running?
25. How do I implement an accelerator key for a text box? [###] *(See Chapter 4.)*
26. How do I force a file dialog box to reread the correct disk?
27. How do I get the number of free bytes on a disk?
28. Data Control is missing from the toolbox when I use VB under NT 3.5. [###]

D. Advanced Visual Basic Programming Issues

1. How do I tell when an application executed using the SHELL command is finished? [###] *(See Appendix B for the (different) ways under the 16- and 32-bit versions of VB.)*
2. How do I access C-style strings?
3. How can I change the printer Windows uses in code without using the print common dialog? How can I change orientation? [###] *(Greatly changed in VB4, it's now pretty easy; see Chapter 6.)*
4. Any tips for speeding up VB?
5. How do I speed up control property access?
6. How much gain in performance will I get if I write my number crunching routines in C instead of Visual Basic?
7. How do you make a TEXTBOX read only? Or, how do I prevent the user from changing the text in a TEXTBOX? [###] *(In VB4, just set the Locked property.)*
8. How can I create a VBX? [###]
9. How do you change the system menu (on the Control-Menu Box)?

10. How do I play MID, WAV, or other multimedia files? [###] *(Use the Microsoft Multimedia control supplied with the Professional and Enterprise editions of VB. See Chapter 13.)*
11. How can I call a 'hidden' DOS program from VB? [###]
12. How do I do drag & drop between applications? [###]
13. How do I use GetPrivateProfileString to read from INI files? [###] *(Win 95 uses a registry rather than INI files.)*
14. How do I implement Undo?
15. How do I create a window with a small title bar as in a floating toolbar? [###]
16. What is Pseudocode? [###] *(Some people use pseudocode to refer to the p-code that VB itself generates.)*
17. Does VB support pointers to functions? [###] *(No pointers to functions, no pointers to anything; do the best you can with arrays :-))*
18. How do I program the Novell NetWare API from VB? [###]
19. Visual Basic 4 news [###]
20. How do you change the icon and otherwise manipulate the DOS box? [###]
21. How do I make the mouse cursor invisible/visible? [####] *(Since custom mouse cursors are allowed, this one is easy in VB 4. See Chapter 3.)*
22. How do I create controls dynamically (at run time)? [###] *(See the section on control arrays in Chapter 10.)*
23. How do I set the Windows wallpaper at run time?
24. How do I call help files from a VB program? [###] *(See Chapter 13.)*

E. Calling the Windows API and DLLs in General

1. What is the Windows API? [###] *(See Chapter 9.)*
2. How do I call a DLL? [###] *(See Chapter 9.)*
3. What about DLL calls that require callbacks?
4. Tips for calling DLLs (such as the Windows API)

F. Visual Basic and Databases

(We do not include any of the database FAQs here.)

1. Why can't I use an index with my VB accessed database? [###]
2. "Can't find installable ISAM" or Why does my compiled VB database app generate an error when it ran just fine in the design environment? [###]
3. Is the Access Engine and Visual Basic Pro good enough for database work? [###]
4. How do you avoid the "Invalid use of null" error when reading null values from a database? [###]
5. What is "NULL"? [###]
6. How can I access a record by record number? [###]
7. How about Access 2.0 compatibility? [###]
8. Tips for VB database programming [###]
9. How come I get a "No Current Record" error when I use a Data Control on an empty table? [###]
10. How can I speed up my VB database application? [###]
11. How do I get a bitmap picture in a field in an Access database? [###]
12. What is "Reserved Error -1209"? [###]
13. "Cannot perform operation. illegal..." with Paradox 3.5 table(s) [###]
14. I'm getting the error message "Reserved Error [-nnnn] ("There is no message for this error")" from Jet Engine 2.0. Huh? [###]
15. Why do I get "object not an array" when I try to reference the fields of a global object variable, which I have set to a table? [###]
16. Steps for securing an Access 2.0 database [**] [###]

G. Distributing Visual Basic Applications

1. What are some tips for using Setup Wizard? [###] *(See Appendix A.)*
2. Are there restrictions on what I can distribute with my VB program?

3. What alternatives to setup wizard do I have? [###]
4. Do I need to worry about users who have Progman replacements such as Norton Desktop and PC Tools? [###] *(Much less important under Win 95.)*
5. Can I distribute my app without vbrunXXX.dll?
6. Why won't my setup program install commdlg.dll et. al.? [###] *(Much less of a problem under Windows 95.)*
7. Where do I install VBXs and DLLs? *(And OCXs of course, in VB4.)*

H. Miscellaneous Tips and Information

1. Multiple identifiers after the DIM statement can be confusing.
2. "Clean up" your project before final EXE compilation.
3. Multiple END statements can be dangerous; or, The program that refused to terminate.
4. What are the latest versions of the various files used by VB? [###]

I. Visual Basic for Applications (VBA)

(We do not include any of the VBA questions either.)

1. Any tips for VB/Win 3 programmers moving to VBA? [###]
2. Does VBA support VBXs? [###]
3. How do I access properties on my dialog boxes in VBA? [###]
4. How do I use database routines from Excel VBA? [###]

A. Preface

This document is a compilation of frequently asked questions and their answers about Visual Basic for Windows and Visual Basic for Applications, which have been gathered from posts to the comp.lang.basic.visual.* newsgroups. Although efforts have been made to find obvious errors, there is no guarantee that the information in this document is error free. Neither the FAQ maintainer nor anyone else associated with this document assumes *any* liability for the content or use of this document. If you find any errors, please report them to the address given below.

jan.haugland@uib.no

This FAQ document is protected by international copyright regulations. Permission is granted to distribute it freely, both in electronic and written format, provided no charge is made. Also, do not make changes to this document without the consent of the maintainer. USENET netiquette applies.

A1. Where to get the VB/Win FAQ

Most FAQs (including this one) are available at the anonymous ftp archive site "rtfm.mit.edu". All parts of the VB FAQ may be found here:

ftp://rtfm.mit.edu/pub/usenet/comp.lang.basic.visual.misc/

The following are alternative sites to rtfm:

North America	ftp.uu.net	/usenet/news.answers
Europe	ftp.uni-paderb/orn.de	/pub/FAQ
	ftp.Germany.EU.net	/pub/newsarchive/news.answers
	grasp1.univ-lyon1.fr	/pub/faq
	ftp.win.tue.nl	/pub/usenet/news.answers
	ftp.sunet.se	/pub/usenet
Asia	nctuccca.edu.tw	/USENET/FAQ
	hwarang.postech.ac.kr	/pub/usenet/news.answers

note: *(FYI: "rtfm" stands for "Read The ******* Manual". I kid you not!)*

[Andre van Meulebrouck (vanmeule@ils.nwu.edu)]

You can also have the VB FAQs e-mailed to you by sending a message to "mail-server@rtfm.mit.edu" with *only* the text:

send usenet/comp.lang.basic.visual.misc/*

in the BODY of the message.

Alternative mail servers for those who have no ftp access are:

ftpmail@decwrl.dec.com or ftpmail@cs.uow.edu.au

bitftp@pucc.princeton.edu or ftpmail@lth.se

bitftp@dearn or to bitftp@vm.gmd.de (Europe only)

ftpmail@ftp.uni-stuttgart.de

ftpmail@grasp.insa-lyon.fr or ftpmail@ieunet.ie

bitftp@plearn.edu.pl or bitftp@plearn (Europe)

ftpmail@doc.ic.ac.uk or ftpmail@sunsite.unc.edu

[thanks to Jakob Faarvang (jakobf@apexsc.com)]

For all mailservers, use the "index" command to get a list of files available at the site. Use the "help" command to get more detailed instructions.

note: *Commands are in the* body *of mail message!*

Also note that a Web-browser such as Netscape or Microsoft Internet Explorer easily can access an ftp site, view, and download files. The ftp address on the top of this point (ftp://...) is formatted for these browsers; just copy and paste the text directly into the "URL" line.

There is currently work going on to make these available in HTML format (for Web-browsers). This work is done by Peter Millard whose address is <millard@buffnet.net>. Look at:

http://www.buffnet.net/~millard/vblinks.htm

or go directly to the copies of his HTML FAQs (when finished!):

http://www.buffnet.net/~millard/vbgenfaq.htm

http://www.buffnet.net/~millard/vbdosfaq.htm

A2. Kudos & comments

In this document, whenever a long line of code must be split into two or more lines of text in the code examples, the _ symbol will precede each line that should be appended to the line above it.

editor's note: *This is now the line continuation character in Visual Basic 4.*

As the FAQ maintainer, I don't have time to explore all of the aspects of Visual Basic. Neither have I time or know-how to personally answer direct technical questions thoroughly. I rely on your submissions to improve the quality and inclusiveness of this document. If you have found a VB hint, tip, trick, work-around, etc., please write it up and send it to me!

Jan Steinar Haugland (Jan.Haugland@uib.no), VB/Win FAQ maintainer

Please note that my first language is not English. You can safely ignore all typos, but if you find an error that is so embarrassing you can't help pulling your hair and screaming loud, just send me a note and I'll correct it quietly. OK?

This document is a collective effort! I would like to thank all contributors, and also all those who have given constructive feedback. This FAQ is now widely distributed in the net community.

Special thanks to the following people who have made many and invaluable contributions to the VB/Win FAQ: Kris Nosack (the previous maintainer), Peter Millard, Nic Gibson, Mr. "D" (the anonymous contributor), George Tatge (gat@csn.org), Andy Dingley (dingbat@codesmth.demon.co.uk), Ayn Shipley (ashipley@hookup.net), and those I may have forgotten (sorry).

John McGuire (jmcguire@jax.jaxnet.com), a long-time VB user, recently went through the FAQ and found lots of things worth his comments. Many of his corrections and suggestions are implemented throughout. Thanks!

Everybody: Your help is *greatly* appreciated!

B. General Visual Basic Questions

This section covers answers to general questions about Visual Basic.

B1. Does VB/Win make standalone .EXE files?

VB/Win produces .EXE files, but they are not standalone. All VB/Win programs must be distributed with the VBRUNx00.DLL file (where x is the major version number). This DLL must accompany all VB/Win programs, but only one such file should reside on every system where VB programs are used.

B3. Where can I get updated VB and other Microsoft files?

The Microsoft Software Library (MSL) is accessible from the following services:

Compu$erve: GO MSL

then

Search for <filename.EXE>

and also the

- Microsoft Download Service (MSDL)

  Dial (206) 936-6735 to connect to MSDL

- Internet (anonymous FTP)

  ftp ftp.microsoft.com

  Change to the \softlib\mslfiles directory

(There are a *lot* of files in this directory! It is not advisable to list all the files unless you have time. See map below.)

B4. Help! I am lost on ftp.microsoft.com, what do I do?

You no longer have to be! The site has been reorganized, and you'll find the file DIRMAP.TXT in root (or whatever it's called on a 3.5 NT server).

note: *Directory and file names at ftp.microsoft.com are* not *case sensitive.*

Thanks to Richard Mason (richard@whitney.demon.co.uk) for the map he made for us before this long overdue reorganization, and thanks for bringing this to my attention.

B5. Where can I get good up-to-date information about VB?

If you do any VB programming at all, you really should get the latest copy of the Microsoft Knowledge Base from one of the sources listed above! The file name is VBKB.EXE or VBKB_FT.EXE for the version with full text searching. The Knowledge Base is a Windows help formatted document that is updated almost monthly. (Beware: The files are huge!) The EXE files on ftp.microsoft.com (and other places) are simple self-extracting files. They don't do any automatic updating of your system, just dump the file(s) inside them in the current directory on your disk, uncompressed and ready for use. Just replace the old files on your system with the new files (same name, usually).

This FAQ (ahem) is a pretty good source as a digest of many of the VB issues that are discussed in the comp.lang.basic.visual.* newsgroups, but as such the information contained in this FAQ may not have been thoroughly tested or verified.

For easier access to and use of this FAQ document, get the Windows Help file format FAQ doc by anonymous ftp to quasar.sba.dal.ca and look under /www/hlp. The .HLP version is made by Tim Roberts (TJR@SBA-COOP.SBA.DAL.CA). This is *highly recommended.*

Dave McCarter puts out a nice Windows help formatted document called "Visual Basic Tips and Tricks"—a good resource with information that isn't found in the Knowledge Base. It can be found by anonymous ftp to ftp.cica.indiana.edu /pub/pc/win3/programr/vbasic/ as VBTIPS??.ZIP, where ?? is the version number (yes, get the one with the highest number).

Mark Schoonover has started a monthly magazine called *VBWin Programmer's Magazine* that is compiled around the Discussion of Microsoft Visual Basic and Related Issues mailing list. This magazine is available at the usual ftp sites like CICA and at his BBS (619) 571-2846. Mark can be contacted at schoon@cts.com. It also has its own anonymous ftp site: ftp.cts.com in the /pub/schoon/VBWM.Issues directory. - ED: this appears to be down, alas.

Jakob Faarvang (jakobf@apexsc.com) maintains the useful CLBV Digest:

http://www.apexsc.com/vb/clbv-digest/

and

ftp.apexsc.com:/pub/cgvb/clbv-digest/

Address for him regarding CLBV Digest is clbv-digest-

editor@apexsc.com

There is presently an effort to put together a VB code library so that VB users can share their best—and trickiest—programming work. The code library project is being spearheaded by Hein Ragas, who has managed to get a directory on CICA for code snippets to be deposited. Stay tuned to comp.lang.basic.visual.misc for more information.

There's a VISBAS-L mailing list for Visual Basic (Thanks to David Liden (DL9U@Virginia.EDU) for tracking it down for me when it moved). You can subscribe to this mailing list by sending an email to

listserv@listserv.tamu.edu

Place the following text in the *body* of the message (no, not the subject line):

SUB VISBAS-L Real Name

Where Real Name is just that, *your full real name* not your email address. Note that the traffic on this list may overflow your mailbox if you have a limited mail buffer. Expect around 40-50 messages every weekday, a bit less during weekends. Also, to unsubscribe, do as above but with "UNSUB" in the body of the message to the LISTSERV address, *not* to the VISBAS-L list address itself. (Believe it or not, we usually receive 2-3 sub/unsub mails every day on the list, and we're really fed up!) Also, this mailserver was split and a new list called VBDATA-L was made for VB database (Jet) related topics. Same procedure for registering (SUB VBDATA-L Real Name).

The address for the MS ACCESS listserver is listserv@indycms.bitnet or listserv@indycms.iupui.edu. The list name is ACCESS-L. To subscribe, you follow the same procedure as for the other lists.

Sorry, I know no mailservers or other Internet resources dedicated to VBA specifically. Send me any information you may have, and I'll bring it on.

There are several USENET newsgroups dedicated to MS Windows programming and use. In fact, far too many to list here :-)

note: *Please don't post VB stuff to comp.lang.visual. This group has *nothing* to do with Visual Basic, and the academics discussing "real" visual programming there are very, very annoyed at what they call "quasi-visual" stuff and postings about those languages to their group.*

If you have a Compu$erve account, you will find a forum for Visual Basic there, including some support from Microsoft on the MS BASIC Forum (GO MSBASIC).

Message Sections Available	Libraries Available
1 Forum News/Info	1 MS Info and Index
2 Setup Wizard/Kit	2 Setup Wizard/Kit
3 Data Access Objects	3 Data Access Objects
4 The Data Control	4 The Data Control
5 Programming Issues	5 Programming Issues
6 ODBC Connectivity	6 ODBC Connectivity
7 SQL Queries	7 SQL Queries
8 ProEdition Controls	8 ProEdition Controls
9 Calling APIs/DLLs	9 Calling APIs/DLLs
10 Using OLE/DDE	10 VBWIN-ODBC/Database
11 MSCOMM control	11 MSCOMM control
12 MCI/MAPI controls	12 MCI/MAPI controls
13 DOS Visual Basic	13 DOS Visual Basic
14 DOS and Mac Basic	14 DOS and Mac Basic
15 Suggestions/Mktg.	15 Suggestions/Mktg.
16 CDK	16 CDK
17 3rd Party Products	17 3rd Party Products

There are magazines dedicated to VB. The best known is Fawcett Technical Publications' *Visual Basic Programmer's Journal* (VBPJ). Phone 800-848-5523 (for U.S. credit card orders) or 303-541-0610 (int'l and U.S. other orders), Email 74003.224@compuserve.com to Shirley Modric for subscription info. Address is 280 Second Street, Suite 200, Los Altos, CA 94022-3603 USA.

From Randy Coates (rcoates@telerama.lm.com):

I currently subscribe to *Inside Visual BASIC for Windows* from the Cobb Group. Although it is a helpful monthly paper (about 14 pages per publication), I find it to be overpriced when compared to *VB Programmer's Journal*. Here is the information anyway:

Domestic $59/yr ($7.00 each); Outside U.S. $79/yr ($8.50 each) Phone: Toll Free: 800-223-8720), Local: 502-491-1900, Customer Relations Fax: 502-491-8050, Editorial Department Fax: 502-491-4200. Address: Inside Visual BASIC for Windows, 9420 Bunsen Parkway, Suite 300, Louisville, KY 40220.

(Note: for completeness, other VB magazines should be listed, and I would like to receive info on those!)

author's note: *I like the "Visual Basic Developer" from Pinnacle Publishing. It's fairly expensive but seems to have high-quality articles on the whole. See Appendix D.*

B6. Are there any WWW pages for VB?

Carl 'n Gary's Visual Basic HomePage is a good place to start:

http://www.apexsc.com/vb/

This page has hotlinks to lots of goodies, including the FAQs, clbv.* archives (with search tool), etc. Send any email inquiries (about the page!) to:

vb-admin@apexsc.com

[Gary Wisniewski (gary@apexsc.com)]

author's note: *The* Visual Basic Programmer's Journal *now has a Web page. The address is*

http://www.windx.com

B7. Are there any examples of commercial applications built using Visual Basic?

Profit, by Microsoft, was written mostly in Visual Basic. In fact, Profit was one of three programs selected as PC Magazine's Editor's Choice among Windows small business accounting packages. Most of the current version of Quicken was written in VB2. The viewer/launcher/installer in the oh-so-popular Way Cool [Topic] for Windows series of CD-ROMs was written in VB3.

Microsoft uses VB extensively for smaller utilities. Three of the small apps in the Windows and Windows for Workgroups Resource Toolkits are written in VB. Also, if you have the Microsoft Bookshelf CD-ROM, you will notice that the MVOPTION.EXE program, which is an "options" program for MS Viewer, is created in VB.

author's note: *UnInstaller, one of the most successful software products of the past few years, was written in Visual Basic as was the Pipeline, a highly rated Internet software access package.*

note: *The existence of VBX files in a package doesn't necessarily mean that it was written in VB. The most popular C++ compilers also support VBXs.*

C. Common Visual Basic Programming Questions

This section covers some common Visual Basic programming questions.

C5. How do I make a text box not beep but do something else when I hit the ENTER key?

Put "something else" in your _KeyPress event, depending on what you really want. This code example makes *nothing* happen, for an extended period of time:

```
Sub Text1_KeyPress (KeyAscii As Integer)
  If KeyAscii = 13 Then   '13 is Key_Return
    KeyAscii = 0
```

```
  End If
End Sub
```

This might not be a very nice thing to do, since your users usually have some intention when they press ENTER. Often they will want to jump to the next control, as the TAB key does. To have the ENTER key emulate the TAB key action, you will need to add the line 'SendKeys "{tab}"' above 'KeyAscii=0' in the example above (Yes, I thought KeyAscii=9 works but it doesn't! TAB is obviously handled by Windows on a lower level).

By the way, you'll also find this in the Microsoft VB Knowledge Base (see KB Q78305 and Q85562).

note: *If MultiLine=True, you will *not* want to disable the normal behavior of the ENTER key.*

C7. How do I get the TAB key to be treated like a normal character?

You must set TabStop = False for *all* controls on the active form. Then you will be able to insert "tab" (chr 9) characters in controls like the text box. If you feel you need the TAB key to behave "normally" (i.e. jump to next control) outside this specific control, it is trivial to emulate its functionality in code:

```
Sub Command1_KeyDown (KeyCode As Integer, Shift As Integer)
If KeyCode = 9 Then
  If Shift = 0 Then
    Command2.SetFocus 'Tab=Next control
  ElseIf Shift = 1 Then
    Command3.SetFocus 'Shift-Tab=Prev.ctrl.
  End If
End If
End Sub
```

C11. Is there any way to pass a variable to a form apart from using global variables?

The standard workaround is to put an invisible text box (or caption or any other control that suits your use) on the target form and access it by Form.textbox = "value". Then you can use the Change event of that control to do anything you want in that form. Also, check out the .Tag property, which is a "what-you-want" property where you can hook any string you want onto a control. This property can also be accessed from other modules.

[Dave Mitton (mitton@dave.enet.dec.com)]

C12. How should dates be implemented so they work with other language and country formats?

If you use i.e. MM/DD/YY format dates in a program, you will get either a run time error (i.e., month>12) or the wrong date (i.e., March 12 instead of December 3) when your program is used in Europe. And vice versa, of course. Even Microsoft's own example programs (like the MAPI sample) make this stupid mistake and fail miserably. Use the Format command to make sure you get the date you want. For example:

strTodaysDate = Format[$](Now, "Short Date")

As a side note, Microsoft has taken much heat on the newsgroup for VB's bad support for internationalization! Just try to make a date literal in source code that works everywhere as a little exercise. Answer elsewhere in this document. No prizes :-)

C14. How do I dial a phone number without using the MSCOMM VBX?

The MSCOMM VBX that comes with VB/Pro is great for creating communication programs, but it's overkill for dialing a phone number. Try the following code:

```
PhoneNumber$ = "(123)456-7890"
Open "COM2:" For Output As #1
'or COM1
Print #1, "ATDT" & PhoneNumber$ & Chr$(13)
Close #1
```

Ian Storrs <exuian@exu.ericsson.se> informed me that he had experienced problems with this when the VB program was run from a network drive. A file named "COM1" was created on the disk! Jeff Rife <jrife@health.org> put in the ":" after COM2 to solve that problem! (This trick is probably not a good idea for bigger applications, but it's nice for small personal utilities.)

C17. How do I get my application on top?

To force a form to the front of the screen, do the following command:

Form1.ZOrder

To make the application *stay* on top, put the ZOrder command in a Timer event repeatedly called, say, every 1000 msecs. This makes a "softer" on-top than other methods, and allows the user to make a short peek below the form.

There are two different "ZOrder's" of forms in Windows, both implemented internally as linked lists. One is for "normal" windows, the other for real "topmost" windows (like the Clock application distributed with MS Windows). The ZOrder command above simply moves your window to the top of the "normal" window stack. To make your window truly topmost, use the SetWindowPos API call like this:

```
'Make these declares:
Declare Function SetWindowPos Lib "user" (ByVal h%, _
ByVal hb%, ByVal x%, ByVal y%, ByVal cx%, ByVal cy%, _
ByVal f%) As Integer
Global Const SWP_NOMOVE = 2
Global Const SWP_NOSIZE = 1
Global Const FLAGS = SWP_NOMOVE Or SWP_NOSIZE
Global Const HWND_TOPMOST = -1
Global Const HWND_NOTOPMOST = -2
'To set Form1 as a TopMost form, do the following:
res% = SetWindowPos (Form1.hWnd, HWND_TOPMOST, 0, 0, |0, 0, FLAGS)
'if res%=0, there is an error
'To turn off topmost (make the form act normal again):
res% = SetWindowPos (Form1.hWnd, HWND_NOTOPMOST, 0, 0, |0, 0, FLAGS)
```

C21. How do I make my applications screen resolution-independent?

There are two methods: Either get a custom control that does the job for you, or you write lots of complicated code in the Load and ReSize events. For the first option, check out VideoSoft's $hareware VSVBX.VBX (download

VSVBX.ZIP from CICA or mirrors). It has a will of its own, as you will experience, but it's generally better than trying what is described below.

For the brave (or stupid), try to write "screen resolution-smart code" in the form's Load event. If the form is resizable (normally it should be), you'll have to put some magic into the Resize event as well. There are 4 rules of thumb:

- Do not trust the form's height and width properties. These measure the entire form, not the client area where your controls are. To see this in action, create a simple applet with the only code being in the ReSize event, which resets a line control from 0,0 to the form's width, height properties. The top left corner is in the client area, the bottom right corner disappears. The API call GetClientRect will return the size of the client area in pixels. You can use the screen object's TwipsPerPixelX and TwipsPerPixelY properties to convert from pixels to twips. If that's not enough, GetWindowRect will return the actual size of the entire form, client and non-client areas combined. GetSystemMetrics will return individual pieces of things like border width/height, caption height, etc.
- Use the TextWidth and TextHeight properties. You can use them off the form if all your controls share the same font, otherwise use them off of the given control. I typically do a TextWidth("X") and TextHeight("X") to get a value that I use as a margin between controls. I grab these values on startup, and multiply them by 2, 1.5, .75, .5, .25 to get varying margin sizes, depending on how close or far apart I want to space things. If your control has an autosize property, you may want to use it, and then calculate the maximum width of a control in a given "column" of controls on your screen and position all of them accordingly.
- Try not to resize your controls in the ReSize event. You will spawn another ReSize event in the process. Of course, you can use a flag to determine whether the ReSize event is the original event or the spawned one. Using the load event, and setting the form's borders to fixed minimizes the amount of work you have to do.
- Make sure you use a consistent scale. I don't even bother with the scale properties, but instead just convert pixels (from API calls) into twips and be done with it. If you do use scale properties, be sure you convert your numbers correctly. I had no end of difficulty when I failed to convert

into twips with one number that was used in a series of calculations to position controls. Also be sure all your controls share the same scale—another nasty problem I had before I gave up on them completely.

[Thanks to our generous anonymous source "D"]

C23. Why doesn't "my string" & Chr$(13) do what I want?

You also need to add a Chr$(10): "my string" & Chr$(13) & Chr$(10) will give you a CR and LF. (Editor's note in VB4, you can use the built-in constant vbCrLf.)

C26. How do I force a file dialog box to reread the current disk?

If you make a simple dialog box modeled after common dialog (normally you should *use* the common dialog VBX!), you will notice that reselecting the diskette drive will not really rescan the disk. Very annoying to change to C:, and to reselect A: just to make it read the directory of a new diskette.

To solve this problem, put

```
drive1.refresh
dir1.refresh
file1.refresh
```

in the code for the "Rescan" button (or whatever).

C27. How do I get the number of free bytes on a disk?

As far as I know, there are three possibilities:

1. SETUPKIT.DLL as mentioned above.
2. Arjen Broeze's VBIO.VBX or something like that, with a lot of options.
3. Make your own DISKINFO.DLL from the example code in VBKB article Q106553.

See Article Q113590 (or Q106553) in Microsoft's VB KnowledgeBase.

A short extract follows:

```
Declare Function DiskSpaceFree Lib "SETUPKIT.DLL" () As Long
Dim free_space& ' Holds number of bytes returned from DiskSpaceFree().
ChDrive "c:"    ' Change to the drive you want to test. free_space& =
DiskSpaceFree()
```

[Geir Tutturen(itfgt@nlh10.nlh.no)]

D. Advanced Visual Basic Programming Issues

This section covers some advanced Visual Basic programming issues.

D2. How do I access C-style strings?

Use the 'lstrlen' and 'lstrcpy' calls found in the Kernel DLL.

D4. Any tips for speeding up VB?

Who said "code in C"???? ;-)

a) When SHOWing a form with lots of bound controls, have a blank frame covering everything. Then, in the Form_Activate event, set the Frame.Visible = False. This greatly speeds the display of the form and hides ugly thrashing as the data controls initialize.

[Christopher Biow (biow@cs.umd.edu)]

b) Try to keep any Global definitions to a minimum. Massive numbers of global variables really seem to slow VB Windows down (besides chewing up memory). In other words, if you've pasted a lot of stuff from the globals.txt file, trim all definitions and variables you don't use in your application.

editor's note: *The remark about global constraints is not relevant to Visual Basic 4.*

c) Keep the total number of controls and forms used to a minimum (you've probably already guessed that).

d) Keep fancy graphics to a minimum (another one you know).

e) Try "pre-processing" in the background (using Do_Events).

Doesn't really speed anything up, but often there is a lot of "idle" time while the user is selecting menus, buttons and such - if you can do some calculations, image loading, or whatever, during this idle time, your user perceives the application is faster than it really is.

f) Hide often-used forms rather than unloading them. Unloading saves memory, but it takes longer to reload a form than simply to "un-hide" it.

[Tips b to f by Galen Raben (galenr@gr.hp.com)]

Bruce Garrett (bruceg@access2.digex.net) had the following tips from his VBITS 93 notes:

a) Polling a control for its properties directly is 10 to 20 times slower than placing the property values you need into variables and testing the value of the variables.

b) Swap tuning: Modules are not loaded until used; put related code in the same modules, reduce the number of intermodule calls, and keep modules small.

c) Binary file I/O is faster then Text/Random.

There was also a lot of discussion about "apparent" speed, i.e., how it looks on the screen as opposed to how fast it's chugging internally. It was noted that the cute little flashing menu items and exploding windows in the Mac amount to a little razzle-dazzle to distract you from how long it takes to actually load something and get it on the screen. Keeping all your forms loaded but hidden until needed was suggested. Other suggestions were the use of progress indicators and a simple quickly loaded and drawn startup form, and preloading data you expect to need.

D5. How do I speed up control property access?

Instead of using a property in a loop, you will be better off using a normal variable in the loop and then assigning the variable once to the property afterwards. Also, when reading a property, you should read it once into a variable instead of using it in a loop.

Sometimes it is not possible to simply put the contents of a property into a variable, for example, if you are using a list box or you need to conserve memory. In these cases you can send the WM_SetRedraw message to the control to prevent redrawing. You can typically increase the speed 6-10 times - or even more.

```
'Add the following declares:
Declare Function SendMessage Lib "User" (ByVal hWnd As
|Integer, ByVal wMsg As Integer, ByVal wParam As
|Integer, lParam As Any) As Long
Const WM_SetRedraw = &HB

'Add this to your code:
Result% = SendMessage(Text1.hWnd, WM_SetRedraw, 0, 0)
'redraw off
'Do your stuff here!
Result% = SendMessage(Text1.hWnd, WM_SetRedraw, 1, 0)
'redraw on
```

This same method applies to list boxes and other controls.

D6. How much gain in performance will I get if I write my number crunching routines in C instead of Visual Basic?

Probably the best solution to the number crunching problem is to write the number crunching routines as a custom control or a DLL, and plug it into a VB app. VB interface handling is not significantly slower than, say C++, and most of the wait is associated with Windows.

Some real world experience speaks volumes about this one:

I wrote some time-consuming code in VB to solve a combinatorial problem. The code consists of one main recursive function, which calls itself very often. It took a night to compute a certain problem. I was rather disappointed and then decided to write the central routine in C++. It was a 1:1 transcription. The routine was compiled with the MS C++-Compiler. It took only 22 minutes for the same problem. Amazing, isn't it? The routine doesn't do any floating point arithmetic, only integer, and handles some arrays. The PC was a

33MHz 486. And the second amazing thing is, that an IBM RS6000 (560)-RISC-machine needed 17 minutes for the same code. I was the only one on the machine. I thought it should be much faster. The MS C++ seems to make very fast, optimized code. The optimization was configured to make fast code.

[Christoph Steinbeck (steinbeck@uni-bonn.de)]

D9. How do you change the system menu (on the Control-Menu Box)?

You can turn off the minimize and maximize menu options by changing properties, but what if you need to remove the "close" option?

```
'Make the following declares.
Declare Function GetSystemMenu Lib "User" (ByVal hWnd _
As Integer, ByVal bRevert As Integer) As Integer
Declare Function RemoveMenu Lib "User" (ByVal hMenu _
As Integer, ByVal nPosition As Integer, ByVal wFlags As _
Integer) As Integer
Global Const MF_BYPOSITION=&H400

'Use the following code to remove the "close" option.
SystemMenu% = GetSystemMenu (hWnd, 0)
Res% = RemoveMenu(SystemMenu%,6, MF_BYPOSITION)
'(also remove the separator line)
Res% = RemoveMenu(SystemMenu%,6, MF_BYPOSITION)
```

Adding menu items to the control menu is more complicated, since you need to respond to the events triggered when the user selects the new options. The newest Message Blaster (msgblast.vbx, see details in beginning of FAQ about how to get files) contains example code.

D14. How do I implement Undo?

For most controls, you will have to keep track of changes yourself. There's no magic involved, just some coding. However, if you use the standard Text box or Combo box, Windows provides a "free" undo function for you!

```
'Do the following declares:
Declare Function SendMessage Lib "User" (ByVal hWnd As _
```

```
Integer, ByVal wMsg As Integer, ByVal wParam As _
Integer, lParam As Any) As Long
Global Const WM_USER = &h400
Global Const EM_UNDO = WM_USER + 23

'And in your Undo Sub do the following:
UndoResult = SendMessage(myControl.hWnd, EM_UNDO, 0, 0)
'UndoResult = -1 indicates an error.
```

editor's note: *If the Text box or the Combo box has the focus, you can use the SendKeys statement.*

D23. How do I set the Windows wallpaper at run time?

I'm surprised this isn't in the FAQ yet. [ED: now it is!] You need the SystemParametersInfo API function and the SPI_SETDESKWALLPAPER constant.

For this you will need the following constants and function declaration:

```
Const SPI_SETDESKWALLPAPER = 20
Const SPIF_SENDWININICHANGE = &H2
Const SPIF_UPDATEINIFILE = &H1
Declare Function SystemParametersInfo Lib "User" _
(ByVal uAction As Integer, ByVal uParam As Integer,_
 lpvParam As Any, ByVal fuWinIni As Integer) As Integer

'You then call the function as follows...
Result% = SystemParametersInfo(SPI_SETDESKWALLPAPER, 0,_
 ByVal BMPFile$, SPIFlags%)
'... where SPIFlags% is 0 if the change is not to be made permanent, or
'(SPIF_UPDATEINIFILE Or SPIF_SENDWININICHANGE) if it is to be carried across
'into future Windows sessions.
```

note: *Please be certain to include the ByVal keyword before the bitmap file name, as this argument is declared as Any,* not *as ByVal String.*

[Luke Webber(webber@werple.apana.org.au)]

E. Calling the Windows API and DLLs in General

This section handles queries concerning DLLs.

E3. What about DLL calls that require callbacks?

VB does not support callbacks, but various extensions can help. Dan Appleman's "Visual Basic Programmer's Guide to the Windows API" comes with a floppy disk containing code samples and tools. It also includes a VBX that supports the callbacks many API calls require. Dan is also founder and president of Desaware, which sells more extensive tools, including SpyWorks, for VB developers.

[Walter Hill (whill@netcom.com)]

E4. Tips for calling DLLs (such as the Windows API)

- Using the BYVAL keyword is critical. Using it when you're supposed to call by reference and (more common) not using it when you are to give a value to the external function are the single most common mistakes. The wrong calling convention can often result in a General Protection Fault (GPF) or, even worse, corruption of another application's data.
- Check return and parameter types. For return types, a C function declared as "void" means you use a Sub not a Function.
- Initialize strings by padding to the necessary length! If you pass a string that is too short to the API, it will happily write past the end of the string and possibly corrupt data.
- Use Option Explicit. A typing error that results in a bug in the VB source will occasionally cause a GPF when you call external code.
- It's a jungle out there! Check parameter values, as there is no type checking outside VB. If you make a mistake, you'll often get a GPF.
- Save before you run! You may even need to restart Windows after a GPF, since DLLs often aren't unloaded properly. As a second option you can check out WPS (Windows Process Status), which is distributed with VB/Pro and placed in the CDK directory. This utility allows you to kick out any module (EXE, DLL) from memory (shooting yourself in the

foot if you want to. WPS is a nice way to find out what DLLs are actually used, but save your work first!).

G. Distributing Visual Basic Applications

This section answers some questions concerning the distribution of Visual Basic applications.

G2. Are there restrictions on what I can distribute with my VB program?

The documentation tells what parts of the Visual Basic kit you can freely distribute: the VBX files, some DLLs, and what the SetupKit includes on your distribution diskettes. Reading software license agreements may be more boring than asking the newsgroup, but is nevertheless a good idea.

There have been some rumors on the newsgroup that you can't redistribute programs written with VB freely. This is nonsense. All applications created with VB can be redistributed freely without royalties (as long as you don't distribute proprietary external files).

The rumors probably originated when Microsoft announced that they will not sell kits allowing third-party software to include the Visual Basic for Applications (VBA) system.

G5. Can I distribute my app without vbrunXXX.dll?

If you are sure that your users have it or can get it, you can easily distribute your app without vbrunXXX.dll. Simply remove the file from your distribution disk or zip file and *also* remove it from the setup.lst file.

[George Tatge (gat@csn.org)]

G7. Where do I install VBXs and DLLs?

Please, this is one place where everybody's life is much easier if you will follow Microsoft's recommendations. All PUBLIC VBXs and DLLs should be installed in the Windows/system directory! A "PUBLIC" DLL or VBX is any that can be purchased on the open market. In other words, if another VB programmer might possibly use the same VBX or DLL, install it in the system directory.

If you have written private VBXs or DLLs that will never be used by any program but yours, you can install them in the same directory where you install your application files.

There are lots of good reasons for doing this, but it makes a short novel to rehearse them all.

[George Tattle (gat@csn.org)]

H. Miscellaneous Tips and Information

This sections contains some general tips and information on Visual Basic.

H1. Multiple identifiers after the DIM statement can be confusing.

Some programmers with background from Pascal can try the following

```
Dim iA, iB, iC as Integer
```

and think that all three variables end up as Integer. In fact, the first two end up as default data type, normally Variant.

Instead you should use

```
Dim iA as Integer
Dim iB as Integer
Dim iC as Integer
```

which takes up more space, but gives you room to comment your variables (hint, hint); *or*

```
Dim iA%, iB%, iC%
```

or

```
Dim iA as Integer, Dim iB as Integer, Dim iC as Integer
```

both of which do the whole job.

H2. "Clean up" your project before final EXE compilation.

When you are ready to compile your VB project into your "finished" EXE, be sure to save the project files, exit VB, restart Windows, run VB, load your project, and go straight to compiling. Otherwise, your EXE may be larger in file size than necessary due to "garbage" getting included in the EXE. For some reason, VB does not fully clean up all of the previously used variables or objects that you may have been playing with while developing your program, so these get included in your EXE even though they aren't used. Other VB users have even advocated saving all the project files as ASCII, then loading the ASCII files before compiling to further "clean up" the resulting EXE file.

editor's note: *The last point is no longer valid in Visual Basic 4.*

H3. Multiple END statements can be dangerous; or, The program that refused to terminate.

Suggestion: put the END statement used to exit your program *only* in the Form_Unload event of the main form. Whenever you want to end the program, just tell the main form to unload.

Some have reported that after their program has (supposedly) terminated, it still appears in the task list. This can happen if you only hide secondary forms and forget to unload them when you end/unload the main form.

Also note that the Stop-button on the button-bar of the integrated development environment doesn't really unload anything. It *nukes* the program, which generally is a good idea since it could be a bug that caused it to be stuck in an eternal loop or something.

Appendix D

Third-Party Tools

and Other Resources

THIRD-PARTY tools can make Visual Basic programs easier, faster, more powerful—or all three. This appendix gives you a quick overview of some of what is available. The number of third-party tools grows monthly; this section can only give you a start. (Of course, probably first on your list should be the upgrade to the Professional edition if you don't already have it.)

note: *Two good sources for the Visual Basic tools mentioned here are Programmer's Paradise (800-445-7899) and VBextras (800-788-4794). Their prices are usually less than that of the actual manufacturer, and the catalogues are very useful.*

Resources

The best resource I know for Visual Basic is the MSBASIC forum on CompuServe. Many knowledgeable people frequent this forum, and Microsoft technical support is omnipresent there as well. Between the two, almost any question will find an answer. If you don't have a CompuServe account, you can also call CompuServe directly to get an account (800-848-8990). (The Internet is becoming much more important—see Appendix C for more on Visual Basic on the Internet.)

Among periodical resources, first, it is hard for me to imagine a serious Visual Basic programmer who won't like (and get a lot out of) the *Visual Basic Programmers Journal* (800-848-5523, 415-833-7100, around $28/year). Their quarterly CD is also very useful ($99.95/year). In addition, they sponsor a conference called VBits that although not cheap (around $700) is an excellent source of information. VBits conferences are held in various locations in both the United States and Europe. They feature lectures by many of the important figures in the Visual Basic community. Another journal whose reviews I like but seems less useful for programming information is *VB Tech Journal* (800-234-0386, 503-747-0800, $24.95/year).

There are two newsletters that have relatively few advertisements and therefore the potential for more "meat" (although at a somewhat higher cost). The one I like the best (disclaimer: it is one I occasionally contribute to) is Pinnacle Publishing Company's *Visual Basic Developer*. It costs $179 for 12 issues and includes a monthly disk of source code (800-788-1900). I find the Cobb Group's *Inside Visual Basic* less interesting overall—but still occasionally useful (800-223-8720, 502-493-3300, $59/year for twelve 16-page issues without the source code—a source code disk is available at an additional charge).

Next, and in many ways the most interesting for developers, is Microsoft's Developer CD Program available by subscription at various levels. It costs $195/year for the lowest level, which consists of four CDs (800-759-5474, Dept. OABB3). The Developer CD Program is not addressed specifically to Visual Basic programmers—it's for Windows developers generally. Nonetheless, there are tens of megabytes of information that a VB programmer will find useful, including the current complete version of the Visual Basic Knowledge Base.

Finally, although they do not focus on Visual Basic, but still have a useful article or two each month, I recommend *PC Techniques* (602-483-0192), *Windows Tech Journal* (800-234-0386), and *Windows/DOS Developer's Journal* (913-841-1631).

Tools

Tools can be divided into groups roughly as follows:

- Those that make the nitty-gritty of design and debugging easier. Included in this are tools to make writing help files easier.
- Tools that, for speed or convenience, add low-level routines or make it easier to use the ones supplied with Windows.
- Custom controls.

Design and Debugging Tools

The first tool that I use to make design and debugging easier is MicroHelp's cross-reference program "VBXRef" (800-922-3383, 404-516-0899). Crescent Software has a good one as well called XRef (800-35BASIC, 617-280-4520).

Cross-reference programs are extremely helpful when doing serious programming (and alas, the concomitant debugging), and both MicroHelp and Crescent's versions are first rate. Both MicroHelp's "Muscle" and Crescent Software's "QuickPak" provide routines for sending debugging information to a secondary (monochrome) monitor. Sheridan Software's "VBAssist" (800-VB-DIRECT, 516-753-0985) enhances the ordinary Visual Basic environment in too many ways to list here. Features include tools to make aligning controls on a form, adding graphics, and accessing data easier. Another feature called the "Code Assistant" makes combining different code fragments trivial as well as helping you with Windows API calls. There are lots of Wizards for doing common tasks; I recommend VBAssist very highly.

I don't know any serious developer who builds help files using RTF tags alone. My favorite tool (and one that has saved me literally hundreds of hours of work) is Blue Sky Software's "RoboHelp" (800-677-4946, 619-459-6365). There are various versions of RoboHelp—all require Word for Windows, but the full package called "WinHelp Office" has many additional tools—for example, ones for building videos. (Besides being an extremely easy-to-use product, the documentation for WinHelp Office is an excellent way to master the intricacies of writing fully Windows 95-compliant help systems.)

Tools for Speed and Convenience

The tools that I use all the time for speedy low-level routines (including adding capabilities such as sound that were mysteriously left out of Visual Basic and would require API calls) are Crescent Software's "QuickPak Professional" and MicroHelp's "Muscle." Both products are essential when porting QuickBasic, the Basic PDS, or even Visual Basic for DOS programs to Visual Basic for Windows. But, in addition, they have hundreds of useful, *fast* routines for everything from matrix handling to swapping variables and arrays.

VideoSoft's "VSVBX" offers three controls, including its extremely useful Elastic control that makes it easier to design forms that are independent of screen size or resolution. Desaware's "SpyWorks-VB" (408-377-4770) is for people who have mastered standard Windows API calls and want to move to full control of Windows at the very lowest levels (call back API functions). For those people, this tool is essential and highly recommended.

Scientists can benefit from two toolkits with scientific routines: Crescent Software's "QuickPak Scientific" and TerraTech's (800-447-9120 x1036) "ProMath VB."

People working in finance can also look at TerraTech's "Financial Library VB" if the Crescent QuickPak doesn't have the appropriate function and it is not built into Visual Basic 3.

Custom Controls

Custom controls probably could use a book of their own. Which control you want to look at depends completely on what you want to do. Doing it yourself is often akin to reinventing the wheel and is an overstated virtue in programming—especially in the nineties. If you need to write an interface to a mainframe, a report generator, or a graphics manipulator, you would be a lot better off looking for a custom control than trying to do it yourself.

tip: *The* Visual Basic Programmers Journal*'s CD offers trial versions of many of the custom controls that are available.*

Chances are someone has developed a tool to make your job easier, your application slicker, or both. Vendors sometimes (as in Crescent Software's "QuickPak Professional") include both custom controls and low-level routines in their packages so that you are getting either one or the other essentially for free.

tip: *There are many shareware custom controls that are inexpensive and can provide a surprising amount of functionality. You can find them on CompuServe and through various CD disks of shareware.*

The *Visual Basic Programmers Journal* is an excellent source for learning which custom controls are being developed and which are already out there. Another place to turn to are the vendors who contributed the custom controls in Visual Basic Professional. If you need to go beyond what those controls can do, chances are the original vendor has a fancier version available. For example, Crescent Software's "PDQComm" offers much more than the controls they supplied for VB Professional. Desaware's (408-377-4770) "Custom Control Factory" (it should be called the "Custom Button Factory") also goes far beyond the animated buttons included in the Professional edition. Similarly, Sheridan Software's Widgets package far exceeds the 3-D controls they supplied to Microsoft in the Professional edition, and Pinnacle Publishing's (206-251-1900) "Chart Builder" goes far beyond the graph control they supplied for Visual Basic Professional.

One of the great failings of Visual Basic is the rather simplistic nature of the grid control and edit controls that are supplied with it. (Even the RichTextBox control requires far too much programming to make it really useful if you need to build a full-featured editor into a Visual Basic project.) For grids you might want to look to FarPoint Technologies (800-645-5913, 919-460-4551) for their "Spread" custom control. (This control has virtually all the functionality of a commercial spreadsheet.) Another possibility is Formula One from Visual Components (800-884-8665, 913-599-6500). As for full-featured edit controls, HighEdit from MicroHelp is my favorite. (They also sell a spell checking custom control.) MicroHelp also sells "OLETools" with around 30 custom controls for common tasks that includes a very useful file viewer. Visual Components has editing/spell checking custom controls that are worth checking out as well.

Database add-ons used to be the biggest add-on area for earlier versions of Visual Basic. With the data access controls added to Visual Basic 4, this area is in flux. There are still tools out there that are vital in special situations. For example, "VB/ISAM MX" from Software Source (510-632-7854) is a wonderful product for small, fast, flat database jobs in which you don't want the overhead (not to mention the disk space) of the relational database Access engine. MicroHelp's "Report Generator" is useful if you need bar codes on mailing labels.

note: *Some people feel that third-party custom controls should not be used because they may not work as planned in new versions of Visual Basic. Be sure you get the newer OLE-aware OCX controls, and you are unlikely to have many problems. In any case, I feel that this is an overstated worry, and the major custom control vendors (such as MicroHelp, Sheridan, Crescent, Visual Components, and so on) are likely to be very quick about upgrading to new versions. On the other hand, it may not be worth using a custom control if all you are getting out of it is a minor improvement—which might very well be obtainable by a clever use of Windows API calls.*

Index

A

B

C

D

E

F

G

H

I

J

K

L

M

N

O

P

Q

R

S

T

U

V

W

X

Y

Z

KNOW UNIX... KNOW the NET

EXPLORE YOUR OPTIONS WITH BOOKS FROM OPEN COMPUTING AND OSBORNE/McGRAW-HILL

Open Computing UNIX Unbound
by Harley Hahn
The consummate guide from the author of the best-selling **The Internet Yellow Pages** and **The Internet Complete Reference**
$27.95 U.S.A.
ISBN: 0-07-882050-2

Open Computing Guide to the Best Free UNIX Utilities
by Jim Keough and Remon Lapid
Includes One CD-ROM
$34.95 U.S.A.
ISBN: 0-07-882046-4

Open Computing Best UNIX Tips Ever
by Kenneth H. Rosen, Richard P. Rosinski, and Douglas A. Host
$29.95 U.S.A.
ISBN: 0-07-881924-5

Open Computing Guide to Mosaic
by Levi Reiss and Joseph Radin
$19.95 U.S.A.
ISBN: 0-07-882088-X

Open Computing Guide to UnixWare
by Levi Reiss and Joseph Radin
$29.95 U.S.A.
ISBN: 0-07-882027-8

BC640SL

WHEN IT COMES TO CD-ROM... WE WROTE THE BOOK

BYTE Guide to CD-ROM,
Second Edition
by Michael Nadeau
Includes One CD-ROM
$39.95 U.S.A.
ISBN: 0-07-882104-5
Available Now

Fully Revised & Expanded!

This Exclusive CD-ROM Package Includes
• Sound Clips and Clip Art
• Samples of CD-ROM Applications
• Multimedia Authoring Tools

Part buyer's guide, part standards guide, and part troubleshooter, the ***BYTE Guide to CD-ROM, Second Edition*** discusses all aspects of this burgeoning technology so you can take full advantage.

BYTE Guide to Telescript
by Cronder Concepcion and
Paul Staniforth
$29.95 U.S.A.
ISBN: 0-07-882119-3
Available December, 1995

BYTE Guide to OpenDOC
by David Berkowitz
$29.95 U.S.A.
ISBN: 0-07-882118-5
Available January, 1996

BYTE Guide to Optimizing Windows 95
by Craig Menefee and Lenny Bailes
$29.95 U.S.A.
ISBN: 0-07-882120-7
Available December, 1995

BC640SL

SURF THE NET WITHOUT GETTING WET!

From the safety and comfort of an easy chair, see what has fascinated millions and held the world spellbound. Now the elusive postings on the Internet are available to every reader—no computer necessary! The one and only INTERNET INSIDER uncovers surprising and sordid details direct from reputable sources on the Net—from the clever, amusing, and often shocking to the touching, sentimental, or sad.

INTERNET INSIDER

by Ruffin Prevost
$14.95 U.S.A.
ISBN: 0-07-882084-7

FIND BIZARRE, STRANGE, AND TITILLATING STUFF THAT WILL MAKE HEARTS POUND...

INTERNET INSIDER HAS IT ALL

"MORE EXCITING THAN CHOCOLATE ICE CREAM... MORE INFORMATIVE THAN THE 7 O'CLOCK NEWS."

SEE WHAT'S FASCINATING MILLIONS OF PEOPLE WORLDWIDE...

The INTERNET YELLOW PAGES
Second Edition

by Harley Hahn and Rick Stout
$29.95 U.S.A.
ISBN: 0-07-882098-7

Schildt's WINDOWS 95 PROGRAMMING in C and C++

by Herbert Schildt
$29.95 U.S.A.
ISBN: 0-07-882081-2

THAT'S EDUTAINMENT! A Parent's Guide to Educational Software

by Eric Brown
Includes one CD-ROM
$29.95 U.S.A.
ISBN: 0-07-882083-9

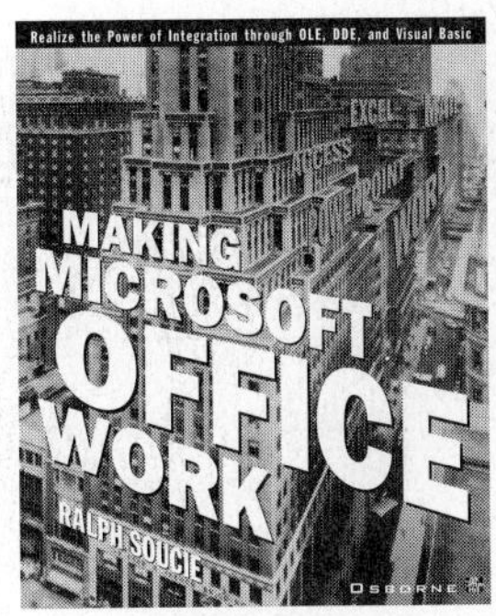

Making MICROSOFT OFFICE Work

by Ralph Soucie
$24.95 U.S.A.
ISBN: 0-07-881188-0

BC640SL

ORDER BOOKS DIRECTLY FROM OSBORNE/McGRAW-HILL

For a complete catalog of Osborne's books, call 510-549-6600 or write to us at 2600 Tenth Street, Berkeley, CA 94710

Call Toll-Free: ***1-800-822-8158***
24 hours a day, 7 days a week in U.S. and Canada

Mail this order form to:
McGraw-Hill, Inc.
Customer Service Dept.
P.O. Box 547
Blacklick, OH 43004

Fax this order form to:
1-614-759-3644

EMAIL
7007.1531@COMPUSERVE.COM
COMPUSERVE GO MH

Ship to:

Name ______________________________

Company ______________________________

Address ______________________________

City / State / Zip ______________________________

Daytime Telephone: ______________________________
(We'll contact you if there's a question about your order.)

ISBN #	BOOK TITLE	Quantity	Price	Total
0-07-88				
0-07-88				
0-07-88				
0-07-88				
0-07-88				
0-07088				
0-07-88				
0-07-88				
0-07-88				
0-07-88				
0-07-88				
0-07-88				
0-07-88				
0-07-88				
	Shipping & Handling Charge from Chart Below			
	Subtotal			
	Please Add Applicable State & Local Sales Tax			
	TOTAL			

Shipping & Handling Charges

Order Amount	U.S.	Outside U.S.
Less than $15	$3.50	$5.50
$15.00 - $24.99	$4.00	$6.00
$25.00 - $49.99	$5.00	$7.00
$50.00 - $74.99	$6.00	$8.00
$75.00 - and up	$7.00	$9.00

Occasionally we allow other selected companies to use our mailing list. If you would prefer that we not include you in these extra mailings, please check here: ❑

METHOD OF PAYMENT

❑ Check or money order enclosed (payable to Osborne/McGraw-Hill)

❑ AMERICAN EXPRESS ❑ DISCOVER ❑ MasterCard ❑ VISA

Account No. ______________________________

Expiration Date ______________________________

Signature ______________________________

In a hurry? Call 1-800-822-8158 anytime, day or night, or visit your local bookstore.

Thank you for your order

Code BC640SL